T0238750

Recent Advances in Computing Sciences

About the Conference

The 1st International Conference on Recent Advances in Computing Sciences (RACS-2022) organized by the School of Computer Application, Lovely Professional University, Jalandhar, Punjab from 4th to 5th November, 2022.

The conference focuses on discussing issues, exchanging ideas, and the most recent innovations towards the advance-ment of research in the field of Computing Sciences and Technology. All technical sessions were predominantly related to Data Science, Artificial Intelligence, Remote Sensing, Image Processing, Computer Vision, Data Forensics, Cyber Security, Computational Sciences, Simulation & Modelling, Business Analytics, and Machine Learning.

The main objective of this conference is to provide a common platform for academia and industry to discuss various technological challenges and share cognitive thoughts. It provided a thought-provoking platform to discuss and disseminate novel solutions for real-world problems in a dynamic and changing technological environment. The main success of RACS-2022 is to give an opportunity for the participants to enhance their knowledge of recent computing technologies.

Recent Advances in Computing Sciences

Proceedings of the 1st International Conference on Recent Advances in Computing Sciences (RACS, 2022)

Edited by

Dr. Sophiya Sheikh

Dr. Sophiya Sheikh is an Associate Professor at Lovely Professional University, Phagwara, Punjab. She has completed her Ph.D. from the Department of Computer Science, Central University of Rajasthan, India. She did her MCA in Computer Science and Applications from Rajasthan Technical University, Kota, and her B.Sc. in Information Technology from Maharshi Dayanand Saraswati University, Ajmer, India. She is a potential reviewer in various reputed journals like IEEE System Journal, Cluster Computing, Scientific Reports, Journal of Supercomputing, etc. Her research interests are Grid/Distributed Computing and Cloud Computing. She regularly writes articles and research papers in reputed National and International magazines and Journals. You can contact her at the School of Computer Applications, Lovely Professional University, Phagwara, Punjab (India) - 144411.

Dr. Manmohan Sharma

Dr. Manmohan Sharma presently serving as Professor in School of Computer Applications, Lovely Professional University, Punjab, INDIA has a vast experience of more than 24 years in the field of academics, research and administration with different Universities and Institutions of repute such as Dr. B.R. Ambedkar University, Mangalayatan University etc. Dr. Sharma has been awarded with his Doctorate degree from Dr. B.R. Ambedkar University, Agra in 2014 in the field of Wireless Mobile Networks. His areas of interest include Wireless Mobile Networks, Adhoc Networks, Mobile Cloud Computing, Recommender Systems, Data Science and Machine Learning etc. More than 50 research papers authored and co-authored, published in International or National journals of repute and conference proceedings comes under his credits. He is currently supervising six doctoral theses. Three Ph.D. and three M.Phil. degrees has already awarded under his supervision. He has guided more than 600 PG and UG projects during his service period under the aegis of various Universities and Institutions. He worked as reviewer of many conference papers and member of the technical program committees for several technical conferences. He is also actively serving several journals related to the field of wireless, mobile communication and cloud computing as editorial board member. He is also member of various professional/technical Societies including Computer Society of India (CSI), Association of Computing Machines (ACM), Cloud Computing Community of IEEE, Network Professional Association (NPA), International Association of Computer Science and Information Technology (IACSIT), and Computer Science Teachers Association (CSTA).

Dr. Amar Singh

Dr. Amar Singh is working as a Professor in the School of Computer Applications, Lovely Professional University, Punjab, India. He did his Ph.D. (Computer Science & Engineering) from IKG Punjab Technical University, Jalandhar, Punjab, India. He has completed his M. Tech. (Information Technology) M.M. University, Mullana, Ambala, Haryana, India. He is a lifetime member of ISCA (Indian Science Congress Association). He has more than 13 years of experience in Teaching and Research. He has published around 80 research articles in various Journals and Conferences. His current research interests are Soft Computing, Machine Learning, and Image Processing. He has successfully guided 02 Ph.D. research scholars and, 08 Ph.D. research scholars are conducting research under his guidance.

CRC Press is an imprint of the
Taylor & Francis Group, an **informa** business

First edition published 2024
by CRC Press
4 Park Square, Milton Park, Abingdon, Oxon, OX14 4RN

and by CRC Press
2385 NW Executive Center Drive, Suite 320, Boca Raton FL 33431

CRC Press is an imprint of Informa UK Limited

British Library Cataloguing-in-Publication Data
A catalogue record for this book is available from the British Library

ISBN: 9781032521954 (pbk)
ISBN: 9781003405573 (ebk)

DOI: 10.1201/9781003405573

Typeset in Sabon
by HBK Digital

Table of Contents

Foreword

The International Conference on Recent Advances in Computing Sciences (RACS 2022) targeted state-of-the-art as well as emerging topics of recent advancement in computing research and its implementation in engineering applications.

The objective of this international conference is to provide opportunities for researchers, academicians, people from the industry, and students to interact and exchange ideas, experiences, and expertise on information and communication technologies. Besides, the participants enhanced their knowledge of recent computing technologies.

We are highly thankful to our valuable authors for their contribution and our Technical Program Committee for their immense support and motivation toward making the first RACS 2022 a success. We are also grateful to our keynote speakers for sharing their precious work and enlightening the delegates of the conference. We sincerely thank our publication partner, Taylor and Francis, for believing in us.

Dr. Manmohan Sharma
Dr. Amar Singh
Dr. Sophiya Sheikh
Convener
Punjab, India RACS-2022

Preface

Introduction

The conference encouraged novel presentations, discussions, and ongoing research by researchers, emerging academics, and members of the more established academic community. The papers contributed the most recent scientific knowledge and research in the field of modern communication systems, sophisticated electronics and communication technologies, artificial intelligence and capsule networks, data transmission, computer networking, and networks for communicative things. With this initiative, we intended to deliver the most recent advancements in all communication technology-related fields.

Putting together international conferences with a focus on computer, communication, and computational sciences to boost research output on a wide scale. Eminent academicians, researchers, and practitioners from around the world are represented on the Technical Program Committee and Advisory Board of the conference. Ten different nations submitted multiple papers to RACS-2022. The conference would not have been as great without their contributions.

Each contribution was checked for plagiarism. Each submission had a thorough assessment by at least two reviewers, with an average of 2-3 per reviewer. A few entries have even undergone more than two reviews. With a 35% acceptance rate, 58 quality articles were chosen for publication in this proceedings volume based on the reviews and plagiarism report. We appreciate the work of all authors and contributors.

Dr. Manmohan Sharma
Dr. Amar Singh
Dr. Sophiya Sheikh
Convener
RACS-2022

Details of programme committee

Conference Chair

Dr. Ashok Kumar
School of Computer Application, Lovely Professional University, Phagwara, Punjab

Convener

Prof. (Dr.) Manmohan Sharma
School of Computer Application, Lovely Professional University, Phagwara, Punjab

Dr. Sophiya Sheikh
School of Computer Application, Lovely Professional University, Phagwara, Punjab

Prof. (Dr.) Amar Singh
School of Computer Application, Lovely Professional University, Phagwara, Punjab

Organizing Committee

Mr. Balraj Kumar
School of Computer Application, Lovely Professional University, Phagwara, Punjab

Mr. Rishi Chopra
School of Computer Application, Lovely Professional University, Phagwara, Punjab

Mr. Sartaj Singh
School of Computer Application, Lovely Professional University, Phagwara, Punjab

Dr. Pawan Kumar
School of Computer Application, Lovely Professional University, Phagwara, Punjab

Mr. Ajay Kumar Bansal
School of Computer Application, Lovely Professional University, Phagwara, Punjab

National Advisory Committee

Prof. (Dr.) R.K.S. Dhakre
Vice-Chancellor, Maharaja Surajmal Brij University, Bharatpur

Prof. CP. Agrawal
Professor and Head, Department of Computer Science and Applications, Makhanlal Chaturvedi National University of Journalism and Communication, Bhopal

Prof. (Dr.) Rajesh Kumar
Thapar Institute of Engineering and Technology, Patiala

Prof. D.C. Sharma
Central University of Rajasthan, Kishangarh, Ajmer

Prof. J.K. Prajapat
Central University of Rajasthan, Kishangarh, Ajmer

Prof. Neeraj Kumar
Thapar Institute of Engineering and Technology, Patiala

Prof. Ravindra Patel
Professor and Head, Department of Computer Applications, UIT, RGPV, Bhopal

Dr. Amit Bhagat
Department of Computer Applications, MANIT, Bhopal

Dr. Dharmendra Singh Rajput
Assoicate Professor, Department of Software and Systems Engineering, Vellor Institute of Technology

Dr. Ghanshyam Singh Thakur
Department of Computer Applications, MANIT, Bhopal

Dr. H. Hannah Inbarani
Professor, Dept of computer Science, Periyar University, Tamilnadu

Dr. Harshita Patel
School of Information Technology and Engineering, VIT University

Dr. Himanshu Aggarwal
Punjabi University, Patiala

Dr. Jagpreet Singh
IIIT, Alahabad

Dr. Kavita Taneja
Panjab University Chandigarh

Dr. Kiranbir Kaur
Department of Computer Science & Engineering, Guru Nanak Dev University, Amritsar

Dr. M. Thangarasu
Data Scientist,OMS Software Solutions, Tamilnadu

Dr. Madan Lal
Punjabi University, Patiala

Dr. Neeraj Sharma
Professor, Deptt. of Computer Science, Punjabi University, Patiala

Dr. Niraj Gupta
Head, School of Corporate Governance and Public Policy, Indian Institute of Corporate Affairs, Minitry of Corporate Affairs, Gurgaon

Dr. Parteek Bhatia
Thapar Institue of Engineering and Technology, Patiala

Dr. Rakesh Kumar
Associate Professor, Central University of Haryana

Dr. Rintu Nath
Scientist F, Division Head, Information Systems & Laboratories, Technology Bhavan, New DelhiSciet

Dr. Seemu Sharma
Computer Science and Engineering Department, Thapar Institute of Engineering & Technology

Dr. Surya Narayan Panda
Chitkara University

Dr. V.K. Saraswat
Director, Institute of Engineering and Technology, Dr. B.R. Ambedkar University, Agra

International Advisory Committee

Prof. (Dr.) Yu-Chen Hu
Providence University, Taiwan

Prof. Abdul Sattar
Griffith University, Australia

Prof. Angelika Klidas
University of Applied Sciences in Amsterdam

Dr. Anish Jindal
Durham University, United Kindgom

Dr. G.A. Preethi
Endicott College of International Studies, Daejeon, South Korea

Dr. Mintu Nath
University of Aberdeen, UK

Mr. Ahmad Taher Azar
Benha University, Egypt

Mr. Gaurav Sharma
Data Engineer, Teck Resources Limited, Canada

Mr. Piyush Gupta
VP Application Development, Essent Guaranty, Inc., Oak Ridge, North Carolina, United States

Mr. Sreelesh Kochukrishnan
Oracle Financial Cloud Consultant, North Carolina, United States

Technical Program Committee

Prof. (Dr.) Anil Sharma
School of Computer Application, Lovely Professional University, Phagwara, Punjab

Prof. (Dr.) Mithilesh Kumar Dubey
School of Computer Application, Lovely Professional University, Phagwara, Punjab

Dr. Ajay Rastogi
School of Computer Application, Lovely Professional University, Phagwara, Punjab

Dr. Amit Sharma
School of Computer Application, Lovely Professional University, Phagwara, Punjab

Dr. Anuj Sharma
School of Computer Application, Lovely Professional University, Phagwara, Punjab

Dr. Apash Roy
School of Computer Application, Lovely Professional University, Phagwara, Punjab

Dr. Avinash Bhagat
School of Computer Application, Lovely Professional University, Phagwara, Punjab

Dr. Deepak Mehta
School of Computer Application, Lovely Professional University, Phagwara, Punjab

Dr. Geeta Sharma
School of Computer Application, Lovely Professional University, Phagwara, Punjab

Dr. Gurpreet Singh Bhatia
School of Computer Application, Lovely Professional University, Phagwara, Punjab

Dr. Jamal Akhtar Khan
School of Computer Application, Lovely Professional University, Phagwara, Punjab

Dr. Mukesh Kumar
School of Computer Application, Lovely Professional University, Phagwara, Punjab

Dr. Pawan Kumar
School of Computer Application, Lovely Professional University, Phagwara, Punjab

Dr. Pooja Chopra
School of Computer Application, Lovely Professional University, Phagwara, Punjab

Dr. Prabhkaran
School of Computer Application, Lovely Professional University, Phagwara, Punjab

Dr. Punam Rattan
School of Computer Application, Lovely Professional University, Phagwara, Punjab

Dr. Ram Kumar
School of Computer Application, Lovely Professional University, Phagwara, Punjab

Dr. Sakshi Dua
School of Computer Application, Lovely Professional University, Phagwara, Punjab

Dr. Sakshi Gupta
School of Computer Application, Lovely Professional University, Phagwara, Punjab

Dr. Shuja Rashid Mirza
School of Computer Application, Lovely Professional University, Phagwara, Punjab

Dr. Sudhakar T
School of Computer Application, Lovely Professional University, Phagwara, Punjab

Dr. Tarandeep Kaur
School of Computer Application, Lovely Professional University, Phagwara, Punjab

Dr. Tarandeep Singh Walia
School of Computer Application, Lovely Professional University, Phagwara, Punjab

Dr. Wasiur Rhmann
School of Computer Application, Lovely Professional University, Phagwara, Punjab

Dr. Yasir Iqbal Mir
School of Computer Application, Lovely Professional University, Phagwara, Punjab

1 Agile estimation: empirical study on critical factors

Ravi Kiran Mallidi[a] *and Manmohan Sharma*[b]

School of Computer Applications, Lovely Professional University, Punjab, India

Abstract

Agile estimations are critical to prioritizing backlog and sprint planning. Estimations are very hard to understand for the developer community to estimate in agile story points—the rule of thumb for estimating story points is to choose the right approach. Agile scrum teams follow estimations in story points. Sprint-level estimation is one where the user stories are broken down into smaller tasks, and estimates story points are assigned to the requirements and their complexity. Story point is measured based on the difficulty of implementation of the given story. The paper presents various deliberation factors used in the agile project to estimate more accurately to complete the task after studying multiple methods. The elements involve complexity, technical/functional requirements, and risks. The story points are more when the complexity is more for the given task. Estimations are essential for resources accountable for each deliverable and a model defined to estimate the agile story point.

Keywords: Agile, critical factors, estimation, model, scrum, story point

Introduction

Estimations for agile projects are critical and have different ways of estimating the product backlog. The crucial principle for agile estimation includes task relative measure and commitment of the team to complete the assigned tasks. Developers are asked to estimate the upcoming work in agile projects. These estimates tend to be too low or too high based on the resource experience on estimations. The estimated efforts should equal the actual time spent on the given task. If the estimates are low, the project delivery expectation is unrealistic. The developer should be confident enough to provide realistic estimates with proper justification to complete the task by the estimated time. Mallidi and Sharma (2021) explained each model's various agile estimation techniques and challenges and provided resolutions. For agile projects, several estimation methods are derived from achieving accurate efforts. Below are the most popular agile estimation models, but these are more towards the expert-based estimations:

- *Story point estimation* – Agile story points estimations roughly estimate the product backlog items with relative sizing. First, the team members, including the product owner, scrum master, developers, testers, and stakeholders, evaluate user stories while grooming sessions. Then, the team provides the story points for a given item from the sequence number defined 0, 1, 1, 2, 3, 5, 8, 13, 21 (the sequence is the sum of the previous two numbers).
- *Planning poker* – Different sizing cards (0, 1, 2, 3, 5, 8, 13, 20, 40 and 100) are distributed cross-team (sized 210), and the team members select a card number for estimation based on the use case and queries answered by the product owner and analyst. Planning poker is relevant for the small number of items and understanding among team members.
- *T-shirt sizing* – The stories are estimated in standard t-shirt sizing (XS, S, M, L, and XL). Story points are assigned to each t-shirt size. T-shirt sizing is relevant for rough estimates, and the team is new to the agile process, more significant backlogs, and early-stage estimates.
- *Dot voting* – User stories are defined and posted on the wall for relative voting. Use pen or markers to create a dot for the vote, which are relevant story points for an item. Dot voting is suitable for well-established teams and a small number of groups.
- *Bucketing system* – Different size buckets are placed with values 0, 1, 2, 3, 5, 8, 13, 20, 40 and 100 on board and assigned the user stores to the appropriate bucket after discussion. Bucketing system is relevant for estimating many stories, quick estimations, and long-term projects.
- *Affinity mapping* – In affinity mapping, the relative sizing cards are placed on the story wall (small to large). The wall is edited according to the appropriate size of the story. Team members place the stories in proper places after the story discussion. T shirt, the Fibonacci series used for estimating relative sizing. Affinity mapping is relevant for long-term projects, mutual understanding of team members, and early-stage estimates process.
- *Analogy* – Story sizes are compared to other relative stories for effort estimation. Relative sizing is good for making assumptions related to agile estimations. In addition, analogy estimates are helpful for a retrospective of stories and highly experienced teams.

[a]ravikiran.mallidi@gmail.com; [b]manmohan.sharma71@gmail.com

- *Three-point method* – Estimation has calculated the average of the best-case scenario, the worst-case scenario, and most likely scenario estimates. The three-point estimation method is relevant for teams new to the agile process, later-stage estimations, and highly prioritized backlogs.

Organizations use the above estimation model to estimate the project. This estimation is more resource experience based. However, resources are not considered the requirement complexity concerning project and task levels. The paper describes various critical factors related to project and task levels for evaluating the effort estimation. This paper is organized as follows: section 2 describes literature review, section 3 describes various critical factors in agile scrum estimations, and section 4 concludes the article.

Literature Review

Canedo and Costa (2018) conducted a systematic review to evaluate nimble project size, time, effort, productivity, and cost based on story point and point of function. Planning poker is a mainly used estimation model for agile projects and promotes average user stories size compared to consensus by Gandomani et al. (2019). Adnan and Afzal (2017) proposed the approach to improve the effort estimations on scrum projects using an ontology model in a multiagent estimation. Validated the process with 12 web-based projects planned on Delphi and planning poker estimation methods and the observations captured using magnitude of relative error (MRE) and PRED (25). Altaleb and Gravell (2019) conducted semi-structural interviews from 18 organizations with different agile projects and concluded that planning poker and expert judgement were used for estimations. Arora et al. (2021) proposed a regression technique to estimate an agile project for considering data pre-processing, model selection, testing, and evolution. Features and user information are used to determine the model hybrid agile software development effort assessment for agile estimations gives promising results by Gupta and Mahapatra (2021). Rosa et al. (2021) define functional and external interfaces for effective sizing measures for early estimates. The stepwise regression model for cost estimation helps the teams significantly reduce errors compared to the use case estimation model by Shams et al. (2019). Hacaloglu and Demirors (2019) investigated the usage of functional size measurement (FSM) for estimating agile and adopted COSMIC FSM to measure measurement accuracy and problems in the COSMIC FSM process. Testing efforts estimation in the agile sprint are complex, and the proposed regression model considers COSMIC FSM. Business applications, real-time software, embedded software, and mobile apps use COSMIC FSM method to achieve better estimations. Defined mobile characteristics like limited memory, CPU, RAM, screen size, connections, application types, and battery power with assigned weights along with the non-functional requirement for measuring mobile testing efforts by Kaur and Kaur (2019). Tool-based application decomposition developed by Shams et al. (2019) to improve the development cost in mobile applications by combining work breakdown and story points might help better estimates in mobile development. The machine learning (ML) technique is used for the effort estimation technique, evaluating the performance of 28 studies using MRE, MMRE, and PRED (25) by Mahmood et al. (2022). Reuse the previous projects with similar scope for estimating. Weights are assigned to each use case point, and the unadjusted actor weights are calculated. Technical factors are defined as a distributed system, end-user efficiency, complex processing, reuse of code, easy to install, easy to use, easy to change, security features, and special training requirements. Environmental factors include familiarity with the rational unified processes, application experience, object-oriented experience, analyst capability, motivation, requirement stability, part-time work, and complex programming language (Rak et al., 2019).

Critical Factors in Agile Scrum Estimations

In agile estimation, most organizations/projects follow the resource-provided estimates to complete the task. The resource which has given the estimate is responsible for completing the story. The product owner, scrum master, developer, and QAs should be part of the estimation exercise in the estimation exercise. For example, search screen on different browsers support might be a two points effort from development, whereas a lot more from a testing perspective. Here, the combined action from the developer and QA must provide to complete the search screen task. Different teams will have various measures of story points based on their experience and the stories they are sizing. The effort required to finish a story by team member A will differ from that needed by team member B in the same group. This difference will reflect in the velocities of team members A and B. Attempting to standardize the point scale across these team members is very important for more extensive programs to handle. Figure 1.1 describes the steps involved in story point estimations.

Each iteration is called a sprint, and the sprint can span from two to four weeks. In the sprint, the team has to complete business functionality and deliver the viable product to the business user to validate. Prioritization of requirements from backlog is critical for project success. Backlog items are divided into segments based on must-have features, should-have features, could-have features, and won't-have features. The sprint cycles divide into these segments and deliver the project within time. Figure 1.2 shows sprint planning activities starting from sprint 0.

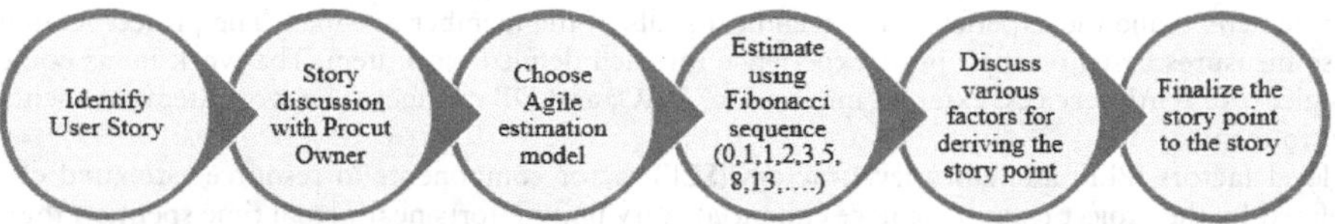

Figure 1.1 Agile story point estimation steps

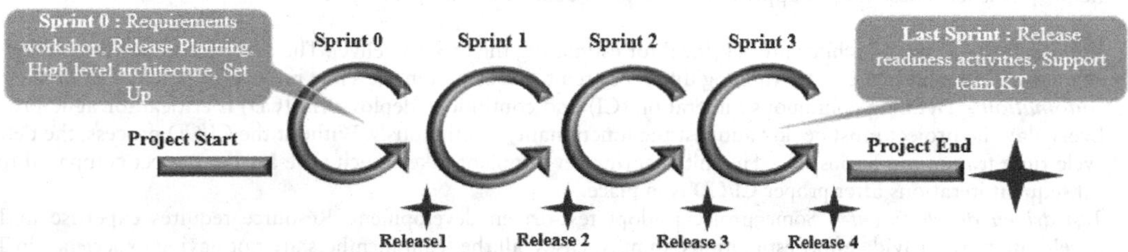

Figure 1.2 Agile sprint planning activities

Standardization of effort estimation between different teams is difficult. The developer is not considering the critical risks while estimating the efforts due to a lack of experience in different scenarios. They recommend adding additional efforts based on various factors identified by the project teams after calculating the developers' efforts in the best-case system to achieve accurate estimations for a given sprint. Nowadays, the application architectures are changing drastically, and the factors defined in functional point estimations and the use case model are insufficient to size stories. The literature review section describes several studies on factors affecting effort estimation—software effort estimation accuracy based on MRE and perdition level p PRED(p). However, the MRE measure is an unreliable accuracy measure.

Consequently, standardized accuracy has been proposed by Idri et al. (2018) along with PRED calculation. Most are use case reuse, traditional techniques like the Constructive Cost Model (COCOMO), and algorithm-based processes. The story point estimations' variance is calculated as MRE.

$$\text{MRE} = \frac{|\textit{Actual Effort} - \textit{Estimated Effort}|}{\textit{Actual Effort}}$$

Plan the project activities correctly, and the effort variance should be zero. Due to resource pressure, the existing estimation models cannot give more accurate estimations. Product backlog prioritization, product owner inefficiency, integration testing cost, estimated sprint duration, and cost quality assurance are the critical influencing factors affecting performance in scrum projects by Alzubaidi et al. (2022). Story point estimations are based on the complexity of

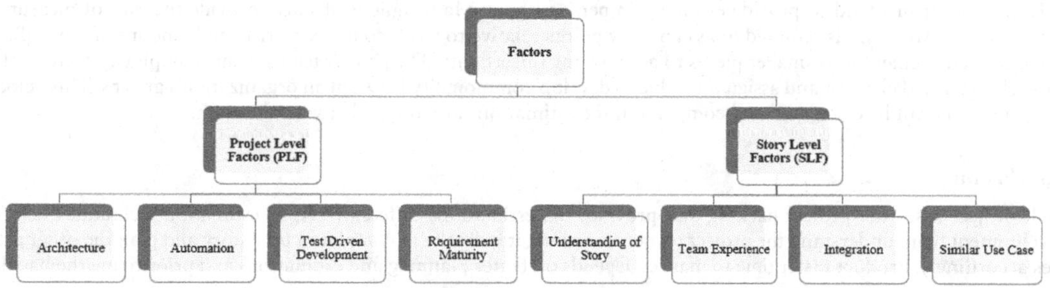

Figure 1.3 Deliberation factors considered to determine story point estimation

the feature work implemented and the experience and technical skills of the member assigned. The project team must identify the raw/base measures based on their prior experience for each defined work item. The work items comprise UI page, business logic, rest/SOAP services, external integration, DAO, and DB changes. The work items elements are changing from team to team.

Add the project level factors (PLF) and story level factors (SLF) factor components to resource estimated efforts/ work item effort defined by the project team to achieve enhanced story point efforts near actual time spent on the task. Figure 1.3 provides critical factors considered to determine story point estimation.

Project level factors (PLF) – Factors related to the project level defined in PLF. Below are the high-level factors described for the project level. These factors apply to all the stores defined in the sprint cycle.

- *Architecture* – Project architecture is critical for estimating the task to deliver. The architectures of the projects are changing daily, and projects are running different architectures within the same project using microservices.
- *Automation* – Defining continuous integration (CI) and continuous deployment (CD) is critical for agile projects. Every day the project must deploy and test the functionality continuously. Without the CI/CD process, the delivery cycle time frames are impossible. The initial sprint development takes much time for the project compared to the subsequent iterations after proper CI/CD is in place.
- *Test-driven development* – Some projects adopt test-driven development. Resource requires expertise in TDD development to provide effort estimations. In most cases, all the team members are not having experience in TDD development. In this case, add additional effort to support TDD.
- *Requirement maturity* – Requirements are documented and explained correctly in the grooming session by the Product Owner. If the requirement is not defined precisely, the estimation may not be accurate.

Story level factors (SLF) – Factors related to the story level rather than the project level. Below are the high-level factors defined for the story level. These factors are applicable for each store defined in the sprint cycle.

- *Understand story* – Some stores are not appropriately defined in a sprint cycle and take more time to complete/ moved to the next sprint cycle. Conversely, illustrated stories take less time to complete.
- *Team experience* – A team member's experience in the particular activity is good, the time required to complete the task is reduced; otherwise, the time is required to complete the job.
- *Integration* – Integrating into other systems takes some significant effort to establish. Therefore, resources must adequately analyze the integration consideration while estimating effort.
- *Similar use case* – A critical factor for effort estimation is identifying similar use cases/business functions. The time taken to complete similar tasks would be less after completing the initial task.

The efforts are not accurate enough to complete the defined task without adding the additional actions measured from PLF and SLF factors. The factors may increase/decrease the efforts defined by the team. After determining the PLF and SLF, the final story point estimation is defined as

$$\textit{Story point} = \textit{Story points defined by the resource in an ideal scenario} \\ + \textit{Efforts defined by PLF} + \textit{Efforts defined by SLF}$$

Figure 1.4 describes the model for complexity factors for agile effort estimations. For each element, define the values concerning low, moderate, and high. The specified values are used to calculate the agile scrum's final effort estimation.

Traditional teams tend to provide estimates in person hours. Many agile teams also provide the unit of measure as person-hours. Adoption is required to assign story points relative to work complexity, risk, and amount of work. Break down the requirement into smaller pieces to address any uncertainty. The project teams define complexity factor values for each described element and assign the value to develop commonality between an organization's groups. This velocity of the projects can be calculated and compared if the estimations are in sync between the team.

Conclusion

Each project asses the project backlog and provides the estimations differently. Agile estimation techniques help the development team understand the project owners how long it will take to complete a user story and plan the other activities accordingly. Product faster time to market depends on better planning and estimations and prioritizing the backlog.

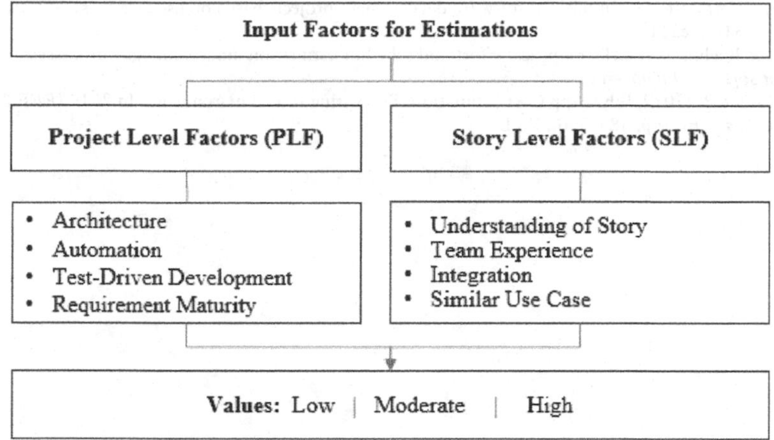

Figure 1.4 Input factors for agile estimations

The user stories are defined as small as possible; the thumb rule is to determine the work item should not exceed 816 hours of work. If any story point exceeds 816 hours, then split the story into multiple smaller tasks to estimate accurately. Moreover, considering the factors related to Project level and Story level is most important for estimation. Without considering the factors while making story points, the efforts may be overestimated or underestimated—in most cases, the team underestimates due to pressure on the project deliverables. Further study can be conducted to define weights for each factor described in the paper and define the model to achieve accurate results and standardization across the organization.

References

Adnan, M. & Afzal, M. (2017). Ontology based multiagent effort estimation system for scrum agile method. *IEEE Access*, *5*, 25993–26005.

Altaleb, A. and Gravell, A. (2019). An empirical investigation of effort estimation in mobile apps using agile development process. *Journal of Software*, *14*(8), 356–369.

Alzubaidi, A. A., Salama, R. M., & Qureshi, M. R. J. (2022). The proposed critical factors to improve the performance of scrum teams. *International Journal of Computer Science and Mobile Computing*, 11(2), 68–74.

Arora, M., Sharma, A., Katoch, S., Malviya, M., & Chopra, S. (2021). A state of the art regressor model's comparison for effort estimation of agile software. In *2021 2nd International Conference on Intelligent Engineering and Management (ICIEM)* (pp. 211–215). IEEE.

Canedo, E. D. & Costa, R. P. D. (2018). Methods and metrics for estimating and planning agile software projects. *Twenty-fourth Americas Conference on Information Systems, New Orleans.*

Gandomani, T. J., Faraji, H., & Radnejad, M. Planning Poker in cost estimation in Agile methods: Averaging Vs. Consensus. In *2019 5th Conference on Knowledge Based Engineering and Innovation (KBEI)* (pp. 066–071). IEEE.

Gupta, N. & Mahapatra, R. P. (2021). An effective agile development process by a hybrid intelligent effort estimation protocol. *Journal of Ambient Intelligence and Humanized Computing*, 1–10.

Hacaloglu, T. & Demirors, O. (2019). Measureability of functional size in Agile software projects: Multiple case studies with COSMIC FSM. In *2019 45th Euromicro Conference on Software Engineering and Advanced Applications (SEAA)* (pp. 204–211). IEEE.

Idri, A., Abnane, I., & Abran, A. (2018). Evaluating Pred (p) and standardized accuracy criteria in software development effort estimation. *Journal of Software: Evolution and Process*, 30(4), e1925.

Kaur, A. & Kaur, K. (2019). A COSMIC function points based test effort estimation model for mobile applications. *Journal of King Saud University-Computer and Information Sciences*. 34(3), 946–963.

Mahmood, Y., Kama, N., Azmi, A., Khan, A. S., & Ali, M. (2022). Software effort estimation accuracy prediction of machine learning techniques: A systematic performance evaluation. *Software: Practice and Experience*, 52(1), 39–65.

Mallidi, R. K. & Sharma, M. (2021). Study on agile story point estimation techniques and challenges. *International Journal of Computer Application*, 174(13), 9–14.

Rak, K., Car, Ž., & Lovrek, I. (2019). Effort estimation model for software development projects based on use case reuse. *Journal of Software: Evolution and Process*, 31(2), e2119.

Rosa, W., Clark, B. K., Madachy, R., & Boehm, B. (2021). Empirical effort and schedule estimation models for agile processes in the US DoD. *IEEE Transactions on Software Engineering*.

Shams, A., Bohm, S., Winzer, P., & Dorner, R. (2019, July). App Cost Estimation: Evaluating Agile Environments. In *2019 IEEE 21st Conference on Business Informatics (CBI)* (pp. 383–390). IEEE.

2 Deepfakes: benefits, threats, and combat strategies

Tawseef Ahmed Teli[1], *Munleef Quadir Bhat*[2], *and Hala Zain*[2]

[1]Department of Computer Applications, Govt Degree College Anantnag, Higher Education Department, Jammu and Kashmir, India

[2]Department of Computer Science, College of Computer Science and Information Technmology, Jazan University, Jazan, Kingdom of Saudi Arabia

[3]Department of Information Technology and Security, College of Computer Science and Information Technmology, Jazan University, Jazan, Kingdom of Saudi Arabia

Abstract

Due to the advent of digitalized technologies, distinguishing between accurate and fraudulent news is getting difficult. Its most new acquisitions to the challenge are deepfakes, which are wacky videos that employ artificial intelligence technology (AI) to portray people speaking or doing something that's not there. When believable deepfakes are paired with the breadth and efficiency of media platforms, they may scope large numbers of people in a moment, posing a serious threat to our country. Although there is no significant research aimed at the field, this work studies 84 online news stories to distinguish between the deepfakes and originals. The study is also focused on techniques to find who makes deepfakes, the advantages and drawbacks of deepfake innovation, and how to avoid them. Whereas techniques pose a significant threat to our civilization, legislative arena, and business, the study suggests that they can be addressed through all the legislations, business governance and personal freedom, training and employment, deepfake sensors, textual certification, and deepfake prevention continuous improvement. The paper examines deepfakes in-depth, as well as the business possibilities for defence and AI firms in the fight against intermediate piracy and fake news.

Keywords: Deepfake, generative adversarial networks, artificial intelligence, security

Introduction

In recent times, fake news has surfaced as a probable issue of social discussion, culture, and politics. Fakes are made with an intention of malice and fraud. On Facebook, incorrect stories spread quickly, reaching thousands of citizens. Based on the ease at which false information can be communicated and made available, it is exceedingly difficult to tell which information to use for strategic decision-making. Humans currently live in a 'post-truth' era, marked by electronic deceit and cyberattacks by hostile actors that utilize bogus information to affect international perception. The recent advances in machine learning (ML) have simplified the process to construct 'deepfakes', or meta films that use face swap and leave a little indication of manipulation. Artificial intelligence (AI) programmes that merge, mix, modify, and try to impose photos and video clips to generate false videos that seem legitimate are known as hoaxes. But without permission of the victim to whom the photo and speaking style are associated, fake data technology is creating, for example, a comedic, sexual content, or governmental video of a person saying something. The extent, complexity, and quality of the advances made in deepfakes are league season since essentially anybody with a keyboard can create fake films that are undistinguishable from legitimate substance. Political leaders, entertainers, comedy acts, and music artists were among the first to have their faces weaved into sexual recordings, investigated intensively will likely be used so often in the future for cyber harassment, bullying, falsified video footage in the high court, electoral destroy, terrorist propaganda, coerce, financial fraud, and rumors. Although it is really easy to communicate false information, it is complex enough to correct the system and combat deepfakes. Deepfakes must be defeated, we must first comprehend them, as well as the causes for their creation and the technology that underpins them. Scholarship study on digital deception in social media, on the other hand, has only lately begun. Because deepfakes first appeared on the Internet in 2017, scientific research on the subject is limited. As a result, the purpose of this research is to examine what deepfakes are and who makes them, the advantages and risks of algorithmic science, existing algorithmics, and how to battle them. The methodology does so by analyzing several deepfake news stories websites of news organizations.

Literature Review

Videos seem to be hyper-realistic recordings digitally edited to represent individuals talking while doing something that has never come true (Ding et al., 2018). They are a mix of 'deep learning' and 'fake'. Deepfakes develop to reproduce a human's facial expressions, activity, voice, and elocution by analyzing massive amounts of data examples (Zhou et al., 2019). The learning technique includes inputting video footage of a couple of individuals into a program to educate it to exchange faces (G'uera et al., 2018). These techniques particularly include the usage of a facial navigation system and AI to supplant an emotion in a videotape with the face of another human (Ding et al., 2019). ML algorithms were

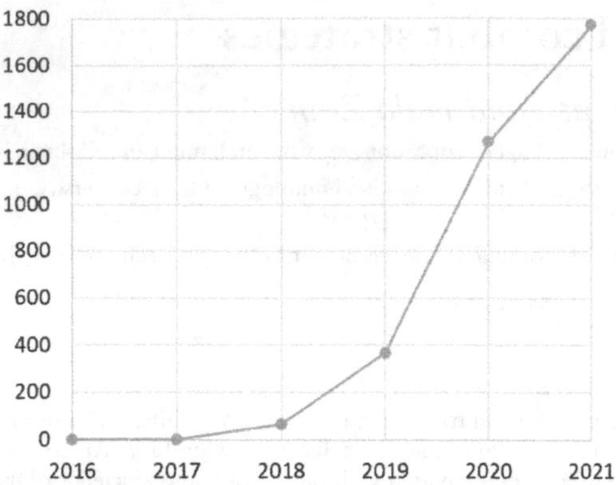

Figure 2.1 Papers related to deepfake from 2016–2021

profoundly used after the instance of a Reddit user releasing audio of personalities having an inappropriate conversation in 2017. And they used genuine films, having separate music, and were meant to spread fast on social media, the images are difficult to notice, and as a result, many viewers believed the film they are watching. Publications related to deepfakes are shown in Figure 2.1.

Deepfakes prey on social media establishments, where hypotheses and misleading information spread swiftly due to peoples' need to follow the herd. Similarly, this 'infopocalypse' pushes everyone to assume that the only credible information comes from online communities, like family members, close friends, or siblings, and that reinforces their previous ideas. Many people are prepared to believe anything that confirms their present ideas, even if they think it is incorrect. Fakes are cheap. quality videos with a little gap in taste. Because low-cost gear, such as efficient GPU, is readily available, doctored genuine content is already ubiquitous (Singh et al., 2018). The availability of open standard tools for making high-quality, accurate deepfakes for misleading is increasing (G'uera et al., 2018). This enables those with little technical skills and creative aptitude to edit videos, swap faces, modify sentiments, and generate speech with vicinity realism (Sabir et al., 2018). A summary of related works is given in Table 2.1.

ML techniques encompass applications in varied fields of cryptography and networks (Masoodi, et al., 2021; Teli, et al., 2021; 2022), navigation (Teli, et al., 2021) and most importantly predictive analysis and healthcare. Deep learning techniques that have applications in secure healthcare (Teli, et al., 2020; 2021; 2022) as well as deepfake detection and generation.

Deepfake Generation

Deepfakes are made using GANs, two Alexnets that help maximize usable content (Ding et al., 2019). Both the 'generation' and 'states' CNN models along the same image, video, or audio datasets (Zhou et al., 2019). The first modelling then attempts to generate new samples to mislead the succeeding network, which is attempting to resolve whether the new video/images it is viewing are real or fake (G'uera et al., 2018). A GAN observes hundreds of pics of an individual and builds a new profile.

Which is similar but not identical to any of the previously examined (Singh et al., 2018). After being educated on fewer data, GANs will soon be able to change heads, full legs, and dialects. Although most deepfakes require a significant number of photographs to be impressive, scholars have developed a way of making a fake movie with just one shot, such as a snapshot. Figure 2.2 provides a flowchart of how deepfakes are generated using GANs.

Benefits of deepfakes

Many sectors, including movies, textbooks and internet technology, gaming and recreation, social media and wellness, bioengineering, and different commercial domains, i.e., fashion and retailing, can benefit from deepfake expertise (Li et al., 2018). Deepfake technology has the potential to benefit movies in many varied ways. It has applications for producing fake voices for actors who are unable to talk as well as saving time to update a particular shot rather than filming a new shot altogether. In addition to this, filmmakers could recreate classic movie segments, make new movies having actors which are dead for years now and elevate unedited video to professional quality. This approach provides

Table 2.1 Summary of deepfake detection

Technology	*Features*	*Pros*	*Cons*	*Dataset*
CNN, RNN (Sabir et al., 2018)	Integration and usage of CNN models with domain-specific face pre-processing techniques	Better performance than the existing state of the art approaches	Poor performance in Multi-layer RNN	Face Forensics++dataset
Deep learning, Face swapping (Ding et al., 2019)	Deep transfer learning for face-swapping detection	Provides uncertainty	Provide less accuracy rate over comparison on human subjects	Generated one of the largest faces swapped dataset
2-Stream neural network, RNN (Zhou et al., 2019)	Detect the tampering artefacts	This approach can learn both manipulated artefacts and hidden noise	Lesser accuracy	Dataset generated by two online face-swapping applications
CNN, RNN (G'uera et al., 2018)	Temporal-aware pipeline to automatically detect deepfake videos	Achieve competitive results in this task while using a simple architecture	Effective with video of size as fewer as 2 seconds.	HOHA dataset

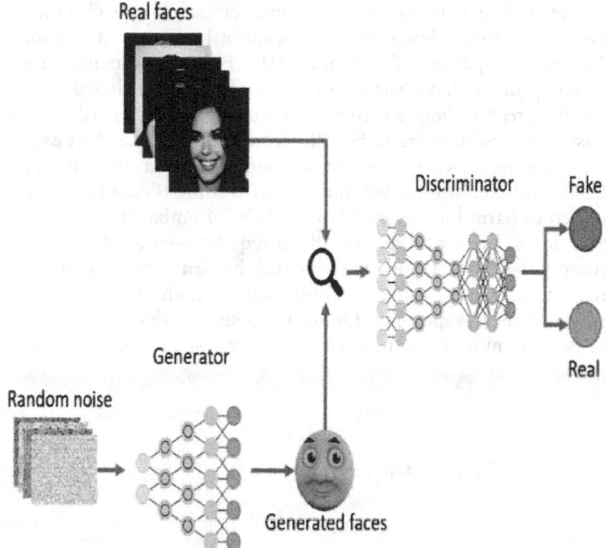

Figure 2.2 Generative adversarial networks

automatic and lifelike voice replication for movies in any nation, increasing public access to films and educational material. Deepfakes technologies enable greater teleconferencing in online graphics and virtual chat settings, as well as pure and believable intelligent assistants and digital doubles of persons. Similarly, knowledge may be useful in the social as well as medical areas. This technology can also aid in the grieving process by artificially bringing a dead friend/family member back to life, helping people to say their last farewell. It could be used to generate a limb for a legless person or help a transgender person to visualize their body in the preferred form. The deepfake technique may allow those with Parkinson's disease to connect with a fresher face. GANs are also being researched for their ability to create simulated chemicals to expedite product and process and pharmaceutical findings. Organizations are enthusiastic about the prospect of manufacturing deepfake science and it has the potential to transform purchasing and advertising (Fernandes et al., 2020).

Deepfakes also provide highly tailored material that turns clients into stars; the tools enable the virtual trial to preview the fitting and liking of an item before purchasing it. The order to appropriately try on men's clothes is an obvious use; the system allows users to not only create model clones of themselves and see these qualitative avatars commute with peers throughout all supermarkets but also to attempt on a crop top dress or suit in binary code and then almost insight a ceremony venue (Sabir et al., 2018). Furthermore, AI may develop distinct virtual voices to differentiate companies and industries, making segmentation easier (Liu et al., 2019).

Possible threats of deepfakes

Deepfakes are more hazardous than 'traditional' alternative facts since they are harder to spot and viewers are so much more prone to believe the counterfeiting is real. The technologies allow for the construction of allegedly genuine news films, jeopardizing the careers of professionals and the medium. Also, a news organization can contest by winning a race to get video footage shot by a victim of an occurrence, although the danger escalates if the material provided is not real. In 2019, with a sudden increase in the tense relationship between India and Pakistan, Reuters identified more than 30 pieces of fake footage on the event; most were old footage from irrelevant occurrences with new scripts. The rise of hoaxes will exacerbate the problem of film misinterpretation, such as a real peaceful demonstration or violent altercation represented as having occurred somewhere else. While looking for video footage of the horrific shootings in Christchurch, New Zealand, CNN broadcasted a video claiming that the suspect was killed by cops moments after the incident. However, the video was from the United States. As per intelligence services, deepfakes are being used to compromise national security by chance to expand disinformation and spoil electoral processes. US security agencies have often worried about foreign interference in American politics, specifically in the primary contest.

The most dangerous aspect of pattern recognition, meanwhile, may not be misleading per se, but how chronic exposure to disinformation leads students to assume that much information, even video, cannot be respected, leading to a condition described as 'communication doomsday' or 'reality apathy'(Sabir et al., 2018). However, the authentic film may be disregarded as phoney (Ding et al., 2019), because others have learnt to think that whatever they don't like is fraudulent (Xuan et al., 2019). To put it another way, the greatest danger is that individuals grow to regard everything as deception (Hsu et al., 2020). Deepfakes could pose a cybersecurity risk. For illustrate, presenting a chief executive using racist or sexist profanity, advocating a bogus partnership, making false claims of monetary costs or ruin, or painting them as though they are breaking the law might be exploited for market and insider trading (G'uera et al., 2018). Deepfake pornography or product debuts might be used to harm businesses, harass CEOs, or embarrass management. However, deepfake tools enable the visual mimicry of a CEO in real-time, for all, to request essential financial assistance or personal details from a staff. Deepfake s might potentially create a false identity by converting an adult image into that of a child or an elderly person in video recordings, raising concerns about convicted child molesters' use of the device. Finally, algorithms can spread malicious code. Experts reportedly found that a section devoted to deepfakes mined bitcoin using the PCs of its visitors. Deepfake fans are more likely to have computer systems, making them candidates for spoofed.

Methods to combat deepfakes

There are four techniques to combat deepfakes, according to the news items examined:

- legal and regulatory requirements
- Business objectives and volunteer action
- growth and investigation
- of the non-system responsible for training, digitally enhanced analysis, media classification, and deepfake rejection.

Deepfakes are deterred by both law and policies. Particular data are technically not subject to criminal and civil laws, while jurists have proposed amending current laws should include libel, harassment, cybercrime, and trying to intimidate a public servant using deepfakes (Zhou et al., 2019). In Virginia, the sharing of fake images and videos has recently been declared a felony (Ding et al., 2019). As AI systems become more advanced, new laws and legal systems shall be needed (Rodriguez et al., 2018).

Officials shall necessarily engage in bringing up a challenging legal environment, including freedom of speech and regulations related to ownership, to not only effectively control the spread of deepfakes as well as have a fair legal reaction to the emergence of malicious deepfakes. While current laws to restrict deepfakes can be implemented, security techniques are also necessary. Today's social media platforms are mostly exempted from the accountability of shared posts from their users. One constitutional option is to take on the social major corporations and take away their legal protection from the materials their users post, making both users and digital platforms more accountable for their actions (Jawadul et al., 2019). But, hostile actors such as international bodies and terrorists who may use social networking sites to launch massive disinformation campaigns against other organizations have had little influence. Corporate standards and volunteer engagement may be more effective ways to combat deepfakes. During electoral politics, politicians could pledge that they shall not make use of unlawful digital campaign strategies or disseminate misinformation. As hate speech, false news, and disinformation have grown more common on digital channels, some corporations have replied by banning login credentials and funding speedier detection technology. On Reddit and Pornhub, deepfake pornographic and other quasi prostitution are prohibited, and users can report such items. Facebook no longer runs ads or makes money on anything that has been reported as false; instead, the corporation has collaborations with over 50 evidence companies, colleges, businesses, and politicians to current progress. Readers will not be encouraged to see everything that's been flagged as 'false' by Facebook's fact-checking systems. Along with many other news organizations, the WSJ and Reuters have created professional crews to assist their correspondents in spotting false information and employing detecting techniques and equipment like Google's dislocation and inverted image scans. People must also understand that as technology advances, fewer photographs of actual people's faces will be designed to establish deepfakes, no one is secure. And anybody who posts a single 30-frame-per-second image or video to a social media website risk being detected as a deepfake. While removing photographs and videos from the internet is preferable, having barriers in the shape of a flying gesture right in front of a person's face may provide some safeguard. Industries, organizations, and institutes that employ biometrics and keep vast amounts of face data for security and authentication must address the danger of cybercrime if this data is compromised. The anti-deepfake approach offers the most comprehensive set of tools for identifying deepfakes, and authentication data and preventing them, avoiding deep fakes and content restrictions to make deepfakes. However, the hurdles of leveraging invention to classify and help detect fakes are increasing, as is the truth that there are far more science assets and personnel looking to develop photoshopped expertise than on catching them (Sawant et al., 2018). Deepfake makers also commonly use insights from previously reported deepfake studies to enhance the techniques and avoid novel approaches (Li et al., 2018). While spy agencies such as the department of defence, Defense Advanced Research Projects Agency (DARPA), provide enough funding for photoshopped researchers, private cybersecurity factories have important trade prospects spoofing a variety of information, building convincing channels, detecting illicit bots, and weapon fraud and online databases pollution (Fernandes et al., 2020). However, increasing ant deepfake capabilities alone is insufficient. Institutions must also embrace technological innovations; any foreign government, for illustration, may be upgraded to face and defend its citizens against deepfake threats.

Conclusion

This study's findings add to the growing corpus of scientific research on deepfakes. This study looked at 84 modern news stories on 'fake news' to learn more about what they are and who builds them, the benefits and hazards of deep learning, present spoofing examples, and how to combat them. As per the study, deepfakes are hyper-realistic films that have been retouched to portray people acting and then doing activities that don't exist. Artificial intelligence is used to create deepfakes, notably (GANs), wherein pit racist biased and creative systems against one another while achieving fantastic performance with each iteration, culminating in a plausible fake. Furthermore, the editors' areas of some of the examined news articles consisted of a great number of reader thoughts and ideas; analyzing those posts can also provide important insights into how deepfakes are construed by the public, and thus what schools should emphasize in their combat strategies. These limitations provide a lot of options for future fake data studies.

References

Bappy, J. H., Simons, C., Nataraj, L., Manjunath, B. S., & Roy-Chowdhury, A. K. (2019). Hybrid LSTM and encoder- decoder architecture for detection of image forgeries. *IEEE Transactions on Image Processing,* 28(7).

Ding, X., Razieiy, Z., Eric, C., Larson, Eli, V., Olinick, K. P., & Hahsler, M. (2019). Swapped Face Detection using Deep Learning and Subjective Assessment. *Research Gate,* 1–9.

Fernandes, S., Raj, S., Ewetz, R., Pannu, J. D., Jha, S. K., Ortiz, E., Vintila, I., & Salte, M. (2020). Detecting deepfake videos using attribution-based confidence metric. *In Proceedings of the IEEE/CVF Conference on Computer Vision and Pattern Recognition Workshops,* (pp. 308–309).

G'uera, D. & Delp, E. J.(2018). Deepfake video detection using recurrent neural networks. *15th IEEE International Conference on Advanced Video and Signal Based Surveillance (AVSS).*

Hsu, C. C., Zhuang, Y. X., & Lee, C. Y. (2020). Deep fake image detection based on pairwise learning. *Applied Science,* 10(1), 370. doi:10.3390/app10010370.

Korshunov, P., Marcel, S. (2018). Speaker inconsistency detection in tampered video. *26th European Signal Processing Conference (EUSIPCO).*

Li, Y., Chang, M. C., & Lyu, S. (2018). Exposing AI created fake videos by detecting eye blinking. *In IEEE International Workshop on Information Forensics and Security (WIFS),* (pp. 1–7).

Liu, F. & Jiao, L. (2019). Task-oriented GAN for PolSAR image classification and clustering. *IEEE Transactions on Neural Networks and Learning Systems,* 30(9).

Masoodi, F., Bamhdi, A. M., & Teli, T. A. (2021). Machine learning for classification analysis of intrusion detection on NSL-KDD dataset. *Turkish Journal of Computer and Mathematics Education*, 12(10).

Rodriguez, A. M. & Geradts, Z. (2018). Detection of deepfake video manipulation. *In Proceedings of the 20th Irish Machine Vision and Image Processing conference*, (pp. 133–136).

Sabir, E., Cheng, J., Jaiswal, A., AbdAlmageed, W., Masi, L., & Natarajan, P. (2018). Recurrent convolutional strategies for face manipulation detection in videos. *In Proceeding of the IEEE Xplore Final Publication,* (pp. 80–87).

Sawant, R. & Sabnis, M. (2018). A review of video forgery and its detection. *IOSR Journal of Computer Engineering (IOSR-JCE)*, 20(2).

Singh, D. R. & Aggarwal, N. (2018). Video content authentication techniques: a comprehensive survey. *Multimedia Systems*, 24, 211–240.

Teli, T. A. & Masoodi, F. (2021). Blockchain in healthcare: challenges and opportunities. *2nd International Conference on IoT Based Control Networks and Intelligent Systems (ICICNIS 2021*). https://ssrn.com/abstract=3882744

Teli, T. A. & Wani, M. A. (2021). A fuzzy-based local minima avoidance path planning in autonomous robots. *International Journal of Information Technology*, 13(1), 33–40. https://doi.org/10.1007/s41870-020-00547-0

Teli, T. A., Masoodi, F., & Yousuf, R. (2020). Security concerns and privacy preservation in blockchain based IoT systems: opportunities and challenges. *International Conference on IoT based Control Networks and Intelligent Systems (ICICNIS 2020)*. https://ssrn.com/abstract=3769572

Teli, T. A., Yousuf, R., & Khan, D. A. (2022). MANET routing protocols, attacks and mitigation techniques: A review. *International Journal of Mechanical Engineering*, 7(2).

Teli, T. A., Masoodi, F. S., & Bahmdi, A. M. (2021). HIBE: Hierarchical Identity-Based Encryption. In K. A. B. Ahmad, K. Ahmad, & U. N. Dulhare, (Eds.). *Functional Encryption* (pp. 187–202). Springer, Cham.

Teli, T. A., Yousuf, R., & Khan, D. A. (2022). Ensuring secure data sharing in IoT domains using blockchain. In M. M. Ghonge, S. Pramanik, R. Mangrulkar, & D. N. Le). *Cyber Security and Digital Forensics.*

Xuan, X., Peng, B., Wang, W., & Dong, J. (2019). On the Generalization of GAN Image Forensics, Computer Vision and Pattern Recognition.

Zhou, P., Han, X., Davis, V. I. M. L. (2019). Two- stream neural networks for tampered face detection. *IEEE Conference on Computer Vision and Pattern Recognition.*

3 Blockchain and big data as emerging solutions for fog challenges: An impeccable study

Rohit[1,a], Sakshi Dua[2,b], Preety Shoran[3,c], and Ajay Nain[1,d]

[1]Research Scholar, Lovely Professional University, Punjab, India

[2]Assistant Professor, Lovely Professional University, Punjab, India

[3]Associate Professor, ADGITM, New Delhi, India

Abstract

In the last few years, a huge expansion has been seen in Internet of things (IoT) devices. With it, the need for computing technologies has emerged as a vast industry to support the execution of various latency sensitive issues of IoTs and computing intensive IoT applications and the IoT ecosystem as a whole. Fog computing, as a result, was introduced to solve latency and computation issues. However, fog computing may pose security and privacy concerns. This paper aims to recognize and discuss the various security issues related to fog computing. This paper also discusses how technologies like blockchain and Big Data can help to mitigate the various challenges of fog computing. The findings of this paper reveal that blockchain can meet the security and privacy issues and big data can help to mitigate the scalability and reliability issues of fog computing. With this study it is also revealed that blockchain and big data come with a number of challenges that need to be looked into more in the context of fog computing.

Keywords: IoT, fog computing, blockchain, Big Data, security, privacy

Introduction

Internet of things (IoT) are technological devices used for the interconnection of multiple kinds of physical gadgets with embedded software, including personal digital assistant (PDAs), cell phones, intelligent transport systems, smart appliances, and sensor systems (Sequeiros and Oliveira, 2022). Cloud computing, in contrast, is a system that offers computing resources on demand. IoT devices rely on the cloud computing to enhance their system's stability, capabilities, flexibility, fault tolerance, cost-effectiveness, novel commercial approaches, and communication capabilities (Dillon et al., 2010). Due to the exponential rise in count of IoT devices, the cloud servers must manage a tremendous volume of data, including sensitive and private data.

Consequently, it necessitates security systems to preserve confidentiality, privacy, and data integrity, and to minimize security risks. Similarly, the usage of cloud computing technology with IoT devices may provide a significant problem for latency in real-time system applications, such as multiplayer activities and emergency and zero-hour services, which may be rendered useless if unforeseen events occur. As a result, fog computing has been introduced to solve these typical disadvantages of cloud computing (Singh et al., 2019a).

Fog computing is a peer-to-peer horizontal design that spreads processing, resource control, storage, and networking/communication operations closer to consumers. Fog computing can assist in addressing several cloud and IoT related data security problems. Fog computing provides the processing and storage of time-critical heterogeneous data on-site by minimizing the volume of sensitive data stored and sent to the cloud data center. Additionally, fog can assist in mitigating latency concerns, lack of location recognition, mobility support, and bandwidth limitations. Fog deployed in close proximity to IoT sensors or devices for locally data processing and storage of IoT-generated data. Also, the enormous amount of data being produced by IoT devices can be stored on the fog servers and this data needs to be analyzed, stored, managed and secured. On the other hand, big data servers can provide better data analysis, data storage, data management, and security of enormous amount of data at a glance (Patel et al., 2012). Big data can considerably help fog computing in improving scalability, reliability, and data integrity. Blockchain (Nofer et al., 2017) on the other hand can provide security, privacy, authentication, and anonymity to the data produced thus helping in maintaining data integrity.

Despite of the above-mentioned qualities of fog computing, it has inherited various issues from cloud computing other than data management and storage, being an extension of it and being close to the IoT devices. Fortunately, the most important challenges cited in the literature survey were privacy and security concerns. This study is carried out to improve the knowledge of the fog computing global problems for future digitalization and how blockchain and big data may limit their impact.

[a]rohitxmalik7@gmail.com; [b]sakshi_nancy@yahoo.in; [c]sunnypreety83@gmail.com; [d]mr.ajaynain@gmail.com

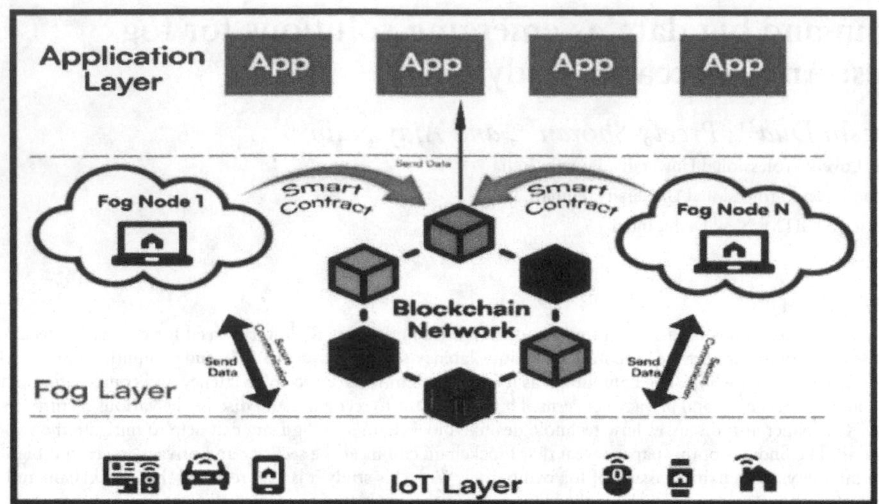

Figure 3.1 Basic architecture for blockchain-enabled fog computing

The contributions of this paper are as follows: i) Examine and assess the security concerns as well as their current solutions and related limits, ii) examine the supportive connection among blockchain and fog computing, and fog computing and big data with blockchain by studying blockchain-based solutions to address the security and privacy problems of a fog-enabled IoT. The rest of this paper is organized as follows. Section 2 discusses the SAS security and privacy challenges owing to the utilization of fog computing. Section 3 discusses how blockchain can assist in resolving the open privacy and security concerns in fog computing. Section 4 discusses how big data can help to reduce the open challenges of fog computing. Section 5 concludes this paper. Moreover, how to improve the overall scenario of current system to increase QoS, is discussed in this study.

In Figure 3.1, it is discussed that blockchain enabled fog paradigm is described in three layers. Layer one describes the IoT layer, or we can say the data creation layer. The data generated is heterogenous in nature and directly forwards the data towards fog nodes. The fog layer is an intermediate layer between the application layer and the data creation layer. The fog layer processes data locally and provides it directly to the application layer, which helps to improve the efficiency of the system. For network security purposes, the system implementation of blockchain with smart contracts will apply protocols on fog nodes for intercommunication between them, which will help to improve data integrity, authenticity, and privacy.

Security and privacy challenges of fog computing

Privacy and security issues and challenges should be addressed before designing any fog computing system. Therefore, we discuss some key privacy challenges for fog computing and try to provide their recommended solutions using big data and blockchain techniques. Here, Table 3.1, describes the various privacy and security concerns with fog computing and how these issues can be mitigated with potential recommended solutions. Various open research challenges and issues for fog computing's security and privacy concerns are mentioned in Table 3.2.

Blockchain as a solution

This section explores how blockchain may assist in mitigating the risks to privacy and security posed by open research in fog computing. Initially, blockchain was developed in 2008 from a paper on bitcoin written by Nakamoto. Blockchain is a sequence of blocks that utilize a shared ledger to record a verified operation/transaction. It has evolved as a disruptive force, a general-purpose technology supporting information transmission and transactions requiring identification and trust (Ali et al., 2021). Blockchain provides a decentralized shared database containing transaction data that are both public and unchangeable. It facilitates peer-to-peer, intermediary-free transfers of digital assets (Tariq et al., 2019).

Table 3.1 Solutions for privacy and security concerns with fog computing

Issue	*Recommended solution*
Access control	Access control (AC) ensures data security. Traditional access control is usually handled in a trusted domain. In the literature review, methods include attribute-based encryptions (ABE) AC (Roman et al., 2018), fine-grained AC (Muthanna et al., 2019), and policy-driven management framework (Guo et al., 2020).
Virtualization	Virtual machine could seize control of fog's hardware with proper security considerations. Multi-factor authentication, isolation restrictions, virtual machine monitoring, detection techniques at network and user level, customer-based permission model are proposed approaches (Li et al., 2018).
Data management	Aggregation, identification, analysis, searching, sharing, and distribution of data are all concerns of fog computing. As data integrity measures, TPM and homomorphic encryption were used. Key distribution, homogeneous, and asymmetric cryptography, and data searchability are used for key-aggregate encryptions (Khan et al., 2017).
Data and user privacy	Fog nodes at the perimeter of the fog system typically collect sensitive data produced by sensors and edge devices. Without decryption, approaches such as homomorphic encryption can provide privacy-preserving aggregation at remote endpoints (Guan et al., 2018).
Intrusion detection	Widespread implementation of intrusion detection (Meng et al., 2018) systems reduce intrusion, insider, overflow, packet inspection, and Virtual machine attacks. IDS can be deployed on the fog node system to detect intrusions by analyzing log files, ACLs, and network packets. They can also be deployed on the fog network to recognize DoS attacks, packet inspection, etc.

Table 3.2 Open research issues for fog computing's security and privacy concerns

Issues	*Open challenges*
Security and privacy	Data following from fog nodes to cloud, and these are computed at fog nodes in network. Therefore, security issue should be kept in mind. A malicious user may imitate a device and access information without proper authorization, resulting in a security breach t5 (Chiang and Zhang, 2016; Dastjerdi and Buyya, 2016).
Connectivity rules	Another important challenge is how all the connected nodes communicate with each other and how these nodes can help in reducing workload (Iorga et al., 2018)
Deployment strategy	Another big challenge is how the workload should be distributed among all fog nodes on fog network (Aazam et al., 2018).
Quality-of-service (QoS)	Fog QoS constraints includes energy constraints, traffic and bandwidth issues; these constraints affect the quality of link as QoS depends on quality of link.
Heterogenous network	The fog nodes deployed at edge comprises of heterogenous devices like IoTs, sensors, mobiles etc. Thus, heterogeneity poses a challenge in FC i.e., how various devices can communicate with one another for handling the duties (Wu and Lee, 2018)
Energy minimization	Since the fog network consists of a huge number of fog nodes in which computations are distributed. Therefore, it can be less energy efficient than other techniques (Wan et al., 2018)

Blockchain technology (Baniata and Kertesz, 2020) possesses properties like decentralization, persistence, anonymization, and auditability. The blockchain persistency feature ensures the capacity to evaluate trust, integrity and provides both consumers and producers with the means to demonstrate the authenticity of their data. Blockchain anonymization can aid in concealing the identities of producers and consumers (Khan and Chishti, 2020). Blockchain's decentralized web registries can detect and avoid harmful activity. Furthermore, blockchain undermines a number of fundamental technologies, including electronic signature, encryption, and distributed consensus methods, which can considerably improve privacy and security issues.

The blockchain's smart contracts feature can provide effective criteria for authentication, so preserving the privacy of IoTs. Additionally, it can aid in detecting infiltration activity and preventing malicious ones. Blockchain facilitates the implementation of secure device-to-device communication, device verification using identity checkers, and the guarantee of secure transactions.

Blockchain can be a viable solution for addressing the aforementioned privacy and security challenges in fog-IoT platforms due to the aforementioned characteristics. It is in an effortless, dependable, and safe method (Ferrag et al., 2019). Blockchain guarantees the confidentiality, authenticity, and data integrity sent by IoT devices that have been cryptographically validated and allotted by the legitimate sender. Blockchain facilitates the secure monitoring of IoT device interactions and provides anonymity to end-users (Safdar and Mateen, 2022).

Big data solutions

This section discusses how big data technologies can considerably help to mitigate fog computing issues in data management, scalability, storage, and reliability (Rajawat et al., 2021). Before any analysis, the data provided by fog devices need specialized management and administration to be of high quality and well-governed. Due to the constant flow of data from and to an organization, it is essential to have reproducible processes for establishing and maintaining data quality standards. A considerable amount of time may be devoted to data cleansing, anomaly removal, and format transformation. Once data is trustworthy, firms should implement a master data management programme that unifies the entire company.

Huge and diversified volumes of data are more cost-effective to store on disc, and Hadoop is an inexpensive alternative for archiving and quickly retrieving huge amounts of data. This framework is capable of storing huge quantities of data and running programmes on commodity hardware clusters. Due to the steady expansion in volume of data and kinds, it has become a crucial business technology, and its distributed system paradigm handles big data quickly. The fact that Hadoop's (IEEE Computer Society et al., n.d.) open-source architecture is free and utilizes minimum resources to store massive amounts of data is an added benefit. Semi-structured and unstructured data types do not usually fit well in relational database-based on structured data-centric traditional data warehouses. Moreover, data warehouses may be unable to meet the workload posed by collections of big data that need to be constantly updated. Therefore, Hadoop's storage system can be used as an additional advantage to store huge amounts of data and helping fog servers to decrease data congestion.

Scalability is yet another crucial aspect of systems development for accommodating workload, system cost, performance, and business requirements (Alzoubi et al., 2021; Singh et al., 2019b). Also, big data technology can help fog servers to increase scalability by providing improved storage systems.

Big data technology can also provide flexibility as it can also by providing flexible storage options.

In Table 3.3 we compared fog, big data and blockchain with various parameters like security, privacy, performance, scalability, energy efficiency and trust and how these technologies perform in them.

Future research directions

Although, sensors and IoT devices are typically inexpensive, if several Fog systems are involved in a large area, the solution involving them may be costly.

Moreover, fog servers can be setup as redundant resources, system reliability is still a major concern when several system components collapse. Given that fog servers can be customized for various applications, the dependability mechanism should be altered according to the application specifications. Performing data analytics on fog is an energy-intensive operation, thus energy efficiency must be achieved, particularly when a significant number of servers are deployed at once.

Even though blockchain has various benefits when used with fog computing, all blockchain consensus mechanisms does not support all applications of fog computing e.g., bitcoin's transaction validation reaction time latency on the blockchain makes it unsuitable for real-world applications. Finally, managing resources is also a difficult task for fog computing.

Conclusion

IoT devices are vulnerable due to a lack of hardware and software security designs and are susceptible to various security assaults. This research investigates potential privacy and security issues identified in fog enabled Internet of Things (IoT) literature. In addition, blockchain as a fresh privacy and security solution for IoT domains enabled by fog was

Table 3.3 **Used parameters and performance of different technologies**

	Parameters					
Technology	*Security*	*Privacy*	*Performance*	*Scalability*	*Energy efficient*	*Trust*
Fog computing	Less	Less	High	Low	High	Low
Blockchain	High	High	High	Moderate	Low	High
Big data	Moderate	Moderate	High	Very high	Moderate	High

presented. This article presents an outline of the unresolved privacy and security issues pertaining to the fog computing. It also explains how blockchain might reduce most of these issues. The blockchain traits that include decentralization, immutability, transparency, encryption techniques can provide a mechanism that improves the security, authenticity, data integration transmitted by IoT devices. Big data characteristics can improve scalability, flexibility and make the system more reliable.

References

Aazam, M., Zeadally, S., and Harras, K. A. (2018). Deploying Fog Computing in Industrial Internet of Things and Industry 4.0. *IEEE Transactions on Industrial Informatics*, 14(10), 4674–4682. https://doi.org/10.1109/TII.2018.2855198

Ali, O., Jaradat, A., Kulakli, A., and Abuhalimeh, A. (2021). A Comparative Study: Blockchain Technology Utilization Benefits, Challenges and Functionalities. *IEEE Access*, 9, 12730–12749. https://doi.org/10.1109/ACCESS.2021.3050241

Alzoubi, Y. I., Al-Ahmad, A., & Jaradat, A. (2021). Fog computing security and privacy issues, open challenges, and blockchain solution: An overview. *In International Journal of Electrical and Computer Engineering*, 11(6), 5081–5088. https://doi.org/10.11591/ijece.v11i6. pp 5081–5088

Baniata, H. & Kertesz, A. (2020). A Survey on Blockchain-Fog Integration Approaches. *IEEE Access*, 8, 102657–102668. https://doi.org/10.1109/ACCESS.2020.2999213

Chiang, M. & Zhang, T. (2016). Fog and IoT: An Overview of Research Opportunities. *In IEEE Internet of Things Journal*, 3(6), 854–864. https://doi.org/10.1109/JIOT.2016.2584538

Dastjerdi, A. V. & Buyya, R. (2016). CLOUD COVER Fog Computing: Helping the Internet of Things Realize Its Potential. *IEEE Computer,* 49(8), 112–116. https://doi.org/10.1109/MC.2016.245

Dillon, T., Wu, C., & Chang, E. (2010). Cloud computing: Issues and challenges. Proceedings - International Conference on Advanced Information Networking and Applications (AINA), 27–33. https://doi.org/10.1109/AINA.2010.187

Ferrag, M. A., Derdour, M., Mukherjee, M., Derhab, A., Maglaras, L., & Janicke, H. (2019). Blockchain technologies for the internet of things: Research issues and challenges. *IEEE Internet of Things Journal*, 6(2), 2188–2204. https://doi.org/10.1109/JIOT.2018.2882794

Guan, Y., Shao, J., Wei, G., & Xie, M. (2018). Data Security and Privacy in Fog Computing. *IEEE Network*, 32(5), 106–111. https://doi.org/10.1109/MNET.2018.1700250

Guo, R., Zhuang, C., Shi, H., Zhang, Y., & Zheng, D. (2020). A lightweight verifiable outsourced decryption of attribute-based encryption scheme for blockchain-enabled wireless body area network in fog computing. *International Journal of Distributed Sensor Networks*, 16(2). https://doi.org/10.1177/1550147720906796

Iorga, M., Feldman, L., Barton, R., Martin, M. J., Goren, N., & Mahmoudi, C. (2018). Fog computing conceptual model. https://doi.org/10.6028/NIST.SP.500-325 (Accessed on January 26, 2023)

Khan, N. S. & Chishti, M. A. (2020). Security Challenges in Fog and IoT, Blockchain Technology and Cell Tree Solutions: *A Review. Scalable Computing: Practice and Experience*, 21(3), 515–542. https://doi.org/10.12694/scpe.v21i3.1782

Khan, S., Parkinson, S., & Qin, Y. (2017). Fog computing security: a review of current applications and security solutions. *International Journal of Cloud Computing,* 6(1). https://doi.org/10.1186/s13677-017-0090-3

Li, J., Jin, J., Yuan, D., & Zhang, H. (2018). Virtual Fog: A Virtualization Enabled Fog Computing Framework for Internet of Things. *IEEE Internet of Things Journal*, 5(1), 121–131. https://doi.org/10.1109/JIOT.2017.2774286

Meng, W., Tischhauser, E. W., Wang, Q., Wang, Y., & Han, J. (2018). When intrusion detection meets blockchain technology: A review. *IEEE Access*, 6, 10179–10188. https://doi.org/10.1109/ACCESS.2018.2799854

Muthanna, A., Ateya, A. A., Khakimov, A., Gudkova, I., Abuarqoub, A., Samouylov, K., & Koucheryavy, A. (2019). Secure IoT network structure based on distributed 2 Fog computing, with SDN/Blockchain. *Journal of Sensor and Actuator Networks*, 8, 15. https://doi.org/10.20944/preprints201901.0305.v1

Nakamoto, S. Bitcoin: A Peer-to-Peer Electronic Cash System. www.bitcoin.org

Nofer, M., Gomber, P., Hinz, O., & Schiereck, D. (2017). Blockchain. *Business and Information Systems Engineering*, 59(3), 183–187. https://doi.org/10.1007/s12599-017-0467-3

Patel, A. B., Birla, M., & Nair, U. (2012). Addressing big data problem using Hadoop and Map Reduce. *In 2012 Nirma University International Conference on Engineering (NUiCONE)* (pp. 1–5). *IEEE.*

Rajawat, A. S., Bedi, P., Goyal, S. B., Alharbi, A. R., Aljaedi, A., Jamal, S. S., & Shukla, P. K. (2021). Fog big data analysis for IoT sensor application using fusion deep learning. *Mathematical Problems in Engineering*. https://doi.org/10.1155/2021/6876688

Roman, R., Lopez, J., & Mambo, M. (2018). Mobile edge computing, Fog et al.: A survey and analysis of security threats and challenges. *Future Generation Computer Systems*, 78, 680–698. https://doi.org/10.1016/j.future.2016.11.009

Safdar Malik, T., Siddiqui, M. N., Mateen, M., Malik, K. R., Sun, S., & Wen, J. (2022). Comparison of Blackhole and Wormhole Attacks in Cloud MANET Enabled IoT for Agricultural Field Monitoring. *Security and Communication Networks*. https://doi.org/10.1155/2022/4943218

Sequeiros, H., Oliveira, T., & Thomas, M. A. (2022). The impact of IoT smart home services on psychological well-being. *Information Systems Frontiers*, 24(3), 1009–1026.

Singh, S. P., Nayyar, A., Kumar, R., & Sharma, A. (2019a). Fog computing: from architecture to edge computing and big data processing. *Journal of Supercomputing*, 75(4), 2070–2105. https://doi.org/10.1007/s11227-018-2701-2

Singh, S. P., Nayyar, A., Kumar, R., & Sharma, A. (2019b). Fog computing: from architecture to edge computing and big data processing. *Journal of Supercomputing*, 75(4), 2070–2105. https://doi.org/10.1007/s11227-018-2701-2
Tariq, N., Asim, M., Al-Obeidat, F., Farooqi, M. Z., Baker, T., Hammoudeh, M., & Ghafir, I. (2019). The security of big data in fog-enabled iot applications including blockchain: A survey. *Sensors*, 19(8). https://doi.org/10.3390/s19081788
Wan, J., Chen, B., Wang, S., Xia, M., Li, D., & Liu, C. (2018). Fog Computing for Energy-Aware Load Balancing and Scheduling in Smart Factory. *IEEE Transactions on Industrial Informatics*, 14(10), 4548–4556. https://doi.org/10.1109/TII.2018.2818932
Wu, H. Y. & Lee, C. R. (2018). Energy Efficient Scheduling for Heterogeneous Fog Computing Architectures, 1, 555–560. https://doi.org/10.1109/COMPSAC.2018.00085

4 Analysis of CNNs built using transfer learning and data augmentation on landmark recognition datasets

Kanishk Bansal and Amar Singh

Department of Computer Applications, Lovely Professional University, Punjab, India

Abstract

Today, there exist highly complex architectures of (CNNs) is in the literature on Image processing. However, constructing such architectures from scratch can be a tedious and time-consuming task. Hence, the concept of transfer learning is used to transfer knowledge from one neural network to another. In this article, the concept of transfer learning is used to transfer the knowledge of a VGG-16 network to train a CNN on landmark recognition datasets. A positive transfer of knowledge is seen in three different landmark recognition datasets. The networks are developed on augmented and non-augmented datasets. The best-trained network had a training accuracy of 90.94% on an augmented dataset in which the network was developed using transfer learning. The minimum accuracy was seen to be the test accuracy of 69.74% on a non-augmented dataset where transfer learning was not used, and a regular three-layered CNN was developed. It was clear from the results that the use of transfer learning and data augmentation should be encouraged on landmark recognition datasets.

Keywords: Transfer learning, VGG-16 network, data augmentation, geographical landmark recognition

Introduction

Landmark recognition is an important area in the field of research. A landmark is any closed area in a pixelated digital image that can be identified distinctly by human eyes. A landmark in a digital image can be most material things, animate or inanimate. This includes animals, plants, buildings, famous monuments, etc (Bansal and Rana, 2021).

Since the definition of a landmark includes a broad range of things, landmark recognition holds an important place in research related to artificial intelligence (AI) and deep learning (DL) (Bansal and Singh, 2023). Landmark recognition refers to the identification of landmarks in a digital image when an AI model is trained on a landmarks dataset (Bansal et al., 2022).

In this article, a geographical landmarks dataset is taken and divided into three parts (Weyand and Leibe, 2015). Then AI models are trained on all three datasets such that one model is trained via VGG-16 transfer learning on each dataset that is augmented to include six-times more data, one without transfer learning on an augmented dataset and one without transfer learning on a non-augmented dataset (Ke et al., 2018).

Transfer learning's fundamental tenet is straightforward: take a model that has been trained on a sizable dataset and apply its knowledge to a smaller dataset (Lu et al., 2015). With a convolutional neural networks (CNNs), we only train the final few layers that produce predictions for object recognition and freeze the network's early convolutional layers (Zhu et al., 2011). The concept is that the convolutional layers extract universal, low-level characteristics that apply to all images, such as edges, patterns, and gradients, while the subsequent layers recognize specific characteristics within an image, such as eyes or nose, windows of a building, etc.

Section 1 of this article introduces the concept of the application of transfer learning on augmented data. Section 2 is the literature survey. Section 3 of the article describes the process of how the data was pre-processed including augmentation. Section 4 describes the process of experimentation; Section 5 describes the results and section 6 concludes the article.

Literature Review

As shown in Figure 4.1, transfer learning is important since we do not need to train complex models again and again. We simply pass down the knowledge of a complex model to train an AI model on a smaller dataset. This not only preserves the generalization of a model but also hastens the process of training a complex AI model on a smaller dataset (Pan and Yang, 2009).

Generalization of AI models is an important task in this field of research since overfitting of models leads to disastrous results. The models seem to perform well on a part of the dataset but when the same AI model is used to predict the results on other parts of the dataset, the AI models miserably fail. This is undesirable since the training of models over a generalized realm can only lead to reliable AI systems (Kumar et al., 2018).

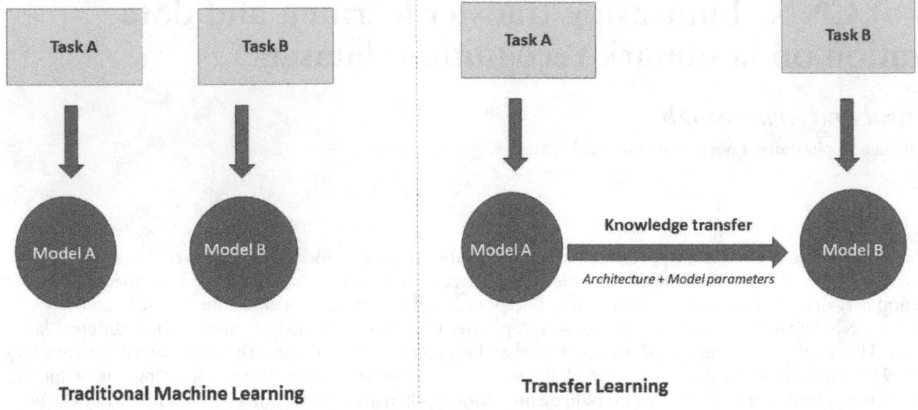

Figure 4.1 Traditional machine learning vs transfer learning

As shown in Figure 4.2, data augmentation is also very important in AI since it helps in the generalization phenomenon. Data augmentation refers to the building up of more data based on the existing dataset (Mikołajczyk and Grochowski, 2018). The existing dataset is subjected to majorly two types of transformations namely position and color augmentations. Position augmentations include scaling, cropping, flipping, padding, rotation, translation, etc. and color augmentations include brightness, contrast, saturation, hue, etc.

Dataset pre-processing

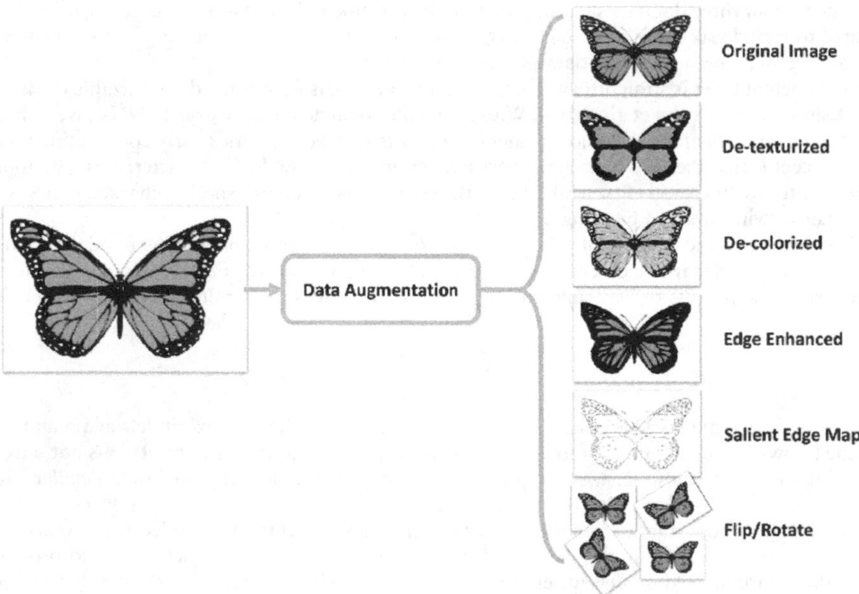

Figure 4.2 The diagrams describing how data is augmented

The Google Landmarks dataset V2 was downloaded from Kaggle (2022). This dataset originally includes more than a million images over a range of more than 100,000 classes. Out of this, around 10,000 images from 200 classes were taken. These were divided into three sets of 50 classes with 50 images in each class (Weyand, 2020).

Each image from each class out of the selected 150 classes was subjected to a size change so that each image consisted of only 64*64 pixels. Also, only the images in RGB format were taken and those in other formats including CMYK were discarded (Hernández and Blum, 2010). Since each image had 3D of RGB, the input tensor X looked like this:

$$X.shape = (7500,64,64,3) \tag{1}$$

This input tensor was further divided into training and test set of ratio 70:30. Hence the training and test set looked like this:

$$X\_train.shape = (5250,64,64,3) \tag{2}$$

$$X\_test.shape = (2250,64,64,3) \tag{3}$$

Both, the training and the test sets were further divided into three datasets manually such that each training data and their specific test datasets had 1750 and 750 images respectively. Hence there existed three training datasets of 50 classes each containing 35 images and three test datasets of 50 classes containing 15 images each.

Experimentation

The experiment was performed on Google Inc.'s publicly available platform Google Colaboratory. It had 12 GB of RAM and allowed working on 1 GB of drive space. The dataset was uploaded to Google Drive and mounted.

The libraries that were used included Keras, Google TensorFlow, SciPy, Image, etc (Abadi, 2016; Ketkar, 2017). The VGG-16 network is also imported from Tensorflow. Keras library. The VGG-16 neural network is used for transfer learning to pass the knowledge to the Augmented Google Landmarks Dataset V2.

The external machine that was used for connecting to Google Colab was an Asus VivoBook S15 with 8 GB RAM and a 2GB Nvidia Graphics Card. It had an 11th Generation Intel i7 processor with a 64-bit operating system. Since Google Colab is available with better configurations and an easy-to-use interface, the Google Colab was used instead of Asus VivoBook.

100 epochs were run for each dataset in 3 modes. The first mode was the VGG-16 transfer learning via Keras's in-built library. This mode had an augmented dataset such that each image was augmented five times with translation, scaling, flipping, rotation, and brightness. This including the original images summed up to a total of 10,500 images from 50 classes.

Mode 2 did not use transfer learning, but an augmented dataset was used. The augmented dataset was the same as in mode 2 but the model trained was a regular 3-layered CNN instead of a VGG-16 network. In mode 3, neither of the two was used. Neither an augmented dataset was used nor VGG-16 transfer learning. A regular 3-layered CNN was trained.

Results

It was found that the best performance in training the network was found in the regular 3-layered CNN applied on an augmented dataset. This accuracy was found to be 99.24%. However, this model showed a lot of over-fitting with

Table 4.1 Accuracies achieved on various datasets with transfer learning, without transfer learning, and on augmented and non-augmented datasets

	TL on Augmented dataset		*3-layered CNN on Augmented dataset*		*3 layered CNN on non-Augmented dataset*	
	Training Accuracy	*Test Accuracy*	*Training Accuracy*	*Test Accuracy*	*Training Accuracy*	*Test Accuracy*
Dataset 1	86.74	85.26	95.17	70.56	95.61	69.74
Dataset 2	90.94	90.05	99.24	78.45	98.69	74.28
Dataset 3	88.78	87.86	97.85	75.86	96.54	75.96

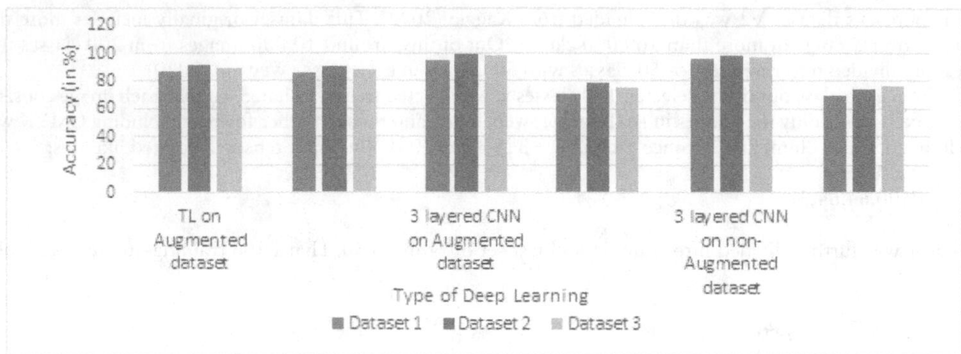

Figure 4.3 Accuracies seen by different types of DL models on three different datasets. Transfer learning is seen on augmented datasets, a regular 3-layered CNN is developed on augmented datasets and the same is developed on a non-augmented datasets.

test accuracy being just 78.45%. It should be because training a simple architecture is easy but generalizing it becomes difficult.

The best network trained was a CNN with VGG-16 transfer learning on an augmented dataset. Though the training accuracy was not the maximum, the test accuracy was maximum and per the training accuracy.

This was achieved on dataset 2 according to our experiment. In general, the maximum accuracies were seen on dataset 2. This was probably because it might have been appropriately augmented and could have a generalized view of the landmarks under consideration.

The maximum accuracy test accuracy achieved was 90.05% along with a training accuracy of 90.94%. This model was trained by a VGG-16 network transfer learning on the augmented dataset although the training accuracy was not maximum, a test accuracy equivalent to training accuracy showed that the model generalized properly.

As described in Figure 4.3, the following observations were made:

- Dataset 2 showed the maximum accuracies in most of the DL realms. Hence, it is taken to be a reliable reference source.
- The maximum training accuracy is achieved by a three-layered CNN on an augmented dataset 2. This shows that three-layered CNN is the easiest to develop.
- However, the best test accuracy is seen in the CNN developed with VGG-16 transfer learning on dataset 2. This means that the best generalization is achieved using transfer learning.
- Also, the training accuracy for the network developed by transfer learning is equivalent to the seen test accuracy, thereby meaning that that model generalizes properly over the dataset.
- It is also seen that in general, more accuracies are seen in an augmented dataset than in a non-augmented dataset. When the 3-layered CNN were compared based on Augmented and non-augmented datasets. The accuracies of the augmented dataset were more.
- Also, it is seen that the models generalize more appropriately on augmented datasets since the training and test accuracies on augmented datasets are seen to be more equivalent, in general.

Hence, we inferred that VGG-16 transfer learning is highly reliable and successful in building more appropriate and well-generalized models for machine learning. It can also be inferred that data augmentation helps in the building of better AI models.

Conclusion

As it is clear from the experiments, it is concluded that VGG-16 transfer learning is a highly preferable DL method that can be used in the realm of image processing. In each of the three datasets used, transfer learning seems to develop highly robust and generalized models for landmark recognition. The training and test accuracies seen in transfer learning mode were highly equivalent concluding that the models were neither under-fit nor over-fit. Also, it is seen, that on all three datasets used, augmentation worked towards increasing the test accuracy. The models built on augmented datasets were more generalizable than models built on non-augmented datasets.

References

Abadi, M. (2016). TensorFlow: learning functions at scale. *Proceedings of the 21st ACM SIGPLAN International Conference on Functional Programming*, 1.

Bansal, K. & Rana, A. S. (2021). Landmark Recognition Using Ensemble-Based Machine Learning Models. In *Machine Learning and Data Analytics for Predicting, Managing, and Monitoring Disease* (pp. 64–74). IGI Global.

Bansal, K. & Singh, A. (2023). Automated evolution of CNN with 3PGA for geographical landmark recognition. *Journal of Intelligent & Fuzzy Systems*, Preprint, 1–12.

Bansal, K., Singh, A., Verma, S., Kavita, Jhanjhi, N. Z., Shorfuzzaman, M., & Masud, M. (2022). Evolving CNN with Paddy Field Algorithm for Geographical Landmark Recognition. *Electronics*, *11*(7). https://doi.org/10.3390/electronics11071075

Hernández, H. & Blum, C. (2010.). Distributed graph coloring: an approach based on the calling behavior of Japanese tree frogs. *Swarm Intelligence*, 6(2), 117–150.

Kaggle, 2021. https://www.kaggle.com/competitions/landmark-recognition-2021 (Accessed on 9 September 2022)

Ke, H., Chen, D., Li, X., Tang, Y., Shah, T., & Ranjan, R. (2018). Towards Brain Big Data Classification: Epileptic EEG Identification With a Lightweight VGGNet on Global MIC. *IEEE Access*, 6, 14722–14733. https://doi.org/10.1109/ACCESS.2018.2810882

Ketkar, N. (2017). Introduction to keras. In *Deep learning with Python* (pp. 97–111). Springer.

Kumar, S., Singh, A., & Walia, S. (2018). Parallel big bang–big crunch global optimization algorithm: performance and its applications to routing in WMNs. *Wireless Personal Communications*, 100(4), 1601–1618.

Lu, J., Behbood, V., Hao, P., Zuo, H., Xue, S., & Zhang, G. (2015). Transfer learning using computational intelligence: A survey. *Knowledge-Based Systems*, 80, 14–23.

Mikołajczyk, A. & Grochowski, M. (2018). Data augmentation for improving deep learning in image classification problem. In *2018 international interdisciplinary PhD workshop (IIPhDW*. IEEE.

Pan, S. J. & Yang, Q. (2009). A survey on transfer learning. *IEEE Transactions on Knowledge and Data Engineering*, 22(10), 1345–1359.

Weyand, T. (2020). Google Landmarks Dataset v2-A Large-Scale Benchmark for Instance-Level Recognition and Retrieval. *Proceedings of the IEEE/CVF Conference on Computer Vision and Pattern Recognition*.

Weyand, T.& Leibe, B. (2015). Visual landmark recognition from internet photo collections: A large-scale evaluation. *Computer Vision and Image Understanding*, 135, 1–15.

Zhu, Y., Chen, Y., Lu, Z., Pan, S. J., Xue, G.-R., Yu, Y., & Yang, Q. (2011). Heterogeneous transfer learning for image classification. *Proceedings of the Twenty-Fifth AAAI Conference on Artificial Intelligence*.

5 A novel framework for the smart healthcare system using load balancing aspired cloud computing and IoT

Navneet Kumar Rajpoot[a], *Prabhdeep Singh*[b], *and Bhaskar Pant*[c]

Department of Computer Science & Engineering Graphic Era Deemed to be University, Dehradun, India

Abstract

Healthcare is one of the most essential aspects of life. There has also been an uptick in the number of hospitals and other medical facilities. But even so, there is always a requirement for immediate medical attention in unexpected circumstances. Healthcare, which provides a variety of services including assessment, treatment, and prevention of mental distress, physical illness, and injury, is one of the cornerstones of human existence. Because they have a such direct impact on a patient's life, healthcare applications are among the most important duties. More computer and storage resources close to medical users are needed for intelligent sensing, processing, and analysis to keep up with rising demands for medical services. Cloud computing is one of the most important technologies that may be used in the healthcare sector. The primary goal of cloud computing in healthcare is to deliver services with minimal latencies between client devices. Load balancing is a crucial part of cloud computing since it ensures that no nodes are either under or overworked. Load balancing is an effective method for enhancing quality of service metrics like resource utilization, throughput, cost, response time, performance, and energy consumption. This paper will discuss the framework of a smart health monitoring system that uses the cloud to reduce latency and bandwidth consumption. First, we provide an overview of the system as a whole. Thereafter, we talk about the difficulties of cloud-based smart health and the ant colony optimization based load-balancing scheme that must be used when a large-scale health monitoring system is put into operation.

Keywords: Cloud computing, Internet of Things, load balancing, smart health care

Introduction

Many facets of our lives have been altered by the advent of cutting-edge technologies. Traditional healthcare has evolved into 'smart healthcare' thanks to the widespread adoption of information and communication technologies in recent years. Enhanced diagnostics, more effective patient care, and life-improving tools are what we mean when we talk about 'smart healthcare'. Integrating patients and medical professionals onto a single platform for intelligent health monitoring through the analysis of day-to-day human activities is central to the concept of smart health (Li. et. al., 2020). It consists of intelligent and linked medical devices, as well as e-Health and m-Health services, electronic record management, smart home services, and more. With the use of the Internet of Things (IoT), a healthcare system facilitates two-way communication between patients and doctors, allowing for the remote interchange of data collected, processed, and monitored from patients' day-to-day activities (Singh et. al., 2021). Smart healthcare aims to assist its users by keeping them informed about their health and providing them with the tools they need to take better care of themselves. A user of a smart healthcare system can handle some medical emergencies on their own.

Cloud computing has numerous advantages in the healthcare industry, which is why more and more hospitals and clinics are using it (Babbar et. al., 2022). Cloud computing's on-demand accessibility, internet-based services, and abundant data have revolutionized the healthcare industry and rebranded it as smart health. The cloud makes it possible to use healthcare technology including EHRs, mobile apps, patient portals, IoT devices, and big data analytics (Hameed et. al., 2022). It makes it easier to make the best possible decisions by providing features such as scalability, adaptability, security, and collaboration with minimal effort. Insights gained from health analytics can be used to better the quality of healthcare records. Doctors and healthcare teams can be helped by clinical applications that allow for continuous treatment. The patient's medical data, laboratory results, and nursing notes are all available to the doctor or nurse via telemedicine.

Distributing tasks and resources across multiple servers in the cloud is called load balancing. [3] With this strategy, a system can achieve the fastest possible responses and the highest possible throughput. Separating the workload between many servers, hard drives, network interfaces, or other computing resources improves resource utilization and system response time (Ahad et. al., 2019).

Load balancing is a method of dispersing a system's burden over multiple servers to guarantee the reliability of the system, boost its performance, and safeguard it against breakdowns. If a server is overburdened with requests from

[a]shubham151515@gmail.com; [b]ssingh.prabhdeep@gmail.com; [c]bhaskar.pant@geu.ac.in

patients but surrounding servers are idle or have fewer requests, the overloaded server's workload will be shared by those with fewer patients' requests. Thus, by dividing up the job in this manner, a system administrator can reduce the wasteful expenditure of energy and materials. Estimation of total load, scalability of servers, throughput, the performance of the system, interaction between servers, quantity of work to be transferred, and best node selection are all important considerations here. Static and dynamic load balancing, as well as periodic and ad hoc decentralized and centralized load balancing, are just some of the options available (Garg et. al., 2021). Unlike the dynamic method, which is dependent on the present state of the network, the load in the static algorithm is known in advance and does not affect the performance of the server. It typically provides superior performance to static algorithms.

In the first section, we discussed the idea of a cloud-based smart healthcare monitoring system. In the second section, we discussed the function of the cloud in smart healthcare, followed by the function of load balancing approaches. In the third section, we discussed earlier relevant research before presenting a framework for smart health using IoT and the cloud. Then in the third section, an ant colony optimization (ACO) approach is described for lowering latency and improving system performance. In the fourth section, we'll discuss the potential applications and future reach of a smart healthcare system.

Related Work

In this section, the challenges of utilizing cloud computing in the healthcare industry, as well as the solutions have been proposed.

Several studies are being conducted on cloud computing as an IT business solution to enhance healthcare services.

(Li. et al., 2020) present a cloud-based system for automatically collecting vital patient signs through a network of sensors coupled with electronic medical devices, with data then being sent to the cloud for storage, real-time processing, and distribution. (Singh et. al., 2021), a ubiquitous cloud initiative, use cloud computing and wireless technologies to provide doctors with on-the-go access to patient health records. (Babbar et al., 2022) presented a three-tiered mobility-enabled IoT infrastructure with sensor nodes, fog nodes for parametric health control, and cloud servers to address aberrant health situations. (Hameed et al., 2022), developed a fog-friendly home healthcare system. This method paves the way for doctors to treat patients in the comfort of their own homes while keeping tabs on their well-being. Ahad et al., 2019 proposed a three-tier system design for remote pain monitoring. Digital signal processing is employed by the smoke node to identify discomfort in this design. The proposed method achieved significantly lower latency than cloud-based implementations. However, the proposed approach does not scale well as the number of patients rises. This occurs because all medical records are processed by a single fog node. (Angurala et al., 2020) also proposed a method for conserving energy. Based on their available processing time and energy usage, tasks are distributed among fog nodes. Simulation results showed that the proposed method significantly reduced application delay, network utilization, and energy consumption. (Singh et. al., 2022) have introduced a LAB scheme for fog computing-based systems to speed up the transfer of IoT data. The LAB scheme offers a workaround by linking the user's device with the most suitable BS for load balancing purposes. (Garg et. al., 2020) a cloud-based emergency medical system prototype was placed into use by the Greek National Health Service. It connects the emergency system to a PHR, so doctors can obtain patient information quickly and efficiently at a cheap cost, no matter where they are.

Proposed Novel Framework for the Smart Healthcare System Using Load Balancing Aspired Cloud Computing and IoT.

To reduce latency and network usage and achieve load balancing with the use of an ACO-based load balancer in cloud computing, a framework for a smart healthcare monitoring system using cloud computing was built in this study. Deploying a smart health monitoring system significantly reduces latency and improves system performance by distributing the load among all the servers in an even manner. All the IoT-based medical devices that are attached to the patients' bodies as well as hospital facilities are connected to cloud servers in this framework for processing and decision-making. The components of the proposed framework are explained below.

Data collection

All wearables and medical sensors attached to patients are part of the data-gathering layer of the proposed health monitoring system that works in tandem with the IoT device network. Measurements of core body temperature, cardiac output, and pulse rate are recorded by the sensors.

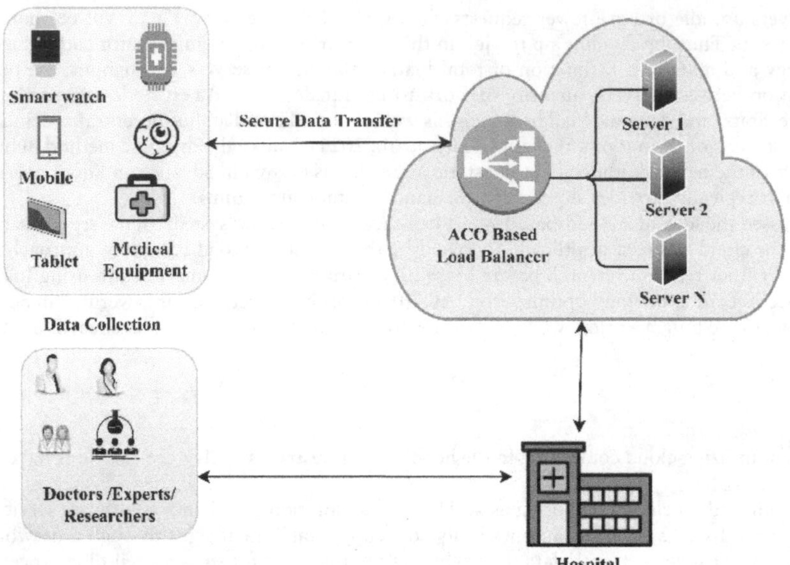

Figure 5.1 Novel framework for the smart healthcare system using load balancing aspired cloud computing and IoT [7].

Cloud server

The cloud enables healthcare technologies which include digital health records, smartphone applications, patient platforms, IoT connected devices, and big data analysis. It facilitates effortless scalability and adaptability, in addition to collaboration and security, which in turn leads to better final decisions.

The healthcare industry can benefit from cloud computing because it simplifies data management and paves the way for more effective ERR management, both of which contribute to the delivery of better care. [2] The clients send requests to the cloud server for data communication and storage, and the server then processes and returns the requests to the clients.

Aco-based load balancer

The ACO algorithm is a paradigm for creating metaheuristic algorithms for optimization problems that were first proposed by Marco Dorigo, 1992. It takes its cues from the foraging behavior of ant colonies. As a method for finding approximations to difficult optimization issues, ACO excels at solving discrete optimization problems and can be easily generalized to continuous optimization problems. Several algorithms that mimic the foraging behavior of ant colonies have recently been used to tackle challenging cases of discrete optimization. [7] Indeed, the ACO algorithm is the most well-known and frequently adopted computational model inspired by ACO. ACO focuses on trying to create algorithms that mimic ants' behavior in one respect their knack for discovering the shortest routes between two points. To manage traffic and distribute load fairly throughout a network, ACO is implemented at the time of data routing. Based on the state of the network, two ants choose different routes for their packets to go. Based on the available bandwidth, energy, mobility, and distance of the network, a decision variable is created to choose an ant to transport packets [8]. For the first ant, the best path is the one with the highest pheromone concentration, but the opposite is true for the second ant.

A pheromone is a substance left by ants when they travel from one location to another. Because ants can smell pheromones and gravitate toward areas with higher concentrations of the chemical, this helps other ants on the team find their way [9]. The program relies on a probabilistic method of selecting nodes and changing the pheromone along the pathways at each one.

Health service providers

The ability of a smart healthcare system to facilitate easy, scalable, and adaptable collaboration benefits the quality of healthcare practitioners' final decisions. [6] Doctors and healthcare teams can be helped by clinical applications that allow for continuous treatment. Doctors and nurses can view lab results for their patients.

Conclusion

Cloud computing makes it easier for numerous healthcare organizations involved in a treatment process to share information. Since load balancing between cloud servers can potentially lessen the delay in providing services to patients. A framework for a smart and intelligent healthcare monitoring system employing cloud computing was developed in this study to reduce latency and network use as well as achieve load balancing with the use of an ant colony optimization -based load balancer. The new study is remarkable because it incorporates load balancing to reduce latency and maximize system performance. This work may enhance several facets of health care by making use of the cloud and various of Internet of Things technologies.

Successful treatment depends on a smart healthcare system that can properly forecast sickness and suggest the optimal treatment. The development of Internet of Things devices has increased the independence of health monitoring. Therefore, the technology has a promising future in providing independent health monitoring and reducing the workload of on-site medical professionals. The quick response capabilities of this framework may be advantageous to patients who are facing a life-or-death crisis. This framework may also incorporate consultation sessions. A patient may have a consultation with the healthcare provider of their choosing via teleconsultation or video conference. One area where the proposed work still needs development is the framework for enabling security, privacy, and trust protocols for healthcare data.

References

Ahad, A., Tahir, M., & Yau, K. L. A., 2019. 5G-based smart healthcare network: architecture, taxonomy, challenges and future research directions. *IEEE Access*, 7, 100747–100762.

Angurala, M., Bala, M., Bamber, S. S., Kaur, R., & Singh, P. (2020). An internet of things assisted drone based approach to reduce rapid spread of COVID-19. *Journal of Safety Science and Resilience*, 1(1), 31–35.

Babbar, H., Rani, S., &AlQahtani, S. A. (2022). Intelligent Edge Load Migration in SDN-IIoT for Smart Healthcare. *IEEE Transactions on Industrial Informatics*, 18(11), 8058–8064.

Garg, N., Wazid, M., Das, A. K., Singh, D. P., Rodrigues, J. J., & Park, Y. (2020). BAKMP-IoMT: Design of blockchain enabled authenticated key management protocol for internet of medical things deployment. *IEEE Access*, 8, 95956–95977.

Garg, N., Obaidat, M. S., Wazid, M., Das, A. K., & Singh, D. P. (2021). SPCS-IoTEH: Secure Privacy-Preserving Communication Scheme for IoT-Enabled e-Health Applications. In ICC 2021-IEEE International Conference on Communications (pp. 1–6). IEEE

Hameed Abdulkareem, K., Awad Mutlag, A., Musa Dinar, A., Frnda, J., Abed Mohammed, M., Hasan Zayr, F., Lakhan, A., Kadry, S., Ali Khattak, H., & Nedoma, J. (2022). Smart Healthcare System for Severity Prediction and Critical Tasks Management of COVID-19 Patients in IoT-Fog Computing Environments. *Computational Intelligence and Neuroscience*. doi: 10.1155/2022/5012962

Li, J., Cai, J., Khan, F., Rehman, A. U., Balasubramaniam, V., Sun, J., & Venu, P. (2020). A secured framework for SDN-based edge computing in IoT-enabled healthcare system. *IEEE Access*, 8, 135479–135490.

Singh, A. & Chatterjee, K. (2021). Securing smart healthcare system with edge computing. *Computers & Security*, 108, 102353.

Singh, P. D., Dhiman, G., $ Sharma, R. (2022). Internet of things for sustaining a smart and secure healthcare system. *Sustainable Computing: Informatics and Systems*, 33, 100622.

6 Convolutional autoencoders-based model for De-novo breast anticancer drug development

Muzaffar Ahmad Sofi[1,a], *Dhanpratap Singh*[1,b], *and Tawseef Ahmed Teli*[2,c]

[1]Lovely Professional University, Punjab, India

[2]Govt Degree College Anantnag, Jammu & Kashmir, India

Abstract

The struggle against disease has been a constant throughout the history of all living things, making the development of treatments more crucial. In this work, the focus is laid on the application of convolutional-based conditional variational autoencoders for de-novo breast anti-cancer drug design with desired properties. Convolutional neural networks (CNNs) are used to fine-tune models by generating molecules with known bioactivities. We show how to efficiently constrain encoder and decoder networks on GI50 (concentration causing 50% cell growth inhibition) and partition coefficient (log P, measures lipophilicity) of a drug molecule. This model can also be used in drug search engines to find biosimilar molecules with target properties. The results demonstrate that adding convolution layers enhance the performance because chemical compounds have cyclic and translation-invariant substructures, which are well captured by CNNs.

Keywords: Cancer, convolutional neural networks, drug discovery, De-novo, machine learning, variational autoencoder

Introduction

Machine learning (ML) techniques encompass applications in varied fields of cryptography and networks (Masoodi et al., 2021; Teli et al., 2021), navigation (Teli et al., 2021), and most importantly predictive analysis and healthcare. Deep learning (DL) techniques (Sidiq et al., 2022) that have applications in secure healthcare (Teli et al., 2020; 2021; 2022) have attained tremendous attention in the recent times. Apart from the prediction of diseases (Shafi, et al., 2022), ML and DL approaches are suitable for drug design. Drug development is a complex process that is time-consuming and expensive (Thomas et al., 2016; Kiriiri et al., 2020). Despite the significant advancements that have been made in drug discovery research, productivity is very low. This is particularly the case in oncology, which only has a 5.1% approval rate following phase-I of its study as indicated by Thomas et al. (2016). Because of high failure rates, drug development research becomes quite expensive and time-consuming. On the other hand, the top cause of death in the 21st century is cancer, and it is estimated that cancer has got more than 200 different types. According to a 2015 WHO report, in more than 90 countries, cancer accounts for the second most reason for death among young people as per the study conducted by Cai, et al. (2021). Researchers are reducing high failure rates and saving a lot of time by repurposing already approved drugs for other similar diseases, a process known as drug repurposing (Yi et al., 2021). Drug repurposing not only saves a ton of time, but these drugs are also safer, resulting in low failure rates. The introduction of artificial intelligence (AI) techniques, such as DL and reinforcement learning, has vastly improved the overall drug development process, particularly the development of cancer drugs. Many biotech companies have made substantial investments in AI due to its promise of rapid and cost-effective drug development. Many researchers are nowadays focusing on using ML techniques for drug target interaction prediction, to find new therapeutic use, property prediction, etc. Given the vastness of chemical space (estimated size is of order 10^{23} – 10^{60}), conventional search methods become either too expensive or impractical for its thorough exploration. ML and DL approaches are increasingly being utilized to explore this huge chemical space. There have been some recent attempts to employ ML models, such as recurrent neural networks (RNNs), variational autoencoders (VAEs), conditional (C-VAEs), generative adversarial neural networks (GANs), etc., to generate completely novel drugs. However, the problem is that the generated drugs have very small chemical validity or, even if they do, some of the properties of these generated molecules are not adequate for testing. Therefore, the primary objective of this study is to generate chemically valid molecules with the required properties.

The organization of the paper is given as follows. The key related literature is presented in the second section. Some insights into VAE and the proposed model are described in sections three and four, respectively. Following that, we present numerical experiments and discuss the results. Finally, we summarize the paper and highlight possible future work.

[a]muzaffarsofi.g@gmail.com; [b]dhanpratap.25706@lpu.co.in; [c]mtawseef805@gmail.com

Related Work

Several important ML models have been utilized for developing novel drug compounds. Gupta et al. (2018) investigated an RNN-based generative model that can build libraries of valid SMILES strings. Transfer learning was utilized to fine-tune models by generating molecules with known bioactivities. Gómez-Bombarelli et al. (2018) presented an RNN-based autoencoder architecture that can design new molecules, and optimize and predict their properties from continuous latent space. Blaschke et al. (2018) have presented many ways to map molecules to continuous representations, in particular, they showed that the VAE, originally proposed by Kingma et al. (2013), is quite good at generating valid molecules since this model allows us to force the encoder to learn a distribution over latent space, which in turn enables the generation of new compounds. Their results show that the model generated 77.4% valid molecules when the model followed a Gaussian distribution. Kadurin et al. (2017) used a 7-layer adversarial autoencoder (AAE) to generate novel compounds from 166-bit Molecular ACCess System (MACCS) chemical fingerprints as inputs. They demonstrate that the generated compounds have anti-cancer properties. In addition to, researchers used generated compounds as a query in PubChem to search for similar compounds among 72 million compounds. The study by Lim et al. (2018) showed how to control molecular synthesis using the conditional variational autoencoder (CVAE) model. CVAE is essentially an extended version of VAE in which we can condition the encoder and decoder to learn and generate new molecular structures similar to reference but with modified properties. They have demonstrated that we can create molecules with the required desired attributes by imposing them in latent space.

The chemical validity of these models remains a significant challenge even though they allow us to develop novel molecules having user-defined properties. The proposed model resembles the model presented by Lim et al. (2018), but we choose to develop CVAE using convolutional layers rather than linear ones because convolutional can consider the spatial and structural characteristics of input molecules. We show how to efficiently constrain encoder and decoder networks on GI50 (concentration causing 50% cell growth inhibition) and partition coefficient (log P, measures lipophilicity) of a drug molecule.

Variational Autoencoder

The VAE is a type of ML model that consists of two parameterized neural networks: an encoder and a decoder. The encoder compresses the input datapoint x to a latent representation z. Mathematically, we can define an encoder as a network which provides parameters (θ) to a Gaussian distribution density, denoted as

$$q_\theta(z|x)$$

as in the study presented by Kingma et al. (2013). The work of the decoder is to restructure the inputs from a latent vector (z), obtained by sampling the Gaussian probability distribution parameterized by the outputs of the encoder. Mathematically, we can define a decoder as a generative network that generates parameters (φ) for a likelihood distribution.

$$p_\varphi(x|z)$$

CVAE incorporates condition (y) into the encoder and decoder networks. The encoder and decoder are represented as

$$q_\theta(z|x,y),\ p_\varphi(x|z,y)$$

respectively. From an application standpoint, the CVAE decoder generates a new sample from the latent representation z and the class embedding vector y, with the class embedding vector (y) acting as a knob to control the generation. We use this class embedding vector (y) to generate molecules with target properties (for example drug molecules with anticancer activities). The CVAE is trained to minimize the following objective:

$$-\mathbb{E}_{z\sim q_\theta(z|x,y)}[\log p_\phi(x|z,y)] + \mathrm{D}_{\mathrm{KL}}\left[q_\theta(z|x,y)\,\|\,p(z\mid y)\right] \tag{1}$$

Minimizing the first part of the objective ensures that reconstruction loss is minimized. The second part is the Kullback-Leibler divergence between the prior and encoder distribution, which when optimized guarantees that the encoder distribution is similar to the prior Gaussian distribution. This term is often viewed as a regularize to avoid over-fitting.

Methodology and Model Specification

- **Dataset:** To conduct experiments, we used NCI-60 growth inhibition data. We used GI50 and calculated log P by RDKit library as indicators of biological sensitivity. The SMILES strings of molecules were converted to one-hot

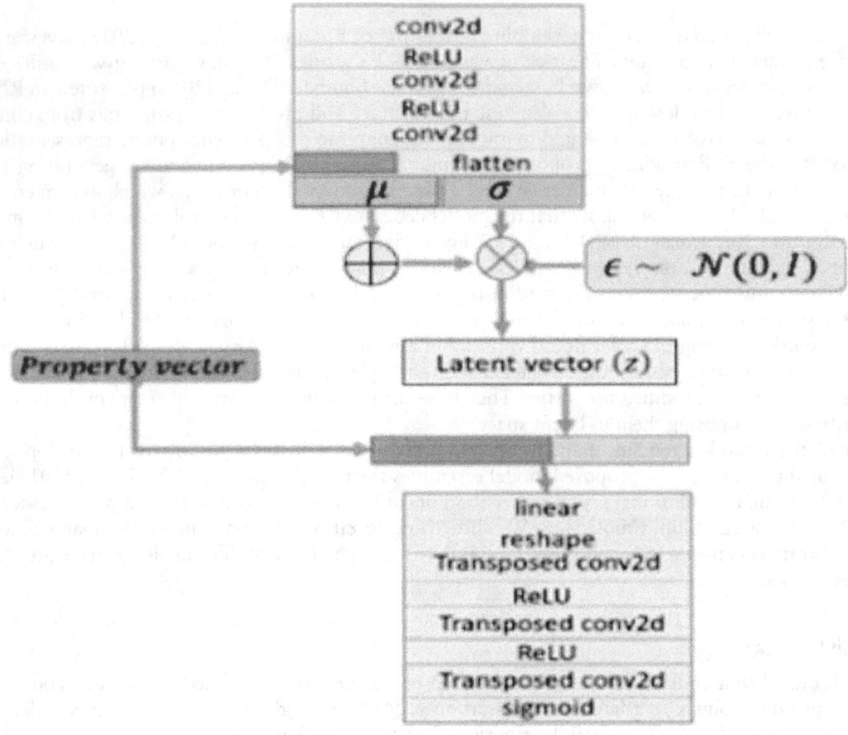

Figure 6.1 CVAE model

encoding matrices of size **60 × 55**, where 55 is the length of unique characters in the SMILES strings dataset and 60 is the maximum allowed molecule string length (shorter strings are padded with 'E'), as presented by Lim, et al. (2018).

- **Model specification:** The proposed model consists of an encoder-decoder architecture. To capture the structural and spatial features, we use three 2D convolutional layers with different filter sizes: 16, 32, and 64. The output of the third convolution layer is flattened and then concatenated with the class embedding vector of dimensions seventeen (16 are for one hot encoding of GI50 and one for log P). The concatenated vector is input into two linear layers, which are the parameters (mean and log variance vectors) of the encoder probability distribution. Following that, we use reparameterization (since it allows gradients to flow in a backward step during training) to sample latent vectors from the distribution parameterized by the encoder outputs.

The decoder consists of a linear layer with an input vector (concatenated latent vector (size = 250) with class embedding vector) followed by three 2D transposed convolutional layers as shown in Figure 6.1. We have also a varied decoder network, where we use stack-GRU and linear layer instead of transposed 2D convolutions block.

The model was trained by optimizing the CVAE objective over the filtered dataset (i.e., the dataset that had SMILES strings that were less than or equal to 60) and the Adam optimizer configured with a rate of 0.00023 for learning for 30 epochs. We observed that using dropout (=0.25) after convolutional layers in the encoder improves model performance.

Experiment and Results

- **Generation:** Some known anti-cancer drugs were fed to an encoder to generate a latent distribution, from which we sampled latent vectors with some perturbations, as shown below:

$$z_{samp} = \alpha * \epsilon + (1-\alpha)\mu, \qquad \epsilon \sim \mathcal{N}(0, I), \qquad \alpha \in [0,1]$$

Then the mean (μ) was obtained from the known FDA-approved breast anti-cancer drug. α was manually varied (0.035, 0.065, 0.085) to perturb the latent representation of known drugs. In simple terms α, controls the perturbation or, in turn, controls the generation. When the value of α is close to zero, the decoder generates a SMILES string that resembles the SMILES string of a reference drug. We used anastrozole, a well-known medicine to treat breast cancer, typically in postmenopausal women, to generate a new anti-cancer drug as shown in Figure 6.2. This served as the encoder's input for generating the latent distribution parameters. In the formula above, the mean (μ) parameter from the encoder output was used. The ϵ was drawn from the standard Gaussian distribution. The latent vector is estimated as a weighted sum of the encoder output epsilon and mean, with weights α and $(1 - \alpha)$, respectively. The latent vector, along with the desired property vector, was given into the decoder to generate the SMILES strings. Figure 6.3, shows some of the samples that were generated for $\alpha = 0.35$. We can infer from the results that generated molecules are modifications of the anastrozole drug molecule. In Table 6.1, we summarized the results of the experiments where we varied the value of α and generated the average Tanimoto similarity forthe target molecule and generated ones. We have also calculated the mean square loss between target properties and the properties of generated molecules. From the results, we can see that the convolutional-based encoder-decoder model generates more valid molecules, and they are slightly less similar to the reference molecule as compared to the convolutional-stack GRU-based model. However, we can see that the average mean square error between target properties and properties of generated molecules is small in the convolutional-stack GRU-based model.

Bio and chemo similar search: We used the novel generated molecules as a query in the PubChem database to find a bio and chemo similar molecules. To find molecules with the desired properties from public databases, we used the above procedure to find novel molecules by generation process. For instance, we generate SMILES strings corresponding to

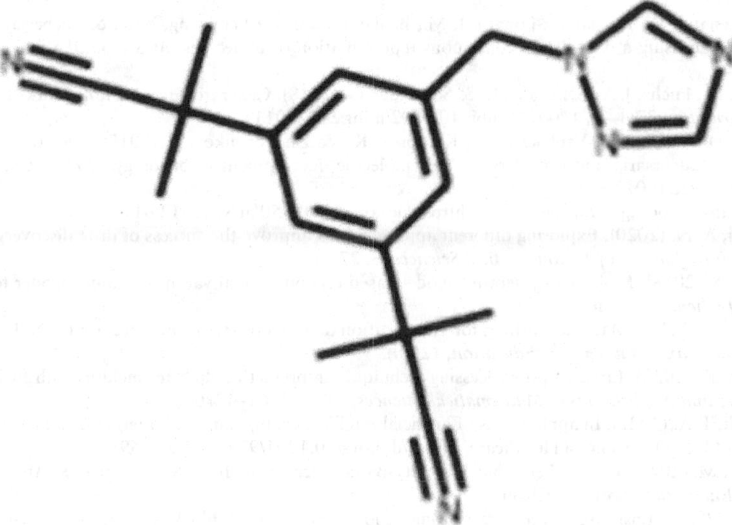

Figure 6.2 Anastrozole

Table 6.1 Performance of convolutional-based condition variational autoencoder for generation of novel anti-cancer drug molecules

Model	$1 - \alpha$	*Number of validly generated molecules (per 1000 trails)*	*The novelty of valid molecules (%)*	*Average Tan moto similarity with target*	*Average Mean-square-error Range concerning target properties*
	0.045	107	100	0.34	33.1%
Conv-based	0.065	56	100	0.51	21%
	0.085	24	100	0.69	11.1%
Conv-stacked GRU	0.045	79	100	0.42	27.3%
	0.065	43	100	0.59	19.2
	0.085	17	100	0.81	9.1%

the FDA-approved Tamoxifen anti-cancer drug at $\alpha = 0.35$. The generated smiles were used as a query to search for biosimilar drugs from public databases. We observe that these queries have successfully been able to identify anti-cancer drugs, some of which are FDA-approved treatments for breast cancer, prostate cancer, anti-allergic, and liver-related diseases. Toremifene, (E)-4-hydroxytamoxifen, phenyltoloxamine, clomifene, doxepin, diphenhydramine, phenoxybenzamine, methantheline, and N,N-diethyl-2-(2-methyl-5-prop-1-en-2-ylcyclohex-2-en-1-yl) oxyethanamine are some of the examples that were found from queries, obtained by perturbation of tamoxifen. For each query, we obtained at least nine compounds with similarity ≥ 0.73. Thus, the results are quite promising, which suggests the model is a nice choice to serve as a drug search engine with targeted properties.

Conclusion

In this paper, we demonstrated the application of convolutional-based conditional variational autoencoders for de novo breast anti-cancer drug design with desired properties. The results signify that adding convolution layers enhances performance because chemical compounds have cyclic and translation-invariant substructures, which are well captured by CNNs. We show how to search public drug databases using novel generated molecules with desired properties. These approaches can quickly provide libraries of molecules for drug repurposing. Drug search engines can also use this model to find biosimilar molecules with target properties. This approach can therefore be used to generate effective anti-cancer drugs having all the required and desired properties.

References

Cai, Z. & Liu, Q. (2021). Understanding the global cancer statistics 2018: implications for cancer control. *Science China Life Sciences*, 64, 1017–1020.

Gómez-Bombarelli, R, Wei, J. N., Duvenaud, D., Hernández-Lobato, J. M., Benjamín Sánchez-Lengeling, B. S., & Sheberla, D. et al. (2018). Automatic chemical design using a data-driven continuous representation of molecules. *ACS Central Science*, 4, 2 268–276.

Gupta, A., Müller, A. T., Huisman, B. J. H., Fuchs, J. A., Schneider, P., & Schneider, G. (2018). Generative recurrent networks for De novo drug design. *Molecular Informatics*. 37(1–2), 1700111. doi: 10.1002/minf.201700111.

Kadurin, A., Aliper, A., Kazennov, A., Mamoshina, P., Vanhaelen, Q., Khrabrov, K., & Zhavoronkov, A. (2017). The cornucopia of meaningful leads: Applying deep adversarial autoencoders for new molecule development in oncology. *Oncotarget*, 8(7), 10883–10890. doi:10.18632/oncotarget.14073

Kingma, D. P. & Welling, M. (2014). Auto-encoding variational bayes. https://doi.org/10.48550/arXiv.1312.6114

Kiriiri, G. K., Njogu, P. M., & Mwangi, A. N. (2020). Exploring different approaches to improve the success of drug discovery and development projects: a review. *Future Journal of Pharmaceutical Sciences,* 6, 27.

Lim, J., Ryu, S., Kim, J. W., & Kim, W. Y. (2018). Molecular generative model based on conditional variational autoencoder for de novo molecular design. *Journal of Cheminformatics*, 10, 31.

Masoodi, F., Bamhdi, A. M., & Teli, T. A. (2021). Machine learning for classification analysis of intrusion detection on NSL-KDD Dataset. *Turkish Journal of Computer and Mathematics Education*, 12(10).

Shafi, O., Sidiq, J. S., Ahmed Teli, T., &, K. (2022). Effect of pre-processing techniques in predicting diabetes mellitus with focus on artificial neural network. *Advances and Applications in Mathematical Sciences*, 21(8), 4761–4770.

Sidiq, S. J., Shafi, O, Zaman, M., & Teli, T. A. (2022). In applications of artificial intelligence, big data and internet of things in sustainable development. Big data and Deep Learning in Healthcare. https://doi.org/10.1201/9781003245469

Teli, T. A., Masoodi, F. S., & Bahmdi, A. M. (2021). HIBE: Hierarchical Identity-Based Encryption. In K. A. B. Ahmad, K. Ahmad, & U. N. Dulhare, (Eds). *Functional Encryption*. Springer, Cham.

Teli, T. A., Yousuf, R., & Khan, D. A. (2022). Ensuring secure data sharing in iot domains using blockchain. In M. M. Ghonge, S. Pramanik, R. Mangrulkar, & D.N. Le). *Cyber Security and Digital Forensics*. https://doi.org/10.1002/9781119795667.ch9

Teli, T. A. & Masoodi, F. (2021). Blockchain in healthcare: challenges and opportunities. *2nd International Conference on IoT Based Control Networks and Intelligent Systems (ICICNIS 2021).* https://ssrn.com/abstract=3882744

Teli, T. A., Masoodi, F., & Yousuf, R. (2020). Security concerns and privacy preservation in blockchain based iot systems: opportunities and challenges. *International Conference on IoT based Control Networks and Intelligent Systems (ICICNIS 2020).* https://ssrn.com/abstract=3769572

Teli, T. A. & Wani, M. A. (2021). A fuzzy based local minima avoidance path planning in autonomous robots. *International Journal of Information Technology (Singapore),* 13(1), 33–40. https://doi.org/10.1007/s41870-020-00547-0

Thomas, B., Olivecrona, M., Engkvist, O., Bajorath, J., & Chen, H. (2018). Application of generative autoencoder in de novo molecular design. *Molecular Informatics,* 37, 1–2.

Thomas, D. W., Burns, J., Audette, J., Carrol, A., Dow-Hygelund, C., & Hay, M. (2016). Clinical development success rates 2006–2015. Amplion, San Diego.

Yi, H. C., You, Z. H., Wang, L., Su, X. R., Zhou, XX., & Jiang, T. H. (2021). In silico drug repositioning using deep learning and comprehensive similarity measures. *BMC Bioinformatics*, 22 (3), 293.

7 Automation using artificial intelligence and machine learning: A study on banking and healthcare

Ravi Kiran Mallidi[1,a], *Manmohan Sharma*[1,b], *Sreenivas Rao Vangala*[2,c], *and Yogeswara Prasad Paladugu*[3,d]

[1]School of Computer Applications, Lovely Professional University, Punjab, India

[2]Senior Enterprise Architect, Wipro Ltd, Hyderabad, India

[3]Associate Director, Cognizent Technologies Ltd, Hyderabad, India

Abstract

Artificial intelligence (AI), machine learning (ML), and deep learning (DL) are widely used programming frameworks in developing digital transformation applications. AI-enabled strategies are more customer-centric and have the well-defined business process flows in new banking systems and healthcare. AI/ML-based baking uses cases are fraud detection, risk management, regularity compliance, and advisory services. The healthcare system's use cases are robotic surgeries, virtual nursing assistance during covid times, precision medicine, and patient care management. The paper presents various technical architectures defined using AI/ML in baking and healthcare applications. After data collection, design the application using predictive modelling, evaluating, enhancing, and deploying the data. Various tools and technologies used in AI/ML process are depicted in real-time case studies. Review the case studies with AI/ML capabilities used in banking and healthcare systems.

Keywords: Artificial intelligence, banking, finance, fraud detection, healthcare, machine learning

Introduction

Most people use the terms artificial intelligence (AI), machine learning (ML), and deep learning (DL) in the digital world. Nowadays, digital applications use AI and ML technologies to change business capabilities with applications like robots, self-driving cars, healthcare management, automated banking systems, and chatbots. AI and ML are closely related and connected. AI mimics human intelligence, which derives from two words, artificial and intelligence, which is human-made thinking power. ML is a subset of AI and deals with learning computers without providing any instruction from humans. ML algorithms are divided into three teaching types: supervised learning, reinforcement learning, and unsupervised learning. ML reads the data from different systems and processes the data to produce accurate predictions/ results. ML algorithms mainly concentrate on patterns in data with accuracy. AI has a broad scope, whereas ML learning has a limited area. Siri, chatbots, and online gaming are examples of AI applications, whereas recommender systems, search algorithms, and auto friend tagging suggestions in social media platforms are examples of ML. DL is part of ML to execute better patterns when unstructured data sets. However, DL overkills if the data is small. DL frameworks like TensorFlow, Torch, and Deep learning 4j are used for analyzing data. AI and ML technologies are reshaping many business processes in the field of banking, telecommunication, and healthcare. Most of the data in organizations are siloes and locked in databases. Data management is the biggest challenge for AI-based analytics. To overcome data challenges, defined AI/ML lifecycle activities appropriately orchestrate the data sets. Before build any AI/ML model requires data sets and historic data for prediction. They are addressing critical challenges by populating data warehouses using streaming engines, defining pipelines on big data, and enriching the data. The Figure 7.1 shows the high-level activities involve in the ML lifecycle.

This paper talks about various business scenarios implemented in real-time applications in banking and healthcare systems using AI/ML. AI/ML is essential for intelligent and automated applications to analyze data from the Internet of Things (IoT), cybersecurity, social media, and healthcare. Sarker (2021) presented ML algorithms to enhance application capabilities and highlighted academic and industry professionals' challenges and real-world situations. Lee and Shin (2020) described categories of ML in enterprise systems, especially in finance systems. Explained the ML algorithm's trade-off between accuracy and interpretability. Software case studies were presented using event based stream ing platforms in payments and trading systems by Vangala et al. (2022). Many banking applications use AI/ML to support customer experience process enhancement, fraud detection, regulatory compliance, and suspected transactions. Hospitals use AI/ML in applications like robotic surgeries, virtual nursing assistance during covid times, precision medicine, and patient care management. For accurate prediction, trained machine learning models use extensive data feeds

[a]ravikiran.mallidi@gmail.com; [b]manmohan.sharma71@gmail.com; [c]sreenivangala@gmail.com; [d]yogeswaraprasad@gmail.com

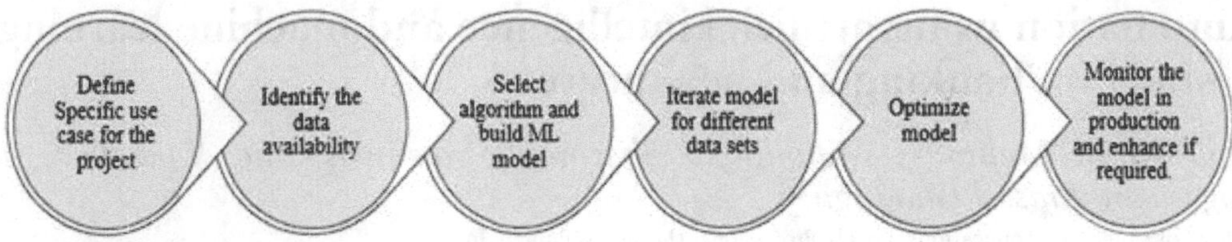

Figure 7.1 High-level lifecycle activities for ML

Table 7.1 Advantages and disadvantages of using AI/ML

	Advantages	*Disadvantages*
Banking	• Enhance banking services and end-user experience • Scam/fraud recognition • Data analysis, prediction, and reporting	• High investment • Bad judgments due to lack of data/improper data
Healthcare	• Real-time data • Precise prediction • Detecting early risk zones • Patient monitoring and streaming activities • Compare previous records and provide an accurate prediction • Surgery assistance	• Requires human surveillance • Lack of human interaction • Defective diagnosis

as the input. AI algorithms behave differently from system to system based on the data provided. Algorithms are literal, and the algorithm learns exclusively from the input data supplied and programmed to do, and DL algorithms predict with extreme precision. Cardiovascular, dermatology, gastroenterology, oncology, pathology, and radiology departments use AI-based applications. The challenge of adopting AI in healthcare is to meet regulatory requirements. Table 7.1 describes the advantages and disadvantages of using AI in the banking and healthcare system.

This paper is organized as follows: Section 2 describes literature review, section 3 describes AI/ML-based case studies in banking, Section 4 describes AI/ML-based case studies in health care, and section 4 concludes the paper.

Literature Review

The adoption of AI and ML plays a crucial role in banks after the covid pandemic to strengthen the market and increase efficiency and revenue growth by Antal-Vaida (2020). AI-based chatbots are popular in the banking industry and still require human inputs for the machine to learn further; challenges are noted in bias, discrimination, and the use of big data by Lui and Lamb (2018). Data is the most critical factor for the success of AI-based solutions. Zohuri and Rahmani (2019) proposed big data solutions are required to adopt AI/ML in a particular industry. Abdulla et al. (2020) presented the central bank of Bahrain prioritizes embracing digital transformation using AI/ML to active suitable operational cost reduction. Suhel et al. (2020) presented that chatbots are used for prompt responses from banks to the customer for various questions. Customer-centric solutions using AI and big data analytics (BDA) to attract new customer onboarding into the bank. Interviewed different bank professionals in Indonesia and proposed AI-based enterprise architecture presented by Indriasari et al. (2019). Agarwal (2019) focused on automating banking operations and customer engagement.

Setiawan et al. (2021) surveyed several questions and concluded that using AI programs in banks gives a more fantastic financial performance. They apply regularity compliance in heath care using AI/ML techniques. The risk is related to regulating medical practice and the developing more medical equipment using ML (Angehrn et al., 2020). Baluprithviraj et al. (2021) proposed an algorithm that identifies whether the person is wearing a mask or not and opens the door accordingly. The person not wearing the mark and willing to come home to the mobile application alerts the user. Gao et al. (2020) constructed Traditional Chinese medicine (TCM) health management model using AI to improve patient recovery during covid time. The use of digital technologies and Industry 4.0 (Fourth Industrial Revolution) tools in the covid pandemic, like digital health/telemedicine, plays a key role, 3D printing for manufacturing masks/PPE kits and automated robots providing contactless services presented by Chandra et al. (2022). Chen et. al. (2021) introduce healthcare models to eliminate existing health inequities and outline ethical considerations using ML. Kushwaha et. al. (2020) describe the use of ML in covid situations to identify the medical images of patients, fever, cough, and cold for patient behavior. Mallidi et al. (2021) conducted a survey and concluded more than 50% growth in developing microservices architecture applications. The usage of DL and conventional neural networks for automating brain tumor detection was presented by Mushtaq et al. (2021). Roy and Ghosh (2021) presented study highlights on applying ML techniques to identify Bengali characters. Deshmukh and Roy (2021) study different AI/ML methods to determine diabetic patients early.

AI/ML-based Case Studies in Banking Systems

The banking industry adopts new technology and innovations very fast. For this context, banks are adopting AI-based solutions in general functions like detecting fraud and more specific use cases like credit scoring and customer onboarding. Below are the essential use cases described:

Customer experience – Customer support activities are moved to AI-based solutions like chatbot to improve customer experience and service. For example, all significant banks worldwide implemented a chatbot for essential banking services, including change of password, balance inquiry, transaction history details, and services provided by the bank.

Customer onboarding – Banks adopt a seamless onboarding experience for customers to open an account using a mobile device without entering bank premises. All the account opening processes would be completed within a few minutes. For example, Singapore's largest bank opens the customer account in a few steps, including verifying the account opening person using social security number. After opening the account, the customer operates the account.

Fraud detection and prevention – Nowadays, the number of customers accessing channels is increasing (mobile, web, social accounts, etc.). When more options are available to operate the account leads to security threats. ML algorithms are crucial in identifying fraudulent transactions rather than traditional rule-based systems. Specific algorithms examine the user's historic card transactions before approval. The transaction will not be processed if any suspicious activity is determined and alert notification triggers.

Portfolio management – Provides solutions to customers for risk analysis dashboards and provides investment decision analytics to invest more efficiently.

Underwriting and credit scoring - ML model helps bankers identify the person's credit risks based on thousands of users' transaction histories to correlate them with various factors to determine credit scoring. Factors include loan repayment history, spending analysis, having children, material status, and level of education of an individual or group.

We present two case studies developed in various banks in Singapore and the US region in the space of fraud detection when login from a mobile and identifying regulatory, compliance, financial fraud, and any other suspected transactions.

Case study 1

The solution has been provided to determine regulatory compliance and financial fraud for suspicious transactions. The answer is implemented for banking customers. Following are the procedural steps for implementing the solution and the architecture diagram depicted in Figure 7.2.

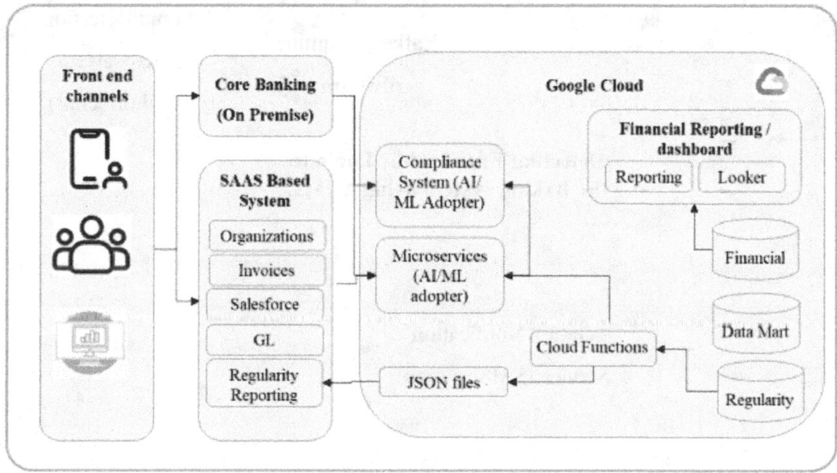

Figure 7.2 End-end Solution for Regulatory Reporting Using AI/ML

- Banking transactions will happen through front-end channels like online or mobile banking portals. Moreover, various related third-party systems will be integrated into the said online banking process.
- Front-end channels will communicate to the core banking system through a file transfer system.
- The file transfer systems will be integrated with an AI/ML-based Python microservice and continuously monitor the solution.
- The Python-based AI/ML microservice is intelligent enough to monitor all unusual transactions like regulatory compliance, financial fraud, and other suspected transactions.
- Any anomalies detected during the banking operations during or outside bank hours will be flashed to the respective reporting sub-systems, and alerts will be sent to concerned bank authorities.
- The sub-systems like regulatory reporting will have business rules to alert the bank officials on a need basis.

Case study 2

Detecting fraud is crucial for banking applications. Figure 7.4 shows the streaming-based AI/ML solutions implemented in Singapore banks to identify fraud while logging into the bank portal using mobile/web. Following are the procedural steps for implementing the solution, as the architecture diagram depicted in Figure 7.3.

- User login is exposed to the end-user using REST API.
- Login requests from mobile/web applications are validated using the IAM service.
- Send the login details to the streaming platform in real-time.
- The microservice program picks the event from the streaming platform in real time and executes the AI/ML algorithm written in Python to validate any fraud login performed using business conditions.
- If there is a deviation in business rules, send a notification to the customer with details.
- All this process is real-time and completes the activity in < 5 ms

Daily, the system processes > 10 million records to identify any fraud login performed. After the AI/ML solution, complaints about unauthorized access were reduced to 50%.

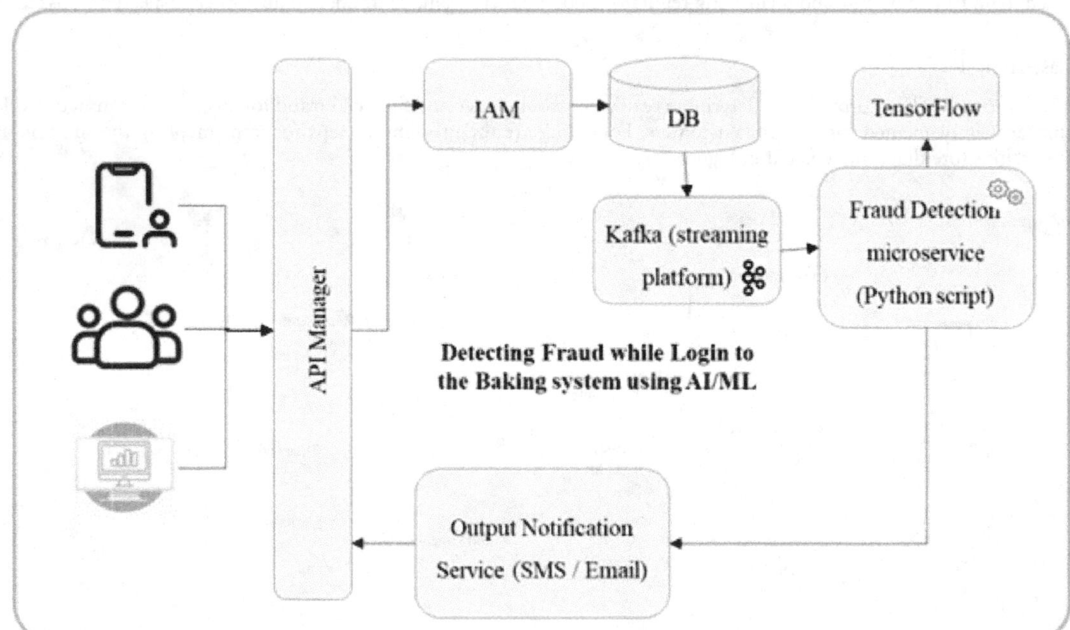

Figure 7. 3 Fraud detection using AI/ML algorithms using real-time processing

AI/ML-based Case Studies in Healthcare

The healthcare industry adopted new technology and innovations due to the pandemic from 2019 onwards. For this context, hospitals are adopting AI-based solutions in functions like medical imaging analysis, drug discovery, forecast disease, emergency medical assistance using video calls, radiation therapy, and patient data analytics. Below are the essential use cases described:

Medical imaging analysis – The case triage AI tool is used to review the clinical image and scan reviews. AI-based solutions eliminate the potential health care records errors for radiologists or cardiologists. In addition, summary reports help doctors identify the patient's past allergies and symptoms and provide proper medication.

Clinical judgement – AI/ML models already developed by different software vendors to identify early detection of cancers and retinopathies.

Precision medicine – Treatment is different from patient to patient. Doctors can use AI-based computing algorithms to identify patients' symptoms and historical records to prescribe the medication.

Drug discovery – AI-based tools/techniques help pharma companies to streamline drug discovery and repurposing. IBM Watson is one of the best AI-based tools for driving oncology drug discovery programs for various pharma companies.

Healthcare data processing – Patient data is produced in various stages and is not visible to others to validate. ML models help to visualize data in a prescribed manner after data is consolidated.

Case study 3

We present a model for managing healthcare data processing in a centralized hub for a major hospital in India. Figure 7.5 shows the detailed flow of events in the healthcare data management system. First, all patient data is consolidated from various sources. Then, AI/ML models are applied to predict care benchmarks, clinical intervention, personalized medication, and asset management using IoT data sets and the architecture diagram depicted in Figure 7.4.

- Patient data like patient records, lab reports, medical reports, IoT data, and social data were collected using streaming platforms Spark and Kafka.
- From the streaming platform, the data ingestion layer picks up the data in real-time and creates data sets using Azure analytics and event hubs.
- Data sets are stored in database/big data systems for reporting purposes.
- Front-end users/doctors view the appropriate data using Azure ML/R-based systems.

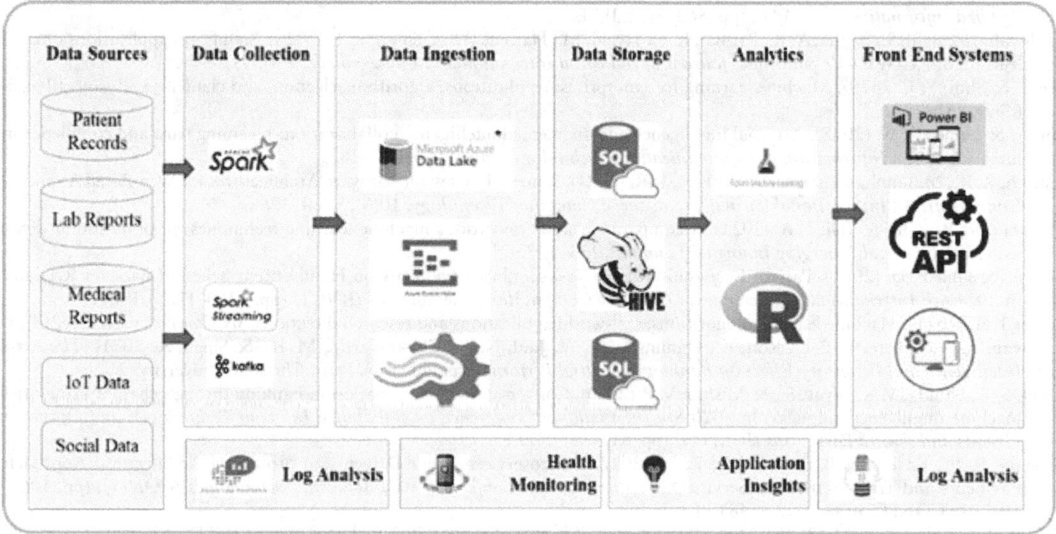

Figure 7. 4 Hospital data processing using Azure-based streaming and AI/ML

Conclusion

Currently, all the business systems are producing a lot of data, which is very important to process appropriately to create reports. Data processing can be made in several ways, and AI/ML methods are beneficial for prediction in industries like banking, telecommunications, automobile, and healthcare. Organizations are creating solutions using streaming platforms along with AI/ML algorithms to solve fraud detection in banking and predict patient health conditions by analyzing various reports using AI/ML. There may be tremendous work for transforming multiple applications to use AI, ML, and Kafka streaming to achieve real-time data for predictions in the next couple of years. Authors have limited the current work scope for AI, ML, and streaming implementations in banking and healthcare domains. The authors would like to extend the work to other business areas like insurance, telecommunication, and automobiles. Also, the authors would like to extend the work to improve data quality algorithms, which may help the prediction process more efficiently.

References

Abdulla, Y., Ebrahim, R., & Kumaraswamy, S. (2020). Artificial intelligence in banking sector: evidence from Bahrain. In *2020 International Conference on Data Analytics for Business and Industry: Way Towards a Sustainable Economy (ICDABI)* (pp. 1–6). IEEE.

Agarwal, P. (2019). Redefining banking and financial industry through the application of computational intelligence. In *2019 Advances in Science and Engineering Technology International Conferences (ASET)* (pp. 1–5). IEEE.

Angehrn, Z., Haldna, L., Zandvliet, A. S., Gil Berglund, E., Zeeuw, J., Amzal, B., ... & Heckman, N. M. (2020). Artificial intelligence and machine learning applied at the point of care. *Frontiers in Pharmacology*, 11, 759.

Antal-Vaida, C. (2022). A review of Artificial Intelligence and Machine Learning adoption in banks, during the COVID-19 outbreak. In *Proceedings of the International Conference on Business Excellence* , 16(1), (pp. 1316–1328).

Baluprithviraj, K. N., Bharathi, K. R., Chendhuran, S., & Lokeshwaran, P. (2021). Artificial intelligence based smart door with face mask detection. In *2021 International Conference on Artificial Intelligence and Smart Systems (ICAIS)*, (pp. 543–548). IEEE.

Chandra, M., Kumar, K., Thakur, P., Chattopadhyaya, S., Alam, F., & Kumar, S. (2022). Digital technologies, Healthcare and Covid-19: insights from developing and emerging nations. *Health and Technology*, 1–22.

Chen, I. Y., Pierson, E., Rose, S., Joshi, S., Ferryman, K., & Ghassemi, M. (2021). Ethical machine learning in healthcare. *Annual Review of Biomedical Data Science*, 4, 123–144.

Deshmukh, S. V. & Roy, A. (2021, March). An Empirical Exploration of Artificial Intelligence in Medical Domain for Prediction and Analysis of Diabetic Retinopathy. *Journal of Physics: Conference Series,* 1831(1), 012012.

Gao, F., Deng, K., & Hu, C. (2020). Construction of TCM health management model for patients with convalescence of coronavirus disease based on artificial intelligence. In *2020 International Conference on Big Data and Informatization Education (ICBDIE),* (pp. 417–420). IEEE.

Indriasari, E., Gaol, F. L., & Matsuo, T. (2019). Digital banking transformation: Application of artificial intelligence and big data analytics for leveraging customer experience in the Indonesia banking sector. In *2019 8th International Congress on Advanced Applied Informatics (IIAI-AAI)*, (pp. 863–868). IEEE.

Kushwaha, S., Bahl, S., Bagha, A. K., Parmar, K. S., Javaid, M., Haleem, A., & Singh, R. P. (2020). Significant applications of machine learning for COVID-19 pandemic. *Journal of Industrial Integration and Management*, 5(4), 453–479.

Lee, I. & Shin, Y. J. (2020). Machine learning for enterprises: Applications, algorithm selection, and challenges. *Business Horizons*, 63(2), 157–170.

Lui, A. & Lamb, G. W. (2018). Artificial intelligence and augmented intelligence collaboration: regaining trust and confidence in the financial sector. *Information & Communications Technology Law*, 27(3), 267–283.

Mallidi, R. K., Manmohan Sharma, & Vangala, S. R. (2021). Sematic Review on Software Architectures for Web-Based Applications. *Compusoft: An International Journal of Advanced Computer Technology*, 10(3), 3960–3968.

Mushtaq, S., Roy, A., & Teli, T. A. (2021). A comparative study on various machine learning techniques for brain tumor detection using MRI. *Global Emerging Innovation Summit,* 125–137.

Roy, A. & Ghosh, D. (2021). Pattern Recognition based Tasks and Achievements on Handwritten Bengali Character Recognition. In *2021 6th International Conference on Inventive Computation Technologies (ICICT)* (pp. 1260–1265). IEEE.

Sarker, I. H. (2021). Machine learning: Algorithms, real-world applications and research directions. *SN Computer Science*, 2(3), 1–21.

Setiawan, R., Cavaliere, L. P. L., Koti, K., Ogunmola, G. A., Jalil, N. A., Chakravarthi, M. K., & Singh, S. (2021). *The Artificial Intelligence and Inventory Effect on Banking Industrial Performance*. PhD diss. Petra Christian University.

Suhel, S. F., Shukla, V. K., Vyas, S., & Mishra, V. P. (2020). Conversation to automation in banking through chatbot using artificial machine intelligence language. In *2020 8th International Conference on Reliability, Infocom Technologies and Optimization (Trends and Future Directions)(ICRITO)* (pp. 611–618). IEEE.

Vangala, S. R., Kasimani, B., & Mallidi, R. K. (2022). Microservices Event Driven and Streaming Architectural Approach for Payments and Trade Settlement Services. *2nd International Conference on Intelligent Technologies (CONIT)*, (pp. 1–6). doi: 10.1109/CONIT55038.2022.9848178.

Zohuri, B. & Rahmani, F. M. (2019). Artificial Intelligence Driven Resiliency with Machine Learning and Deep Learning Components. *International Journal of Nanotechnology & Nanomedicine*, 4(2), 1–8.

8 Comparative study of deep learning-based clustering techniques for brain tumor segmentation

Shabir Ahmad Rather[1], Arshad Hussain Bhat[1], Jaibir Singh[1], and Muzaffar Rasool[2]

[1]Department of Computer Applications, OPJS University, Rajasthan, India

[2]Department of Computer Applications, IUST, Jammu and Kashmir, India

Abstract

Image segmentation, a digital image can be divided into several segments, thereby reducing image noise. The information returned from the image segmentation process has been used to train various machine learning models and indeed solved many business problems. One of the notable areas where image segmentation has had a big impact is brain tumor segmentation. Brain tumors have long been a fatal disease. Even in today's technologically advanced era, a brain tumor can be dangerous if we don't recognize it at the initial stage. Detecting tumor cells early could save millions of lives. The segmentation of brain tumors by automated methods has become difficult in the field of medical sciences. There are many algorithms and techniques for segmenting brain tumor images, but there is still a need to develop a rapid, accurate and efficient brain tumor segmentation technique. This paper is an overview of the segmentation of brain tumors using several clustering algorithms. We compared these algorithms to understand the mechanism of different parameters of medical imaging as well as those of deterministic algorithms which have a great influence on the overall process. Our discussion concluded that a technique has a number of notable advantages, certainly some weaknesses which make its implementation difficult individually in practice. We have also shown that it is relatively preferable to integrate one segmentation technique into another to take advantage of each. The work can be of great benefit to anyone wishing to enter the vast area of deep learning, segmentation and clustering.

Keywords: Image segmentation, brain tumor segmentation, clustering, deep learning

Introduction

Brain tumors are brought on by the aberrant cell growth that is escalating in the brain. It can be one of kind; malignant or benign. It is important to note that the shape of tumor determines the severity of tumor. Let us see how these automated techniques are developed and improved. Imagine being given an image with a single object and we want to find that object. One way to accomplish this task would be to develop a simple model and predict that there is such an object in a given image. But what if we have two different types of objects in a picture? Yes, we can train a multi-label classifier, in this case. Now there's another problem: we don't know the position of either object within the object. This is where the concept of image localization comes in. It helps us find the position of a single object in the image. But before classifying the image, we need to divide the image into parts called segments. This is how image segmentation works and what it is used for. The combination of different pixels constitutes the image. We use a clustering algorithm to segment MRI images of the brain so that it can automatically detect tumor cells definitely yes. Many researchers have used different clustering algorithms to segment brain tumors and have achieved remarkable results. While there are many other techniques to perform automated brain tumor segmentation, clustering techniques are some of the best techniques to accomplish the same thing. This is because the advantages outweigh their disadvantages. Because clustering algorithms are easy to implement, it is easy to interpret the results of clustering, and these techniques are also relatively faster and more efficient than other technologies in terms of computational cost. The MRI images of the brain tumor being analyzed came from very large data sets, and the aggregation worked very well for large data sets. In fact, clustering techniques have flexibility with respect to granularity. This paper elucidates the functional and important parameters of several clustering techniques, namely k-means, spectral and fuzzy c-means clustering.

Literature Review

The National Brain Tumor Society claims that brain tumors have more than 120 different types, some of which are fast-growing and others are slowly. This evolving nature of brain tumors has made automated segmentation of brain tumor the latest field of research. Several academics have proposed several methods and algorithms for automatically segmenting brain tumors. The application of fuzzy c-means (FCM) segmentation approach is one of the publications

(Phillips et al., 1995), fuzzy technique for brain tumor segmentation was initially used by the authors. The FCM algorithm gives a better result. K-means clustering is a well-known clustering method for segmenting brain tumors (Tuhin et al., 2012). Also, the K-means clustering approach was proposed by Bandyopadhyay and Paul (2013) for brain tumor segmentation. To be separated into two sections, the region of the brain tumor. The first section contains the typical brain cells, which are made up of the cerebral spinal fluid (CSF), grey matter (GM), and white matter (WM). The brain tumor cells are found in the second segment. The GMM is widely used to model an unsupervised brain tumor segmentation approach (Liang et al., 2012). To address the GMM's optimization issue, expected maximization (EM) is used. Just a few years back, many researchers (Jeetashree et al., 2016) have shown how to improve the performance of image segmentation. On the other hand, several other researchers proposed some hybrid picture segmentation techniques. For instance, combined k-means and fuzzy c-means (Christe et al., 2010), and it reduces within-class sum square errors, but when used on images with noise distortion, its performance suffers. The authors performed a preprocessing step to find a solution to this issue. Machine learning (ML) techniques encompass applications in varied fields of cryptography and networks (Masoodi et al., 2021; Teli et al., 2021; 2022), navigation (Teli et al., 2021) and in areas of predictive analysis and healthcare. Deep learning (DL) techniques (Sidiq et al., 2022) that have applications in secure healthcare (Teli, et al., 2020; 2021; 2022) have attained tremendous attention in the recent times. Apart from the prediction of diseases (Shafi, et al., 2022), ML and DL approaches are suitable for drug design.

In this work, the processing performance of three different clustering techniques in aspects of processing, accuracy, handling of noise etc. is investigated. This comparison would give you an idea about how we can go deep into the challenging aspects of automated brain tumor segmentation problems and come up with some notable results.

Discussion

A method of unsupervised image segmentation called clustering divides an image into a group of smaller clusters; total clusters to generate is either be determined by an expert or an algorithm. Pixels in each cluster (also known as a segment) should display some common characteristics because of the categorization process. There are no training phases in this method; instead, it trains itself by utilizing the data at hand. The pixels are gathered into a cluster according to specific criteria. Value initializations are necessary, and the effectiveness of the segmentation is significantly influenced by these initializations. There are numerous clustering algorithms employed in the segmentation of images of brain tumors; in this article, we will talk about K-means, FCM, and spectral clustering. Usually, the major phases include:

Color conversions and filtering

It is not uncommon to convert a color image to grayscale; doing so effectively simulates the result of using various colored photography filters on the cameras to capture black and white film. To represent any color's luminance in grayscale, one must first get the RGB primaries' linear intensity encoding values. Edge detection, noise reduction, sharpening, and edge smoothing are just a few of the uses for image filtering.

Pre-processing stage: Pre-processing involves either reducing undesirable distortions or increasing some key picture attributes. The given MRI image is not always ready for clustering; hence this phase involves applying a number of preliminary processing approaches to the image before any special purposes processing. Noise is reduced, and image quality is improved. The images should be as crisp and high-quality as possible because the brain is more sensitive than other medical organs. Denoising is carried out here because, among other disruptions, MRI images are commonly contaminated by Gaussian and Poisson noise. White additive Gaussian noise is the default assumption in most denoising methods. The free version of de-result noise. Clustering step: The MRI image is de-noised and skulls are removed before it is supplied to the desired clustering stage.

Brain tumor segmentation using K-means clustering

The algorithm, Figure 8.1, is the most frequently employed clustering techniques. A batch of data is often divided into k groups of data. A centroid is used to identify a cluster and its data member. The centroid is the point in the cluster where all the components' combined distances are at their shortest. Because K-means minimizes the overall distances between each object and its cluster, it is an iterative method.

Look at an image with a k-cluster density and an x*y-resolution. Let c stand in for the cluster centers and p(x,y) for the input pixels. The following is the k-means clustering algorithm:

i. Initialize the cluster count to k.
ii. Randomly choose the k cluster centers (centroid).

iii. Determine the separation between the centers of each cluster and each pixel. Calculate the Euclidean distance d for each pixel in a picture using the formula d = ||p(x,y)-ck||, where p(x,y) is the pixel at position (x,y)th of the input image and ck is the centre of the kth cluster.
iv. Based on Euclidean distance d, assign each pixel to the centre that is closest to it, i.e., if the space is almost the middle then move thereto cluster. Otherwise, move to the next cluster.
v. The new position of the centre has been computed, or re-estimated after all pixels have been assigned.
vi. The process should be continued until the tolerance value or error value is reached.

In addition to being simple to use, K-means may perform computationally more quickly when dealing with a large number of variables (if k is small). Tighter clusters may also be produced via K-means'-means has some disadvantages despite being simple to use and having benefits. K's value is difficult to anticipate. Various initial partitions could lead to various final clusters. With clusters (in the original data) of varied sizes and densities, K-means do not perform well. The initial selection of the starting centroid of the clusters affects the quality of the K-means algorithm's ultimate segmentation output. To address these issues, numerous algorithms have been developed. A novel hybrid technique for dynamic particle swarm optimization was put out by Haiyang et al. (2015).

Fuzzy C-means clustering

Each datum might belong to more than one cluster, which is the main driving force behind FC algorithms. The non-FC, in which each datum can only be a member of one particular cluster, is the opposite. Data points may potentially belong to more than one cluster in fuzzy clustering. An apple, for instance, is frequently red or green (in non-fuzzy clustering). In this case, the apples are frequently to a certain extent both red and green. Consequently, membership ratings are assigned to each of the information points in fuzzy clustering (tags). The degree to which each data point is a member of each cluster is shown by the membership grades. For instance, apples are frequently both red and green to varying degrees. The apple can belong to green [0.5] and red [0.5] Therefore, points at the sting of the cluster may be more or less within the cluster than points at the centre of the cluster depending on their membership grade. One of the most

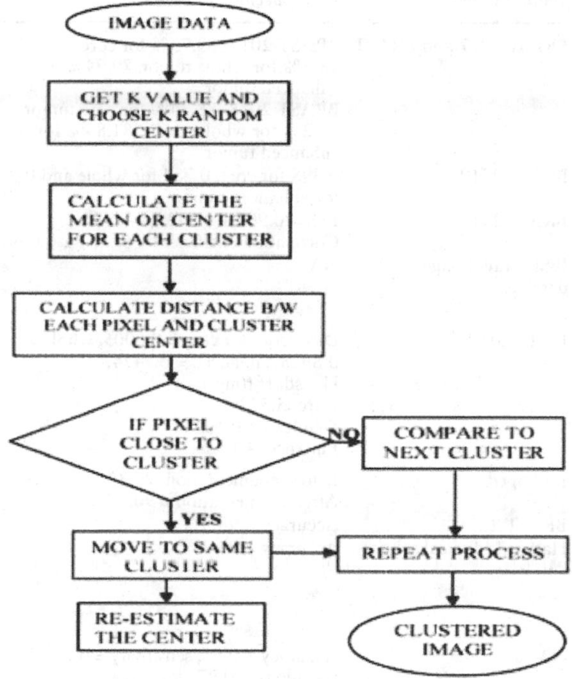

Figure 8.1 The diagrammatic representation of K-means

popular and commonly used FC methods is FCM, which was created by JC Dunn. The way this method operates is by determining each datum's membership based on the distance between the datum and each cluster centre. The closer the information is to the cluster centre, the closer it is to the real cluster centre. It is obvious that adding together each datum's membership should equal at least 1. Membership and cluster centers are updated after each iteration. The general steps of FCM are:

- Select a range of clusters.
- Randomly assign coefficients to each datum for inclusion in the clusters.
- Continue until the algorithm reaches a point of convergence, or until between two iterations, the coefficients change. does not reach the specified sensitivity threshold.
- Make a centroid calculation for each cluster.
- Calculate each datum's coefficients of inclusion in the clusters for each datum.

The centroid is the mean of all points, weighted according to how much they are part of the cluster. Accurate detection may be improved by FCM with an automatically decided number of clusters. It offers the best outcome for a set of overlapped data and performs somewhat better than the k-means method. The best results are awarded to objects in the dataset rather than forcing them to fully belong to at least one of the classes. FCM clustering has issues with large data sets and a large number of prototypes.

Comparative study of performance of different deep learning-based clustering algorithms

We compared different DP-based algorithms on different datasets to know the result accuracy and to understand the mechanism of different parameters of medical imaging as well as those of deterministic algorithms which have a great influence on the overall process, shown in Table 8.1.

Table 8.1 Comparative analysis

Ref	*Techniques/algorithm used*	*Dataset used*	*Result accuracy*
Sharif et al. (2020)	Effective DL dependent feature selection method	BRAST 2017 and BRAST 2018	BRAST 2017- 83.73% for core tumor, 93.7% for whole tumor, 79.94% for enhanced tumor. BRAST 2018- 88.34% for core tumor, 91.2% for whole tumor, 81.84% for enhanced tumor
Murugesan et al. (2019)	2D and 3D segmentation model	BRATS 2019	0.898 for core, 0.784 for whole and 0.779 for enhanced tumor
Bruse et al. (2017)	Pipeline processing	BRATS 2019	F- S= (0.902 ± 0.042), Correlation coefficient = (0.851 ± 0.064),
Huang et al. (2019)	Novel image segmentation approach by fusing FCM clustering with rough set theory	IBSR brain image database	NA
Liu et al. (2020)	Encoder-decoder NN that is DSSE-V-Net	BraTS 2017	Dice score for core = 0.8005, whole = 0.8928, enhanced = 0.7474. Hausdorf f(mm) Core=5.5724, Whole=4.5295, Enhance=4.1977
Sajjad et al. (2019)	Novel CNN dependent on multigrade brain tumor classification system	Radiopedia	Before augmentation=87.38 After augmentation = 90.67
Raja et al. (2020)	Classification (DAE) along with (BFC)	BRAST 2015	Accuracy = 98.5%
Samanta et al. (2018)	Intelligent computer-aided method for automatic brain tumor detection from the MR image, K-mean clustering gray level co-occurrence matrices (GLCM) and SVM	Harvard Medical school database	Accuracy = 99.28%
Senthil Kumar et. al. (2019)	Hybrid SFC for brain tumor segmentation without noises and artifacts	NA	Accuracy = 0.98, sensitivity = 0.88, specificity = 0.97

Table 8.1 Comparative analysis

Ref	*Techniques/algorithm used*	*Dataset used*	*Result accuracy*
Rezende et al. (2018)	Malware family classification method using VGG16 bottleneck features' of deep neural network	NA	Accuracy = 92.97%
Tiwari et al. (2019)	Agglomerative clustering which is an enhanced version of weblog extraction technique and forecasting online navigation pattern	www.getglobalindia.com	Effectiveness = 18.44%
Rodrigues et al. (2017)	Method for artifact and noise detection in ECG depend on time agglomerative clustering	Fantasia, motion artifact contaminated dataset, PhysioNet/CinC challenge 2014: Test set	Sensitivity = 88%, specificity = 92%, accuracy = 91%
Liu et al. (2017)	VGG16 depend fully convolutional neural system to categorize weld defect image	ImageNet	Test accuracy= 97.6%, Train accuracy =100% Time= 0.012s

Conclusion

Brain tumor segmentation methods are challenging in the medical field due to the diverse nature of tumor size. Among various segmentation methods, the unsupervised segmentation methods provide high accuracy in less amount of time as it requires no training. Thus, our current work focused on a few deep learning-based unsupervised clustering methods for improving the segmentation of brain tumors—K-means, C-means, VGG16, 2D and 3D segmentation models etc.

References

Abdelmaksoud, E., Elmogy, M., & Al-Awadi, R. (2015). —Brian tumor segmentation based on a hybrid clustering technique.

Bandhyopadhyay, S. K. & Paul, T. U. (2013). Automatic segmentation of brain tumour from multiple images of brain MRI. *International Journal of Application or Innovation in Engineering & Management.* 2(1), 240–248.

Bruse, J. L. (2017). Detecting clinically meaningful shape clusters in medical image data: metrics analysis for hierarchical clustering applied to healthy and pathological aortic arches. " *IEEE Transactions on Biomedical Engineering*, 64(10), 2373–2383.

Christe, S. A., Malathy, K., & Kandaswamy, A. (2010). Improved hybrid segmentation of brain MRI tissue and tumor using statistical features. *Journal of Image Video Process*, 1(1), 43–49.

Dhanachandara, J. (2017). A survey on Image segmentation methods using clustering techniques.

Huang, H., Meng, F., Zhou, S., Jiang, F., & Manogaran, G. (2019). Brain image segmentation based on FCM clustering algorithm and rough set. *IEEE Access*, 7, 12386–12396.

Jeetashree, A., PradiptaKumar, N., & Niva, D. (2016). Modified possibilistic fuzzy Cmeans algorithms for segmentation of magnetic resonance image. *Applied Soft Computing*, 41, 104–119.

Li, H., He, H., & Wen, Y. (2015). Dynamic particle swarm optimization and k-means clustering algorithm for image segmentation. *Optik*. 126, 4817–4822.

Liang, Z., Wei, W., & Jason, J. C. (2012). Brain tumor segmentation based on GMM and active contour method with a model-aware edge map. *In: Proceedings of MICCAI-BRATS*, (pp. 24–32).

Liu, B., Zhang, X., Gao, Z., & Chen, L. (2017). Weld defect images classification with VGG16-Based neural network. *Digital TV and Wireless Multimedia Communications*, (pp. 215–223.

Liu P., Dou Q., Wang Q., and Heng P. A., "An Encoder-Decoder Neural Network with 3D Squeeze-and-Excitation and Deep Supervision for Brain Tumor Segmentation," IEEE Access, 2020.

Masoodi, F., Bamhdi, A. M., &Teli, T. A. (2021). Machine Learning for Classification analysis of Intrusion Detection on NSL-KDD Dataset. In Turkish Journal of Computer and Mathematics Education (Vol. 12, Issue 10).

Murugesan G. K., "Multidimensional and Multiresolution Ensemble Networks for Brain Tumor Segmentation," bioRxiv, p. 760124, 2019.

Phillips, W., Velthulzen, R., Phuphanich, S., Hall, L., Clarke, L., & Silbiger, M. (1995). Application of fuzzy c-means segmentation technique for tissue differentiation in MR images of a hemorrhagic glioblastoma multiforme. *Magnetic Resonance Imaging*, 13(2), 277–290.

Raja, P. S. (2020). Brain tumor classification using a hybrid deep autoencoder with Bayesian fuzzy clustering-based segmentation approach. *Biocybernetics and Biomedical Engineering*, 40(1), 440–453.

Rezende, E., Ruppert, G., Carvalho, T., Theophilo, A., Ramos, F., & de Geus, P. 2018). Malicious software classification using VGG16 deep neural network's bottleneck features. *Information Technology-New Generations,* 51–59.

Rodrigues, J., Belo, D., & Gamboa, H. (2017). Noise detection on ECG based on agglomerative clustering of morphological features. *Computers in Biology and Medicine*, 87, 322–334.

Sajjad, M., Khan, S., Muhammad, K., Wu, W., Ullah, A., & Baik S. W. (2019). Multi-grade brain tumor classification using deep CNN with extensive data augmentation. *Journal of Computational Science*, 30, 174–182.

Samanta, A. K. & Khan A. A. (2018). Computer aided diagnostic system for automatic detection of brain tumor through MRI using clustering based segmentation technique and SVM classifier. *International Conference on Advanced Machine Learning Technologies and Applications*, 343–351.

Samir, B., Shahnawaz, A. & Samer, M. (2014). Optimized K-Means Algorithm. *Mathematical Problems in Engineering*, 14.

Senthil Kumar, C. & Gnanamurthy, R. (2019). A fuzzy clustering based MRI brain image segmentation using back propagation neural networks. *Cluster Computing*, 22(5), 12305–12312.

Shafi, O., Sidiq, J. S., & Teli, T. A. (2022). Effect of pre-processing techniques in predicting diabetes mellitus with focus on artificial neural network. *Advances and Applications in Mathematical Sciences,* 21(8).

Sharif, M. I., Li, J. P, Khan, M. A., & Saleem, M. A., (2020). Active deep neural network features selection for segmentation and recognition of brain tumors using MRI images. *Pattern Recognition Letters*, 129, 181–189.

Sidiq, S. J., Shafi, O., Zaman, M., and Teli, T. A. (2022). Applications of artificial intelligence, big data and internet of things in sustainable development. CRC Press, Boca Raton. Teli, T. A. & Masoodi, F. (2021). Blockchain in healthcare: challenges and opportunities. *2nd International Conference on IoT Based Control Networks and Intelligent Systems (ICICNIS 2021).* https://ssrn.com/abstract=3882744

Teli, T. A. & Wani, M. A. (2021). A fuzzy-based local minima avoidance path planning in autonomous robots. *International Journal of Information Technology*, 13(1), 33–40. https://doi.org/10.1007/s41870-020-00547-0

Teli, T. A., Masoodi, F., & Yousuf, R. (2020). Security Concerns and privacy preservation in blockchain based IoT systems: opportunities and challenges. *International Conference on IoT based Control Networks and Intelligent Systems (ICICNIS 2020).* https://ssrn.com/abstract=3769572

Teli, T. A., Masoodi, F. S., & Bahmdi, A. M. (2021). HIBE: Hierarchical Identity-Based Encryption. In K. A. B. Ahmad, K. Ahmad, & U. N. Dulhare, (Eds.) *Functional Encryption.* Springer, Cham. https://doi.org/10.1007/978-3-030-60890-3_11

Teli, T. A., Yousuf, R. & Khan, D. A. (2022). Ensuring secure data sharing in IoT domains using blockchain. In M. M. Ghonge, S. Pramanik, R. Mangrulkar, & D. N. Le (Eds.). *Cyber Security and Digital Forensics*. https://doi.org/10.1002/9781119795667.ch9

Teli, T. A., Yousuf, R., & Khan, D. A. (2022). MANET routing protocols, attacks and mitigation techniques: A review. *International Journal of Mechanical Engineering*, 7(2).

Tiwari, S., Gupta, R. K., & Kashyap, R. (2019). To enhance web response time using agglomerative clustering technique for web navigation recommendation. *Computational Intelligence in Data Mining*. Springer, (pp. 659–672).

Tuhin, U. P. & Samir, K. B. (2012). Segmentation of brain tumor from brain MRI images. Reintroducing k-means with advanced dual localization method. *International Journal of Engineering Research and Applications*. (3), 226–231.

9 Leukemia detection: An overview of different artificial intelligence based approaches

Navpreet Kaur[1,a] *and Amar Singh*[1]

[1]School of Computer Science and Engineering, Lovely Professional University, Punjab, India

Abstract

The detection of leukemia at the early stage is challenging as the symptoms of leukemia like flu, weight loss, tiredness, fatigue etc. are quite common. Leukemia is generally detected by the pathologist after analyzing the blood smear through a microscope. The number of different types of cells is analyzed by the pathologists to detect leukemia. When the count of the immature leukocytes increases abnormally and the count of the other blood cells is reduced, it may indicate leukemia. This conventional method of detecting the leukemia takes much time, and the results can also be affected by the skills of the medical experts who are involved in the diagnosis process. To detect the leukemia quickly and automatically, the microscopic smear images can be observed using various methods and approaches based on image processing. It has been shown in different research that the imaging of blood cells helps to detect leukemia. The analysis of different artificial intelligence-based approaches for the detection of leukemia at early phase is done in this paper and the accuracy of different approaches is discussed.

Keywords: Leukemia, pathologist, conventional method, artificial intelligence

Introduction

Blood cancer generally occurs due to the abnormal and excessive growth of the white blood cell (WBCs). The oxygen is transferred from lungs to the tissues and the other parts of the body by red blood cells (RBCs). WBCs consist of a nucleus and cytoplasm, and play an important role in fighting against infections. Platelets are useful as they help in forming blood clots, and blood loss is prevented with platelets. Plasma is a liquid medium of the blood through which the nutrients, proteins and other molecules are transferred, responsible for the functioning of different body parts. Essential components of human blood are depicted in Figure 9.1.

The new WBCs are continuously generated in the bone marrow of a healthy body, replacing the old and dying WBCs. The excessive growth of the WBCs leads to blood cancers (Blood Cancer and Its types. Johnny Ottesen*(2021) Department of Science and Environment (2021)).

Leukemia is a hematological disorder initiated in the bone marrow which is the spongy tissue inside most bones. The bone marrow starts producing WBCs abnormally in the patients suffering from leukemia, leading to the decrease in immunity. WBCs are further classified into different parts as represented in Figure 9.2.

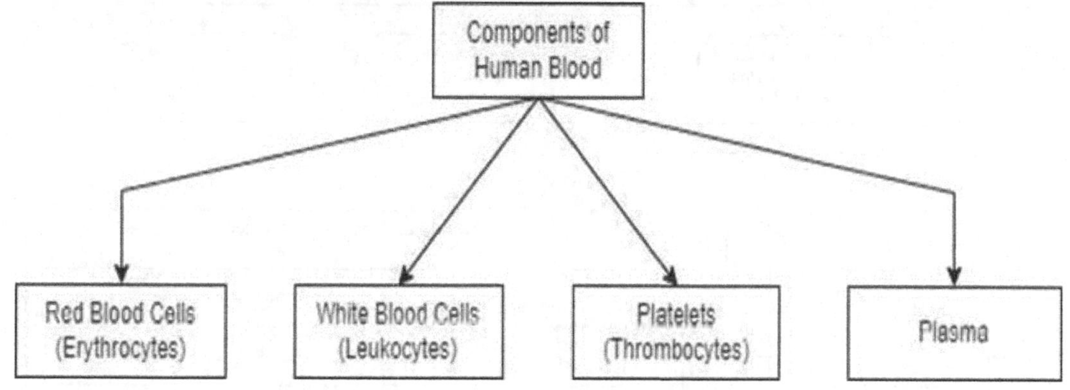

Figure 9.1 Components of human blood

[a]Navkaur21191@gmail.com

Leukemia is a cancer of leukocytes which is also called blood cancer. Leukemia is categorized into lymphoid leukemia or myeloid leukemia (Figure 9.3) based on the types of the cells which can become cancerous and it is also categorized to two types i.e., chronic, and acute based on the rate at which it grows. The lymphoid cells, also called lymphocytes are the part of the immune system and are affected in lymphocytic leukemia and the myeloid cells of the bone marrow are affected in the myeloid leukemia.

The overproduction of a category of lymphocyte is called B-cells. Myeloid cells are helpful in producing the WBCs, RBCs and the platelets. In acute leukemia, the blood cells which are abnormal grow quickly, whereas in chronic leukemia, the abnormal blood cells grow slowly. The overproduction of WBCs can be understood from Figure 9.4.

Mainly, there are four types of leukemia i.e., acute myeloid leukemia (AML), chronic myeloid leukemia (CML), acute lymphoid leukemia (ALL), and chronic lymphoid leukemia (CLL). Other than these types, there are some rarer types

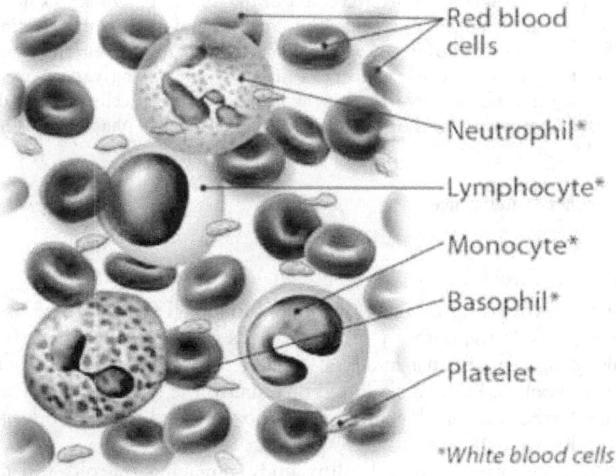

Figure 9.2 Healthy blood cells (cancercenter.com)

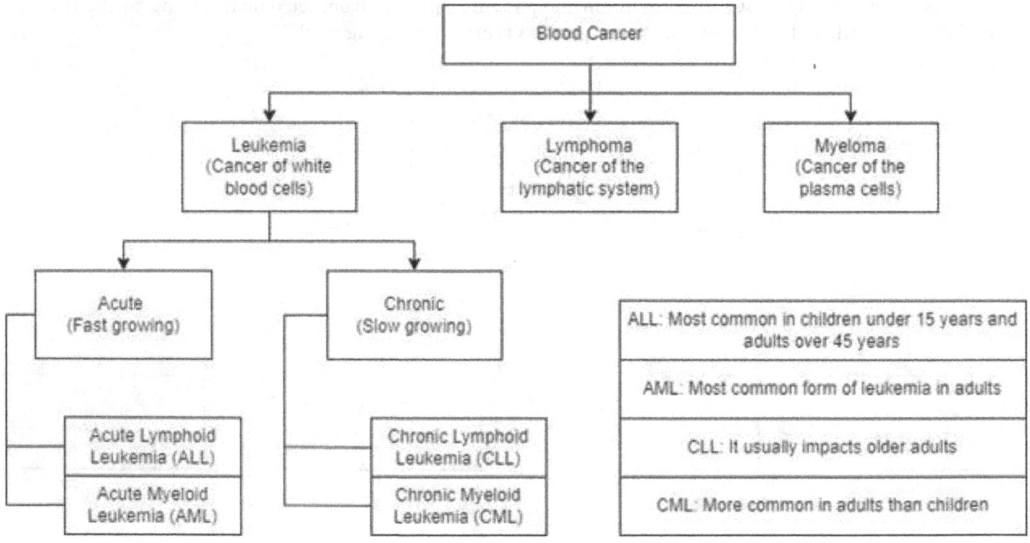

Figure 9.3 Blood cancer types (Yale Medicine. Blood cancers, fact sheets)

of leukemia i.e., Hairy cell leukemia (HCL), chronic myelomonocytic leukemia (CMML), large granular lymphocytic leukemia, B-cell prolymphocytic leukemia etc. In the entire world, leukemia cases are increasing rapidly as compared to the other types of the cancer. Some Studies suggest that in reported cases of Blood Cancer, India ranks third highest after USA and China. As per American Cancer Society, the estimated cases of leukemia in 2021 are represented in Figure 9.5. If anyone had already diagnosed with some other type of cancer, then the chances of occurrence of leukemia is 30% (Iswarya et al., 2022).

Different artificial intelligence (AI) and machine learning (ML) based algorithms as mentioned in Figure 9.6 can be used for the detection of leukemia based on the images of blood cell (Hossain et al., 2022).

The subsets of AI, i.e., ML, neural network, and DL, are being used for segmentation, clustering, and classification. In this study, section 1, is representing the introduction, section 2 is discussing about various techniques, model design and performance of various systems, and section 3 revealing the detailed conclusion of the study.

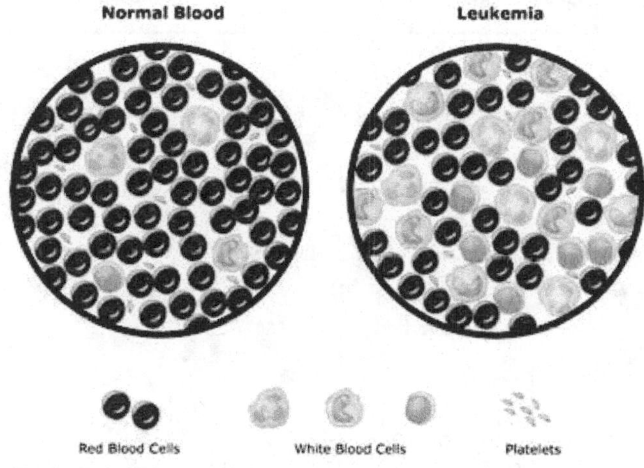

Figure 9.4 Normal blood cells vs leukemia blood cells (OrthoInfo – AAOS)

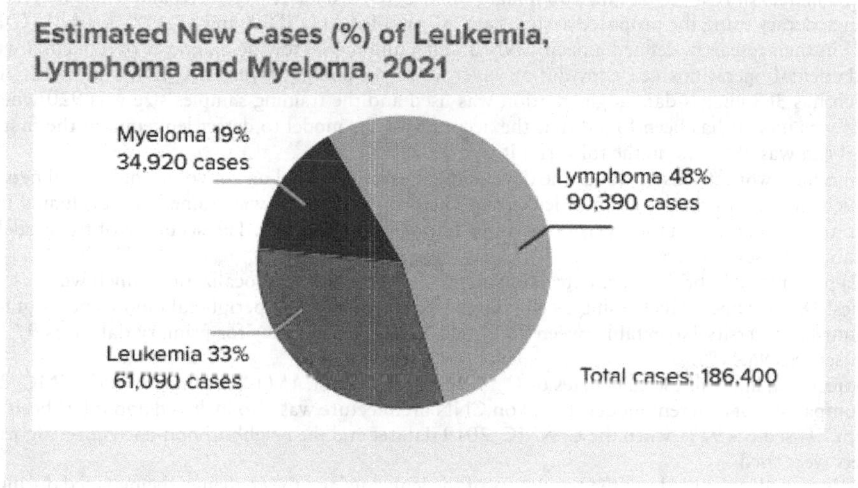

Figure 9.5 Normal blood cells vs leukemia blood cells
Source: Cancer facts and figures 2021. American Cancer Society; 2021

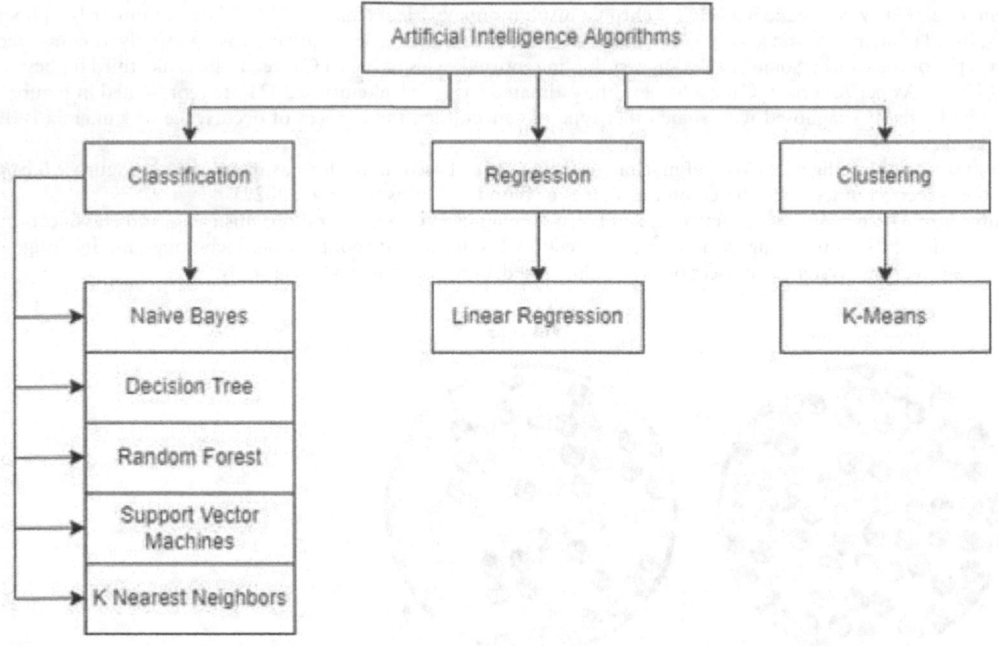

Figure 9.6 AI algorithms (Kallem, 2012)

Review of Literature

The literature associated with this article is taken from different sources. Some indispensable sources contributing to a review of the literature regarding leukemia detection include articles, research papers, and books.

Abunadi and Senan (2022) described in detail about the challenges in the detection of leukemia using manual diagnosis systems and the diagnosis systems based on ANN, feed forward neural network, convolutional neural network, and SVM. A total of 108 images of ALL_IDB1 and 260 images of ALL_IDB2 dataset were used and it has been found that leukemia detection accuracy using the proposed systems are 90.91% for ALL_IDB1 and 98.11% for ALL_IDB2.

Bukhari et al. (2022) in their research, defined a deep CNN architecture model for the diagnosis of leukemia which included the two fundamental operations i.e., convolution layer and max-pooling layer. ALL_IDB1 and ALL_IDB2 dataset were used which has 368 images data augmentation was used and the training samples size was 920 whereas the testing samples size was nine. It has been found that the accuracy of the model to detect leukemia in the first run was 96%, in the second run was 98% and in the third run it was 99.98%.

Anagha et al. (2021) in their work discussed about the development of a tool based on convolutional neural network and DL techniques which can be used in detection of leukemia. The proposed model was trained and evaluated using C_NMC_2019 dataset and the implementation was done using TensorFlow and keras. The accuracy of the model for the training was 91% and for testing was 87%.

Elhassan et al. (2022) presented a hybrid feature extraction method CMYK-moment localization which was based on deep learning techniques. 18,365 expert-labeled single-cell images were obtained from peripheral blood smears of more than 90 patients at Munich University Hospital between 2014 and 2017. The accuracy for primary data was 97.57% and for Secondary dataset was 96.41%.

Gupta et al. (2022) presented in detail the challenges of C_NMC_2019 dataset. 15114 cell images of C_NMC_2019 dataset was taken. A comparison of different models based on CNN architecture was also included and it has been analyzed that the maximum F1- score is 91% when the C_NMC_2019 dataset and the neighborhood-correction algorithm with fine-tuned ResNets were used.

Iswarya et al. (2022) discussed in detail about the symptoms of the leukemia and the challenges being faced during the early detection of leukemia using traditional methods. The segmentation and the classification on the collected images were performed using the machine learning based algorithms for the detection of leukemia at the early phases.

Hossain et al. (2022) proposed a supervised machine learning model for the detection of leukemia at early stage. ALL-IDB dataset and seven different ML models i.e., ANN, random forest, decision tree, adaboost classifier, K-nearest neighbor, logistic regression classifier and Naïve Bayesian classifier were used in this supervised model and it has been analyzed that the accuracy of all these different machine learning model lies in between 85.55–97.74%.

Rajaraman, (2021) discussed that the process for detection of leukemia using the manual method is long and it also requires the expert skills. A new approach for the detection of leukemia was proposed which is based on random forest classifier. A total of 370 images from Kaggle, UCI repository, and cancer image archive were used. The accuracy of this proposed model which is based on random forest classifier is 91%.

Ranjitha and Duth (2021)) defined a methodology for the diagnosis of leukemia using K-means algorithm which includes image acquisition, image preprocessing, image segmentation and feature extraction. A total of 360 sample data images and 76 pictures of contaminated cells were taken from Kaggle Public Data Collection. It has been found from the results that that accuracy is 90%.

Oliveira & Dantas (2021) proposed the modifications in the standard neural network architectures. Xception and VGGNet were the tested architecture used. C_NMC_2019 dataset with 15114 images were used and it has been found that the F1 score value is 92.60%, the precision value is 91.14%, the sensitivity value is 94.10% and the specificity value is 90.86%.

Boldú et al. (2021) presented a DL-based system with two modules (ALNet) which can be used for the detection of leukemia. The first module was designed to find the abnormal blasts and the second module was designed to categorize whether the blast is lymphoid or myeloid. 16450 blood cell images of dataset from Hospital Clinic of Barcelona were used in this system to evaluate VGG16, ResNet101, DenseNet121 and SENet154. It has been found that the accuracy with VGG16 is 88.4% and with SENet154 it is 87.2%.

Ramaneswaran et al. (2021) discussed in detail about the classification of leukemia based on slow growing and fast growing. In this study, a hybrid Inception v3 XGBoost model was introduced in which XGBoost was used as a classification head. The data was taken from the Laboratory Oncology, AIIMS, New Delhi and 10661 images were used. It has been found that with the proposed model the F1 score is 0.986.

Pałczyński et al. (2021) described an architecture which is based on deep neural network using the AlexNet model from CNN to differentiate the subtypes and the normal state of leukemia. ALL-IDB dataset with 260 segmented images was used and the algorithms used were XGBoost, CNN and random forest. It was found that the accuracy to detect leukemia as per different types was 90%.

Sahlol et al. (2020) presented an improved hybrid approach for the classification of WBCs leukemia. In this study, feature extraction from images was done using VGGNet and after that the features which were extracted were filtered with statistically enhanced Salp Swarm Algorithm (SSA). 260 images from ALL-IDB dataset and 10661 images from C_NMC_2019 dataset were used and the accuracy found was 90%.

Conclusion

Different studies conducted so far for the detection of leukemia have been analyzed in this paper. A review of different approaches based on machine learning and deep learning to detect the leukemia at the early phase has been presented and the datasets, algorithms, classifiers etc. which are used for the development of various models are also mentioned. With the artificial intelligence approaches, the image-based leukemia detection can improve accuracy, reduce the diagnosis time, and provide the safe services for diagnosis. It has been concluded that the results of the algorithms and the classifiers are not stable and vary as per the size of the dataset, so in the near future, the challenges being faced can be overcome for the reliable detection of leukemia.

References

Abunadi, I. & Senan, E. (2022). Multi-Method diagnosis of blood microscopic sample for early detection of acute lymphoblastic leukemia based on deep learning and hybrid techniques. *Sensors*, 22(4), 1629. https://doi.org/10.3390/s22041629

Anagha, V., Disha, A., Aishwarya, B., Nikkita, R., & Biradar, V. (2021). Detection of leukemia using convolutional neural network. *Emerging Research in Computing, Information, Communication and Applications*, (pp. 229–242). https://doi.org/10.1007/978-981-16-1338-8_20

Boldú, L., Merino, A., Acevedo, A., Molina, A., & Rodellar, J. (2021). A deep learning model (ALNet) for the diagnosis of acute leukaemia lineage using peripheral blood cell images. *Computer Methods and Programs in Biomedicine*, 202, 105999. https://doi.org/10.1016/j.cmpb.2021.105999

Bukhari, M., Yasmin, S., Sammad, S., & Abd El-Latif, A. (2022). A deep learning framework for leukemia cancer detection in microscopic blood samples using squeeze and excitation learning. *Mathematical Problems in Engineering*, (pp. 1–18). https://doi.org/10.1155/2022/2801227

Elhassan, T., Rahim, M., Swee, T., Hashim, S., & Aljurf, M. (2022). Feature extraction of white blood cells using CMYK-moment localization and deep learning in acute myeloid leukemia blood smear microscopic images. *IEEE Access*, 10, 16577–16591. https://doi.org/10.1109/access.2022.3149637

Gupta, R., Gehlot, S., & Gupta, A. (2022). C-NMC: B-lineage acute lymphoblastic leukaemia: A blood cancer dataset. *Medical Engineering & Physics*, 103, 103793. https://doi.org/10.1016/j.medengphy.2022.103793

Hossain, M., Islam, A., Islam, S., Shatabda, S., & Ahmed, A. (2022). Symptom Based Explainable Artificial Intelligence Model for Leukemia Detection. *IEEE Access*, 10, 57283–57298. https://doi.org/10.1109/access.2022.3176274

Iswarya, M., A, S., R, A., & A, K. (2022). Detection of leukemia using machine learning. *2022 International Conference on Applied Artificial Intelligence and Computing (ICAAIC)*. https://doi.org/10.1109/icaaic53929.2022.9792725

Kallem, S. (2012). Artificial Intelligence Algorithms. *IOSR Journal of Computer Engineering*, 6(3), 1–8. https://doi.org/10.9790/0661-0630108

Ottesen, J. (2021). Blood cancer and its types. *Allied Journal of Medical Research*.

Pałczyński, K., Śmigiel, S., Gackowska, M., Ledziński, D., Bujnowski, S., & Lutowski, Z. (2021). IoT application of transfer learning in hybrid artificial intelligence systems for acute lymphoblastic leukemia classification. *Sensors*, 21(23), 8025. https://doi.org/10.3390/s21238025

Rajaraman, A. (2021). An automated detection of leukemia. *International Journal for Research in Applied Science and Engineering Technology*, 9(8), 1977–1981. https://doi.org/10.22214/ijraset.2021.37670

Ramaneswaran, S., Srinivasan, K., Vincent, P., & Chang, C. (2021). Hybrid inception v3 XGBoost model for acute lymphoblastic leukemia classification. *Computational and Mathematical Methods in Medicine*, (pp. 1– 10). https://doi.org/10.1155/2021/2577375

Ranjitha, P. & Duth, S. (2021). Detection of blood cancer-leukemia using k-means algorithm. *5Th International Conference on Intelligent Computing and Control Systems (ICICCS)*. https://doi.org/10.1109/iciccs51141.2021.9432244

Sahlol, A., Kollmannsberger, P., & Ewees, A. (2020). Efficient classification of white blood cell leukemia with improved swarm optimization of deep features. *Scientific Reports*, 10(1). https://doi.org/10.1038/s41598- 020-59215-9

Yale Medicine. Blood cancers, fact sheets.

10 Industry 5.0 centric curriculum and pedagogy adoption capability of educational institutions—remodeling technical education in India

Ajay Chandel[1,a], *Jasneet Kaur*[1,b], *Neeraj Bhanot*[1,c], *Tejbir Kaur*[2,d], *and Anesu Felicity Chekera*[3,e]

[1]Assistant Professor, Mittal School of Business, Lovely Professional University, Punjab, India

[2]HR Business Partner in a Leading North American E-Commerce Company, Ontario, Canada

[3]Student, Mittal School of Business, Lovely Professional University, Punjab, India

Abstract

It has been claimed worldwide that academic curriculum must conform to developments posed by the transition from Industry 4.0 to Industry 5.0, however, more extensive strata of engineering graduates battle with conventional technical expertise. The current study attempts to unearth critical factors that can enable educational institutes to bring in the necessary curriculum and pedagogical reform to nurture engineering graduates ready to take up challenging roles in Industry 5.0. Considering the strategic role of educators, this study is also a unique attempt to determine the gap between the expectation and perception of educators in terms of the preparedness of educational institutions to take an active role in creating an industry 5.0-ready workforce. The trade-off between expectations and perceptions of educators was determined by circulating a questionnaire to 280 educators in public and private universities in Punjab. The study concludes with clear standings of private and public universities' preparedness towards Industry 5.0-centric curriculum adoption capability.

Keywords: Industry 5.0, education, curriculum, institutional strategy, institutional infrastructure, educator upskilling, leadership, institutional culture, academia-industry partnerships, quality education

Introduction

Industrial revolution 4.0 took 40 years, while the first three took 100. Despite Industry 4.0's infancy, industry visionaries and tech leaders are looking forward to Industrial Revolution 5.0: a machine-human interface-based production approach. Industry 4.0 ignores the human cost to improve process efficiency—Industry 4.0's biggest challenge in a few years. Labor groups and lawmakers will oppose Industry 4.0, reducing its employment benefits (Nahavandi, 2019). Industry 4.0's benefits include security risks, the need for experienced workers, and the fear that humans will be replaced rather than empowered, leading to a dystopian future (Pereira et al., 2020). Even though AI algorithms have been used to explore sustainable business practices (Papadimitriou et al., 2019), Industry 4.0 has not shown a strong inclination towards environmental preservation or focused on technology that supports environmental sustainability. Prior research linking AI algorithms to environmental protection paved the way, but a lack of attention and commitment requires a superior technology approach to protect the environment and promote sustainability (Yetilmezsoy et al., 2011). Industry 5.0 focuses on personalization and the 'Human Touch' By activating and harnessing human brains in machines, we can achieve personalization (Zhang et al., 2020). Automated procedures, intelligent devices, and machine-cooperation systems will replace people. Because more students are opting for engineering programmes due to better career prospects, disciplines involving human, machine, and AI collaboration are in high demand. A synergistic human-AI cooperation for next-generation industrial automation is also pushing it (Broo et al., 2022). As time passes, it is thought that graduates should be taught Industry 5.0-driven know-how instead of just producing goods or providing services for profit (Collins, 2018). The current study aims to identify critical factors that can help educational institutes reform curriculum and pedagogy to prepare engineering graduates for Industry 5.0. Educators are the key to this success. This study is a unique attempt to determine the gap between educators' expectations and perceptions of educational institutions' readiness to create industry 5.0-ready workforces. The section below reviews key subthemes from existing literature as critical enablers for engineering education in India to be Industry 5.0 ready.

[a]ajay.chandel@lpu.co.in; [b]jasneet.16413@lpu.co.in; [c]neeraj.27064@lpu.co.in; [d]kaurtejbir@gmail.com; [e]chekeranes@gmail.com

Review of Literature

Despite India's size, teaching is the art of supporting discovery. Indian higher education encourages guarded, solo work with too many limits, unlike top universities. This requires a liberal approach to changing outdated norms and regulations to match higher education's global dynamics.

Academia-industry partnerships-breaking the firewall between academia and industry: Academics and practitioners have studied academia-industry collaboration for 20 years because academia-industry cooperation improves science implementation. 'Manufacturing the Future Workforce' calls for innovative educational techniques, including modular content, to meet revised and new skill needs (Collier and Shakespeare, 2020). It discusses business-academic co-creation (Collier and Shakespeare, 2020). Industry-academia cooperation and an excellent regulatory environment are needed to commercialize Industry 5.0 solutions (Chitkara et al., 2020).

Upskilling educators: Engineers in the 21st century must be able to handle change in a hypercompetitive market. Industry 5.0 should let engineers move from technology to solutions to processes. Various skills are needed (Mitchell and Guile, 2021). Teachers must learn 21st-century skills. Those skilled in 21st-century technologies like Industry 5.0 can work on tasks that are hard to automate because they require human skills to work with machines. Educators must be data miners, analysts, organizers, partners, curriculum specialists, synthesizers, critical thinkers, and researchers to personalize student experiences. Institutions must engage educators in faculty exchange, faculty development, industry-academia partnership initiatives, and research to understand and apply Industry 5.0 dynamics in pedagogy and curriculum (Mitchell and Guile, 2021).

Institutional strategy: Education is viewed as resistant to change despite criticism for inadequately preparing graduates for the workforce. Academic institutions should upgrade pedagogy and evaluation procedures to promote Industry 5.0 curriculum (OECD, 2021). Institutional and industrial strategies must align for a tech-savvy workforce. These strategic objectives can communicate an institution's commitment to exceptional teaching, establish a unified set of institutional, departmental, and program-level activities, and track progress toward improved results (OECD, 2021). Academic institutions should create synergies to promote Industry 5.0.

Institutional culture: Industry 5.0 helps companies leverage technology and data in fast-changing industries. People and cultures need training and growth to continue in industry 5.0. Influential institutional culture matches the external environment, resources, values, and goals. Indian higher education encourages guarded, secretive work with too many limitations, unlike top universities. Academic, financial, and administrative independence lead to restrictions, hierarchies, and traditions. Industry 5.0 requests a permissive approach to modifying old norms and regulations to reflect higher education is changing global dynamics (Mitchell and Guile, 2021). Academic leaders must reassure teachers about Industry 5.0's benefits. Industry 5.0 skills include data analytics, IT, software, and HMI (Mohelska and Sokolova, 2018).

Institutional infrastructure: Immersive, interactive tools and pedagogy are the future of education and learning, blending Education 5.0 and Industry 5.0 equipment to engage today's digital-age learners. Teachers need the technology and infrastructure to create immersive, interactive lessons. This is made worse by schools' failure to invest in tech-based teaching content and infrastructure (Mustafa Kamal et al., 2019). Industry 5.0 needs money to improve school technology. Industry 4.0/5.0 learning environments are the most expensive for instructors and infrastructure (Brown-Martin, 2017).

Leadership: Leaders can inspire innovation. Academic leaders should hire people with diverse experiences and talents to inspire creativity and innovation in curriculum and pedagogy (OECD, 2021). Some academics may feel they need to do it better for years, even though interactive, immersive, and engaging pedagogy is more effective in meeting industrial demands. This could stifle change. Research, not teaching, defines academics. Institutions must value educational innovation and recognize educational innovators and successful researchers to effectively implement creative learning and teaching strategies. Research professors may be hesitant to be educational reformers. Any subtle opposition can be overcome if the change leader is prominent and many people, departments, and staff support the change and leadership (IMHE, 2012).

Methodology

An in-depth literature review (2016–2022) from Google Scholar, ProQuest, and JSTOR was conducted to identify critical aspects of the Industry 5.0 curriculum and pedagogy. This created a 29-item survey. The questionnaire was sent to 280 academics from four private and state universities in Punjab (70 from each university). Punjab was chosen because its government is working to strengthen higher education and promote education despite a 20% drop in enrolment each year (The Tribune, 2018; Indian Express, 2020). Subpar education and lack of innovation contribute. A 5-point Likert scale questionnaire was used to collect educators' expectations and perceptions of educational institutions' ability to embrace the industry. The trade-off score compares expectations to reality. Higher trade-off scores indicate less change readiness.

Analysis and Discussion

Reliability statistics examined internal consistency. All items were subjected to an exploratory factor analysis with Promax rotation and maximum likelihood extraction to study educational institutions' ability to embrace curricular and pedagogical innovation (particular sample). KMO = 0.883 confirmed sample adequacy and factor reduction. Bartlett test of Sphericity = 0.000, indicating adequate EFA data set correlations. Maximum likelihood factor analysis using a cut-off point of 40 and Kaiser's Eigen values greater than 1 (Field, 2009) provided a six-factor solution accounting for 69.53% variance. Organizational support, innovation, strategy, communication, leadership, and structure may help schools adopt Industry 5.0. Confirmatory factor analysis was needed to validate the measuring model/scale after EFA revealed six characteristics that could help educational institutes adopt Industry 5.0 curriculum and pedagogy. Fornell-criterion Larcker measures latent variable variance. AVE should be above 0.5 to assess convergent model validity. CR above 0.7 is good (Hair et al., 1995). Composite reliability and average variance explained for institutional culture (CR = 0.847, AVE = 0.581), institutional strategy (CR=0.931, AVE=0.729), upskilling educators (CR=0.905, AVE= 0.657), academia-industry partnerships (CR=0.918, AVE= 0.736), leadership (CR=0.928, AVE=0.766), and institutional infrastructure (CR = 0.888, AVE = 0.665) were within acceptable bounds, indicating An FCM summarizes discriminant validity results. These values surpassed construct correlations. Thus, discovered criteria (items) assessed educational institutions' ability to implement Industry 5.0-centric curriculum and pedagogy. Fitness indexes in CFA measure model fit. Absolute (RMSEA = 0.33, GFI = 0.910), incremental (CFI = 0.983, NFI = 0.932), and parsimonious model fits were satisfactory. As mentioned, the results validated the CFA model fit indices.

Trade-off calculation

This section demonstrates and discusses the stepwise process followed to calculate trade-off scores of selected public and private universities.

Step 1: Average scores of various universities on 'Industry 5.0 centric curriculum and pedagogy adoption capability' dimensions

In this step, average scores (statement-wise as well as an average of each dimension) of expected and perceived (observed) Industry 5.0-centric curriculum and pedagogy adoption capability dimensions were demonstrated.

Table 10.1 Comparative score analysis of industry 5.0 centric curriculum and pedagogy adoption capability' dimensions

Expectation [E]			*Perception [P]*				
Sr. No	*Institutional culture*	E	*Institutional culture*	*PSU-A*	*PSU-B*	*PU-A*	*PU-B*
1	S1*	4.51	S1	3.61	3.02	4.32	3.79
2	S2*	4.52	S2	3.58	3.04	4.76	3.86
3	S3*	4.33	S3	3.36	3.78	3.69	3.74
4	S4*	4.28	S4	3.76	3.59	3.32	3.79
	Average score	4.41		3.57	3.35	4.02	3.79
	Institutional strategy		*Institutional strategy*	*PSU-A*	*PSU-B*	*PU-A*	*PU-B*
5	S5*	4.44	S5	3.21	3.50	4.12	3.84
6	S6*	4.43	S6	4.02	3.72	4.16	4.02
7	S7*	4.32	S7	3.82	3.83	3.88	3.89
8	S8*	4.39	S8	3.06	3.70	4.02	3.42
	Average score	4.39		3.52	3.68	4.04	3.79

Table 10.1 Comparative score analysis of industry 5.0 centric curriculum and pedagogy adoption capability' dimensions

	Upskilling educators		*Upskilling educators*	*PSU-A*	*PSU-B*	*PU-A*	*PU-B*
9	S9*	4.22	S9	3.22	3.08	4.01	3.65
10	S10*	4.28	S10	3.06	3.26	3.58	3.62
11	S11*	4.80	S11	3.22	3.38	3.62	3.82
12	S12*	4.52	S12	3.38	3.66	3.44	4.24
13	S13*	4.36	S13	3.5	3.26	4.14	3.52
	Average score	4.43		3.27	3.75	3.68	3.76
	Academia-industry partnerships		*Academia-industry partnerships*	*PSU-A*	*PSU-B*	*PU-A*	*PU-B*
14	S14*	4.08	S14	3.30	3.12	3.32	3.78
15	S15*	3.98	S15	3.62	3.62	3.34	3.46
16	S16*	3.76	S16	3.52	3.28	3.10	3.84
17	S17*	4.06	S17	3.42	3.88	4.06	4.14
18	S18	4.02	S18	3.58	3.74	4.04	4.02
	Average score	3.98		3.48	3.52	3.57	3.82
	Leadership		*Leadership*	*PSU-A*	*PSU-B*	*PU-A*	*PU-B*
19	S19*	4.02	S19	3.62	3.10	3.84	3.22
20	S20*	4.12	S20	3.48	3.44	4.07	4.06
21	S21*	3.88	S21	3.46	3.24	3.84	3.33
22	S22*	4.22	S22	3.68	3.84	4.02	3.56
	Average score	4.06		3.51	3.40	3.94	3.54
	Institutional infrastructure		*Institutional infrastructure*	*PSU-A*	*PSU-B*	*PU-A*	*PU-B*
23	S23*	4.42	S23	3.58	3.48	3.92	3.52
24	S24*	4.43	S24	3.52	3.52	4.02	3.82
25	S25*	4.51	S25	3.64	3.88	3.82	3.70
26	S26*	4.24	S26	3.26	3.76	3.72	3.88
	Average Score	4.40		3.50	3.71	3.87	3.73

(S1, S2…. Represent statements used to capture the perception of educators while S1*, S2*…. Represent statements used to capture expectations of educators, public state university (PSU), private university (PU).

Step 2: Trade-off score calculations

This section calculates and compares the trade-off scores (E-P) between the expectations and perception of educators regarding Industry 5.0 centric curriculum and pedagogy adoption capability of their respective institutions:

PU-A had the lowest trade-off score (0.42). Institutional culture (1.06) in PSU-B, curriculum, pedagogy, and evaluation (0.87), upskilling educators (1.16), academia-industry relationships (0.5) in PSU-A, leadership (0.66) in PSU-B, and institutional infrastructure (0.9) in PSU-A have the most significant trade-off. These colleges must correct the gap between expected and perceived Industry 5.0 curriculum and pedagogy adoption. Innovation in curriculum, pedagogy,

Table 10.2 Comparative trade-off score of universities

Sr. No.	*Dimension*	*PSU-A [E-P]*	*PSU-B [E-P]*	*PU-A [E-P]*	*PU-B [E-P]*
1	Institutional culture	0.84	**1.06***	**0.39****	0.62
2	Institutional strategy	**0.87***	0.71	**0.35****	0.6
3	Upskilling educators	**1.16***	0.68	0.75	**0.67****
4	Academia-industry partnerships	**0.5***	0.46	0.41	**0.16****
5	Leadership	0.55	**0.66***	**0.12****	0.52
6	Institutional infrastructure	**0.9***	0.69	**0.53****	0.67
Total		4.82	4.26	2.55	3.24
Average Un-weighted Trade-off score (Total/6)		**0.80***	0.71	**0.42****	0.54

(* Shows the highest trade-off score, whereas ** shows the lowest trade-off score in a particular dimension)

and evaluation must be part of the company's strategy. Innovation in curriculum, pedagogy and evaluation is important for government institutions' future growth. Today, students choose universities based on quality, not cheap fees. Private universities teach innovative courses. These colleges adapt their curricula to global workforce needs. Teachers can create their course curriculum. Private universities offer innovative, high-quality education. Government universities lag in innovative teaching. Companies must prioritize innovation to achieve this (Kirsch et al., 2010). These universities must strengthen institutional culture for innovative curriculum and teaching. Leadership, infrastructure, upskilling educators, and academia-industry relationships are key. PU-A had the lowest trade-off in four of the six Industry 5.0-centric curriculum and pedagogy adoption capability dimensions (institutional culture, 0.39; strategy, 0.35; leadership, 0.12; institutional infrastructure, 0.53) and must lower its trade-off in academia-industry partnerships (0.41) and educator upskilling (0.75) just like PU-B, which has the lowest trade-off in these dimensions (academia-industry partnerships, 0.16 and educator upskilling, 0.67). PU-A must support industry-academia partnerships and teacher upskilling (Mitchell and Guile, 2021; Collins, 2018). The rest of the universities must benchmark with PU-A in four dimensions (Institutional Culture, Curriculum, pedagogy and evaluation, leadership, and institutional infrastructure) and PU-B in two dimensions (academia-industry partnerships and educator upskilling). No public institution had the lowest trade-off score in any of the six Industry 5.0 curriculum and pedagogy adoption capability characteristics, challenging their readiness to implement Industry 5.0 and compete with private colleges.

Step 3: Assigning weights

This stage expands weighted scoring. Twenty experts received a 6D response sheet. Experts ranked six dimensions. The experts were requested to elaborate on the most critical aspect of the Industry 5.0 curriculum and pedagogy.

Step 4: Calculation of weighted score

Using steps two and step 3, the weighted trade-off score calculation has been listed in Table 10.4.

Table 10.3 Weights assigned to industry 5.0 centric curriculum and pedagogy adoption capability dimensions

S. No.	*Dimensions*	*Points*
1	Institutional strategy	0.28
2	Institutional infrastructure	0.12
3	Educator upskilling	0.15
4	Leadership	0.14
5	Institutional culture	0.08
6	Academia-industry partnerships	0.23
	Total	1

Table 10.4 Weighted trade-off scores of selected universities

Sr. No.	*Dimension*		*PSU-A [E-P]*	*(WTS) PSU-A*	*PSU-B [E-P]*	*(WTS) PSU-B*	*PU-A [E-P]*	*(WTS) PU-A*	*PU-B [E-P]*	*(WTS) PU-B*
1	Institutional culture	0.08	0.84	0.0672	1.06	0.0848*	0.39	0.0312**	0.62	0.0496
2	Institutional strategy	0.28	0.87	0.2436*	0.71	0.1988	0.35	0.098**	0.6	0.168
3	Upskilling educators	0.15	1.16	0.174*	0.68	0.102	0.75	0.1125	0.67	0.1005**
4	Academia-industry partnerships	0.23	0.5	0.115*	0.46	0.1058	0.41	0.0943	0.16	0.0368**
5	Leadership	0.14	0.55	0.077	0.66	0.0924*	0.12	0.0168**	0.52	0.0728
6	Institutional infrastructure	0.12	0.9	0.108*	0.69	0.0828	0.53	0.0636**	0.67	0.0804
Total weighted trade-off score (TWAS)				0.7848		0.6666		0.4164**		0.5081

*US – Un-weighted score, *WTS – Weighted Trade-off score, *WTAS- Total weighted trade-off score, *Score in bold represents the minimum weighted Trade-off score

Table 10.4 shows that PU-A had the lowest total weighted trade-off score (TWAS, 0.41) between expected and perceived innovation-supportive qualities, including institutional culture (WTS, 0.0312), institutional strategy (WTS, 0.098), leadership (WTS, 0.0168), and institutional infrastructure (WTS-0.0636). PU-B scored lowest on Upskilling educators (WTS, 0.1005) and Academia-industry cooperation (WTS-0.0368). The trade-off score represents expected and perceived industry 5.0 curriculum and pedagogy adoption capabilities. The highest trade-off score demonstrates institutions' inability to adapt the industry 5.0 curriculum and methodology. As seen, public sector universities had the highest weighted trade-off score in all six dimensions (institutional culture, PSU-B, WTS-0.0848; institutional strategy, PSU-A, WTS-0.2436; upskilling educators, PSU-A, WTS-0.174; academia-industry partnerships, PSU-A, WTS-0.115; leadership, PSU-B, WTS-0.0924; institutional infrastructure, PSU-A.

Conclusion

The study found six key Industry 5.0 curriculum and pedagogy adoption characteristics. As discussed above, institutional strategy is the most important component for education institutions to embrace Industry 5.0 curriculum, pedagogy, and evaluation approaches. Institutions must set strategic objectives that prioritize implementing Industry 5.0 to create industry-ready workers. These strategic goals must be shared as KPIs to show institutional commitment to innovative education. If resistance arises, the entire organization must be involved. The strategy must develop Industry 5.0-ready professionals. This study concluded that academia-industry ties are the second most important enabler of Industry 5.0-ready academic changes. Industry-academia partnerships are crucial for technological innovation and advancement. While industry concentrates on solutions with immediate commercial benefits and academia on research and education, the two can work together to hasten discoveries. Upskilling educators is the third most crucial Industry 5.0 curriculum enabler. Instructors are directly involved in curriculum development, pedagogy, and evaluation, so they need training and assistance. Implementing an industry-ready curriculum will depend on instructors' ability to provide pupils with industry-ready inputs, which will require upskilling. Leadership is the fourth Industry 5.0 enabler. Developing institutions into thriving learning communities demands strong leadership. Leaders can act as change agents to help educational institutions implement the Industry 5.0 curriculum. Adopting the future curriculum requires modern infrastructure that allows students to put theory into practice and be job-ready from day one. The fifth significant driver of curriculum innovation is institutional infrastructure. Institutional culture followed. Encouraging a quality institutional culture that empowers instructors and students to defy traditional mindsets and be inventive will determine if educational institutions can adopt Industry 5.0 and build tomorrow's workforce. Academic leaders should heed the study's conclusions. The mismatch between educators' expectations and perceptions of their institutions' readiness calls for a thorough rethinking and reengineering of technical education in India. Since public colleges scored top on all six key enablers, they have a long way to go to compete with private universities in Industry 5.0 readiness.

Limitations and Scope for Future Research

The current study included 280 educators from two public and two private universities in Punjab, India. This is a tiny fraction of India's 12,84,755 higher education academics and 907 universities (399 state, 126 deemed-to-be, 48 central, and 334 private). Future studies can use a larger sample to generalize results. Future research might compare Industry 5.0 curriculum and pedagogy uptake across countries to learn what drives innovation at top schools worldwide.

References

Broo, D. G., Kaynak, O., & Sait, S. M. (2022). Rethinking engineering education at the age of industry 5.0. *Journal of Industrial Information Integration*, 25, 100311.

Brown-Martin, G. (2017). Education and the fourth industrial revolution. Groupe Média TFO, 1.

Chitkara, M., Kanwar, V. S., & Dutta, H. (2020). Redefining Indian Universities: An Insight of Education Sector towards Evolution of Industry 4.0 and 5.0. *University News*, 58, 33.

Collier, I. & Shakespeare, P. (2020). Manufacturing the future workforce. High-Value Manufacturing Catapult/Gatsby Foundation. https://hvm. Catapult. Org. UK/tfw.

Collins, A. and Halverson, R. (2018). Rethinking education in the age of technology: The digital revolution and schooling in America. Teachers College Press, New York, (NY)

Field, M. and Golubitsky, M. (2009). Symmetry in chaos: a search for pattern in mathematics, art, and nature. Society for Industrial and Applied Mathematics.

Fornell, C. and Larcker, D. F. (1981). Structural equation models with unobservable variables and measurement error: Algebra and statistics.

Hair Jr, J. F., Anderson, R. E., Tatham, R. L., & William, C. (1995). Multivariate data analysis with readings. Prentice Hall, New Jersey.

IMHE (2012). Fostering quality teaching in higher education: policies and practices. https://www.oecd.org/education/imhe/QT%20policies%20and%20practices.pdf.

Indian Express (2020). COVID-19 pandemic pauses Punjab students' foreign dream. https://www.newindianexpress.com/nation/2020/aug/03/covid-19-pandemic-pauses-punjab-students-foreign-dream.

Kirsch, L. J., Ko, D. G., & Haney, M. H. (2010). Investigating the antecedents of team-based clan control: Adding social capital as a predictor. Organization Science, 21(2), 469–489.

Mitchell, J. & Guile, D. (2021). Fusion Skills and Industry 5.0: Conceptions and Challenges.

Mohelska, H. & Sokolova, M. (2018). Management approaches for Industry 4.0–the organizational culture perspective. *Technological and Economic Development of Economy*, 24(6), 2225–2240.

Mustafa Kamal, N. N., Mohd Adnan, A. H., Yusof, A. A., Ahmad, M. K., & Mohd Kamal, M. A. (2019, January). Immersive interactive educational experiences–adopting education 5.0, industry 4.0 learning technologies for Malaysian universities. *In Proceedings of the International Invention, Innovative & Creative (InIIC) Conference*, (pp. 190–196).

Nahavandi, S. (2019). Industry 5.0—A human-centric solution. *Sustainability*, 11(16), 4371.

OECD. (2021). The future of education and skills Education 2030, https://www.oecd.org/education/2030/E2030%20Position%20Paper%20(05.04.2018).pdf

Papadimitriou, F. (2012). Artificial Intelligence in modelling the complexity of Mediterranean landscape transformations. *Computers and Electronics in Agriculture*, 81, 87–96.

Pereira, A. G., Lima, T. M., & Charrua-Santos, F. (2020). Industry 4.0 and Society 5.0: opportunities and threats. *International Journal of Recent Technology and Engineering*, 8(5), 3305–3308.

The Tribune, (2018). Crisis in higher education in Punjab https://www.tribuneindia.com/news/comment/crisis-in-higher-education-in-punjab/575515.html.

Yetilmezsoy, K., Ozkaya, B., & Cakmakci, M. (2011). Artificial intelligence-based prediction models for environmental engineering. *Neural Network World*, 21(3), 193.

Zhang, X., Yang, S., Srivastava, G., Chen, M. Y., & Cheng, X. (2020). Hybridization of cognitive computing for food services. *Applied Soft Computing*, 89, 106051.

11 Soil inspecting smart machine

Mohmmad Umer Farooq[1,a], *Shivanshu Sharma*[1,b], *Rakshak*[1,c], *Harsh Vardhan Khati*[1,d], *and Nitin Kumar*[2,e]

[1]School of Agriculture, Lovely Professional University, Punjab, India

[2]Assistant Professor, School of Electronics and Electrical Engineering, Lovely Professional University, Punjab, India

Abstract

A soil test is fundamental in modern agriculture for streamlining the creation, shielding climate from over utilization of composts, and setting aside money and energy. In this undertaking, an independent versatile stage with soil examining gadgets was created for agriculture. Soil samples are investigated to decide the structure, attributes, and supplement levels of the soil. A basic hand-held field-testing unit can be utilized by small landholder farmers. In enormous homesteads, where plants are developed on many hectares, an independent portable stage with a soil sampler would be the most ideal choice. New creation and the board strategies considering information gathered about unambiguous areas and harvest assortments are called accuracy cultivating. Utilizing the robot referenced above can expand asset and cost-effectiveness in information obtaining. By utilizing the robot's installed frameworks, farmers can get continuous data about soil properties from the field. An effective creation process is empowered by information advances and soil assortment frameworks. Agribusiness is no special case for the dynamic digitization of all parts of our lives, including the utilization of robots. We will depict the centerline of the soil-examining robot.

After portraying accessible business answers for soil testing and information stockpiling. The versatile robot looks like a six-wheeled stage with an off-road suspension framework. The soil examining gadget is mounted and installed and comprises a drill pipe with a fold toward the finish to hold the soil inside, keeping up with its entire cross-segment. It is presently being created how soil tests can be put away and broken down. The consequences of tests and reviews show that such a robot could upgrade creation productivity. Examining gathered examples gives exact data about supplement accessibility.

Keywords: ArduinoUNO, hand-held probe, soil moisture, weather monitor

Introduction

The characterization of soil texture depends on the mixture of particles of minerals in the soil with a few kinds of recovery systems. The global characterization system separates soil texture into four gatherings (sand, clay-loam, clay, and loam) and 13 levels.

The electrical properties of soil allude to the electrical and physical properties of soil, which are not quite the same as its electrochemical properties, including the natural electric field (electric potential), resistance (conductivity), electro-osmosis, and dielectric constant of different soils. Likewise, soil resistance is the inverse of soil conductivity. Deciding the soil moisture or saltiness and the dispersion limit of specific soils is normally utilized. These soil properties give a hypothetical premise for estimating soil moisture.

Soil properties are gathered and analyzed involving numerous particular machines in farming. Current cultivating puts a high worth on soil quality. A restricted agriculture workforce and expanding natural debasement make soil examination vital. Checking soil debasement requires a soil test. Offering better types of assistance to farmers would empower them to successfully deal with their territories more. Worldwide cultivating will profit from

In agribusiness, however, robotized guiding frameworks, information applications, and versatile stages are scant on farmers. The idea of shrewd cultivating includes the reconciliation of rural advances with current information innovation. We present our answer to the soil testing issue in this paper.

Available Solution

Hand-held soil probes are the most affordable commercial solution. Surface samples are commonly collected with this device. It takes time to examine the soil in a laboratory after it is collected. In large farms covering hundreds of hectares, these methods are not sufficient. (Carlson T 2007).

[a]mohdumer7m@gmail.com;[b]shivanshus669@gmail.com;[c]rakshakchoudhary332@gmail.com;[d]harshkhati123@gmail.com;[e]nitin.14652@lpu.co.in

Figure 11.1 Hand-held soil probe

Figure 11.2 On-board platform during activity

Agriculture doesn't have many motorized arrangements. These days, reaping robots are more popular than soil-monitoring robots. There are a couple of portable science labs in space missions, like the Mars Science Lab (Interest wanderer) and the Yutu Lunar Meanderer. Such arrangements ought to be executed on the planet. An example of a soil sampling device on a mobile platform comes from the well-known University Rover Challenge. Based on a similar method to the Curiosity rover, Figure 11.2 presents the designed solution. It is a driller equipped with self-sealing containers. We could use such a solution in agriculture and add applications to store soil properties data. (Fares A, Polyakov V. 2006)

The device can collect up to 30 g of loose soil in 30 s. For further analysis, the sample is taken to a lab. The laboratory must analyze soil samples for the above-mentioned examples. We will create a 'laboratory on wheels'. Data will be stored in the base after samples are examined in situ using the mobile platform.

Design of the Mechanism

A wide range of territory can be taken care ofby our answer for profound soil tests. The suppositions were to convey soil tests from various geographical layers, furnish the stage with lab gadgets, and mount a mechanical arm on the stage. An illustration of a planned stage with a dirt driller is displayed in Figure 11.3.

To gather profound soil tests, a unique driller is utilized. Appended to the meanderer body, it is a singular module. A steel pipe fills in as the foundation of the penetrating part, which conveys the heap during the cycle and finishes with a centre drill that is uncommonly planned. PVC pipe is utilized as s supplement. There is a longer cut in the steel pipe that permits you to see what's inside (the ground layers). Two sensors are situated inside the line to screen temperature and dampness. Two straight aides are driven by DC engines connected to trapezoidal screws. With the development, it is feasible to take an example 35–40 cm subterranean level with layers noticeable. Variolation was likewise used to guarantee that response powers were isolated from the stage (J. P. Grotzinger et al., 2012). Figure 11.4 outlines a suspension framework suggestive of a rocker-boogie. The suspension estimates 890 mm wide × 1200 mm long × 400 mm high and weighs under 23 kg. Utilizing aluminium profiles welded together, it accomplishes a lightweight and strong design.(Kargas G, Soulis K X 2012)

Planned locally available soil driller. The differential system permits each wheel to be lifted to 40 cm while the other wheels stay on the ground. Different high deterrents can be overwhelmed by the stage. A plain holding on for an aluminium profile connected to two strung poles shapes the actual differential. A supported bind withrotating conjuncture interfaces bars to swingarms. Utilizing this methodology, we had the option to nullify.

Conventional incline gears, expand differential dependability while keeping a smooth Top of the undercarriage framework development over impediments without extra dampers. The edge was additionally upheld by this instrument. Swingarms are associated with the edge through the plain plastic direction. The arrangement gives an oil-free, soil-safe, and truly solid association. (Kinzli K D, Manana N, Oad R 2012). To further develop driveability, the centre arrangement ofthe wheels is moved around 5 cm to the outside (Figure 11.4).

Figure 11.8 represents the fc28 hygrometer and the sensor called DHT11 these two are used to measure soil moisture humidity and temperature respectively the data is read by the sensor and sent to the microcontroller board. Then the board processes and the data are mapped according to the code and at last, finally, the result is displayed on the LCD unit.

Test

An image of the soil testing portable stage in real life should be visible in Figure 11.5. It has been tried in various fields on our university campus and outside the campus. The soil tester has been tried for humidity and temperature tests in the O-humus layer of the soil horizon. (M. Rećko and J. Tolstoj-Sienkiewicz 2017)

Figure 11.3 A platform with a soil driller

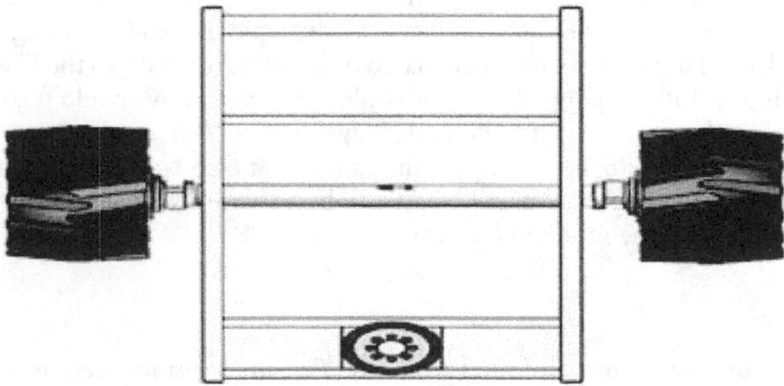

Figure 11.4 Suspension framework

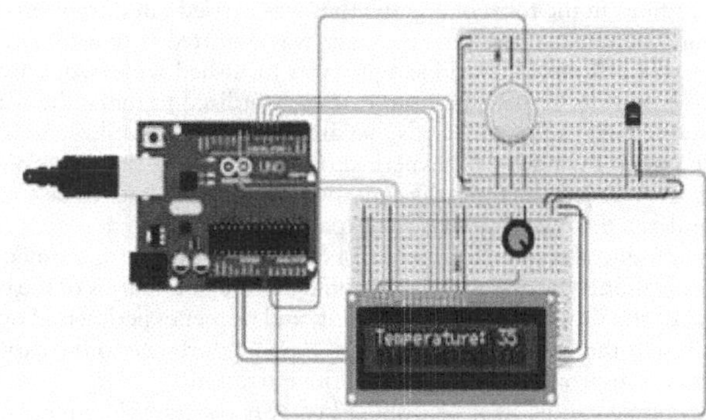

Figure 11.4a Arduino connected to sensors

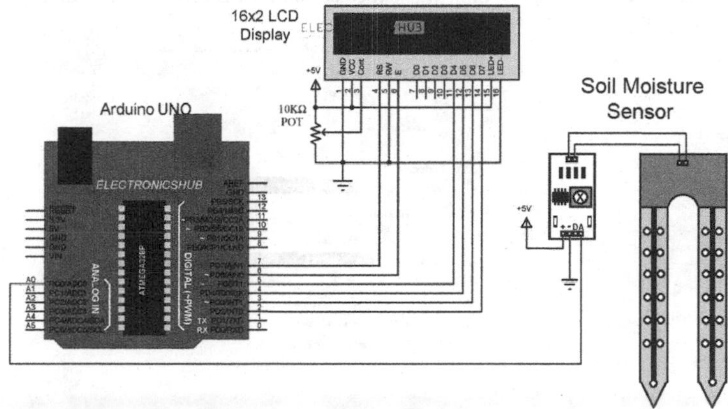

Figure 11.4b a-Arduino Uno with the soil moisture sensor

Figure 11.5 Soil test gadget on a versatile stage during activity

Coming up next is temperature and humidity readings in the form of a graph that was carried out during this activity notwithstanding GPS, magnetometers and surrounding sensors, the versatile stage was outfitted with a camera. A test with a temperature sensor and a humidity sensor was utilized. The drill sampler was furnished with two sensors. The robot was controlled from a distance from the base station in this situation. Python is utilized to make the war room application (Figure 11.6). The application is partitioned into a few sub-cards that are not difficult to utilize. A GPS scroll map shows the area of the meanderer in the fundamental window. All experimentally fascinating tangible estimations are gathered in the lab segment. The design board, another part, permits the condition of the meanderer to be controlled. A joystick with various buttons controls the meanderer. Each has a particular capability and activity.

The information from the sensors is saved in the produced report (Figure 11.7.a & 11.7.b) after the assessment on the picked site. Thusly, the administrator can acquire a genuinely necessary understanding of the boundaries of the example that has been gathered. There is a precise portrayal of the site, current air conditions, and primer experimental outcomes remembered for the report. The specialist can choose if the gathered examples have any importance to the exploration completed, as well as whether the gathered material is appropriate for additional investigation.

As per the administrator's primer choice, the example can be kept or disposed of. It is conceivable, in any case, for one more example to become debased with pollutants from the past example on the off chance that the material is discarded. The unloading technique might prompt misleading positive or bogus adverse outcomes if it is intruded on or not finished accurately. Subsequently, another emphasis of the plan was expected to address this imperfection

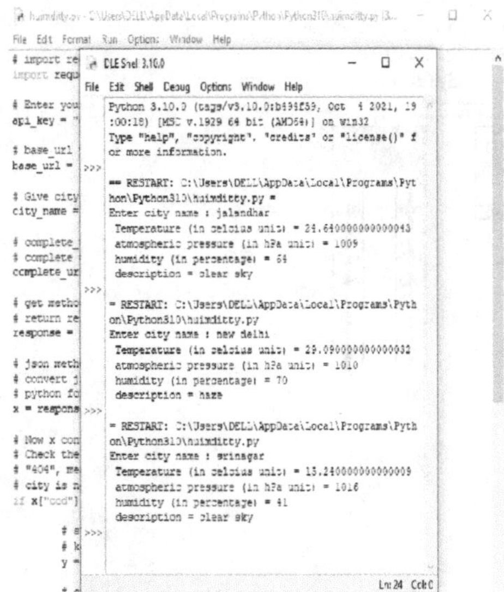

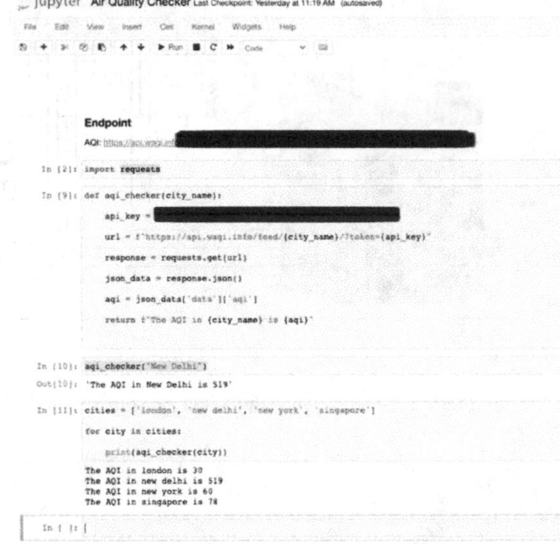

Figure 11.6 Real-time application interface

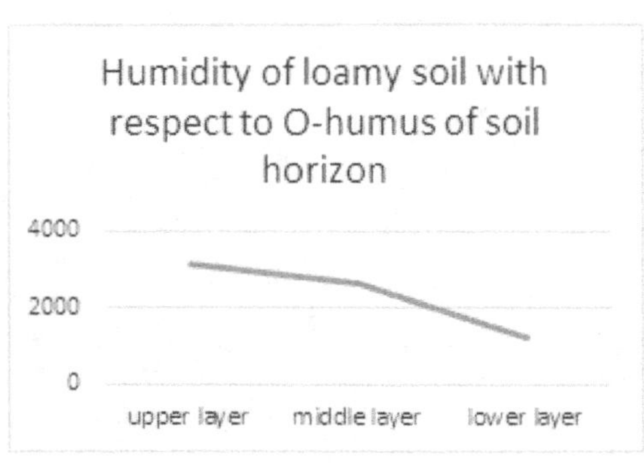

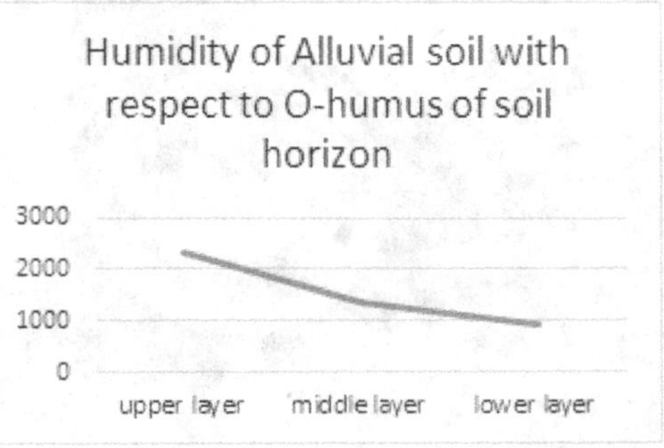

Figure 11.7a Report created on the analyzed site

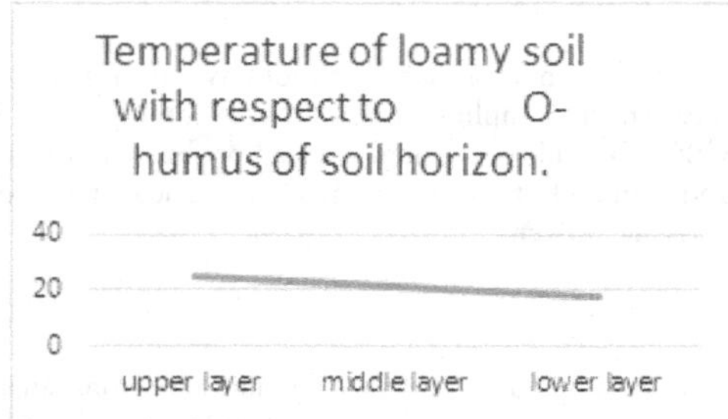

Temperature of Alluvial soil with respect to O-humus of soil horizon.
40
20
0
upper layer
middle layer
lower layer

Figure 11.7b Report created on the analyzed site

Representation of model

Figure 11.8a Shows a side view of the on-board platform

Figure 11.8b Shows side view of the on-board platform

Figure 11.8c Shows a side view of the on-board platform

Result

The control unit is programmed to act in a sequence to achieve the best performance. But the robot navigation platform is still experimental. The control unit has the power to navigate between the sampling points slower than the operator with ATV approximately two times. If a human-based operator with ATV and the manually based probe can approximately collect 50 composite samples per hour at max while the robot can collect 75 samples per hour. The difference is due to the faster processor and the traditional beat method while driving slower.

References

Carlson, T. (2007). An overview of the triangle method for estimating surface evapotranspiration and soil moisture from satellite imagery. *Sensors*, 7(8), 1612–1629.

Fares, A. & Polyakov, V. (2006). Advances in crop water management using capacitive water sensors. *Advances in Agronomy*, 90, 43–77.

Grotzinger, J. P., Crisp, J., Vasavada, A. R., Anderson, R. C., Baker, C. J., Barry, R., et al. (2012). Mars Science Laboratory mission and science investigation. *Space Science. Reviews*, 170, 5–56, 2012.

Kargas, G. & Soulis, K. X. (2012). Performance analysis and calibration of a new low-cost capacitance soil moisture sensor. *Journal of Irrigation and Drainage Engineering*, 138(7), 632–641.

Kinzli, K. D, Manana, N., & Oad, R. (2012). Comparison of laboratory and field calibration of a soil-moisture capacitance probe for various soils. *Journal of Irrigation and Drainage Engineering*, 138(4), 310–321.

NagAhage, E. A. A. D., Nagahage, I. S. P., & Fujino, T. (2019). Calibration and validation of a low-cost capacitive moisture sensor to integrate the automated soil moisture monitoring system. *Agriculture*, 9(7), 141. doi: 10.3390/agriculture90701

Njoku, E. G. & Entekhabi, D. (1996). Passive microwave remote sensing of soil moisture. *Journal of Hydrology*, 184(1–2), 101–129.

Peng, S. Q., Zhong, Y. H., Cui, Y., & Yang, C. R. (Technical manual of farmland soil moisture monitoring.

Raper, T. B. (2014). In-season drought monitoring: Testing instrumentation and developing methods of measurement analysis. *Doctoral dissertation*, 2014; 158p.

Rećko, M. & Tolstoj-Sienkiewicz, J. (2017). Versatile soil sampling system capable of collecting transporting storing and preliminary onboard analysis for mars rover analogue. Solid State Phenomena, 260, 59–65.

Su, S. L., Singh, D. N., & Baghini, M. S. (2014). A critical review of soil moisture measurement. *Measurement*, 54, 92–105.

Thomas, A. M. (1966). In situ measurement of moisture in the soil and similar substances by 'fringe' capacitance. *Journal of Scientific Instruments*, 43(1), 21–27.

Van Bavel, C. H. M., Underwood, N., & Swanson, R. W. (1956). Soil moisture measurement by neutron moderation. *Soil Science*, 82(1), 29–42.

Yu, H., Xie, D. T., Luo, Y. Z., Zhang, Z. L., Zhang, S. R., Li, W. L., et al. Accuracy analysis and evaluation of four common soil moisture sensors.

Zazueta, F. S., & Xin, J. N. (1994). Soil moisture sensors. Florida Cooperative Extension Service, Bulletin, 292, 1–11.

Zhang, Y., Ma, Y. H., Jiang, Z. H., Tan, C. J., & Wang, C. S. Progress on research and application of rapid measurement of soil moisture sensor.

12 Study and comparison of various substrate integrated waveguide fed antenna technology for X-band applications

Vishakha Tomar[a]

Assistant Professor, ECE Department, Maharaja Surajmal Institute of Technology, Delhi, India

Abstract

This research work proposes substrate integrated waveguide-fed antennas with different design structures that operate in the license-free spectrum of X-band (9-10 GHz). With respect to the configuration of antenna design the issue of obtaining narrower return loss bandwidth is addressed by the initiation of different shaped slots in the rectangular waveguide section of the empty substrate integrated waveguides antenna design. empty substrate integrated waveguides design uses a more enhanced and promised technique i.e., absence of dielectric material from the substrate design while upholding and keeping their advantages of low-cost and low-profile characteristics intact. This paper describes the impact and control of the design parameters on the characteristics like insertion losses and fractional bandwidth. The results obtained from simulation using Ansys HFSS environment confirms the design approach which confirms the attainment of return loss value better than 10 dB in the operating bandwidth for all systems.

Keywords: Empty substrate integrated waveguide, dielectric, slot, bandwidth

Introduction

Rapid revolution and advancement in the emerging field of wireless communication system demand allocation of unoccupied frequency bands and thus the advancement in antenna design having wider bandwidth, low profile, and improved efficiency. In the initial field of communication, microwave guiding structures used for application in microwave frequency bands were conventional metallic waveguides with high power, low loss, and high Q-factor but had the drawback of being bulky, voluminous, and non-planar in nature. Microstrip and CPW technologies when used in the microwave frequency domain are generally used for low-power applications which necessitate very firm tolerances for wavelengths of smaller value and such waveguide devices undergo an elevated amount of manufacturing costs.

As an alternative a viable technique of implementing substrate integrated waveguide (SIW) structures has been placed upfront, which gets the better of the issue of the backside radiation and enhances the bandwidth value by making acceptable modifications in the parameters like size and shape of the slots in the design of the antenna (El Khamlichi et al., 2021). Technology involving the use of SIW structures, has been employed in a diversity of microwave devices and circuits, over a last decade which involves devices like active and passive circuits. Mostly invented devices and circuits using this technology have been filters, couplers, and antennas. Likewise, active circuits have been made consisting of oscillators, active antennas, and mixers (Tomar, 2021).

Cavity-backed slot antennas were proposed using SIW technology. This design topology is used in the fabrication of devices operating at high frequencies i.e., in (X and Ku bands) and further can be utilized for millimeter-waves applications. They suffer from the disadvantage of narrow bandwidth which is confronted by some authors. Belenguer et al. (2014) proposed an improvement in cavity-backed single-slot antenna design parameters like bandwidth by allocation of hybrid cavity modes in SIW design. However, Bozzi et al. (2011) proposed an antenna based on cavity-backed dual-slot technique attaining 8.5% of bandwidth i.e., (0.8 GHz in the X-band). It was indicated that if a slot of bow-tie is used, the bandwidth is augmented to an additional of 1 GHz (9.4%). Raghavan and Kumar proposed a planar cavity-backed circular patch that delivers the bandwidth more than 2.31 GHz i.e., 23.1% (Deslandes and Wu, 2003).

In addition to the above, cavity-backed slot antennas suffer from minimal values of gain (El Khamlichi et al., 2021). The antenna fabricated in achieved good bandwidth but with a minimal gain of 3.7 dbi. When the design is excited using a SIW cavity with slots being bilateral, it achieves wider bandwidth besides high gain.

Slots size and shape along with the feed network type affects the bandwidth immensely. In this paper, we delve into the potentiality of combining several slots of variable shapes and dimensions over a substrate of lossy in nature to accomplish an improvement in the bandwidth (Dashti et al., 2003). The antenna is realized on a Neltec NH9348 substrate. Gain, insertion loss, reflection coefficient, bandwidth and radiation pattern are calculated and verified using EM simulation. The designed and simulated antenna design shows a gain which is in quasi-stable state over the frequency band ranging from 9.1 – 10 GHz and attaining the highest gain value of 9 dBi.

[a]vishakhatomar@msit.in

Design Procedure

The design structure of SIW, to be made perfectly, needs to stipulate the parameters required for the waveguide designing by considering certain conditions provided by the equations to find the accurate value of diameter 'd' of the vias and spacing 's' to be considered between the two adjacent vias.

$$d < \frac{\lambda_g}{5}, \tag{2(a)}$$

$$s \leq 2d \tag{2(b)}$$

Rectangular waveguide dimensions are obtained by the empirical equation

$$W_{SIW} = W_{eq} + \frac{d^2}{0.95 * s} \tag{2(c)}$$

$$L_{SIW} = L_{eq} + \frac{d^2}{0.95 * s} \tag{2(d)}$$

W_{SIW} and L_{SIW} represents the waveguide's width and length, similarly, W_{eq} and L_{eq} represents in its equivalent waveguide.

Solid rectangular waveguide filled with dielectric material required cut-off frequency is calculated by the empirical equation given,

$$f_{c_{mn}} = \frac{c}{2\sqrt{\mu_{r}\epsilon_r}}\sqrt{\left(\frac{m}{a}\right)^2 + \left(\frac{n}{b}\right)^2} \tag{2(e)}$$

$$fc_{10} = \frac{c}{2\sqrt{\mu_r \epsilon_r}} \frac{1}{\left(W_{SIW} - \frac{d^2}{0.95s}\right)} \tag{2(f)}$$

Parameters a and b signifies waveguides width and height, $f_{c_{mn}}$ indicates general cut-off frequency expression, $f_{c_{10}}$ represents the fundamental cut-off frequency mode (El Khamlichi et al., 2021).

Initial values of width and length i.e., W_{eq} and L_{eq} are obtained using the above-mentioned equations which are then optimized in the Electromagnetic simulation so as to achieve the effective characteristics of the corresponding rectangular waveguide apprehended in the technology based on SIW technique.

Bandwidth Improvements

Proposed antenna designs are designed and simulated using ANSYS HFSS environment with Neltec NH9348 as substrate having relative permeability of $\epsilon_r = 3.48$ and thickness of 0.760 mm. Performance of an antenna is optimized by taking its parametric study into consideration about the dimensions and the number of slots including the feedline as well. The detailed description of the study is followed below.

Slots effect

Number of slots effect

Initially the design of the SIW antenna was designed without adding any slots. Further, taking this study into consideration some slots were added in SIW cavity backed slot antenna-based design with different parameters and dimensions. The same parametric analysis or designing is executed to govern the slots to be used, to attain the parameters like optimal gain and efficiency at the preferred frequency band to operate. Results are obtained as anticipated and shown in the figure. It is evident from the analysis that better insertion loss and increased resonating frequency of the antenna is achieved as the slots are introduced in the design of SIW antenna. Figure certifies the positive outcome of including slots on the bandwidth in the designing of SIW. Impedance's real part i.e., Re (Z_{11}) is equivalent to 50 Ω on the resonating band of the antenna [9.4–10.5 GHz]. Likewise, the imaginary part i.e., Im (Z_{11}) value is equivalent to zero on this band of frequency (Belenguer et al., 2014)

Slots dimension and shape effect

Studies by various authors have summarized that the variation being made in the positioning and dimensions of slots have a great impact on the parameters like bandwidth and insertion loss of antenna, so this alteration made allows us to widen the bandwidth of the antenna design. Variables like feedline's length, position and number of the slots have an influence on the gain and bandwidth of the antenna. To upgrade the operational bandwidth, antenna design is augmented with three slots of different parameters like shape and size.

Design of square (length and width of 12 mm) and circular shaped slot (with radius of 6 mm) and the third slot of plus sign (length 14 mm and width 5.5 mm) are etched on the top of the substrate. The length of these slots is maximized keeping the constraints that they accommodate within the length of the antenna. The dimensions of the square slot are determined by analyzing the cavity resonator with its mode. The radius taken for the circle slot is kept such that it follows the condition $\lambda_g/20$ to sustain the resonance frequency.

Position and the size of the slots determines total current flow and its resonating frequency. The distribution of current over the surface is severely affected by the dimensions like shape and size of the slots. Performance analysis is described in the tabular form in Table 12.1 below for the various configurations of SIW antenna design.

Table 12.1 Performance analysis summary of different configurations

Configuration	*Return loss*	*Bandwidth*	*Insertion loss*
C1	>20 db	2.07 GHz	<1.07 db
C2	>15 db	2.03 GHz	<0.97 db
C3	>20 db	2.20 GHz	<1.04 db
C4	>10 db	100 MHz	<1.90 db

Source: Author's compilation

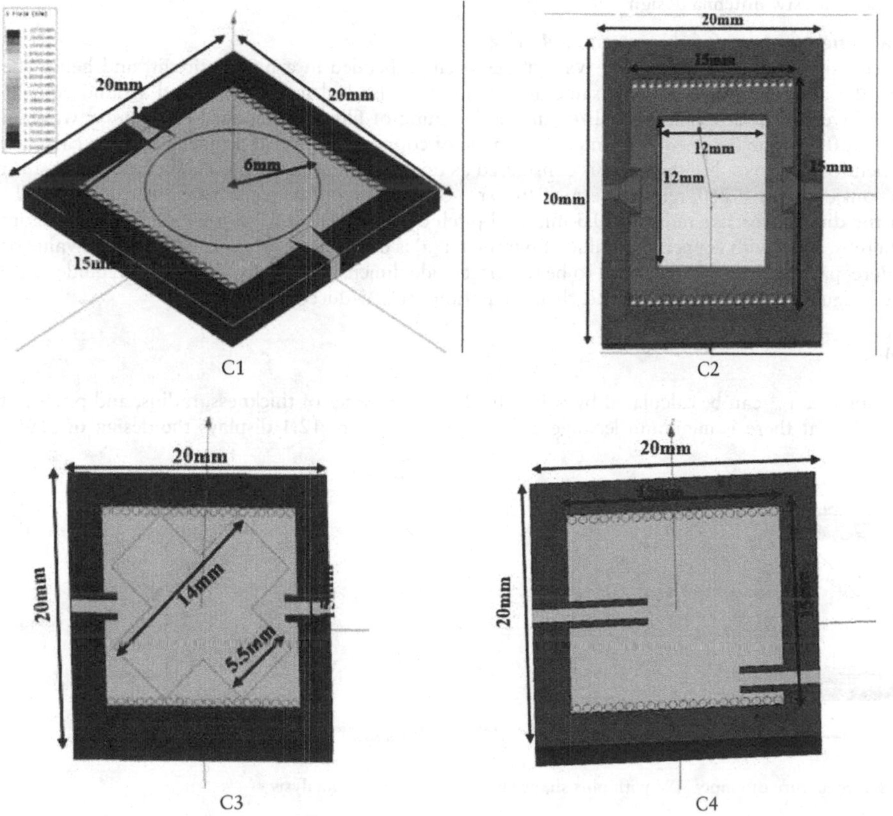

Feedline effect

Feedline length has its own effect and allows the resonance mode to excite i.e., TE_{140} of the cavity and instantaneously the slots. Therefore, it is essential to shift the operating frequency of the specific slot in the required and desirable X-band, to achieve higher gain and efficiency with better radiation performance. Indeed, parametric analysis and simulation is executed to optimize the parameters such as feedline length L, width W, which in turn has a slight influence on the results of gain and bandwidth of the antenna. Figure demonstrates the result for the different slot structures and empty dielectric configuration antenna with different values of length and width. The important thing noticed in the different configurations is that slot and feedline has an evident role in the improvement of bandwidth and gain of antenna.

Parametric Analysis

SIW cavity backed slot antenna design configurations have influence on the bandwidth which is analyzed with the optimization being done at the simulation tool i.e., ansys HFSS. Analyzation is necessary to determine both the resonance frequency boundaries i.e., upper, and lower. Parameter's affecting the input impedance and bandwidth of the rectangular slot antenna are its length and width dimensions (L_s, W_s). The width considered for the slots is considered very low in comparison to the resonating antenna's wavelength. The position and width of the slots plays an important role in determining certain conditions of the antenna like impedance matching. Input impedance is affected in an immense manner by increasing the width of the slot. To radiate maximum energy, the length of the slot is kept at a value which is half the wavelength value of resonance frequency. The major shift caused in the bandwidth and resonance frequency of the SIW based cavity backed antenna is due to the alteration done in the dimensions of length of the rectangular slot (Deslandes and Wu, 2013). The antenna, designed with the rectangular and various other shaped slots, attain the value of bandwidth varying in the range of 2 – 3 GHz. On comparing it with an SIW antenna with no cavity backed slot-based antenna the huge difference is noticeable, when it comes to the bandwidth and resonance frequency parameters.

Parametric study of esiw antenna design

Empty ESIW design for cut-off frequency of 9.44 GHz

ESIW filters are similar to the rectangular waveguides been embedded in a planar circuit, and hence the procedure conducted in the designing these filters is same as that used in classical method centered around equivalent circuits comprising of invertors and resonators utilized in the designing of filters in standard rectangular waveguide (Kumar and Raghavan, 2017). The designed SIW antenna is made of copper. The cut-off frequency can be calculated from the equation 3 mentioned above. The thickness is considered as tm = 0.760 mm etched on Neltec NH9348 substrate whose thickness is considered as 0.760, relative permittivity εr = 3.48 and had loss constant value of 0.003. All the vias are etched with the dimensions like radius of 0.3 mm and pitch equivalent to 0.75 mm for different configuration styles, which are thereby, filled with copper. The value of parameter 'a' is determined by approximating the value of resonating frequency. Here, parameter 'a' is considered to be the larger side dimension of conventional waveguide (air-filled). If the considered waveguide is filled with dielectric, then the parameter is deduced to 'ad'.

$$f_c = c/2a \quad 3(a)$$

SIW dimensions i.e., a_{SIW} can be calculated by using the 2(a). The values of thickness, radius, and pitch of the vias are considered such that there is minimum leakage across the vias. Figure 12.1 displays the design of SIW with all the

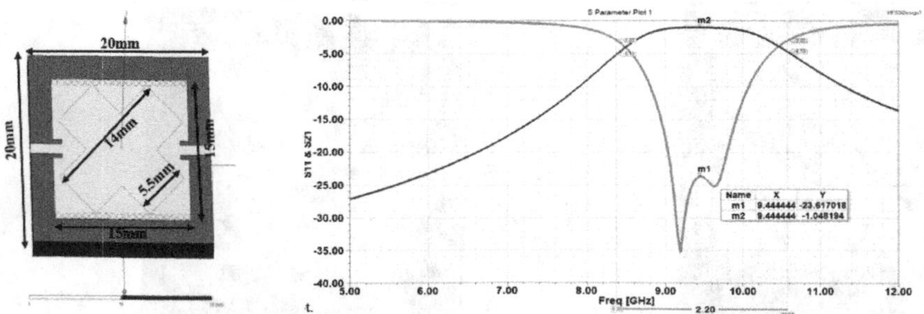

Figure 12.1 Structure of empty SIW with plus shape slot and S parameter analysis

calculated parameters. Proper selection of the parameters like pitch and diameter of the vias reduces the leakage of the field (Chen et al., 2016)

The S11 parameter i.e., the reflection coefficient of the cavity slot antenna is obtained and verified with simulation software (HFSS). The value of reflection coefficient calculated by the simulation results concludes a better adaptation to the resonating frequency in the bandwidth of about 9.0–10.0 GHz.

Figure 12.1 explains the behavior of plus shaped slot SIW antenna and the working of SIW antenna can be obtained by the S11 parameter as shown in Figure 12.1 in the X-band.

Empty substrate integrated waveguide design with no slot

The reason to consider the substrate without any dielectric is to attain an improvement in the efficiency of the gain by minimizing the loss due to substrate. The substrate comprising air aids to match simply with the impedance of the free space, which makes the requirement nil at the end of the transition (Kumar et al., 2018).

No slot based ESIW antenna design is kept like the ESIW antenna with slots to realize the changes, improvement, and significance of both the structures. Table 12.3 shows the several parameters of no slot ESIW antenna. On finding the S11 parameter from the Figure 12.2, it is evident that the antenna consisting of no slot resonates at a frequency of 5.88 GHz. The insertion and return loss obtained in this structure is less as compared to the ESIW design as mentioned in Figure 12.1.

Figure 12.1 explains the resultant change in the S11 parameter when the ESIW antenna was designed with no slot and all the changes in the value of insertion and return loss can be calculated and are mentioned in the Table 12.3. Specifications of both the antennas are kept the same. By the comparison between the antenna designs it can be clearly seen that slot has a major effect on the resonance frequency, return loss and insertion loss parameters of the antenna.

Table 12.2 Optimal values of antenna parameters

S. No	*Specifications*	*Value*	*Parameter*	*Value*
1	Ground plane	20 mm × 20 mm × 0.2 mm	Cutoff frequency (f_c)	9.44 GHz
2	Top patch	15 mm × 15 mm × 1.5 mm	Bandwidth	2.20 GHz
3	Slot in substrate	14 mm × 5.5 mm	Insertion loss (dB)	<1.04
4	Via radius	0.3 mm	Return loss (dB)	>20
5	Loss tangent (δ)	0.003	Dielectric constant (ε_r)	3.48
6	pitch	0.75 mm		

Source: Author's compilation

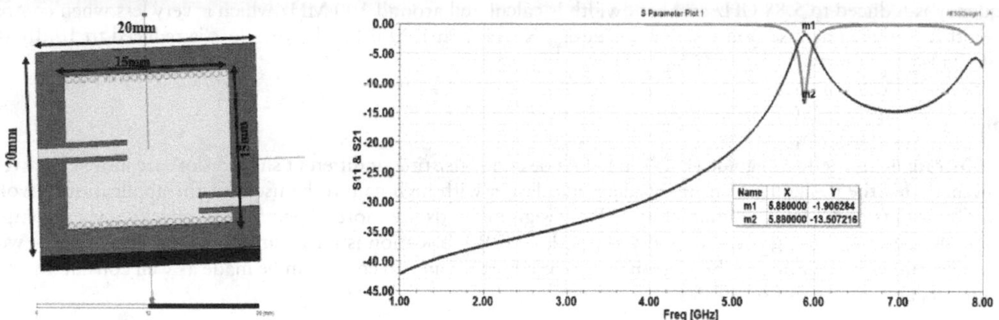

Figure 12.2 Structure of SIW for same dimension without slot in substrate and its parameter analysis

Table 12.3 Optimal values of antenna parameters with no slot

S.No	*Specifications*	*Value*	*Parameter*	*Value*
1	Ground plane	20 mm × 20 mm × 0.2 mm	Cut off Frequency (f_c)	5.88 GHz
2	Top patch	15 mm × 15 mm × 1.5 mm	Bandwidth	100 MHz
3	Slot in substrate	No slot	Insertion loss (dB)	<1.90
4	Via radius	0.3 mm	Return loss (dB)	>10
5	pitch	0.75 mm	Loss tangent (δ)	0.003

Source: Author's compilation

Result and Discussion

To compare the ESIW antennas with slot and no slot, we have plotted S11 parameter and calculated both insertion and return losses.

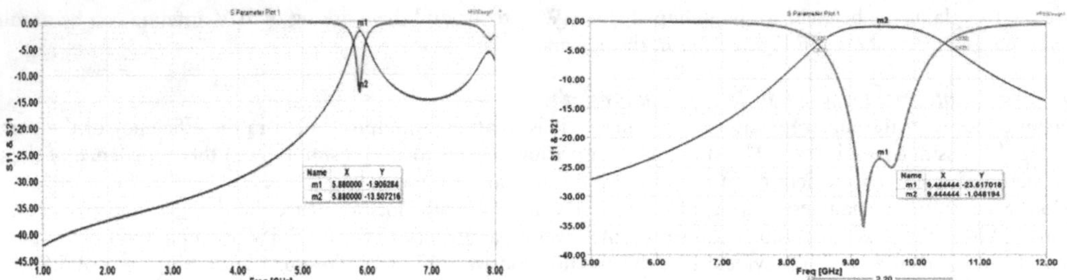

Figure 12.3 S parameter analysis (a) without slot (b) with plus slot

Table 12.4 Comparison of parameters of both the designs

Parameters	*Design 1 (Slot)*	*Design 2 (No slot)*
Substrate	14 × 5.5 mm^2	No slot
Cut off frequency	9.44 GHz	5.88 GHz
Bandwidth	2.20 GHz	100 MHz
Insertion loss	1.04 dB	1.09 dB
Return loss	>20	>10

Source: Author's compilation

In design 1, plus shape slot is created in substrate of 14 × 5.5 mm^2. The cut off frequency is 9.44 GHz and bandwidth is 2.20 GHz. For the given design insertion loss is less than 1.04 dB and return loss is better than 20 dB. The simulated results are shown in Figure 12.3 (b) whereas in design 2, no slot is considered in the substrate of the same size. The cut off frequency is reduced to 5.88 GHz and bandwidth is calculated around 100 MHz which is very less when compared with the other design. The insertion loss for this design is less than 1.09 dB and return loss is reduced to 10 dB as the earlier design.

Conclusion

Empty substrate integrated waveguide (ESIW) antenna design consisting of different shaped slots are more effective and better methods for the designing of front-end antenna design with high gain to be used for the applications involving X-band. The results and analysis obtained by ESIW design methods are more impactful and effective when compared to the antenna designing using conventional waveguide. ESIW fabrication is much simpler and is very light as well in weight which makes installation of this antenna very easy. Further improvement can be made as well considering different design cuts and analysis of substrates.

References

Belenguer, A., Esteban, H., & Boria, V. E. (2014). Novel empty substrate integrated waveguide for high-performance microwave integrated circuits. *IEEE Transactions on Microwave Theory and Techniques*, 62(4), 832–839.

Bozzi, M., Georgiadis, A. & Wu, K. (2011). Review of substrate-integrated waveguide circuits and antennas. *IET Microwaves, Antennas & Propagation,* 5, 909–920.

Chen, Z. N., Liu, D., Nakano, H., Qing, X., & Zwick, T. (2016). *Handbook of antenna technologies*. Springer, Singapore.

Dashti, H., Shahabadi, M., & Neshati, M. H. (2013). SIW cavity-backed slot antennas with improved gain. 21st Iranian Conference on Electrical Engineering (ICEE), (pp. 1–4). IEEE.

Deslandes, D. & Wu, K. (2003). Single-substrate integration technique of planar circuits and waveguide filters. *IEEE Transactions on Microwave Theory and Techniques*, 51(2), 593–596.

El khamlichi, D., Touhami, N. A., Elhamadi, T., & Ali Ennasar, M. (2021). High-gain and broadband SIW cavity-backed slots antenna for X-band applications. *International Journal of Microwave and Wireless Technologies*, 13(10), 1078–1085.
El Khamlichi, D., Touhami, N. A., Elhamadi, T., & Badaoui, I. (2020). Broadband antenna SIW for X-band application. *Procedia Manufacturing*, 46, 808–813.
Kumar, A. & Raghavan, S. (2017). Wideband slotted substrate integrated waveguide cavity-backed antenna for Ku–band application. *Microwave and Optical Technology Letters*, 59(7), 1613–1619.
Kumar, A., Chaturvedi, D., & Raghavan, S. (2018). SIW cavity-backed circularly polarized square ring slot antenna with wide axial-ratio bandwidth. *AEU-International Journal of Electronics and Communications*, 94, 122–127.
Tomar, V. (2021). Analysis of SIW filter with less dielectric substrate. *International Conference on Industrial Electronics Research and Applications (ICIERA)*, (pp. 1–5). IEEE.

13 A comparative study on access control mechanism for blockchain enabled scalable systems in health care

Prince Arora[1] *and Avinash Bhagat*[2]

[1]Assistant Professor, School of Computer Applications, Lovely Professional University, Punjab, India

[2]Associate Professor, School of Computer Applications, Lovely Professional University, Punjab, India

Abstract

Blockchain has been one of the most interesting areas for a long time and it is also being used in various industries. Healthcare is one sector where blockchain technology can be used due to its security, privacy and decentralized nature, which benefits the healthcare system in many ways. The electronic health systems face different issues related to security, scalability, and integrity. In this paper, we discuss how the blockchain-enabled system can find the solution to the issues. We present a framework which reduces the load on the nodes by using some special calculations and also provides secure storage of the electronic records. Moreover, the framework also discusses the scalability problems faced by blockchain technology. The framework provides a scalable electronic healthcare system that solves the problems related to the scalability of blockchain.

Keywords: Blockchain, scalability, framework

Introduction

The health industry is currently facing various challenges regarding the maintenance of data. Maintenance of the medical history of the patient is a huge challenge because the use of different attribute-based smart healthcare devices has increased over the years. The data related to various patients' treatments and medicines needs to be integrated so that it can be easily accessible. The estimation is that 1 out of 13 students has been affected by medical identity theft in the last 5 years from 2015 to 2019. The limitations have also led to fraud in medical claims, so the importance of the data becomes even greater as compared to the various applications of the blockchain. A blockchain is a technology where the database is decentralized and shared across various network nodes. The information is stored in electronic form securely in a decentralized format where track of all the transactions is kept. The main advantage of using blockchain is that the transaction is completed without any third-party involvement. The technology is highly secure and follows various properties like irreversibility and immutability. When the block is filled in, the chain's time stamp is associated with it, and it is added to the chain. The technology offers peer-to-peer communication between two parties where the intervention of a third party is not required for the transaction to be completed.

Literature Review

Design Based Research

Wang et al. (2018) conducted a study based on various smart contract enabled frameworks. One of the frameworks is a parallel blockchain based on using multiple chains at one time. Various layers of the blockchain are discussed that allow the smart contract to be written in it. The code is also shared in it. The paper also focuses on insights on the applications and challenges faced by various frameworks. The network intends to have two separate modules. Kuo et al. (2017) created a review study of the blockchain-based network at the medical level. Various advantages and disadvantages of the blockchain-based network are discussed. Decentralization and immutability are various advantages of the blockchain network. The limitations of the blockchain-based network are confidentiality, speed, and scalability. To improve this, various virtual private networks have been created and encryption techniques have been introduced to store medical-related data.

Vujicic et al. (2018) conducted a study on Ethereum and bitcoin. The author has defined the change in technology as benefiting information systems. Blockchain mining is also considered in this concept. The paper also focuses on various dependencies of the blockchain and differentiates various blockchain models.

Implémentation Based Research

Ayache et al. (2022) proposed a Decentralised Accessible, Scalable, and Secure (DASSCare 2.0) model that works on real-time health monitoring that routes all the data from various resources and makes it available to various end users, which allows collaborative health monitoring and maintains the bills paid by the patient. The model gives an extra edge to other frameworks. Using a distributed database is a consensus of shared and synchronized digital data spread along a set of nodes. Contrary to popular belief, however, not all decentralized ledgers are in fact distributed ledger technology (DLT). The duplicity is high when the data is shared across various blocks.

Zhang et al. (2018) proposed a model that is based on the scalability of the blockchain where the clinics are required to be online through the blockchain based model. The study works on DAPP and focuses on how the FHIR chain model can be improved by using various techniques. The study also focuses on various parameters like blockchain, scalability, and other factors that work on blockchain.

Al-Karaki (2019) proposed the DASS Care framework, which is a scalable and highly accessible framework that is capable of getting real-time access to live data. This model is highly used in the healthcare sector where the clinical data is signed after it is generated from various sources. The integration of the data is done to ensure that the data is available to all the concerned hospitals and clinics.

Hafid et al. (2020) proposed a micro-payment transaction model which records only important transactions. The off-chain trading channel is established for offline trading. The transactions are performed via a private channel. If the offline chain is required to be closed, the recently signed message is transferred to the chain and the result is finalized.

Kim et al. (2018) proposed a survey-based model which is used for diagnosis system EHR. The study is primarily based on two factors: creating and storing the data gathered by various questionnaires. The validated questionnaires are then forwarded to a specific format which allows the data to be converted from the arbitrary model to a fixed model. The permission model can also be added to the mechanism to ensure that the data is secure and can't be updated by any other party.

Sahoo et al. (2018) proposed a model that is based on the Hadoop map-reduce framework that emphasizes the scalability problem to ensure that the availability of the data is at each end. A SHA-256 model is used to generate a unique hash for every transaction. The model works like a normal blockchain network with one modification: it stores the data in the Hadoop network.

Materials and Methods

The dataset which is being used for the implementation is taken from kaggle.com which has a wide attribute based database.

www.kaggle.com/datasets/davidechicco/chronic-kidney-disease-ehrs-abu-dhabi

Data is collected so that the operations like fetch, insert, update, and delete can be performed. The data set consists of various attributes which can be primarily divided into three categories. First attribute is based on the patient id which carries a lot of record. Second major attribute related to the work is history of the various patient records that is related to diabetic, smoking and vascular history. Third attribute is the baseline which formulates the average of various attributes and provides the current state of the patient.

Data Type: Chronic Kidney DiseaseEHRsfromAbu Dhabi (2)
Syntax:[Subgroup][PatientName][Doctor][Medicine]Time (3)

The data set is based on chronic kidney disease of the patients which requires the medical history of the patients to be stored so that if the patient is undergoing to some surgery or treatment the data can be accessed from EHR's quickly. This is a data set of electronic medical records of 491 patients collected at Tawam Hospital in Al-Aincity (Abu Dhabi, United Arab Emirates). The patients included 241 women and 250 men, with an average age of 53.2 years. Each patient has a chart of 22 clinical variables, that expresses her/his values of laboratory tests and exams or data about her/his medical history. Various attributes like patient and doctor are used in the data set which ensures that based on the parameters the data can be fetched.

Proposed Methodology

The model of access control ensures the arbitrary data comes from diverse resources. The data is difficult to handle due to its heterogeneous nature. The major role of the model is to convert the arbitrary data into fix type of data. To ensure this, various parameters like:- permission level, consensus level models are created.

Consensus level: Consensus level provides access to single or group of users. The level maintains there cord of all the users.

Permission level: The level grants various permission types. There are three permission types:- read, write and read/write.

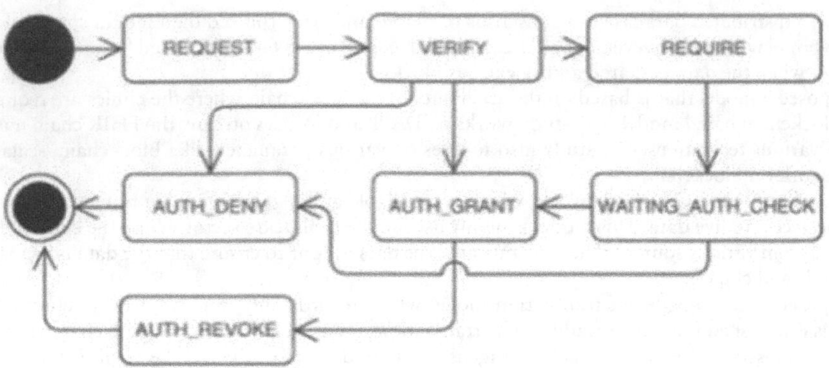

Figure 13.1 The grant-based model of proposed framework

Data keeper: It ensure that the access granted to various levels is as per the permission level or not. It also keeps track of all the access granted.

Policies: Certain defined policies are created, under these policies establishes a relation between the data keepers and various permission levels granted to them.

Comparison of Proposed Framework with Existing Frameworks

Scalability

Scalability refers to the ability to perform all the functions well even if the volume of transactions increases or decreases. Scalability is an important factor which should be addressed while working on technology like blockchain. The proposed model uses the log file model to ensure scalability, which focuses on the logic that the blockchain is not required to pass the complete chain instead of the total blockchain. As a result, the chain uses less gas to pass the chain from one node to the other node. Scalability can allow the information to be passed from one node to other node. With this, if huge amounts of patient records are to be stored, the degradation of the model is not there. It also ensures that while solving the scalability of the model, the security is not compromised.

Integrity

Integrity is measured by the trustworthiness of the system, and it is also ensured that the system is temper-proof and reliable. The information is accurate and cannot be changed by any unauthorized person. Doctors and patients are given access to the information. No third-party people have the right to change any type of information. Various access rules and regulations are associated with this to ensure that the data is not made available to everyone. The proposed model also assures that the security of the system is not degraded while focusing on its integrity. Different access controls can be provided to the system so that the data can be restricted to the users.

Access control

Access control is a role-based access mechanism that allocates a role to each step. There is two-step verification done. One by the access mechanism that itself is a secure model, and the second by the blockchain technology that makes the network more secure. The role-based system has defined roles and they use those definitions to grant and deny access to various requests coming forward to them. The parameters also ensure that patients' medical data is not compromised when access is provided to only authorized users.

Security of data

The patient's records are kept safe from any kind of third-party intervention. The patient's data includes various confidential data such as X-Rays, MRI, and blood group. All of this information is beneficial not only to patients but also to

Table 13.1 Comparison of different models

Parameter	*H-Base chain*	*FHIR-Chain*	*Questionnaire*	*Proposed model*
Scalability	High	High	Low	High
Integrity	High	High	High	High
Access Control	Low	High	High	High
Security	High	Moderate	Low	High

hospitals. A well-written smart contract is very helpful for the system to ensure transparency. If any third party wants to access the system, access is denied and hits the privacy as well. Information is kept private.

Conclusion

In this paper, different models are discussed that works on scalability, integrity, access control and security. These models are compared with the proposed model. The results are evaluated with the proposed model. The model is a collection of different attributes and high quality of scalability, integrity, access control is achieved by the model. The model basically focuses on two key points to ensure scalability: one is the conversion of arbitrary values to fix values, that is done by using the access control mechanism and the second is the block size construction that allows the model to be more precise and scalable. By access control mechanism, integrity can also be achieved in the model.

References

Al-Karaki, Jamal, N., Gawanmeh, A., Ayache, M. & Mashaleh, A. (2019). International wireless communications and mobile computing conference (IWCMC). *IEEE.*

Ayache, M., Gawanmeh, A., & Al-Karaki, J. N. (2022). DASS-CARE 2.0: blockchain-based healthcare framework for collaborative diagnosis in CIoMT ecosystem. *5th Conference on Cloud and Internet of Things (CIoT)*, (pp. 40–47). doi: 10.1109/CIoT53061.2022.9766532.

Hafid, A., Hafid, A. S., & Samih, M. (2020). Scaling blockchains: A comprehensive survey. *IEEE Access*, 8, 125244–125262. doi:10.1109/ACCESS.2020.3007251.

Kim, M. G., Lee, A. R., Kwon, H. J., Kim, J. W., & Kim, I. K. (2018). Sharing medical questionnaires based on blockchain. *2021 IEEE International Conference on Bioinformatics and Biomedicine (BIBM).* (pp. 2767–2769).

Sahoo, M. S. & Baruah, P. K. (2018). HBasechainDB - A scalable blockchain framework on Hadoop ecosystem. *Supercomputing Frontiers,* (pp.18–29).

Vujičić, D. Jagodić, D., & Randić, S. (2018). Blockchain technology, bitcoin, and Ethereum: A brief overview. *17th International Symposium Infoteh-Jahorina (INFOTEH).* (pp.1–6).

Wang, S., Yuan, Y., Wang, X., Li, J., Qin, R., & Wang, F. Y. (2018). An overview of smart contract: Architecture, applications, and future trends. *IEEE Intelligent Vehicles Symposium.* 4, (pp. 108–113).

Zhang, P., White, J., Schmidt, D. C., Lenz, G., & Rosenbloom, S. T. (2018). FHIRChain: Applying blockchain to securely and scalably share clinical data. *Computational and Structural Biotechnology Journal.* 16, 267–278.

14 A comprehensive study on student's academic performance prediction using artificial intelligence

Kajal Mahawar[1] *and Punam Rattan*[2]

[1]Ph.D. Scholar, Lovely Professional University, Punjab, India

[2]Faculty School of Computer Application, Lovely Professional University, Punjab, India

Abstract

Student academic performance prediction with the help of artificial intelligence (AI) is one of the challenging and popular research topics in educational data mining. Many known and unknown factors influence the academic performance of the student. Therefore, early detection and prevention measures are important in educational institutions. Several studies have been proposed by researchers in the field of educational data mining (EDM) and AI, in which it is challenging to predict the academic performance of students. Also, it is a major challenge for researchers to identify which machine learning techniques are very accurate in determining a student's academic success. To solve this challenge, in our study, we explored surveys and studies of 18 papers in this area. These surveys and studies mainly focus on trying to identify effective potential features and predictive models of students' academic performance prediction. It focuses on various important hidden features that may affect students' academic performance. This study will provide researchers with a quick review of some important and hidden features and AI techniques that can be used in this area.

Keywords: Student academic performance prediction, artificial intelligence, machine learning, features

Introduction

In artificial intelligence (AI) and educational data mining, for developing or evaluating models, choosing effective parameters are a difficult task. Educational data mining (EDM) employs AI and data mining approaches to sift through data from educational settings in search of patterns and predictions that describe students' actions and performance. It enhances students' brains and personalities. Predicting academic achievement in advance is a key part of the future perspective in education. Since learners are the key participants in academic institutions, academic institutions can respond to the changing requirements of the community by studying learner facts and finding various judgments from them. Additionally, the outcomes of projections might be useful for developing plans to raise educational standards. Intuitively, EDM was used to unearth facts concealed in the information that raised the standard of the entire educational system. A machine learning (ML) technique in EDM are increasingly being used to investigate educational data and identify hidden relevant patterns for predicting students' grades. The main goal of educational data mining is to propose models to enhance the quality of education. In data mining, EDM is a study area having applications of artificial intelligence, machine learning, deep learning, and statistics for the education sector. For the examination of data sets, many statistical methods, approaches, visualization software, and data mining tools are employed.

In this study, we have focused on the major difficulties of researchers to perform students' academic performance prediction research. To perform student's academic performance prediction research, identifying machine learning techniques and hidden features is a significant challenge for researchers. To solve this problem, we conducted a methodical literature review of 18 research articles from the year 2015–2022 to identify the effective hidden features and techniques of machine learning. From the methodological overview, the following research concerns were answered:

Which machine learning techniques are suitable for predicting students' academic success?

What are some hidden features that can be used to determine students' success?

Followed by these research concerns, to conduct this survey, we devised taxonomy of research directions and classified the relevant publications accordingly. The outline of the review paper is as follows: section 2 presented a related literature review with a comparative study table; section 3 presented the results and discussion on findings, section 4 presented the research gaps and recommendations. At last, in section 5, the conclusion is presented.

Literature Review

Research approach

In this paper, (Khan and Ghosh, 2021) research approach is used to conduct the study. As a result, as part of the survey strategy, we first constructed taxonomy of study directions. After defining the taxonomy, we used a hybrid strategy to find relevant literature. Using the letters 'student academic performance prediction', 'artificial intelligence' 'student academic performance parameters', and 'machine learning' in Google Scholar, we find papers. We were able to uncover 34 different studies connected to our survey using this method. We scan the abstract and keywords in each one for additional screening, and it filters out 16 papers that aren't relevant. Following that, we reviewed the complete text and attempted to determine whether the study's contribution is critical to the survey's research goal. This procedure aids us in weeding out research that is unrelated to academic performance prediction or parameters for students. Due to these criteria, 16 studies fail the eligibility test, leaving only 18 eligible publications for this review. The nominated papers are added to Mendeley tool as the next step in the qualitative synthesis. Finally, we organize and prepare a literature review of pertinent papers (Khan and Ghosh, 2021).

State-of-the-art studies

This section contains the 18 research articles that mainly contributed to this research paper.

Studies proposed in 2015: Alharbi et al. (2015) conducted research using nine different prediction algorithms to predict course grades for public university students. In the paper, two algorithms: decision tree and k-mean are used to forecast the achievement of the algorithms (Saxena, 2015).

Studies proposed in 2016: Using supervised machine learning techniques implemented using Rapid Miner researchers performed opinion mining on student responses generated through surveys (Dhanalakshmi et al., 2016).

Studies proposed in 2017: Gowri et al. (2017) analyzed EDM applications for students' academic performance prediction.

Studies proposed in 2018: Harvey and Kumar (2018) focused to provide a technique for grade k-12 students by finding out the important parameters used for the prediction of academic performance. Chui et al. (2018) suggested a reduced training vector-based support vector machine that can identify at-risk and marginal students. To forecast kids at risk of dropping out of high school (Chung and Lee, 2018) applied machine learning supervised classification algorithms. Additionally, Sugiyarti et al. (2018) focused on the issue of student scholarship.

Studies proposed in 2019: A study conducted by Tomasevic et al. (2019) aims to provide an analysis of supervised machine learning techniques and applied techniques to solve the problem of students' academic performance and students' future achievements prediction. One research conducted by Kamal and Ahuja, (2019) aims to investigate the reasons behind the big list of dropouts and less percentage rate of first-year students and highlighted the parameters which influence the academic rate.

Studies proposed in 2020: Yousafzai et al. (2020) analyzed the student grades and marks and proved that one subject mark can be used in the prediction of a student's previous academic marks. Tsai et al. (2020) study was based on analyzing how big data and AI are helpful for universities or colleges to learn about students' backgrounds and then interventions can be developed. Shankhdhar et al. (2020) created web-based software that allows students to choose a career path based on their personality traits, interests, and ability to complete the course, as well as find the top universities in their area depending on their location and tuition structure.

Studies proposed in 2021: A research by Agnafors et al. (2021) was conducted to test whether students' mental health parameter was useful to predict their academic performance or not and vice-versa, and also to investigate the relation between the mental health with academic performance during the development period (age 12–20). The study was conducted for students who are at risk and not able to pass their end-term exams (Rivas et al., 2021).

Studies proposed in 2022: Guterres et al. (2022) conducted one study and the scope of the study was to discover the important parameters and predict the students' academic performance rate in an online class environment during the COVID-19 pandemic. Study by Middleton et al. (2022) aims to provide an approach for testing the various in-formal networks among college faculty members and for estimating faculty potential results on work. Using the logistic regression model of machine learning, (Shaga et al., 2022) paper predicts the performance of 137 postgraduate students based on feedback.

The comparative studies of each paper with factors are presented in Table 14.1.

Table 14.1 A comparative study of papers

References	*Sample size*	*Techniques*	*Highest Accuracy technique*	*Gaps*	*Tools*
Alharbi et al. (2015)	213	SVD (SVDPP (SO (BO (non-negative matrix factorization (Normal Predictor (KNNBasic (KNNWithZscore (and CoClustering.	K- NN with ZScore = 84% in terms of PTA	Few Samples	NA
Saxena (2015)	NA	DT (J48) and K-means.	J48 = 87.75%	Dataset NA	WEKA
Dhanalakshmi et al. (2016)	6433	SVM (Naïve Bayes (KNN (and ANN.	NB= 99.11%	NA	Rapid Miner
Gowri et al. (2017)	100	Apriori Algorithm and k-means.	Both Apriori algorithm (k-means	Few Samples	WEKA
Harvey and Kumar (2018)	403	NB (LR (and DT.	NB = 71%	Few Samples	R
Chui et al. (2018)	32,593	RTV-SVM	RTV-SVM = 92.2%-93.8%	Influx Samples	VLE platform
Chung and Lee (2018)	165,715	RF	RF= 95%	Influx Samples	R
Sugiyarti et al. (2018)	19	Interview and DT (C4.5).	DT (C4.5) = 94.7%	Few Samples	WEKA
Tomasevic et al. (2019)	3166	K-NN (SVM (ANN (DT (NB (and LR	ANN = 96.6% with RMSE = 12.12	NA	Matlab
Kamal and Ahuja (2019)	480	Regression and DT (ID3).	ID3	Few Samples	SAS (Rapid Miner.
Yousafzai et al. (2020)	80,000	DT (K-Fold CV (Regression (KNN (and GA.	GA= 96.64% with RMSE= 5.34	Influx Samples	NA
Tsai et al. (2020)	3552	LR and Multilayer perceptron algorithm.	Multilayer perceptron= 77 %-90%	NA	TensorFlow (Keras
Shankhdhar et al. (2020)	270	DT (ID3 (CART (CHAID) (and NB.	ID3 = 66.37%	Few Samples	Python
Agnafors et al. (2021)	1700	LR and Statistics Techniques.	Mental health problems in early childhood increase the risk of poor result.	NA	SPSS
Rivas et al. (2021)	32,593	DT (RF (EGB (and ANN.	ANN = 78.2 %	Influx Samples	VLE platform
Guterres et al. (2022)	487	DT (ID3 and J48).	ID3= 84.80 %	Few Samples	Moodle
Middleton et al. (2022)	80	Snowball sampling (directed graph (and SNA.	Faculty culture parameter is related to quality practice.	Few Samples	Matlab 1015b bi-ograph
Shaga et al. (2022)	137	LR	Questionnaire (LR= 72%	Few Samples	Gnomio (Python.

Discussion

Relevant state-of-the-art studies: The Figure 14.1 shows the percentage of most relevant literature. Only 53% of the publications are relevant after the taxonomy is defined.

Number of state-of-the-articles (years): The Figure 14.2 shows the total number of research articles discussed in this paper from the year 2015 to the year 2022.

AI techniques used in state-of-the-art studies: To answer the first research question, the review of the literature revealed that many researchers used regression and classification algorithms in their studies, as shown in Figure 14.3. Decision tree 26%, logistic regression 20%, naive Bayes 14%, artificial neural network 13%, k- nearest neighbours 7%, support vector machine and random forest 5%, are the most popular regression and classification AI algorithms among researchers.

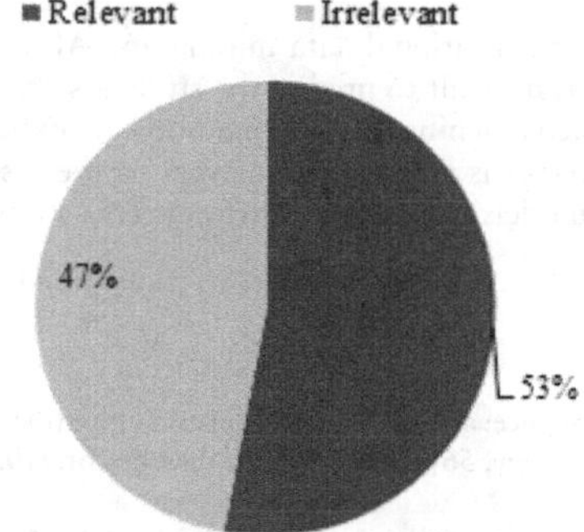

Figure 14.1 % of relevant literature

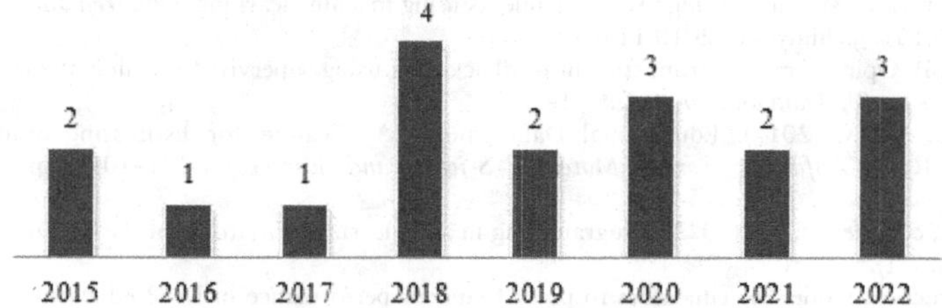

Figure 14.2 Number of state-of-the articles (years)

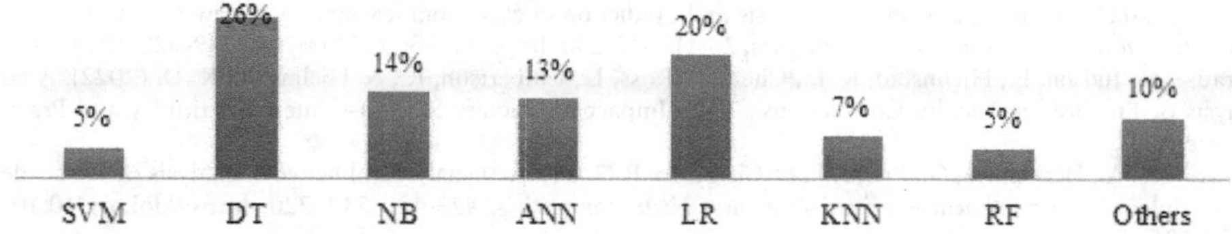

Figure 14.3 AI techniques used in state-of-the-art studies

Research Gaps and Recommendations

One core disadvantage is that the size of the dataset considered by many researchers is varying in nature. Additionally, in study, the authors worked on scholarship features in students' academic performance prediction (Sugiyarti et al., 2018). They worked on majors, parent income, parental responsibility, academic achievement, and non-academic achievement features. In this study, scholarship considerations feature such as religion, gender, single girl child, area they lived (urban or rural), category (EWS, UR, SC, ST, and OBC), etc. was not considered. In student-faculty interaction study, the authors used before COVID-19 pandemic data to test faculty-to-student and faculty-to-faculty interactions (Middleton et al., 2022). Researchers' study findings may affect because of the pandemic.

Recommendations

In order to answer the last research question, some more important features such as the 'number of hours spent playing video games', 'child life trauma' 'transportation facility', 'career awareness', and 'course satisfaction' should be used to predict the student's academic performance. Additionally, to generate prediction models, additional regression and classification algorithms should be explored in the future.

Conclusion

Predicting students' academic success is one of the difficult study subjects in educational data mining and AI. Experts in the field of artificial intelligence have put out several studies, in which it is difficult to predict the student's academic achievement. Additionally, it is quite difficult for researchers to pinpoint which machine learning methods are extremely precise in determining a student's academic success. The purpose of this paper is to provide answers to the research questions raised and to identify effective potential features and predictive models of machine learning. This study also uncovered several obscure features that previous studies have missed.

References

Agnafors, S., Barmark, M., & Sydsjö, G. (2021). Mental health and academic performance: a study on selection and causation effects from childhood to early adulthood. *Social Psychiatry and Psychiatric Epidemiology*, 56(5), 857–866. https://doi.org/10.1007/s00127-020-01934-5

Alharbi, B., Assiri, F., & Alharbi, B. (2015). A comparative study of student performance prediction using pre-course data. *Advances in Distributed Computing and Artificial Intelligence Journal*, 3, 1–14.

Chui, K. T., Chun, D., Fung, L., Lytras, M. D., & Lam, T. M. (2018). Predicting At-risk University Students in a Virtual Learning Environment via a Machine Learning Algorithm. *Computers in Human Behavior*. https://doi.org/10.1016/j.chb.2018.06.032

Chung, J. Y. & Lee, S. (2018). Dropout early warning systems for high school students using machine learning. *Children and Youth Services Review*, 1–35. https://doi.org/10.1016/j.childyouth.2018.11.030

Dhanalakshmi, V., Bino, D., & A. M., S. (2016). Opinion mining from student feedback data using supervised learning algorithms. *IEEE, 3rd MEC International Conference on Big Data and Smart City*, 1–5.

Gowri, G. S., Thulasiram, R., & Baburao, M. A. (2017). Educational Data Mining Application for Estimating Students Performance in Weka Environment. *IOP Conference Series: Materials Science and Engineering*, 1–10. https://doi.org/10.1088/1757-899X/263/3/032002

Guterres, J. de D., Laksitowening, kusuma A., & Sthevanie, F. (2022). Programming in an E-learning Environment Using Decision. *Syntax Literate: Jurnal Ilmiah Indonesia*, 7(1).

Harvey, J. L. & Kumar, S. A. P. (2018). A practical model for educators to predict student performance in K-12 education using machine learning. *Academia*, 2–9.

Kamal, P. & Ahuja, S. (2019). Academic Performance Prediction Using Data Mining Techniques : Identification of Influential Factors Effecting the Academic Performance in Undergrad. *Advances in Intelligent Systems and Computing*, 835–843. https://doi.org/10.1007/978-981-13-0761-4

Khan, A. & Ghosh, S. K. (2021). Student performance analysis and prediction in classroom learning: A review of educational data mining studies. *Education and Information Technologies*, 26(1), 205–240. https://doi.org/10.1007/s10639-020-10230-3

Middleton, J. A., Krause, S., Judson, E., Hjelmstad, K. L., Chen, Y., Ross, L., Culbertson, R., & Hjelmstad, K. D. (2022). A Social Network Analysis of Engineering Faculty Connections : Their Impact on Faculty Student-Centered Attitudes and Practices. *Education Sciences*.

Rivas, A., González-Briones, A., Hernández, G., Prieto, J., & Chamoso, P. (2021). Artificial neural network analysis of the academic performance of students in virtual learning environments. *Neurocomputing*, 423(40), 713–720. https://doi.org/10.1016/j.neucom.2020.02.125

Saxena, R. (2015). Educational Data Mining : Performance Evaluation of Decision Tree and Clustering Techniques Using WEKA Platform. *International Journal of Computer Science and Business Informatics*, 15(2).

Shaga, V., Gebregziabher, H., & Chintal, P. (2022). Predicting Performance of Students Considering Individual Feedback at Online Learning Using Logistic Regression Model. *Lecture Notes in Networks and Systems*, 191(2020), 111–120. https://doi.org/10.1007/978-981-16-0739-4_11

Shankhdhar, A., Sharma, D., Pushkarna, M., Agrawal, A., & Chaturvedi, S. (2020). Intelligent Decision Support System Using Decision Tree Method for Student Career. *International Conference on Power Electronics & IoT Applications in Renewable Energy and Its Control (PARC)*, 140–142.

Sugiyarti, E., Jasmi, K. A., Basiron, B., & Huda, M. (2018). Decision support system of scholarship grantee selection using data mining. *International Journal of Pure and Applied Mathematics*, 119(15), 2239–2249.

Tomasevic, N., Gvozdenovic, N., & Vranes, S. (2019). An overview and comparison of supervised data mining techniques for student exam performance prediction. *Computers & Education*, 103676. https://doi.org/10.1016/j.compedu.2019.103676

Tsai, S., Chen, C., Shiao, Y., Ciou, J., & Wu, T. (2020). Precision education with statistical learning and deep learning : a case study in Taiwan. *International Journal of Educational Technology in Higher Education*.

Yousafzai, B. K., Hayat, M., & Afzal, S. (2020). Application of machine learning and data mining in predicting the performance of intermediate and secondary education level student. *Education and Information Technologies*.

15 Detection of COVID-19 in CT scan images using intelligent methods

Ritika Mahajan[1,a], *Amritpal Singh*[1,b], *and Aman Singh*[2,c]

[1]Lovely Professional University, Punjab, India

[2]Universidad Europeadel Atlántico, Spain

Abstract

The objective of this study was to diagnose coronavirus lung illness using CT scan images of patients. We trained five image classification models based on neural networks using over 2800 photos infected with COVID-19 and non-infected with covid containing Inception V3, ResNet50, convolutional neural networks (CNN), and VGG16. Once trained for at least 50 epochs, all of the algorithms achieved more than 75% accuracy. Performance metrics improve with an increase in epochs, according to the accuracy and loss curves. As a result of the study, CNN performed at 84%, DenseNet121 at 88.73%, VGG19 at 81.08%, InceptionV3 at 77.87%, and ResNet50 at 90.14% on the CT scan dataset. Results indicate that the proposed model outperforms previous deep learning techniques.

Keywords: Covid, non-covid, CT scan, Inception V3, ResNet50, convolutional neural networks, VGG19, DenseNet121

Introduction

There has been constant devastation throughout the world since a new coronavirus caused a rapid outbreak in Wuhan, China, in 2019. Even the most advanced countries' healthcare systems were strained and crumbled by the disaster, not just their economies.

The respiratory tract can be infected by coronavirus infections, however the timing of these infections varies. Common viral symptoms like colds, coughs, fever, sore throats, and body pains are also associated with COVID-19. Breathlessness, chills, loss of smell, nausea, and diarrhea are further signs of the infection. It was initially thought that COVID-19 was pneumonia. There is also a connection between coronavirus and pneumonia. A lot of similarities were observed between pneumonia and COVID-19, for example, both of which are classified as respiratory illnesses and they both have the potential to cause severe illness. Breathlessness, coughing, chest pain, and chills are symptoms of the pneumonia virus, which also causes lung inflammation. It also results in a cold and fever, as well as chills and exhaustion. The flu or cold are the most frequently to blame for pneumonia, while COVID-19 can also be to blame. Based on CT scans, image analysis distinguishes COVID-19 from normal pneumonia. One part of the lung becomes infected with COVID 19, while another part becomes infected with pneumonia. Furthermore, COVID-19 spreads much more quickly than pneumonia. By infecting other organs and body parts, COVID-19 can cause damage.

A chest X-ray, a lung CT scan, and RT-PCR are currently the three most commonly used procedures for diagnosing COVID-19 infection. However, it lacks sensitivity and stability, which makes the RT-PRT test ineffective.

Furthermore, developing nations have faced a shortage of test kits due to the lack of testing capacity for COVID-19. COVID-19 can be identified using a lung CT scan image as an alternative to the RT-PRT test-based COVID-19 identification. Individuals with COVID-19 infection often have patchy shadows on both sides of their lung CT scans. Additionally, chest CT scans are inexpensive, quick, and highly sensitive methods of prescreening for COVID-19. As a result of the lack of testing capabilities, COVID-19 diagnosis requests have increased in underdeveloped countries. COVID-19 detection with image segmentation and RT-PRT tests is discussed below.

The current pandemic crisis has increased the number of infections and suspected cases, making manual annotation and contouring diseased lesions a critical and time-consuming task for health specialists. In order to diagnose individuals infected with coronavirus and increase treatment accessibility, it is crucial to segment these infections using an automated approach.

With the rise of coronavirus infections, it is more critical than ever to get early detection and treat them effectively. CT scans and X-rays are the two techniques for identifying the virus in the lungs. As a result, the proposed study intends to increase the precision of CT scans in identifying coronavirus infections. Also, it makes a distinction between people with pneumonia and those who have the coronavirus.

[a]ritikamahajan2010@gmail.com; [b]amritpal.17673@lpu.co.in; [c]amansingh.x@gmail.com

Literature Review

Using convolutional neural networks (CNN) for diagnosing coronavirus cases across all the chest X-rays was proposed by (Ozturk et al., 2020). In principle, they proposed a parallel classifier with two possible outcomes, coronavirus positive or negative. In addition to a multi-class classifier for coronavirus positivity or negativity, the authors also proposed a pneumonia-specific model. Their order accuracy was 96% and 98% in each case.

Keles et al. (2020) trained a deep transfer learning algorithm to categorize COVID-19 cases using chest X-ray image data using a ResNet architecture. This method had a high accuracy rate of 94.28%.

Hu et al. (2020) proposed an artificial Intelligence-based ShuffleNet V2 system. We supplemented the dataset with images to increase the number of photos for training. As a result, transfer learning applications were trained quickly and accurately. There was an average of 90.52% specificity, 91.58% sensitivity, and 0.9689% area under the curve (AUC).

The CTnet-10 binary classifier model had an accuracy of 82.1% when compared to the pre-trained VGG-19 model (Khan et al., 2020).

For categorizing COVID-19 positive and negative photos, Barstugan et al. (2020) used machine learning techniques. In addition to GLSZM and DWT, a support vector machine (SVM) was used to categorize the extracted features. An accuracy of 99.68% was achieved by combining the GLSZM approach with SVM.

Amyar et al. (2020) developed a model architecture based on the encoders and convolutional layers. AUC of 0.93% was achieved after training the model on three datasets.

Another study by Wang et al. (2020) used Unet for lung area segmentation training and pretrained UNets for CT volume testing to obtain lung masks. We concatenated all CT volumes with their corresponding lung masks and uploaded them to DeCoVNet. For this network, the AUC-ROC was 0.959.

The CT volumes were concatenated with their lung masks and uploaded to DeCoVNet. The AUC-ROC for this network was 0.959. CNN, ANFIS, and ANN models did not perform better than the suggested technique on any of the measures considered.

The COVID-19 images were classified using pre-trained networks and augmented data (Ahuja et al., 2020). As a means of enhancing CT scan images, stationary wavelets were combined with random rotation, translation, and shearing operations.

It was suggested that deep learning (DL) could be used to differentiate between COVID-19 and pneumonia (Wang et al., 2020). As part of the suggested technique, it was necessary to segment, suppress unnecessary regions, and analyze COVID-19. DenseNet121-FPN was used to segment lungs based on COVID 19 NET classification. According to AUC-ROC curves for two test sets, 0.87 and 0.88 were obtained for each.

According to Xu et al. (2020), relative position information of the lung patch is included in the CT scan classification process, in addition to preprocessing and ResNet18 image segmentation. In total, 86.7% of the tests were accurate.

The DRE-Net is based on the pre-prepared ResNet-50, as suggested by Ying et al. (2020). We compared the proposed network with ResNet, DenseNet, and VGG16 models previously developed. Based on AUC-ROC scores for image level characterization and human level grouping, the proposed network was found to perform better than all of the other models.

Rajagopal (2021) discussed in cooperation with deep learning and machine learning techniques, the researchers developed a system to identify COVID-19 positive X-ray images, pneumonia, and normal X-ray images.

Based on the CT images, Gozes et al. (2020) developed a new DL-based approach for diagnosing COVID-19 infection. Besides determining the severity of an infection, the algorithm can also determine the type of infection. AUC of 0.948 was obtained from the classification of the dataset.

Proposed Model

Coronavirus infections are on the rise, making it more important than ever to diagnose them correctly so that cases may be treated as soon as possible. Medical imaging equipment, such as CT scans, can be used to identify viruses in the lungs. This study aims to improve CT scan accuracy in diagnosing coronavirus infections. Furthermore, we want to distinguish patients with coronavirus from those with pneumonia. After comparing performance with the current approach, the new technique will be evaluated.

Following are the stages involved in the suggested technique:

Data: Among the data collected from reputable websites are CT scan images of the lungs. CT scan images of the lungs will be included in the data collected from reputable web sources.

Pre-processing: The preprocessing of the photographs in the acquired dataset will be the main emphasis of this section of the technique. It will eliminate unwanted characteristics in addition to noise. On the dataset containing the images, data cleansing and transformation will be performed.

Data partitioning: The dataset will be split into training and validation sets using cross-validation methods.

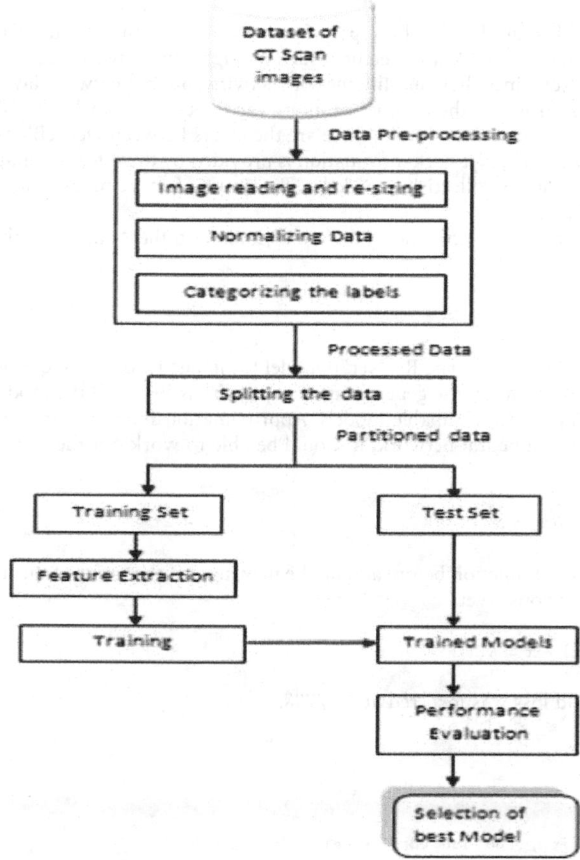

Figure 15.1 Phases of proposed methodology

Feature selection: To extract various features from the photographs, a variety of feature extraction/filtering techniques will be applied. This will allow for more accurate categorization of photos.

Model building: COVID-19 positive images, COVID-19 negative images, or pneumonia images will be categorized using classification.

Performance evaluation: We will use accuracy, precision, recall evaluation metrics to evaluate the performance of our suggested technique:

Selection of the best model: The effectiveness of different classification algorithms will be compared to choose the optimal model for this use case.

Proposed Algorithm

Artificial intelligence applications are increasingly relying on DL. Among the fields where deep learning can show state-of-the-art results are computer vision, natural language processing, and speech recognition. As a result, DL has become increasingly popular, as has research in the field. Deep learning is excellent at classifying images, one of its applications. Data can be trained on the model after preprocessing and separating it into training and validation sets. Data sets are trained using five different models, and their performances are compared. Models include the following:

DenseNet121

Training is conducted using the DenseNet-121 model. The gradient and the path from the input to the output layers vanish as the number of layers in the network increases. Network architectures such as highway networks, residual networks, and fractal networks can benefit from denseNets since they simplify the connectivity patterns between layers. DenseNets are divided into blocks called DenseBlocks, in which the number of filters varies between blocks, but the dimension of the feature maps does not change. Known as transition layers, these are the layers between DenseBlocks. Each layer of a features map grows in size as it is concatenated. Network information is provided by these feature maps. By accessing the previous layer's feature maps, each layer gains collective knowledge. By creating feature maps of information, each layer contributes to this collective knowledge.

A total of 50 epochs with a 64-point size is used to train. The activation function *softmax* and the Adam optimizer are used to build the DenseNet121 model.

ResNet50

Following ResNet50, the model has been trained using ResNet50. The ResNet50 model for image recognition consists of 50 layers of ResNet. Whenever the VGG model goes too deep, the generalization capability is lost, and the model's performance suffers. ResNet was studied in order to make more capable models. Approximation functions are good for neural networks. When given the input and output of a neural network, it should be able to work out the identify function independently.

$$f(x) = x$$

A neural network model can predict the previously learned function before adding the new input if the input of the first layer is circumvented and taken as the output of the previous layer.

$$f(x) + x = h(x)$$

Using this model, accuracy was achieved at 90.14% and loss was incurred at 23.77%.

```
#using DenseNet121 Model
def build_densenet():
    densenet = DenseNet121(weights='imagenet', include_top=False)

    input = Input(shape=(SIZE, SIZE, N_ch))
    x = Conv2D(3, (3, 3), padding='same')(input)

    x = densenet(x)

    x = GlobalAveragePooling2D()(x)
    x = BatchNormalization()(x)
    x = Dropout(0.5)(x)
    x = Dense(256, activation='relu')(x)
    x = BatchNormalization()(x)
    x = Dropout(0.5)(x)

    # multi output
    output = Dense(2,activation = 'softmax', name='root')(x)

    # model
    model = Model(input,output)

    optimizer = Adam(lr=0.002, beta_1=0.9, beta_2=0.999, epsilon=0.1, decay=0.0)
    model.compile(loss='categorical_crossentropy', optimizer=optimizer, metrics=['accuracy'])
    model.summary()

    return model
```

Figure 15.2 DenseNet121 model building

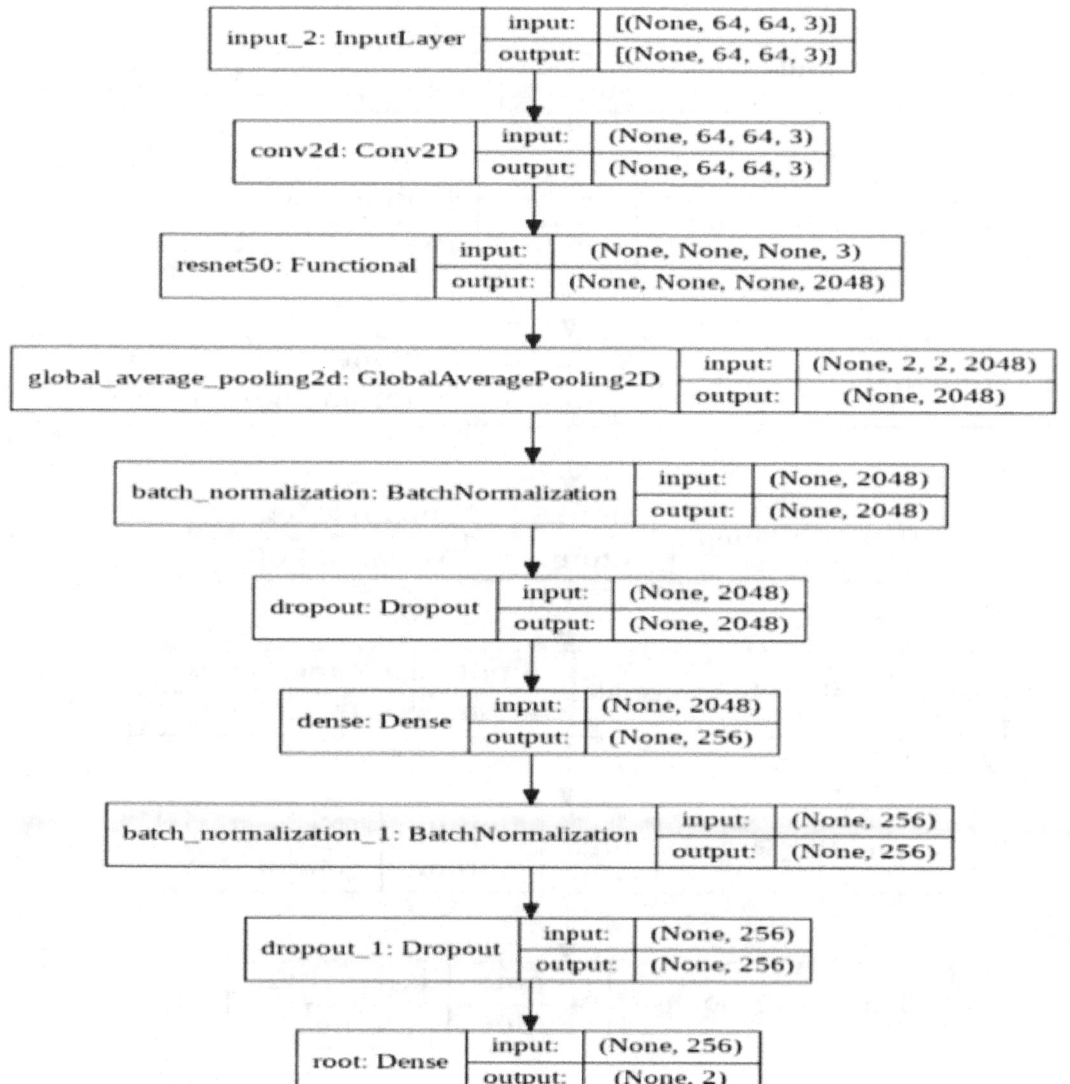

Figure 15.3 ResNet50 model plotting

Convolutional neural network

An image segmentation and recognition algorithm based on convolutional neural networks. While processing, weights and biases are assigned to images as inputs and outputs. Image recognition and classification are performed using convolutional neural networks (CNNs).

A model's assessment metric, such as precision, recall, F1 score, and support, is calculated. The model summary is displayed in the graphic below.

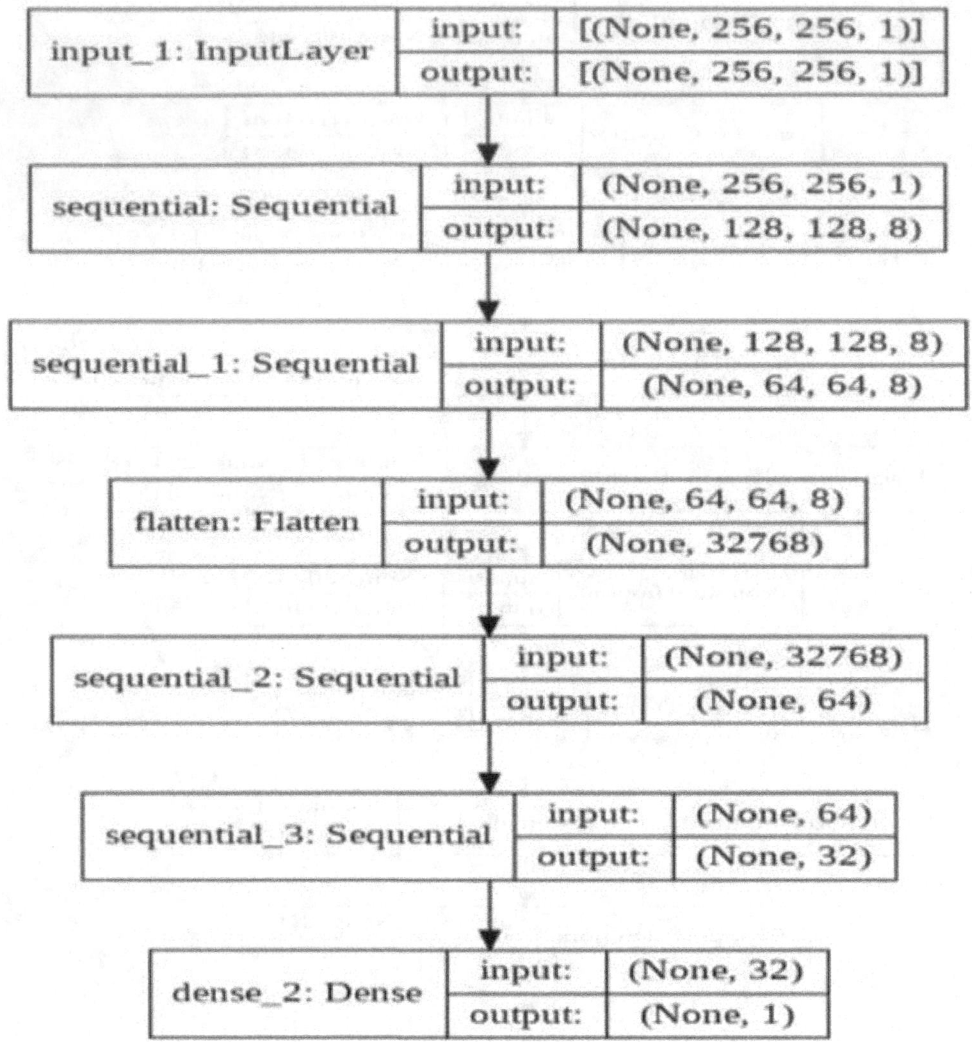

Figure 15.4 CNN model plotting

4.4 Inception V3

It is made up of a model of a convolutional neural network with label smoothing, convolutional factorization, and auxiliary classifiers. It is used for image analysis and detection. Neural networks are widely used for image recognition, including Inception V3. A 78.1% accuracy rate was obtained with the Inception V3 model on the ImageNet dataset. Szegedyet originally proposed this model in his paper. The theme of the paper is 'Rethinking the Inception Architecture for Computer Vision'. Convolutions, dropouts, maximum pooling, average pooling, contacts, and fully connected layers form the Inception V3 model, which consists of both symmetric and asymmetric building blocks. The model uses Batchnorm extensively, and its activation inputs are affected by it as well. For this model, we use Softmax as the loss function.

This model achieves an accuracy of 77.87% and a loss of 51.45%

```
# inception V3
def build_in():
    inception = InceptionV3(weights='imagenet', include_top=False)

    input = Input(shape=(SIZE, SIZE, N_ch))
    x = Conv2D(3, (3, 3), padding='same')(input)

    x = inception(x)

    x = GlobalAveragePooling2D()(x)
    x = BatchNormalization()(x)
    x = Dropout(0.5)(x)
    x = Dense(256, activation='relu')(x)
    x = BatchNormalization()(x)
    x = Dropout(0.5)(x)

    # multi output
    output = Dense(2,activation = 'softmax', name='root')(x)
    # model
    model = Model(input,output)

    optimizer = Adam(lr=0.002, beta_1=0.9, beta_2=0.999, epsilon=0.1, decay=0.0)
    model.compile(loss='categorical_crossentropy', optimizer=optimizer, metrics=['accuracy'])
    model.summary()

    return model
```

Figure 15.5 Inception V3 model building

4.5 VGG19

An image classification and recognition model based on CNN, VGG19. In their paper '*Very Deep Convolutional Networks for Large-Scale Image Recognition*', Simonyan and A. Unlike traditional convolutional networks, deep neural networks can be used to resolve complex problems involving large volumes of data. Based on the ImageNet dataset, the researchers achieved 92.7% top-5 accuracy. A RGB image of 224 × 224 is used as an input to the first convolutional layer in VGG16.

```
def build_vgg():
    vgg = VGG19(weights='imagenet', include_top=False)

    input = Input(shape=(SIZE, SIZE, N_ch))
    x = Conv2D(3, (3, 3), padding='same')(input)

    x = vgg(x)

    x = GlobalAveragePooling2D()(x)
    x = BatchNormalization()(x)
    x = Dropout(0.5)(x)
    x = Dense(256, activation='relu')(x)
    x = BatchNormalization()(x)
    x = Dropout(0.5)(x)

    # multi output
    output = Dense(2,activation = 'softmax', name='root')(x)

    # model
    model = Model(input,output)

    optimizer = Adam(lr=0.002, beta_1=0.9, beta_2=0.999, epsilon=0.1, decay=0.0)
    model.compile(loss='categorical_crossentropy', optimizer=optimizer, metrics=['accuracy'])
    model.summary()

    return model
```

Figure 15.6 VGG19 Model Building

Table 15.1 Comparison b/w various classification techniques

	Accuracy	*Loss*
DenseNet121	88.73%	0.2379
ResNet50	90.14%	0.2378
CNN	84%	0.56
Inception V3	77.87%	0.5140
VGG19	81.08%	0.48

Result Analysis

Analyzing CT scan images allowed us to determine whether cases were COVID positive or not. These images were trained using five different algorithms. The model was trained using DenseNet121, ResNet50, Inception V3, VGG 16, and CNN. A ResNet50 model achieves the greatest accuracy, and a DenseNet121 model achieves the lowest loss. We can thus conclude that ResNet 50 is the most effective model in this particular scenario. It is likely that the results will improve further as the number of epochs increases.

Conclusion

Since COVID-19 is still spreading, it needs to be diagnosed and analyzed rapidly and effectively in the current situation. In nucleic acid detection, hysteresis and false negatives are common. In addition, it cannot determine the severity of the condition. A CT scan can be used as an auxiliary diagnostic tool and to monitor disease progression. In this study, we propose a method for automatically detecting COVID-19 in lung CT scans in order to facilitate rapid diagnosis and interpretation of lung CT scans. COVID-19 was distinguished from non-COVID-19 using the collected datasets. To train the false positive screening network, we use DenseNet121, CNN, ResNet50, VGG19, and Inception V3.

ResNet50 model showed 90.14% of accuracy, on the other hand the accuracy for the other four models was 77.87%, 81.08%, 84%, and 88.73%, respectively.

References

Apostolopoulos, I. D. & Mpesiana, T. A. (2020). COVID-19: Automatic detection from X-ray images utilizing transfer learning with convolutional neural networks. *Physical and Engineering Sciences in Medicine*, 43(2), 635–640. https://doi.org/10.1007/s13246-020-00865-4

Armato, S., McLennan, G., McNitt-Gray, M., Meyer, C., Reeves, A., Bidaut, L., Zhao, B., Croft, B., & Clarke, L. (2010). WE-B-201B-02: The lung image database consortium (LIDC) and image database resource initiative (IDRI): A completed public database of CT scans for lung nodule analysis. *Medical Physics*, 37(6Part6), 3416–3417. https://doi.org/10.1118/1.3469350

Barstugan, M., Ozturk, S., & Ozkaya, U. (2020). Classification of coronavirus images using shrunken features. https://doi.org/10.1101/2020.04.03.20048868

Berrimi, M., Hamdi, S., Cherif, R. Y., Moussaoui, A., Oussalah, M., & Chabane, M. (2021). COVID-19 detection from xray and CT scans using transfer learning. *2021 International Conference of Women in Data Science at Taif University (WiDSTaif)*. https://doi.org/10.1109/widstaif52235.2021.9430229

Chaplin, S. (2020). COVID-19: A brief history and treatments in development. *Prescriber*, 31(5), 23–28. https://doi.org/10.1002/psb.1843

Coronavirus (COVID-19) overview. (August 2013, 7). WebMD. https://www.webmd.com/lung/coronavirus#4-8

Dansana, D., Kumar, R., Bhattacharjee, A., Hemanth, D. J., Gupta, D., Khanna, A., & Castillo, O. (2020). Early diagnosis of COVID-19-affected patients based on X-ray and computed tomography images using deep learning algorithm. *Soft Computing*. https://doi.org/10.1007/s00500-020-05275-y

Depeursinge, A., Vargas, A., Platon, A., Geissbuhler, A., Poletti, P., & Müller, H. (2012). Building a reference multimedia database for interstitial lung diseases. *Computerized Medical Imaging and Graphics*, 36(3), 227–238. https://doi.org/10.1016/j.compmedimag.2011.07.003

Elkorany, A. S. & Elsharkawy, Z. F. (2021). Covidetection-net: A tailored COVID-19 detection from chest radiography images using deep learning. *Optik*, 231, 166405. https://doi.org/10.1016/j.ijleo.2021.166405

Farooq, M. S., Rehman, A. U., Idrees, M., Raza, M. A., Ali, J., Masud, M., Al-Amri, J. F., & Kazmi, S. H. (2021). An effective Convolutional neural network model for the early detection of COVID-19 using chest X-ray images. *Applied Sciences*, 11(21), 10301. https://doi.org/10.3390/app112110301

Frid-Adar, M., Amer, R., Gozes, O., Nassar, J., & Greenspan, H. (2021). COVID-19 in CXR: From detection and severity scoring to patient disease monitoring. *IEEE Journal of Biomedical and Health Informatics*, 25(6), 1892–1903. https://doi.org/10.1109/jbhi.2021.3069169

Gozes, O., Frid-Adar, M., Sagie, N., Kabakovitch, A., Amran, D., Amer, R., & Greenspan, H. (2020). undefined. *Thoracic Image Analysis*, 84–93. https://doi.org/10.1007/978-3-030-62469-9_8

Guan, W., Ni, Z., Hu, Y., Liang, W., Ou, C., He, J., Liu, L., Shan, H., Lei, C., Hui, D. S., Du, B., Li, L., Zeng, G., Yuen, K., Chen, R., Tang, C., Wang, T., Chen, P., Xiang, J., … Zhong, N. (2020). Clinical characteristics of coronavirus disease 2019 in China. *New England Journal of Medicine*, 382(18), 1708–1720. https://doi.org/10.1056/nejmoa2002032

Hu, R., Ruan, G., Xiang, S., Huang, M., Liang, Q., & Li, J. (2020). Automated diagnosis of COVID-19 using deep learning and data augmentation on chest CT. https://doi.org/10.1101/2020.04.24.20078998

Iqbal M. N., H., Romero-Castillo, K. D., Bilal, M., & Parra-Saldivar, R. (2020). The emergence of novel-coronavirus and its replication cycle - An overview. *Journal of Pure and Applied Microbiology*, 14(1), 13–16. https://doi.org/10.22207/jpam.14.1.03

Jaiswal, A., Gianchandani, N., Singh, D., Kumar, V., & Kaur, M. (2020). Classification of the COVID-19 infected patients using DenseNet201 based deep transfer learning. *Journal of Biomolecular Structure and Dynamics*, 39(15), 5682–5689. https://doi.org/10.1080/07391102.2020.1788642

Jia, H., Zhao, J., & Arshaghi, A. (2021). COVID-19 diagnosis from CT images with Convolutional neural network optimized by marine predator optimization algorithm. *BioMed Research International*, 1–9. https://doi.org/10.1155/2021/5122962

Jin, C., Chen, W., Cao, Y., Xu, Z., Zhang, X., Deng, L., Zheng, C., Zhou, J., Shi, H., & Feng, J. (2020). Development and evaluation of an AI system for COVID-19 diagnosis. https://doi.org/10.1101/2020.03.20.20039834

Kang, H., Xia, L., Yan, F., Wan, Z., Shi, F., Yuan, H., Jiang, H., Wu, D., Sui, H., Zhang, C., & Shen, D. (2020). Diagnosis of coronavirus disease 2019 (COVID-19) with structured latent multi-view representation learning. *IEEE Transactions on Medical Imaging*, 39(8), 2606–2614. https://doi.org/10.1109/tmi.2020.2992546

Keles, A., Keles, M. B., & Keles, A. (2021). COV19-cnnet and COV19-resnet: Diagnostic inference engines for early detection of COVID-19. *Cognitive Computation*. https://doi.org/10.1007/s12559-020-09795-5

Khan, A. I., Shah, J. L., & Bhat, M. M. (2020). CoroNet: A deep neural network for detection and diagnosis of COVID-19 from chest X-ray images. *Computer Methods and Programs in Biomedicine*, 196, 105581. https://doi.org/10.1016/j.cmpb.2020.105581

Lei, J., Li, J., Li, X., & Qi, X. (2020). CT imaging of the 2019 novel coronavirus (2019-nCoV) pneumonia. *Radiology*, 295(1), 18–18. https://doi.org/10.1148/radiol.2020200236

Li, X., Li, C., & Zhu, D. (2020). COVID-mobilexpert: On-device COVID-19 patient triage and follow-up using chest X-rays. *2020 IEEE International Conference on Bioinformatics and Biomedicine (BIBM)*. https://doi.org/10.1109/bibm49941.2020.9313217

Loey, M., Smarandache, F., & M. Khalifa, N. E. (2020). Within the lack of chest COVID-19 X-ray dataset: A novel detection model based on GAN and deep transfer learning. *Symmetry*, 12(4), 651. https://doi.org/10.3390/sym12040651

Malek, A. (2008). Applications of recurrent neural networks to optimization problems. *Recurrent Neural Networks*. https://doi.org/10.5772/5556

Narin, A., Kaya, C., & Pamuk, Z. (2021). Automatic detection of coronavirus disease (COVID-19) using X-ray images and deep convolutional neural networks. *Pattern Analysis and Applications*, 24(3), 1207–1220. https://doi.org/10.1007/s10044-021-00984-y

Ozturk, T., Talo, M., Yildirim, E. A., Baloglu, U. B., Yildirim, O., & Rajendra Acharya, U. (2020). Automated detection of COVID-19 cases using deep neural networks with X-ray images. *Computers in Biology and Medicine*, 121, 103792. https://doi.org/10.1016/j.compbiomed.2020.103792

Rajagopal, R. (2021). Comparative analysis of COVID-19 X-ray images classification using Convolutional neural network, transfer learning, and machine learning classifiers using deep features. *Pattern Recognition and Image Analysis*, 31(2), 313–322. https://doi.org/10.1134/s1054661821020140

Shah, V., Keniya, R., Shridharani, A., Punjabi, M., Shah, J., & Mehendale, N. (2020). Diagnosis of COVID-19 using CT scan images and deep learning techniques. https://doi.org/10.1101/2020.07.11.20151332

Siddiqui, M. K., Morales-Menendez, R., Gupta, P. K., Iqbal, H. M., Hussain, F., Khatoon, K., & Ahmad, S. (2020). Correlation between temperature and COVID-19 (Suspected, confirmed and death) cases based on machine learning analysis. *Journal of Pure and Applied Microbiology*, 14(1), 1017–1024. https://doi.org/10.22207/jpam.14.spl1.40

Singh, D., Kumar, V., Vaishali, & Kaur, M. (2020). Classification of COVID-19 patients from chest CT images using multi-objective differential evolution–based convolutional neural networks. *European Journal of Clinical Microbiology & Infectious Diseases*, 39(7), 1379–1389. https://doi.org/10.1007/s10096-020-03901-z

Tiwari, S. (2020). A comparative study of deep learning models with handcraft features and non-handcraft features for automatic plant species identification. *International Journal of Agricultural and Environmental Information Systems*, 11(2), 44–57. https://doi.org/10.4018/ijaeis.2020040104

16 Comprehensive review on digital image forgery detection methods

Nishigandha N Zanje[1,a], *Gagandeep Kaur*[2,b], *and Anupkumar M Bongale*[3,c]

[1]M.Tech Scholar, SIT Pune, Symbiosis International (Deemed University), India

[2]Assistant Professor, SIT Pune, Symbiosis International (Deemed University), India

[3]Associate Professor, SIT Pune, Symbiosis International (Deemed University), India

Abstract

Owing to the current times of quick advancement, several methods used to create and alter digital information today offer an extremely high level of authenticity. The line separating authentic and artificial content has shrunk significantly. It presents serious cyber security risks. Anybody can produce incredibly believable bogus photos using software applications that are readily accessible online. Such fake images can be utilized to defraud individuals, defame, or extort someone, as well as to manipulate public perception about certain individuals amid campaigns. Automated systems which can identify fake digital content are thus urgently needed in order to limit the circulation of harmful misleading data. The purpose of this survey work is to explore Digital Image Forgery Detection (DIFD) methods. The new trend of Deepfakes, fake multimedia produced using deep learning algorithms, as well as contemporary data-driven forensics techniques to combat them will receive close attention.

Keywords: Multimedia, fake images, digital image forgery detection, Deepfakes, deep learning.

Introduction

Since the introduction of so-called 'Deepfakes', or fake multimedia that has been altered using robust and user-friendly deep learning (DL) technologies such as generative adversarial networks (GAN) or autoencoders (AE) where false media has emerged as a major issue. If someone has access to a lot of information, using this technique to create realistically modified multimedia content might well be relatively simple. Software for photographs, online gaming, augmented world, and might soon include filmmaking. Yet the exact technique might also be employed for wrongdoing, such as making false pornographic recordings to extort individuals or fabricating media stories to distort public sentiment. Over time, it might also undermine belief in genuine and trustworthy forms of news. Several popular deepfakes that have been circulated online are shown in Figure 16.1. Because these were created for entertainment and feature popular celebrities and leaders in absurd circumstances, such forgeries are simple to recognize. Additionally, retrieving the genuine as well as the altered form is typically available online, dispelling any uncertainty regarding legitimacy. Today, alterations made with DL techniques have grown to be a serious problem. How simple it is for fairly untrained people to produce bogus information is disturbing, given that there is enough information accessible. These days, DL relying on assaults mostly try to create totally artificial pictures using GAN variant networks and also to fabricate digitized pictures in order to alter their identification or meanings.

The rest of the paper is structured as follows. Section 2 includes different types of DIFD methods and approaches. Section 3 reviews the literature works and shows the literature survey details. Section 4 concludes the overall review done in this paper.

Digital Image Forgery Methods

Electronic images are the subject of digital picture forgeries. Since the advent of strong PC graphics modifying applications like Corel Paint Shop, GIMP, Adobe Photoshop, etc., several of them are freely accessible; the procedure for generating photoshopped pictures has become incredibly easy. The following are some of the digitized picture forgeries methods.

Image splicing: As seen in Figure 16.2, photograph splicing is a method that includes creating a collage from two or even more real photos.

[a]zanje123n@gmail.com; [b]gagandeep.kaur@sitpune.edu.in; [c]anupkumar.bongale@sitpune.edu.in

Figure 16.1 Deepfakes manipulated images

Figure 16.2 Photograph splicing

Copy-move method: It is similar to image splicing. However, a copy and move technique copies, moves, then paste portions in the actual picture. It is typically intended to hide particular information or replicate specific elements of a picture. Figure 16.3 shows the copy-move attack.

Figure 16.3 Copy-move attack

Morphing: A smooth shift from one photograph or pattern to the other, where special effects are employed in movies and animations. It is typically utilized to represent an individual technologically changing into some other or as a portion of a fantastical or strange scenario. Figure 16.4 depicts the Morphing method.

There are two types of DIFD approaches: active and passive.

Figure 16.4 Morphing method

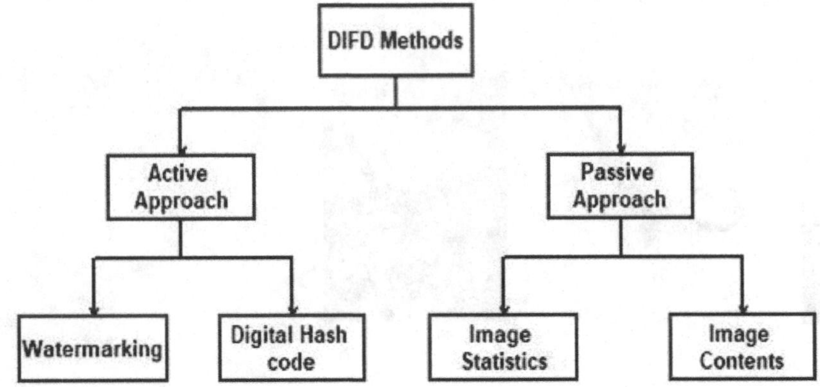

Figure 16.5 DIFD approach classification

A special marker is required in the active approach, like electronic watermarking and hash codes, so that manipulation could be recognized by a distorted watermark picture. In the passive approach, image features are extracted after image preprocessing such as image statistics and contents. The Figure shows the approaches for detecting digital image forgery.

Related Works

A basic approach that can identify both manipulated photos, as well as GANs, created pictures was developed by Zhang et al. (2019). This work proposes a broad strategy for concurrently identifying manipulated photos plus pictures produced by GAN. To begin, utilize the Scharr tool to retrieve the picture's edges details. Then resize the picture while not losing any picture data by converting the edge picture data matrices to the grayish level co-occurrence matrix (GLCM). Kim and Cho (2021) introduced a composite facial forensics system built on a convolutional neural network (CNN) that combines dual forensics methodologies. To identify altered photos and recordings, Verdoliva (2020) set out to give an assessment and overview of the techniques for graphical multimedia authenticity validation. The new trend of false content produced using DL systems, as well as a contemporary data-based forensics tool to combat these would garner significant consideration. Employing DL techniques, Barad and Goswami (2020) presented an overview of picture fabrication recognition. Most of the customized elements were used in conventional approaches for detecting picture counterfeiting.

Minimal cost forgery approach was developed by Zhao et al. (2021) utilizing current DL methods to modify useful documents and used groups of networking architecture ideas to overcome the shortcomings of the textual altering methods used today when dealing with intricate backgrounds and symbols. Several key discoveries to the creation of whole face pictures, where kind of face manipulation—were first presented by Neves et al. (2020). In an attempt to fool face modification detecting methods whilst maintaining the aesthetic clarity of the produced photographs, a new method to erase GAN 'fingerprints' off artificial false pictures built on AE is presented. With the utilization of the suggested GAN-fingerprint Removing method (GANprintR) to artificial false photos that are generally incredibly convincing, a brand-new open dataset called iFakeFaceDB was created. JPEG is the more widely employed standard for electronic photos and digitized photography equipment, where Shailaja Rani and Kumar (2019) contrasted computerized picture fraud. To recover certain digitized pictures having originality and fidelity and also to identify electronic picture forgeries utilizing active as well as passive approaches, these acts are carried out in Adobe Photoshop utilizing the picture safety contents. Fernando et al. (2021) developed a Hierarchical Attention Memory Network (HAMN) framework for the identification of false and counterfeit facials, which was inspired by the societal sight and socio cognitive mechanisms of the human mind.

According to Ahmed et al. (2020), the AlexNet and GoogLeNet architectures of CNN, which are employed in both extracting features and information to pass methods, have demonstrated that systems are capable of comprehending the sequential modifications in the content of digital pictures which are procured from the exact source. Camera trace is a distinctive disturbance generated during the digital imaging session. Forensic techniques currently in use typically examine camera traces to pinpoint portrait roots. The above article by Chen et al. (2020) examines a brand-new low-level vision issue called camera trace erasing to highlight the shortcomings of trace-based forensic techniques. An extensive analysis of current anti-forensic techniques discloses that it's challenging to successfully remove camera traces without compromising the product message. The structure of known GAN-based facial manipulative tactics is examined in this study by Huang et al. (2022). They find out the inadequacy of the up sampling techniques contained therein may be utilized as a significant resource for GAN synthesized fraudulent picture identification and localization in forgery. Based on this fundamental finding, they developed the FakeLocator innovative method to produce strong positioning accuracy at high resolution on altered facial photographs. A study on DeepFake identification by Malik et al. (2022) utilized by deep neural networks (DNNs) has drawn more attention to recognize and categorize Deepfakes. DeepFake is essentially the media that has been generated again through the injection or replacement of data into the DNN model. Based on their outcomes, performances, employed methodologies, and style of detection, the DeepFake detection techniques in face photographs and videos will be discussed in this review.

A brand-new ensemble forensic detection method with two unique discriminators as well as two identical generators was presented by Baek et al. (2020). It can improve forensics identification outcomes depending on the integrated discriminators' forecast. This approach focuses primarily on enhancing discriminating skills over picture-generating skills. Research concerning the identification of pictures altered using GAN-based picture-to-picture conversion was given by Marra et al. (2020) DNNs, like XceptionNet, that continue to function relatively well despite in the midst of train-test discrepancies, are effective at maintaining resilience. The research, which used a database of 36,302 photos, demonstrates how the traditional and DL classifiers would reach recognition levels of accuracy near 95%. Fake Colorized Image Detection (FCID) was the novel issue that Guo et al. (2018) set out to solve in the realm of fraudulent picture recognition. To overcome this identification issue, two straightforward yet efficient schemes—FCID-HIST, which uses histogram-based identification, and FCID-FE, which uses feature-encoding-based detection were developed.

Literature Survey Details

Table 16.1 Literature survey details

S. No	*Paper title and year*	*Method*	*Tampering method*	*Pros/Cons*
1	No One Can Escape: A General Aapproach to Detect Tampered and Generated Image. 2019	GLCM, DNN	GAN technique	Both altered and GAN-synthesized photos were recognized.
2	Exposing Fake Faces Through Deep Neural Networks Combining Content and Trace Feature Extractors. 2021	CNN-based face authenticity classifier	Deepfakes and Face2Face created by GAN & AE	Excellent accuracy for lossless compressed videos.
3	Media Forensics and Deepfakes: An Overview. 2020	Conventional detection and DL methods	GAN based PRNU	DL methods performed better than traditional ML methods.
4	Image Forgery Detection using Deep Learning: A Survey. 2020	Block-based, and DL methods.	Copy-move, cut-paste	To autonomously recognize altered areas, DL techniques can understand conceptual & sophisticated attributes.

Table 16.1 Literature survey details

S. No	*Paper title and year*	*Method*	*Tampering method*	*Pros/Cons*
5	Deep Learning-Based Forgery Attack on Document Images. 2021	DL based ForgeNet	Forge and Recapture	The documentation pictures now pose a serious safety threat due to DL textual altering methods.
6	GANprintR: Improved Fakes and Evaluation of the State of the Art in Face Manipulation Detection. 2020	GANPrintR based on Convolutional AE	GAN based iFakeFaceDB	Keeps a close graphical resemblance to the source picture.
7	Digital Image Forgery Detection Techniques: A Comprehensive Review. 2019	DIFD-based active and passive methods	JPEG, Adobe Photoshop	For the simplest DIFD, use active and passive picture detection methods including copy-move, splicing, and re-sampling.
8	Detection of Fake and Fraudulent Faces via Neural Memory Networks. 2021	HAMN	FFW, FaceSwap, Face2Face	Potential to use its acquired depiction with various, but more critically, invisible face alteration techniques.
9	Temporal Image Forensic Analysis for Picture Dating with Deep Learning. 2020	(NTIF), CNN and Deep learning.	Deepfakes Creation and Detection	During image dating, various CNN models as well as productivity indicators will be evaluated.
10	Camera trace erasing. 2020	Siamese Trace Erasing (SiamTE)	Image anti-forensics	Effectively erase camera trace without visible detection of the content signal.
11	FakeLocator: Robust Localization of GAN-Based Face Manipulations. 2022	Forgery Localization	Upsampling methods	Accurate SOTA location is achieved using fakeness mapping in monochrome.
12	DeepFake Detection for Human Face Images and Videos: A Survey. 2022	Deep learning, DeepFake, CNNs, GANs	ZAO, Auto FaceSwap, and FaceApp	Existing DeepFake is autonomous detection and evaluation of the visual media's integrity
13	Generative Adversarial Ensemble Learning for Face Forensics. 2020	ResNet and DenseNet	Neural Textures	Minimal distortion across a variety of collections of actual and artificial pictures.
14	Detection of GAN-Generated Fake Images over Social Networks. 2018	DenseNet, Inception v3 and XceptionNet	Cycle-GAN image-to-image translation	Deep NNs, like XceptionNet, is great at maintaining durability.
15	Fake Colorized Image Detection. 2018	FCID-HIST and FCID-FE	Colorization and image generation	Authentic colors were used to colorize gray-scale photographs.

Conclusion

In this paper, surveys on various papers regarding DIFD methods are done, most of them use deep learning (DL)-based techniques and some use convolutional neural networks (CNN)-based models in the detection of fake images. Many of the algorithms used are of DL, specifically CNN-based and few are ensemble learning techniques. The fake images are being generated by the GAN in most cases. Most of the DL algorithms give an accuracy of more than 85% and some give low accuracy based on the image dataset used. The various DL and ensemble learning algorithms are efficient when compared to conventional machine learning algorithms in the detection of Deepfakes, fake images, digital image forgery etc, and can be applied on various datasets. Each category's various existing approaches have been examined, and it has been found that they all have one or more of the following shortcomings: Accurate detection, complex computation, open to many attacks, including rotation, scaling, JPEG compression, blurring, and brightness manipulation, among others, numerous incorrect matches with a consistent backdrop. The limited range of application of these detection techniques, which excludes methods created for copy-move forgery from working with picture splicing or resampling and vice versa, is a serious problem, in addition to the constraints noted above. Even though there is a lot of research being done in the area of identifying image forgeries, no detection technique can be utilized as a general-purpose tool to identify all kinds of forgeries. To overcome the aforementioned restrictions, a strong, sophisticated forgery detection technique is urgently needed. Additionally, scientists could develop these methods to find fake videos.

References

Ahmed, F., Khelifi, F., Ashref, L., & Ahmed, B. (2020). Temporal image forensic analysis for picture dating with deep learning. *2020 International Conference on Computing, Electronics & Communications Engineering (ICCECE)*, (pp. 119–114).

Baek, J. Y., Yoo, Y. S., & Bae, S. H. (2020). Generative adversarial ensemble learning for face forensics. *IEEE Access*. 18, 45421–45431.

Barad, Z., J. & Goswami, M., M. (2020). Image forgery detection using deep learning: a survey. *International Conference on Advanced Computing and Communication Systems (ICACCS)*, 978(1), 571–576.

Chen, C., Xiong, Z., Liu, X., & Wu, F. (2020) Camera trace erasing. *26th IEEE Conference on Computer Vision and Pattern Recognition, (CVPR)*, 11, 2950–2959.

Fernando, T., Fookes, C., Denman, S., & Sridharan, S. (2021). Detection of fake and fraudulent faces via neural memory networks. IEEE Transactions on Information Forensics and Security, 16, 1973–1988.

Guo, Y., Cao, X., Zhang, W., & Wang, R. (2018). Fake colorized image detection. *IEEE Transactions on Information Forensics and Security*. 13(8), 1932–1944.

Huang, Y., Juefei-Xu, F., Guo, Q., Liu, Y., & Pu, G. (2022). FakeLocator: Robust localization of GAN-based face manipulations. *IEEE Transactions on Information Forensics and Security*. 17, 2657–2672.

Kim, E. & Cho, S. (2021). Exposing Fake Faces Through Deep Neural Networks Combining Content and Trace Feature Extractors. *EEE Access*. 9, 123493–123503.

Malik, A., Minoru, K., Abdullahi, M. S., & Khan, N. A. (2022). DeepFake Detection for Human Face Images and Videos: A Survey. *IEEE Access*. 10, 18757–18775.

Marra, F., Gragnaniello, D., Cozzolino, D, & Verdoliva, L. (2018). Detection of GAN-Generated Fake Images over Social Networks. *IEEE Conference on Multimedia Information Processing and Retrieval (MIPR)*, 213, 384–389.

Neves, J., C., Tolosana, R., Vera-Rodriguez, R., Lopes, V., Proença, H, & Fierrez, J. (2020). GANprintR: Improved Fakes and Evaluation of the State of the Art in Face Manipulation Detection. *IEEE Journal of Selected Topics in Signal Processing*, 14(5), 1038–1048.

Shailaja, Rani, P., B., & Kumar, A. (2019). Digital image forgery detection techniques: a comprehensive review. *International Conference on Electronics, Communication and Aerospace Technology (ICECA)*, 5, 959–963.

Verdoliva, L. (2020). Media Forensics and Deepfakes: An Overview. *IEEE Journal of Selected Topics in Signal Processing*, 255, 1 1.

Zhang, K., Liang, Y., Zhang, J., Wang, Z., & Li, X. (2019). No One Can Escape: A General Approach to Detect Tampered and Generated Image. *IEEE Access*, 7, 129494–129503.

Zhao, L., Chen, C. and Huang, J. (2021). Deep learning-based forgery attack on document images. *IEEE Transactions on Image Processing*, 30, 7964–7979.

17 Model for home automation system through FPGA

Ravi Payal[1,a] *and Amit Prakash Singh*[2,b]

[1]PHD scholar, Guru Gobind Singh Indraprastha University, Joint Director, CDAC Noida, India

[2]Professor, Guru Gobind Singh Indraprastha University, New Delhi, India

Abstract

Home automation system is now a days is very popular in industry. It consists of intelligent control systems which can make life very easy. Now a days in the era of smart city this concept is very popular. This system detects the fire and thief through the different entry point of house. Controlling of light and temperature of the house can be done through this. A full home automation system model is considered here and for coding language used is Verilog hardware description language (HDL). Xilinx FPGA technology is used for the synthesis. Concepts of FSM designing is used and coding was done in Verilog HDL. Coding was done in Questa Sim tool and simulation waveform was obtained and verified.

Keywords: Automation system, finite state machine, mealy machine, Moore machine, synthesis, simulation, Verilog, FPGA

Introduction

Security and comfort these are the two main points or we can say two main features which everyone wants at any cost at home. Currently concepts of Smart home is very popular. The term smart home means that a home which is equipped with all the devices which can be fully disciplined by some laptop or smartphone or desktop system. Whenever a home is considered then security and comfort are on priority (Liu, 2021). In a smart home concept or modern home both the features are very important. The security and comfort module were written in Verilog hardware description language (HDL). Verilog code activates the comfort and security module which allows the owner to relax, and owner will not worry about the security. Security module will be activated only after entering the correct password. Comfort module will be activated only when motion signal is high and password module gets triggered when owner is not at home. FPGA used in this project is Xilinx Spartan 3E. The project concerns about to design and implement a comfort and security features for smart home. In the project coding was done to control the entry point of houses like door and window, garage. Also, the features like smoke detection, temperature, and luminosity control were verified.

Theory

In this project the HDL used for a coding of different module is Verilog. For making a system various different submodule were written and then connected with each other (Liu, 2021). The FPGA used in this project is Xilinx Spartan 3E and all the synthesis results are targeted to this FPGA library. Synthesis tool used in this project is Xilinx ISE14.7.

Hierarchy

The entire 'home automation module' is divided into two sub modules. They include 'top security' and 'comfort module'. Top security module is further break into 'password', and 'security module'. Module password consists of 11-bit password which when entered correctly, allows the proprietor to make into the house. If wrong password is entered by the stranger the 'alarm' will ring. As soon as the proprietor enters inside the house security module will turn ON. Security module is further subdivided into 'room door' module, 'room window' module, 'garage door' module and 'smoke' module. If door of room, garage or window remains open then 'door alarm', 'garage alarm' or 'window alarm' will ring respectively. If smoke is detected then 'fire alarm' will ring.

When proprietor enters inside the room 'comfort module' will be activated. 'heater' will turn ON if temperature is less than 15°C. If temperature is more than 28°C then 'air conditioner' will turn ON. 'Dim light' will turn ON if luminosity is greater than 250 Lux. Whenever luminosity will go below 200 Lux then 'bright light' will turn ON.

[a]ravi.payal@gmail.com, ravipayal@cdac.in; [b]amit@ipu.ac.in

Flowchart

It starts with start state. An application is installed on mobile phone based on Android (Kamelia, Lia, 2014). This application is based on JAVA platform which must be downloaded from Google play store. The application provides a graphical user interface for homeowner to provide the required commands. With the Bluetooth module HC05 is paired. Then a

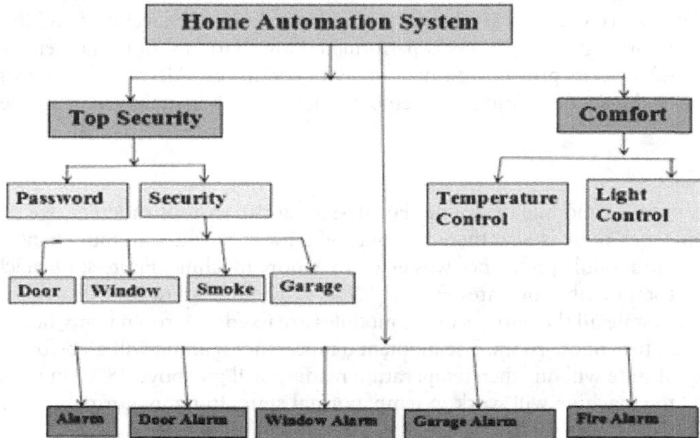

Figure 17.1 Block diagram of home automation system

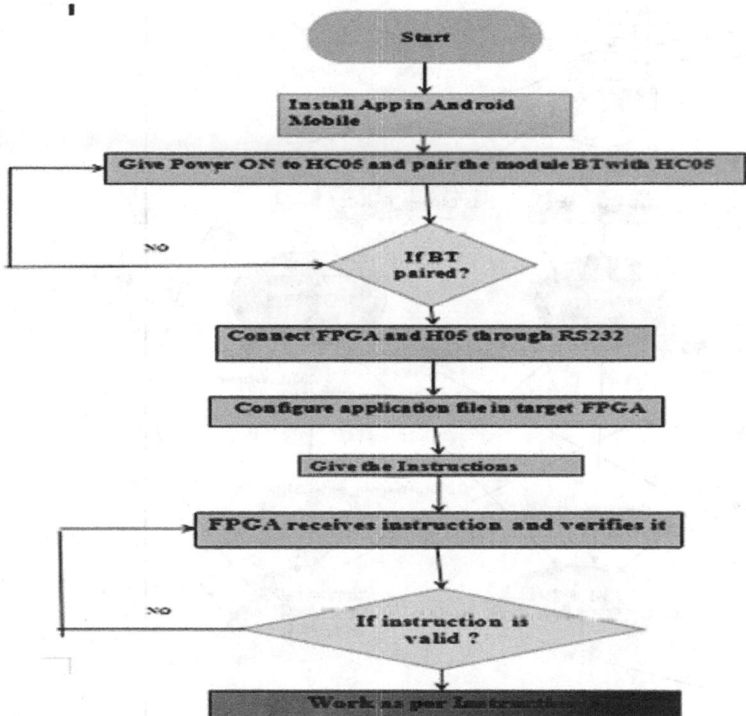

Figure 17.2 Home automation project flow diagram

condition is checked that is if Bluetooth is paired or not. If Bluetooth is not paired then control will go back to previous stage, where it waits for Bluetooth to be paired with HC05. If it is paired then FPGA is connected to HC05 through RS232. The desired application file is then downloaded into the FPGA (Negi et al., 2021). FPGA after receiving the instructions and verifies it. In case of any invalid instructions command will not execute and FPGA will wait for another set of instructions. Module will work only for valid instructions as per instructions. Bluetooth technology is used in this project as it has various advantages over other technologies. It does not require any form of wires for transmission of data. It is easily available in smart phones. It is easy to use and effective technology. For connection through Bluetooth we require UART that is universal asynchronous receiver transmitter (Yu et al., 2021). Home automation module is developed and .bit file is loaded in the FPGA. Instructions are given accordingly and process is performed. Flowchart is simple and depicts the whole process in detail. It is shown in Figure 17.2. Sensors provide information about conditions. Alarms are alerts which ring for different conditions. A four-digit password is set for pairing of Bluetooth which is confidential for homeowner.

State Diagram for Comfort Module

In this project finite state machine (FSM) is used for module designing. For designing the various modules, we prefer the Moore machine. Although Mealy machine technique is also there but since in Moore machine output changes on every clock edge. So during designing of different module preference was given to Moore machine. Finite state machine is shown in Figure 17.3 for comfort module. Total number of states in this FSM is 7. The first state is the starting state which is also equivalent to reset state and in this state all the outputs of the modules are fixed to zero. In temp_heat state temperature sensor is checking the state temperature of the room. The moment temperature reading will go below 15°C heater of room will in ON state. The temp_cool state will on when temperature reading will go above 28°C. In this case AC of the room will start. Between 15–28°C the machine will work in temp_normal state. In temp_normal state both

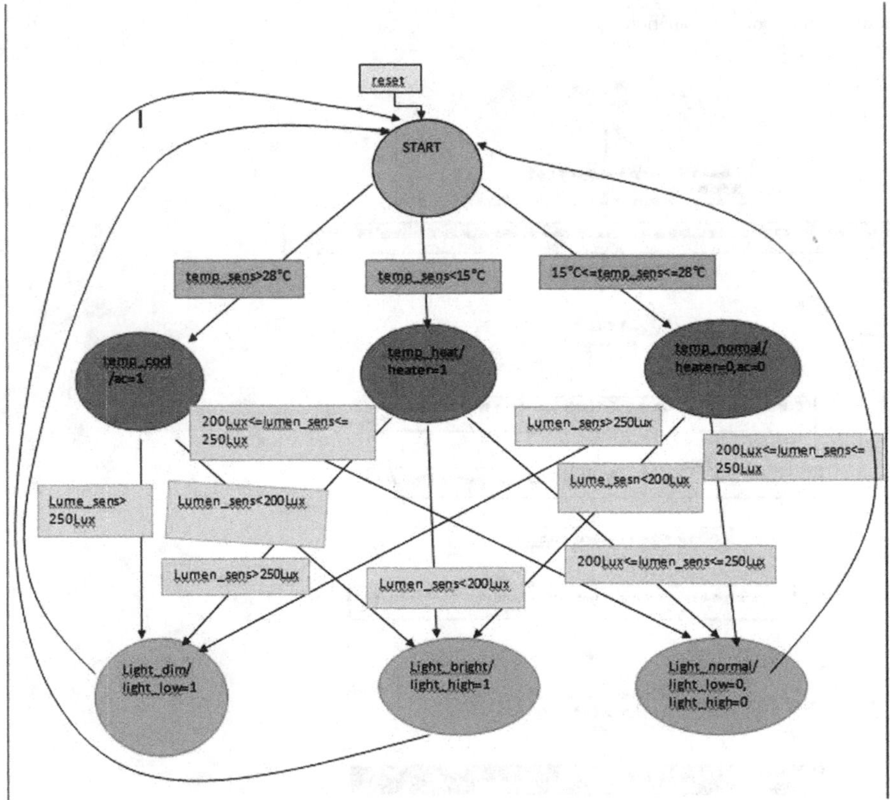

Figure 17.3 State diagram for comfort module

air conditioner and heater will remain in off. In every state light will get get turn ON when the owner arrives inside the toom. There are other states also named light_bright, light dim and light_normal. If the system is getting bright light when luminosity is less than 200 Lux then we are in light_bright state, if dim light is coming then we are in dim light state when luminosity is more than 250 Lux and for normal luminosity we are in light_normal state when range of luminosity is between 200–250 Lux. After light_dim state, light_bright state and light_normal state it will go to start state. Comfort module gets turn ON as soon as the owner enters the room. Temperature of room can be easily adjusted by heater and cooler. Luminosity of light can also be controlled by dim and bright lights. Specifically, 15–28°C is chosen as it is the human comfort zone. 200–250 Lux luminosity is taken as it is the luminosity range of normal light in the room. A Verilog code can be developed keeping in mind the concepts of finite state machine.

Implementation

Given below the code for garage module is written. Here when reset is high then at positive edge of clock garage state and garage alarm are considered at low state. When reset is low then garage_state will search for door and there will be an alarm if garage state is high and when garage state is low then no alarm will ring. Just like below modules other modules were also designed.

```
always @(posedge clock)
begin
if(reset==1'b1)
begin
garage_state=1'b0;
garagealarm=1'b0;
end
else
begin
garage_state = garage_door ? 1'b1 : 1'b0; // go to burglary state if garage is on
garagealarm = (garage_state == 1'b1) ? (flag?1'b1:1'b0): 1'b0; // if burglary state, signal a burglary
end
end
```

Result

When wrong password is entered by stranger then alarm will ring. For correct password is entered by the homeowner then module of security become activated. Security module keeps check on room door, garage door, window, and fire. Whenever one finds broken magnet of door of room or garage or window then door alarm, garage alarm or window alarm will ring respectively. If there is smoke in the room the fire alarm will ring. When the person enters into the room comfort module will work. Comfort module will be activated only when motion_sensor is at one(on) state. Whenever there will be a positive edge of clock then at that time luminosity sensor, temperature-sensor and motion-sensor are checked. For verifying the main module code different test cases were written and all the outputs were checked. Various modules like comfort, security, top security, door, window, smoke and garage modules RTL schematic were shown below. After simulation desired waveform were obtained. The code written for various module are synthesizable.

Table 17.1 Inputs for module

S. No	*Variable (input)*	*Size*	*Function*
1	Data_in	12	Password
2	lumen sens	7	Light sensor
3	temp_sens	7	temperature sensor
4	Clock	1	Clock signal
5	room_door	1	Represent magnetic door sensor
6	Smoke	1	smoke detector sensor
7	Garage_door	1	garage sensor
8	motion_sens	1	Determine human presence
9	Reset	1	For restart the FSM

RTL schematics

For generating the RTL schematic view first initialize all the outputs at zero. A virtual model was considered, and sensors were interfaced. RTL schematic shown at Figure 17.4 includes inputs and outputs ports.

Some of the main output signals are described below in the Table 17.2.

Table 17.2 Outputs for module

S. No	*Variable (output)*	*Size*	*Function*
1	Door	1	Door operations
2	Fire	1	Checking smoke
3	Window	1	Window operations
4	Garage	1	Garage operations
5	Alarm	1	Alarm operations
6	Flag	1	Detecting the owner

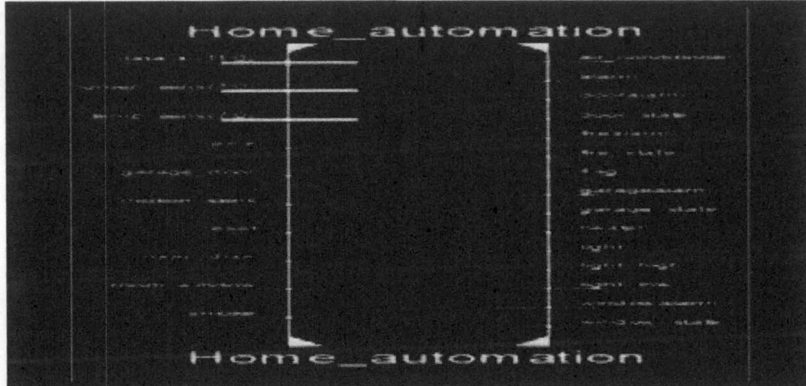

Figure 17.4 Home automation module

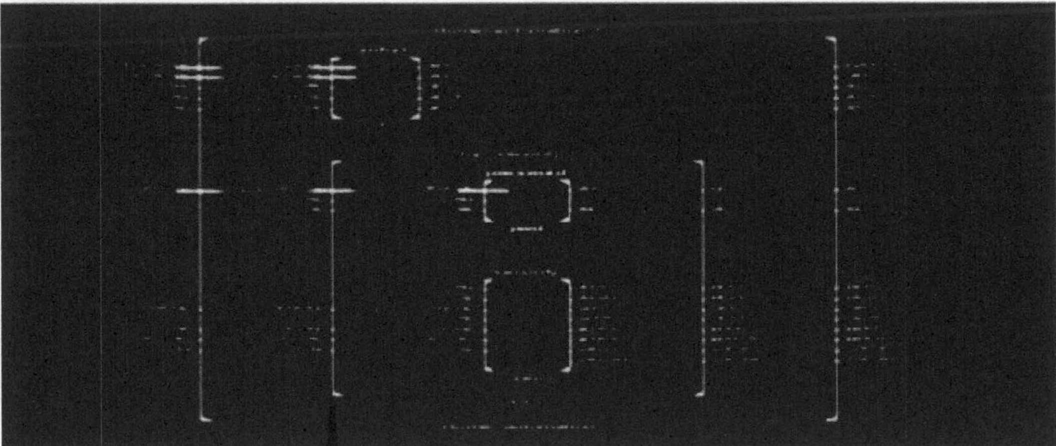

Figure 17.5 RTL schematic for comfort, password, and security system

Simulated waveforms

The RTL code written in Verilog is simulated by generating various test cases. Different conditions were tested, and waveform were generated. The value of input variables was fixed for different conditions and output response was verified based on waveform.

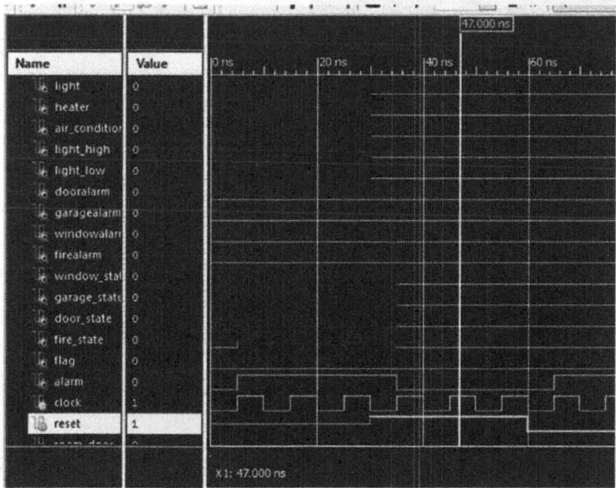

Figure 17.6 Waveform1 output with respect to testcase 1

The waveform 1 is with respect test case 1 where considering the situation where variable room_door =0, garage_door=0, room_window=0, smoke=0, data_in=11'd00000001988, motion_sense=1, temp_sense=8'd00000032 and lumen_sens=8'd00000035

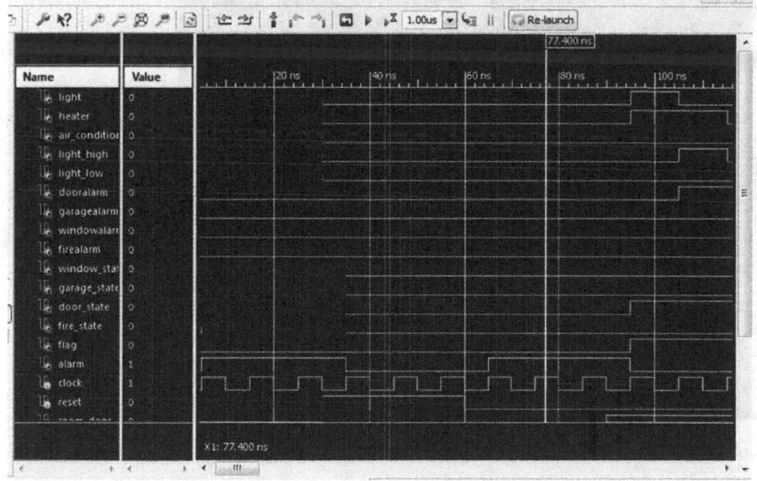

Figure 17.7 Waveform 2 output with respect to testcase 2

The waveform 2 is with respect test case 2 where considering the situation where variable room_door =0, garage_door = 0, room_window = 0, smoke = 0, data_in = 11'd00000001990, motion_sense = 0, temp_sense = 8'd00000023 and lumen_sens = 8'd00000040

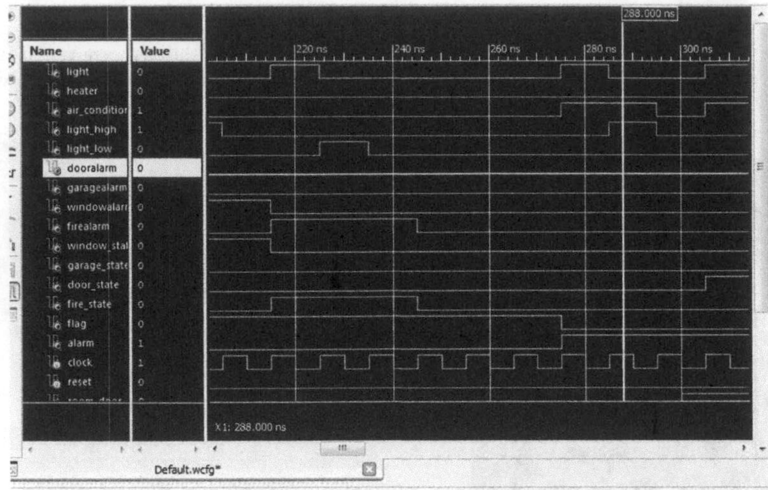

Figure 17.8 Waveform3 output with respect to testcase 3

The waveform 3 is with respect test case 3 where considering the situation where variable room_door =0, garage_door = 0, room_window = 0, smoke = 1, data_in = 11'd00000001980, motion_sense=1, temp_sense = 8'd00000067 and lumen_sens = 8'd00000100.

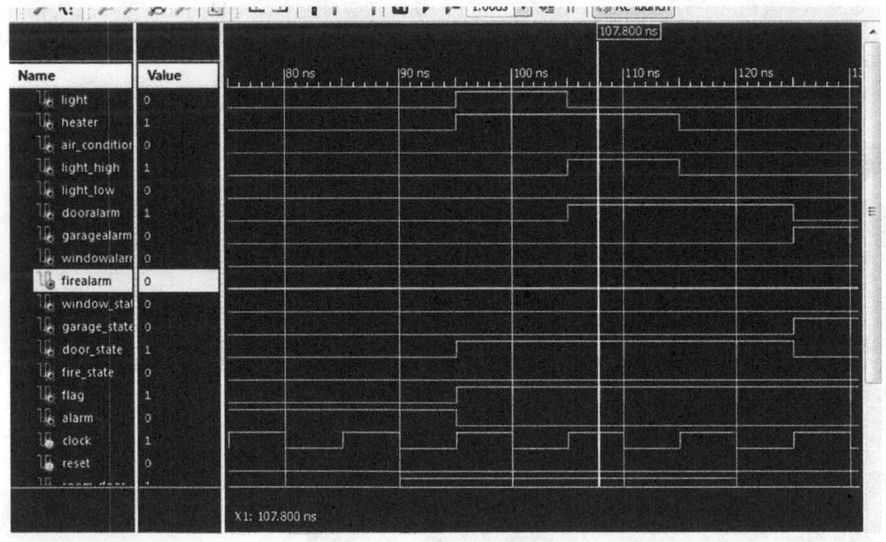

Figure 17.9 Waveform4 output with respect to testcase 4

The waveform 4 is with respect test case 4 where considering the situation where variable room_door =0, garage_door = 0, room_window = 0, smoke = 0, data_in = 11'd00000001987, motion_sense = 1, temp_sense = 8'd00000015 and lumen_sens = 8'd00000252

The device utilization summary was given in Table 17.1. The RTL code is synthesized wrt to Xilinx FPGA Baysys3e

Table 17.3 Device utilization summary

Slice logic utilization	*used*	*Available*	*Utilization*
Flip flops	264	4800	5.5%
Luts	180	2400	7.5%
Occupied slices	33	600	5.5%
Bonded IOBs	50	102	49%

Conclusion

In the implementation of smart home projects. All the modules were implemented successfully without any fault. Coding part was done by Verilog HDL and for most of the modules FSM techniques were used. RTL description was successfully tested by running various cases and finally desired waveform was obtained. Target FPGA was Xilinx Spartan 3E and al the schematic was generated in ISE14.7 version of tool.

References

Kamelia, Lia, et al., "Door-automation system using bluetooth-based android for mobile phone." *ARPN Journal of Engineering and Applied Sciences* 9.10 (2014): 1759–1762.

Liu, Y., 2021. Simulation of art design of indoor furnishings based on FPGA and internet of things system. Microprocessors and Microsystems, 83, p.104023.

Negi, A., Raj, S., Thapa, S. and Indu, S., 2021. Field Programmable Gate Array (FPGA) Based IoT for Smart City Applications. In Data-Driven Mining, Learning and Analytics for Secured Smart Cities (pp. 135–158). Springer, Cham.

Yu, R., Zhang, X. and Zhang, M., 2021, March. Smart home security analysis system based on the internet of things. In *2021 IEEE 2nd International Conference on Big Data, Artificial Intelligence and Internet of Things Engineering (ICBAIE)* (pp. 596–599). IEEE.

18 K-means algorithm to cluster the Internet autonomous systems into tiers

Abdul Azeez R. Alobaid[1,a] *and Zinah N. Nuimi*[2,b]

[1]Department of Computer Techniques Engineering, Faculty of Information Technology, Imam Ja'afar Al-Sadiq University, Baghdad, Iraq

[2]Department of Electrical Engineering, Faculty of Engineering, University of Mayasan, Mayasan, Iraq

Abstract

The Internet autonomous system (AS) diagram can gain more insight into how the Internet infrastructure is evolving. To construct this AS, the relations between ASes must be harvested. Subsequently, diagram theory must be leveraged to study the characteristics of the constructed diagram. One of the main properties of the AS diagram is the type of relations between the ASes and their classification. In this paper, AS graph has been constructed from two data sources: locking glass servers and PeeringDB. Subsequently, Gephi has been utilized to extract the characteristic of the constructed diagram. Finally, the extracted characteristics have been fed into a K-mean model that clusters the ASes in the diagram into three tiers according to the relations inferred. The obtained results show that K-mean can infer the tier of each AS with an accuracy of 88%. Moreover, the Eigen value diagram metric can be utilized as the clustering feature without other features.

Keywords: Diagram theory, K-means, Eigen value, centrality metrics, autonomous system

Introduction

Internet is defined as a complex massive network of networks. These networks are connected with different fiber optics and satellites connections all over the globe. Moreover, Internet is the infrastructure of the Internet of things (IoT) and Internet of everything (IoE) paradigms (Delgado-Segura et al., 2018). Internet carries different applications, data, and information all over the world. To gain more insight into the Internet infrastructure, its development, and its future, this massive network should be modeled (Baldi et al., 2003).

Modeling the Internet has many methods and layers. It can be modeled as an overlay application as in peer-to-peer applications, such as PPTV (Liu, 2003), crypto-currencies (Delgado-Segura et al., 2018). It can be modeled also as several networks companies' that provided services to other networks and users. These networks or enterprises are called autonomous systems (ASes). These ASes are under the administration of a single entity, and they offer different services to the users. Internet service providers (ISPs) are an example of these ASes. Each one of these ASes has a unique identifier number, called ASN. This number is utilized to route the traffic between these ASes since the exterior gateway protocol (EGP) does not leverage IP addresses for routing. The de facto EGP protocol on the Internet is the border gateway protocol (BGP) that creates an AS path between any two ASes over the Internet (Green et al., 2018). A third and final method to model the Internet is at the router level. This level is complex, and it can gain more insight into the technical details of the Internet and how to route the data inside the ASes and between them. However, it is hard if not impossible to create a complete router model of the Internet. To study the AS model of the Internet, the relations between ASes must be harvested. Subsequently, diagram theory must be utilized to study the properties of the constructed diagram (Jaiswal et al., 2004). These properties have shown the small world phenomenon of the Internet, relation types, and even how the Internet is converting to a flat structure (Masoud et al., 2013).

In this paper, we attempted to cluster the ASes in the AS diagram into their tiers based on an unsupervised K-means machine learning algorithm. An AS diagram has been constructed from two main sources: locking glass servers and PeeringDB. Subsequently, Gephi has been utilized to analyze the constructed diagram to extract five different diagram metrics: Node degree, triangles, closeness, betweenness, and Eigen value. Finally, the calculated diagram metrics have been used as features of the K-means algorithm to cluster the ASes into one of three tiers. Our contribution to this work can be summarized as follows:

Constructing an AS diagram. Python has been utilized to telnet 32 locking glass servers to save the BGP dumps located in these servers. Subsequently, another Python code has been written to harvest the data from Peering DB to enhance the accuracy of the constructed diagram.

[a]abdulazeez.riyadh@sadiq.edu.iq; [b]zeina.nazar@yahoo.com

Gephi has been leveraged to construct the diagram to calculate different diagram metrics.

A K-means algorithm has been trained with the data extracted from Gephi to cluster the ASes into one of three tiers. The model has been written in Python.

The rest of this paper is organized as follows; section 2 summarizes some of the related works that have been conducted in the area of AS modeling on the Internet. Section 3 overviews our proposed system. Section 4 details the experiment and the results. Finally, we conclude this paper in section 5.

Related Works

Studying the Internet and modeling it as AS relations have attracted many researchers over the years. In (Nemmi et al., 2021), the authors have shown a study of AS evolution utilizing data harvested over 17 years. Many insights have been shown of Internet ASes. However, the authors of this work did not generate diagrams of their data and did not study the relations between the ASes. In (Silva et al., 2018), the author is interested in studying the Latin America AS connections over public and private exchange points (IXPs). In (Witono et al., 2022), the author surveyed all the works that have been conducted in the area of studying the Internet at the AS level and they have shown the opportunities and the challenges that encounter this modeling of the Internet. However, none of these studies attempted to study the Internet as a mathematical diagram. In (Barabási, 2013), the authors attempted to find the AS relations type utilizing diagram theory and machine learning. A soft clustering algorithm has been utilized in this work. However, the author utilized an uncompleted list of AS relations for the AS relations calculations. Moreover, they have shown that betweenness and closeness centralities are good metrics in AS clustering process. Our work differs from this work in three main folds. Firstly, the constructed diagram is bigger and constructed from more sources, such as PeeringDB that have been utilized in studying the AS peering relations (Böttger et al., 2018). Secondly, the comparison list in this work is more competitive. Finally, we have shown in this work that only the Eigen value can be utilized for the clustering purpose of AS into their tiers.

Proposed System

The proposed system utilizes unsupervised machine learning clustering algorithms. Two unsupervised clustering algorithms will be utilized in this work: k-means and soft-clustering with EM algorithms. In addition, several AS diagram features will be calculated and supplied into these algorithms to cluster ASes into three layers. Subsequently, the links between ASes in the same cluster will be classified as peering or horizontal links. On the other side, the link between two ASes in different clusters will be classified as crossing or vertical links. Our contributions to this work are as follows:

- An AS diagram will be built from BGP dumps collected from different routers in the world. Consequently, different diagram features will be calculated; such as; node betweenness, closeness, eigenvector centrality, node-local cluster coefficient, and node degrees. Finally, Information Gain (IG) will be utilized to select features for the ASes clustering process.
- Two unsupervised clustering algorithms will be used in this work: k-means and soft-clustering with EM algorithms. In the EM approach, maximum likelihood estimation (MLE) will be used to estimate the mean and variance values of each cluster.

The proposed method will be deployed on the clustered ASes and the classified links will be compared with CAIDA AS ranking data.

A diagram

A diagram is a data structure that consists of nodes and links or relations that connects these nodes. Any two nodes are connected if a relation occurs between them. The diagram is classified as directed and undirected. In the directed diagram, the relations between the nodes are directed from one node as a parent to the second node as a child. In other words, the relation can be passed in only one direction. On the other hand, the relations in the undirected diagram can be passed from both sides. The diagram data structure is one of the most data structures in computer science. It is the main theory in the network science field. Many mathematical properties have been proposed over the years to study this data structure (Barabási, 2013). These properties are called the diagram metrics. Each one of these properties has a physical meaning after calculation. In this work, we will focus on five diagram metrics which are: node degree, Eigen value, betweenness centrality, closeness centrality, and triangles. The definition of these metrics is as follows.

Table 18.1 shows the definitions of the variables utilized in these metrics.

Table 18.1 Variables' definitions

Variable	*Definition*
n	Total number of nodes in the diagram
$d(N,y)$	The shortest path between node N and node y
$\partial_{st}(N)$	The shortest path between node S and node T that passes through node N
$E(a,b)$	The distance between data point a with the features (x1,x2,x3...) and data point b with the features (x1,x2,x3....)

- Node degree: A measure of the number of links that start or end at the node. The node degree can be general as in the undirected diagram or it can be divided into in-degree and out-degree. In this work, the constructed diagram is undirected. This means that a general degree is used.
- Eigen value: The Eigen value of nodes in the diagram is the Eigen values of the adjacency matrix. The adjacency matrix on the other hand is a square matrix that has zeros if no relation occurs between nodes an equal a value, called the weight if a relation occurs. The Eigen value and Eigenvector have an important role in understanding linear systems.
- Betweenness: It is defined as the number of shortest paths in the diagram that passes through the node. Equation 1 shows how to calculate the betweenness.

$$b(N) = \sum_{s \neq N \neq t} \frac{\partial_{st}(N)}{\partial_{st}} \tag{1}$$

- Closeness: It is defined as the sum of all the shortest paths between any node and all other nodes in the diagram. If this number is small, the node is more central than other nodes. Equation 2 shows how to calculate this metric.

$$C(N) = \frac{n}{\sum_y d(N,y)} \tag{2}$$

- Triangles: is the number of triangles that any node in the diagram participates in. A triangle means that the neighbors of a node are neighbors. The number of triangles is an important metric in the calculation of the clustering coefficient of a diagram.

K-means

K-means is one of the oldest well-known unsupervised machine learning algorithms utilized for clustering purposes (Likas et al., 2003). This algorithm works on data features as input parameters only without the target labels as in the supervised algorithms. The algorithm requires a second input with the data features, the number of required clusters 'K'. After entering the number of clusters and the data into the algorithm, the algorithm creates 'K' random values called centroids. Each one of these centroids will be at the center of one of the 'K' clusters. As with any machine learning algorithm, the K-means algorithm has a training step that consists of several iterations. The training step differs from other supervised algorithms in the calculation process and what to calculate. In this algorithm, the training process is utilized to optimize the location of the random centroid by calculating the distance between these centroids and all other data nodes in the dataset. After calculating these distances, the dataset rows are classified to be in the cluster of the nearest centroid. Subsequently, the data nodes in each cluster are averaged to construct a new centroid rather than the random one. This process is iterated until no new updates occur on the calculated centroids. The Euclidean distance is the most popular method for distance calculations in the K-means algorithm. Equation 3 shows this metric.

$$E(a,b) = \sqrt{(a_{x1} - b_{x1})^2 + (a_{x2} - b_{x2})^2 + \dots} \tag{3}$$

Experiment and Results

Our experiment in this work consists of two parts. In the first part, the AS diagram must be constructed from dump data. The data must be harvested from the Internet and should contain the AS and their connections with each other. In the second part, the constructed AS diagram must be analyzed to extract nodes' metrics, such as closeness, betweenness,

Eigen value, degrees, and the number of triangles. Finally, the nodes' calculated metrics must be utilized as features for the K-mean algorithm to cluster the nodes into three clusters: tier 1, tier 2, and tier 3.

To construct the AS diagram, first, BGP table dumps have been collected from 32 different locking glass servers that can be found in (Traceroute, 2021). A Python code has been written to create a telnet connection to these servers and execute 'show BGP tables' and save the telnet output into files. Subsequently, the saved outputs must be analyzed to extract the last field in the BGP table 'AS path'. Finally, the extracted 'AS paths' have been written to find the connections between different AS numbers. This operation has been repeated 32 times to reach all servers. The output of these 32 operations has been merged and duplicated connections have been deleted. To enhance the accuracy of the constructed AS diagram, the AS peering connections have been harvested as in (Böttger et al., 2018). The harvested connections have been added to the constructed list with removing of the duplicated links. Finally, A list of the AS connection types that has been reported by CAIDA and can be found in (Nemmi et al., 2021) has been downloaded. The connections in this list have been added to our constructed AS diagram. Moreover, the list extracted from PeeringDB has been added to the CAIDA list for the type of relations between ASes. This new list has been constructed to compare our K-mean algorithm clustering output in the last step to calculate its accuracy.

The constructed AS diagram has 62051 nodes and 189980 connections. Only 42070 ASes have been found in the CAIDA list. However, with the list extracted from PeeringDB, the number increased to approximately 50,000 AS. The constructed list has been fed as an undirected diagram into Gephi, the diagram analyzer tool, to find its features, metrics, and different statistics. Gephi (Bastian et al., 2009), has been utilized widely in studying direct and undirected diagrams in different areas, such as WSN (Van Geenen, 2020), Internet diagram Wikipedia and social media. Table 18.2 shows the characteristics of the constructed diagram. Figure 18.1 shows a visualization of the constructed diagram.

Figure 18.2 (a) shows the nodes' degree of the ASes in the diagram. We can observe from the log scale in Figure 18.2 (a) that few nodes have a massive node degree while the rest of the nodes have a small node degree value. This shows that the diagram follows the small world phenomenon. The second prove of this is the value of the global clustering coefficient and the average path length calculated from the diagram as shown in Table 18.2.

Figure 18.1 The constructed diagram in Gephi

Table 18.2 Constructed diagram properties

Diagram type	*Undirected*
Number of nodes	62051
Number of links	189980
Average degree	4.622
diagram diameter	9
Average path length	5.733
Global cluster Ccoefficient	0.333

The most important metric in categorizing ASes is the nodes' Eigen value. We have studied the Eigen value of the nodes in this work to show the relationship between this value and other diagram metrics. Figure 18.2 (b) shows the relation between Eigen value and node degree. We can observe from Figure 18.2 (b) that nodes with a high degree have a high Eigen value. However, some nodes with a high Eigen value have a small node degree as we observe on the left of Figure 18.2 (b). Figure 18.2 (c) shows the relation between the betweenness centrality and Eigen value. We also can observe from Figure 18.2 (c) that nodes with a higher betweenness value than other nodes have a higher Eigen value. However, it is easy to find nodes with a high Eigen value with a low betweenness value. Finally, Figure 18.2 (d) shows the relationship between closeness centrality and Eigen value. We can observe from Figure 18.2 (d) that with a small closeness value a high Eigen value occurs. This means that the relationship between closeness and Eigen value is the opposite of the other metrics.

To cluster the ASes into tiers, the constructed AS diagram with all its metrics have been fed into a K-mean algorithm. The K-mean algorithm has been written in Python. Five diagram metrics have been utilized as features for clustering purposes. These metrics are: closeness, betweenness, Eigen value, node degree, and the number of triangles. Each one of these metrics has been leveraged as a feature of the K-mean algorithm. This means that the algorithm has clustered the AS according to these features five times. In the last time, these metrics have been fed to the algorithm as five features. The output clusters of each run of the algorithm have been compared to the second list that has been constructed from PeeringDB and CAIDA as mentioned. Finally, the comparison has been utilized as the accuracy measure of the clustering process. To enhance the accuracy of the K-mean clustering process, 30 runs have been used for each metric and an averaging of all the 30 runs have been used.

Figure 18.3 shows the number of ASes in each clustering process according to the five metrics that have been leveraged. We can observe from Figure 18.3 that the number of ASes in each of the tiers varies according to the metric.

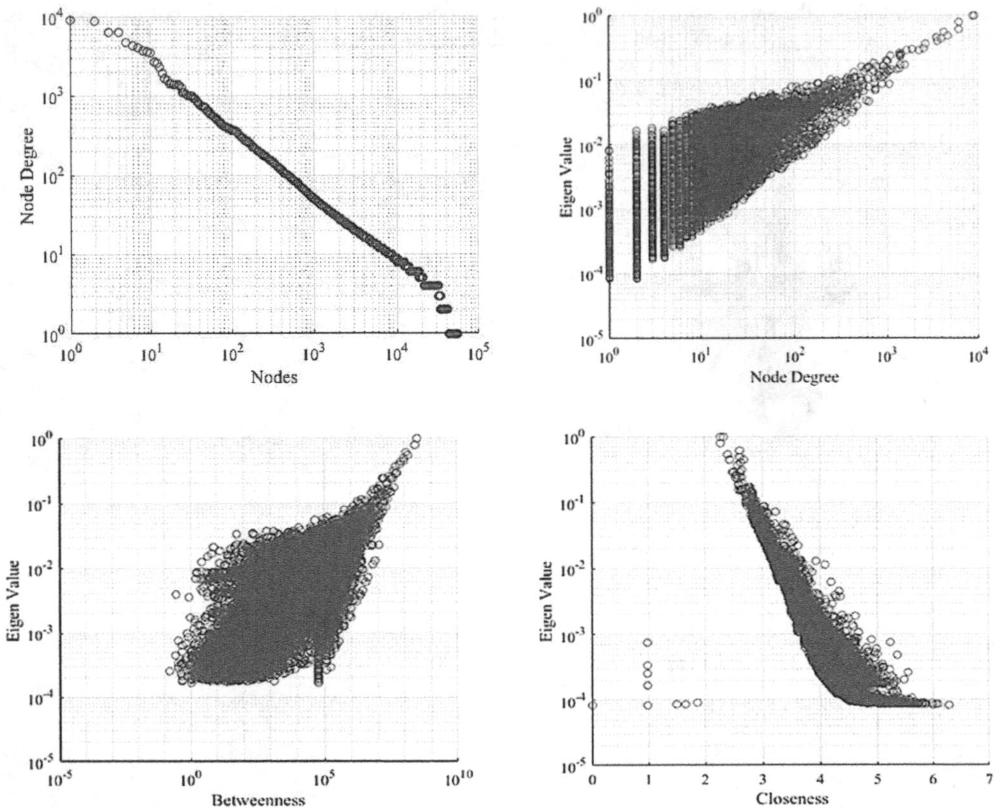

Figure 18.2 Experiment results: (a) Node degree distribution; (b) Node degree vs Eigen value; (c) Betweenness vs Eigen value; (d) Closeness vs Eigen value

Figure 18.3 is logged scale to show the small numbers in the other tiers. For example, when the degree metric is used, the number of ASes in tier 1 is 11295, tier 2 is 27996, and tier 3 is 20527. These numbers are far from the real numbers since the list of tier 1 ASes that has been constructed consists of only 17 AS. However, when the Eigen value metric is utilized, the number of ASes in these tiers are 54545, 5257, and 15 respectively, which is very close to the real numbers. To calculate the accuracy of our clustering process, a simple mean square error (MSE) has been calculated for each clustering process. The calculated accuracies have been given in Table 18.3. From Table 18.3 we can observe that the Eigen value is the best feature to cluster the ASes since the accuracy is 88% which is higher than other metrics.

Finally, Figure 18.4 shows the convergence process of the K-mean with the Eigen value feature. The algorithm has executed 50 iterations. However, the convergence occurred at 10 iterations.

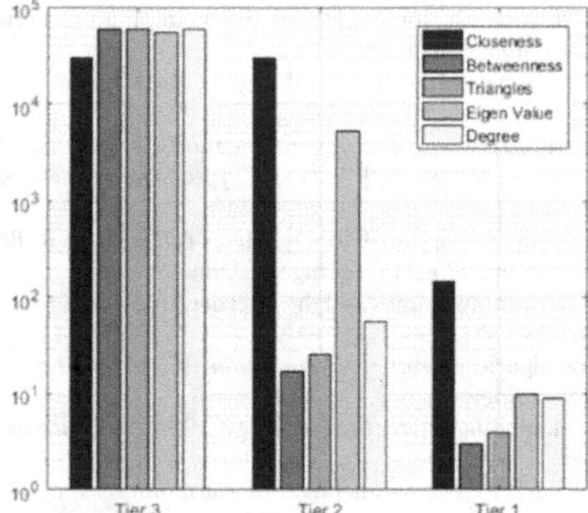

Figure 18.3 K-mean clustering output

Table 18.3 The accuracy of the diagram metrics clustering process

Metric	*Accuracy*
Degree	55%
Betweenness	69%
Closeness	62%
Eigen value	88%
Triangles	63%
All metrics	69%

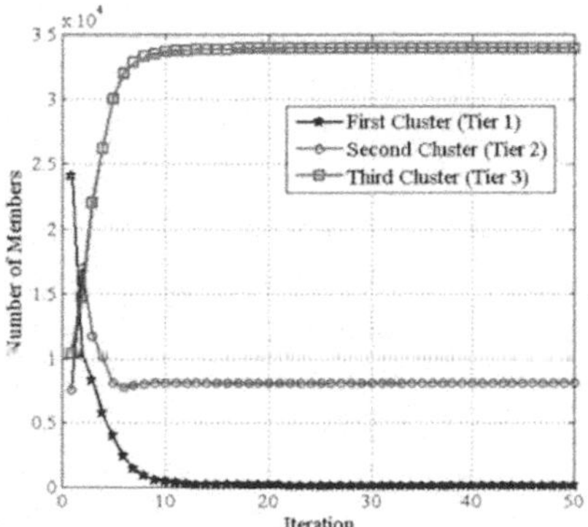

Figure 18.4 K-means convergence

Conclusion

Studying the AS relations has attracted researchers over the years. In this work, the AS diagram has been constructed from locking glass servers and PeeringDB harvested data. The constructed diagram has been analyzed to find five important metrics which are: degree, triangles count, Eigen value, betweenness, and closeness. Subsequently, the extracted metrics have been fed as features to the K-means algorithm to cluster the Internet ASes into one of three tiers. This classification is an important process in studying the properties of the internet. Our results show that the Eigen value is the only diagram metric that can be leveraged to classify the ASes into their tiers. An accuracy of 88% has been recorded for the Eigen value feature in the K-means clustering algorithm.

References

Baldi, P., Frasconi, P., & Smyth, P. (2003). Modeling the Internet and the Web. Wiley, New York.

Bastian, M., Heymann, S., & Jacomy, M. (2009). Gephi an open source software for exploring and manipulating networks. *Proceedings of the International AAAI Conference on Web and Social Media*, 3, 361–362.

Barabási, A. L. (2013). Philosophical transactions of the royal society A: Mathematical, physical and engineering sciences. *Network science*, 371, 20120375.

Böttger, T., Cuadrado, F. & Uhlig, S. (2018). Looking for hypergiants in PeeringDB. *Computer Communication Review*, 48, 13–19.

Delgado-Segura, S., Pérez-Solà, C., Herrera-Joancomartí, J., Navarro-Arribas, G., & Borrell, J. (2018). Cryptocurrency networks: A new P2P paradigm. *Mobile Information Systems*, e2159082.

Green, T., Lambert, A., Pelsser, C., & Rossi, D. (2018). Leveraging Inter-domain Stability for BGP Dynamics Analysis. In R. Beverly, G. Smaragdakis, & A. Feldmann, (Eds.). *Passive and Active Measurement.* pp. 203–215. Springer, Cham.

Jaiswal, S., Rosenberg, A. L., Towsley, D. (2004). Comparing the structure of power-law graphs and the Internet AS graph. *Proceedings of the 12th IEEE International Conference on Network Protocol* (pp. 294–303).

Likas, A., Vlassis, N., J. & Verbeek, J. (2003). The global k-means clustering algorithm. *Pattern Recognition*. 36, 451–461.

Liu J. (2021). Case study on PPTV. *The Frontiers of Society, Science and Technology*, 3.

Masoud, M. Z., Hei, X., & Cheng, W. (2013). A graph-theoretic study of the flattening Internet AS topology. *19th IEEE International Conference on Networks (ICON)*. (pp. 1–6).

Nemmi, E. N., Sassi, F., La Morgia, M., Testart, C., Mei, A., & Dainotti, A. (2021). The parallel lives of autonomous systems: ASN allocations vs. BGP. *Proceedings of the 21st ACM Internet Measurement Conference*. (pp. 593–611).

Silva, B., S. & Valera Pintor, F. (2018). Radiography of internet autonomous systems interconnection in Latin America and the Caribbean. *Computer Communications*. 119, 15–28.

Traceroute. http://traceroute.org/. (Accessed on 23 March, 2021).

Van Geenen, D.(2020). Critical affordance analysis for digital methods: *The Case of Gephi*. 1–21.

Witono, T. & Yazid, S. (2022). A Review of internet topology research at the autonomous system level. *Proceedings of Sixth International Congress on Information and Communication Technology*. 581–598).

19 A comparative analysis of machine learning techniques for effective heart disease prediction

Ab Qayoom Sofi[1,a] *and Ram Kumar*[2,b]

[1]Research Scholar, Department of Computer Applications, Lovely Professional University, Punjab, India

[2]Faculty, School of Computer Applications, Lovely Professional University, Punjab, India

Abstract

Cardiovascular diseases (CVD) are the biggest challenges and problems faced worldwide by the people in general and doctors/ clinicians in particular. Heart disease is the leading cause of death in the world and the mortality rate has increased after COVID-19, affecting the individual productivity and national economies badly. Owing to variety of risk factors and types of the disease, it becomes very difficult for the clinicians to diagnose the type of heart disease quickly and accurately. So, there is a dire need that the mortality rate is brought down and the precious lives be saved by effectively predicting the disease early and on time. In this paper, we have compared the performance of different machine learning/deep learning techniques. The experimental results indicated that the K-nearest neighbor with K = 5 achieved the best performance especially in Bi-class mode followed by ensemble algorithm random forest.

Keywords: artificial neural networks, cardio-vascular disease, classification, deep learning, ensemble algorithms, heart disease, K-nearest neighbor, machine learning, random forest, support vector machine

Introduction

As per the WHO, cardiovascular disease (CVD) is spreading like an epidemic. Any condition affecting the heart indicated by the chest pain, abnormal pulse rate and other symptoms is a heart disease (HD). A huge loss is caused to the economy by the HD. Further, the individual suffering from the disease leads a poor-quality life and the overall productivity decreases significantly. So, the heart diseases need to be prevented and checked. If the disease is diagnosed early on time accurately, it can be controlled, and the patients can be given good treatment to prevent the huge losses and the precious lives can be saved. Hence, it is very important to predict the HD early, efficiently, and accurately. Since there are several different types of HD (Swathy and Saruladha, 2021), there is a need to employ the latest machine learning (ML) techniques for earliest identification of the disease with its type to increase the survival rate.

Systems already designed for the prediction of the HD using ML techniques have achieved very good accuracies. But a lot of research can be still done to find the improved techniques for use with a particular data type. More research can be done to select the most significant feature subset after comparison and analysis of several feature selection (FS) algorithms. This paper is an effort to compare some of the popular ML techniques employed for prediction of the heart disease.

Literature Review

Swain et al. (2018) analyzed various ML techniques and obtained best accuracy of 97.5% in artificial neural networks (ANN) technique with 13 features. Panicker (2020) reviewed varied ML algorithms successfully and noted support vector machine (SVM) as popular algorithm used for classification followed by neural networks and ensembles with high accuracy. Convolutional neural networks (CNNs) and deep learning (DL) techniques also have high accuracies of over 95%. Krittanawong et al. (2020) found that SVM and boosting algorithms have been commonly used but comparison of various ML algorithms with conventional classifiers is required for selection of the best algorithm. Mehanović et al. (2020) applied ANN, K-nearest neighbor (KNN), and SVM. They used evaluation methods - percentage split (66:34) and 10-fold cross validation in two ways- multiclass (5 outputs) and bi-class (2 outputs) with majority voting having highest accuracy (87.37%) in bi-class method and 61.16% in multi-class method with percentage split found to be better than 10-fold cross validation. In Bi-class algorithm using 10 fold cross validation, ANN performed better than the ensemble method indicating that NNs can be explored to obtain even better results. Gao et al. (2021) applied PCA and LDA to obtain significant features from the Cleveland dataset and compared ensemble methods (boosting and bagging) with five classifiers (KNN, SVM, NB, DT, and RF). Bagging ensemble algorithm achieved the best performance in case of DT and PCA FS methods. Nayak et al. (2021) used NB and KNN classifiers and optimized values for NN using Salp

[a]abqayoom@gmail.com; [b]ram.26209@lpu.co.in

Swarm Algorithm. They applied Bayesian optimization to optimize the weight and kernel function of SVM. The optimized SVM method achieved a maximum accuracy of 93.3% highest than the other methods. This study (Chowdary, 2020) analyzed several classifiers including LR, RF, ANNs, XGBoost, SVM and KNN and found the RFA as most powerful technique with 100% accuracy score. Wang et al. (2021) demonstrated that LSTM is a feasible and powerful DL method to predict HD. Tasneem et al. (2021) classified CVD/CAD/HVD and highlighted the contributing risk factors. Investigated the datasets comprehensively and recorded detailed information about each dataset. Demonstrated that SVM, ANN, and MLP are the most used algorithms; but best performance is achieved by combining these methods with other algorithms. Katarya and Meena (2021) compared the performance of several ML techniques on UCI data set and found RFA achieved the best accuracy 95.6% proving it better and accurate than others. However, DL based algorithms can outperform RFA. Mansur Huang et al. (2021) compared the performance of RF, SVM, NB, and LR techniques using a publicly available dataset from Kaggle to show that RF produced the highest performance score, 0.88 compared to SVM, NB, and LR. They indicated that all 13 features were significant. However, Pal et al. (2022) demonstrated that MLP performed better with an accuracy of 82.47% than KNN with 73.77% accuracy.

Machine Learning Algorithms

Naïve Bayes (NB) Working on the Bayes theorem, it is a simple and yet effective classification algorithm where the features are assumed to be independent or unrelated and contribute to the probability independently.

Support vector machine (SVM) is a supervised learning algorithm which has been very popular in the prediction of the heart disease. It uses a hyperplane in the feature space to differentiate between the classes.

K-nearest neighbor (KNN) is a classification type supervised learning algorithm. The classifier classifies the new data point using the most similar classes.

Decision tree (DT) is a type of supervised ML algorithm used for classifications on both continuous and categorical attributes. It calculates the entropy of each attribute and splits the data set using predictors with minimum entropy.

Random forest (RF) is a supervised learning technique which can be used for both classification and regression. Its performance is better in classification problems. It creates multiple decision trees and forms their ensemble to reach to the outcome. It uses a majority voting system in classification and mean of all outputs in regression.

Ensemble of different ML algorithms (base classifiers) have been constituted and used for the prediction of HD with accuracies generally more than that of individual classifiers.

Deep learning (DL) is a subset of ML in which machines automatically learn from the data from features and tasks directly without any human intervention.

Artificial neural networks (ANN) is a type of DL which simulates human brain. It is a system which comprises of multiple nodes that processes information in parallel. Each node is like a neuron of the human brain and has a weight associated with it. It is organised in several finite layers with at least one layer for input, several hidden layers and one layer for output. ANN's have already been utilized in several areas of medicine including cardiology, etc. **convolutional neural network** (CNN) is a type of neural networks.

Methodology

Data sets: The data set used in the experiments is the Cleveland dataset.

Data pre-processing and features selection: Data pre-processing is required to clean, normalize and transform the data. The missing values and data inconsistencies were removed before applying the algorithms. However, FS techniques have not been applied in these experiments as most of the researchers have selected the 13 features out of 76 as the subset and treated as significant features or symptoms, which are shown below in Table 19.1.

Table 19.1 Features in the cleveland dataset

Index	*Age*	*Sex*	*cp*	*trestbps*	*chol*	*fbs*	*restecg*
thalach	exang	oldpeak	slope	ca	thal	class	

Classification methods: A very large number of ML techniques have been applied so far on various heart disease data sets and the results have been recorded. It has been observed that even same algorithm has yielded different results at different times using the same data set. The result has also been found to change with the change in data set i.e., when same algorithm has been applied on a different data set of the same health problem, the results (accuracy) have been found to be varying. This problem has been taken as multi class as well as Bi-class and the results of the techniques differ in these cases also using the same data sets.

Results and Discussion

So far as medical diagnostic is concerned, accuracy is the most significant factor as it involves the life a patient in addition to the precious cost, time, money, and efforts of the doctors. In our experiments done using Co-lab environment using Sci-kit learn library, we applied ANN, SVM, KNN, and RF algorithms on the Cleveland data set (processed data) using 13 significant features first in multi-class and then in bi-class mode to compare the accuracy of these algorithms on the given dataset and obtained the results shown below in Table 19.2, 19.3, and Figure 19.1.

Table 19.2 Accuracy results based on experiments

Method/classification algorithm	*ANN (Epochs=150, Batch size=10)*	*SVM*	*KNN (K=5)*	*Random forest*
Multiclass	53.3%	48%	56.6%	50.0%
Bi-class	85%	85%	88%	87%

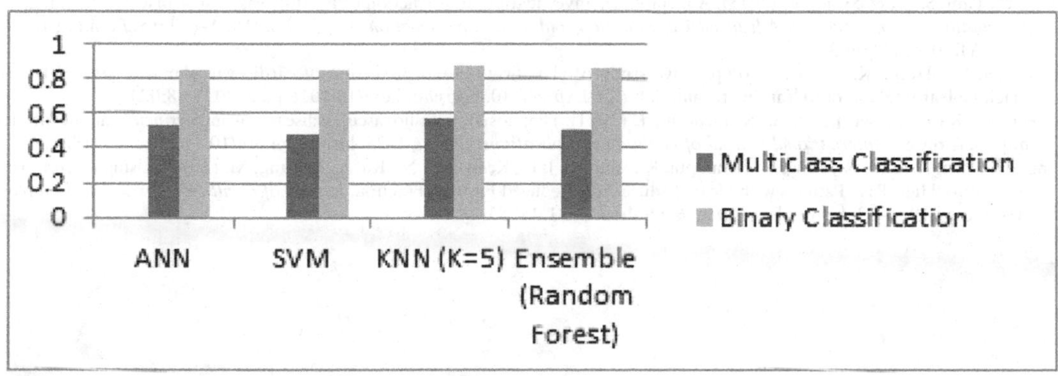

Figure 19.1 Accuracy comparison of the classifier algorithms

Table 19.3 Comparison of results (precision/recall/F1-score)

Method/algorithm	*SVM*	*KNN (K=5)*	*RF*
Precision/recall/F1-score (Multiclass)	0.48	0.57	0.50
Precision/recall/F1-score (Bi-class)	0.85	0.88	0.87

Conclusions

Cardiovascular diseases are a major threat to the humans as a huge no. of persons die because of heart diseases since doctors/clinicians are unable to predict the disease on time owing to the number and variety of risk factors and types of the disease. A number of machine learning and deep learning algorithms have already been employed on different datasets in different modes for the prediction of the disease and the results have been found to vary from dataset to dataset. This paper compares the performance of K-nearest neighbor, random forest, artificial neural networks (ANN) algorithms in the experiments done on Cleveland dataset (htt) using 13 features in multi-class and bi-class modes and it has been found that in bi-class mode, KNN (K=5) has the best accuracy followed by ensemble algorithm RF. In future, this research can be extended by performing experiments applying the various feature selection methods which is expected to improve the performance of the algorithms further.

References

Chowdary, G. J. (2020). Prediction of cardiovascular disease using machine learning Algorithms. *International Journal of Engineering and Advanced Technology*, 9(3), 2404–2414. https://doi.org/10.35940/ijeat.b3986.029320

Gao, X. Y., Amin Ali, A., Shaban Hassan, H., & Anwar, E. M. (2021). Improving the Accuracy for analyzing heart diseases prediction based on the ensemble method. *Complexity*, *2021*. https://doi.org/10.1155/2021/6663455

Katarya, R. & Meena, S. K. (2021). Machine learning techniques for heart disease prediction: A comparative study and analysis. *Health and Technology*, 11(1), 87–97. https://doi.org/10.1007/s12553-020-00505-7

Krittanawong, C., Virk, H. U. H., Bangalore, S., Wang, Z., Johnson, K. W., Pinotti, R., Zhang, H. J., Kaplin, S., Narasimhan, B., Kitai, T., Baber, U., Halperin, J. L., & Tang, W. H. W. (2020). Machine learning prediction in cardiovascular diseases: a meta-analysis. *Scientific Reports*, 10(1), 1–11. https://doi.org/10.1038/s41598-020-72685-1

Mansur Huang, N. S., Ibrahim, Z., & Mat Diah, N. (2021). Machine learning techniques for heart failure prediction. *Malaysian Journal of Computing*, *6*(2), 872. https://doi.org/10.24191/mjoc.v6i2.13708

Mehanović, D., Mašetić, Z., & Kečo, D. (2020). Prediction of heart diseases using majority voting ensemble method. *IFMBE Proceedings*, 73, 491–498. https://doi.org/10.1007/978-3-030-17971-7_73

Nayak, G. S., Patro, S. P., & Padhy, N. (2021). Heart disease prediction by using novel optimization algorithm: A supervised learning prospective. *Informatics in Medicine Unlocked*, 100696. https://doi.org/10.1016/j.imu.2021.100696

Pal, M., Parija, S., Panda, G., Dhama, K., & Mohapatra, R. K. (2022). Risk prediction of cardiovascular disease using machine learning classifiers. *Open Medicine (Poland)*, 17(1), 1100–1113. https://doi.org/10.1515/med-2022-0508

Panicker, S. (2020). Use of Machine learning techniques in healthcare: A brief review of cardiovascular disease classification. *SSRN Electronic Journal*. https://doi.org/10.2139/ssrn.3681833

Swain, D., Pani, S. K., & Swain, D. (2018). A metaphoric investigation on prediction of heart disease using machine learning. *2018 International Conference on Advanced Computation and Telecommunication, ICACAT 2018*, 1–6. https://doi.org/10.1109/ICACAT.2018.8933603

Swathy, M. Saruladha, K. (2021). A comparative study of classification and prediction of cardio-vascular diseases (CVD) using machine learning and deep learning techniques. *ICT Express*, 40. https://doi.org/10.1016/j.icte.2021.08.021

Tasneem, T., Kabir, M. M. J., Xu, S., & Tasneem, T. (2021). Diagnosis of cardiovascular diseases using artificial intelligence techniques: A review. *International Journal of Computer Applications*, 183(3), 1–25. https://doi.org/10.5120/ijca2021921313

Wang, Z., Chen, X., Tan, X., Yang, L., Kannapur, K., Vincent, J. L., Kessler, G. N., Ru, B., & Yang, M. (2021). Using Deep Learning to Identify High-Risk Patients with Heart Failure with Reduced Ejection Fraction. *Journal of Health Economics and Outcomes Research*, *8*(2), 6–13. https://doi.org/10.36469/jheor.2021.25753

20 Sample size estimation techniques for classification – A review

Yogesh Mahawar[a] *and Tanima Thakur*[b]

School of Computer Science & Engineering, Lovely Professional University, Punjab, India

Abstract

The biggest problem for researchers, machine learning engineers, and data scientists when it comes to classification is to decide the sample size used for training their classification model. As the quantity of algorithms for machine learning and the amount of the training data both keep growing, it is becoming harder for the researchers to determine how much dataset should they use for their research, and it becomes tedious for them to do trial and error to achieve the required performance. This paper provides an overview on many methods discussed in the past studies for sample size estimation in classification problems and discusses the research gap in those methods. At the end, it concludes with the best technique that can be used for sample size estimation.

Keywords: Sample size estimation, classification, machine learning, deep learning

Introduction

The research on machine learning (ML) techniques like classification, regression, and clustering keeps getting popular and there are more and more disciplines which are starting to apply ML concepts which some challenges along the way. One of the biggest challenges is how to calculate the sample size used for training dataset in classification. This paper aims to provide background on the terms related to classification and discusses the various methods being researched to estimate the sample size of classification.

According to the founder of artificial intelligence (AI), John McCarthy, who first used the phrase AI in 1956, AI is the synthesis of science and engineering to create intelligent machines for human wellbeing. There are claims that it has an intelligence that is much more intelligent than the finest human brain in almost every subject, including computer science and linguistic reasoning. In general, it combines problem-solving, learning, perception, and linguistics (Rupali and Amit, 2017).

According to Lantz (2019), the research area of ML focuses on the creation of computer algorithms for turning data into intelligent action. ML is an application of AI that deals with making a machine learn by providing it with some data. There are many popular real-world applications of ML such as Siri by Apple, Watson by IBM, Cortana by Microsoft, Self-Driving Cars, and Humanoid Robots such as Valkyrine and ASIMO (Rupali and Amit, 2017).

Supervised learning, unsupervised learning, and reinforcement learning are the three categories of ML approaches, which are further classified into classification, regression, association, and clustering as provided in Table 20.1 below. When a model is being learned using labelled data then the learning is called supervised learning and otherwise unsupervised learning. Reinforcement learning deals with making an agent take a set of actions in the environment and based on the feedback it is given rewards and punishments.

As shown in Figure 20.1 above, the general process to apply ML is to first collect the data that will be used by an algorithm for training purpose, then the data is explored and prepared in such a way that it is most beneficial to the learning algorithm. Once the data is prepared, the ML model which represents the learning algorithm will be trained on that data and then its performance will be evaluated. If the desired performance is not obtained, then advanced strategies are utilized to obtain better performance (Goodfellow et al., 2016).

Deep learning (DL) is a sort of ML in which models are made more complicated by incorporating representations that are stated in terms of other simpler representations to address the issue in representation learning (Goodfellow et al., 2016). Between the input layer and the output layer, DL models are built utilizing many hidden layers. Multilayer PERCeptron's (MLPs), recurrent neural networks (RNNs), convolutional neural networks (CNNs), and long short-term memory networks (LSTMs) are a few of the widely used DL techniques. The Figure 20.2 below shows how AI, ML, and DL are correlated. In general, DL is a part of ML, which in turn is a part of AI.

The remainder of the paper is structured as follows: The literature review related to the domain of this study is included in section 2 of this paper, followed by section 3 which discusses the various results obtained from the literature review and the research gap associated with it. This paper ends in section 4 which concludes this study by mentioning the best approach to follow.

[a]yogeshdmc.ym@gmail.com; [b]tanima.23532@lpu.co.in

Table 20.1 Types of ML techniques

	Discrete data	*Continuous data*
Supervised	Classification	Regression
Unsupervised	Association	Clustering

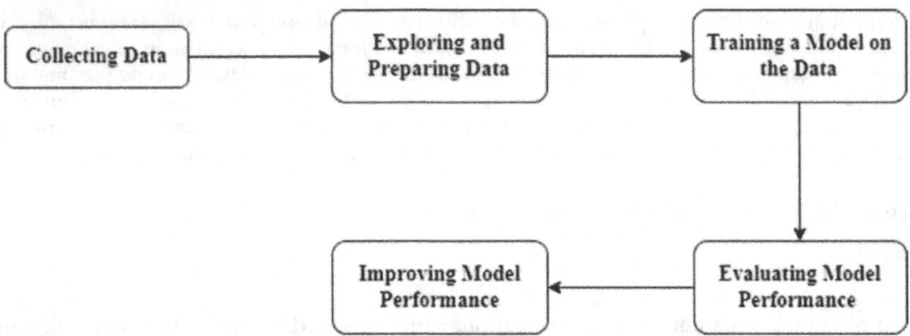

Figure 20.1 Steps to apply machine learning

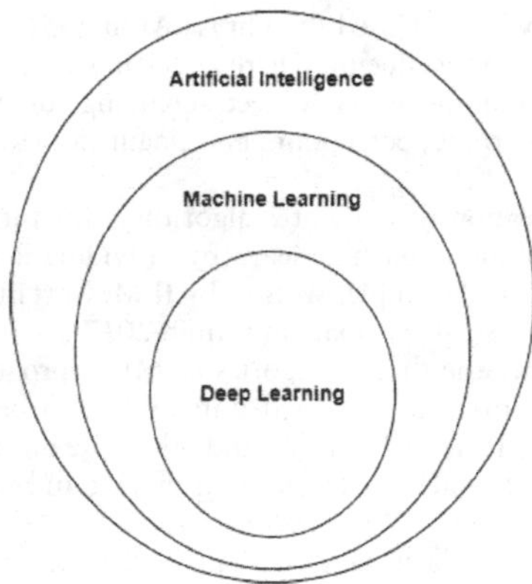

Figure 20.2 AI, ML, and DL venn diagram

Literature Review

Dobbin et al. (2005) provided formulas to calculate sample size for microarray investigations to compare classes and create prognostic indicators. A total of 240 patients' biopsy samples were used to validate these formulas. The results showed that their formulae were appropriate for determining the sample size of microarray data.

Sordo et al. (2005) analyzed a dataset of extracts taken from the narrative reports of a hospital to determine the link between sample size and accuracy of classification using support vector machines (SVMs), Naive Bayes (NB), and decision trees (DTs). The results showed that SVM and DTs greatly increased their accuracy in increasing the sample size of the dataset while Naïve Bayes showed a small and abrupt change in accuracy.

Hua et al. (2005) investigated the ideal number of characteristics needed for classification when the sample size is held constant. Patient information from research using microarrays to classify cancer served as the dataset for this project. It was discovered that, for given sample sizes, a classifier's classification error sometimes initially drops and then rises as the number of features grows.

Dobbin et al. (2008) offered a model-based method to establish the necessary sample size for effective classifier training. The presented approach was applied to four different datasets and the results showed that three quantities are required for the determination of sample size which are the amount of features on arrays, class predominance, and standardized fold change.

Foody (2009) stated some basic statistical principles for determining the size of the testing set used for assessing the accuracy and comparison for classification of remote sensing images. The equations discussed in this paper were compared based on the issues they have, and it was found that the size of the data used for testing cannot be determined using a technique that is generally recognized but rather careful planning should be done regarding which method to use based on their merits and demerits.

de Valpine et al. (2009) devised a method for linear discriminant analysis (LDA) that combines approximation approaches and Monte Carlo approaches to investigate the dependence of validation error rate on informative features, non-informative features, sample size, and individual feature length. The findings demonstrated that size of the sample and individual feature size are the most crucial variables in pattern discovery.

Hess et al. (2010) used diagonal LDA, three nearest neighbors, and SVMs to examine the learning curves in the categorization of microarray data. The models were trained on four different large clinical genomic cancer datasets. Out of the 12 experiments, some experiments showed a rapid and continuous increase in performance as the dataset size increased while others showed very little improvement.

Figueroa et al. (2012) created and put into use a technique that forecasts a classifier's effectiveness and confidence interval for bigger sample numbers. They used a non-linear weighted curve fitting method for evaluation of 568 different models trained on three different datasets with four different sampling methods in each one of them and prediction validations were done by comparing predicted performance with actual observed performance. Their weighted fitting approach surpassed a benchmark un-weighted approach covered in earlier research.

Beleites et al. (2013) experimented to observe the learning curves which helps in determining the size of the training sample required to reach better accuracy in a classifier. The experiment was done on a dataset of around 2550 single-cell Raman spectra, then it was determined that to evaluate an effective classifier, 75–100 samples for each class would be required and calculating the necessary sample sizes for classifiers needs breadth of the confidence interval and a model to contrast with.

Prusa et al. (2015) examined the impact of dataset size on categorizing tweet sentiments using the C4.5 DT algorithm, NB algorithm, five NB algotirhm, and Radial Basis Function neural network (RBFN) to determine how many instances of the dataset are needed before there is no more significant improvement with the increase in dataset size. Seven different datasets were used for this study with instances ranging from 1000–243,000. Naïve Bayes was found to be the best performing learner and it achieved its optimal performance at 81,000 instances of tweet sentiments.

Althnian et al. (2021) looked at the influence of the training data size on classification accuracy in the medical sector. 20 different datasets were used to train six different classification models and their average accuracies were noted down. The average accuracy of classifiers where smaller training data was used for training ranged from 62–99%, while the average accuracy across datasets ranged from 79–82%. This indicates that given a smaller training data, classifier performance is generally similar, but that performance varies across small training datasets for each classifier. For large datasets, the sample size was reduced, and accuracy was checked on each reduction showed that some models' accuracy dropped drastically, some remained nearly the same, and some increased their accuracy. It was concluded that, rather than its size, the dataset's ability to accurately capture the original distribution affects the classifier's overall performance.

Valpine et al. (2021) developed an approach that is effective for calculating the oversampling size, which is smaller than the sample size required to achieve class balance based on the complexity of the imbalanced dataset because oversampling the minority class to make it equal to the majority class can induce overfitting. Instead of broad oversampling research that propose where to add new samples, how to create new samples, and how to eliminate noise, this study focused on how much oversampling is necessary to obtain excellent accuracy. The assessment was conducted on 16 distinct unbalanced datasets using a variety of boosting algorithms and other oversampling techniques. The findings revealed that the sample size computed using their approach outperforms the sample size required to restore the dataset's balance.

Alshammari et al. (2021) investigated how the amount of the dataset affected the predictability of software defects. They mentioned that the statistical approach is weak against outliers, high dimensionality, and imbalanced classes which are why they used a ML approach using SVM using four different datasets of different sizes from the NASA MDP website, and four different feature selection algorithms. It was found that dataset size directly affects the performance of the SVM model in defect prediction, having fewer features made it perform well but it does not guarantee a shorter execution time.

Table 20.2 Literature review summary

S. No	*Author(s)*	*Objective*	*Tools*	*Dataset*	*Result*
1.	Dobbin et al. (2005)	To devise formulae to determine sample size in microarray experiments	Prognostic Markers, Significance Level, Power	240 patients' biopsy samples	Formulas were accurate for finding the microarray data sample size
2.	Sordo et al. (2005)	To examine the relationship among sample size and classification accuracy	NB, SVM, DT	Extracts dataset taken from a hospital's narrative reports	SVM and DT got a greater performance increase than Naïve Bayes with an increase in dataset size
3.	Hua et al. (2005)	To get the optimum number of features in classification as a function of training sample	3NN, Gaussian Kernel, Linear SVM, Polynomial SVM, Perceptron, Regular Histogram, LDA	Patient data from a cancer classification research using microarrays	By increasing the number of characteristics, classification error lowers initially and later rises
4.	Dobbin et al. (2008)	To calculate the size of the training set required to create a classifier for microarray data	Mathematical Model-based approach	Four different datasets from past studies	Amount of features, class predominance, standardized fold change are sample size determination quantities
5.	Foody (2009)	To state some basic statistical principles for determining the testing set size in remote sensing image classification	Meaningful Difference, Significance Level, Power	Datasets from original papers that were discussed in this paper	There is no commonly acknowledged technique for determining the testing set size
6.	de Valpine et al. (2009)	To provide a simulation-approximation method for choosing sample size in data with high-dimension	Monte Carlo methods, Approximation approaches for LDA	Several different datasets were used	Sample size and feature length are the most essential parameters in pattern discovery
7.	Hess et al. (2010)	To study the learning curves in classification with microarray data	Learning Curve Estimation, Progressive Sampling, DNDA, k-NN3, SVM	Four clinical genomic cancer datasets from the Oncomine website	Rapid and continuous increase in performance in some experiments as the dataset size increased
8.	Figueroa et al. (2012)	To develop a method that predicts performance of a classifier and confidence interval with greater sample sizes	Learning Curve Weighted Fitting, DIST, DIV, CMB, RAND, Mean Absolute Error, RMSE	Smoking-related sentences from patient discharge summaries and Waveform-5000 dataset	Discussed weighted fitting approach surpassed a benchmark un-weighted approach
9.	Beleites et al. (2013)	To examine the learning curves and identify the training sample size required for effective classifier performance	The learning curve, Confidence interval width, LDA, ggplot2	2550 single-cell Raman spectra	A decent classifier requires 75100 samples each class to be tested
10.	Prusa et al. (2015)	To investigate the impact of dataset size on tweet sentiment classification	C4.5, NB, 5-NN, RBF, Cross Validation	6 datasets from the sentiment140 corpus and one self-constructed dataset	Naïve Bayes was found to be the best performing learner with optimal dataset instances of 81,000
11.	Althnian et al. (2021)	To study the influence of the training data size on classification accuracy in the medical sector	Ada Boost, NB, SVM, Neural Network, DT, RF	20 different datasets from the UCI data repository	Classifier's overall performance is determined more by how closely the dataset captures the original distribution than by its size
12.	Lee et al. (2021)	To provide an effective strategy for calculating the oversampling size that is below the sample size required to achieve class balance	Oversampling, Adaptive Boosting, Ensemble Learning, Imbalance ratio, Classification complexity	13 datasets from the UCI repository, 2 from a NASA repository, and 1 from existing research	Compared to the sample size required to balance the dataset, the computed sample size performed better
13.	Alshammari et al. (2021)	To investigate how dataset size affects software fault prediction model precision	SVM, Feature Selection, Cross Validation, WEKA, DTREG Predictive Modelling Software	Four different datasets from the NASA MDP website	Fewer features in the dataset can make a model perform well but a shorter execution time is not guaranteed

Discussion

From the literature survey (Table 20.2) we can see that the studies by Dobbin and Simon (2005), Foody (2009), and de Valpine et al. (2009), we can see that the estimation of sample size was only done using statistical approaches and mathematical formulas but not using a ML model to predict the accuracies that a particular model will give when trained on a particular dataset with a larger sample size. Observing the learning curve as mentioned by Beleites et al. (2013) will not tell you any prediction that the learning curve will have after increasing the sample size and you can only guess the additional sample size by looking at the curve itself. In the study by Althnian et al. (2021) the progression of research is mentioned as the investigation of the smallest dataset size each classifier need to operate at its best which makes it a research gap that needs to be investigated which can help in automating the task of sample size determination instead of explicitly calculating the sample size using formulas, guessing it from the learning curve or doing trial and error.

The accuracies gained by increasing the size of the training data is a number sequence and the best networks to find a pattern in number sequences are recurrent neural networks (RNN). The method discussed by Dobbin et al. (2008) does not use an RNN to predict the accuracies for larger sample sizes. The studies of Prusa et al. (2015), Althnian et al. (2021), and Alshammari et al. (2021) didn't consider an important factor when examining how the dataset affects the categorization accuracy. The factor is the number of distinct classes the dataset contains; as the number of classes in a dataset rises, so does the ambiguity in the data, and the model's accuracy will suffer as a result.

Conclusion

The need of predicting the size of the sample required by a model in training to perform well on a specific dataset can be seen in the literature review itself. There are a lot of ML models in existence to choose from and every one of them converges at a different rate for different datasets, the task of determining the size of dataset for a particular model is very much time consuming. There are many methods to predict the needed sample size given by the researchers in the past studies, but they all have advantages and disadvantages which makes it harder to determine which method to use and most of them require the researcher to do a lot of time-consuming manual work. As the results of estimating the sample size varies for different models and datasets, we can say that a better approach for this task will be to design a framework which takes the model and dataset as input and predicts the required sample size without requiring any extra effort or manual work by the user.

References

Alshammari, M. A., & Alshayeb, M. (2021). The Effect of the Dataset Size on the Accuracy of Software Defect Prediction Models: An Empirical Study. *Inteligencia Artificial*, 24(68), 72–88.

Althnian, A., AlSaeed, D., Al-Baity, H., Samha, A., Dris, A. B., Alzakari, N., Elwafa, A. A., & Kurdi, H. (2021). Impact of dataset size on classification performance: an empirical evaluation in the medical domain. Applied Sciences, 11(2), 796.

Beleites, C., Neugebauer, U., Bocklitz, T., Krafft, C., & Popp, J. (2013). Sample size planning for classification models. *Analytica Chimica Acta*, 760, 25–33.

de Valpine, P., Bitter, H. M., Brown, M. P., & Heller, J. (2009). A simulation–approximation approach to sample size planning for high-dimensional classification studies. *Biostatistics*, 10(3), 424–435.

Dobbin, K. & Simon, R. (2005). Sample size determination in microarray experiments for class comparison and prognostic classification. *Biostatistics*, 6(1), 27–38.

Dobbin, K. K., Zhao, Y., & Simon, R. M. (2008). How large a training set is needed to develop a classifier for microarray data?. *Clinical Cancer Research*, 14(1), 108–114.

Figueroa, R. L., Zeng-Treitler, Q., Kandula, S., & Ngo, L. H. (2012). Predicting sample size required for classification performance. *BMC Medical Informatics and Decision Making*, 12(1), 1–10.

Foody, G. M. (2009). Sample size determination for image classification accuracy assessment and comparison. *International Journal of Remote Sensing*, 30(20), 5273–5291.

Goodfellow, I., Bengio, Y., & Courville, A. (2016). Deep learning. MIT press.

Hess, K. R. & Wei, C. (2010, February). Learning curves in classification with microarray data. *Seminars Oncology*, 37(1), 65–68).

Hua, J., Xiong, Z., Lowey, J., Suh, E., & Dougherty, E. R. (2005). The optimal number of features as a function of sample size for various classification rules. *Bioinformatics*, 21(8), 1509–1515.

Kamusoko, C. (2019). Remote sensing image classification in R. Springer, Singapore.

Lantz, B. (2019). Machine learning with R: Expert techniques for predictive modeling. Packt, Birmingham, UK

Lee, D. & Kim, K. (2021). An efficient method to determine sample size in oversampling based on classification complexity for imbalanced data. *Expert Systems with Applications*, 184, 115442.

Prusa, J., Khoshgoftaar, T. M., & Seliya, N. (2015, December). The effect of dataset size on training tweet sentiment classifiers. *In 2015 IEEE 14th International Conference on Machine Learning and Applications (ICMLA)*. (pp. 96–102).

Rupali, M. & Amit, P. (2017). A review paper on general concepts of artificial intelligence and machine learning. *International Advanced Research Journal in Science, Engineering and Technology*, 4(4), 79–82.

Sordo, M. & Zeng, Q. (2005). On sample size and classification accuracy: A performance comparison. In International Symposium on Biological and Medical Data Analysis (pp. 193–201). Springer, Berlin, Heidelberg.

21 Detection of early-stage symptoms of diabetic retinopathy prediction performance in machine learning algorithms

Aruna Kumari[1,a], *Avinash Bhagat*[2,b], *and Santosh Kumar Henge*[3,c]

[1]Research Scholar, Lovely Professional University, Punjab, India

[2]Associate Professor, Lovely Professional University, Punjab, India

[3]Associate Professor, Manipal University, Jaipur, India

Abstract

Diabetics is a very common chronic disease it occurs either when the body cannot effectively use the produces insulin or when pancreas does not produce sufficient insulin. Diabetic retinopathy is a difficulty of diabetes that touches eyes. Diabetic retinopathy may cause through impairment to the blood vessels. The back of the eye tissue impairment in the blood vessels, blood sugar is a risk factor. The dataset contains the 520 observations and with 16 characteristics, the prediction of early stages of diabetes causes the sixteen signs, they are polyuria, polyphagia, genital thrush, sudden weight loss, visual blurring, itching, irritability, delayed healing, partial paresis, muscle stiffness, alopecia, obesity, age, sex, weakness, class. And proposed method of most effective prototypical is calculated by 2D convolution neural network model, and it has an accuracy of 99% over the 10 epochs representation for train and test set.

Keywords: Diabetes risk, early stage, symptom, hyperparameter tuning

Introduction

Diabetic is a disease continuing metabolic syndrome, it disturbs the capability of the body in producing the hormone insulin. They two types of diabetics, type 1 and type 2. Type 1 is insulin dependent diabetes, this reaction destroys the cells of pancreas that makes the insulin the process can develop the months or years before symptoms occurs (Reddy et al., 2022). When the blood glucose level is too high and the body is not producing the hormone called insulin, it is called type 1 diabetes. Type 2 is the long-term condition, too much sugar circulating in the blood, it can lead the elevated blood sugar levels. High blood sugar levels remain the reason of disorder of circulatory, immune system, and nervous (Kumari et al., 2022) system. Type 2 diabetes common causes are overweight, obesity, and inactive lifestyle. The dataset collected using straight surveys and analysis consequences from patients in clinic Sylhet, Bangladesh. Outstanding to occurrence of a comparatively extensive symptomless, early detection of diabetes is continuously anticipated for a clinically expressive outcome (Canto et al., 2021). Almost 50% of people suffering from diabetes are undiagnosed.

Literature Review

The proposed method is step by step procedure for circle cropping algorithm, it refers the all the sides of eye image, when image can be rotate all the direction. The directions of image should be up, top, bottom, corners and edges. They are two types type 1 and type 2, and stages of diabetes is proliferated diabetic retinopathy and non-proliferate diabetic retinopathy. On-proliferate have four stages, they are normal, mild, moderate, severe and it takes threshold values as 0,1,2,3 correspondingly for no diabetic retinopathy, if threshold value is 4 it is proliferative diabetic retinopathy (Kumari et al., 2022).

The diabetic mellites mainly divided into two types, they are type 1 and type 2. The proposed methodology is single field digital monochromatic non-mydriatic photography, the proposed method main aim is before being examined by an ophthalmologist using ophthalmoscopy having 30 degrees color stereoscopic Ansari et al. (2022).

The author is mainly focus on early detection of diabetic retinopathy, in his study they are of two types: type 1 and type 2, and it can be non-proliferate, proliferate. In non-proliferate can be mild, moderate, severe and proliferate. The proposed method can estimate the automatically in 3D-MGRF model based spatial occurs (Mohamed et al, 2022).

The proposed methods built on segmentation, A method can be modified by U-Net algorithm, the similarities between blood vessels, retinal hemorrhage, contextual work of original images, the segmentation of images with digital fund images are segmentation (Skouta et al, 2022).

---

[a]aruna2k4@gmail.com; [b]avinash.bhagat@lpu.co.in; [c]hingesantosh@gmail.com

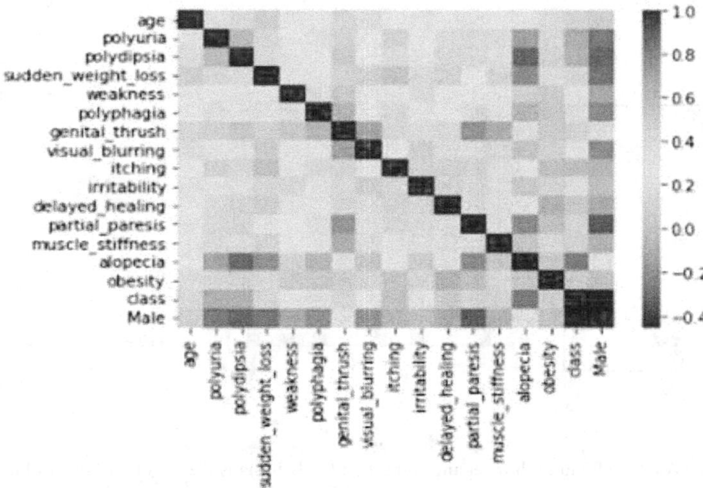

Figure 21.1 Shows the 16 symptoms of diabetic retinopathy

Existing Methodology

ML algorithms-Navi Bayes is supervised learning algorithm can be adapted by Bayes' theorem through robust independence exceptions among landscapes obtain outcomes. Logistic regression is supervised and important machine learning algorithm, this algorithm also called as binary classifier, it is supports the or it predicts the yes or no event occurring. Decision tree (DT) is supervised learning algorithm, it can use the tasks as classifications and regressions, the DT consists of tree structure, hierarchical. Random forest (RF) is multipurpose supervised algorithm, that produces and associations many decision trees to generate a forest. support vector machine most common supervised learning algorithm, it can use problems for classification and regression. K-nearest neighbor (KNN) is a parameter can refer the nearest neighbor with popular voting process. Extreme Gradient Boosting back-to-back built superficial decision trees to generated exact outcomes and it uses the extremely adaptable training technique to avoid overfitting. Voting classifier trains ensemble of various models and predictions of output. voting classifier have two classification problems-hard voting classifier, soft voting classifier.

There are differences between diabetic and non-diabetic in polyuria, polydipsia, sudden-weight-loss, weakness, polyphagia, visual-blurring, partial-paresis, alopecia, gender. Figure 21.1 shows the 16 symptoms of early detection of diabetic retinopathy polyuria the most common caused by uses of diuretics and uncontrolled diabetes mellitus and urine volume is high. Polydipsia symptoms is feeling of extreme thirstiness. Sudden weight loss is a perceptible, drop-in body weight. Weakness of diabetic retinopathy encompass of unclear vision. Polyphagia diabetic mellitus due low blood sugar. Genital thrush disease with specific problematic diabetes because glucose aids candida grows. Visual blurring can occur the over time, diabetes harm minor blood vessels throughout eye as well as retina. Itching if person have diabetes, more likely to have dry skin due to glucose. Irritability is a feeling of a person, delayed healing when person have diabetes. Partial paresis person can struggle concentrating or dual vision. Muscle stiffness causes the joint pain to move person joints. Alopecia may lead to the loss of hair on the head. Obesity causes diabetes to worsen faster.

Methodology and Model Specifications

Convolution neural network comes under the subdomain of machine learning. The purpose of using filters in convolution neural network, filters can exist of some dissimilar kinds conferring to persistence. Filters can support to utilize the dimensional located of specific image by implementing a local connection pattern among neurons. the convolution principally a point-by-point reproduction of binary functions to generate tierce function, unity function is image pixels matrix and other one is filters. Figure 21.2 shows the model of ROC-score.

Description of model framework

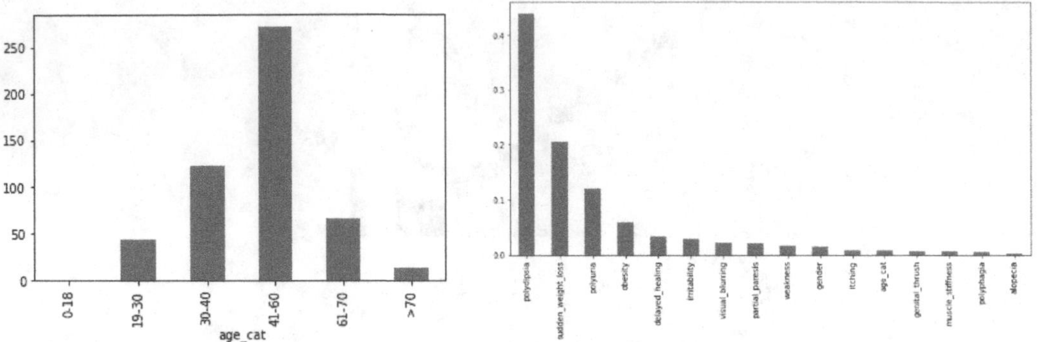

Figure 21.2 Shows the model of ROC-score is 0.99 in both train and test set and polydipsia is the major variable to build the model and feature engineering values

Dataset and processing stages

Dataset: https://archive.ics.uci.edu/ml/datasets/Early+stage+diabetes+risk+prediction+dataset

Stage1: Diabetic person
Stage 2: Non-diabetic person
Stage 3: Class represents the positive, negative values of diabetic symptoms
Stage 4: Classification of diabetic symptoms ->polyuria, polyphagia, genital thrush, sudden weight loss, visual blurring, itching, irritability, delayed healing, partial paresis, muscle stiffness, alopecia, obesity, age, sex, weakness, class.
Stage 5: Hyperparameters and their min and max values.
Stage 6: n_estimators can be shows the number of boosting stages and default value = 100
Stage7: Step size compress the subscription of every tree by their value and default value = 0.1. The trade-off among step size and n_estimators.
Stage 8: Max_depth can be shows the extreme depth of discrete regression evaluate and default value = 3. The max depth restrictions in quantity of nodes in the tree.
Stage 9: Under sampling, can define the segment of trials used for correct the separate base learners and default value=1.0
Stage 10: Max_features can indicate the number of landscapes to be reflect for best split, possible values are auto, sqrt, log2 and default value = None.

Transformed into numerical. All the missing values are removed and the data cleaning number is 480. Data transformation for the dataset is applied.

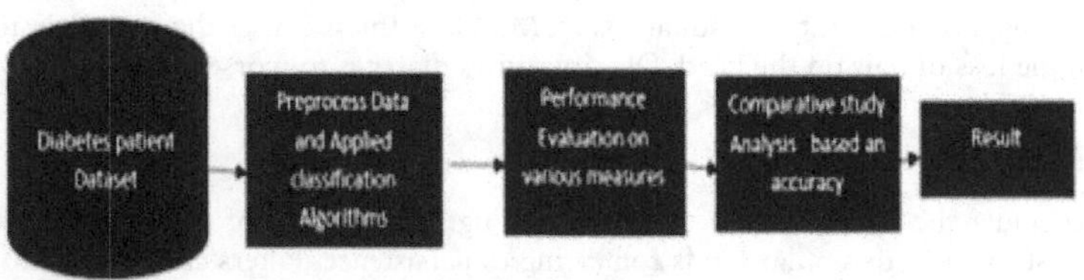

Figure 21.3 Shows the process flow of data and measures

Experimental Results

All the machine learning models stand executed the diabetic risk prediction dataset, the outcomes can evaluate f-score in Table 21.1, according to the results and evaluation of model, the maximum classification accuracy is accomplished by 2D convolutional neural network, an accuracy of dataset measured classification is 99% performance comparison with Figure 21.4 shows chi squared test, for best categorical input and categorical output, the best models for predicting the diabetes in dataset are XGBoost, RF, DT.

Comparative study

Summary statistics: The various ML algorithms, F-score and chi square test Table 21.1.

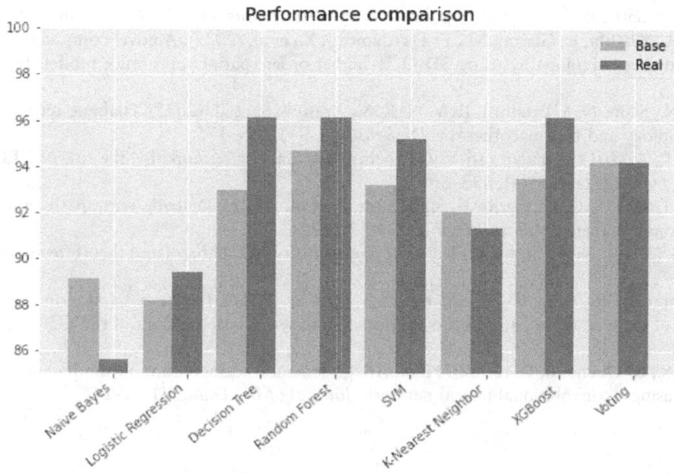

Figure 21.4 Shows the feature selection with chi squared test

Table 21.1 Comparative study of machine learning algorithms, F-score and chi square test

S. No	*ML algorithms*	*F-score*	*Chi square test*
1	Naïve Bayes	85.57%	85.57%
2	Logistic regression	89.42%	88.46%
3	DT	96.15%	96.15%
4	RF	96.15%	97.11%
5	SVM	95.19%	93.26%
6	KNN	91.34%	89.42%
7	XGBoost	96.15%	97.11%
8	Voting classifier	94.23%	94.23%

Conclusion

There are 320 people in diabetes and 200 people in non-diabetes, people who have diabetes are heavily distributed between 40–60-year-old and are distributed over 80-years old, then those who don't have diabetes are distributed between 25–70-year old. Early-stage diabetes risk forecast dataset can apply eight machine learning algorithms, The results can be compared by in relationships of performance metrics, they are accuracy, recall, precision and F-score. The effective typical is XGBoost with f score is 96.15% and random forest is 96.15%, decision tree is 96.15%. And proposed method of maximum positive model is designed by 2D convolution neural network model, and it has an accuracy of 99% over the 10 epochs in schema for train and test set. In future work we can take age, age is continuous variable and we can consider the feature engineering factor as age categorical variable by extracting the age as variable.

References

Borodina, T., Kostyushev, D., Zamyatnin, A. A., & Parodi, A. (2021). Nanomedicine for treating diabetic retinopathy vascular degeneration. *International Journal of Translational Medicine*, 1(3), 306–322.

Cantó, A., Martínezet, J., Perini-Villanueva, G., Miranda, M., & Bejarano, E. (2021). Early neural changes as underlying pathophysiological mechanism in diabetic retinopathy." *International Journal of Translational Medicine*, 2(1), 1–16.

Cushley, L. N., Curran, K., Quinn, N. B., Bell, A., Muldrew, A., & Graham, U. M. et al. (2021). Diabetic retinopathy screening programme: attendance, barriers and enablers amongst young people with diabetes mellitus aged 12–26 years. *International Journal of Translational Medicine*, 1(3), 154–162.

Gardiner, T. A. & Stitt, A. W. (2022). Juxtavascular microglia scavenge dying pericytes and vascular smooth muscle cells in diabetic retinopathy. *International Journal of Translational Medicine*, 2(1), 41–50.

Kumari, A. & Kumar Henge, S. (2022). A hybrid model on deep learning for the diagnosis of diabetic retinopathy using image cropping. *Intelligent Sustainable Systems,* pp. 515–525. Springer, Singapore.

Kumari, A. & Kumar Henge, S. (2023). Comparative analysis of machine learning approaches of prediction of diabetes consequences in pregnancy with implications of data matrices. *Soft Computing for Security Applications*. pp. 613–626. Springer, Singapore.

Mohamed, E., Sharafeldeen, A., Soliman, A., Khalifa, F., Ghazal, M., El-Daydamony, E., et al. (2022). A novel computer-aided diagnostic system for early detection of diabetic retinopathy using 3D-OCT higher-order spatial appearance model. *Diagnostics*, 12(2), 461.

Prawej, A., Tabasumma, N., Snigdha, N. N., Siam, N. S. Panduru, R. V. N. R. S., Azam 4, S. et al. (2022). Diabetic retinopathy: An overview on mechanisms, pathophysiology and pharmacotherapy. *Diabetology*, 3(1), 159–175

Rafael, S., Sundstrom, J. M., & Antonetti, D. A. (2014). Ocular anti-VEGF therapy for diabetic retinopathy: the role of VEGF in the pathogenesis of diabetic retinopathy. *Diabetes care,* 37(4), 893–899.

Reddy, N. G., Venkatesh, R., Jayadev, C., Gadde, S. G. K., Agrawal, S., Mishra, P. et al. (2022). Diabetic retinopathy and diabetic macular edema in people with early-onset diabetes." *Clinical Diabetes,* 40(2), 222–232.

Saw, M., Wong, V. W., Ho, I.-V, & Liew, G. (2019). New anti-hyperglycaemic agents for type 2 diabetes and their effects on diabetic retinopathy. Eye 33(12), 1842–1851.

Santos, A. R., Ribeiro, L., Bandello, F., Lattanzio, R., Egan, C., Frydkjaer-Olsen, U. et al. (2017). Functional and structural findings of neurodegeneration in early stages of diabetic retinopathy: cross-sectional analyses of baseline data of the EUROCONDOR project. *Diabetes*, 66(9), 2503–2510.

Skouta, A., Elmoufidi, A., Jai-Andaloussi, S., & Ouchetto, O. (2022). Hemorrhage semantic segmentation in fundus images for the diagnosis of diabetic retinopathy by using a convolutional neural network. *Journal of Big Data*, 9(1), 1–24.

22 Smart contract-based access control in file sharing

Shallu Sharma[1,a], *Balraj Singh*[2,b], *and Ranbir Singh Batth*[2,c]

[1]School of Computer Application, Lovely Professional University, Punjab, India

[2]School of Computer Science and Engineering, Lovely Professional University, Punjab, India

Abstract

Smart contract is the core of blockchain networks. It eliminates the requirement for third-party services. They are the self-executing contracts that compose rules and terms of transactions that should be agreed upon by every participating node. Smart contracts are executed in a decentralized environment of blockchain. The conditions of an agreement are written in a code that is coded using various programming languages. With more advancement in technology, access control to data has become increasingly difficult. The users need to have access to their assets and resources to complete the job even if the location is remote. We proposed smart contract-based system architecture to implement contract policies to manage access control over the given data. This will help in maintaining data security and integrity and avoid unauthorized attacks.

Keywords: Access control, blockchain technology, distributed system, smart contract

Introduction

With more advancement in technology, access control to data has become increasingly difficult. The users need to have access to their assets and resources to complete the job even if the location is remote. Access control systems are required to protect the resources from unauthorized attacks. There are some access control models designed based on system policies, level of data sensitivity, and security requirements within the group.

Process of access control

To secure the network information, the following procedure is followed:

- To grant permission through user id and password to enter the network.
- To permit access to resources such as files, hardware, or software required by the user.
- To ensure that the user has the suitable level of permissions to complete his task. There are four access control models to grant permissions to the user as per his role and duties:
- **Mandatory access control (MAC):** In MAC model, the ownership privilege is specified by the resource owner. The requestor at the other end has no control over the data or the transaction.
- **Role-based access control (RBAC):** In this model, the access privileges are managed according to the positions an entity acquires in the organization. With this model, it is convenient to handle the security of the same information at different levels.
- **Discretionary access control (DAC):** This model is the least restricted compared to MAC. DAC allowed the requestor to control the privilege level for other users too. This gives the users more privilege than the owner.
- **Rule-based access control (RBAC or RB-RBAC):** The rule-based access control assigns the role dynamically to the users depending on the role conditions followed by the system manager. This model is programmed as a code in the system by the administrator.

Table 22.1 discusses all four access control models in brief.

Table 22.1 Comparison between different access models

Attributes	*MAC*	*RBAC*	*DAC*	*RB-RBAC*
Performance	Level dependency	Good	Low	Good
Controller	Low	Medium	High	Medium
organized	System	Role based	Owner	User attributes
Single point of failure	Low	Low	No authorization	Low
Restrictions	High	Medium	Low	Medium

[a]shallujoshii@gmail.com; [b]balraj.13075@lpu.co.in; [c]ranbirbatth@ieee.org

The remaining part of this paper is planned as follows. Section 2 reviews the available literature. Section 3 describes the smart contract for access control and proposed architecture. Section 4 concludes the work accomplished till now and upcoming work plans.

Literature Review

Various articles have been published on using blockchain technology for access control over confidential data and information. This literature review has focused on outlining the articles on blockchain implementation for access control in different domains.

Zeng et al. (2019) introduced an inner campus book-sharing system using blockchain. In their proposal, every user can trace the book of interest, and thus, the loss of the book is potentially reduced. Sharples and Domingue (2016) discussed the advancement of blockchain technology for education records, rewards, and reputation. It explains various sectors of education where blockchain can make remarkable updates as a distributed system. Naz et al. (2019) detailed the present data sharing platforms which use arbitrary services to transfer the resources. He explains how blockchain can eliminate the problem of single failure and distrust amongst the users. Shrestha and Vassileva (2018) shows the approach to using blockchain technology for research data collection, its accountability for access, verification of records, data ownership, and research data sharing. Rajalakshmi et al. (2018) proposed a framework using blockchain and IPFS to a secure and tamperproof design of academic record keeping using access control methods. Ouaddah et al. (2016) proposes an innovative framework for securing access in IoT based on blockchain technology and named it 'FairAccess'. Table 22.2 summarizes the literature review for use of blockchain in access control.

Smart Contract for Access Control

The smart contract is the core of the blockchain networks when seen from a more macro perspective. A blockchain, which inalterably records the histories of all transactions, and a world state, which stores the present value of these states, could both be accessed programmatically by the smart contract. Both performing actions on the stages that are recorded in the state DB and querying the records of transactions that are maintained in the blockchain are within the capabilities of the programmed smart contract. Programs running outside the blockchain works with the contract, to carry out actions on the blockchain network (Khan et al., 2021). The programmable contract could be put into a container and then uploaded to a blockchain. It is possible to specify many smart contracts inside the same package, and after that package has been deployed, all the smart contracts that it contains would become accessible to applications. Two smart contracts would be sent out into the blockchain. The policy contract establishes a particular rule list that is used to regulate access to resources. This is accomplished by linking a policy with the contract that determines whether the user is authorized to access or modify the resources that are managed by the blockchain network. These three organizations adhere to three separate sets of rules about permits. Accessibility control for administrative changes made to a network is referred to as network access control, while access control for resources housed inside a business network is referred to as business network access control. This difference is made by a policy contract (business access control). Figure 22.1 shows the smart contract for blockchain network interaction and access policies.

Table 22.2 Literature review for blockchain technology in access control

References	*Type*	*Year*	*Access Control*	*Platform*
Shrestha and Vassileva (2018)	Non permissioned	2018	×	Ethereum
Sharples and Domingue (2016)	Non permissioned	2016	✓	Ethereum
Naz et al. (2019)	Non permissioned	2019	×	Ethereum
Zhao and Nie (2018)	Permissioned	2018	×	Hyperledger
Zhang et al. (2018)	Non permissioned	2018	×	Ethereum
Ocheja et al. (2018)	Non permissioned	2018	✓	Ethereum
Daraghmi et al. (2019)	Non permissioned	2019	×	Ethereum
Zeng et al. (2019)	Permissioned	2019	✓	Not specified
Ranka et al. (2018)	Non permissioned	2018	×	Ethereum

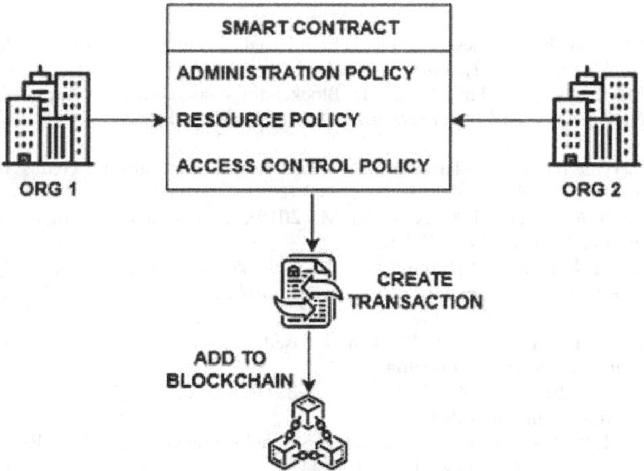

Figure 22.1 Smart contract for access control policy in blockchain network

Table 22.3 Pseudo code for access control in file sharing

```
Program start
Input UserID and AdminID for respective login
if (AdminID is valid)
{
User request for a resource;
Get Resource information;
Read registered user credentials;
if (UserID is valid)
{
Create Private and Public Key to encrypt the data;
Grant access to the requested data;
}
Else
Access denied to unauthorized attempt;
}
Else
Return:'Admin Not registered";
End program
```

Proposed system

In the proposed model, the user and admin are assigned their respective access privileges over the data. The admin has the right to limit the users' permissions to maintain the data security and avoid unauthorized access. If the user is verified, the requested data will be shared with him in encrypted form. this will ensure the integrity of data and avoid attacks and loss of data. The pseudo-code for smart contract-based access control is shown in Table 22.3.

Conclusion and Future Work

In this paper, we have discussed the various access control models along with their features. We proposed smart contract-based system architecture to implement contract policies to manage access control over the given data. This will help in maintaining data security and integrity and avoid unauthorized attacks. Upcoming, we will design a model using the proposed architecture and pseudo code and evaluate its performance with the given parameters.

References

Daraghmi, E. -Y., Daraghmi, Y. A., & Yuan, S. M. (2019). UniChain: A design of blockchain-based system for electronic academic records access and permissions management. *Applied Sciences*, 9 (22), 4966.

Khan, S. N., Loukil, F., Ghedira-Guegan, C., Benkhelifa, E., & Bani-Hani, A. (2021). Blockchain smart contracts: Applications, challenges, and future trends. *Peer-to-Peer Networking and Applications*. 14, 2901–2925. https://doi.org/10.1007/s12083-021-01127-0

Lee, D. & Song, M. (2021). MEXchange: A privacy-preserving blockchain- based framework for health information exchange using ring signature and stealth address. *IEEE Access*, 9, 158122–158139.

Naz, M., Al-zahrani, F. A., Khalid, R., Javaid, N., Qamar, A. M., Afzal, M. K., & Shafiq, M. (2019). A secure data sharing platform using blockchain and interplanetary file system. *Sustainability*, 11(24), p.7054.

Ocheja, P., Flanagan, B., & Ogata, H. (2018). Connecting decentralized learning records: a blockchain based learning analytics platform. In *Proceedings of the 8th International Conference on Learning Analytics and Knowledge (LAK '18)*, (pp. 265–269). https://doi.org/10.1145/3170358.3170365

Ouaddah, A., AbouElkalam, A., & Ait Ouahman, A. (2016). FairAccess: a new Blockchain-based access control framework for the Internet of Things. *Security and Communication Networks,* 9(18), 5943–5964.

Qi, X., Emmanuel, S., Abla, S., Sandro, A., & Xiaosong, Z. (2017). BBDS: Blockchain-based data sharing for electronic medical records in cloud environments. *Information*, 8, 44. 10.3390/info8020044.

Rajalakshmi, A., Lakshmy, K. V., Sindhu, M., & Amritha, P. P. (2018). A blockchain and IPFS based framework for secure Research record keeping. *International Journal of Pure and Applied Mathematics*, 119, 1437–1442

Ranka, Y., Bagrecha, J., Gandhi, K., Sarvaria, B., Chawan, P., & Student, U. G. (2018). A survey on file storage & retrieval using blockchain technology. *International Research Journal of Engineering and Technology*, 5(10), 763–766.

Sharma, S. & Batth, R. S. (2020). Blockchain technology for higher education sytem: A mirror review. *2020 International Conference on Intelligent Engineering and Management (ICIEM)* (pp. 348–353).

Sharma, S. & Batth, R. S. (2022). BLOCKLIB: Blockchain enabled library resource sharing. *Journal of Discrete Mathematical Sciences and Cryptography*, 25(3), 839–857.

Sharples, M. & Domingue, J. (2016). The blockchain and kudos: A distributed system for educational record, reputation and reward. *In European conference on technology enhanced learning* (pp. 490–496). Springer, Cham.

Shrestha, A. K. & Vassileva, J. (2018). Blockchain-Based Research Data Sharing Framework for Incentivizing the Data Owners. In S. Chen, H. Wang, L. J. Zhang (Eds). Lecture Notes in Computer Science, Springer, Cham.

Zeng, J., Dai, X., Xiao, J., Yang, W., Hao W., & Jin, H.. (2019). BookChain: Library- free book sharing based on blockchain technology. *15th International Conference on Mobile Ad-Hoc and Sensor Networks (MSN)*, (pp. 224–229), Shenzhen, China, doi: 10.1109/MSN48538.2019.00051.

Zhao, W. & Nie, L. (2018). Exploration of library technology application prospect under the concept of blockchain. *Library Science Research*, 21, 7–9.

Zhang, P., White, J., Schmidt, D. C., Lenz, G., & Rosenbloom, S. T. (2018). FHIRChain: applying blockchain to securely and scalably share clinical data. *Computational and Structural Biotechnology Journal*, 16, 267–278.

23 JSON Web Token Jumble Render Technique based authentication scheme for android applications

Er. Sarvesh Chopra[1,a], *Amritpal Singh*[1,b], *and Aman Singh*[2,c]

[1]Department of Computer Science, Lovely Professional University, Punjab, India

[2]Faculty of Engineering, Universidade, Cuito-Bie, Angola

Abstract

Information and Communication Technology (ICT) combines a variety of hardware and software that is directly linked to Internet connections. In the current technological era, the development of customer server systems, such as Internet of Things (IoT)-based, cloud-based, and smart home systems, are accelerating. For many apps, user authentication is a major concern and due to increase in client server queries, server load has increased (Kumar P et al., 2016). To counter this problem, we propose JSON Web Token Jumble Render Technique (JWTJRT) for JSON Web Token (JWT) based authentication. Here, login can be done without making repeated visits to a secured resource server or database. JWT are utilized to authenticate subsequent consumer requests. Case examples show that the complexity of time and space improve the effectiveness of the suggested strategy.

Keywords: JSON Web Token Jumble Render Technique, client-side authentication, JSON Web Token, O-auth network-security

Introduction

Security and privacy of user data is a prime concern in today's digital world. User authentication, access to services and access to services and time taken with repeat to Internet of Things (IoT) application, mobile application and web or closed application. While communicating with clients, servers maintain customer identity during customer-server interaction (Kumar P et al., 2016). If vital security checks are not performed to protect client identity, it can lead to serious misuse of personal data. Real data access becomes complicated when the same user accesses a resource server from different devices such as mobile phones, tabs, personal computers etc. using a different operating system such as IOS, Android, Windows, Linux, etc. (Janardanan et al., 2018).

Header Payload Signature

This is how a JSON Web Token (JWT) actually looks like:

eyJhbGciOiJIUzI1NiIsInR5cCI6IkpXVCJ9.eyJuYW1lIjoiSm9obiBEb2UiLCJ1c2VX25hbWUiOiJq b2huLmRvZSIsImlzX2FkbWluIjpmYWxzZX0.kSttjHFaqlNtyuyQ8VufrD84YIuhqFfD67XkEam0_aY

1. Metadata info such as algorithm used for signature and type of JWT are contained in the header:
   {
   e. g. "algo": "HS384", "type": "JWT
2. Information about the uses that is verified by the application is contained in the Payload. A sample token is given as follows:
   {
   "id": "Sarvesh"
   "u_name": "Sarvesh_ch"
   "is_admin": false
   }
3. *At last, we have signatures, it is a base 64 url encoding which uses a secret key depending on what algorithm we are using (Kumar P et al., 2016). For example: we can use SHA-512 so its encryption and encoding process may be as follows:*
   HMACSHA512(base64URLEncode(header)+"."+base64UrlEncode(Payload+data), secret)
   This signature is appended to the base64url encoded header which looks like:
   kSttjHFaqlNtyuyQ8VufrD84YIuhqFfD67XkEam0_aY

[a]er.sarveshchopra@gmail.com; [b]amritpal.17673@lpu.co.in; [c]amansingh.x@gmail.com

Until a user logs out of the system, a server typically uses the same JWT for all requests. A universally applicable solution must be put up for all applications. To eliminate client authentication risk completely, the generalized solution should protect JWT (Ethelbert O et al., 2017). Therefore, we are suggesting the following:

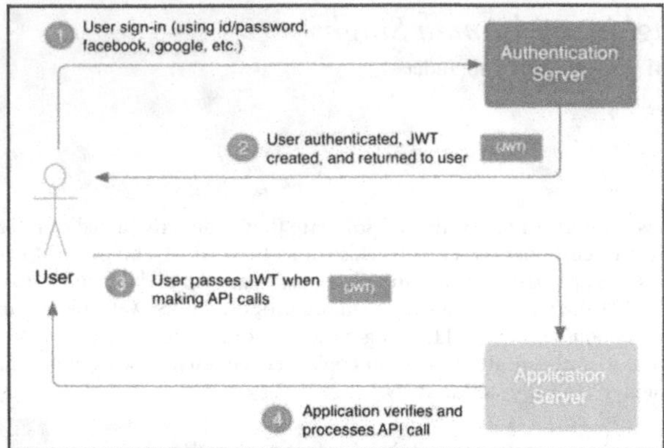

Figure 23.1 How JWT technique works

Table 23.1 JWT authentication techniques

HS-256	HMAC with SHA-256
HS-384	HMAC with SHA-384
HS-512	HMAC with SHA-512
RS-256	RSASSA-PKCS1-v1_5 with SHA-256
RS-384	RSASSA-PKCS1-v1_5 with SHA-384
RS-512	RSASSA-PKCS1-v1_5 with SHA-512
ES-256	ECDSA with P-256 and SHA-256
ES-384	ECDSA with P-384 and SHA-384
ES-512	ECDSA with P-521 and SHA-512
PS-256	RSASSA-PSS with SHA-256 and MGF1 with SHA-256
PS-384	RSASSA-PSS with SHA-384 and MGF1 with SHA-384
PS-512	RSASSA-PSS with SHA-512 and MGF1 with SHA-512

Problem statement

The two major problem statements are as follows:

i. *After the token has been allocated to the client, any change in the user role results in a considerable value loss. It is hack able to take advantage of the permissions the user was provided on the initial attempt. A server resource must be safe and inaccessible to users without authorization or users whose permissions have been revoked.*
ii. *In the majority of get/post/put request and response situations involving client and server interaction, the access token or the JWT remains the same. Attacker can foresee this weakness and can modify the JWT (Kumar P et al., 2016) (Janardanan et al., 2018).*

The number of concurrent clients is the only other aspect that can affect the system because client session lengths are provided. We can divide the population into various groups, each of which employs a different JWT secret, to reduce this number. As a result, only clients belonging to the same group would be impacted by the revocations (Kumar P et al., 2016)

A group identification data component that is accessible to all services could be used to implement this segmentation. This enables the service to obtain the correct JWT secret for the token's decoding. Initial group allocations can be made at random, with the use of a hash function, or with the aid of a personalized algorithm depending on client behavior.

Garbage collection is one area where a unique algorithm could find inspiration. In order to make gathering easier, 10 things, for instance, are categorized into 'generations' based on their current or anticipated lifetime. By assigning clients who log out more frequently to the same group, the same might be done for clients. This allows one to skip the real secret update in the event of numerous revocation occurrences (Jones M et al., 2015).

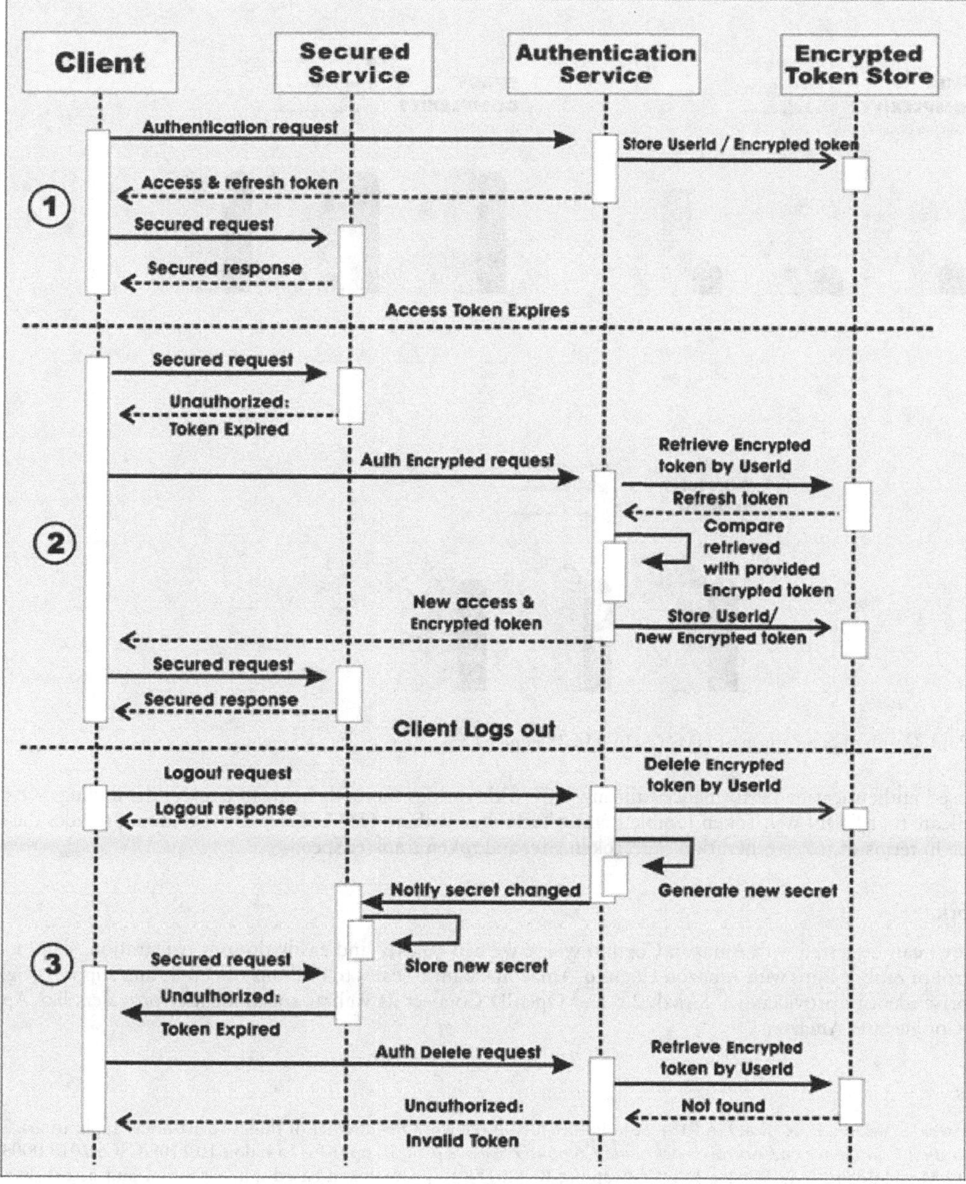

Figure 23.2 Basic working of the proposed solution based on JSON Web Token Jumble Render Technique [Kumar P et al., 2016]

Conclusion

We have improved the JSON Web Token (JWT) access control solutions for various platform-based applications, including mobile apps and cloud systems. Every time a client makes a request, the server creates a new token so that any attempt by an attacker to read the client's signature can be denied. We have put in place a method that application developers can utilize to protect server resources from revoked access rights and unauthenticated requests. The comparison

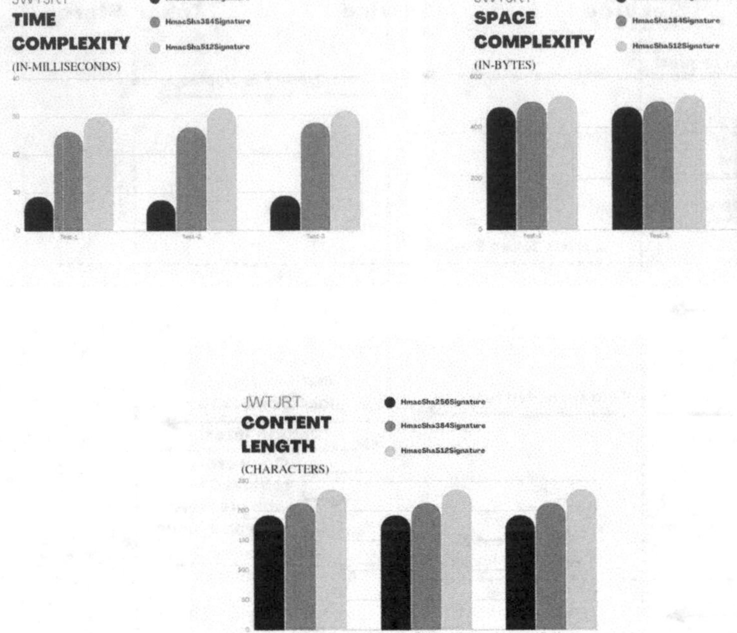

Figure 23.3 Graph of comparison of HMACSHA-256,384 and 512

of token-based authentication performance utilizing JWT with various methods helps to explain the findings. Overall findings indicate that JSON Web Token Jumble Render Technique with an HMACSHA-256 signature provides the best performance in terms of token generation time, token size, and token transfer speed.

Future Work

Our technique can be tested with Amazon Cognito where we can quickly and easily do user registration, sign-in, and access control of mobile apps with Amazon Cognito. Amazon Cognito scales to millions of people and supports sign-in with enterprise identity providers via SAML 2.0 and OpenID Connect as well as social identity providers like Apple, Facebook, Google, and Amazon.

References

Chifor, B., Arseni, S., Matei, I., & Bica, I. (2019). Security-oriented framework for internet of things smart-home applications. *22nd International Conference on Control Systems and Computer Science (CSCS)*, pp. 146–153. doi: 10.1109/CSCS.2019.00033.

Ethelbert, O., Moghaddam, F. F., Wieder, P. & Yahyapour, R. (2017). A JSON token-based authentication and access management schema for cloud SaaS applications. *2017 IEEE 5th International Conference on Future Internet of Things and Cloud (FiCloud), Prague*. (pp. 47–53). doi: 10.1109/FiCloud.

Gomez, C. & Paradells, J. (2010). Wireless home automation networks: A survey of architectures and technologies. *IEEE Communications Magazine*, 48(6), 92–101.

Gutzmann, K. (2001). Access control and session management in the HTTP environment. *In IEEE Internet Computing*, 5(1), 26–35. doi: 10.1109/4236.895139.

Hong, N., Kim, M., Jun, M., & Kang, J. (2017). A study on a JWT-based user authentication and API assessment scheme using IMEI in a smart home environment. *Journal of Sustainability*, 9(7).

Janardanan, Ajil Paul C, Anju P, Eldiva Thomas V and Davis D, "Android Application for Car Wash Services," 2018 International Conference on Emerging Trends and Innovations In Engineering And Technological Research (ICETIETR), Ernakulam, 2018, pp. 1-3. doi: 10.1109/ICETIETR.2018.8529025.

Jones M, Bradley J, and Sakimura N, "JSON Web Token (JWT) RFC 7519", http://www.rfc-edi tor.org/rfc/rfc7519.txt, RFC Editor 2015.

Kim J. E., Boulos, G., Yackovich, J., Barth, T., Beckel, C., & Mosse, D. (2012). Seamless integration of heterogeneous devices and access control in smart homes. In Proceeding *8th International Conference on Intelligent Environments*, (pp. 206–213.

Kumar P, Gurtov A, Iinatti J, Ylianttila M., & Sain, M. (2016). Lightweight and secure session-key establishment scheme in smart home environments. *IEEE Sensors Journal*, 16(1), 254–264, doi: 10.1109/JSEN.2015.2475298.

Liu, Z. & Gupta, B. (2019). Study of secured full-stack web development. *Proceedings of 34th International Conference on Computers and Their Applications*, 58, 317–324. doi: 10.29007/jpj6.

Mantas, G., Lymberopoulos, D., & Komninos, N (2006). Security in smart home environment. In A. Lazakidou, K. Siassiakos, & k. Ioannou. *Wireless Technologies for Ambient Assisted Living and Healthcare: Systems and Applications*. Hershey, PA, USA.

Viktor Jánoky, L., Levendovszky, J., & Ekler, P. (2018). An analysis on the revoking mechanisms for JSON Web Tokens. *International Journal of Distributed Sensor Networks*, 14. doi: https://doi.org/10.1177/1550147718801535.

Yuan, X., Borkor, E., Beal, S., & Yu, H. (2014). Retrieving relevant CAPEC attack patterns for secure software development. *In Proceedings of the 9th Annual Cyber and Information Security Research Conference (CISR '14)*. pp. 33–36. https://doi.org/10.1145/2602087.2602092.

24 A review on deep learning techniques for detecting COVID-19 from X-rays and CT scans

Nisar Ahmad Kangoo[1,a] and Apash Roy[2]

[1]Research Scholar at Lovely Professional University, Punjab, India

[2]Associate Professor at Lovely Professional University, Punjab, India

Abstract

The corona virus (COVID-19) outbreak has created havoc in the entire world with its high prevalence. Although the mortality rate of this disease is low, the percentage of the population affected by this disease is a concern for scientists, doctors, and others. So, for the most broadly used procedure for COVID-19 is real-time reverse transcription-polymerase chain reaction (RT-PCR). In this paper, the different profound gaining methods for recognizing COVID-19 from X-beams and computer tomography (CT) filters have been dissected and this gives bits of knowledge on notable informational indexes used to prepare these organizations. Additionally, it illustrates the many performance measurements and data collection strategies created by researchers in this area. It finishes by discussing the difficulties associated with using deep learning techniques for COVID-19 recognition and potential upcoming trends in this field of study. This paper aims to assist professionals (whether medical or non-medical) in comprehending how deep learning approaches are applied in this viewpoint and how these might be applied further to fight the COVID-19 epidemic.

Keywords: Deep learning, X-ray, computer tomography scan, COVID-19

Introduction

Originally started in China at Wuhan city in December 2019, severe acute respiratory syndrome corona virus 2 (SARS-CoV-2) also called COVID-19 spread to the whole world with its high spread speed. Although the mortality rate of this virus is low as compared to other deadly viruses found worldwide. While writing this review paper the population infected by this virus globally is 638,070,984 and the total number of deaths caused is 6,595,100 (Worldmeters). The extensive spread of COVID-19 leads to quarantine of a significant section of the whole population of the world, destroyed a number of industrial sectors, and sparked a global financial crisis. In Geneva, Professor of International Economics Richard Baldwin at the Graduate Institute stated, 'This virus is as economically contagious as it is medically contagious' (Pandemic, 2020). On February 11, 2020, the World Health Organization (WHO) coined the term COVID-19 for this viral disease' (Holshue et al., 2019). COVID-19 was stated as an epidemic by the World Health Organization (WHO) on April 18, 2020.

COVID-19 being an extremely communicable (Wang et al., 2020; Jiang et al., 2020), it is essential to swiftly and precisely spot viruses to halt the disease's transmission and give appropriate treatment. CT scanning and the finding of nucleic acid reagents are common COVID-19 detection methods. Examining recent developments in COVID-19 detecting systems based on deep learning (DL) and information acquired from medical imaging samples is the main objective of the study. Patients frequently show symptoms of infection such as fever, shortness of breath, cough, sputum, and tightness in the chest, tiredness, and wooziness. Patients with chronic pneumonia may face complexity in breathing and/or hypoxemia once exhibiting symptoms for a week. Rapid illness progression can lead to the development of coagulopathy, metabolic acidosis, septic shock, and acute respiratory distress syndrome (Huang et al., 2019).

The most recent advancements in deep learning-based COVID-19 detecting systems from X-ray and CT scan medical imaging specimens are outlined in this review paper.

Deep learning

To transform inputs into features that may be used to predict matching outputs, a subfield of machine learning called DL [7] stresses the use of numerous connected layers. At each layer in the network, a set of parameters are fine tuned. Given an adequately enough database of input-output pairs, a training algorithm may be trained by mapping inputs to outputs without human assistance (Rumelhart et al., 1986). Due to their flexible architectural design, DL models may be modified to handle any type of data. Back-propagation training of DL models on examples typically results in well-organized inner presentation of the material being used for a task (LeCun et al., 1998). This preprogrammed feature learning

[a]nisarphd2020@gmail.com

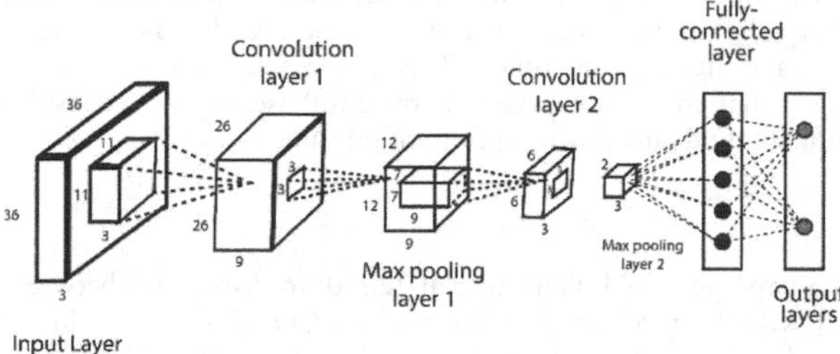

Figure 24.1 Convolutional neural network structure diagram

eliminates most of the human feature engineering, a difficult and possibly error-prone procedure requiring specialised domain expertise. The most effective DL applications to date have been in sectors where incredibly large numbers of examples are accessible (Kumar and Roy, 2021). DL models, however, simply have an enormous number of domestic parameters and hence are data hungry.

Convolutional neural networks

Convolutional neural networks (CNN), architecture, was developed to process input that is frequently spatially dependent (like the pixels in a digital image). A CNN layer exploits this promptness by applying the identical set of neighboring convolutional filters from corner-to-corner different places in the data. This has two virtues: it is transformation invariant and avoids the over-fitting problem by requiring only a few weight adjustments related to the dimensionality of input layer and following layer. To give the nodes in subsequent layers greater receptive fields and the ability to learn more complicated features, a CNN module often comprises numerous consecutive CNN layers.

Transfer learning

A ML technique called transfer learning (Jain et al., 2020) makes use of prior knowledge to address issues in various but related disciplines. Every human endeavor makes considerable use of transfer learning. Transfer learning is made easier by the number of factors that are shared by two disparate domains. Otherwise, it could be harder or perhaps have a faulty transfer that has an adverse effect. By transferring a range of source domain-related knowledge to the target domain, this method intends to resolve the learning issue of inadequate sample trainings of target domain.

Residual neural network

A pooling layer for attribute processing and a convolutional layer for attribute extraction make up the residual neural network (ResNet). Multiple-layer neural networks can address issues like gradient fading and deprivation. The CNN's gradient steadily vanishes as the network gets deeper, making it impossible to update the network's surface parameters. The way shortcut relations are structured ensures that the back propagation parameters are revised, preventing the challenge of gradient disappearance brought on by back propagation. The ResNet facilitates deep model optimization.

Image Databases

Cohen JP [25], Kaggle's Chest X-ray images [26], GitHub Repository [27-28], The Cancer Imaging Archive (TCIA) [29-30], Italian Society of Radiology (SIRM), and Japanese Society of Radiological Technology (JSRT) are a few of the image databases used by various DL techniques for the revealing COVID-19. Websites like Figure 24.1.com and Radiopedia.org [31, 34] have also been utilized as image database resources.

Methodology and Model Specifications

Transfer learning with convolutional neural network

A CNN that has previously been trained on a dataset of brand-new images for the model and has saved weights is overloaded and retrained in the transfer learning advance (Kumar and Roy, 2021). The benefit of implementing transfer learning to guide the CNN is that the original layers of the network, which would other-wise be exceedingly challenging to guide because of disappearing gradient issue, have already been learned. The network already has a strong understanding of basic features like detecting shape and image edges, among others. The pre-trained model gets benefit from this awareness of the essential properties of the images that are already present in the database. As just the last layers of the network want to be taught, this network training method cuts down on computing time.

Augmentation and generation techniques

An effective multi-class DL method is described in a paper reported (Panwar et al., 2020) to distinguish between pneumonia and COVID-19 from normal chest X-rays (CXR). They collected 295 pictures of COVID-19 in all. In addition, they gathered 98 cases for pneumonia screening and 65 examples of typical cases. To get over the limitations of the COVID-19 dataset, they employed a fuzzy color approach as a pre-processing pace to reorganize the dataset's data classes, and the images that were produced in tandem with the novel ones were layered. They found that COVID-19 picture classification had a high proportion of success and that the categorization of normal and pneumonia images had a 99.27% success rate. In less than 5 s, the model correctly predicted a COVID-19 patient with only a 2.03% mistake, and it had a 97.62% accuracy rate for COVID-19 positive patients.

DarkCovidNet model

Building a model using existing models is a more balanced advance than preparing from scratch with deep model development. As a result, the Darknet-19 model (Panwar et al., 2020) is selected as the initial spot when creating the deep model employed in this work. The classifier model known as Darknet-19 serves as the foundation of the YOLO (You Only Look Once) real-time entity recognition system (Agarap, 2018). This system's design is cutting-edge in terms of object recognition. The DarkNet classifier serves as the foundation of this effective design. The DarkCovidNet design (available at https://github.com/muhammedtalo/COVID-19) was motivated by the DarkNet idea, which itself has established in DL [Roy, 2019; Haque and Abdelgawad, 2020), rather than creating a model from scratch.

Combined CNN-long short-term memory network

Utilizing three different kinds of X-ray pictures, a combination technique was created to automatically identify COVID-19 instances (Roy and Manna, 2015). The method used to create this design was joining CNN and LSTM networks, with CNN being utilized to remove complicated properties from images and LSTM being utilized as a classifier. The network consists of 20 layers in total: twelve convolutional layers, five pooling layers, 1FC layer, 1 LSTM layer, and one output layer along softmax function. Each one of the convolution blocks are connected by one pooling layer, 2 or 3 2D CNNs, and a dropout layer with 25% dropout rate. For feature extraction, the 3 X 3 kernel size convolutional layer is activated by the ReLU function. By employing max-pooling layer, which has a size of 2 X 2 kernels, the size of an input image is reduced. In order to demand time data, function map is relocated to LSTM layer in the final design step. The output form is discovered to be following the convolutional block to be (none, 7, 7, and 512).

Lightweight deep learning models

Karakanis and Leontidis, 2021 have suggested a deep CNN model for the binary categorization instance for the recognition of COVID-19. The model was created to perform effectively while being compact and devoid of transfer learning. It can make accommodations for any irregularities in the distribution of the data and the classes' constrained access to training images. A Max Pooling layer, ReLU [18] activation function, and input representation down sampling are added after one and only one convolutional layer with a filter size of 32 and kernel size of 4 X 4 has been applied. Features can be extracted thanks to this. Following a flatten layer, a dropout layer, and an ending dense layer using softmax activation software, a binary output is created using a dense layer of magnitude 128.

Details relation extraction neural network on CT scans

A DL-based CT analysis method was created by Song Y. et al. (2021) to identify the pneumonia-causing COVID-19 strain and to focus on the primary lesions. As shown in Figure 24.3, three important procedures were used to build the completely automated lung CT diagnosis technique. To evade noises brought on by various lung shapes, the main portion of the lung was first excised and crammed with the blank of lung segmentation. A DRENet was used to derive the image-level conjectures after that. The image-level conjectures were used to create the individual-level diagnoses.

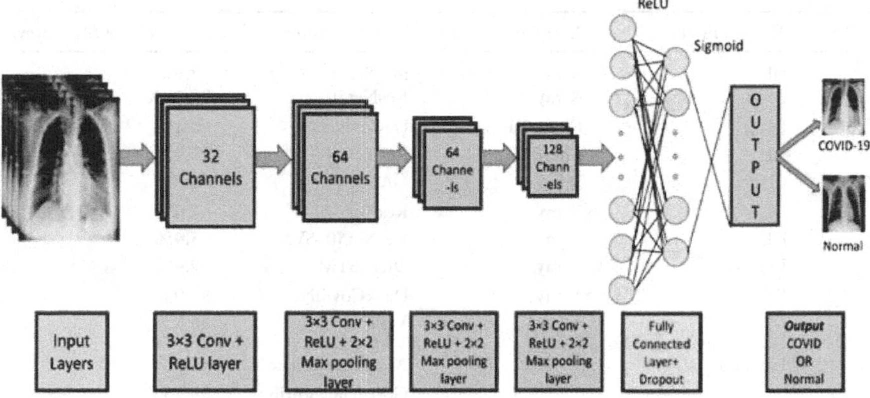

Figure 24.2 A sketch of the planned hybrid network for COVID-19 recognition

Source: Haque, K. F., & Abdelgawad, A. (2020). A deep learning approach to detect COVID-19 patients from chest X-ray images. AI, 1(3), 27.

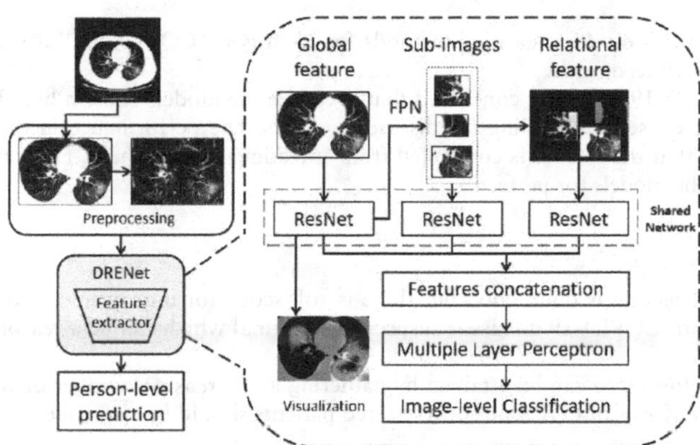

Figure 24.3 The planned training design including (1) Pre-processing: (2) Image-level classifications (3) Individual-level prediction (Roy and Manna, 2012)

Source: Song, Ying, et al. "Deep learning enables accurate diagnosis of novel coronavirus (COVID-19) with CT images." IEEE/ACM transactions on computational biology and bioinformatics 18.6 (2021): 2775–2780.

Evaluation Index

The metrics utilized to evaluate the model performances are accuracy, specificity, sensitivity, F-score, and Matthews' correlation coefficient.

Accuracy is the main well-known evaluation index. More the accuracy, the model performs better. The approach is as under:

Accuracy = [TP + TN] / [TP + TN + FP + FN]   Sensitivity = TP / [TP + FN]

Recall = TP/[TP+FN]   F-score = [2 × TP] / [2 × TP + FP + FN]

The number of specimens that were accurately identified to be positive and were positive is referred true positive (TP). The amount of specimens that were accurately identified as negative and turned out to be negatives is true negatives (TN). Additionally, false positive (FP) denotes the amount of specimens that were actually negative but were mis predicted and false negative (FN) denotes the amount of specimens that were really positive but were mis predicted.

Table 24.1 Performance in detecting COVID-19 by DL techniques

Reference	*Method used*	*X-ray or CT scan*	*Training model*	*Performance (Accuracy)*
Panwar et al. (2020)	DL	X-ray	nCOVnet	97.97 %
Bukhari et al.(2020)	DL	X-ray	ResNet50	98.18%
Wang et al. (2020)	DL	Chest CT	DeCovNet	90.1%
Ahuja et al.(2020)	DL	Chest CT	ResNet18	99.4%
Karakanis et al. (2020)	CNN	X-ray	GAN	98.7%
Albahli (2020)	DL	X-ray	ResNet	87.0%
Sethy (2020)]	DL	X-ray	ResNet50+SVM	95.4%
Islam, MZ. Et al. (2020)	LSTM	X-ray	DL+LSTM	99.4%
Ozturk et al. (2020)	DL	X-ray	DarkCovidNet	87.0%
Civit-Masot (2020)	DL	X-ray	VGG16	86.0%
Apostolopoulos et al. (2020)	Deep transfer earning	X-ray	VGG19	97.8%
Zhou et al. (2020)	Ensemble DL	CT scan	Alexnet-softmax	98.16%
			Googlenet-softmax	98.25%
			ResNet-softmax	98.56%

Conclusion

Following is a survey of numerous research articles on deep learning methods for identifying COVID-19. Table 24.1 summarizes the effectiveness and precision of various models.

Keeping in view the high prevalence of COVID-19, it can be concluded that even if some models show a high level of accuracy but still little dropouts can be the cause of spreading the disease to others. The performance in case of COVID-19 detection must be 100% to ensure that the disease is controlled from spreading to the others. This can be achieved by getting huge data and fine tuning the models for perfection.

Future Aspects

The overall performance of deep learning in detecting is quite good but there is still scope for improvement so that 100% accuracy is achieved hence no patient with COVID-19 disease is suspected as normal which can be a reason for the spread of this disease.

In order to properly train the model, the performance can be attained by gathering an increasing number of X-ray and CT scan images of infected individuals. The X-ray and CT scans of recovered patients should be also collected and used in the models for improving performance.

Future deep learning models may be expanded to recognize other viruses, such as H1N1, SARS, MERS, and severe acute respiratory syndromes (SARS), Acquired Immunodeficiency Syndrome (AIDS), and Middle East Respiratory Syndrome (MERS).

References

Agarap, A. F. M. (2018). Deep learning using rectified linear units (Relu). arXiv preprintarXiv:1803.08375.

Ahuja, S., Panigrahi, B. K., Dey, N., Rajinikanth, V. & Gandhi, T. K. (2021). Deep transfer learning-based automated detection of COVID-19 from lung CT scan slices. Applied Intelligence, 51(1), 571–585.

Albahli, S. (2021). A deep neural network to distinguish COVID-19 from other chest diseases usingx-ray images. Current Medical Imaging, 17(1), 109–119.

Apash Roy, N. R. Manna, "Handwritten Character Recognition Using Block wise Segmentation Technique (BST) in Neural Network", Proceedings of First International Conference on Intelligent Infrastructure, held during 1-2 December, 2012 at Science City, Kolkata.

Apash Roy, N. R. Manna, "Handwritten Character Recognition with Feedback Neural Network", "International Journal of Computer Science & Engineering Technology (IJCSET 2229–3345)", Vol. 5, Issue1, 2014. Keja Publication

Apash Roy, N. R. Manna, "Recognition of Handwritten Text: Artificial Neural Network Approach"- International Journal of Advanced and Innovative Research (2278–7844), Volume 2, Issue 9, 2013. Publisher Spring S Technologies

Apostolopoulos, I. D. & Mpesiana, T. A. (2020). Covid-19: automaticdetectionfromx-rayimages utilizing transfer learning with convolutional neural networks. Physical and Engineering Sciences in Medicine, 43(2), 635-640.

Bukhari, S. U. K., Bukhari, S. S. K., Syed, A., & Shah, S. S. H. (2020). The diagnostic evaluation of convolutional neural network (CNN) for the assessment of chest X-ray of patients infected with COVID-19. medRxiv.

Civit-Masot, J., Luna-Perejón, F., Domínguez Morales, M., & Civit, A. (2020). Deep learning system for COVID-19 diagnosis aidusing X-ray pulmonary images. *Applied Sciences*, 10(13), 4640.

Cohen, J. P. & Morrison, P. (2020). *COVID-19 image data collection*. https://github.com/ieee8023/covid-chestxray-dataset2020.

Goodfellow, I., Bengio, Y., Courville, A., & Bengio, Y. (2016). Deep learning. MIT Press, Cambridge.

Haque, K. F., & Abdelgawad, A. (2020). A deep learning approach to detect COVID-19 patients from chest X-ray images. *AI*, 1(3), 27.

Holshue, M. L., DeBolt, C., Lindquist, S. (2019). First case of 2019 novel coronavirus in the United States. New England Journal of Medicine, 382(10), 929–936.

Huang, C. L., Wang, Y. M., Li, X. W., Ren, L. L., Zhao, P. et al. (2019). Clinical features of patients infected with 2019 novel corona virus in Wuhan, China. *Lancet*, 395(10223), 497–506.

Islam, M. Z., Islam, M. M., & Asraf, A. (2020). A combined deep CNN-LSTM network for the detection of novel coronavirus (COVID-19) using X-ray images. *Informatics in Medicine Unlocked*, 20, 100412.

Islam, M. Z., Islam, M. M., & Asraf, A. (2020). A combined deep CNN-LSTM network for the detection of novel corona virus (COVID-19) usingX-ray images. *Informatics in Medicine Unlocked*, 20.

Jain, G., Mittal, D., Thakur, D., & Mittal, M. K. (2020). A deep learning approach to detect Covid-19 coronavirus with X-Ray images. *Biocybernetics and Biomedical Engineering*, 40(4), 1391–1405.

Jiang, X., Coffee, M., Bari, A., Wang, J., Jiang, X., Huang, J. et al. (2020). Towards an artificial intelligence frame work for data-driven prediction of coronavirus clinical severity. *Computers, Materials & Continua*, 63(1), 537–551.

Karakanis, S. & Leontidis, G. (2021). Light weight deep learning models for detecting COVID-19 from chest X-ray images. *Computers in Biology and Medicine*, 130, 104181.

Kumar, J. & Roy, A. (2021). DograNet- A comprehensive offline Dogra handwriting character dataset. International Conference on Robotics and Artificial Intelligence.

LeCun, Y., Bottou, L., Bengio, Y., & Haffner, P. (1998). Gradient-based learning applied to document recognition. Proceedings of the IEEE, 86(11), 2278–2324.

Mooney P. Chest x-ray images (pneumonia); Online, https://www.kaggle.com/paultimothymooney/chest-xray-pneumonia, tanggal akses2018.

Ozturk, T., Talo M., Yildirim, E. A., Baloglu, U. B., Yildirim, O., & Acharya, U. R.(2020). Automated detection of COVID-19 cases using deep neural networks with X-ray images. *Computers in Biology and Medicine*, 121, 103792.

Pandemic, A. E. (2020). Coronavirus disease (covid-2019). https://foreignpolicy.com/2020/03/09/coronavirus-economic-pandemic-impact-recession/Lastac-cessedonMar2020

Panwar, H., Gupta, P. K., Siddiqui, M. K., Morales-Menendez, R., & Singh, V. (2020). Application of deep learning for fast detection of COVID-19 in X-Rays using COVnet. *Chaos, Solitons & Fractals*, 138, 109944.

Panwar, H., Gupta, P. K., Siddiqui, M. K., Morales-Menendez, R., & Singh, V.(2020). Application of deep learning for fast detection of COVID-19 in X-Rays using nCOVnet. *Chaos, Solitons & Fractals*, 138, 109944.

Roy, A. & Ghosh, D. (2021). Pattern recognition based tasks and achievements on handwritten bengali character recognition. *2021 6th International Conference on Inventive Computation Technologies*, pp. 1260–1265. doi: 10.1109/ICICT50816.2021.9358783.

Roy, A. & Manna, N. R. (2012). Character recognition with multi scale training. https:// https://www.jstage.jst.go.jp/browse/jjrt

Roy, A. & Manna, N. R. (2012). Competitive neural network as applied for character recognition. *International Journal of advanced research in Computer science and Software Engineering*, 2(3).

Roy, A. & Manna, N. R. (2012). Handwritten character recognition using mask vector in competitive neural network with multi-scale training. International Journal of Advanced and Innovative Research, 1(2).

Roy, A. & Manna, N. R. (2012). Handwritten character recognition using mask vector input (MVI) in neural network. International Journal of Advances in Science and Technology, 4(4).

Roy, A. & Manna, N. R. (2015). An approach towards segmentation of real time handwritten text. International Journal of Advanced and Innovative Research, 4(5).

Roy, A. (2019). Handwritten Bengali character recognition- A study of works during current decade. Advances and Applications in Mathematical Sciences, 18(9), 867–875.

Rumelhart, D. E., Hinton, G. E., & Williams, R. J. (1986). Learning representations by back-propagating errors. Nature, 323(6088), 533–536.

Sethy, P. K., Behera, S. K., Ratha, P. K., & Biswas, P. (2020). Detection of coronavirus disease (COVID-19) based on deep features and support vector machine. *Preprints*.

Song, Ying, et al. "Deep learning enables accurate diagnosis of novel coronavirus (COVID-19) with CT images." IEEE/ACM transactions on computational biology and bioinformatics 18.6 (2021): 2775 2780.

Togaçar, M., Ergen, B., Comert, Z. (2020). Covid-19 detection using deep learning models to exploit so cialmimic optimization and structured chest x-ray images using fuzzy color and stacking approaches. *Computation Biol.* Med.

Transfer Learning Model Using Chest X-Ray Dataset, 2020arXivpreprintarXiv:2004.01184.

Wang, D. W., Hu, B., Hu, C., Zhu, F. F., Liu, X. et al. (2020). Clinical characteristics of 138 hospitalized patients with 2019 novel coronavirus–infected pneumonia in Wuhan, China. *Journal of the American Veterinary Medical Association*, 323(11), 1061–1069. http://dx.doi.org/10.1001/jama.2020.1585.

Wang X, Deng X, Fu Q, Zhou Q, Feng J, Ma H, et al. (2020). A weakly- supervised framework for COVID-19 classification and lesion localization from chest CT. *IEEE Trans Med Imaging*, 39(8), 2615

Welcome to the cancer imaging archive – the cancer imaging archive (TCIA). https://www.cancerimagingarchive.net/. [Accessed19 June 2020].

Worldmeters. Accessed September. 10, 2022. https://www.worldometers.info/coronavirus/

Zhou, T., Lu, H., Yang, Z., Qiu, S., Huo, B., & Dong, Y. (2021). The ensemble deep learning model for novel COVID-19 on CT images. *Applied Soft Computing*, 98, 106885.

25 Gamification applications: A new perspective

Balraj Kumar[a] *and Cephas Iko-Ojo Gabriel*[b]

School of Computer Application, Lovely Professional University, Punjab, India

Abstract

Gamification is the buzzword and gaining acceptance day by day all around the globe. The sway of gamification can be observed using gaming rules to enhance the learners' interest in problem-solving. Gamification is continuously fascinating the researchers' fraternity with its amazing results and that is the reason why there is an exploration of its potential in diverse areas. Technology-driven gamified systems such as augmented reality, virtual reality, and IoT-based systems provide a more immersive learning experience and lead to a great need in the market. In education field, the use of gamified learning kits is a favorable method that not only strengthens knowledge but also develops essential skills such as problem-solving, teamwork, and healthy competition. Moreover, gamification helps financial institutions to motivate employees, provide outstanding customer service, meet goals or targets and sell services, track performance, and adopt digital transformation. This article aims to present a review study on the increasing use of gamification in various fields such as technology, education, business, and banking, and also analyses its impact in these areas.

Keywords: Gamification, game elements, gamified approach, learners' engagement, gamification application areas

Introduction

Gamification has attained wide popularity and attention in recent years. The authors (Deterding et al., 2011) have defined gamification as 'the use of game design elements in non-game contexts'. Gamification can lead to various developments, such as technological, educational, economic, and societal. It may provide several benefits like playfulness, engagement, creativity, happiness, motivation, and overall growth.

There are two terms, game-based learning, and gamification, that are extensively used in literature. The difference between game-based learning and gamification lies in the way game components are incorporated into the learning process. Both standings syndicate gaming and learning but differ in how gaming is integrated into learning. For games, the goal is to use the game to achieve a skill or learn a goal. A few examples are bingo and puzzle games integrated into lessons (Wright, 2018). Gamification is the application of structured gamified attributes to inspire and encourage learners to attain desired learning objectives. Examples include leaderboards, badges, trophies, rating systems, and "unlocking" more content after defeating prior content.

The entire course is based on the concept of a game, but not the game itself. It aims to develop skills using techniques. Our lives are gamified and learning is becoming more and more fashionable (Saleem et al., 2021). But as there is a constant change in the world, in what way will gamification develop to meet the unstable desires of today's modern users? Has gamification attained its peak? In what way can one apply these patterns to plan or develop better-gamified

Figure 25.1 Gamification in everything

[a]balraj_kr@yahoo.co.in; [b]cephas.iko.ojo@gmail.com, cephas.12110883@lpu.in

programmes? In this article, as shown in Figure 25.1, appended is a carefully summarized significant trend that is going to impact the gamification as a whole over the subsequent years (Growth, 2021).

Related Work

The study of game functions and mechanisms is a scientific come back for analyzing the enhancement and prevalence of the gamified applications (Konzack, 2007; Propaganda, 2007). The article by Walsh (2009) concluded that young people would not pay enough attention if a website did not have gaming functionality. This results in believing that the mechanics and features of the games strongly influence human behavior and these games (inventions) play a major role in attracting users. So, the computer has software evolution with game characters that allows for a trending form called gamification. This new perspective blends the concept of facilitating human-his-machine interaction, bringing elements such as eye-catching design, compelling, and gameplay mechanics. Gamification is likely to turn out to be the leading technology in the development of software applications, incorporating gaming features that users value (Meloni and Gruener, 2012). Gamification is therefore a new way to think, design, develop, and deploy software applications to change user attitude and behavior.

Classes of gamification features such network architecture, oversight, interaction, competition, leadership, badges, goals or objectives, incentives, prizes, rules, interfaces, and motivations are summarized by Deterding et al. (2011). Gamification entails giving e-learning, e-banking, e-commerce, e-campaigns, and e-health a 'game' layer. It enables users to carry out tasks, learn more, promote alternative perspectives, and alter individual's action.

Using the context of information technology, beliefs are well-defined as influences on individuals that can produce behavioral change. Intervene at the time of decision making and provide rewards for the expected behavior and motivation (Fogg, 2002). Game mechanics is a technology that transforms routine consumer interactions in games that serve strategic corporate goals. and science (Zichermann and Linder, 2010). Such mechanisms are necessary to create entertaining environments and gaming experiences in software that makes incremental improvements according to consumer feedback, add new features and use new game mechanics (Hamari and Lehdonvirta, 2010). Online gaming has become such a common practice that the research fraternity and the software developers have started to examine and monitor the development of gamification (Juul, 2010).

Methodology

The study is narrowed to reviews from 2022–2026. This research was conducted using the following preferred electronic sources to provide a global perspective: Web of Science, Google Scholar and IEEE Xplore, Science Direct, and Springer. To find relevant works distributed across all databases, data and information were collected using the following keywords: Gamified, Gamification, Gamification Elements, and Gamification Components. The following sentence is applied to

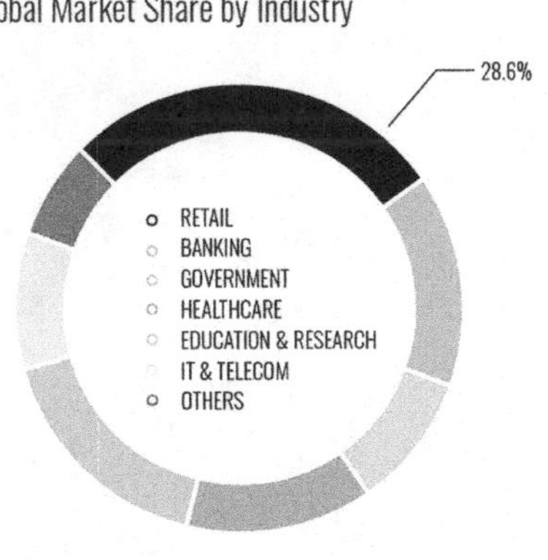

Figure 25.2 Global market shared by industry

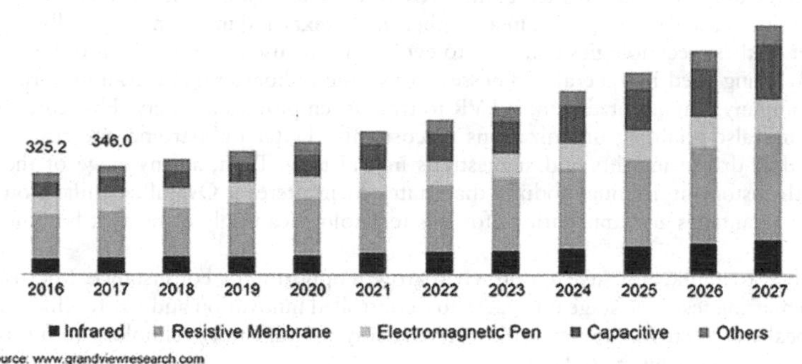

Figure 25.3 Asia pacific whiteboard market size (2016–2027)

find similar studies in Google Scholar and databases in the present field of study. 'Gamified' or 'Gamification' and 'Gamification Elements', or 'Gamification Components' and 'Technology' or 'Education' or 'Business', or 'E-Banking'.

A growing interest in gamification has been growing in modern society as a result of universal consumer and entertainment psychology. As per Growth (2021), it is becoming progressively common for games to be incorporated into all spheres of life: technology, business, education, healthcare, and banking as indicated in the chart shown in Figure 25.2. On the other side, Figure 25.3 shows that these areas will be in top gear in gamification in the next five years as the need for gamified systems increases (Growth, 2021).

Results and Discussion

Gamification is frequently used to improve the efficiency of numerous processes because its major goal is to change how a person or audience behaves as a whole (Alsawaier, 2018). Nowadays, gamification is applied in every aspect of human life. Its advantage is recognised as the foundation for quick feedback: a big aim is broken down into numerous smaller ones, and the user always sees even the smallest improvement. The game's design includes both internal and extrinsic motivation to keep players engaged. The game allows for limitless time involvement since 'you cannot only win or lose but also play' (Alsawaier, 2018; McCombes and Van Den Eertwegh, 2019). The rewards and objectives imposed on players are a distinctive feature of games. No textual content has the capacity for offering such a high level of involvement without the need for prompt feedback or decision-making.

Gamification is effective for the structure of learning materials, the management of community tournaments, and the visual recognition of accomplishments. It's a very effective tool for influencing human interest by utilizing human participation and motivation. The analysis revealed that technology, business, education, banking, and health are the top gamification application areas (Figol et al., 2021).

Technology

India alone had 1.2 billion mobiles phone users in 2021, out of which about 750 million are smartphone users; and it is expected to become the runner-up of smartphone producers by 2026 (Deloitte, 2022). According to Deloitte's 2022 Global TMT (technology, media and entertainment, telecom) forecast, 'the smartphone market is expected to reach one billion smartphone users by 2026'. This helps to elucidate why present-day manufacturers are adopting mobile-first gamified solutions. The need for smartphones is projected to raise as internet penetration increases. This increase in demand is driven by the need to embrace fintech, e-health, e-learning and e-commerce'(Deloitte, 2022). It is only reasonable to assume that new businesses will adopt the mobile-first design philosophy throughout the course of the next five years to cater to the demands of today's users. The growth of the engineering learning app and the microlearning solution, which uses gamification to promote and improve knowledge retention across all organizations of various shapes and sizes, provide compelling examples of how soon gamification of mobile learning solutions will grow the levels of engagement of its users.

Immersive technologies like virtual reality (VR), augmented reality (AR), and mixed reality (MR) will be connected by gamification. These interactions will encourage participation in a number of contexts and may fundamentally alter how gamification is done in the market as these technologies continue to evolve and be used by a range of different firms. Immersive innovations are already being used by several businesses to execute onboarding and training procedures. ExxonMobil is an example of a company that adopted gamified VR to train its employees in safety (Phaneuf, 2022).

Gamified systems in AI-driven are also enabling organizations to customize better onboarding and training programmes. AI engines can deliver data-driven insights and suggestions in real time. Then, at any stage of their programme, learners are provided with custom-fit training modules that match their interests. Overall, gamification fueled by AI has endless potential. More advantages and applications for this technology can only come as it becomes more sophisticated (Growth, 2021).

Game mechanics connected with IoT can likewise give a more vivid growth opportunity. For instance, Microsoft has made a virtual stage, a foundation matting test. The stage interfaces IoT-controlled innovation and Azure Kinect sensors to make a 3D 'virtual' stage for speakers. There are innumerable alternate ways of adjusting technology to future gamified programs; the possibilities are endless (Growth, 2021).

Business

The integration of advanced technologies into gamification solutions and the increasing use of AR and VR in gamification solutions for education will lead to great demand in the market. The global gamification market is projected to grow by US$ 27.77 billion between 2022 and 2026, reaching a CAGR of 29.15% during the forecast period. Gartner reports that gamification is presently utilized by more than 70% of the companies that make up the Worldwide 2000 list of companies. As more businesses incorporate gaming into their commerce forms, this slant will continue to evolve (Growth, 2021). Large businesses are anticipated to own a dominant market share because many of them used the programme early on. It's likely that businesses like IBM, Google, HP, and Oracle will invest in more creative gamified solutions to support this trend. In fact, small firms will gamify their negotiations and contracting efforts in response to increased competition among small and medium-sized businesses (SME) in general. As a result, it is anticipated that social media will be used more frequently in this field to implement gamification tactics (Meloni and Gruener, 2012).

Education

Conventional schooling is perceived as unproductive and uninteresting by many students of this age in science technology engineering and mathematics (STEM). Although teachers continuously seek innovative instructional methods, it is largely agreed that the key problem faced by schools' majors is centered on student motivation and engagement (Saleem et al., 2021). The implementation of learning kits such as educational games is a favorable ideal. Due to the teaching abilities of educational games, implementing learning kits like these is a good idea. This is especially true given the assurance that it will improve not just knowledge but also crucial skills like problem-solving, teamwork, efficient communication, and healthy competitiveness (Alsawaier, 2018). Games have amazing motivational power; employing several mechanisms to incite people engage with them, most times without reward, just for the pleasure of playing and the possibility to win (Radu, 2021; Kumar and Khurana, 2012; Kumar and Sharma, 2018). However, creating highly engaging and complete learning games is difficult, time-consuming, and costly. It's also usually aimed at only one learning goal, chosen by the game designer (Deterding et al., 2011). Moreover, effective introduction into the classroom requires a certain technological infrastructure and proper educational integration. Unlike elaborate games that require significant effort to design and develop, the 'gamification' approach uses game thinking and elements of game design to increase learner engagement and motivation (Szopiński and Bachnik, 2022).

Banking

The concept of gamification doesn't mean literally turning a banking app into a game. Rather strengthen traditional methods with game elements. Examples of gamification in banking emanate from diverse spheres: talent management, sales, marketing, and innovation management. Banks launch web or mobile applications that in the form of a challenge teach users how taxes are paid and or conduct online transactions (Zichermann and Linder, 2010). As successful as the gamification of corporate banking services has been so also it is in retail banking services. The same is true for both traditional and digital banks. Fierce competition levels the odds as shown in Figure 25.4 (Growth, 2021). At the forefront of gamification are banks that use game design elements and principles judiciously and systematically. After all, a bank's size and assets are not the decisive factors in attracting and retaining customers. According to a recent Juniper Research,

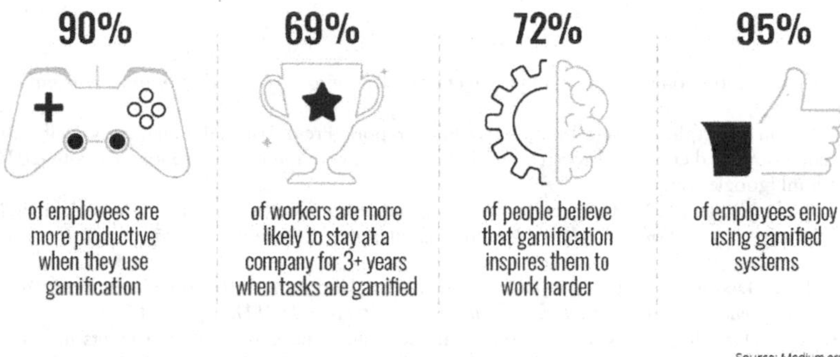
The Impact of Gamification
90%
of employees are more productive when they use gamification
69%
of workers are more likely to stay at a company for 3+ years when tasks are gamified
72%
of people believe that gamification inspires them to work harder
95%
of employees enjoy using gamified systems
Source: Medium.org

Figure 25.4 Impact of gamification

approximately 4.2 billion people would be using digital banking services by 2026, up from 2.5 billion in 2021, or 53% of the world's populace (Phaneuf, 2022). Research updates on digital banking, banking as a service, market changes, and hence forecasts China will overtake the U.S. as the top digital banking market between 2021 and 2026 By 2026, 25% of people will be using digital banking. In order to compete with a wide range of competitors, the report advises banks to combine several services into a single seamless digital experience (Hamari and Lehdonvirta, 2010).

Gamification helps financial institutions to motivate employees, improve regulatory compliance, boost innovations, provide outstanding customer service, reach personal development goals, meet targets and sell services, track performance, and adopt digital transformation. There are many ways banks have incorporated game elements into their financial app. Here are some best practices of gamification in the banking sector; accomplishment strategy, winning competition, better service experience, edutainment, customer insights, and client loyalty. A skilled method of analyzing this data enables banks to better understand their clients and provides an accurate snapshot of user activity and the amount of interest in banking services. Additionally, it is no longer about rewards, accolades, or currency but rather about insightful analytical data, a larger clientele, and a desirable reputation (Phaneuf, 2022; Kumar, 2019).

Miscellaneous

Apart from the above-mentioned areas, gamification is also used in many other fields such as healthcare systems, advertisement, tourism, online surveys, housekeeping, etc. Here, the findings revealed that gamification literature is available in abundance mainly in education sector (Kumar, 2019).

Conclusion

Since it has been discovered that as gamified solutions become more advanced, so does their influence, and hence the emergence of gamification in numerous fields will continue to be observed. Large companies continue to innovate existing gamified practices. With the assistance of social media and access to additional digital tools, small businesses are also entering the fray. The need for gamified mobile solutions will rise in response to the explosive expansion in smartphone usage. This is also made possible by emerging technological trends like remote employment and flexible scheduling in the classroom. An important technique that businesses can use to boost employee engagement and business impact is gamification. The influence of gamified software will only rise as it develops and scales. This generates a fresh set of gamification advantages and application cases that will be researched in the next years. What could make gamification so potent and successful? Because it draws on the neuroscience of human motivation and behavior.

Gamification as a topic of academic research is relatively young, with few founded theoretical backgrounds or unified discourses. This literature review included only studies that explicitly addressed gamification and motivational offers. Therefore, work related to other topics conceptually or theoretically close to gamification (such as studies on intrinsic motivation) or reporting similar research results is limited in terms of measured results. Also, there may be studies that explore similar phenomena but treat them differently, and thus are harder to find. Studies relied on inclusion criteria that were explicitly investigated. Therefore, this article provides a comprehensive insight into the research being done specifically about the gamification.

References

Alsawaier, R. S. (2018). The effect of gamification on motivation and engagement. *International Journal of Information and Learning Technology*.

Deloitte. (2022). India to have 1 billion smartphone users by 2026: Deloitte report, Press Trust of India, New Delhi. Business Standard. https://www.business-standard.com/article/current-affairs/india-to-have-1-billion-smartphone-users-by-2026-deloitte-report-122022200996_1.html#google_vignette

Deterdinga, S., Dixon, D., Khaled, R., & Nacke, L. (2011, September). From game design elements to gamefulness: defining" gamification". *In Proceedings of the 15th International Academic Mindtrek Conference: Envisioning Future Media Environments*, (pp. 9–15).

Deterdingb, S., Khaled, R., Nacke, L., & Dixon, D. (2011). Gamification: Toward a definition. *CHI 2011 Gamification Workshop Proceedings. In 2011 Annual Conference on Human Factors in Computing Systems (CHI'11),* (pp. 12–15).

Deterdingc, S., Sicart, M., Nacke, L., O'Hara, K., & Dixon, D. (2011). Gamification: using game-design elements in non-gaming contexts. In CHI'11 Extended Abstracts on Human Factors in Computing Systems (pp. 2425–2428), ACM, New York.

Figol, N., Faichuk, T., Pobidash, I., Trishchuk, O., & Teremko, V. (2021). Application fields of gamification. *Amazonia Investiga*, 10(37), 93–100.

Fogg, B. J. (2002). Persuasive technology: using computers to change what we think and do. *Ubiquity*, 2.

Growth, E. (2021). 19 Gamification trends for 2022-2025: Top stats, facts & examples. *Growth Engineering*. https://www.growthengineering.co.uk/19-gamification-trends-for-2022-2025-top-stats-facts-examples/

Hamari, J. & Lehdonvirta, V. (2010). Game design as marketing: How game mechanics create demand for virtual goods. *International Journal of Business Science & Applied Management*, 5(1), 14–29.

Juul, J. (2010). A casual revolution: Reinventing video games and their players. MIT press. Cambridge, England

Konzack, L. (2007). Rhetorics of computer and video game research. The Players' Realm: studies on the culture of video games and gaming, 110–130.

Kumar, B. (2019). Gamification–doing things with fun: A broader perspective. *Think India Journal*, 22(17), 1760–1767.

Kumar, B. & Khurana, P. (2012). Gamification in education-learn computer programming with fun. *International Journal of Computers and Distributed Systems*, 2(1), 46–53.

Kumar, B. & Sharma, K. (2018). A gamified approach to achieve excellence in programming. *In 2018 4th International Conference on Computing Sciences (ICCS)*, (pp. 107–114). IEEE.

McCombes, S. & Van Den Eertwegh, L. (2019). Courses of nature. *Junctions: Graduate Journal of the Humanities*, 4(1).

Meloni, W. & Gruener, W. (2012). Gamification in 2012: Market update, consumer and enterprise market trends. *Gaming Business Review*, M2 Research.

Phaneuf, A. (2022) The future of retail, mobile, online, and digital-only banking technology in 2022. *Insider Intelligence*. https://www.insiderintelligence.com/insights/future-of-banking-technology/

Propaganda, P. (2007). The Players Realm: Studies on the Culture of Video Games and Gaming. In J. Patrick Williams and J. H. Smith (Eds). (pp. 91–109), Jefferson, NC: McFarland & Company,

Radu, A. (2021) Key Difference Between Game-based Learning and eLearning Gamification. eLearning Industry. https://elearningindustry.com/key-differences-between-game-based-learning-and-elearning-gamification

Saleem, A. N., Noori, N. M., & Ozdamli, F. (2021). Gamification applications in E-learning: A literature review. *Technology, Knowledge and Learning*, 1–21.

Szopiński, T. & Bachnik, K. (2022). Student evaluation of online learning during the COVID-19 pandemic. *Technological Forecasting and Social Change*, 174, 121203.

Walsh, M. J. (2009). Futuretainment: Yesterday the world changed, now it's your turn. Phaidon Press.

Wright, C. (2018). Game-based Learning vs Gamification: What's the Difference? MIND Research Institute, https://blog.mindresearch.org/blog/game-based-learning-vs-gamification

Zichermann, G. & Linder, J. (2010). Game-based marketing: inspire customer loyalty through rewards, challenges, and contests. John Wiley & Sons.

26 In-depth analysis of key task scheduling algorithms and inception of real-time EPSO-BAT model

Parvaz Ahmad Malla[1], *Sophiya Sheikh*[1], *and Tawseef Ahmad Teli*[2]

[1]Department of Computer Applications, Lovely Professional University, Punjab, India

[2]Higher Education Department J&K, Jammu and Kashmir, India

Abstract

Cloud computing operates on a 'pay-as-you-go' basis and offers users various services that can be customized to their needs. One of the biggest challenges for cloud service providers is lowering energy consumption without sacrificing performance in a virtualized cloud environment. The expenses of providing a service can be reduced, the effectiveness of the system can be improved, and the environment can be protected all by using less energy. Both cloud service providers and researchers are primarily interested in finding ways to maximize performance while minimizing energy consumption in cloud computing. It can be achieved in a real-time paradigm by properly allocating jobs to the virtual machines (VMs) to be serviced more effectively. Consequently, many scheduling systems have been developed to accomplish these objectives efficiently. This work aims to provide a comparative evaluation of the popular scheduling methods. The time it takes to finish various tasks using alternate methodologies is compared. The paper also details the steps that need to be taken in the future to complete a real-time energy-aware scheduling model.

Keywords: Scheduling, completion time, bandwidth-aware divisible task, particle swarm algorithm, realtime

Introduction

Providing consumers with a variety of pay-as-you-go services relies heavily on cloud computing. With cloud computing, problems may be resolved devoid of any form of physical infrastructure. The services are delivered using a variety of approaches under the service level agreement (SLA) and the anticipated timeframes. Scheduling is one of the biggest issues today (Panda et al, 2015; 2016), mapping tasks to the available resources. There are several distinct categories of cloud computing services, one of the important services is infrastructure as a service (IaaS). In IaaS, customers utilize virtual machines (VMs) set up in their data centers to access cloud services (Singh et al., 2016; Panda et al., 2016). The geographically dispersed data centers are present in the cloud ecosystem (Boveiri et al, 2019). The data centre has thousands of servers, each partitioned into several virtual machines with memory, processor, and other allied resources. The cloud users are given a VM/VMs, to utilize, to, accomplish the tasks. The need for cloud computing is increasing daily and quickly. The ecology is negatively impacted by the excessive usage of cloud computing systems since they produce a significant amount of green house gases (GHG). It has been calculated that 0.3% of all crbon dioxide (CO_2) emissions come from data centers of cloud (Malla et al., 2022). Therefore, the ultimate objective of a cloud user is to rent resources at the lowest possible cost. On the other hand, a cloud service provider's goal is to maximize profit through efficient resource allocation. The management of cloud resources is a big issue. The performance of cloud computing systems will improve, and energy consumption will decrease if the resources are managed effectively and efficiently. Task scheduling is essential for enhancing performance and lowering energy usage. Finding the best techniques for task scheduling in the cloud context has been described as a very hard problem (NP-hard) (Tianle et al., 2011). The purpose of the work is to carry out a result-based comparative study among various strategies that include Shortest Job First (SJF), First Come First Serve (FCFS), round robin (RR) algorithm and the particle swarm algorithm (PSO). In the computation analysis, the task completion time of various algorithms is calculated and compared using the Cloudsim 3.0 environment.

Literature Review

Energy usage, execution cost, Makespan, deadline, job priority, waiting time, etc., are some factors that are considered for the ideal task scheduling. Several optimizing techniques augment the scheduling of the work to be done in the cloud given that we are aware that scheduling tasks are an NP-hard problem (Mesbani et al., 2013). The first stage in cloud scheduling is to find an optimal mapping for the n workloads that will be assigned to the m virtual machines. The hierarchy process method for resource scheduling was put out by the authors (Ergu et al., 2013). The goal of the hierarchical process is to optimize decisions based on the many factors. Incoming jobs are prioritized by the hybrid algorithm using the cloud hierarchy procedure. In this strategy, the ranking of tasks determines how the computer resources are allocated. The authors introduced multiple priority queues genetic algorithm-based cost-aware job scheduling solution for heterogeneous systems (Xu et al., 2014). Additionally, a search method is suggested to discover a solution utilizing the earliest finish time algorithm to minimize the Makespan. The authors have not taken resource utilization and reliability into consideration. In the context of a multi-cloud system, the authors (Panda et al., 2016) have given four job scheduling methods based on the normalization technique. The methods are effective in reducing the Makespan, execution time and utilization costs but the reliability and transfer costs across many clouds were not evaluated. An energy-efficient task scheduling hybrid method, developed by authors (Azad et al., 2017), combines two meta-heuristic algorithms that reduce Makespan and energy usage. The use of resources was not considered as an evaluation parameter. The authors (Sreenu et al, 2019) created a cost-effective meta-heuristic task scheduling method to allocate work to VMs. The technique reduces both Makespan and cost to a minimum. Execution time and resource utilization, however, were not taken into consideration. Security is also a big issue in cloud environments and many machine learning techniques encompass applications in varied fields of cryptography and networks (Masoodi et al., 2021; Teli, et al., 2021; 2022), navigation (Teli et al., 2021) and most importantly predictive analysis and healthcare. Deep learning techniques that have applications in secure healthcare (Teli, et al., 2020; 2021; 2022) can also have cloud security applications.

Key Scheduling Algorithms

A given set of n tasks (T_1, T_2..., T_n) must be allocated to a variety of accessible m machines (M_1, M_2, ..., M_m) in an optimum and energy-efficient way while considering the stated target functions or metrics. This is the challenge of task scheduling. The scheduler's goal is to use the resources to speed up the processes of completion time, system throughput, waiting time, turnaround time, and response time (Sharma et al, 2015). Different scheduling strategies have been presented to achieve the goal in an optimized and energy-efficient manner. In this study, we have focused on traditional task scheduling (TTS) which is a fairly straightforward method since it is predicated on knowledge of the system's overall state. The TSS algorithms include the RR, FCFS, and SJF algorithms. One of the main evolutionary task scheduling (ETS) algorithms known as PSO which is the most recent meta-heuristic algorithm has also been implemented in this work due to its relative maturity and greater popularity, especially with complicated large-scale issues in the context of cloud computing, this is the essential approach that came under the swarm intelligence umbrella (Rjoub et al., 2017).

Experiment and Results

The simulation was done on Cloudsim 3.0, which was initialized with a configuration of having five virtual machines and five data centers.

The range of tasks to be completed was set at 30 to 50, with a space of five tasks. The task completion time for all the techniques is given in Table 26.1. SJF and RR performs better in traditional techniques, while particle swarm optimization performs extremely well, as shown in the performance chart in Chart 1. The task completion time is used as the criteria of performance for these techniques. The findings unequivocally demonstrate the importance and potential of evolutionary algorithms in addressing job scheduling issues in cloud computing.

Discussion and Future Work

In its simplest rudimentary form, PSO has clearly shown better performance in task scheduling surpassing all traditional methods. However, PSO has a low convergence rate in large-scale optimization issues.

The PSO method has a slow rate of convergence during the iterative process, and it is easy to get stuck in a local optimum in a high-dimensional environment. The PSO algorithm requires some fine-tuning as the size of the work grows (Elbes et al, 2019). Moreover, the PSO does not consider bandwidth requirements when scheduling a task. The goal is to get around these restrictions and achieve successful outcomes. This research proposes combining the PSO meta-heuristic with the bandwidth-aware divisible task (BAT) scheduling model (Lin et al., 2014) for a real-time setting in

Table 26.1 Task completion time

No. of tasks	*PSO*	*RR*	*FCFS*	*SJF*
30	5000.34	9336.7	10607.32	12423.38
35	5449.93	9542.74	10543.99	9003.34
40	7190.74	15109.39	11486.36	17487.45
45	5322.78	9016.32	8518.67	14089.6
50	5063.11	9757.94	10473.53	9171.25

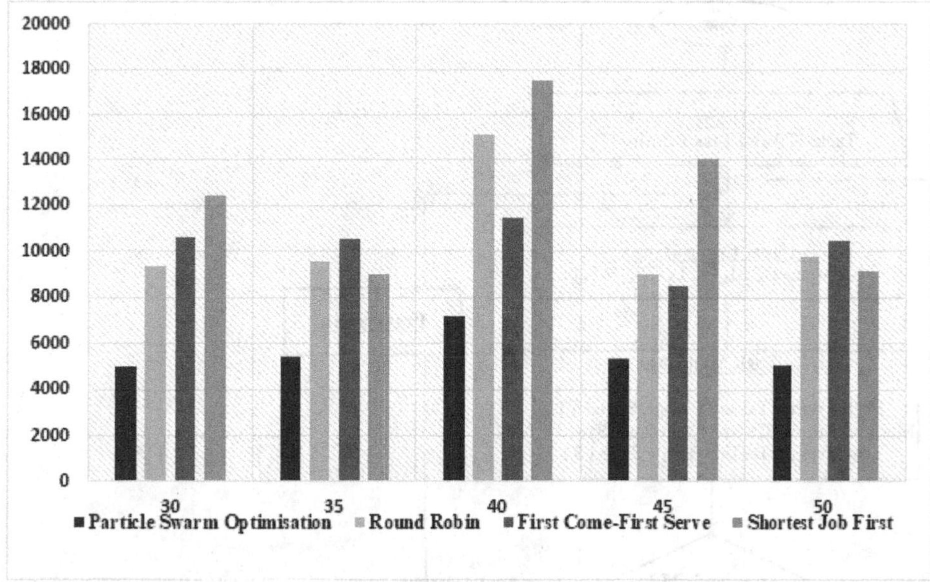

Chart 26.1 Performance chart (y-axis task completion time)

Table 26.2 Notions and their meaning

Notion	*Meaning*
T_i	i_{th} task submitted by the user.
T_{ip}	Priority of the i_{th} task.
B_j	The bandwidth of the j_{th} VM.
M_j	Memory utilized by the j_{th} VM.
C_j	CPU utilization of the jt_hVM.
T_{Si}	Size of the i_{th} task.
V_{Sj}	Computation speed of jt_h VM.
L_j	Current load of the j_{th} VM.

an energy-aware manner. The new model integrates the best features of the mentioned approaches in a real-time setting to consume less energy with proficient performance. The notions behind the forthcoming model are laid forth in Table 26.2, and its flowchart is depicted in Figure 26.1. The new method shall overcome the limitations of PSO and other TTS algorithms as well as produce better results that are in line with energy efficiency and quality of service.

Conclusion

Maximizing resource utilization while minimizing task execution time and other performance optimization criteria is the primary goal of task scheduling. The total time to complete a job is used as a performance metric in First Come First Serve (FCFS), Shortest Job First (SJF), round robin (RR) algorithm, and bandwidth-aware divisible task (PSO). The results provide unmistakable proof of the significance and potential of evolutionary algorithms in dealing with job scheduling challenges in the cloud. Traditional methods like the SJF and RR fare slightly better, but PSO fares far better. The EPSO-BAT model is proposed as an additional energy-aware scheduling tactic for time-sensitive information. In the future, that model will be used to fine-tune a wide range of parameters.

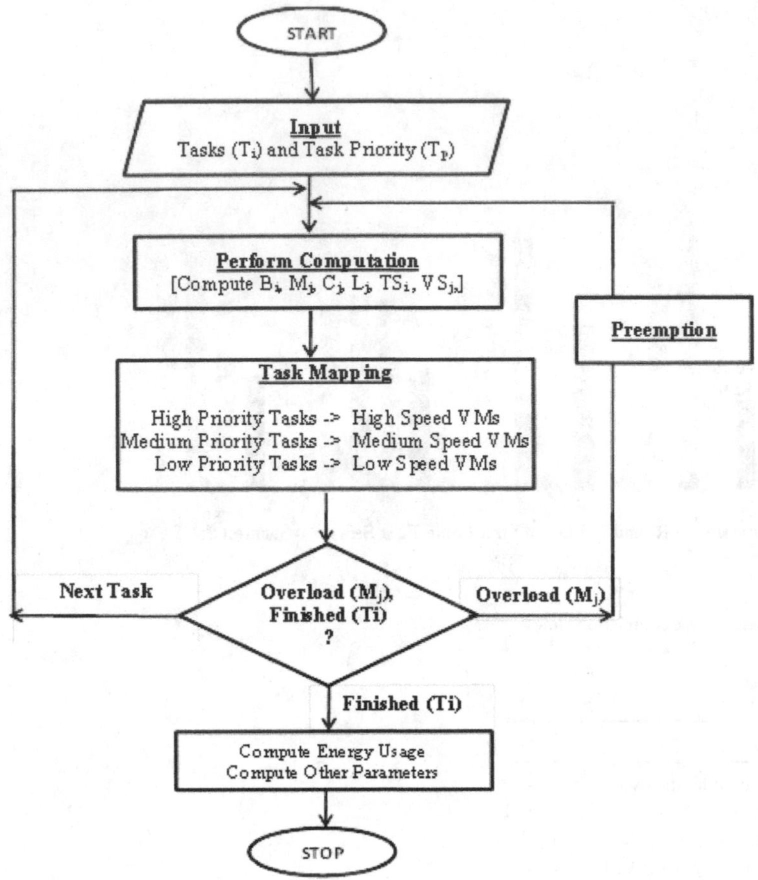

Figure 26.1 Flowchart for real-time EPSO-BAT model

References

Azad, P. & Navimipour, N. J (2017). An energy-aware task scheduling in the cloud computing using a hybrid cultural and ant colony optimisation algorithm. *International Journal of Cloud Applications and Computing*, 7, 20–40.

Boveiri, H. R., Khayami, R., Elhoseny, M., & Gunasekaran, M. (2019). An efficient Swarm-Intelligence approach for task scheduling in cloud-based internet of things applications. *Journal of Ambient Intelligence and Humanized Computing*, 10(9), 3469–3479.

Eberhart, R. & Kennedy, J. (1995). A new optimiser using particle swarm theory, in: MHS'95. *Proceedings of the Sixth International Symposium on Micro Machine and Human Science, IEEE*, pp. 39–43.

Elbes, M., Alzubi, S., Kanan, T., Al-Fuqaha, A., & Hawashin, B. (2019). A survey on particle swarm optimisation with emphasis on engineering and network applications. *Evolutionary Intelligence*, 12(2), 113–129.

Ergu, D., Kou, G., Peng, Y., Shi, Y., & Shi, Y. (2013). The analytic hierarchy process: task scheduling and resource allocation in cloud computing environment. *Journal of Supercomputing*, 64(3), 835–848

Lin, W., Liang, C., Wang, J. Z., & Buyya, R. (2014). Bandwidth-aware divisible task scheduling for cloud computing. *Software: Practice and Experience*, 44(2), 163–174.

Malla, P. A. & Sheikh, S. (2022). Analysis of QoS aware energy-efficient resource provisioning techniques in cloud computing. *International Journal of Communication Systems*, e5359. doi:10.1002/dac.5359

Masoodi, F., Bamhdi, A. M., & Teli, T. A. (2021). Machine learning for classification analysis of intrusion detection on NSL-KDD dataset. *Turkish Journal of Computer and Mathematics Education*, 12(10).

Mesbahi, M. R., Rahmani, A. M., & Hosseinzadeh, M. (2018). Reliability and high availability in cloud computing environments: a reference roadmap. *Human-centric Computing and Information Sciences*, 8, 20.

Panda, S. K. & Jana, P. K. (2015). An efficient resource allocation algorithm for IaaS cloud. *19th International Conference on Distributed Computing and Intelligent Technology*, 8956, 351–355.

Panda, S. K. & Jana, P. K. (2016). An efficient task consolidation algorithm for cloud computing systems. *19th International Conference on Distributed Computing and Intelligent Technology*, 9581.

Panda, S. K. & Jana, P. K. (2016). Normalisation-based task scheduling algorithms for heterogeneous multi-cloud environment. Springe, New York, N Y.

Rjoub G. & Bentahar J. (2017). Cloud task scheduling based on swarm intelligence and ma- chine learning. *2017 IEEE 5th International Conference on Future Internet of Things and Cloud (FiCloud)*, pp. 272–279.

Sharma, M. K. & Bansal, K. K. (2015). Fuzzy analysis of shortest job first. *International Journal of Engineering Research & Management Technology*. 125–128

Singh, S. & Chana, I. (2016). A survey on resource scheduling in cloud computing: Issues and challenges. *Journal of Grid Computing*. 14, 217–264.

Sreenu, K. & Sreelatha, M. (2019). W-Scheduler: whale optimisation for task scheduling in cloud computing. *Cluster Computing*. 22, 1087–1098.

Teli, T. A. & Wani, M. A. (2021). A fuzzy-based local minima avoidance path planning in autonomous robots. International Journal of Information Technology, 13(1), 33–40. https://doi.org/10.1007/s41870-020-00547-0

Teli, T. A., &Masoodi, F. (2021). 2nd International Conference on IoT Based Control Networks and Intelligent Systems (ICICNIS 2021) Blockchain in Healthcare: Challenges and Opportunities. https://ssrn.com/abstract=3882744

Teli, T. A., Masoodi, F., & Yousuf, R. (2020). International Conference on IoT based Control Networks and Intelligent Systems (ICICNIS 2020) Security Concerns and Privacy Preservation in Blockchain based IoT Systems: Opportunities and Challenges. https://ssrn.com/abstract=3769572

Teli, T. A., Masoodi, F. S., & Bahmdi, A. M. (2021). HIBE: Hierarchical Identity-Based Encryption. In: K. A. B. Ahmad, K. Ahmad, U. N. Dulhare (Eds). Functional Encryption. *EAI/Springer Innovations in Communication and Computing*. Springer, Cham.

Teli, T. A., Yousuf, R. & Khan, D. A. (2022). Ensuring secure data sharing in iot domains using blockchain. In M.M. Ghonge, S. Pramanik, R. Mangrulkar, & D.-N. Le (Eds. *Cyber Security and Digital Forensic*. https://doi.org/10.1002/9781119795667.ch9

Teli, T. A., Yousuf, R., & Khan, D. A. (2022). MANET routing protocols, attacks and mitigation techniques: A review. *International Journal of Mechanical Engineering*, 7(2).

Tianle, Z., Zhihui, D., Yinong, C., Xiang, Ji, c., & Xiaoying, W. (2011). Typical virtual appliances: An optimised mechanism for virtual appliances provisioning and management. *Elsevier Journal of Systems and Software*, 84(3).

Xu, Y., Li, K., Hu, J., & Li, K. (2014). A genetic algorithm for task scheduling on heterogeneous computing systems using multiple priority queues. *Journal of Information Science*, 270, 255–287.

27 Improved BEENISH protocol using fuzzy rules to reduce energy consumption in wireless sensor networks

Devika[1,a] *and Inderpal*[2,b]

[1]Research Scholar, CT. Institute of Technology & Research, Jalandhar, India

[2]Assistant Professor, Department of CSE, CT. Institute of Technology & Research, Jalandharer, India

Abstract

The exhaustion of power is an important parameter of wireless sensor networks. The hierarchical clustering is an approach which prolongs the working period of radio networks. The concern related to energy consumption is addressed in this paper and BEENISH protocol is improved using fuzzy interface system. The cluster head is picked by thinking over node power, mobility, pause time, and density. The node with least power, least mobility, maximum pause time, and maximum density is picked up as cluster head. In the obtained simulation-based outcomes, that projected system does better in comparison to existing system in the context of power consumed, and the number of packets transmitted to base station.

Keywords: Wireless sensor networks, cluster head, fuzzy rule, energy consumption

Introduction

Research and development in wireless sensor networks (WSNs) are driving advancements in multiple different applications ranging from warzone surveillance to home security passing by smart homes, environmental observing and object detection. In WSNs, plenty of tiny and independent nodes are installed for environmental sensing and monitoring (Benaddy et al., 2017). The nodes through radio channel communicate with each other so that the acquired information can be delivered to the base station via one or several hops. The sink node or base station has extra power to interface the WSN with the ultimate client, as it typically sends the obtained info to the server. In WSN, each sensing mote has four sections as depicted in Figure 27.1. power unit supplies energy to the sensing mote. This unit may contain a mini battery. The sensor node can sense different physical parameters like temperature, light intensity and water level from the environment by means of an appropriate already loaded sensor unit (Banđur et al., 2019). The outcome of the sensor unit which is an analog signal will be converted into a digital signal. The microcontroller module dependent on ADC unit recognizes this signal. The sensed outcome is further forwarded to the base station via communication unit.

Energy consumption in WSN

Owing to cost effectiveness and miniaturization requirements, WSN nodes are lack of resources with insufficient memory and computation capacity. Furthermore, nodes generally get power from battery, so energy is the most restricting aspect as it has a direct impact on the service cycle of the network (Ali et al., 2017). The three tasks of sensing, computation, and data transmission consume maximum energy of nodes. Among them, transmission is the most energy-exploiting task. For meeting design goals for example, the sensor node's size must be suppressed. The energy consumption in a WSN depends on three main elements which are sensing (Benaddy et al., 2017), processing and transmission. In contrast, $E_{i,k}^{proc}$ (processing energy consumption) for sensor node i and task k is proportionate to the intricacy of task k and the E_i^{ins} (average energy consumption per instruction) belonging to node i.

This relationship can be defined like below:

$$E_{i,k}^{proc} = I_k \times E_i^{ins} \tag{1}$$

Besides this, two crucial aspects which are the transmission and reception energy consumption must be considered as well (Nguyen et al., 2013).

$$\begin{cases} P_{ij}^{T} = P_i^{To} + P_i^{A}\left(\delta_{ij}\right) = P_i^{To} + \dfrac{P_i^{Tx}\left(\delta_{ij}\right)}{\eta_i} \\ P_j^{R} = P_j^{Ro} \end{cases} \tag{2}$$

[a]devbadyal290@gmail.com; [b]inderpal13@gmail.com

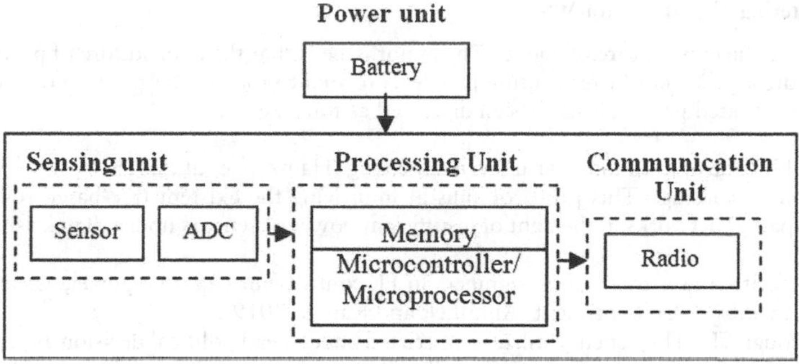

Figure 27.1 Sensing mote design

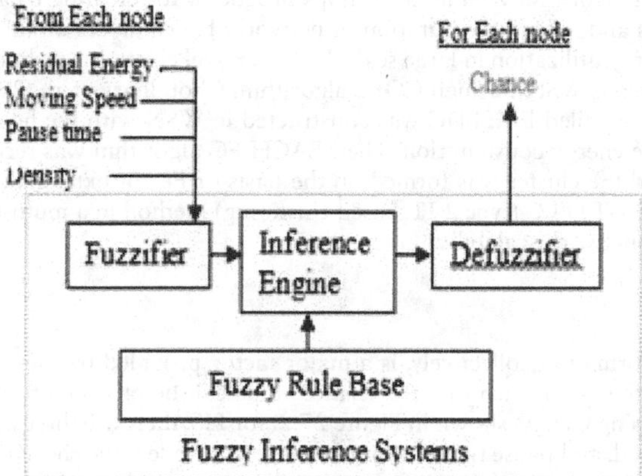

Figure 27.2 Proposed FIS-specific probabilistic reasoning for selecting CH

Where P_{ij}^{T} and P_{j}^{R} represent the radio frequency power consumption values respectively for transferring and receiving. Also, $P_{i}^{A}\left(\delta_{ij}\right)$ is the power exhausted by the power amplifier (PA). It is based on the distance δ_{ij} between transmitting node i and receiving node j; P_{i}^{T0} and P_{j}^{R0} respectively denote the mechanisms of power consumption of the transmitting and receiving circuitry (Pushpalatha and Nayak, 2015); P_{i}^{Tx} denotes the output power at node iantenna which, for trustable transmission relies upon the distance δ_{ij}; η_i indicates the drain efficacy of the power amplifier at node i.

Fuzzy logic for reducing energy consumption in WSN

The approaches based on fuzzy logic (FL) are widely implemented in WSNs due to their ability of handling doubts in network design and management. FL may assist at network level to split the network into clusters. CH aggregate the data gathered by the cluster nodes. This means that the clustering upscale the communication efficacy and network scalability. In addition, CHs closer to the sink exploit large amount of power as they establish communication with the sink more often. To deal with this issue, disparate clustering algorithms have been proposed. These algorithms seek network splits so as to make the clusters adjacent to the sink lesser than clusters farther from it. At the data link level, fuzzy-logic centric solutions can be implemented to coordinate channel availability. Furthermore, rather being active constantly, a mote can be power-efficient by detecting and collaborating at regular time intervals, i.e., with correct sampling and snoozing times (Pankaj et al., 2021).

Fuzzy logic-based energy efficient clustering algorithms for WSN

The clustering has the potential to reduce the expenditure of energy. The major issue is that the expenditure of power is cluster head centric. To eliminate this drawback, the cluster routing problems related to the apt distribution of energy consumption should be addressed. Some related protocols have been discussed as follows:

- EAUCF: EAUCF scheme adopts a FL controller to discover uneven clustering (Hamzah, et al., 2019)
- FEAR (Fuzzy energy aware tree-based routing): This protocol aims at improving the existent tree-based routing protocols and extends the service span of networks in the light of insufficient power of sensors nodes (Balakrishnan, and Balachandran 2017).
- Fuzzy-LEACH: The fuzzy leach algorithm uses three fuzzy signifiers in FL controls for example power, attention, and importance to improvise the scheme of CH assortment (Abhishek and Kanika 2019).
- CHEF (CH election mechanism through FL). This scheme utilizes a restricted bunch head political decision approach that doesn't need the base station to accumulate information from all nodes.

Literature Review

Mohamed et al. (2021) projected a FL specific clustering algorithm with multiple hops broadcast for creating balance amid load allotted, mitigate the power utilized by nodes and extend the duration of network. Fattoum, et., al. (2020) discussed that clustering was efficient to decrease the energy utilization in large scale WSN. A novel clustering technique was introduced by Mohamed et al. (2020) for heterogeneous WSN through COFL algorithm. Choudhary et al. (2017) selected the CH in WSN. A new data collection algorithm called EMFLDC was constructed in WSN with the help of moving components by Ch et al. (2020) for lessening the energy consumption. The LEACH-FC algorithm was recommended by Lata, et al. (2020). The CH was selected and the cluster was formed on the basis of FL for extending the duration of network. Mohamed et al. (2021) constructed a TTFLC (type 2 FL-based clustering) method in a multi-hop WSN for mitigating the energy usage and enhancing the network scalability.

Proposed Model

The handling of numerical data as well as linguistic information collectively, is a major factor provided by the fuzzy inference systems. The utilization of FIS is proposed in this work such that the chance value can be provided to each node to minimize the uncertainties that occur while choosing CH. As shown in Figure 27.2, for FIS, there are three input variables provided which are residual energy, moving speed, and pause time. The probability of a node to be chosen as a cluster head is the one output parameters provided. This is names as 'chance'. The probability that a node can be chosen as cluster head is higher if the value of chance is higher than other nodes (Choudhary, et al., 2017). In Figure 27.3(a), the fuzzy set through which the remaining power input variable is seen, is presented. For this fuzzy set, the provided language variables are VL (very low), M (medium), H (high) and VH (very high). The speed at which the CH candidate is moving is given as another fuzzy input variable. In Figure 27.3(b), the fuzzy set through which the moving speed input variable is shown, is presented. VS (Very slow), S (slow), M (medium), F (fast), and VF (very fast) are the linguistic variables provided for this fuzzy set. The pause time of the CH candidate is given as another fuzzy input variable. In Figure 27.3(c), the fuzzy set through which the gap time input variable is shown, is presented.

VS, S, M, large, and very large are the linguistic variables used in this fuzzy set. In Figure 27.3(d), the fuzzy set through which the node density is input variable is seen, is presented. For this fuzzy set, the provided language metrics are VL, M, H and VH. The event of a CH applicant is given as an output variable, the fuzzy set of which is shown in Figure 27.3 (e). VL, L, RL, ML, M, MH, RH, H and VH are the nine linguistic variables given in this set. The triangular membership functions are utilized here for minimizing the computational load. To handle any kinds of uncertainties, the predefined fuzzy if-then inference rules are utilized to calculate chance. As per the three fuzzy input variables, there are 125 inference rules achieved which are shown in Table 27.1. With the help of rules, the fuzzy output variable event can be calculated. To bring this utilization under practice, the fuzzy variable needs to be transformed into one crisp number. The center of a region defuzzification approach is adopted here, in the proposed mechanism. Thus, there will be various crisp values generated in between 0 and 1 even when there are numerous sensors that involve similar linguistic variables. All the sensors will be chosen as CHs in case various numbers of sensors have similar crisp value of chance. Based on LEACH architecture, the LEACH-MF technique is proposed. Here, the numbers of clusters are assumed to be around 5% of the nodes within the network (Ch, et al., 2020). Either by utilizing the human heuristics or the experimental data, the fuzzy rules can be generated generally. A novel heuristic rule is created in this paper. The basic principle of this rule is that the likelihood of a mote to be chosen as a CH is higher if the amount of residual energy is higher, the mobility

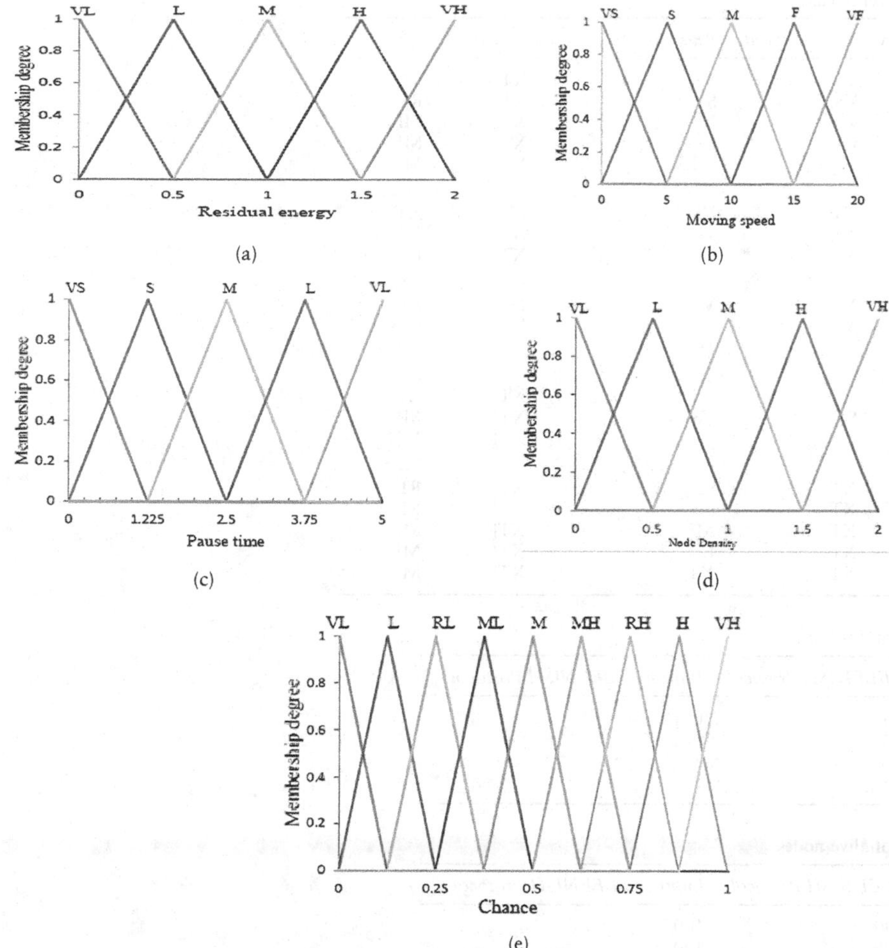

Figure 27.3 Fuzzy sets for input variables (a) residual energy, (b) moving speed, and (c) pause time, and for the output variable (d) Node density (e) chance

speed is less, and the pause time involved is longer. Rule 105 shown in Table 27.1 is the perfect example of this scenario whereas, rule 21 is complete opposite of it.

Results and Discussion

A 100-node network is deployed within this simulation. Within a (100×100)-square-meter area, there is a random distribution of initial locations of mobile nodes in uniform manner. At the position (50, 175) m a stationary base station is placed in this network. For each node, the initial energy provided is 2 (J), 1–20 m/s is the moving speed it is given and 0–5 s is the pause time. MATLAB environment is installed for conducting the simulations. There were on average 100 self-regulating simulation scores made along with a 95% confidence interval when almost all the results were achieved for this technique.

Figure 27.4 exhibits that the no. of dead nodes-based comparison is made between BEENISH and improved BEENISH protocol. As shown in Figure 27.5, BEENISH protocol is compared with the improved BEENISH protocol in context of alive nodes.

Table 27.1 Fuzzy inference rules

Rule	*Residual energy*	*Moving speed*	*Pause time*	*Density*	*Chance*
1	XT	VS	VS	XT	RL
2	XT	VS	S	XT	RL
3	XT	vs	M	XT	ML
4	XT	vs	L	XT	ML
5	XT	vs	XT	XT	M
…					
21	XT	XT	VS	XT	XT
22	XT	XT	s	XT	XT
23	XT	XT	M	XT	L
…					
61	M	M	VS	M	RL
62	M	M	s	M	RL
63	M	M	M	M	ML
…					
105	XU	VS	XT	XT!	XU
106	XU	S	VS	XT{	M
107	XU	s	s	XT!	MH
…					
121	XU	XT	vs	XT{	RL
122	XU	XT	s	XT!	RL
123	XU	XT	M	XT{	ML
124	XU	XT	L	XT!	ML
125	X'H	XT	XT	XT{	M

Table 27.2 Number of dead nodes

No of Rounds	*BEENISH Protocol*	*Improved BEENISH Protocol*
20	1	0
40	1	0
60	3	1
100	8	2

Table 27.3 Number of alive nodes

No of Rounds	*BEENISH Protocol*	*Improved BEENISH Protocol*
20	99	100
40	99	100
60	97	99
100	92	98

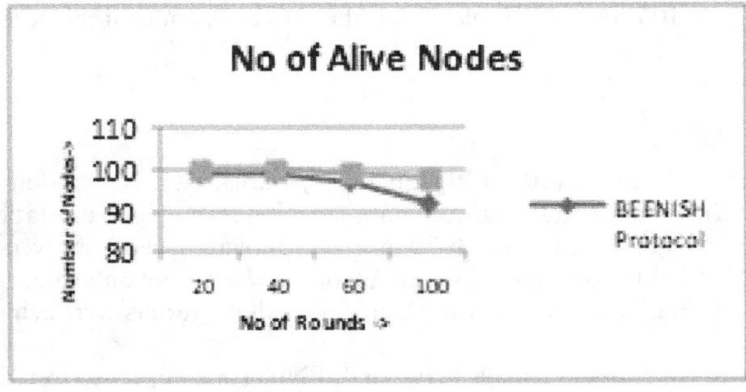

Figure 27.4 No. of dead nodes analysis

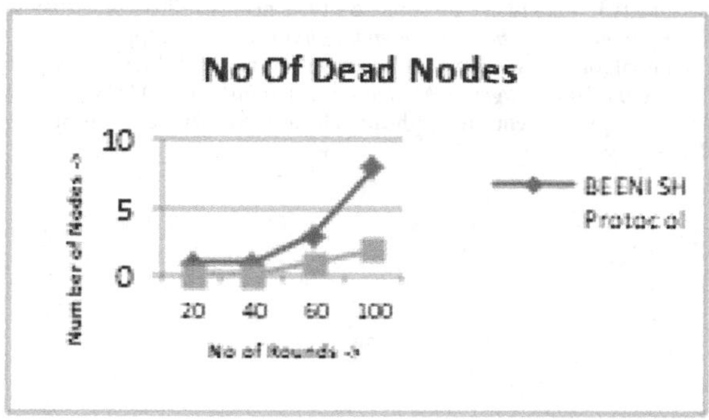

Figure 27.5 No. of alive nodes

Conclusion

Power exhaustion is an important challenge of wireless sensor networks. The wireless sensor networks which support mobility can face the issue of density and topology change. The improvement in Improved BEENISH protocol is proposed here to increase lifetime and count of transmitted packets in the network. In the proposed system, the technique of fuzzy logic is applied for selecting CH. The mote which has higher energy, less mobility, long pause time and maximum density has the maximum chances to be selected as CH. The simulation is done in MATLAB and results indicate that energy consumption is reduced.

References

Adnan, M., Ahmad, T., & Yang, T. (2021). Type-2 fuzzy logic based energy-efficient cluster head election for multi-hop wireless sensor networks. *2021 IEEE Asia Pacific Conference on Wireless and Mobile (APWiMob)*, (pp. 32–38).

Adnan, M., Yang, L., Ahmad, T., & Tao, Y. (2021). An unequally clustered multi-hop routing protocol based on fuzzy logic for wireless sensor networks. *IEEE Access*, 9, 38531–38545.

Ali, N. F., Said, A. M., Nisar, K., & Aziz, I. A. (2017). A survey on software defined network approaches for achieving energy efficiency in wireless sensor network. *2017 IEEE Conference on Wireless Sensors (ICWiSe)*, (pp. 1–6).

Balakrishnan, B. & Balachandran, S. (2017). FLECH: fuzzy logic based energy efficient clustering hierarchy for nonuniform wireless sensor networks. *Wireless Communications and Mobile Computing.*

Banđur, Đ., Jakšić, B., Banđur, M., & Jović, S. (2019). An analysis of energy efficiency in Wireless Sensor Networks (WSNs) applied in smart agriculture. *Computers and Electronics in Agriculture*, 156, 500–507.

Benaddy, M., El Habil, B., El Ouali, M., El Meslouhi, O., & Krit, S. (2017, May). A mutlipath routing algorithm for wireless sensor networks under distance and energy consumption constraints for reliable data transmission. In *2017 International Conference on Engineering & MIS (ICEMIS)*, (pp. 1–4).

Ch, S. & Budyal, V. R. (2020). Expectation maximization and fuzzy logic based energy efficient data collection in wireless sensor networks with mobile Elements. *2020 7th International Conference on Signal Processing and Integrated Networks (SPIN)*, (pp. 21–26).

Choudhary, D. & Sharma, I. (2017, July). Using fuzzy logic for clustering in wireless sensor networks. *2017 International Conference on Intelligent Computing, Instrumentation and Control Technologies (ICICICT)*, (pp. 861–866).

Fattoum, M., Jellali, Z., & Atallah, L. N. (2020). Fuzzy logic-based two-level clustering for data aggregation in WSN. *2020 17th International Multi-Conference on Systems, Signals & Devices (SSD)*, (pp. 360–365).

Hamzah, A., Shurman, M., Al-Jarrah, O., & Taqieddin, E. (2019). Energy-efficient fuzzy-logic-based clustering technique for hierarchical routing protocols in wireless sensor networks. *Sensors*, 19(3), 561.

Lata, S., Mehfuz, S., Urooj, S., & Alrowais, F. (2020). Fuzzy clustering algorithm for enhancing reliability and network lifetime of wireless sensor networks. *IEEE Access*, 8, 66013–66024.

Mishra, P. K. & Verma, S. K. (2021). FFMCP: Feed-forward multi-clustering protocol using fuzzy logic for wireless sensor networks (WSNs). *Energies*, 14(10), 2866.

Mohamed, A., Saber, W., Elnahry, I., & Hassanien, A. E. (2020). Coyote optimization based on a fuzzy logic algorithm for energy-efficiency in wireless sensor networks. *IEEE Access*, 8, 185816–185829.

Nayak, P. & Devulapalli, A. (2015). A fuzzy logic-based clustering algorithm for WSN to extend the network lifetime. *IEEE Sensors Journal*, 16(1), 137–144.

Nguyen, T. T., Shieh, C. S., Dao, T. K., Wu, J. S., & Hu, W. C. (2013, December). Prolonging of the network lifetime of WSN using fuzzy clustering topology. *2013 Second International Conference on Robot, Vision and Signal Processing*, (pp. 13–16).

Pushpalatha, D. V. & Nayak, P. (2015, December). A clustering algorithm for WSN to optimize the network lifetime using type-2 fuzzy logic model. *2015 3rd International Conference on Artificial Intelligence, Modelling and Simulation (AIMS)*, (pp. 53–58).

Rai, A. & Sharma, K. (2019). A fuzzy based techniques for energy efficient cluster head selection for wireless sensor network. *International Journal of Engineering and Advanced Technology*.

28 An optimized model for apple leaf disease detection and performance comparison with state-of-art techniques using indigenous dataset

Arshad Ahmad Yatoo[1,a] *and Amit Sharma*[2,b]

[1]Research Scholar, School of Computer Applications, Lovely Professional University, Punjab, India

[2]Associate Professor, School of Computer Applications, Lovely Professional Universiy, Punjab, India

Abstract

As plant diseases reduce crop yield, their early detection can help farmers to control them and hence prevent economic loss. The manual detection process is a complex task as the symptoms developed by these diseases have similar appearances. Due to similarity in color, shape, and texture of symptoms, farmers feel it difficult to detect and classify the diseases accurately. As deep learning has recently gained a lot of interest in image identification and classification it is being vehemently tested as a tool for automated disease detection in plant leaves. This study presents a review of research work done in the field of phytopathology aided by deep learning. Moreover, it offers an optimized model for the automated identification of leaf diseases in apple crops. The main impediment faced by these techniques is the unavailability of a huge data set capable of representing the diverse conditions in the field. This study proposes an indigenous dataset constructed by capturing apple-leaf images from the real field. It uses histogram equalization and other image data-augmentation methods to enhance the diversity of the data set to make it more suitable for disease detection and to control the issue of over-fitting. Moreover, it leverages transfer learning and fine-tuning to compare the performance of state-of-the-art techniques on the given data set consisting of more than seven thousand images in three classes and investigates the effect of hyperparameters.

Keywords: Apple leaf disease, convolutional neural networks, deep learning, automatic disease detection, fine-tuning

Introduction

Crop production is severely affected by plant diseases. They not only reduce the crop yield by 40% but also affect the shape, size, and texture of the fruits by developing ugly cosmetic effects. This results in the loss of the fruit's economic value and poses a significant threat to world food security. So, these diseases need to be detected early to apply control measures to ensure a sustained food supply to a world with a growing population. Traditionally, botanists, agriculturists or plant pathologists used to manually inspect leaves through the naked eye to reach a decision. This method of disease detection is unreliable as it often suffers from human error resulting in misuse and overuse of pesticides.

Moreover, this manual approach is unavailable as experts are mostly not available in hard-to-reach areas. Artificial intelligence (AI), especially the advancements in soft computing, has been used in several initiatives to farmers accurately detect the disorders that influence their productivity. These interventions also help them to measure the severity of disease symptoms. Any farmer with a smartphone may benefit from professional knowledge in a useful and affordable manner (Esgario et al., 2022). Like machine learning, AI is a field of deep learning (DL) (Lecun et al., 2015) which is used in many areas like health care, robotics, entertainment, computer vision etc. DL is a subfield of artificial intelligence which deploys multiple layers of data processing and classification (Deng and Yu, 2014).

Additionally, it is also being used in computer vision, natural language processing (NLP), and speech and audio processing (Deng and Yu, 2014; He et al., 2016). DL is also being leveraged in fields like business, agriculture, the automobile industry, and image classification (Mohanty et al., 2016; Arsenovic et al., 2019). Research and progress in computer vision through DL has found scope in agriculture (Mohanty et al., 2016; Sladojevic et al., 2016). Image-based disease diagnosis and categorization using DL algorithms is now possible. Different DL-based methods are now being utilized to identify plant diseases (Mohanty et al., 2016; Sladojevic et al., 2016). As per Perroy (2015) the continuously growing world population will be nearly 10 billion by 2050, so it is important to maintain a sustained food supply. The continuous and extensive research in deep learning has led to the use of convolutional neural networks for object recognition and image categorization. The advantage of using deep learning over traditional machine learning is that it does not require feature extraction. It merges feature extraction with classification and works on a huge volume of data

[a]arshadyatoo@gmail.com; [b]amit.25076@lpu.co.in

Significance of the study

Manual methods are not accurate as they involve the naked eye. However, they can be made reliable using a microscope, allied optical equipment, and technical expertise. Due to their non-availability in hard-to-reach areas, mobile phones can play an important role as the penetration of mobile phones is increasing daily. A farmer can detect the disease by photographing an affected leaf and feeding it to the DL-based classification system. The technique presented in this paper boosts performance and accuracy significantly by building an enhanced indigenous data set. The primary findings of this research are:

- It presents a real and indigenous data set of more than seven thousand images in three different classes. Images are captured by mobile phones and digital cameras with varying resolutions.
- Image processing procedures are applied to increase the coverage and diversity of the data set. This is done to handle varying lighting situations, item sizes, and background alterations expected in the physical field.
- An optimized DL model is presented by applying transfer learning and fine-tuning the hyperparameters.
- The new model is evaluated by comparing its performance with the state-of-the-art models.
- A comparison of the improved model with state-of-the-art models is also presented to demonstrate the impact of hyperparameters and to emphasize the viability of the proposed indigenous dataset.

Related Works

Esgario et al. (2022) deploys DL models to classify and categorize biotic stress in coffee leaves. It uses RestNet50 convolutional neural networks (CNN) model and achieves an accuracy of 97%. Brahimi et al. (2017) uses CNN for pest detection and classification in tomatoes. It uses a data set comprising 14,828 images affected with nine diseases. It achieved an accuracy of 99%. Thenmozhi and Srinivasulu Reddy (2019) uses different CNN models for pest classification. It uses data set containing images of different insects to train various CNN models and compares their performance. The study also investigates the role of hyperparameters like batch size, epoch, learning rate etc., to boost the model performance. Ferentinos (2018) uses an openly available data set of 87,848 leaf images of 25 different plant species. The study investigates the performance of various DL models on the given data set and finds VGG as the best model based on accuracy. Garcia and Barbedo (2019) tries to increase data variability by considering individual lesions rather than adding images to the data set. The study claims 12% higher accuracy. Fuentes et al. (2017) deploys VGG and ResNet as deep feature extractors and subsequently combines them with meta-architecture, which are faster region-based CNN. The system is then used to detect pets in tomatoes using a database built by collecting images with devices of varied resolution. Uses an ensemble model and achieves an accuracy of 96% to classify the leaves into four different classes. Amara et al. (2017) uses LeNet model for the classification and categorization of diseases in the leaves of banana plants. The authors try to demonstrate the viability of the proposed model for automating detection and classification of phytopathology related problems. Turkoglu et al. (2019) proposes a two-stage model for the purpose of detection and classification of fruit diseases. It uses some models at the first stage for feature extraction, then with the help of an added layer performs classification by taking majority voting into consideration. Johannes et al. (2017) proposes model for wheat crop. Table 28.1 lists some of the prominent studies that have used deep learning for automated disease detection

Table 28.1 Some prominent studies for automated disease detection

Ref.	*CNN model used*	*No. of layers*	*Parameters (Million)*	*Crop type*	*Data set*	*Number of classes*	*Total No. of images*	*Accuracy*
Esgario et al. (2022)	RestNet	50	25	Coffee	BRACOL (Krohling et al., 2019)	5	500	97%
Brahimi et al. (2017)	AlexNet, GoogLeNet	8,22	61,6.9	Tomato	PlantVillage (subset)	9	14,828	98%
Ferentinos, (2018)	VGG, AlexNetOWBTn	---	--	Multiple	Open	57	87,848	99.53
Garcia and Barbedo (2019)	GoogleNet	22	--	Multiple	Own data set	Different in different crops	46,409	88%
Amara et al. (2017)	LeNet	7	6	Banana	PlantVillage	3	5,757	81%
Turkoglu et al. (2019)	Hybrid Model	-	-	Apple	Own dataset	4	1,192	96%

in different crops. Yatoo and Sharma (2021) presented a fine-tuned model for the detection of leaf diseases in apple crop. The model classifies the detected disease into three classes.

Materials and Methods

Data set

Several data sets are publicly available free of cost. But the existing data sets have the following limitations.

- The existing data sets mostly belong to China, the Philippines and other countries. They also lack authenticity.
- India being the 5th largest producer of apples, a comprehensive and authentic dataset to deal with the local condition is the need of the hour.
- Available datasets lack diversity as they have mostly been built by acquiring images under controlled conditions and with a homogenous background.
- The images in the available data sets have been modified by removing the background.
- Apple leaves vary in size and shape depending on the apple variety. Existing datasets do not contain images across apple varieties.
- In some authentic datasets, the number of images per disease or class is much less. And datasets having small size in terms of the number of images do not properly fit for the training of the CNN models.

Due to the above reasons the models which are trained on the publicly available datasets do not perform well on the unseen data collected from the actual apple orchards. This is called as covariate shift, and this should not exist if a model must perform well while addressing the issues of farmers. The dataset presented in this paper contains images of healthy leaves and leaves with the symptoms of Apple-Mosaic and Alternaria. It has been built by collecting images from the apple orchards. The diversity has been added by capturing the images using different devices and under different environmental conditions e.g., sunny days, cloudy days, and rainy days. Figure 28.1 shows the methodology adopted for building the data set.

Authors have visited various apple fields in Kashmir Valley in India for image acquisition. To accommodate all possible conditions reflected by an apple orchard following caution has been exercised while recording image data:

- Images of a particular disease or class have been collected at different stages of the symptom development,
- As the shape, size and texture of a leaf vary from one variety of apple to other, leaves having symptoms of a particular disease have been collected from different types of apple trees.
- Images with various illuminations and heterogeneous backgrounds have been collected.
- Images have been captured using cameras and other handheld devices having different optical characteristics.

Cleaning and labeling of data

The images, once collected, were subjected to manual scrutiny to examine the region of interest (ROI) by the experts. On minute examination, it was found that some images had mechanical damage resembling Alternaria's symptoms. All

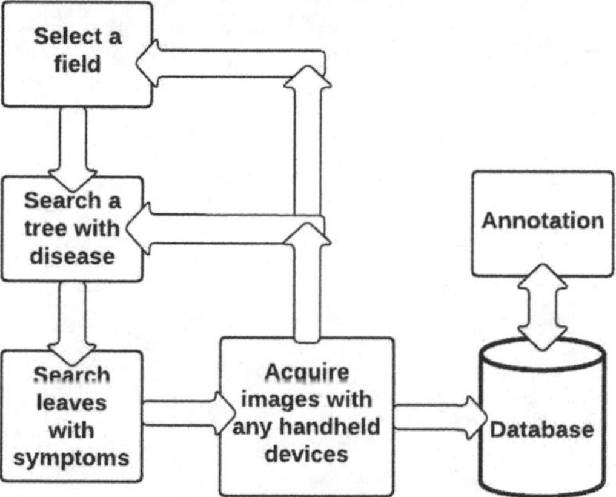

Figure 28.1 Procedure followed for building a dataset

such images were removed from the data set. The images were classified into three classes: healthy, Apple-Mosaic and Alternaria. Moreover, Image preprocessing techniques have been applied to enhance the data quality.

Data augmentation

A common problem with DL models is over-fitting. Over-fitting means when a model perfectly fits the training data but fails to generalize and performs badly on the unseen data. It often happens when sufficient training data is not available (Ying, 2019). This is because an over-fitted model finds it challenging to handle data from the testing set that may differ from the training set. In contrast to learning the features hidden in the data, over-fitted models have a tendency to remember all the data, including inherent noise in the training set. Different processing methods and techniques have been leveraged to enlarge the data set and infuse diversity in the samples to avoid such problems. Using ImageDataGenerator class of the Keras library following transformations were applied to the dataset to create new samples.

Translations: This means to move an image in a rectilinear fashion. For t_x *and* t_y values of shift along the x-axis and y-axis, we apply the following transformation matrix for translation.

$$\begin{pmatrix} 0 & 1 & t_x \\ 1 & 0 & t_y \end{pmatrix}$$

Rotation: The new coordinates (x_{new}, y_{new}) of a point (x_{old}, y_{old}) after rotation through an angle $\propto$ with respect to (x_0, y_0) are given as under:

$$x_{new} = \cos(\propto) \times (x_{old} - x_0) + \sin(\propto) \times (y_{old} - y_0) \tag{1}$$

$$y_{new} = -\sin(\propto) \times (x_{old} - x_0) + \cos(\propto) \times (y_{old} - y_0) \tag{2}$$

Shearing: It means to bring dis-formation in the image. This can be applied in x-direction, y-direction, z-direction, in any 2D or 3D).

Image flipping: The leaf images are flipped through different angles to generate new images in the data set. The operation includes horizontal and vertical flipping.

Zooming: We zoom in to make the objects in the image more visible. The technique is applied through pixel replication or the zero-order hold method. However, it is used in research to guarantee that the data set contains all feasible captures of the same scene.

Resizing: Resizing is done to make the images in the data set applicable to the individual deep learning models. For example VGG16 models accept image size of 224 × 224.

Table 28.2 Number of images in the dataset in different classes

S. No	*Sample type*	*No. of images*
1.	Healthy	2523
2.	Alternaria	2523
3.	Apple-Mosaic	2523

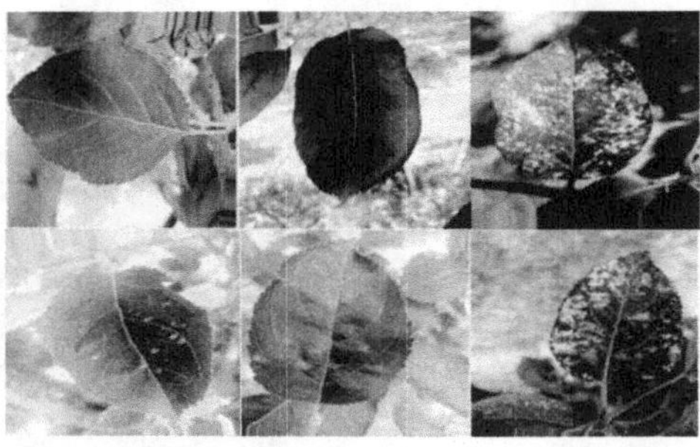

Figure 28.2 Sample images from the dataset

Besides the above pre-processing techniques, variations in brightness, contrast, color, and sharpness were also applied to widen the dataset. The number of images in the final data has been kept uniform to avoid bias.

The sample images from the data set from three different classes are given as under.

Experimental Results

Different CNN models were executed on the dataset discussed above on google co-laboratory with Tesla K80, 12GB DDR5 VRAM, IntelXeon with two cores 2.30GHz, 13 GB RAM. The following metrics were used for the evaluation and analysis of performance of the models.

$$\text{Accuracy} = \frac{\text{TP}+\text{TN}}{\text{TP}+\text{TN}+\text{FP}+\text{FN}} \times 100 \quad (3)$$

$$\text{Precision} = \frac{\text{TP}}{\text{TP}+\text{FP}} \times 100 \quad (4)$$

$$\text{Recall} = \frac{\text{TP}}{\text{TP}+\text{FN}} \times 100 \quad (5)$$

$$\text{Precision} = \frac{\text{TP}}{\text{TP}+\text{FP}} \times 100 \quad (6)$$

$$\text{F1 Score} = 2 \times \frac{\text{Recall} \times \text{Precision}}{\text{Recall}+\text{Precision}} \times 100 \quad (7)$$

Optimized model

The study initially deployed VGG16 on the given data set. VGG16 was presented by Simonyan and Zisserman (2014). It uses convolution layers *(with 3×3 filter size, a stride value of one (1))* and maxpool layer of 2×2 filter. Maxpool layers follow the convolution layers and at the end two fully connected layers are followed by a softmax layer for output.

The dataset is divided into training and testing sets using 80% for training and 20% for testing by following the study (Mohanty et al., 2016). The model yielded an accuracy of 86%. However, the model performance was improved by applying fine-tuning. In fine-tuning, VGG16 was used as a feature extractor. Its first twelve layers were freeze, and the rest were retrained on the above dataset by unfreezing them and allowing them to update their weights on new training data. Some additional layers were then added for classification purposes. The model after unfreezing is retrained on the dataset discussed above by taking 80:20 as the training to testing ratio with the hyperparameters given in Table 28.3. The model leverages the benefits of transfer learning as it has already been trained on the ImageNet database, which contains millions of images of different objects that one expects to see in a real-world scene. The transfer learning also relieves the programmers from training a CNN model from scratch.

The model yielded an accuracy of 99.21% with a loss value of 0.017. Figure 28.3 below shows model accuracy (left sub-graph) and model-loss (right sub-graph).

Subsequently, other models AlexNet, InceptionV3 and ResNet were trained and tested on the same dataset using 80:20 ratio for training and testing. The models were run with the same value for hyperparameters as mentioned in

Table 28.3 Parameter/hyper-parameter values

Parameter	*Value*
Learning rate	0.0001
Minimum learning rate	0.000001
Patience	3
Epochs	20
Batch size	32
Iterations per batch	110
Optimizer	Stochastic gradient descent
Decay	Default
Momentum	0.9

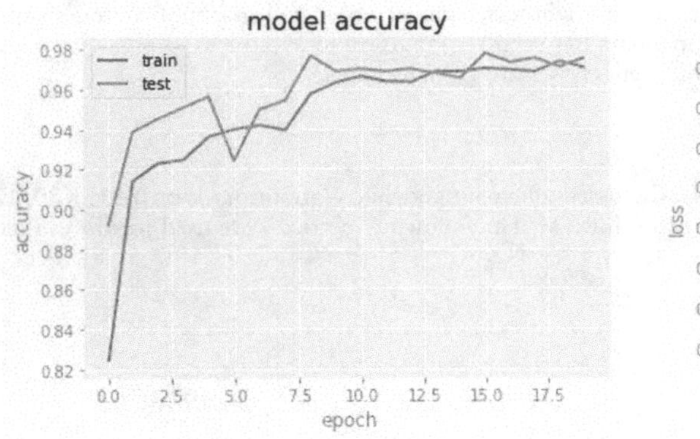

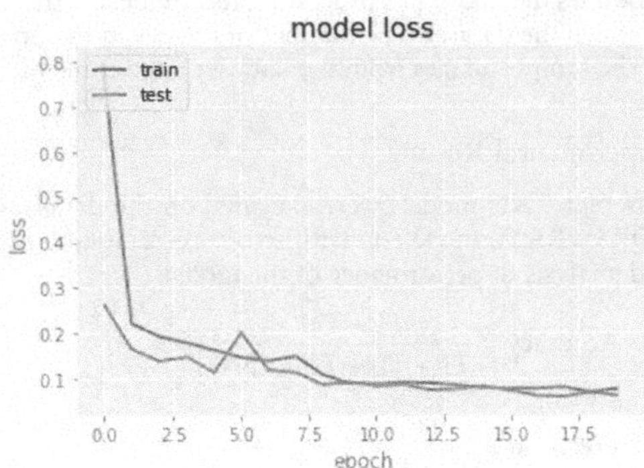

Figure 28.3 Accuracy (left sub-graph) and loss (right sub-graph) of the improved model

Table 28.4 Models and their performance

Model name	*Accuracy*	*Loss*
VGG16	86%	0.027
Improved VGG16	99.21%	0.017
AlexNet	78%	0.043
InceptionV3	86%	0.034
ResNet	65%	0.055

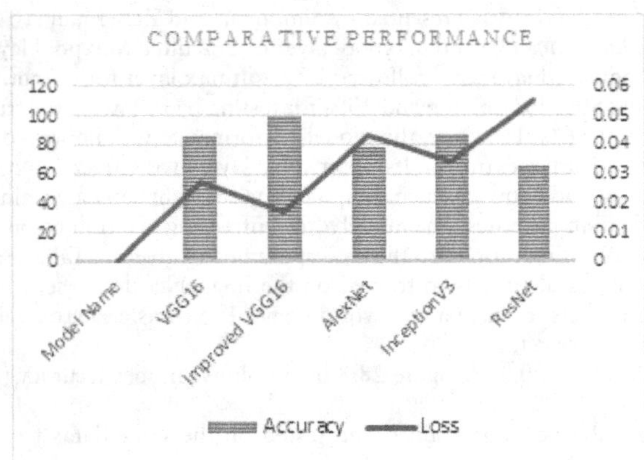

Figure 28.4 Comparative performance of the models

Table 28.3. The models yielded varied values for accuracy and loss, as given below in Table 28.4. From the contents of Table 28.4, it is clear that improved-VGG16 delivered the best performance with 99.21% accuracy compared to all the other models tested in the study.

The comparative performance of all the models tested on the dataset is plotted in the graph shown in Figure 28.4.

Conclusion

This study proposed an original and indigenous data set specific to the Indian horticulture sector, built by collecting leaf images in real-time from apple orchards. The data set presented has been widened to include all diversities and scenes possible in the real world. As the leaf images have a non-uniform and heterogeneous background, the models trained on this data set do not suffer from covariate shifts or performance degrading when tested on real-time data in the field. Moreover, the study also checks the viability of this data set by trying some state-of-the-art deep learning models on it and proposes an improved convolutional neural networks model for classifying leaf images into three classes Healthy, Alternaria and Apple-Mosaic. The study also concludes that the optimized model performs better than other models considered in experimental work.

References

Amara, J., Bouaziz, B., & Algergawy, A. (2017). A deep learning-based approach for banana leaf diseases classification. *Lecture Notes in Informatics (LNI), Proceedings - Series of the Gesellschaft Fur Informatik (GI)*, 266, 79–88.

Arsenovic, M., Karanovic, M., Sladojevic, S., Anderla, A., & Stefanovic, D. (2019). Solving current limitations of deep learning based approaches for plant disease detection. *Symmetry*, 11(7). https://doi.org/10.3390/sym11070939

Brahimi, M., Boukhalfa, K., & Moussaoui, A. (2017). Deep Learning for Tomato Diseases: Classification and Symptoms Visualization. *Applied Artificial Intelligence*, 31(4), 299–315. https://doi.org/10.1080/08839514.2017.1315516

Deng, L. & Yu, D. (2014). Deep learning: methods and applications. *Foundations and Trends® in Signal Processing*, 7(3–4), 197–387.

Esgario, J. G. M., de Castro, P. B. C., Tassis, L. M., & Krohling, R. A. (2022). An app to assist farmers in the identification of diseases and pests of coffee leaves using deep learning. *Information Processing in Agriculture*, 9(1), 38–47. https://doi.org/10.1016/j.inpa.2021.01.004

Ferentinos, K. P. (2018). Deep learning models for plant disease detection and diagnosis. *Computers and Electronics in Agriculture*, 145, 311–318. https://doi.org/10.1016/j.compag.2018.01.009

Fuentes, A., Yoon, S., Kim, S. C., & Park, D. S. (2017). A robust deep-learning-based detector for real-time tomato plant diseases and pests recognition. *Sensors*, 17(9). https://doi.org/10.3390/s17092022

Garcia, J. & Barbedo, A. (2019). ScienceDirect Plant disease identification from individual lesions and spots using deep learning. *Biosystems Engineering*, 180, 96–107. https://doi.org/10.1016/j.biosystemseng.2019.02.002

He, K., Zhang, X., Ren, S., & Sun, J. (2016). Deep residual learning for image recognition. *Proceedings of the IEEE Conference on Computer Vision and Pattern Recognition*, (pp. 770–778).

Johannes, A., Picon, A., Alvarez-Gila, A., Echazarra, J., Rodriguez-Vaamonde, S., Navajas, A. D., & Ortiz-Barredo, A. (2017). Automatic plant disease diagnosis using mobile capture devices, applied on a wheat use case. *Computers and Electronics in Agriculture*, 138, 200–209. https://doi.org/10.1016/j.compag.2017.04.013

Krohling, R. A., Esgario, J., & Ventura, J. A. (2019). BRACOL–a Brazilian Arabica Coffee Leaf images dataset to identification and quantification of coffee diseases and pests. *Mendeley Doi*, 10.

Lecun, Y., Bengio, Y., & Hinton, G. (2015). Deep learning. *Nature*, 521(7553), 436–444. https://doi.org/10.1038/nature14539

Mohanty, S. P., Hughes, D. P., & Salathé, M. (2016). Using deep learning for image-based plant disease detection. *Frontiers in Plant Science*, 7, 1419.

Perroy, R. (2015). *World Population Prospects. United Nations*, 1(6042), 587–92.

Simonyan, K. & Zisserman, A. (2014). Very deep convolutional networks for large-scale image recognition. *ArXiv Preprint ArXiv:1409.1556*.

Sladojevic, S., Arsenovic, M., Anderla, A., Culibrk, D., & Stefanovic, D. (2016). *Deep Neural Networks Based Recognition of Plant Diseases by Leaf Image Classification*.

Thenmozhi, K. & Srinivasulu Reddy, U. (2019). Crop pest classification based on deep convolutional neural network and transfer learning. *Computers and Electronics in Agriculture*, 164, 104906. https://doi.org/10.1016/J.COMPAG.2019.104906

Turkoglu, M., Hanbay, D., & Sengur, A. (2019). Multi-model LSTM-based convolutional neural networks for detection of apple diseases and pests. *Journal of Ambient Intelligence and Humanized Computing*, 0123456789. https://doi.org/10.1007/s12652-019-01591-w

Yatoo, A. A. & Sharma, A. (2021). A Novel Model for Automatic Crop Disease Detection. *2021 Sixth International Conference on Image Information Processing (ICIIP)*, 6, 310–313.

Ying, X. (2019). An Overview of Overfitting and its Solutions. *Journal of Physics: Conference Series*, 1168(2). https://doi.org/10.1088/1742-6596/1168/2/022022

29 Recent trends and challenges in malware analysis and detection-A comparative study

Chandini S B[1,a] *and Rajendra A B*[2,b]

[1]Assistant Professor, Department of Information Science and Engineering, Vidyavardhaka College of Engineering, Gokulam III stage, Mysuru, Karnataka, India

[2]Professor and Head, Department of Information Science and Engineering, Vidyavardhaka College of Engineering, Gokulam III stage, Mysuru, Karnataka, India

Abstract

In current era, Internet is the main source of information exchange which involves online banking, e-commerce, social networking, and many more where data security is the primary concerns because data is precious. But cyber threats are posing challenges like Ransomware attack which caused havoc on individual and organization and this trend continued in 2022. Sova is an Android banking trojan malware that steals personnel information which pose a threat to online banking.

Detection of malware has become more and necessary due to the enormous and rapid usage of the internet. One of the major challenges in malware detection is to find out the malicious software with obfuscated behavior. The purpose of the malware is almost the same but the syntactic structure varies due to code obfuscation which incorporates changing behavior techniques like metamorphic and polymorphic. This changing behavior poses a challenge for the detection of a new type of malware. The existing techniques which include signature and behavior are not so effective in detecting the new type of malwares, so this paper gives us an insight into the existing techniques, machine learning, and deep learning techniques to detect the malware along with the comparison of the same.

Keywords: Polymorphic, obfuscated, malware, signature based, behavior based, heuristic based, application program interface, opcode, control flow graph, machine learning, deep learning, convolutional neural networks, KNN, random forest

Introduction

Malware (malicious software) is the malformed program or code that is intended to impair computer, network, or server. Some variants of malware include Ransomware which deactivates victim's access to data until ransom is remunerated, fileless malware creates fluctuations to files that are inherent to the operating systems; spyware collects information about the victims user activity without their knowledge and send it to another entity with motive to compromise the user privacy; adware displays or serves undesirable advertisements such as pop-ups or banners; trojans masquerades itself as legitimate software and opens the backdoors to the hackers to steal victims information; worms can replicates on its own without human intervention and spreads through a network; rootkits hides inside the computer and gives hackers remote control of a victim's device; keyloggers captures and records users' keystrokes to steal sensitive information like password; bots harms the host system and connects back to its central server which acts as commander and controls all the compromised devices and this network is called botnet, polymorphic malicious software can change or morph its features or identification similarly metamorphic virus changes its code and signature pattern to evade detection, mobile malware infects mobile devices[1]. According to Fortinet, 97% of viruses employ polymorphism and 40% of the malware detected is zero day or previously unknown. It is also predicted that the cybercrime may cause damage of six trillion dollars annually by 2021. According to Crowdstrike threat report 63% of incidents reported are financially motivated threat players. According to McAfee Labs Threats-Report (November 2020) malware threats have been increased due to pandemic situation. According to Sophos, threat report working from home due to pandemic situation have present new challenge which intensifying an organization's security perimeter to thousands of home networks protected by widely variable levels of security. The recent trend solutions to the various security threats particularly to malware is to train the systems using various learning models of machine learning (ML) techniques such as supervised, unsupervised, and reinforcement learning as such systems will become more and more perfect over time.

The paper consists of the below section where in: Section 1 focus on introduction of different kinds of malwares followed by section 2 which tells about challenges faced in malware analysis, detection, and the research challenges. section 3 and 4 discuss about the existing systems and tools used in malware analysis and detection. Section 5 and 6 discuss about the contribution of ML and AI in the field of malware classification and the section 6 is the conclusion.

[a]Chandini@vvce.ac.in; [b]abrajendra@vvce.ac.in

Challenges

Malware is growing in terms of numbers which throws big challenges in analyzing and detection. Realtime malware detection is still more challenging because of the changing behavior of the unknown malwares. Some of the major challenges are as follows (Chandini et al., 2019):

- Lack of context understanding in the existing detection techniques.
- Complication in attack analysis.
- Dynamic nature of the malicious files.
- Lack of effective detection system.
- The gap between the identification of the threat and the fixing the issue will give a sufficient time to successfully initiate an attack which is known as zero-day attack for which has no signature exists.
- Some of the variants of malware which changes its behavior throws a major challenge for the traditional antivirus for detection.
- Finding dataset or appropriate malware samples for the experiment.
- Due to the IPR issues many of the organization do not share the complete information regarding the detection methodology which as a result limits the researchers from real time solution comparison (Botacin et al., 2022).
- Identification of features and attribute consideration for the classification of good ware and malware.
- Sandbox limitation and environment constraints.
- Security tools and technique requires frequent updates.

Generally, the challenges mentioned above are faced in malware analysis and detection. Existing antiviruses are not smart enough to understand the context and the intelligent systems used are not dynamic enough to identify the new threats and as a result this will lead to false positive and false negative results which will reduce the effectiveness in the detection system. Finding the relevant dataset for the research and for the scientific investigation to produce a reproducible solution to the problem is difficult because of the intellectual property rights constraints and privacy issues. There are some constraints on the testing environment like sandbox has storage limitation and some sophisticated malware will use sandbox evasion technique and evade from detection system.

Malware Analysis

Analysis of malware is a process to know and understand the function, behavior, intention, purpose, and potential impact of the malicious code on the given system. It is an investigation of the malicious code to mitigate or identification of the potential threats. There are static and dynamic means of malware analysis and the explanation is as discussed below:

In static analysis the analysis is done without the actual execution of the program. This is one of the safest means of malware analysis. Malware are examined using the attributes like portable executable (PE) which is a file format for executables which includes dynamic library references with the attributes like file name, hashes, IP address, domain name and byte codes etc.

In dynamic analysis process of analyzing or testing the malicious or the suspicious software the codes are executed in the safe or isolated environment like sandbox. Sandbox is a security tool which helps in preserving the integrity of the system and helps (eSecurity Planet) to test the suspicious code without risking the host system with features like threat analysis, memory forensics which helps in analyzing the malicious behavior. The Table 29.1 briefly discuss about the tools and techniques that are used in the malware analysis some of the tools discussed are PE studio for static analysis of any files, virus total and virus share provides malware sample and used for analysis likewise many other tools are discussed in the table.

Malware Detection

Malware detection are broadly classified as signature based, behavior based and heuristic.

Signature based

This technique uses pattern matching which uses the unique features like byte code patterns or system calls traces of the known malicious software which is stored in the databases and it is blacklisted as shown in Figure 29.1. This technique is fast, simple, and effective.

Table 29.1 Tools used in malware analysis

Malware analysis tools	*Description*
PE studio	It's a free open-source tool used for the static malware analyses. It retrieves the details of executable files and analyses the registry, process, threads, files and embedded files for suspicious incidence.
Virus total	Used to analyze malicious or the suspicious files, IP or URL for the detection of the any kind of security breaches. It includes the features like: • Intelligence to build smart detection system. • Hunting the new variants of malware • VT graph to identify the relationship on the given data and synthesize the findings in an ongoing investigation (VIRUSTOTAL).
Wireshark	It's a network protocol analyzer tool. It helps in deep inspection of the network protocol, packet capture and analysis (VIRUSTOTAL).
Virusshare	This is a website which helps research scholar by providing the malware samples to access the resource we need to take permission by sending email (VirusShare.com).
Fiddler	Tool for analyzing end to end behavior like traffic capture and inspect (Fiddler Everywhere).
REMnux	It's a free Linux toolkit which helps in reverse engineering and malware analyzing it includes free tools which analyst can use to investigate the malware behavior (REMnux).
Zeek	It's a free software platform which helps in network traffic analyzing and providing transaction logs, file content, security, performance and audit content for investigating malicious activity (Zeek)
Intezer	Helps both new and experienced analysts to quickly identify malware families and extract behavior for the detection and classification (INTEZER).
Kali Linux	It's a Linux based system used for penetration testing, digital forensics and for various security assessments (KALI).
Process hacker	Helps to analyze the behavior of processes running on the device and assist the malware analyst by displaying the activity of malware which are attempting to hide (Process Hacker).
Cuckoo sandbox	Automatic malware analysis which helps in analyzing the suspicious file and provides the report (Cuckoo Sandbox).

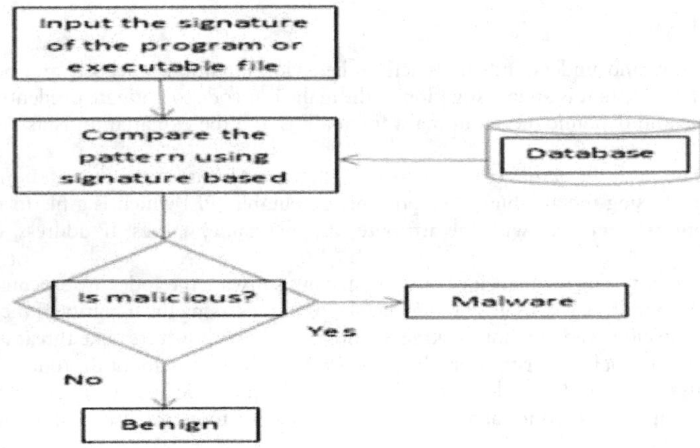

Figure 29.1 Signature based malware detection

Behavior based

This model observes the behavior of code to classify it as malicious or benign and monitors the behavior of executable file rather than just considering signature or fingerprints. The behavior pattern is extracted and is used to analyze the potential suspicious activity. Some of the behavior which is considered in these techniques are process control behavior, network behavior, register behavior, and file operation behavior (Zhao et al., 2019) as shown in the Figure 29.2. This

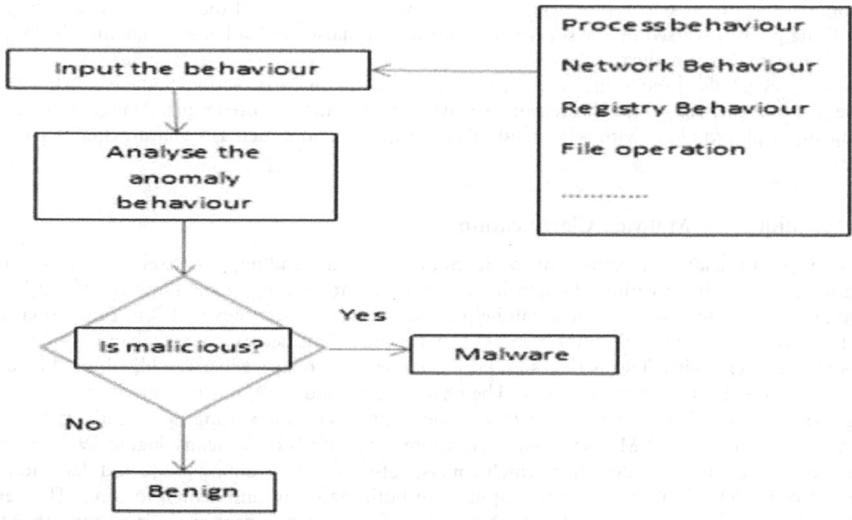

Figure 29.2 Behavior based malware detection

will analyze the potential behavior for abnormal activities like altering boot record, disabling security control, installing rootkits, requesting for restart, modifying files, deleting files, encrypting files, altering user account, connecting to black-listed websites, opening backdoors and downloading malicious software (Cyberdefensemagazine). Behavior-based identify whether a program is malicious or not by observing and analyzing the behavior by what it does rather than what it says. Protects against the new unknown malware and helps in collecting detailed information about the malware which helps further to train the system for better detection. Some of the limitations are that it is not as fast as signature-based and requires more hardware resources.

Heuristic based

Heuristic detection is the hybrid technology which adopts both static and dynamic methods to detect the malware. This will identify the vulnerability in the system using the several decision rules or evaluation methodologies (Forcepoint). The threats are identified effectively and it uses the different scanning techniques like file analysis, file emulation and pattern matching.

- File analysis used for detailed analysis of the file and obtain its purpose (Wikipedia).
- File emulation is used for dynamic scanning or sandboxing which is used to test the behavior of the code in the controlled environment (Wikipedia).
- Signature-based detection used to identify the known treats.

Some of the features used in the heuristic methods to classify the benign and malware code are:

API call are the application program interface which is used to create the interface between internal and external code. The API call sequence can be extracted and used to analyze the dynamic behavior of the code.

Opcode is also called as instruction code or an part of machine language which specify the operation to be performed by the machine. Opcode mining can be used to detect the obfuscated malware (Santos, et al., 2010). Opcode sequence and their frequency of appearance are calculated for malware and benign and used for the detection of malware using similarity check.

N-Gram is a technique which use substring that is a part of a string of a larger string with a dimension of N. The words can be segmented into several grams lets take an example string for 2-grams “malware”:”ma”,”lw”,”ar”, ”re” etc. N –grams can be used to build classifier based on artificial neural network (ANN) or K-nearest-neighbor (KNN) classifier for malware detection.

CFG is called as control flow grams which represent the graphical representation of the program code using graph notation and shows all the paths traversed by the source code. Graph similarity and subgraph matching is done using graph isomorphism property to detect malwares.

Many other hybrid features are also used in the heuristic techniques for malware detection. Some of the limitation of this techniques is false positives rate is high for this reason, heuristic implements are often typically used as value added services. They are typically deployed along with other methods of virus detection, such as signature analysis and other proactive technologies.

Machine Learning Techniques for Malware Classification

Machine learning is a part of artificial intelligence that can learn automatically and improve from the previous experience without programming explicitly or without human intervention (great learning). Collaboration of the ML technique with the existing malware detection techniques can help in improving the accuracy and detect unknown or new malware effectively. The model is build based on the sample data set which is called as training data in order to make decision without programming explicitly. This is the essential prerequisite in today's cyber world, where thousands of new malware are reported every day (Imran et al., 2016). The basic idea behind the ML is to train the system based on the historical or the previous data and classify/categorize/cluster new data accordingly using suitable algorithm like linear regression, support vector machines (SVM), Naïve Bayes, random forest, kNN or K-means. Figure 29.3 depicts how ML techniques can be used in the malware detection which consists of two-phase training phase and detection phase. In training phase predictive model is built based on the input from both malicious and benign features. The very first step is the feature extraction which can be achieved using N-grams, principle component analysis or any other feature extraction algorithm. The expectation from the feature extraction algorithm is to select the attribute or features which are considered to be useful and non-redundant.

The features selected should be contributing for the better result prediction hence the selected features from the dataset needs to be relevant and appropriate. Further prepare the training model and build the predictive model. The next phase is the detection phase where it takes the unknown executable and classifies the code as malicious and benign. The

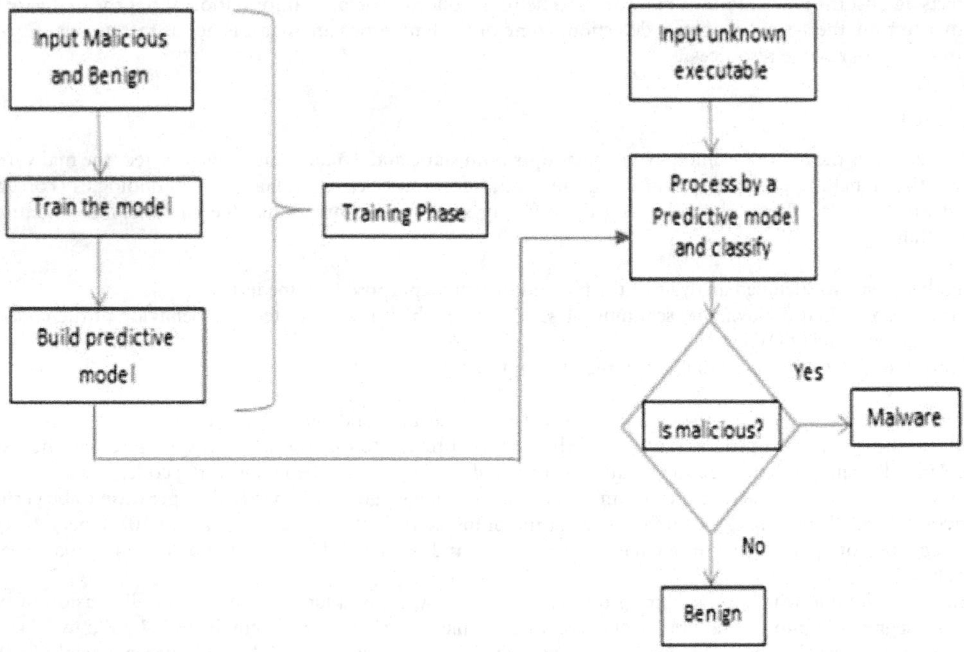

Figure 29.3 Machine learning model for detection of malware

classification can be done using the classifier algorithms like KNN, Naïve Bayes and J48 decision tree and Random. The malware is classified as malware and benign.

Deep Learning for Malware Classification

Traditional machine learning techniques faces a challenge in extraction of meaningful features to improve effectiveness in detection. Rare or occasional attacks are designed for high profile organization and convention system will have less evidence to prove the malicious behavior. In this kind of cases deep learning-based models are more efficient in identifying the malicious behavior and classifying (Zhong and Gu, 2019). These deep learning models mainly use three types of neural network architectures: Convolutional neural network (CNN) which will work based on translation invariance characteristics it is inspired by biological process it consist of three layers input, hidden and output layer to differentiate one from other and this is how it classify, recurrent neural network (RNN) works based on feedforward neural network which uses internal state to process input and Fully connected feedforward neural network (FC) this technique is different from recurrent neural network the information moves in only one direction and they do not form loops every input neuron is connected to every neuron in next layer which helps in better segmentation (Xiao et al., 2019). Some of the papers were studied to understand the existing models of machine learning and its contribution towards malware classification and the same is discussed in the Table 29.2.

Table 29.2 Literature survey on malware detection machine learning

Author	*Methodology*	*Advantage*	*Limitation*	*Performance measure*
Zhao et al. (2019)	The feature extraction method of hybrid gram for malicious behavior based on machine learning.	The effectiveness malicious behavior analysis is achieved using H-gram when compared with the fixed-length n-gram in all four performance indexes of the classification algorithm such as AdboostM1, Bagging, ID3 and Random Forest.	Tracking all the API's and identifying all the behavioral characteristics of the sample in the actual process is challenging because of the enormous API functions.	Accuracy, AUC, FPR and TPR.
Naeem et al. (2020)	Deep learning models and hybrid image visualization.	In depth analysis of malware is done using color image visualization and deep convolution neural network. and this technology is used to design the architecture to detect malicious on the Industrial Internet of Things.	Computation power and resources are the shortcomings of conventional malware detection techniques and they are not suitable for IIOT devices. Hence in future combined blockchain and machine learning memory less are recommended to develop.	Precision, accuracy and f-measure.
Nisa et al. (2020)	Deep learning models such as deep convolution neural network and segmentation-based fractal texture analysis which forms hybrid technic for malware classification.	Here in this work technic called AlexNet and Inception-V3 which is deep neural network is used for feature extraction which is segmentation-based fractal texture analysis of images and later the classification is done using the SVM, KNN and DT and methodology achieve a high level of accuracy.	Deep learning model requires large data set to train the model which reduces the efficiency of the system by consuming lot of time and computational resources.	Accuracy, recall, AUC and ER.
Zhang et al. (2021)	Android malware detection using natural language processing and hybrid sequence-based technology.	Android malwares are effectively detected using features like opcode and system call along with Natural language processing. Prediction is done using deep learning models such as CNN and LSTM.	But, the analysis of native compiled libraries and more rich dynamic features of the sandbox cannot use in real devices.	Accuracy, precision, recall and F1-score.
Rahul et al. (20220)	Analysis of machine learning models for malware detection.	Analysis of malware is done using efficient machine learning models.	But, the method required high computational time and also failed to detect new variants.	Accuracy, precision, recall and f1- measure.
Raff et al. (2018)	Raw bytes sequence are analyzed using neural networks	In this approach it address batch normalization which has linear complexity dependence on the sequence length.	Due to the extreme memory use of the architecture, this could not be performed on a single GPU.	Accuracy, recall, AUC and ER.

Conclusion

In this paper we have discussed about the malware analysis and detection issues and research challenges and also covers the existing malware detection techniques and discuss about the pros and cons of the same. The existing techniques such as signature, behavior and heuristic are not so effective in the detection of new unknown malware. So we discussed about the smarter and intelligent based system like data mining, machine learning techniques and learning deep learning techniques which comes under the domain of artificial intelligence for the more effective classification. In the future work will be working on effective detection of malware by considering all the literature survey related to malware classification.

References

Botacin, M., Ceschin, F., Sun, R., & Oliveira, D. (2022). Challenges and pitfalls in malware research. *Computers & Security*, 122.

Chandini, S. B., Rajendra, A. B., Nitin Srivatsa, G. (2019), A research on different types of malware and detection techniques. *International Journal of Recent Technology and Engineering*, 8(2), 8, 1792–1797.

CrowdStrike. https://www.crowdstrike.com

Cuckoosandbox. https://cuckoosandbox.org/

Cyberdefensemagazine. https://www.cyberdefensemagazine.com/advanced-malware-detection/

eSecurity Planet. https://www.esecurityplanet.com/endpoint/sandboxing-advanced-malware-analysis/

Fiddler Everywhere. https://www.telerik.com/fiddler/fiddler-everywhere

Forcepoint. https://www.forcepoint.com/cyber-edu/heuristic-analysis

Fortinet. https://www.fortinet.com/content/dam/fortinet/assets/white-papers/wp-covering-the-bases-for-advacned-threat-intelligence.pdf

Great Learning. https://expertsystem.com/machine-learning-definition/

Imran, M., Afzal, M. T., & Qadir, M. A. (2016). A comparison of feature extraction techniques for malware analysis. *Turkish Journal of Electrical Engineering & Computer Sciences*, 25(2), 1173–1183. doi:10.3906/elk-1601-189

Infosecurity-magazine. https://www.infosecurity-magazine.com/opinions/malware-detection-signatures

INTEZER. https://www.intezer.com

KALI. https://www.kali.org/

McAfee Labs Threats-Report (November 2020). https://www.mcafee.com/enterprise/en-us/assets/reports/rp-quarterly-threats-nov-2020.pdf

Naeem, H., Ullah, F., Naeem, M. R., Khalid, S., Vasan, D., Jabbar, S., & Saeed, S. (2020). Malware detection in industrial internet of things based on hybrid image visualization and deep learning model. *Ad Hoc Networks*, 105, 102154.

Nisa, M., Shah, J. H., Kanwal, S., Raza, M., Khan, M. A., Damaševičius, R., & Blažauskas, T. (2020). Hybrid malware classification method using segmentation-based fractal texture analysis and deep convolution neural network features. *Applied Sciences*, 10(14), 4966.

Process Hacker. https://processhacker.sourceforge.io/

Raff, E., Barker, J., Sylvester, J., Brandon, J., Catanzaro, B., & Nicholas, C. K. (2018). Malware detection by eating a whole EXE, AAAI Conference on Artificial Intelligence. https://doi.org/10.48550/arXiv.1710.09435

Rahul, Kedia, P., Sarangi, S., & Monika (2020). Analysis of machine learning models for malware detection. *Journal of Discrete Mathematical Sciences and Cryptography*, 23(2), 395–407.

REMnux: A Linux toolkit for malware analysis. https://remnux.org/

Santos, I., Brezo, F., Nieves, J., Penya, Y. K., Sanz, B., Laorden, C., & Bringas, P. G. (2010). Idea: Opcode-sequence-based malware detection. *Engineering Secure Software and Systems Second International Symposium*. doi:10.1007/978-3-642-11747-3_3

SOPHOS. https://www.sophos.com/en-us/medialibrary/pdfs/technical-papers/sophos-2021-threat-report.pdf

VirusShare.com. https://virusshare.com

Virustotal. https://www.virustotal.com

Wikipedia. https://en.wikipedia.org/wiki/Heuristic_analysis

Wireshark. https://www.wireshark.org/

Xiao, F., Lin, Z., Sun, Y. & Ma, Y. (2019). Malware detection based on deep learning of behaviour graphs, *Mathematical Problems in Engineering*.

Zahra Bazrafshan; Hashem Hashemi; Seyed Mehdi Hazrati Fard; Ali Hamzeh, (2013). A survey on heuristic malware detection techniques, *IEEE Conference on Information and Knowledge Technology*, pp 113–120.

Zeek. https://zeek.org/

Zhang, N., Xue, J., Ma, Y., Zhang, R., Liang, T., & Tan, Y. A. (2021). Hybrid sequence-based Android malware detection using natural language processing. *International Journal of Intelligent Systems*, 36(10), 5770–5784.

Zhao, Y., Bo, B., Feng, Y., Xu, C., & Yu, B. (2019). A feature extraction method of hybrid gram for malicious behavior based on machine learning. *Security and Communication Networks*.

Zhong, W. & Gu, F. (2019). A multi-level deep learning system for malware detection. *Expert Systems with Applications*, 133(8).

30 Robust cloud-based Internet of Things authenticated key agreement scheme for wireless sensor networks

Sartaj Singh[1,a], *Amar Singh*[2,b], *Ashok Sharma*[3,c], *Geeta Sharma*[4,d], *and Sandeep Kaur*[5,e]

[1]Research Scholar, School of Computer Applications, Lovely Professional University, Punjab, India

[2]Professor, School of Computer Applications, Lovely Professional University, Punjab, India

[3]Professor, Department of Computer Science and & IT, University of Jammu, India

[4]Assistant Professor, School of Computer Applications, Lovely Professional University, Punjab, India

[5]Assistant Professor, Dept of Computer Science, Guru Nanak College for Women, Banga, India

Abstract

With the recent advancements in mobile and wireless technology, cloud computing and Internet of Things (IoT) paradigms have transformed way of exchange of information using diverse technologies making intelligent detection and management a reality. Wireless sensor networks (WSNs) for IoT have numerous applications such as smart healthcare, military, agriculture. The IoT devices deployed in these applications generates enormous amount of data. This data is sent to cloud for later processing and use. Thus, to guarantee secure access of data in WSNs, user authentication is of utmost importance. Authenticating users in WSNs is still an open challenge. This paper proposes an efficient and robust user authentication and key agreement scheme for WSNs in distributed cloud-IoT applications. The comparative analysis with related schemes confirms that our scheme is secure for WSNs.

Keywords: Authentication, cloud, Internet of Things, security, wireless sensor networks

Introduction

The Internet of Things (IoT) aid things (objects) to exchange data using the Internet, radio frequency identification technology (RFID), microelectronics, embedded technologies, and sensors. Cloud and IoT has emerged as powerful paradigms to envision intelligent identification and management. Wireless sensor network (WSN) dispenses data to the IoT applications. WSN comprises of several low-cost and low-power sensors. These sensors communicate with each other over wireless means. They are employed to monitor the environmental conditions of a specific area via the information collected from sensor nodes. WSNs are widely used in industries, such as healthcare monitoring (Shah et al., 2013), intelligent transportation (Xiong et al., 2012), and environmental monitoring (Mois et al., 2016). The architecture of WSNs consists of three participants, users, gateway node and sensor nodes. Sensor nodes are deployed in the specific region to collect and sense data. This sensed data is sent to the gateway node using open networks. This data is stored on the cloud for later use. This data is required by industries, companies, and every sector of the economy.

The proposed framework is shown in Figure 30.1. In this paper, the proposed framework of WSN is based on the concept of the IoT in which all sensor nodes and the gateway node are interconnected through the Internet. WSNs cover a wide range of application fields and thus, plays a vital role in the IoT. In such an environment, a user can access any sensor node that is part of a WSN through a gateway node. As the communication takes place in unreliable public environments, intruders can access and manipulate the data easily. Thus, user authentication is one of the crucial design factors in such environments. Additionally, sensor nodes have limitations of computational power, battery power and communication capability. The security mechanism employed to authenticate remote user must be computationally lightweight.

Several user authentication mechanisms have been proposed in the literature (Yeh et al., 2011; Das et al., 2012; Xue et al., 2013; Xu and Wang, 2013; Turkanovic and Hölbl, 2013; Li et al., 2013; Turkanovic et al., 2014; Farash et al., 2016; Amin and Biswas, 2016; Sharma and Kalra, 2020; Dolev and Yao, 1983). Yeh et al. (2011) presented an elliptic curve cryptography (ECC) based user authentication protocol. However, the scheme has memory overhead. Das et al. (2012) and Xue et al. (2013) suggested password based and temporal credential based authentication schemes respectively for WSNs. Later, in two different papers Xu and Wang (2013) and Turkanovic and Hölbl (2013) found Xue et al. (2013) failed to resist forgery attacks. They proposed improvised schemes. The claims made by Xue et al. (2013) were nullified by Li et al. (2013). They also found security flaws in the scheme. Turkanovic et al. (2014) suggested authentication for

[a]sartaj.singh@lpu.co.in; [b]amar.23318@lpu.co.in; [c]drashoksharma@hotmail.com; [d]geeta.26875@lpu.co.in; [e]sandeep_nagra@yahoo.com

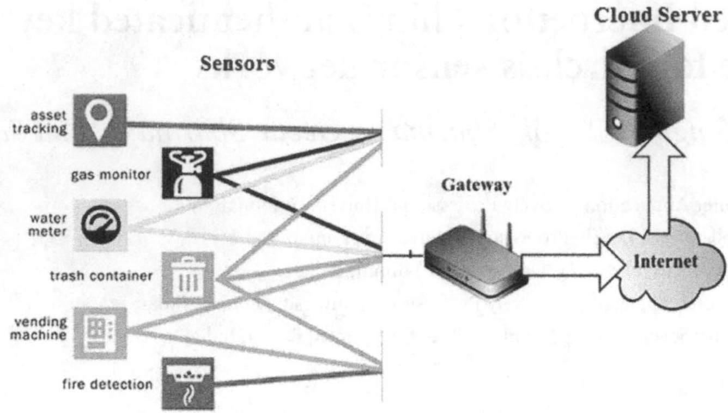

Figure 30.1 Proposed framework of WSNs in cloud-IoT applications

Table 30.1 Notations

Symbol	*Meaning*
U_t	t^{th} user
SN	Sensor node
GW	Gateway node
ID_t	Unique identity of user U_t
X	Secret parameter known only to SN
PS_t	Strong user password
SM	Smart card
R_1, R_2, R_3	Secret random nonces
SK_{SN}	Calculated session key by SN
SKu	Calculated session key by U_t
H(·)	Hash operation
||	Concatenation operation
⊕	XOR operation

ad-hoc WSNs. They claimed their scheme has low computation cost and attack resistant. But Farash et al. (2016) and Amin and Biswas (2016) found scheme insecure to impersonation and forgery attacks (Turkanovic et al., 2014).

Organization of the paper

The paper is organised as follows. Section 1 explains the need for authentication in cloud-IoT environment and related work in the field of WSNs. Section 2 proposes a secure user authentication scheme. Section 3 shows the security analysis of the proposed scheme. Section 4 presents the results obtained on implementing the scheme using AVISPA. Section 5 concludes the paper.

Proposed Key Agreement Scheme

This section proposes a secure remote user authentication scheme for WSNs in IoT deployment. Table 30.1 shows notations.

Pre-deployment phase

This phase facilitates gate way nodes and sensor nodes to establish secure connections.

Step 1: The GW submits its identity ID_{GW}, pseudo-identity MID_{GW} to SN through secure channel.

Step 2: Further, SN calculates $C_1 = H(MID_{GW} \| ID_{SN} \| X)$, $C_2 = H(ID_{GW} \| X)$ stores ID_{GW} and transmits $\{C_1, C_2, ID_{SN}\}$ to GW.

Step 3: GW stores $\{C_1, C_2, ID_{SW}, ID_{GW}, ID_{SN}\}$.

Registration phase

Step 1: Ut selects his/her identity ID_t, PS_t. Ut generates random nonce $R_1$and computes masked identity $MID_t = H(R_1 \| ID_t)$, $MPS_t = H(R_1 \| PS_t)$ and transmits $\{ID_t, MID_t\}$ to SN.

Step 2: SN verifies submitted ID_t. If ID_t is invalid, the process will be terminated. Else, SN computes $A_1 = H(MID_t \| ID_{SN} \| X)$, $A_2 = H(ID_t \| X)$, stores ID_t in its database and communicates $\{M_1, M_2, ID_{SN}\}$ to U_t using secure channel.

Step 3: U_t calculates $B_1 = A_1 \oplus MPS_t$, $B_2 = A_2 \oplus H(ID_t \| MPS_t)$, $B_3 = R_1 \oplus H(ID_t \| PS_t)$ and stores $\{B_1, B_2, B_3, MID_t, ID_{SN}\}$ in the smart card.

Authentication phase

Step 1: When U_t wish to access the services, U_t inserts smart card and enters $\{ID_t, PS_t\}$. U_t generates a random R_2 and fresh pseudo-identity MID_{tnew}, calculates $D_t = B_3 \oplus H(ID_t \| PS_t)$, $MPS_t = H(PS_t \| D_t)$, $A_1 = B_1 \oplus MPS_t$, $A_2 = B_2 \oplus H(ID_t \| MPS_t)$, $E_1 = A_1 \oplus R_2$, $E_2 = H(R_2 \| MID_t \| ID_{SN}) \oplus ID_t$, $E_3 = A_2 \oplus H(ID_t \| MPS_t) \oplus MID_{tnew} \oplus H(R_2 \| ID_t)$, $E_4 = H(ID_t \| MID_t \| MID_{tnew} \| R_2 \| E_3)$. U_t transmits $\{MID_t, E_1, E_2, E_3, E_4\}$ to SN.

Step 2: GW chooses fresh MID_{GWnew}, random nonce R_3, calculates $E_5 = C_1 \oplus R_3$, $E_6 = H(R_3 \| ID_{GW} \| ID_{SN}) \oplus ID_{GW}$, $E_7 = C_2 \oplus MID_{GWnew} \oplus H(R_3 \| ID_{GW})$, $E_8 = H(MID_{GW} \| ID_{GW} \| MID_{GWnew} \| R_3 \| E_7)$. GW transmits $\{MID_t, E_1, E_2, E_3, E_4, ID_{GW}, E_6, E_7, E_8\}$ to SN.

Step 3: SN calculates $R_2 = E_1 \oplus H(MID_t \| ID_{SN} \| X)$, $ID_t = E_2 \oplus H(R_2 \| MID_t \| ID_{SN})$, $MID_{tnew} = E_3 \oplus H(Id_t \| X) \oplus H(R_2 \| ID_t)$. It checks ID_t and $E_4 = H(ID_t \| MID_t \| MID_{tnew} \| R_2 \| E_3)$?. If true, $R_3 = E_5 \oplus H(ID_{GW} \| ID_{SN} \| X)$, $ID_{GW} = E_6 \oplus H(R_3 \| ID_{GW} \| ID_{SN})$, $ID_{GWnew} = E_7 \oplus H(ID_{GW} \| X) \oplus H(R_3 \| ID_{GW})$, verifies ID_{GW} and $E_8 = H(ID_{GW} \| ID_{GW} \| ID_{GWnew} \| R_3 \| E_7)$?. If it fails, session is terminated.

Step 4: Else, SN generates random R_{SN} to calculate $SK_{SN} = H(R_2 \oplus R_3 \oplus R_{SN})$, $E_9 = H(ID_{GWnew} \| ID_{SN} \| X) \oplus H(R_3 \| ID_{GWnew})$, $E_{10} = H(ID_{GWnew} \| R_3 \| ID_{GW}) \oplus H(R_2 \| R_{SN})$, $E_{11} = H(SK_{SN} \| E_9 \| E_{10} \| H(ID_{GW} \| X))$, $E_{12} = H(MID_{tnew} \| ID_{SN} \| X) \oplus H(R_2 \| MID_{tnew})$, $E_{13} = H(MID_{tnew} \| R_2 \| MID_t) \oplus (R_3 \oplus R_{SN})$, $E_{14} = H(SK_{SN} \| E_{12} \| E_{13} \| H(ID_t \| X))$ and transmits $\{E_9, E_{10}, E_{11}, E_{12}, E_{13}, E_{14}\}$ to GW.

Step 5: GW calculates $(R_2 \oplus R_{SN}) = E_{10} \oplus H(ID_{GWnew} \| R_3 \| ID_{GW})$, $SK_{GW} = H(R_3 \oplus R_2 \oplus R_{SN})$, verifies $E_{11} = H(SK_{GW} \| E_9 \| E_{10} \| C_2)$?. If true, GW computes $C_{1new} = E_9 \oplus H(R_3 \| ID_{GWnew})$ and replaces C_1 with C_{1new} and ID_{GW}withID_{GWnew}. Further, sends $\{E_{12}, E_{13}, E_{14}\}$ to U_t.

Step 6: SM calculates $(R_3 \oplus R_{SN}) = E_{13} \oplus H(MID_{tnew} \| R_2 \| MID_t)$, $SK_U = H(R_2 \oplus R_{GW} \oplus R_{SN})$. It validates $E_{14} = H(SK_U \| E_{12} \| E_{13} \| A_2)$?. If true, SM proceeds $B_{1new} = E_{12} \oplus H(R_2 \| MID_{tnew}) \oplus MPS_t$. It replaces B_1 with B_{1new} and MID_t with MID_{tnew}.

Table 30.2 Security feature comparison

Security Features	*Yeh et al. [4]*	*Das et al. [5]*	*Xue et al. [6]*	*Turkanovic and Hölbl [81*	*Farash et al. [11]*	*Proposed scheme*
Provides mutual authentication	Yes	No	Yes	Yes	Yes	Yes
Resists malicious user attack	No	No	No	No	No	Yes
Provides forward secrecy	No	Yes	Yes	Yes	Yes	Yes
Resists user anonymity	No	No	No	No	Yes	Yes
Resists replay attack	Yes	No	No	Yes	Yes	Yes
Resists online password guessing attack	No	No	No	No	No	Yes
Resists insider attack	No	No	No	No	Yes	Yes
Provides smart card revocation	No	No	No	No	Yes	Yes
Resists hidden server attack	No	No	No	No	No	Yes

```
% OFMC
% Version of 2006/02/13
SUMMARY
SAFE
DETAILS
BOUNDED_NUMBER_OF_SESSIONS
PROTOCOL
/home/avispa/web-interface-computation/
./tempdir/workfilevOpMGm.if
GOAL
as_specified
BACKEND
OFMC
COMMENTS
STATISTICS
parseTime: 0.00s
searchTime: 0.31s
visitedNodes: 179 nodes
depth: 11 plies
```

Figure 30.2 Simulation results on OFMC

Security Analysis

The security comparison with the related schemes shows that our scheme achieves all security attributes and is resistant to attacks. Table 30.2 shows the comparison of security features.

Experimental Results

The proposed scheme has been simulated using automated validation of internet security protocols and applications (AVISPA) (Dolev and Yao, 1983). It is extensively employed to verify security of the security protocols. AVISPA employs High Level Protocol Specification Language to validate resilience of protocols. For our proposed scheme, it has been simulated on on-the-fly model-checker (OFMC). The results obtained are shown in Figure 30.2.

Conclusion

The advent of wireless sensor networks has led the growth of numerous applications using which users can access data anywhere. Consequently, authenticating user is of paramount significance. This paper proposes a robust user authentication scheme. The security analysis and simulation of the scheme is AVISPA confirms its resilience to attacks. In future, we will simulate our scheme for the other back-ends of the AVISPA.

References

Amin, R. & Biswas, G. P. (2016). A secure light weight scheme for user authentication and key agreement in multi-gateway based wireless sensor networks. *Ad Hoc Networks*, 36, 58–80.

Das, A. K., Sharma, P., Chatterjee, S., & Sing, J. K. (2012). A dynamic password-based user authentication scheme for hierarchical wireless sensor networks. *Journal of Network and Computer Applications*, 35(5), 1646–1656.

Dolev, D. & Yao, A. (1983). On the security of public key protocols. *IEEE Transactions on information theory*, 29(2), 198–208.

Farash, M. S., Turkanović, M., Kumari, S., & Hölbl, M. (2016). An efficient user authentication and key agreement scheme for heterogeneous wireless sensor network tailored for the Internet of Things environment. *Ad Hoc Networks*, 36, 152–176.

Li, C. T., Weng, C. Y., & Lee, C. C. (2013). An advanced temporal credential-based security scheme with mutual authentication and key agreement for wireless sensor networks. *Sensors*, 13(8), 9589–9603.

Mois, G., Sanislav, T., & Folea, S. C. (2016). A cyber-physical system for environmental monitoring. *IEEE transactions on instrumentation and measurement*, 65(6), 1463–1471.

Shah, S. H., Iqbal, A., & Shah, S. S. A. (2013). Remote health monitoring through an integration of wireless sensor networks, mobile phones & cloud computing technologies. *2013 IEEE Global Humanitarian Technology Conference (GHTC)*, pp. 401–405.

Sharma, G. & Kalra, S. (2020). Advanced lightweight multi-factor remote user authentication scheme for cloud-IoT applications. *Journal of Ambient Intelligence and Humanized Computing*, 11(4), 1771–1794.

Turkanović, M., Brumen, B., & Hölbl, M. (2014). A novel user authentication and key agreement scheme for heterogeneous ad hoc wireless sensor networks, based on the Internet of Things notion. *Ad Hoc Networks*, 20, 96–112.

Turkanovic, M., & Holbl, M. (2013). An improved dynamic password-based user authentication scheme for hierarchical wireless sensor networks. *Elektronika Ir Elektrotechnika*, 19(6), 109–116.

Xiong, Z., Sheng, H., Rong, W., & Cooper, D. E. (2012). Intelligent transportation systems for smart cities: a progress review. *Science China Information Sciences*, 55(12), 2908–2914.

Xue, K., Ma, C., Hong, P., & Ding, R. (2013). A temporal-credential-based mutual authentication and key agreement scheme for wireless sensor networks. *Journal of Network and Computer Applications*, 36(1), 316–323.

Xu, S. & Wang, X. (2013). A new user authentication scheme for hierarchical wireless sensor networks. *Int. Rev. Comput. Softw*, 8(6), 197–203.

Yeh, H. L., Chen, T. H., Liu, P. C., Kim, T. H., & Wei, H. W. (2011). A secured authentication protocol for wireless sensor networks using elliptic curves cryptography. *Sensors*, 11(5), 4767–4779.

31 Relevance of cloud computing in health industry- A critical study

Reeti Jaswal[a]

Assistant Professor, University of Computing, Chandigarh University, Chandigarh, India

Abstract

In the existing time, cloud computing is working as a very collaborative tactic that can be useful in almost all domains either it is public or private. Apart from playing a vital role in public and private domains cloud also plays a significant part in healthcare sector by storing large amount of patients' data, as patients' lives totally depend on their past records. In healthcare sector, very large amount volume of data is produced on the daily basis. The data are not just only vital for making decisions but also necessary for offering the best facilities to the patients. Wholly these features were not achievable by using traditional conducts. Cloud computing is the most feasible way to manage vast amount of data. Cloud computing and healthcare organization being working together for providing appropriate monitoring and collecting patient health record. The main aim of writing this paper is to discusses the cloud technology in healthcare sector. Also, it discusses the main key advantages, glitches, and applications of cloud computing in healthcare sector.

Keywords: Blockchain, cloud computing, electronic health record, IoT, personal health record

Introduction

Cloud computing is one of the greatest latest innovative technologies in all domains. The demand of cloud computing is quickly growing in day by day. Healthcare sector and non-IT organizations also take full benefit of cloud computing. Adopting cloud computing in healthcare sector reduces the overhead of tasks like upgrading records. In daily basis large number of data collected and processed in healthcare organizations. These data are vital and very necessary for delivering the appropriate treatment to patients and for making better decisions. Still, most of the healthcare organizations depend on paper healthcare records, and due to this there is limiting cooperation and synchronization between patients and doctors. By using cloud technology, the medical sector can develop a proper plan for monitoring patients remotely.

Cloud-based service offers provision and support the health infrastructure by improving the availability and interoperability of data (Javaid et al., 2022). Cloud-based healthcare is the process of integrating cloud computing technology into healthcare services for the purpose of data sharing, reduced costs, increase patient data availability improved secrecy, and enabling improved patient care through teamwork and interoperability, modified treatment, health apps, and many more profits. Healthcare sector covers very challenging procedures of the diagnosis, treatment, and preclusion of disease, and also other physical and psychological weakening in humans. The medical organization is reckless-rising portion of the economy of almost all countries in recent civilization so the appropriate gathering, administration and use of medical data play a serious part for the purpose of recognizing advanced ideas and detecting medical difficulties (Jensen et al., 2012), allocating resources to treat patients. So, to improve and enhance the quality of healthcare facilities cloud computing are broadly working. To solve the challenges like "big data" cloud is the best solution (Murdoch and Detsky, 2013). The key features regarding cloud computing are to deliver limitless storage facility and eases the method of sharing patients' records among different medical sector. It also offers an active medical facility and management technique and decreasing massive functioning costs.

Healthcare Sector before Cloud Computing

A health care organization service would require devoting significantly on the infrastructure and maintenance to handle all the inside tasks or jobs related to storage, data processing, transfer, and collaboration. Main limitations of traditionally health care system is, it is less user-friendly paralleled to cloud computing because at that time data cannot be retrieved from anywhere and user need to save that data on external storage medium if he wants to access it. Also, it provides a lesser amount of storage as compared to cloud computing. In medical sector, huge amount of data and records are utilized on daily basis. The main challenges face by healthcare companies are high cost, accessibility, and security of data.

[a]reeti.e13367@cumail.in, reetijaswal2204@gmail.com

Healthcare Sector after Cloud Computing

All the things have reformed significantly with the initiation of cloud computing, although much progress is even now taking place in health care organizations. This results in growth of services, facilities and substructures and has also initiated novel ways in medical research. Cloud computing in medical sector has brought forth revolution for the industry while altering it for good- from creation, storage and sharing of medical data in cost effective manner. There are so many explanations for keen health or good health that can be 'the medical and public health exercise maintained by smart mobile devices' (Aziz, 2015), or 'the intellectual health management and medical service using information technology (IT)' (Fabian, 2015), and another can be 'the best usage of advance technologies such as robots, smart cards, sensors, and tele-health systems via Internet for finest medical practices' (Sharma et al., 2018). Today, it provides a connected, accessible, secured, and collaborative environment for patients. Cloud computing usage in healthcare industry has improved a lot by far. Electronic medical records (EMR) helps medical companies or provide best solutions to store and secure their patient records by using cloud computing.

How Cloud Computing Helps the Healthcare Industry?

Cloud computing in healthcare sector means put on remote servers using internet. So, by using this healthcare sector store, handle, and process medical information. Also cloud computing help healthcare sector to increase patient engagement and provide them access to their medical data, tests, results and many more information from anywhere. Cloud computing help healthcare sector to increase patient engagement and provide them access to their medical data, tests, results and many more information from anywhere. As stated by Health Information and Management System Society (HIMSS) analytics (Amron et al., 2017) and ISO/TS 18308 standards (Mukherjee, 2019), medical health record (MHR), personal health record (PHR), and electronic health record (EHR) are the furthermost significant technologies that are designed to deliver improved services in healthcare area. EHR system is designed to collect patient's medical record, plus the history of medical problems and treatment for those problems, analysis results, vaccinations, results of X-rays, ultrasounds, and descriptions of special and chronic conditions and many more. Cloud computing offers a shared platform for all EHR systems among isolated hospitals with the support of cloud database that acts as the data bank for all cooperating healthcare industry while validation server allowances access to approved users and denies access to unauthorized users on the system. Personal health record is a medical data or record which is created by an individual provides a centralized ways for patients to manage their own medical records, which significantly enables the storage, access and sharing of personal health data.

Cloud Computing-based Healthcare Service

Healthcare industry uses cloud computing to streamline their processes and to deliver better healthcare facility. Despite the use of information technologies, medical sector faces many challenges such as increase demand of collaboration, high infrastructure management expenses, scalability of human resources, and dynamic needs for computational resources.

There are some important features of the cloud computing that effectively address these challenges.

- **Services required by users:** By means of service required by user can be provisioned deprived of any social involvement.
- **Resource pooling:** With the help of resource pooling numerous users may utilize the services at the same time.
- **Measured service:** With the help of this service facility customers pay only basis of their use.
- **Elasticity:** With the term elasticity means based on structural requirements resources can be added or removed.
- **Wide-ranging network access:** With the help of this, facilities can be retrieved from anyplace at any time.

The cloud healthcare system is shown in Figure 31.1, (Alzoubaidi, 2016). The patient's data may be of private and sensitive in nature and collective by smart phones, wearable sensors, and healthcare monitoring devices. But direct access from the real data provides risks of disclosing patients' position, action behavior and other health related private information. In this system, these models are not denoted to any specific person, including doctors, patients, researchers, can generate machine learning models to full fill requirements from people in the system. In adding, regarding the secrecy conserving topic, the in-between method results of the model will not expose any relevant patient information but can reflect the information about the training data and learning model.

Key Aspects Influencing the Cloud Computing System Implementation

By using internet, cloud computing supports in providing numerous modules, tools, and applications. Cloud computing is a very helpful application that provides easy accessibility of data and long-term cost saving to help any association

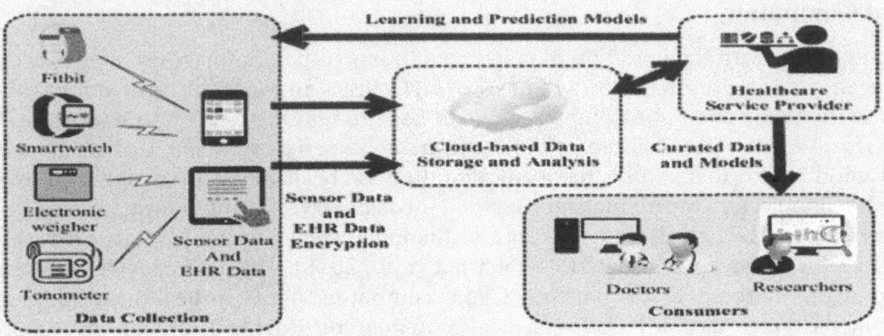

Figure 31.1 Cloud-based e-healthcare system framework

(Sultan, 2014). To manage large amount of data and information. It is finest step taken by any organization to manage data in efficient manner. Various organizations elect cloud computing for the cost efficiency and easy approach of data with the aim of match with the existing financial situation. Cloud computing also provides benefits to organizations for quick facts that can be attained with few mouse clicks from the service. The implementation of cloud is somewhat motivated by administration interests including data, information integration, and price efficiency. Table 31.1 presents some important aspects influencing the cloud computing system implementation.

Cloud Computing Advantages - Healthcare Sector

Now a days, with the help of cloud computing healthcare sector totally transforming. Today's healthcare industry is gradually focusing toward cloud computing for its inspiring qualities such as efficiency, security, collaboration, accessibility along with security, storage, and scalability. In Software as a Service (SaaS), it offers services on demand to healthcare sector, permitting immediate approach toward data and information. In infrastructure as a service (IaaS), it can proposal health services with computing according to their demand and large storage and in Platform as a Service (PaaS), it offers a safe atmosphere for web facilities and cloud application distribution (Devadass et al., 2017).

The cloud computing facility turn out to the critical matter in IT in recent years. Cloud computing provides huge benefits like security benefits, scalability, and servers accessible remotely, resources on- demand (e.g., hardware, software, and networking) to users. On the word of research (Masrom and Rahimli, 2014) cloud has lately developed as pillar of IoT healthcare organizations. Cloud computing allows healthcare facilities to interoperate between them to provide a faster and effective reply that helps healthcare organizations to recover the patient worth of service through sharing information across healthcare industries. So, healthcare organizations, hospitals, clinics, pharmacies, imaging centers, and insurance companies can efficiently share patient's medical records, prescription information, X rays, test results, physicians' availability, references, etc. can be retrieved from anywhere and all over the place by approved entities. Wholly these data would help healthcare sector for making decisions, scheduling physician's appointments, obtaining better diagnosis and treatments to produce better outcomes, fast moving assurance approval, etc. which extremely recovers patient's value of facilities. Also, cloud computing -based facilities support improve the health organization by creation data more reachable and interoperable. There are numerous key advantages of cloud computing technology used in healthcare organization (Javaida et al., 2022).

Discussion- Recent Progress

In recent technology, the implementation of active health care organization is mandatory to satisfy the requirements of different patients and support health care experts to deliver best treatment to their patients (Muhammad et al., 2021). The combination of cloud computing and IoT sensors, offers best health care real-time results with security, cost saving, increasing efficiency and, virtualization, high productivity, and scalability (Sultan, 2014). Almost all countries have using cloud computing in healthcare sector for better treatment, diagnosis, resource providing, patient monitoring and controlling. After several researches, it has been found out that for financial growth of any country, healthcare sector plays a major role.

Challenges and Glitches in Applying Cloud Computing for Healthcare

Security and privacy, organizational inertia, and loss of data governance are the key glitches of cloud computing in healthcare sector. Despite the advanced strategies, security remains the biggest challenge for cloud implementation process. Unrealized cloud potential is another challenge in cloud implementation. The biggest challenges when healthcare organizations moving to the cloud service is interoperability. This is because of the huge existence of different protocols, programming languages, data format, different platforms, O. S, databases and methods that different healthcare sector have been using. The switching between the cloud suppliers have also been created as the supplementary barriers for healthcare sector. The causes of cyber-attacks, use of smart keys, the flexibility of the overall system, following the rules and regulations and laws, etc. have additional given an advantage to the whole cooperating and remarkable execution of cloud computing technology for the healthcare sector (Somula et al., 2019). The main concern in cloud computing is to process and analyze vast amount of data composed from Bluetooth devices and sensors. Therefore, it is vital for healthcare sector to utilize newly developed skills such as fog computing and big data to sustain with this enormous arrival of data. Other technical challenges related to the use of cloud computing includes data transfer bottlenecks, resource exhaustion, unpredictability of performance, data lock-in and bugs in large-scale distributed cloud system.

The major barrier for cloud computing is that it offers minor constraint over its infrastructure. This is a foremost difficulty for organizations, but the service suppliers take care of this also and offering assurances and guarantees. The resources controlling and management is the core matter of concern or problem when different techniques like cloud computing and healthcare are involved in a system (Rawassizadeh et al., 2015). Healthcare sector needs to deal with a large amount of data of different persons who share the similar resources. Thus, there may be slightest interruption in data processing. Consequently, when implementing cloud computing in healthcare sector, different issues that disturb the resources allocation must be sensibly analyzed.

Cloud Computing Applications in Healthcare Sector

Cloud computing works on the principle of Interoperability. It collects, analyses also share the records from several sources of data such as hospitals, clinics, chemist's, insurance companies. Cloud services help to make a bridge between the centralized and decentralized data base systems and provides smooth connectivity among the two. Cloud service provide clinical/non-clinical data of patients, easy reorganizing and informing schedules of patients and monitoring the condition of patient, economic management/planning, and also caring the patient records. Cloud-based keen routing organizations can effortlessly grip patient support (Hussain et al., 2018). Some of the cloud computing applications in healthcare sector are:

High worth treatment facility

The cloud computing supports patients to gain high-excellence based treatment facility without ever moving to a health center with advanced mobile applications on the way to observe the current condition of the patient and mobile applications to retain their specialist knowledgeable and medical support. Healthcare system is now shifting towards expense methods for worth-based action. Earlier the cloud computing, it was a sluggish and difficult method to found complete health information of a patient. Nevertheless, after cloud computing all the information are combined with the help of compact cloud structural design to offer fast access to information from all over the place.

Rapid backup and recovery substitutions

The cloud computing provides the benefit of rapid backups and recovery substitutions that dropping weighty data damage dangers. With help of big data and machine learning cloud computing improves the capability to quickly identify, distinguish, approximation, and response to data mandates. By using cloud medical organizations practice their healthcare record and information to handle critical healthcare glitches.

Upgrading of medical organizations

By using cloud connectivity, we will also enhance the communications among different medical sectors with the mutual motive when a pandemic rises and physicians are under pressure. Without wasting time, medical organizations can speedily upgrade software applications and tools in cloud computing. When an innovative skill technology program arises into business, a medical advance improvement technology will raise the system as healthcare people at organizations run this freely. Mobile applications are constructed into cloud-friendly services that produce system programs understandable and functional on small gadgets.

Servers accessible remotely

To store huge volume of data in safest environment cloud is a best decision that enables healthcare sector to usage a network of remotely reachable servers. The meaningful way to protect the client's interaction data is to use electronic medical records in an efficient manner. With the help of this improves health care medical facilities in safety, and effectiveness in quality, including patients and families, ensuring privacy and security, and enhancing the coordination of care of patients.

Reduce dependency

By using patient records independently access from any location cloud computing helps healthcare industry to decreases the addiction of a specific device. Medical staffs should continuously be capable to transfer data related to patient conditions. As we all know that medical information is very vital for health research. So, there is the opportunity for doctors to study data and use those records for new treatment and therapy. This type of software might be helps in decision making and contributes to medical error checking.

Latest Industry Trends of Cloud Computing in Healthcare

Market by component

Hardware

The rapid growth of cloud computing and the growing number of cloud-based applications in medical have strained greatly attention from healthcare investors, researchers, and commercial holders. Also, to the continued growth of cloud computing in healthcare sector by presenting innovative technologies huge amount of start-up firms are actively sponsoring. In the healthcare industry market, the classification of the cloud computing into three coresets, components, applications, and end-user. In Figure 31.2, there are latest industrial development in cloud computing that helps healthcare services organizations to improve their services. Now a days, in term of health sector the smartwatch is an important wearable device. Because it presented several disruptive technologies that have prolonged the demand of wearable devices. Along with operational as a reliable device, a smart watch is also a wrist-worn 'general purpose, networked computer with a collection of sensors'

Software

Blockchain resolutions

To offer a safest mechanism for storing, maintaining, and delivering of medical records in health care department the blockchain technology is used. By using blockchain medical and medical specialists, and patients have better constraint over their data, and the confidential information are strongly protected from unauthorized users and hackers.

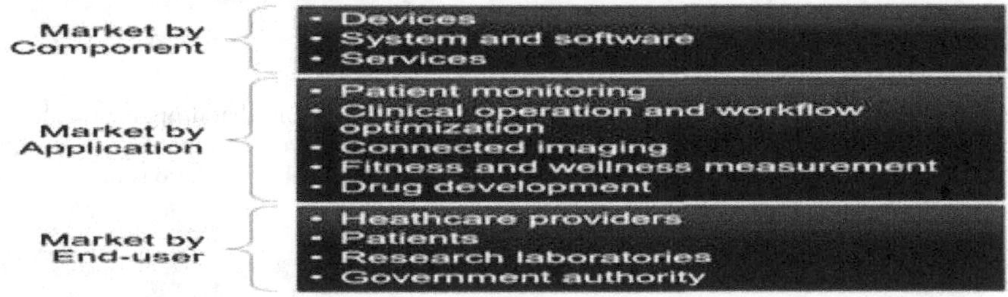

Figure 31.2 The modern industrial development in cloud computing that helps healthcare services organizations to improved their services

Table 31.1 Presents some important aspects influencing the cloud computing system implementation

Factors	*Descriptions*
Cost effectiveness	Adopting cloud computing helps healthcare sector to reduce software cost, hardware cost and data storage cost.
Information combination	Cloud computing structure acceptance based on the discussion with health care department and recollecting their specific information to efficiently confer system difficulties.
Confidentiality	This factor confirm that patient data remains hidden through communications between cloud and devices in the e-health organization.
Data integrity	In the exchange of data between receiver and sender evaluation of the integrity of the nodes involved.
Access control	It confirms limiting and monitoring user access to keep private data protected
Medical image exchange	With the help of cloud-based e-health system we can exchange medical images during communications.

Patient 24-hour monitoring
Physicians and healthcare providers can observe patients remotely with the help of patient monitoring applications and cloud computing technology have shown a vital role in remote patient monitoring applications. This technique helps in operation cost reduction, fewer admissions in hospitals and more comfortable services.

Future scope

It is true that the cloud in health care have a challenging future. Cloud computing services will allow doctors, surgeons to form best-in-class patient journeys maintained by tech-permitted care delivery areas such as remote monitoring and telehealth. Several healthcare organizations realize that developments or advancement in healthcare delivery with the of technology to advance treatment, management, and effectiveness are now straightaway required as an urgency. Healthcare opportunities are even now escalating on market advances. Medical trial scientists struggle to decide for a specific patient cluster which medicine perform well. The important research related to medical surgeries will be easily accessed and stored. In the future, all medical record will be protected and retrieved on the cloud whenever required. Cloud computing technology will extremely transform how the health professional works by streamlining data access to backup and recovery.

Conclusion

By using cloud computing, it is feasible for patients to obtain improved action, information, and interaction. Also by using cloud computing-based method patients can change an inclusive system of healthcare. Cloud-based Internet of things helps in certation of databases, and merging the cloud computing with intellectual information systems for healthcare sector. These devices are connected to hospital system through various procedures and locations. Also, research communities, administration and different organizations from the world are carefully collaborating to confirm a unified transformation that cloud computing bring to a medical business. To utilize their network remotely the cloud computing is the only greatest and reliable solution. Nowadays all healthcare industry is starting to grip the solution to protection patient's medical records. Healthcare sector maintains patient's medical information electronically and cloud makes it feasible for patients to take improved treatment and interaction. In hospitals to collect all client's information, including documents, pictures, videos electronically, cloud with IoT performs best role. The cloud computing provides the tools for installing, retrieving, and applying networked of the rising requirements and expectations. Now medical data, applications, and resources in on-demand computing. Also, it is true the healthcare organizations handle numerous new difficulties because organizations might measure lots of electronic patient records by using cloud computing and it also joins medical records and facilitates in clinics, surgical and hospital journeys. With the help of this research readers can understand and learn different aspects and phases of cloud computing in the healthcare sector. Sooner or later, all the data will be kept on the cloud and retrieved from the cloud whenever required. Cloud technology will radically transform how the medical industry operates by making more efficient information access to backup and recovery.

References

Alzoubaidi, A. R. (2016). Cloud computing national e-health services: data center solution architecture. *International Journal of Computer Science and Network Security*, 16(9), 1.

Amron, M. T., Ibrahim, & R., Chuprat, S. (2017). A review on cloud computing acceptance factors. *Procedia Computer Science*, 124, 639–646.

Aziz, H. A. (2015). Health informatics – introduction. *Clinical Laboratory Science Journal*. 28, 238–239.

Devadass, L., Sekaran, S. S., & Thinakaran, R. (2017). Cloud computing in healthcare. *International Journal of Students' Research in Technology & Management*, 5(1), 25–31.

Du, Jun & Jiang, Chunxiao & Gelenbe, Erol & Xu, Lei & Li, Jianhua & Ren, Yong. (2018). Distributed Data Privacy Preservation in IoT Applications. *IEEE Wireless Communications*. 25. 68–76. 10.1109/MWC.2017.1800094.

Fabian, B, Ermakova, T, & Junghanns, P. (2015). Collaborative and secure sharing of healthcare data in multi-clouds. *Information Systems*, 48, 132–150

Hussain, S. R., Mehnaz, S, Nirjon, S., & Bertino, E. (2018). Secure seamless bluetooth low energy connection migration for unmodified IoT devices. *IEEE Transactions on Mobile Computing*, 17, 927–944.

Javaid, M., Haleem, A., Singh, R. V., Rab, S., Suman, R., & Khan, I. H. (2022). Evolutionary trends in progressive cloud computing based healthcare: Ideas, enablers, and barriers. *International Journal of Cognitive Computing in Engineering*, 3, 124–135

Jensen, P. B., Jensen, L. J., & Brunak, S. (2012). Mining electronic health records: towards better research applications and clinical care. *Nature Reviews Genetics*, 13 (6) (2012) 395–405

Masrom, M. & Rahimli, A. (2014). A review of cloud computing technology solution for the healthcare system. *Research Journal of Applied Sciences, Engineering and Technology*, 8(20), 2150–2153.

Muhammad, G., Hossain, M. S, & Kumar, N. (2021). EEG-based pathology detection for home health monitoring. *IEEE Journal on Selected Areas in Communications*, 39(2), 603–610.

Mukherjee, S. (2019). Benefits of AWS in modern cloud. doi:10.5281/zenodo.2587217

Murdoch, T. B. & Detsky, A. S. (2013). The inevitable application of bigdata to health care. *Journal of the American Medical Association*, 309(13), 1351–1352.

Rawassizadeh, R., B. A. Price, & Petre, M. (2015). Wearables: Has the age of smartwatches finally arrived? *Communications of the ACM*, 58(1), 45–47.

Sharma, S. Chen, K., & Sheth, A. (2018). Towards practical privacy-preserving analytics for IoT and cloud-based healthcare systems. *IEEE Internet Computing*, 99, 1–1.

Somula, R., Anilkumar, C., Venkatesh, B., Karrothu, A., Kumar, C. P., & Sasikala, R. (2019). Cloudlet services for healthcare applications in mobile cloud computing. *Proceedings of the 2nd International Conference On Data Engineering and Communication Technology*, pp. 535–543.

Sultan, N. (2014). Making use of cloud computing for healthcare provision: Opportunities and challenges. *International Journal of Information Management*, 34, 177–184.

32 Review of Internet of Things and its enabling technologies

Syed Mohtashim Mian[a] *and Ms Sushma*[b]

Assistant Professor, University Institute of Computing, Chandigarh University, Chandigarh, India

Abstract

The term 'physical objects' or 'groups of such items' with sensors, processing power, software, and other technologies are referred to as the Internet of Things (IoT) when they link to other systems and devices through the Internet or other communications networks and exchange data with them. Devices simply need to be linked to a network and be individually addressable; they do not need to be connected to the public internet, which has led to the term 'internet of things' being used. Given that the IoT is the final stage of the Internet's growth and is hierarchically growing, it is crucial to understand the numerous implicit domains for IoT applications and the research issues that go along with them. The IoT is predicted to permeate part of daily life, including smart agriculture, smart cities intendance, and smart agriculture.

Keywords: Internet of Things, wireless sensor network, IoT application, IoT security, radio frequency identification, authentication, GPS

Introduction

The most revolutionary innovations are the ones that vanish. They become so ingrained in daily life that it is impossible to keep them apart. Mark Weiser's main contention in his essay was that 1991's landmark article [Weis 91] in Scientific American. Our modern world is starting to take on an IoT form. Considering a regular man's existence in society, a future where gadgets of all sizes and shapes are made with 'smart' features that enable them to engage and communicate with people as well as other gadgets but also with people, trade data, and create independent judgments and, do out beneficial duties on a set of parameters. IoT is gaining popularity. Notion across a variety of vertical and horizontal markets with its wide range of uses. To illustrate how the IoT may impact our daily lives: You go in the grocery store and receive a text notification from your refrigerator (Madakam, et al., 2015). You are out of milk' said sensors in the dairy area. You have a milk carton in your supermarket trolley. As you approach towards the pharmacist, your fitness bracelet vibrates as it collects your vitals and sends the data to you your doctor to modify your medication. When you're done shopping, you just walk out the door. When you leave the grocery, your credit card is charged. Your automobile communicates with you as you drive home to avoid collisions with other vehicles on the road (Tuen).

Machine to machine (M2M) connectivity was the foundation of the early IoT. M2M interaction refers to two devices interacting with one other, generally without the intervention of a person. The communication platform is not specified, and it can be either wireless or wired. M2M is derived from telecommunication systems. Various destinations in these platforms needed to exchange information, such as the identification of the caller. This data was delivered between the

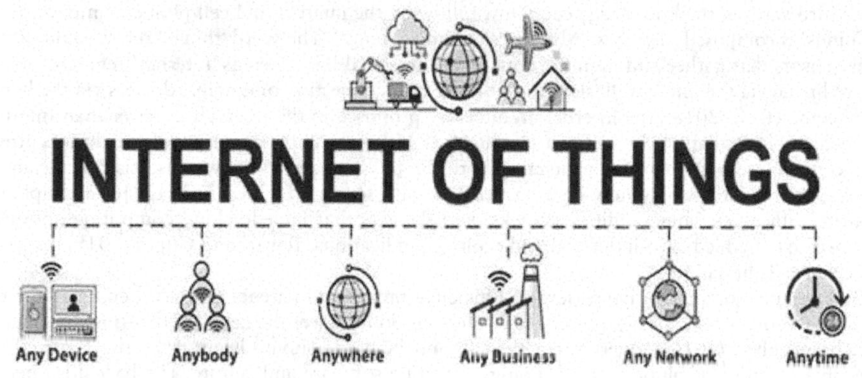

Figure 32.1 Application areas of IoT

[a]syedmohtashim15@gmail.com; [b]sushldh676@gmail.com

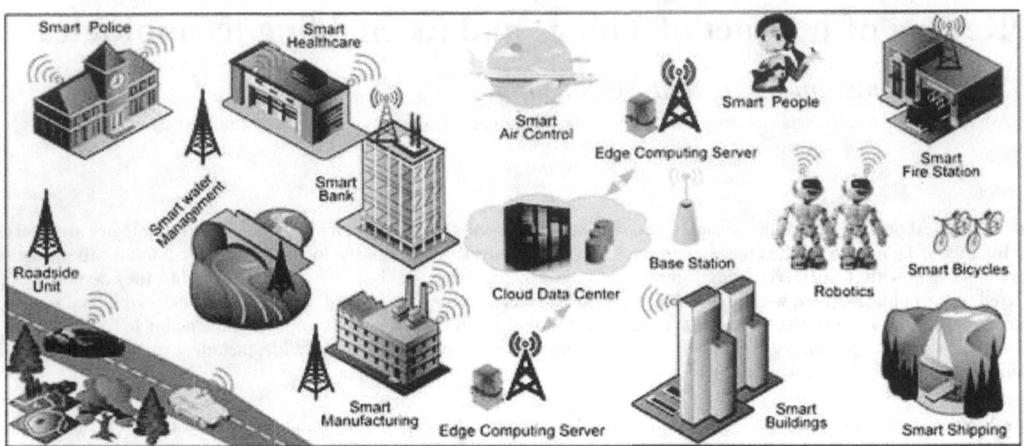

Figure 32.2 IoT application areas

ends without the requirement for a person to begin the transmission. The term M2M is still widely used, particularly in the industrial industry, and is often viewed as a subset of IoT (Tuen).

The idea of a digital world is expanded into the physical world through the IoT. The human will be guided by this addition to be safer, more at ease, and happier than before. The IoT idea is the result of several technologies, therefore numerous research obstacles are unavoidable. The term IoT refers to a type of network that uses the internet to connect numerous devices together. IoT helps with data transmission between devices, device tracking and monitoring, and other things. The IoT is quickly developing into a disruptive technological business potential. Standards are largely forming for wireless communication between sensors, actuators, and gadgets used in daily life, collectively referred to as 'Things,' and which are all referred to as such. The current advancement of IoT technology, as well as upcoming applications and research difficulties, are discussed in this study (Mian et al., 2019; MohtashimMian and Kumar, 2020).

Literature Review

The IoT refers to the interconnection of numerous sensors and items that communicate with one another without the intervention of people.

According to Oladayo Bello et al., the majority of the specifications addressed are focused on application areas within the IoT. Lin et. al. (2017) provided an in-depth examination of IoT, considering enabling technologies. According to Cui et. al. (2018), IoT is the third wave in the knowledge economy, following the internet and cell phone communication. The term 'Internet of Things' is composed of two words: 'Internet' and 'Things'. The word 'things' refers to numerous physical devices such as sensors that gather and monitor data linked to social life, whereas 'Internet' refers to diverse hardware objects that are linked via the internet. Basically, that is the interconnection of tangible devices via the hyper-space. According to Sangeetha et. al. (2018), the Internet architecture proposed in the research is better than Internet-mediated straight remote-control installation. According to K. Sha et al. [5,] as the implementation of IoT devices grows, preservation becomes a censorious component for protecting both the physical and cyber worlds. Via advancements in smartphone technology, multiple items may now be a part of IoT with sensors (Lin et. al., 2017) [6] attempted to demonstrate many security difficulties, vulnerabilities, attacks, and dangers that impede cloud computing adoption. Talavera et al. [7] examined IoT- enabled agro-industrial and ecology applications. Tewari and Gupta (2018) discussed security problems with other IoT difficulties.

Trappey et. al. (2017) present a comprehensive review of Efficiency ranges and patents as crucial enablers for this next high-tech. According to Verma et. al. (2017), present IoT solutions do not meet the needs of real-time IoT analytics. According to Weyrich and Ebert (2016), governments throughout the world should begin using the digitized IoT network since it has become the most revolutionary technology, affecting software and culture. The basic idea behind IoT is to allow the self-ruling swap of valuable facts between unseen fix different quirky identifiable real-world devices surrounding, encourage by key technologies such as wireless technologies (WSNs) and radio frequency identification (RFID) (Tuen,), that is felt by sensor devices and then additionally analyzed for decision making, on the premise of which an automated activity is taken.

Figure 32.3 Radio-frequency identification

In 2005, the ITU predicted an omnipresent networking age in which all connections will be linked and everything from tires to clothing would be a component of this massive network (Tewari and Gupta, 2018). Consider yourself conducting a web search for a watch that you have misplaced someplace in your home. So, the basic goal of IoT is an ecosystem in which items can communicate and its data can be analyzed to fulfil specified activities using machine learning (Trappey et al., 2017). A soon-to-be-released twine, a tiny and limited hardware working along with real-time web software that makes this vision come true (Verma et al., 2017), demonstrates a viable application of IoT. However, various people and organizations have diverse views for the IoT (Weyrich and Ebert, 2016).

An article was published in world of networking showed prominent IT suppliers' IoT strategy; they conducted interviews with important IT vendors. According to HP's vision, they see a world in which individuals are always linked to their information. IBM envisions a smarter planet by remotely managing gadgets through secure servers (Syed et al., 2019).

Analyze the Responsibility of Layers

Architecture of IoT is a collection of many layers that make up an IoT services including networking services, sensor technology, cloud service and different protocols. It often consists of distinct levels that let official assess, keep an eye on, and uphold the consistency of the system. Conceptually, an IoT architecture is made up of four parts: infrastructure, security, and applications and analytics. There isn't a single agreed-upon IoT design since many architectures have been put out by various academics (Chen, 2012; Wu et al., 2010).

Coding layer: This is the IoT base layer, which gives target items their identity. Each item is given a distinct ID in this layer, which makes it much simpler to distinguish between the objects.

Perception layer: It also translates the information that has already been acquired or obtained from sensor devices connected to each item into digital signals so that they may be sent to the network layer for further action.

Network layer: Through sensors, it transports and communicates the data gathered from real things. Both wireless and wired technologies can be used as the communication medium. It also assumes responsibilities for interconnecting networks, network devices, and smart objects. That is extremely accessible to attacks coming from the side of attackers. Regarding the authenticity and integrity of the information being transferred across the network, it contains serious security flaws.

Middleware layer: Information for this layer is obtained via its sensor devices. It has technologies like ubiquitous computing that ensure immediate access to its database so that all the crucial information may be gathered there. The processed information, as well as a completely automatic action, have been performed utilizing the intelligent processing equipment (IPE), which is based on its information for its processed outcomes.

Application layer: The formatting and display of the data are handled by this layer. The HTTP protocol is often the foundation of the Internet's application layer. However, because to its excessive weight and high parsing cost, HTTP is not appropriate in environments with limited resources. Therefore, a variety of alternative protocols have been created for IoT contexts.

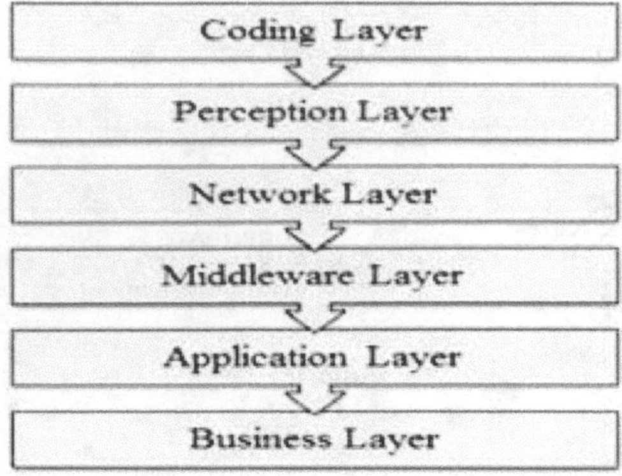

Figure 32.4 Six layer architecture of IoT

Business layer: Different business models are created in this layer to influence company tactics. Every organization seeks to gain insight from data to help it achieve certain goals and objectives. Business owners and other stakeholders utilize historical and current data to make accurate future plans. Businesses are vying with one another to collect more data for analysis and decision-making.

Application of IoT

IoT application run on IoT devices and can be built to almost every industry and workspace including smart-city, healthcare, agriculture, education, smart-home, industrial etc. IT play an important role in artificial intelligence (AI) and ML. IoT devices can also be used inside the hospitals to track location of medical devices, monitoring the environment and temperature regulation (Abdmeziem and Tandjaoui, 2014).

Smart city: - The IoT is present in every commercial and government sector today, from industrial applications to emergency services. Smart lighting, smart government, digital citizens, security, open data, smart health, traffic monitoring, water-management, climate change and flood modelling, smart infrastructure, and other smart cities applications (Syed et al., 2019).

- **Traffic monitoring:** In traffic monitoring system IoT play a major role to easily identify any incident with help of cameras.
- **Water management:** Use digital IoT device to save water.
- **Fire and smoke detection:** Cameras and video analytics that detect smoke and fire.
- **Smart lighting:** Now a day's sensors are more valuable in street light to make a smart cities in which lights are automatically on and off with the help of IoT.
- **Smart CCTV:** Use for minor detector like vehicle plate recognition, illegal instrument.
- **Facial recognition:** Cameras and others storage device like laptops with stored data used to identify backlisted individuals.
- **Smart infrastructure:** Overweight detector system on the bridge, highway monitoring system.

Agriculture: IoT based smart farming improves the entire farming system by real-time monitoring. With the help of IoT devices like sensor and interconnections, in agriculture not only saves farmers time but also reduces resources such as water and electricity (TongKe, 2013).

Healthcare: IoT plays a major role in healthcare like in logging the temperature, humidity of vaccines, blood coagulation system which allows patients to check how their blood clots (Islam et al., 2015).

Education: There are some important areas where the internet of things application in education like smart school transportation, smart classroom with projector, smart stream lab, student activity tracking, digital minimart, student IoT project management, improve admission records, attendance monitoring system, monitoring health of students and staff. Distance learning, enhanced interaction and productivity plays and important role at that time in education.

Vehicle industry: The company launched smart cars complete with self-driving capabilities and even the ability to open the garage door its only possible with the help of IoT. GPS navigation, Lidar, video cameras, radars, ultrasonic sensors, position sensors and so many IoT devices which we used in vehicle industry (Abdmeziem and Tandjaoui, 2014).

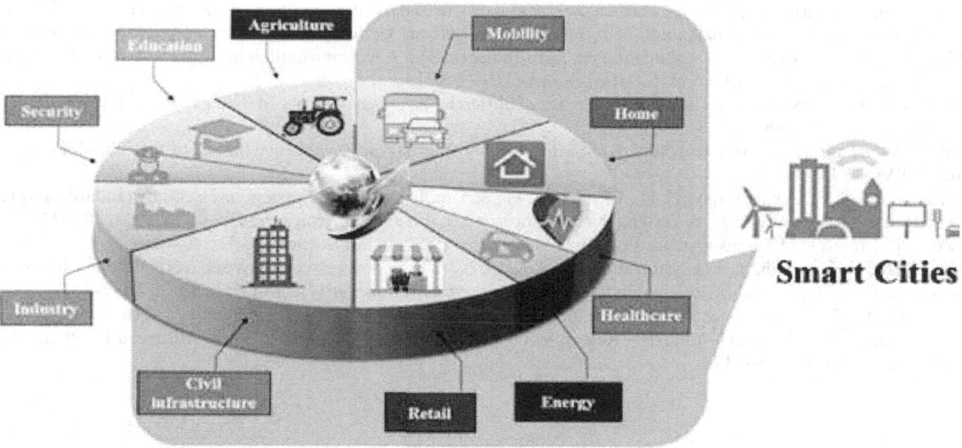

Figure 32.5 IoT applications for smart cities

Conclusion

In this paper, we discussed the architecture of Internet of Things (IoT), applications of IoT and its basic concept. The term refers to a type of network that uses the Internet to connect numerous devices together. IoT helps with data transmission between devices, device tracking and monitoring, and other things. The IoT is predicted to permeate almost every angle of daily life, as well as smart agriculture, health care, smart cities, education, and vehicle industries. The future of IoT will be predicted to be integrated and the paper presented review of the basic concept.

References

Abdmeziem, R. & Tandjaoui, D. (2014). Internet of Things: concept, building blocks, applications and challenges. Computers and Society. arXiv:1401.6877

Bello, O., & Zeadally, S. (2013). Communication Issues in the Internet of Things (IoT). In: Chilamkurti, N., Zeadally, S., Chaouchi, H. (eds) Next-Generation Wireless Technologies. Computer Communications and Networks. Springer, London. https://doi.org/10.1007/978-1-4471-5164-7_10

Chen, W. (2012). An IBE based security scheme of internet of things. *Cloud Computing and Intelligent Systems*, 1046–1049.

Cui, Y., Ma, Y., Zhao, Z., Li, Y., Liu, W., & Shu, W. (2018). Research on data fusion algorithm and anti-collision algorithm based on internet of thin. *Future Generation Computer Systems*. 85, 107–115.

Islam, S. M. R., Kwak, D., Kabir, M. H., Hossain, M., & Kwak, K. (2015). The Internet of Things for healthcare: A comprehensive survey. *IEEE Access*, 3, 678–708.

Lin, J., Yu, W., Zhang, N., Yang, X., Zhang, H., & Zhao, W. (2017). A survey on Internet of Things: architecture, enabling technologies, security and privacy, and applications. *IEEE Internet of Things Journal*, 4, 1125–1142.

Madakam, S. Ramaswamy, R., & Tripathi, S. (2015). Internet of things (IoT): A literature review. *Journal of Computer and Communications*, 3, 164–173

Mian, S. M. & Kumar, R. (2019). Review on intend adaptive algorithms for time critical applications in underwater we less sensor auditory and multipath network. *2019 International Conference on Automation, Computational and Technology Management*. pp. 469–472. https://doi.org/10.1109/ICACTM.2019.8776782

MohtashimMian, S. & Kumar, R. (2020). Reduced Time Application (RTA) in Distributed Underwater Wireless Sensor in Multipath Routing Network. *International Conference on Computation, Automation and Knowledge Management*, pp. 14–17. doi:10.1109/ICCAKM46823.2020.9051480.

Sangeetha, A. L., Bharathi, N., Ganesh, A. B., & Radhakrishnan, T. (2018). Particle swarm optimization tuned cascade control system in an Internet of Things (IoT) environment. *Measurement*, 117, 80–89.

Sha, K., Yang, T., Wei, W., & Davari, S. (2019). A survey of edge computing based designs for IoT security. Digital Communications and Networks. 6. 10.1016/j.dcan.2019.08.006

Syed, M., Mohtashim, & Kumar, R. (2019). Intend adaptive algorithms for time critical applications in underwater wireless sensor auditory and multipath network. *IJSRD–International Journal for Scientific Research & Development (IJSRD)*, 7(3), 1307–1310.

Syed, M., Mohtashim, & Kumar, R. (2019). Security analysis and issues in underwater wireless sensor auditory and multipath network (2019). *International Journal of Analytical and Experimental Modal Analysis*, 11(10). https://ssrn.com/abstract=3896925

Talavera, J.M., et al. (2017). Review of IoT Applications in Agro-Industrial and Environmental Fields. Computers and Electronics in Agriculture, 142,283-297. https://doi.org/10.1016/j.compag.2017.09.015

Tewari, A. & Gupta, B. (2018). Security, privacy and trust of different layers in Internet-of-Things (IoTs) framework. *Future Generation Computer Systems*.

TongKe, F. (2013). Smart agriculture based on cloud computing and IoT. Journal of Convergence Information Technology. 8(2). doi: 10.4156/JCIT.VOL8.ISSUE2.26

Trappey, A. J., Trappey, C. V., Govindarajan, U. H., Chuang, A. C., & Sun, J. J. (2017). A review of essential standards and patent landscapes for the Internet of Things: A key enabler for Industry 4.0. *Advanced Engineering Informatics*, 33, 208–229.

Tuen, C. D. Security in Internet of Things systems. PhD diss., Norwegian University of Science and Technology.

Verma, S., Kawamoto, Y., Fadlullah, Z. M., Nishiyama, H., & Kato, N. (2017). A survey on network methodologies for real-time analytics of massive IoT data and open research issues. *IEEE Communications Surveys Tutorials*. 19(3), 1457–1477.

Weyrich, M. & Ebert, C. (2016). Reference architectures for the Internet of Things. *IEEE Software*. 33, 112–116.

Wu, M., Lu, T. -L, Ling, Y., Sun, L., Du, H.-Y. (2010). Research on the architecture of Internet of Things. *Advanced Computer Theory and Engineering (ICACTE)*, 484–487.

33 A robust DNN-based model for diabetes mellitus

Ovass Shafi[1], *Avinash Baghat*[1], *and Tawseef Ahmad Teli*[2]

[1]Department of Computer Applications, Lovely Professional University, Punjab, India

[2]Higher Education Department J&K, Jammu and Kashmir, India

Abstract

Diabetes mellitus prediction using machine learning techniques is not a new feat. However, deep neural network (DNN)-based models are still employed to achieve higher accuracies and better results. The prediction of diabetes mellitus does not simply count toward the process of training a model and achieving results. It is a complex process that involves careful consideration of many techniques at different stages of going through the complex process of correctly predicting this disease. In this research work, a robust and unbiased DNN-based model to predict diabetes mellitus on the PIMA dataset is proposed. Techniques like spearman correlation and polynomial regression are employed for feature importance and selection. Missing value imputation techniques to make the dataset unbiased and then use the DNN in tandem with a hyperparameter optimizer to accurately classify the data have also been implemented.

Keywords: Diabetes mellitus, deep neural network, hybrid, robust, hyperparameter

Introduction

Usually, diabetes mellitus disease is tested by calculating the content of glucose in the human body using measures like BIM, hemoglobin A1C, and OGTT. However, with the advancement of new AI-based techniques, enough research has been carried out to assist in the early prediction of diabetes disease. With the availability of huge volumes of data from various medical organizations like hospitals, polyclinics, nursing homes, primary and secondary health centers and community health centers, it is possible to use the concept of data mining to extract useful information from the data and use that information for early prediction and diagnosis of diabetes. The researchers have developed deep neural network (DNN) models that may help to predict the disease before its onset and subsequently improve the quality of human life. However, such models are still in their infancy and need refinements and further research to make more accurate and reliable predictions. This could profoundly help patients with diabetes to cater to different symptoms that come with the disease and live a normal life. This is only possible if the disease is diagnosed at an early stage and the treatment starts right at its onset. In this work, a more promising field of DNN shall be employed to help achieve greater accuracies and develop an unbiased and robust framework to deal with different uncertainties and biases in the data.

Literature Review

Naz et al. (2020) developed a framework for the prediction of diabetes mellitus by implementing several algorithms. Thaiyalnayaki et al. (2021) carried out a research study for the diagnosis of diabetes on PIMA using deep learning (DL) perceptron and a support vector machine (SVM). The authors selected 18 parameters for classification and the proposed methodology using DL gives an accuracy of 77.4% whereas SVM-based classification gives an accuracy of 65.1%. Zhu et al. (2020) reviewed various studies from time to time for diabetes diagnosis. The researchers found that DL-based classification outperforms traditional ML techniques. The researchers (Ashiquzzaman et al., 2017) proposed a framework using the dropout method to address the issue of overfitting. The authors used NN architecture with fully connected layers and dropout layers. The authors (De-Bois et al., 2021) use the concept of transfer learning and propose a glucose forecasting model using a convolutional neural networks (CNN). The authors (Rahman et al.2020) developed a model based on CNN-LSTM on the PIMA dataset. The researchers (Ayon et al., 2019) developed a strategy with the help of a deep neural network and the application of cross-validation techniques. Patil et al. (2020) studied the application of breath to monitor and diagnose the levels of glucose in the blood. Naito et al. (2021) carried out a research study and proposed a DEEP HLA based on a DL method to impute HLA genotypes. The works by Lu et al. (2021) showed that the random forest model outperformed other models. Zhou et al. (2020) in a research study, they propose a method for early prediction of diabetes in addition to determining the type of disease a patient suffers from. The proposed method tries to differentiate between type I and type II diabetes and proposes a proper treatment for the disease. The model works mainly using the latent layers of DNN. The developed model performs better than any of the trivial

ML-based methods. The authors Lin et al. (2022) studied and reached the conclusion that the Long short-term memory model is not a stable model and is more complex. The researchers (Mushtaq et al., 2022) used a dataset from an online repository and applied techniques like Tomek and SMOTE to eliminate outliers from the dataset. After pre-processing the dataset, the authors applied two-stage model selection methodologies. The authors (Barriada et al., 2022) proposed a model in which they apply the coronary artery calcium (CAC) score as an indicator and train a DL-based model for early prediction of diabetes mellitus. The researchers (Padmavathi et al.2019) studied the impact of data pre-processing for building classification models to predict diabetes mellitus. The authors (Ismail et al., 2022) studied the taxonomy of risk factors associated with diabetes mellitus and evaluated 35 machine-learning algorithms. They employ three diabetes datasets along with nine algorithms of feature selection. The authors (Lim et al., 2022) carried out a review of various traditional ML algorithms and DL algorithms. ML techniques encompass applications in varied fields of cryptography and networks (Masoodi, et al., 2021; Teli, et al., 2021; 2022), navigation (Teli, et al., 2021) and in areas of predictive analysis and healthcare. Deep learning techniques (Sidiq et al., 2022) that have applications in secure healthcare (Teli et al., 2020; 2021; 2022) have attained tremendous attention in the recent times. Besides predicting diseases (Shafi, et al., 2022), ML and DL approaches are suitable for drug design.

Proposed Methodology

The proposed methodology starts by handling null values in the PIMA dataset and focusing on the significance of features. Then the most vital features are selected and pre-processing is applied as well. The dataset is divided into two subsets; training and testing data which are used for training and prediction accuracy respectively. An optimizer is also used for hyperparameter optimization. To carry out the research study for early prediction and diagnosis of diabetes mellitus we have chosen one of the benchmarks and standard datasets namely the PIMA India diabetes dataset. Data pre-processing is done by employing the missing value imputation technique. The dataset is searched for the most significant features and the selected features shall be used to train the model. Using correlations, it was observed that glucose, bp, and insulin are essentially related to the prediction variable. We have also used a threshold of 5% null values to apply polynomial regression continuously. We have also employed a grid search to optimize the hyperparameters. The

```
Model: "sequential"
_________________________________________________________________
 Layer (type)                Output Shape              Param #
=================================================================
 normalization (Normalizatio  (None, 4)                9
 n)

 dense (Dense)               (None, 8)                 40

 dense_1 (Dense)             (None, 8)                 72

 dense_2 (Dense)             (None, 16)                144

 dense_3 (Dense)             (None, 16)                272

 dense_4 (Dense)             (None, 3)                 51

=================================================================
Total params: 588
Trainable params: 579
Non-trainable params: 9
_________________________________________________________________
```

Figure 33.1 Deep neural network architecture

outcome of this step avoids the dimensionality problem which is followed by cross-validation and stratification to fine-tune hyperparameters. The DNN architecture and layers organization is given in Figure 33.1.

It has a total of five layers as well as a normalization layer. The total number of trainable parameters is 579 and nine non-trainable parameters.

The complete methodology is depicted in the flowchart given in Figure 33.2.

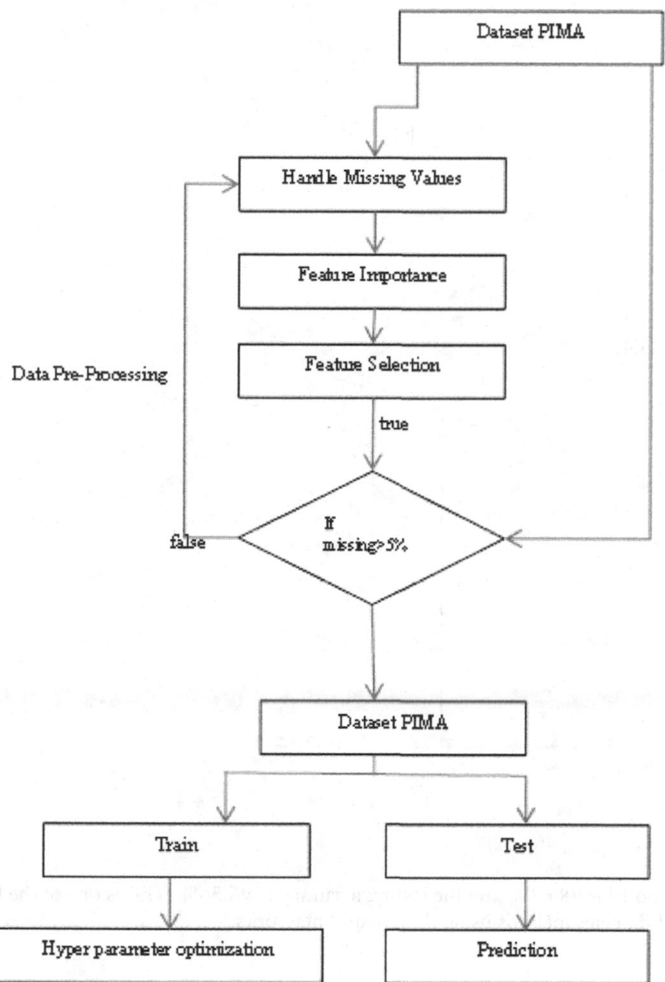

Figure 33.2 Proposed methodology

Experiment and Results

The experiment was done on TensorFlow and Keras libraries on the PIMA dataset. The above-discussed DNN was trained and tested for accuracy and the following results have been achieved:

1. The loss graph is given in Figure 33.3.

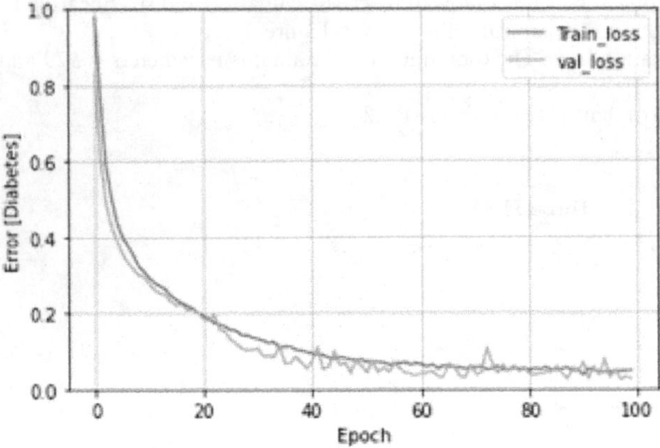

Figure 33.3 Loss

2. The accuracy graph is given in Figure 33.4.

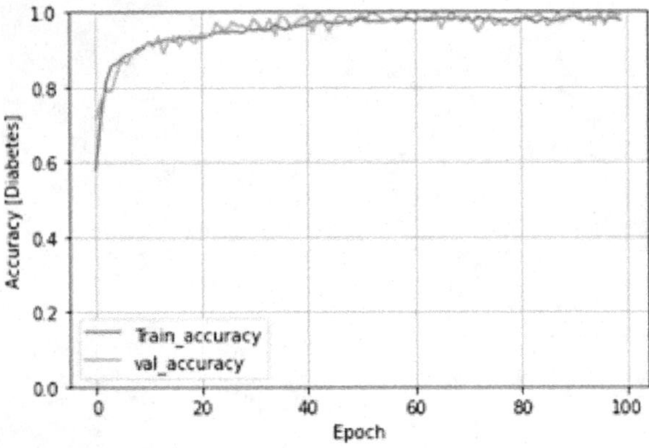

Figure 33.4 Accuracy

The training accuracy for the proposed model is 98.62% and the testing accuracy is 96.36%. This is one of the highest achieved accuracies in the prediction of diabetes mellitus using deep neural networks.

Conclusion

Diabetes mellitus accounts for a common and life-threatening disease which has a time-critical significance as far as its prediction and subsequent treatment are concerned. The paper focused on developing a robust deep learning-based framework to cater to almost all the issues involved in the prediction of diabetes mellitus correctly without any bias. The proposed model achieved excellent accuracy of 96.36%. Many techniques were integrated to remove the drawbacks or limitations of classifying the data. There are two facets of diagnosing the disease; data pre-processing involving a plethora of methods to deal with different kinds of problems and the actual training and classification. Both were taken care of robustly. In an extended version of this paper, the whole methodology shall be discussed in detail, describing each technique with adequate explanation and comprehensive results.

References

Ashiquzzaman, A. et al. (2017). Reduction of overfitting in diabetes prediction using deep. doi: 10.1007/978-981-10-6451-7.

Ayon, S. I. & Islam, M. (2019). Diabetes prediction: A deep learning approach. 21–7. doi: 10.5815/ijieeb.2019.02.03.

Barriada, R. G., O. Simó-Servat, A. Planas, C. Hernández, R. Simó, & D. Masip (2022). Applied sciences deep learning of retinal imaging: A useful tool for coronary artery calcium score prediction in diabetic patients.

De-Bois, M., El, M. A., & Ammi M. (2021). Computer Methods and Programs in Biomedicine Adversarial Multi-source Transfer Learning in Healthcare: Application to Glucose Prediction for Diabetic People. *Computer Methods & Programs in Biomedicine*, 199, 105874. doi: 10.1016/j.cmpb.2020.105874.

Huma, N. & Ahuja, S. (2020). Deep learning approach for diabetes prediction using PIMA Indian dataset deep learning approach for diabetes prediction using PIMA Indian dataset. *Journal of Diabetes & Metabolic Disorders*, 19(1), 391–403. doi: 10.1007/s40200-020-00520-5, PubMed: 32550190.

Ismail, L., Materwala, H., Tayefi, M., Ngo, P., & Karduck, A. P. (2022). Type 2 Diabetes with artificial intelligence machine learning: Methods and evaluation. *Archives of Computational Methods in Engineering*, 29(1), 313–33. doi: 10.1007/s11831-021-09582-x.

Lim, W. X., Chen, Z. H, & Ahmed, A. (2022). The adoption of deep learning interpretability techniques on diabetic retinopathy analysis: A Review. *Medical & Biological Engineering & Computing*, 60(3), 633–42. doi: 10.1007/s11517-021-02487-8, PubMed: 35083634.

Lu, H., Uddin, S., Hajati, F., Ali, M., & Matloob, M. (2021). A patient network-based machine learning model for disease prediction: The case of type 2 diabetes mellitus.

Masoodi, F., Bamhdi, A. M., & Teli, T. A. (2021). Machine Learning for Classification analysis of Intrusion Detection on NSL-KDD Dataset. *Turkish Journal of Computer and Mathematics Education*, 12(10).

Mushtaq, Z., Ramzan, M. F., Ali, S., Baseer, S., Samad, A., & Husnain, M. (2022). Voting classification-based diabetes mellitus prediction using hypertuned machine-learning techniques. *Mobile Information Systems*, 1–16. doi: 10.1155/2022/6521532.

Padmavathi, M. S. & Sumathi, C. P. (2019). A New method of data preparation for classifying diabetes dataset. *Indian Journal of Science & Technology*, 12(22), 1–9. doi: 10.17485/ijst/2019/v12i22/144929.

Patil, A., Patil, A. Kad, A., & Kharat, S. (2020). Non-Invasive method for diabetes detection using CNN & SVM classifier. *International Journal of Scientific Research and Engineering Development*, 3(3).

Rahman, Motiur, Dilshad Islam, Rokeya Jahan Mukti, and Indrajit Saha. (2020). A deep learning approach based on convolutional LSTM for detecting diabetes. *Computational Biology & Chemistry*, 88. 107329. doi: 10.1016/j.compbiolchem.2020.107329, PubMed: 32688009.

Shafi, O., Sidiq, J. S., Ahmed Teli, T., & -, K. (2022). Effect of pre-processing techniques in predicting diabetes mellitus with focus on artificial neural network. *Advances and Applications in Mathematical Sciences*, 21(8).

Shih-Lin, L. (2022). Application of Empirical Mode Decomposition to Improve Deep Learning for US GDP Data Forecasting. *Heliyon*, 8, e08748. doi: 10.1016/j.heliyon.2022.e08748, PubMed: 35146147.

Sidiq S. J., Shafi O, Zaman M., & Teli T. A. (2022). Big Data and deep learning in healthcare. *Applications of Artificial Intelligence, Big Data and Internet of Things in Sustainable Development*.

Tatsuhiko, N., Suzuki, K., Hirata, J., Kamatani, Y., Matsuda, K., Toda, T, & Okada, Y. (2021). A deep learning method for HLA imputation and trans-ethnic MHC fine-mapping of type 1 diabetes. *Nature Communications*, 12(1), 1639. doi: 10.1038/s41467-021-21975-x, PubMed: 33712626.

Teli, T. A., & Masoodi, F. (2021). 2nd International Conference on IoT Based Control Networks and Intelligent Systems (ICICNIS 2021) Blockchain in Healthcare: Challenges and Opportunities. https://ssrn.com/abstract=3882744

Teli, T. A. & Wani, M. A. (2021). A fuzzy-based local minima avoidance path planning in autonomous robots. *International Journal of Information Technology*, 13(1), 33–40. https://doi.org/10.1007/s41870-020-00547-0

Teli, T. A., Masoodi, F., & Yousuf, R. (2020). Security Concerns and Privacy Preservation in Blockchain based IoT Systems: Opportunities and Challenges. *International Conference on IoT based Control Networks and Intelligent Systems (ICICNIS 2020)*. https://ssrn.com/abstract=3769572

Teli, T. A., Yousuf, R., & Khan, D. A. (2022). MANET Routing protocols, attacks and mitigation techniques: A review. *International Journal of Mechanical Engineering*, 7(2).

Teli, T. A., Masoodi, F. S., Bahmdi, A. M. (2021). HIBE: Hierarchical identity-based encryption. In K. A. B. Ahmad, K. Ahmad, U. N. Dulhare, (Eds). *Functional Encryption*. Springer, Cham.

Teli, T. A., Yousuf, R, & Khan, D. A. (2022). Ensuring Secure data sharing in IoT domains using blockchain. In M. M. Ghonge, S. Pramanik, R. Mangrulkar, & D.-N. Le (Eds.). *In Cyber Security and Digital Forensics*,

Thaiyalnayaki, K. (2021). Classification of Diabetes Using Deep Learning and SVM Techniques. *International Journal of Current Research & Review*, 13(1), 146–149. doi: 10.31782/IJCRR.2021.13127.

Zhou, H., R. Myrzashova, & R. Zheng. (2020). Diabetes Prediction Model Based on an Enhanced Deep Neural Network. *EURASIP Journal on Wireless Communications & Networking*, 1. doi: 10.1186/s13638-020-01765-7.

Zhu, T., S. Member, a& K. Li. (2020). Deep Learning for diabetes: A systematic review. 2194, 1–14. doi: 10.1109/JBHI.2020.3040225.

34 Role of load balancing algorithms in cloud environment

Navneet Kumar Rajpoot[a], *Prabhdeep Singh*[b], *and Bhaskar Pant*[c]
Department of Computer Science & Engineering, Graphic Era Deemed to be University, Dehradun, Uttrakhand, India

Abstract

Cloud computing, which offers online computer services, has gained popularity in recent years. With the advancement of computer technology, a new paradigm in user services has emerged cloud computing, which enables on-demand, pay-as-you-go access to a wide range of IT services. Many businesses are moving their operations to the cloud because of the scalability of cloud services, and many service providers are opening new data centers to meet the growing demand. The number of people are using the cloud that go into the billions. But it's crucial to offer efficient use of resources and cost-effective task execution. In cloud computing, load balancing becomes essential because of the continually growing user base and service needs. Allocating the millions of requests from users to the cloud's distributed resources is the core function of load balancing in the cloud. To maximize performance and resource utilization, several strategies have been described in the literature, including load balancing, task scheduling, resource management, quality of service, and task management. To prevent performance deterioration and maximize resource efficiency, data centers can use load balancing in the cloud to distribute the workload among available virtual machines. For this reason, it is crucial to employ a powerful load balancing algorithm in the data centre when choosing virtual machines to carry out activities. It presents a difficulty for researchers working in cloud computing. Because of this, developers and researchers must find a way to create a load balancer that works well in parallel and dispersed cloud system.

Keywords: Cloud computing, dynamic load balancing, load balancing, static load balancing

Introduction

With the advent of new IT, cloud computing has replaced more traditional computing methods, allowing users to use a shared pool of programmable computing resources from any location and at any time (servers, storage, networks, applications). Through a variety of different providers, users can access these cloud-based service (Arul et al., 2021). Cloud computing's core goal is the efficient utilization of distributed resources for maximum throughput and performance (Kumar et al., 2020). In this way, the cloud can handle complex calculations and solve difficult problems. Distributed computing also enables the use of multiple data centers to speed up service delivery to customers. All the benefits of grid computing, Software as a service (SaaS), and utility computing are available through cloud computing (Neelima et al., 2020). The idea of virtualization is used, because of their dispersed and parallel nature, cloud computing systems are well-suited to meeting the needs of a wide variety of users. Cloud computing makes it possible to distribute a huge amount of related resources as well as share information. Users are only charged for the exact amount of resources they consume. In cloud computing, data and resources are stored and managed centrally, with the latter growing rapidly to accommodate ever-increasing data needs. As a result, load balancing is the primary responsibility of the cloud. Distributing a variable workload over numerous nodes helps prevent any single node from becoming overburdened. The unpredictable arrival of jobs in a cloud computing environment, each with its unique CPU service time requirements, might cause one set of resources to become significantly occupied while the rest remain mostly unutilized (Mishra et al., 2020). Consequently, load balancing and resource management pose significant difficulties in the cloud computing environment. Load balancing is a technique that uses a network's available bandwidth to balance a task's processing load among many computers or other resources (Garg et al., 2021). This maximizes resource utilization, shortens the amount of time it takes to process data, and prevents overload. The objective of load balancing is to distribute processing tasks evenly across all available system and network resources. The primary goal of load balancing is to maximize cloud resource availability, while the secondary goal is to maximize performance.

Load Balancing in Cloud Computing

The cloud computing industry has been one of the most rapidly expanding sectors of IT in the last decade. Cloud computing is gaining popularity as a means of data storage and management because of its apparent ease of use and adaptability (Mishra et al., 2020). Thus, more and more people are moving to the cloud. With the rate at which

[a]shubham151515@gmail.com; [b]ssingh.prabhdeep@gmail.com; [c]bhaskar.pant@geu.ac.in

technology is advancing, there are a great many users on the internet, and it's becoming increasingly important to meet their needs. To do so efficiently, administrators employ load balancing strategies, which guarantee that the load is distributed evenly across all available servers (Kaur et al., 2019). By spreading the workload across multiple cloud nodes, load balancing is a modern approach that both prevents virtual machines (VMs) from being over- and underutilized and maximizes the time they are used. Maximum throughput, optimal resource usage, and minimum response time are the primary goals of load balancing. Load balancing is essential for optimizing cloud performance and making effective use of available resources (Jodayree et al., 2019).

Classification of Load Balancing Algorithms

Based on this decision-making process, load balancing approaches can be broken down into two primary forms: static and dynamic [4, 6].

Static load balancing techniques

- In contrast to their dynamic counterparts, static algorithms are much easier to implement.
- It should be necessary to know the current state of the entire distributed system in advance.
- When distributing work, it ignores a node's present status and behavior.
- The traffic is distributed fairly among all the available servers and VMs (Hota et al., 2019).
- In addition to these benefits, they are also: use fewer resources, increase predictability, and boast a high degree of stability.

Dynamic load balancing techniques

The characteristics of dynamic load balancing are as follows:

- It is not necessary to be familiar with the state of the distributed system in advance.
- It provides a more pleasant experience for widely dispersed systems like cloud computing.
- It distributes the load so that it is evenly distributed among all physical and VMs.
- The failure of a single node will not bring down the entire system, but rather will have a negligible impact on overall performance.

The benefits include

- High adaptability is an advantage.
- This system has a high response time and is very fault tolerant.
- It has a very high degree of dependability.

Current load balancing strategies

Although many different load-balancing methods have been presented in the field of cloud computing research, this paper will only cover the three that are now available in the cloud.

Round robin

Time slicing is the mechanism used by round robin. The algorithm's name implies that it operates in a round robin fashion, wherein each node receives a time slice and then waits for its turn. Each node receives a certain time allocation and interval within that period. Each node has a certain amount of time to complete its work. In comparison to the other two algorithms, this algorithm is less complicit. This algorithm simply distributes work among machines in a round-robin fashion without considering the current workload of the system as a whole (Garg et al., 2020). The round-robin method employs a random sampling strategy. If some servers are already at capacity and others are relatively underutilized, it will randomly allocate the load among the remaining servers.

Active monitoring load balancing

A dynamic process, load balancing with active monitoring is always evolving to meet new demands. When the limit for the number of requests granted to a certain VM is reached, a new VM is allocated [11]. This information is stored. If more than one VM is present, AMLB will select the first one it finds and send that VMs id back to the data center's

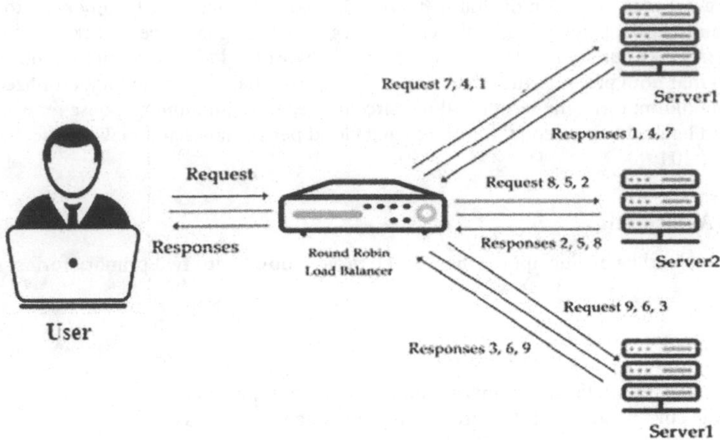

Figure 34.1 Round robin algorithm
Source: (Neelima et al., 2020)

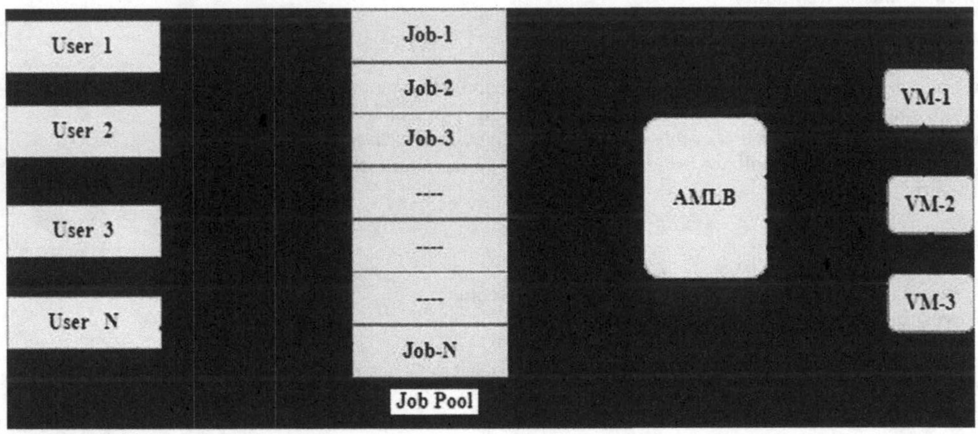

Figure 34.2 Active monitoring load balancing
Source: (Hota et al., 2019)

master controller. Based on the VM id, the data centre manager will then send the request to the relevant virtual machine VM. The AMLB is alerted by the datacenter controller of the new allocation, and a request is made to it.

Throttled load balancing
In comparison to the two current policies, the throttled algorithm provides the best performance and response time. The behavior is also very dynamic. All incoming processes are effectively distributed to VM.

It finds the best VM to use for a given task. The job manager keeps track of all the VMs and uses an index to send work to the one that can handle the workload most effectively [12]. If the job specifications match those of a specific VM, the manager will allocate it to that machine immediately, otherwise it will be placed in a queue until a client requests its processing.

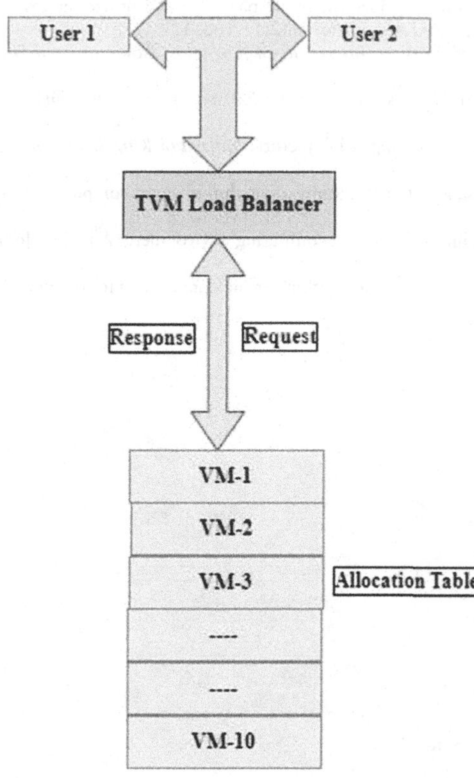

Figure 34.3 Throttled load balancing
Source: (Mishra et al., 2020)

Conclusion

The field of cloud computing is growing quickly on a global scale. Load balancing is a crucial task in cloud computing for effective resource usage. Increased client experience, optimal resource usage, and improved cloud system performance are the key objectives of load balancing. The effectiveness of the three load balancing techniques—round robin, throttled, and active monitoring was discussed in this paper. We conclude that throttled load balancing works more cost-effectively for load balancing in the cloud since it reduces the cost of utilization.

References

Arul Kumar, V. & Bhalaji, N. (2021). Performance analysis of nature inspired load balancing algorithm in cloud environment. *Journal of Ambient Intelligence and Humanized Computing*, 12(3), 3735–3742.

Garg, N., Obaidat, M. S., Wazid, M., Das, A. K. & Singh, D. P. (2021). SPCS-IoTEH: Secure privacy-preserving communication scheme for IoT-enabled e-health applications. *ICC 2021-IEEE International Conference on Communications*, pp. 1–6.

Garg, N., Wazid, M., Das, A. K., Singh, D. P., Rodrigues, J. J., & Park, Y. (2020). BAKMP-IoMT: Design of blockchain enabled authenticated key management protocol for internet of medical things deployment. *IEEE Access*, 8, 95956–95977.

Jodayree, M., Abaza, M., & Tan, Q. (2019). A predictive workload balancing algorithm in cloud services. Procedia Computer Science, 159, 902–912. In A. Hota, S. Mohapatra, & S. Mohanty. Survey of different load balancing approach-based algorithms in cloud *computing: a comprehensive review. Computational Intelligence in Data Mining*, 99–110.

Kaur, A. and Kaur, B., 2019. Load balancing optimization based on hybrid HeuristicMetaheuristic techniques in cloud environment. *Journal of King Saud University Computer and Information Sciences.*

Kumar, M. & Sharma, S. C. (2020). Dynamic load balancing algorithm to minimize the makespan time and utilize the resources effectively in cloud environment. *International Journal of Computers and Applications*, 42(1), 108–117.

Mishra, K. & Majhi, S. (2020). A state-of-art on cloud load balancing algorithms. *International Journal of Computing nd Digital Systems*, 9(2), 201–220.

Mishra, K. & Majhi, S., 2020. A state-of-art on cloud load balancing algorithms. *International Journal of Computing and Digital Systems*, 9(2), 201–220.

Mishra, S. K., Sahoo, B., & Parida, P. P. (2020). Load balancing in cloud computing: a big picture. *Journal of King Saud University-Computer and Information Sciences*, 32(2), 149–158.

Neelima, P. & Reddy, A. (2020). An efficient load balancing system using adaptive dragonfly algorithm in cloud computing. *Cluster Computing*, 23(4), 2891–2899.

Shafiq, D. A., Jhanjhi, N. Z., & Abdullah, A. (2021). Load balancing techniques in cloud computing environment: A review. Journal of King Saud University-Computer and Information Sciences.

Shafiq, D. A., Jhanjhi, N. Z., Abdullah, A., & Alzain, M. A. (2021). A load balancing algorithm for the data centres to optimize cloud computing applications. *IEEE Access*, 9, 41731–41744.

35 Software-defined network: An emerging solution for IoT-CC-edge paradigm—An impeccable study

Ajay Nain[1,a], Sophiya Sheikh[2,b], and Rohit[1,c]

[1]Research Scholar, Lovely Professional University, Punjab, India

[2]Assistant Professor, Lovely Professional University, Punjab, India

Abstract

The exponential rise of the Internet of Things (IoT) devices and applications have been popular in the recent decade. For the computation and storing services, the IoT integrates with different technology for better efficiency and increase the scalability, robustness of the system, and its changes with time for improvement and overcoming limitations. In this paper, we are discussing the Cloud of Things (CoT) and its limitations that are overcome by edge computing. After that, we discussed a new paradigm Internet of things-cloud computing-edge computing (IoT-CC-EC) with its benefits and limitations. We also analyze that software-defined network (SDN) can be used in the IoT-CC-EC paradigm to optimize the Quality of service (QoS) parameter and better management of resources and network.

Keywords: Cloud of Things, internet of thing, edge computing, Internet of Things-cloud computing-edge computing, software-defined network

Introduction

The exponential rise of the Internet of Things (IoT) devices and apps have been popular in the recent decade. The number of devices is increasing regularly, as a result, these devices hold an enormous amount of data but do not have computation and storage capacity of their own. In a centralized infrastructure, the IoT devices integrate with the cloud for better computation and storage capabilities. Besides, clouds provide four types of services to the user, i.e., Infrastructure as a Service (IaaS) (Abdullah et al., 2020), Software as a Service (SaaS), Networks as a Service (NaaS), and Platform as a Service (PaaS). The user can utilize multiple networks as they need, with the desired segmentation and policy enforcement. However traditional cloud servers are unable to handle this massive volume of data efficiently. As a result, the necessity of edge computing as an optimized compute management system is unavoidable for real-time IoT applications.

Any computational and network resources that are positioned between data sources and data centers are referred to collectively as 'edge' resources. Edge computing is based on the idea that processing should happen close to where the data comes from, like on a user's smartphone, which is the boundary between their real world and the cloud. It is meant to overcome the limitations of a centralized architecture by bringing computing capabilities to the network's edge. The data came from heterogeneous sources to the multiple edge server. To improve resource utilization and enhance the capabilities of edge computing, a software-defined network (SDN) controller that facilitates improved resource management and enhanced Quality of service (QoS) parameters is required. Furthermore, SDN is a network technology that decouples the plane of the forwarding devices such as router switches, etc. It takes all control planes in its hand and manages the resource and the network accordingly. With its decoupling power of planes, it helps to overcome the limitation of the IoT with edge computing (EC) and cloud computing (CC) paradigm and improve the performance, resource utilization, and QoS parameters.

Our contribution: In this article, we talk about the challenges of the cloud of things (CoT) that can be overcome by edge computing. We also discussed improvements provided by edge computing in the distributed architecture. Besides, the subsequent IoT-CC-EC paradigm has some limitations. Therefore, we employed a new technology in the IoT-CC-EC paradigm called SDN that helps to improve the QoS parameter and the management of network resources efficiently.

The remaining portion of the paper is structured as follows: Section 2 of the paper is the literature review. Section 3 describes a brief introduction to the integration of IoT and CC called CoT and the challenges in IoT and CoT. Section 4 depicts the challenges and utility of edge computing. Moreover, it defines the IoT-CC-EC paradigm with its efficiency and consequences. Section 5 illustrates the SDN and its potential to overcome the challenges in the previous paradigm.

Literature Review

Intense literature has already been conducted on efficient resource utilization in CC, IoT, and EC. However, they possess various limitations while using this architecture independently or within the integration of other technologies. Besides,

[a]mr.ajaynain@gmail.com; [b]sophiyasheikh@gmail.com; [c]rohitxmalik7@gmail.com

very limited literature has analyzed and explored the limitations in the CoT and IoT-CC-EC environment. It is important to identify how these technologies can overcome the existing problems to improve QoS and resource utilization. Moreover, to improve the overall system efficiency, integration with the other technologies is highly needed.

Gokhale et al. (2018) presents the architecture of IoT devices, and the services provided by the internet of things. Wu et al. (2017) focuses on the security of IoT devices, mechanisms, architecture, various attacks, and implementation challenges. Atlam et al. (2017) discussed the importance of developing cloud based IoT strategies. The study also focused on IoT cloud architecture, use cases, barriers to effective integration, transparency, and directions for future research. Singh and Chatterjee (2017) discussed the fundamental characteristics of cloud computing and security issues because of virtualized, distributed, shared, and public nature of the cloud. Abdullah et al. (2020) uses cloud computing to deploy an enterprise human resource management system (EHRMS). Several technologies, including the CodeIgniter framework, were combined to develop the system. Zeebaree et al. (2019) suggested doing a review on security methods for the effectiveness of enterprise-wide systems. Weisong et al. (2019) provided snipping discussion of edge computing issues, highlighting present challenges and potential solutions, and the potential and implementation of edge computing. This paper by Atlam et al. (2017) provides an overview of various risk estimation techniques technique, selection of the most suitable risk estimation method, and risk variables. Existing risk-based access control models' evaluation areas are also reviewed and contrasted. The expanding use of IoTs and their integration with cloud computing for better and more helpful service supply to consumers and effective resource utilization are discussed by the authors (Mohammad et al., 2014). In order to bring the idea of edge computing into practice, this study Shi et al. (2016) explains it and provides numerous case examples, spanning from cloud offloading to smart homes and cities, as well as collaborative edge. This article by Cao et al. (2020) contrasts edge and cloud computing research and results. It also describes edge computing, keyword technology, security, and privacy. This research created a mobility-aware flow-table implementation technique to maximize software-defined IoT network performance (Bera et al., 2016). The suggested approach reduces network power usage and message overhead.

Motivation: After intense analysis, the motivation of the research work is how the new technologies are used to overcome the limitations of existing technology. Moreover, this study identifies the basis of the introduction of new technology, and how these can be used to overcome the limitations of the existing technologies.

Cloud of Things Integration of IoT and CC

The term 'cloud of things' refers to the integration of IoT and CC. The phrase 'Internet of Things' can be defined as a collection of various technology kinds operating in a network autonomously and without the assistance of human contact. Additionally, the term 'Internet of Things' (IoT) refers to the link created by two internets of computing devices that are implanted in common things and allow them to send and receive data (Gokhale et al., 2018). Radio Frequency Identification (RFID) (Wu et al., 2017) tags are the primary method of data exchange between things and the Internet (Atlam et al., 2017). These things are very small in size and not able to perform computation and storage of data. To overcome these limitations of IoT, it engaged with another ubiquitous technology that has the capability of infinite storage and computation, i.e., cloud computing. Cloud computing refers to the process of providing a variety of services using the internet (Singh and Chatterjee, 2017). Data storage, servers, databases, networking, and software were shown. Cloud-based storage enables files to be stored on a distant database rather than a personal hard drive or local storage device (Chopra and Dhote, 2019). Cloud computing provides a scalable, reliable, and efficient setting for the real-time aggregation of data from disparate sources due to its ubiquity and scalability. As a result, cloud computing partially solved the IoT problem. Both the IoT and the cloud are advanced technologies that, when combined, will affect the way in which we use the internet in the near and distant future.

A framework called the IoT in the cloud enables the economical and intelligent use of architecture, data, and applications. Although IoT and cloud computing is distinct from one another, their characteristics are almost complementary. However, the cloud of things is facing certain challenges which are discussed as follows:

- Privacy and security: Data security would be a concern on both the IoT and cloud sides. The information of one country is virtually stored in another country, so it's a matter of concern if the data of the user is not stored in the user's country (Abdullah et al., 2020; Zeebaree et al., 2019).
- Latency: IoT applications require real-time performance optimization. Classical cloud computing involves apps sending data to the data center and waiting for a response. This raises system latency and reduces system performance (Weisong et al., 2019).
- Reliability: Integration of IoT with cloud computing is implemented for mission-critical applications. Once apps are utilized in real-time scenarios with limited resources, several difficulties related to devise failure or non-permanent device accessibility exist (Tayyaba et al., 2020).

- Energy: A huge data transfer by said technology consumes a lot of energy. It is impossible with the usage of billions of sensors, energy consumption minimized. However, efficient energy consumption is a dire need in today's world (Chen, 2012). The sensors may get power from sustainable sources, like solar energy, vibration, and airflow.
- Heterogeneity: A significant challenge in integrating the cloud with the IoT model is the wide heterogeneity of things, operational systems platforms, and available services (Atlam et al., 2017). Managing such a heterogeneous cloud environment is an additional and significant concern.
- Bandwidth: Real-time transmission of massive amounts of data created by edge devices to the cloud would strain network bandwidth (Mohammad et al., 2014). Bandwidth between a satellite and an aircraft must accommodate real-time communication.
- Protocol Support: Different protocols will be used to connect different things to the Internet and different sensors might use different protocols, such as Wireless HART, ZigBee, IEEE 1451, and 6LOWPAN (Mohammad et al., 2014). Standardized protocols may be mapped in the gateway to solve this kind of problem.

To overcome these challenges a new computing environment is required that stores and processes the data locally and has high performance and that is edge computing.

IoT-edge-CC Paradigm

Edge computing is the term for the technology that enables computation to be done on downstream data for cloud services and upstream data for IoT services at the network's edge (Weisong et al., 2019). Any computer and network resources that are situated in between cloud data centers and data sources are referred to as 'edge' resources. For instance, the cloud and body things are on opposite sides of the smartphone. The idea behind edge computing is that computation should take place close to data sources.

Things in the paradigm of edge computing are both data consumers and data producers (Shi et al., 2016). Things at the edge can not only request cloud-based services and content but also execute cloud-based computing operations (Cao et al., 2020). Edge computing can offload cloud-based computing, data storage, caching, processing, request distribution, and service delivery to the user. Therefore, the edge must be properly constructed to meet service requirements, including reliability, security, and privacy protection.

In CC, there is huge data storage for a long time and the response time could be high. In EC, there is temporary limited storage with the minimized response, i.e., milliseconds.

Edge computing came into use as a complementary technology of cloud computing which helps to overcome the challenges in the IoT-CC paradigm (Jazaeri et al., 2021). However, the IoT-edge-CC paradigm also faces some challenges which are discussed below:

- Uninterrupted communication: The movement of users from one edge network coverage region to another edge network coverage area causes communication to be disrupted.
- Privacy and security: Because the data of end users is processed remotely, end users are primarily concerned with protecting their privacy and maintaining their security.
- Real-time data processing: The connectivity of a wide variety of devices, such as sensors, smartphones, tablets, smart bracelets, or laptops, results in an overwhelming amount of data being generated. The computation of these data in real time presents a significant challenge.
- Heterogeneity and resource management: The request came from multiple sources for task execution, so resource management and load balancing are big issues in edge computing. It is also very difficult to communicate between heterogeneous edge networks without common standardization.

Edge computing helps to solve several challenges in a centralized architecture. However, the computational offloading, resource management, QoS parameter optimization, and overcoming existing challenges of IoT-CC-edge, a new technology for network controlling and better management system is introduced, i.e., SDN.

Software Defined Network

The traditional networking infrastructure contains various networking devices such as switches, routers, and other intermediate devices. Integrated circuits that are designed to do certain tasks are put into these devices. All these devices use a set of rules (protocol) to communicate with each other. Real-time applications use devices that are different from each other. So, it is very hard to get these devices to communicate with each other. In the IoT-CC-edge environment, the data creation layer and the application layer communicate with each other through different edge nodes. The data

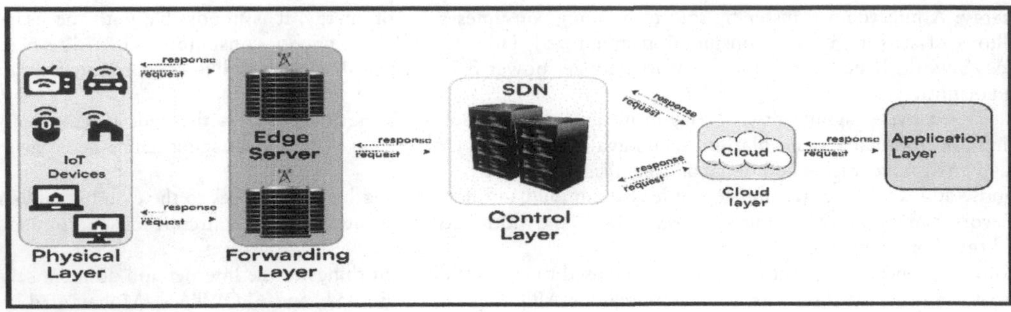

Figure 35.1 SDN based edge paradigm

came from heterogeneous devices to the heterogeneous nodes. Setting up communication between these devices is very complex. A new term called SDN is introduced to overcome these limitations.

The SDN-based edge paradigm is divided into five layers as described in Figure 35.1. The first layer is the physical layer, or data creation layer, which contains all the data generated by IoT devices. IoT devices connect with the edge servers in the second layer, called the forwarding layer. The forwarding layer is controlled by the SDN at the control layer that helps to manage the edge servers, improving the efficiency of the system, and maximizing the use of resources. SDN is directly connected to the cloud and gateways (cloud layer), which sends data to the user on the application layer. The whole system is controlled by the control layer that controls the data flow of a network.

SDN is a new network architecture that allows network control to be decoupled from traditional hardware devices (Jazaeri et al., 2021). Thus, the major objective of SDN is to isolate the control plane from the data plane, which consists of forwarding devices (Software-Defined Networking, 2012). Various application program interfaces (APIs)—northbound, southbound, eastbound, and westbound—improve SDN's layer-wise framework. The application layer and the control layer are linked via the northbound API, enabling communication between them. The northbound API also offers the application layer the virtualized view of the network. The southbound API serves as an interface between the control and infrastructure layers, enabling controllers to install various policies in forwarding devices like routers and switches and for those same devices to interact in real-time with the controller. OpenFlow is the most widely used protocol for facilitating communication across the control and data planes.

SDN may be defined as it is a technology that can help bridge the gap between the integration of edge computing and clouds (Amadeo et al., 2016; Bera et al., 2017; Yanget. Al., 2015; Samaresh et al., 2017; Samaresh et al., 2017). The SDN has access to all the control planes in the networking environment which helps to manage the traffic, load balancing, and resource allocation. In SDN based edge environment the SDN is directly connected with all the edge nodes which help in maximum use of resources and enhances the QoS parameter. As a result, SDN aids in network administration, network function virtualization, energy optimization, resource utilization, security, and privacy.

Conclusion

Internet of Things (IoT) devices have gained huge attention in recent years, they generate a lot of raw data which is needed to be stored, computed, and managed. Since the data is enormous in amount therefore it is difficult for the centralized cloud system to handle the data in real-time. To overcome these challenges, integration of Cloud of Things (CoT) and edge computing came into existence. However, CoT and EC have various networking limitations, and software-defined network (SDN) can overcome these issues. SDN provides better management of networks and resources. It also helps to make the more reliable and efficient, robust and has good Quality of service parameters.

References

Abdullah, P. Y., Zeebaree, S. R., Jacksi, K., & Zeabri, R. R. (2020). An HRM system for small and medium enterprises (SME)s based on cloud computing technology. *International Journal of Research-GRANTHAALAYAH*, 8, 56–64.

Amadeo, M. et al. (2016). Information-centric networking for the Internet of Things: Challenges and opportunities. *IEEE Network magazine*, 30(2), 92–100.

Atlam, H. F., Alenezi, A., Walters, R. J., & Wills, G. B. (2017). An overview of risk estimation techniques in risk-based access control for the Internet of Things. *2nd International Conference on Internet of Things, Big Data and Security*, pp. 1–8

Atlam, H. F. et al. (2017). Integration of cloud computing with internet of things: challenges and open issues. *2017 IEEE international conference on internet of things (iThings) and IEEE green computing and communications (GreenCom) and IEEE cyber, physical and social computing (CPSCom) and IEEE smart data (SmartData).*

Bera, S. Misra, S., & Obaidat, M. S. (2016). Mobility-aware flow-table implementation in software-defined IoT. *IEEE Global Communications Conference*, pp. 1–6.

Cao, K., Liu, Y., Meng, G., & Sun, Q. (2020). An overview on edge computing research. *IEEE Access*, 8, 85714–85728.

Chen, Y.-K. (2012). Challenges and opportunities of internet of things. *2012 17th Asia and South Pacific, Design Automation Conference (ASP-DAC)*, pp. 383–388.

Chopra, M. & Dhote, V. (2019). A comparative study of cloud computing through IoT. *International Journal of Engineering Development and Research*, 7(2), 259–266.

Gokhale, P., Omkar, B., & Bhat, S. (2018). Introduction to IoT. *International Advanced Research Journal in Science, Engineering and Technology*, 5(1), 41–44.

Jazaeri, S. S., et al. (2021). Edge computing in SDN-IoT networks: a systematic review of issues, challenges and solutions. *Cluster Computing*, 24, 4, 3187–3228.

Khattak, S. K., Almogren, H. A., Shah, A., Din, M. A., Alkhalifa, I. U., et al. (2020). 5G vehicular network resource management for improving radio access through machine learning. *IEEE Access*, 8, 6792–6800

Mohammad, A. et al. (2014). Cloud of things: Integrating Internet of Things and cloud computing and the issues involved. *Proceedings of 2014 11th International Bhurban Conference on Applied Sciences & Technology (IBCAST) Islamabad, Pakistan.*

Samaresh, B., Misra, S., & Vasilakos, A. V. (2017). Software-defined networking for internet of things: A survey. *IEEE Internet of Things Journal*, 4, 6, 1994–2008.

Singh, A. & Chatterjee, K. (2017). Cloud security issues and challenges: A survey. *Journal of Network and Computer Applications*, 79, 88–115.

Shi, W., Cao, J., Zhang, Q., Li, Y., & Xu, L. (2016). Edge computing: Vision and challenges. *IEEE Internet Things Journal*, 3(5), 637–646.

Software-Defined Networking (2012): The New Norm for Networks. Open Netw. Foundation White Paper.

Weisong, S., Pallis, G., & Xu, Z. (2019). Edge computing [scanning the issue]. *Proceedings of the IEEE*, 107(8), 1474–1481.

Wu, G, Y., Yin, L., Li, L., & Zhao, H. (2017). A survey on security and privacy issues in Internet-of-Things. *IEEE Internet of Things Journal*, 4(5), 1250–1258.

Yang, M., Li, Y., Jin, D., & Zeng, L. (2015). Software-defined and virtualized future mobile and wireless networks: A survey. *Mobile Networks and Applications* , 20, 1, 4–18.

Zeebaree, S., Zebari, R. R., Jacksi, K., & Hasan, D. A. (2019). Security approaches for integrated enterprise systems performance: A review. *International Journal of Scientific & Technology Research*, 8.

36 Optimized prediction model using support vector machine for classification of infection in Tulsi leaf

Manjot Kaur[1,a], *Someet Singh*[1,b], *and Anita Gehlot*[2,c]

[1]School of Electrical & Electronics Engineering, Lovely Professional University, Punjab, India

[2]Uttaranchal Institute of Technology, Uttaranchal University, Dehradun, India

Abstract

Tulsi (*Ocimumtenuiflorum*) herb is highly susceptible to diseases that can hinder plant growth and impact the farmer's ability to learn about the environmental factors affecting plant development. A prediction model integrating machine learning and image processing techniques can be constructed to expedite the approach of disease detection and classification with high-performance indicators to find any type of plant infection at a very initial stage. Machine learning and computer vision are developing technologies that enable computers to recognize and comprehend information from digital images. The purpose of this research is to assess and investigate the use and implementation of supervised machine learning image classifier models support vector machine (SVM) utilizing histograms of gradients as feature extraction and for categorization and classification of Tulsi leaf diseases. Finally, computations from the confusion matrix are used to compare the two models for better accuracy. The accuracy of the classification of the leaf disease using SVM is calculated. The proposed prediction model performs well with an increased training dataset with an accuracy of 96.714%.

Keywords: Image processing, machine learning, *Ocimumtenuiflorum*, support vector machine

Introduction

Productive recognition and identification of leaf infection is an enduring research work in computer vision (CV) due to its substantial applications in agribusiness and agrarian frugality as per Barbedo (2013). Numerous infections exist in horticulture that has an impact on the development and nature of plants. Many of these infections are decided according to a specialist in this space considering their side effects. However, it is expensive due to the difficulty in reaching specialists and higher costs as described by Jasim et al. (2020). In this way, the processing scientists have developed several calculations for the automated discovery of infections in plants in collaboration with agricultural experts. To distinguish the infections in a few types of plants, leaf side effects are a valuable source of information. The major herb plant *Ocimumtenuiflorum* is well known for its nutritional benefits. But the attack of numerous infections damages both its creation and quality. Therefore, it is crucial to develop an automated framework for early phase symptom finding and categorizing of *Ocimumtenuiflorum* leaf symptoms. Finding the lesion spot is an active research subject in computer vision Vishnoi et al. (2021) and numerous methods for plant disease diagnosis using image processing and machine learning algorithms have recently been introduced Dhingra et al. (2018). Characteristics like color, texture, and form are crucial for classifying leaf diseases since the plant lesion spots are typically evaluated by their appearance. A prediction model for plant leaf infection detection and classification using quick computer vision technology and machine learning techniques are proposed widely.

Need for *Ocimumtenuiflorum* Infection Classification

Like any restorative plant, ideal development, collecting, safeguarding, and stockpiling strategies are expected for *Ocimumtenuiflorum's* therapeutic and profound qualities as mentioned by Mishra et al. (2021). It is essential to guarantee the quality principles and cycles for solid *Ocimumtenuiflorum* leaves according to Roopashree et al. (2020) It turns out to be critical to recognize the sound and contaminated infection passes on and take fundamental estimations to further develop the creation quality and harvest yield. The *Ocimumtenuiflorum* plant is filled normally in sodden soil all over globe. It is filled in mild environment, and it tends to be effectively impacted by contagious, bacterial microorganisms, and nematodes. Unpredictable dull spots and round spots on leaves with faint light habitats, yellow, withering leaves, staggered development, dying leaves dropping from plant, sores on *stem* are caused because of parasite. Yellowing leaves are regularly viewed as supplement lack; however, they are spread by tainting of seeds. Sporadic brown or dark water-drenched spots or rakish spots on leaves, streaks on stems are caused because of microbes as illustrated

[a]manjotkaur.hpk@gmail.com; [b]someet.17380@lpu.co.in; [c]anita.ri@uttaranchaluniversity.ac.in

by Gowans (2021). The principal illnesses which can influence the plant development are fine mold, seedling scourge and root rot.

It can be concluded that crop disease, which results from changes in climatic and environmental conditions, is a natural occurrence. An important herbal and ayurvedic plant called *Ocimumtenuiflorum* has had very little effort done to identify the infected area in its leaf. It is essential to have precise disease detection and control measures to prevent disease occurrence in time and propose relevant preventative activities for the infected leaves to ensure that good quality and high output crop is available in the market.

Prediction Model for Infection Classification

Using test data from known categories, predictive modelling creates a model that classifies fresh interpretations. The basic goal is to categorize diseases into either healthy or infected leaf classifications. Any open-source or licensed machine learning tool can be used with the model, and the output can be evaluated in terms of performance measures. Although it is important to re-educate the model and evaluate the set to be verified every minute we put up or delete a feature or collection of characteristics on or after the given data. When given a leaf image, ML models with computerization and computational abilities can quickly detect whether the plant is infected with a certain disease or not. A system that combines various classifier models to generate decisions using a multi-functional approach can be suggested to improve recognition success rate and accuracy. Prediction model system consists of five different processes: image pre-processing, image segmentation, feature extraction, disease detection, and identification (training and testing the designed model). Image pre-processing is the major technique to extricate suitable features from the image. The images, which have noise are always not acceptable irrespective of what image acquisition devices are used as demonstrated by Naikwadi and Amoda, (2013). For example, there are noises in the test image, the area of significance in the test image is not apparent, ecological considerations exist or other entities' interference exists in the image, and so on than different pre-processing methods can be chosen for different image applications.

At this point, the methods that can be employed for leaf infection identification are data image resizing, image enhancement, segmentation, noise removal filtering, grayscale conversion, thresholding, and binarization. The steps followed for the implementation of classification of infection using support vector machine (SVM) model is shown in Figure 36.1. SVM outputs an optimal separate hyperplane which categorize data points (new ones) into classes. The accuracy of the model can be improved, parameter is tuned by Azlah et al. (2019). Kernel and method of regularization are two important parameters. Kernel decides for separation to be linear or non-linear. A greater value of regularization for minimal classification of training samples chooses small hyperplane margins. SVM computations are based on computational intelligence predictions and have a solid mathematical assumptions base and extensive hypothesis research, which has the advantage of predictions completion, global efficiency, versatility, and significant system more effective. The previous problems with selecting a machine learning model, over-fitting, non-linearity, locally optimal locations, etc. have been greatly resolved. It reduces the observational concern while also significantly boosting the calculation's prediction performance as described in the model by Oo et al. (2018).

Experimental Results and Discussions

We have carried out our implementation work using computer vision (CV) learning studio. We have categorized images in CV studio which is an open-source computer vision application that is quick, simple, and collaborative. The datasets

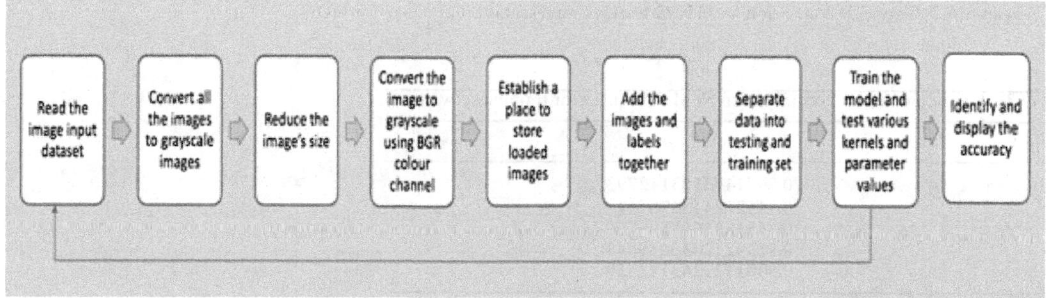

Figure 36.1 Flowchart for implementation of SVM model

are uploaded and labelled into four categories namely fungal, bacterial, insects and healthy leaves. The system is trained on dataset with four classes and 10169 images. Histogram of gradients (HOG) each localized region's histogram is generated by HOG. The image is first converted to a grayscale image to construct HOG features. Then the image is reconfigured to a lower size to help the algorithm run more quickly, and further to grayscale the images to fewer channels. Since OpenCV interprets images as BGR, we have used that color channel to translate the image to grayscale. HOG gives an array of features when we run it, and we use the Image/output feature to tra'n the SVM model. After this the images are loaded in CV studio and creation of a training/testing dataset is done. to vertically stack arrays for wrangling after creating an array of the images. The array will be set to (label size, 1). The array will appear as follow [[1],[0] ... [0]]. The images and labels are concatenated, and data is divided into training and testing set as done by Bao et al. (2020).

Hyperparameters are to be utilized as the kernel type, and radial base function is used as kernel type. In the SVM, C functions are used as a regularization parameter. The C parameter compromises between correctly classifying the training examples and maximizing the margin of the decision function. A narrower margin will be acceptable for greater values of C if the decision function is more accurate at accurately classifying all training points. A lower C will promote a greater margin and, as a result, a more straightforward decision function at the expense of accuracy. Using the validation data, we decide on C and the ideal kernel as done by Mingqiang et al. (2020). The RBF kerne"s parameter gamma can be viewed as the spread of the kernel and, thus, the decision on region. Low values indicate 'far,' while high values indicate 'near'. The gamma parameter has a significant impact on how the model behaves. The radius of the support vector sphere of effect only includes the support vector itself if gamma is too large.

Once the training is complete, predictions can be made using the trained model. SVM will be used to categorize the images. A sample image in Figure 36.3. is attached which was correctly classified by the model as fungal label.

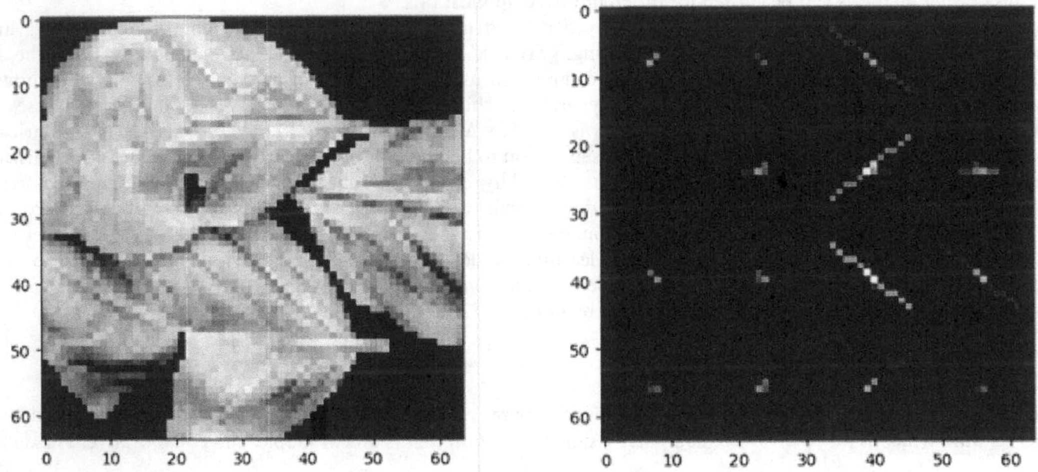

Figure 36.2 Grayscale conversion and HOG features representation of image for HOG

Table 36.1 Comparison of accuracy with SVM with different training set values

Train %	*Accuracy*
80	0.9671473503112793
75	0.945272445678711
70	0.8551883697509766
65	0.8134222030639648
60	0.8091521263122559

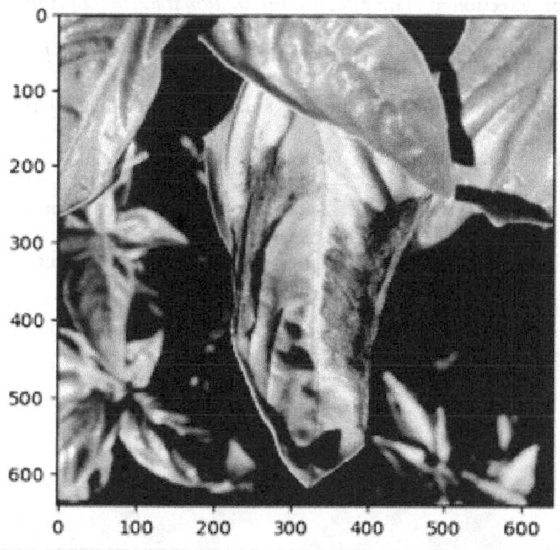

Figure 36.3 Test image correct classification illustration

Conclusion

In this study, we have demonstrated the effectiveness of employing training and testing dataset combinations, as opposed to image data, the de facto automated diagnosis methodology, to do field diagnosis of disease. The use of more of training dataset in experiments has significantly improved the accuracy of disease prediction. This study has demonstrated the reliability of training dataset. Since they are reliable, accurate, and work well even with a tiny training sample, they have grown in popularity and have their roots in statistical learning theory. Support vector machines are fundamentally binary classifiers by nature, but they can be used to handle the many classification tasks that are frequently encountered in remote sensing investigations. The foundation for our future efforts will be designing a novel prediction model with better accuracy.

References

Azlah, M. A. F., Chua, L. S., Rahmad, F. R., Abdullah, F. I., & Wan Alwi, S. R. (2019). Review on techniques for plant leaf classification and recognition. *Computers*, 8(4), 77. http://dx.doi.org/10.3390/computers8040077.

Bao, Q. T., Kiet, N. T. T., Dinh, T. Q., & Hiep, H. K. (2020). Plant species identification from leaf patterns using histogram of oriented gradients feature space and convolution neural networks. Journal of Information and Telecommunication 4(2), 140-150. doi: 10.1080/24751839.2019.1666625.

Barbedo, J. G. A. (2013). Digital image processing techniques for detecting, quantifying and classifying plant diseases. *SpringerPlus*, 2(1), 1–12.

Dhingra, G., Kumar, V., & Joshi, H. D. (2018). Study of digital image processing techniques for leaf disease detection and classification. *Multimedia Tools and Applications*, 77(15), 19951–20000.

Ganatra, N., Patel, A. (2020). A Multiclass Plant Leaf Disease Detection using Image Processing and Machine Learning Techniques. International Journal on Emerging Technologies 11(2), 1082–1086.

Gowans M. (2021). Brownish yellow spots on a holy basil plant. https://homeguides.sfgate.com/brownish-yellow-spots-holy-basil-plant-71343.html

Jasim, M. A. & Al-Tuwaijari, J. M. (2020). Plant leaf diseases detection and classification using image processing and deep learning techniques. *In 2020 International Conference on Computer Science and Software Engineering (CSASE)*, pp. 259–265.

Ji., M., Yu., Y., Zheng, Y., Zhu, Q., Huang, M., & Ya, G. (2020). In-field automatic detection of maize tassels using computer vision. *Information Processing in Agriculture*, 8, 87–95. https://doi.org/10.1016/j.inpa.2020.03.002.

Mishra: T. & Rai, A. (2021). Antimicrobial potential of *Ocimumsantum* and *Adhatodavasica*: The medicinal herbs. *International Journal of Pharmacy and Biological Sciences*, 1191, 17–28. doi:10.21276/ijpbs.2021.11.1.3.

Naikwadi, S. & Amoda, N.(2013). Advances in image processing for detection of plant diseases. *International Journal of Application or Innovation in Engineering & Management,* 2(11).

Oo, Y. M., & Htun, N. (2018). Plant leaf disease detection and classification using image processing. *International Journal of Research and Engineering* 5, 516–523.

Rhoades, H. (2021). Diseases and problems with growing basil. https://www.gardeningknowhow.com/edible/herbs/basil/basil-diseases.htm.

Roopashree, S., Anitha, J. (2020). Enrich Ayurveda knowledge using machine learning techniques. *Indian Journal of Traditional Knowledge,* 19(4), 813–820.

Sakhamuri, S. &Kompalli, V. S. (2020). An overview on prediction of plant leaves disease using image processing techniques. *In IOP Conference Series: Materials Science and Engineering,* 981(2), 022024.

Vishnoi, V. K., Kumar, K. & Kumar, B. (2021). Plant disease detection using computational intelligence and image processing. *Journal of Plant Diseases and Protection,* 128(1), 19–53.

37 Mapping landslide vulnerability in Kali Khola catchment: A frequency ratio approach with integrated machine learning ensembles

Sumon Dey[a] *and Swarup Das*[b]

Department of Computer Science and Technology, University of North Bengal, Darjeeling, India

Abstract

Every year, the mountainous regions face substantial loss of human lives, properties, and a huge damage to infrastructure due to one of the most disastrous and frequent intrinsic catastrophes, landslides. Darjeeling Himalayan region is non-exceptionally, highly prone to the most dangerous geo-hazards due to the incoherent geo-environmental planning and heavy tropical rainfall. The present assessment is intended to recognize the landslide vulnerable zones in Kali Khola River catchment in Darjeeling district using a knowledge driven frequency ratio model with the integration of support vector machine ensemble. In total, 107 landslide locations have been picked out through field survey and satellite images collected from Google earth imagery. Among the identified locations, 75% of the landslide sites are arbitrarily selected as the training data and the rest as validation dataset. Five classes; namely, very high, high, moderate, low, and very low vulnerability, have been established for the susceptibility area. Finally, the findings have been intensely evaluated through the AUC-ROC curves, which show the prediction rate, ranging from 72–75% in terms of accuracy.

Keywords: Landslide susceptibility zonation, frequency ratio, support vector machine, AUC-ROC curve

Introduction

Landslides are among the most treacherous and costly catastrophes on the earth and a type of rock movement and soil down slope under the effect of the earth's gravitational force (Kalantar et al., 2017). Landslides are discovered as the most dangerous cataclysms in the Darjeeling Himalayan region because of the topology of rug cliffs, which has an unjustified purpose of land use-landcover and destructive rainy seasons (Pattanaik et al., 2018). For the current study, a knowledge driven Frequency Ratio model with the integration of support vector machine (SVM) ensembles has been proposed for slope instability analysis. The vulnerability analysis for landslides is foremost to ensure safeguard to human lives and alleviate the adverse effect on territorial and national economy of a country.

Area of Study

Kali Khola is a small tributary of West Bengal state which flows through the Darjeeling district. The catchment extends from 26°49' N to 26°58' N and 88°20' E to 88°30' E, approximately 151.91 km^2. The study region is composed of Precambrian, Miocene, Permian rocks (Pawde and Saha, 1982). Geomorphologically, the study area comprises active flood plain, piedmont alluvial plain, moderately, and highly dissected hills and valleys (Chawla et al., 2019). The region, pedologically, is categorized by various soil types; namely, humic acrisols, dystric regosols, humic cambisols, and eutric fluvisols (Pramanik, 2016). Figure 37.1 delineates the study area for Kali Khola catchment.

Materials and Methodologies

The study comprised the following methodology: (i) the previous landslide features were collected using the Google Earth Imagery and verified through field observations; (ii) preparation of the data layers for the landslides conditioning factors; (iii) analysis of the correspondence between the landslide conditioning constituents and previous landslides has been carried out; (iv) applying the frequency ratio approach along with the SVM ensemble learning approach; (v) application of AUC-ROC to find out the precision of the framework.

[a]sumon.csa.nbu@gmail.com; [b]sd.csa@nbu.ac.in

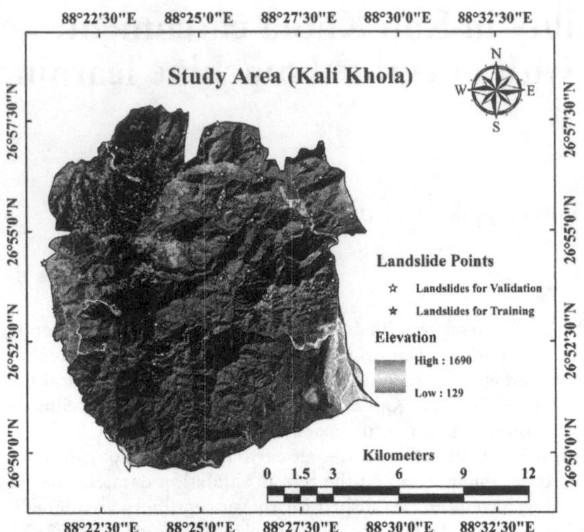

Figure 37.1 Study area location map of Kali Khola river basin

Data Preparation

Construction of landslide inventory

For the fulfilment of current study, several important data have been accumulated from various sources viz. SRTM DEM from USGS Earth Explorer, drainage and road networks from Open Series Topological Maps, LULC Map from Environmental Systems Research Institute (ESRI). For the susceptibility mapping of the landslides, fifteen landslide conditioning factors are chosen through FR and FR-SVM ensemble.

Occurrence factors for landslides

In Kali Khola basin, the factors selected for the susceptibility study were (1) surface factors (elevation, slope, aspect, curvature), (2) erosion factors (drainage density, lineament density), (3) anthological factors (distance to roads), (4) geological or lithological factors (soil type, geology), (5) hydrological factors (SPI, TWI, STI), (6) Hydro-morphological factors (geomorphology), (7) land use factors (LULC, NDVI).

Multicollinearity Analysis of the LCFs

Multicollinearity analysis is a widely accepted and indispensable method to recognize and pick out pertinent landslide conditioning factors for mapping landslide vulnerability in the study zone (Tien Bui et al., 2015; Roy and Saha, 2019).

The findings of multicollinearity assessment exhibit that the lowest and highest value in terms of tolerance is represented by 0.351 (TWI) and 0.969 (slope) respectively and in terms of variance inflation factor (VIF), the minimum and maximum values are 1.032 (slope) and 2.851 (TWI). Table 37.1 illustrates the multicollinearity diagnostics of the selected factors for landslide occurrence.

Applied Models with Exhibits

Frequency ratio analysis

One of the recurrently used bi-variate statistical techniques, also known as the likelihood ratio model, the FR analysis is established on the interdependence between the spatial sites of the landslides and the influencers responsible for landslide occurrence (Pal and Chowdhuri, 2019). The following equation has been utilized to produce the FR value for each group of the data layers:

$$FR = \frac{Proportion\,of\,landslide\,in\,a\,feature\,class}{Area\,of\,feature\,class\,as\,a\,proportion\,of\,the\,total\,area} \quad (1)$$

Table 37.1 Analysis of multicollinearity of LCFs

LCFs	*Collinearity statistics*	
	Tolerance	*VIF*
TWI	0.351	2.851
Elevation	0.493	2.028
Aspect	0.535	1.869
NDVI	0.559	1.790
Curvature	0.566	1.766
Soil map	0.611	1.637
Geomorphology	0.620	1.612
SPI	0.661	1.513
STI	0.687	1.456
Geology	0.688	1.453
Distance to roads	0.810	1.235
Drainage density	0.866	1.155
Landuse/Landcover	0.920	1.087
Lineament density	0.950	1.052
Slope	0.969	1.032

The FR methodology illustrates that 23.31 km^2 (15.34%) and 77.29 km^2 (50.88%) areas are covered under very high and highly vulnerable areas in terms of landslide occurrence.

SVM ensemble

SVM is a predominant supervised machine learning algorithm and has exhibited significant potential in solving regression and classification problems (Chen et al., 2017). SVM segregates formation of the hyperplane from the given data for training and is responsible to pick out the optimized hyperplane which can categorize the training data into two classes viz. slides and no-slides as represented by {+1,−1}. The map produced by the SVM classification were further segregated into five classes; very high, high, moderate, low, and very low vulnerability to landslides, and it was completed by utilizing the GIS environment's natural break categorization. The produced map for landslide susceptibility using the SVM ensemble has been illustrated in Figure 37.2.

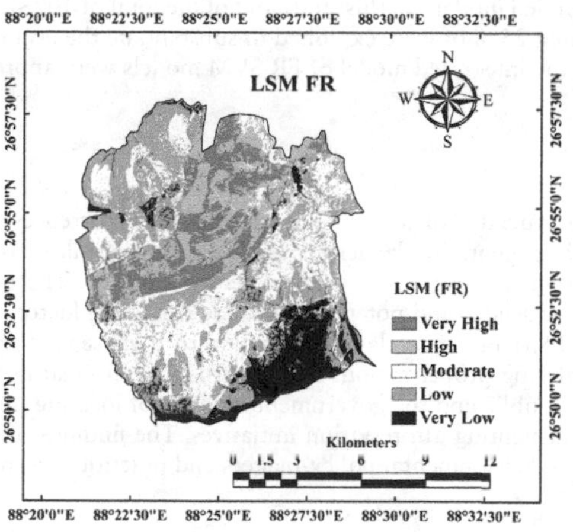

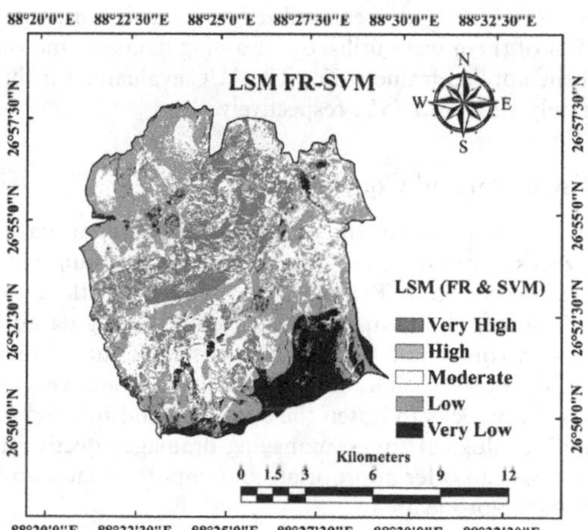

Figure 37.2 Landslide susceptibility map developed by FR (left) and FR-SVM (right)

The SVM ensemble depicts that 25.70 km^2 (16.92%) and 78.49 km^2 (51.67%) of the study region are covered under very high and high susceptible zones for landslide occurrence. The areal distribution of the LSMs produced by FR and FR-SVM ensemble models are illustrated and depicted in Table 37.2 as follows.

Table 37.2 Areal distribution of LSMs

Susceptibility	*FR-SVM*		*FR*	
	Area (Percentage)	*Total area*	*Area (Percentage)*	*Total area*
Very high	16.92	25.70	253	15.34
High	51.67	78.49	839	50.88
Moderate	26.08	39.61	470	28.50
Low	3.94	5.99	57	3.46
Very low	1.39	2.12	30	1.82

(a)

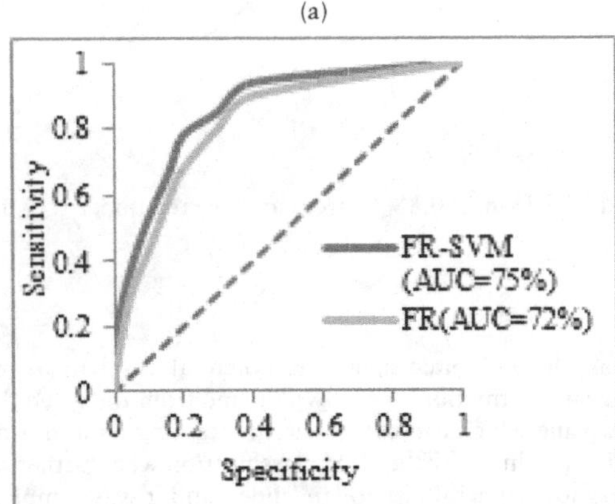

(b)

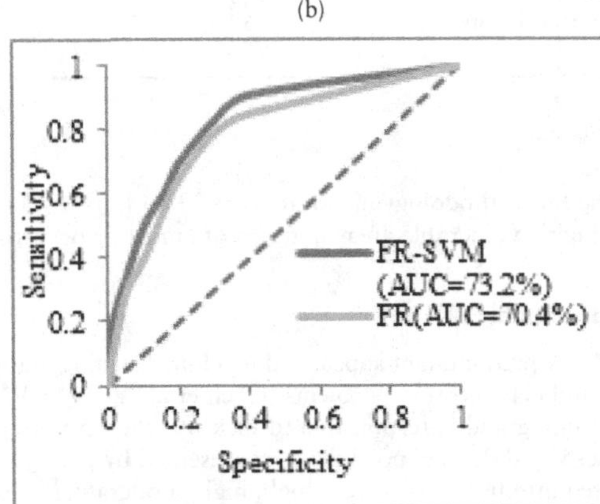

Figure 37.3 Performance evaluation of the proposed methodology using AUC-ROC curve- (a) Training datasets, (b) Testing dataset

Accuracy validation for the applied models

The ROC curve has been utilized for the substantiation of the applied models. In this study, out of the total of 107 slides, 75% of them were utilized as training datasets, and the remaining 25% of were exploited to substantiate the accuracy of the applied frameworks. The AUC evaluated for the FR and the integrated model of FR-SVM models were approximately 72% and 75% respectively.

Discussion and Conclusion

This study's assessment of landslide hazards using LSMs is a crucial tool for mitigating landslide occurrences and hazards, sustaining the eco-system, and assisting inhabitants in potentially dangerous landslide susceptibility zones. The present study exploits the ensembled methodologies of frequency ratio and support vector machine. The landslide susceptibility maps were developed using data from 107 landslides and potential landslide occurring factors (15 geo-environmental factors). The ensemble model divided the LSM into five classes according to their sensitivity to landslides: very high, high, moderate, low, and very low. By offering proper actions and hazard mitigation strategies, this study seeks to lessen the effects of landslides on the general public and the government in terms of locating faults, weak geological zones, managing drainage effectively, and implementing afforestation initiatives. The findings of this analysis can offer appropriate and important facts and figures to developmental policy-makers and practitioners in the landslide-prone areas.

References

Chawla, A., Pasupuleti, S., Chawla, S., Rao, A. C. S., Sarkar, K., & Dwivedi, R. (2019). Landslide susceptibility zonation mapping: A case study from Darjeeling District, Eastern Himalayas, India. *Journal of the Indian Society of Remote Sensing*, 47(3), 497–511.

Chen, W., Xie, X., Peng, J., Wang, J., Duan, Z., & Hong, H., (2017). GIS-based landslide susceptibility modelling: a comparative assessment of kernel logistic regression, Naïve-Bayes tree, and alternating decision tree models. *Geomatics, Natural Hazards and Risk*, 8(2), 950–973.

Kalantar, B., Pradhan, B., Naghibi, S. A., Motevalli, A., & Mansor, S., (2017). Assessment of the effects of training data selection on the landslide susceptibility mapping: a comparison between support vector machine (SVM), logistic regression (LR) and artificial neural networks (ANN). *Geomatics, Natural Hazards and Risk*, 9(1), 49–69.

Pal, S. C. & Chowdhuri, I., (2019). GIS-based spatial prediction of landslide susceptibility using frequency ratio model of Lachung River basin, North Sikkim, India. *SN Applied Sciences*, 1(5).

Pattanaik, A., Singh, T. K., Saxena, M., & Prusty, B. G., (2018). Landslide susceptibility mapping using AHP along Mechuka Valley, Arunachal Pradesh, India. *Springer Series in Geomechanics and Geoengineering*. (pp. 635–651), Springer, Cham.

Pawde, M. B. & Saha, S. S., (1982). Geology of the Darjeeling Himalaya. *Geological Survey of India Miscellaneous Publication*, 41(11).

Pramanik, M. K. (2016). Site suitability analysis for agricultural land use of Darjeeling district using AHP and GIS techniques. *Modeling Earth Systems and Environment*, 2(2).

Roy, J. & Saha, S. (2019). Landslide susceptibility mapping using knowledge driven statistical models in Darjeeling District, West Bengal, India. *Geoenvironmental Disasters*, 6(1).

Tien Bui, D., Tuan, T. A., Klempe, H., Pradhan, B., & Revhaug, I., (2015). Spatial prediction models for shallow landslide hazards: a comparative assessment of the efficacy of support vector machines, artificial neural networks, kernel logistic regression, and logistic model tree. *Landslides*, 13(2), 361–378.

38 A review for identification and detection of plant disease using machine learning

Angelina Gill[1,a], *Tarandeep Kaur*[2,b], *and Yendrembam K. Devi*[3,c]

[1]Research Scholar, School of Computer Application, Lovely Professional University, Punjab, India

[2]Assistant Professor. School of Computer Application, Lovely Professional University, Punjab, India

[3]Assistant Professor, School of Agriculture, Lovely Professional University, Punjab, India

Abstract

Plant disease detection is an important part of the agricultural section owing to the natural phenomena of occurrence of plant disease identification for timely management. If this area is not adequately cared for, it might have an important effect on the plant's productivity, product quality, and quantity. The leaf is an essential part of plants for rapid growth and increased crop yield. Crop diseases infected on leaves can reduce the yield and quality of the product. Farmers are facing difficulties in identifying diseases in plant leaves, fruits, and any other parts of the plants. Early crop health and disease detection can aid in suppressing disease infection and dissemination by implementing proper management practices. In this paper, we described many algorithms which are used for identifying and classifying plant diseases through image processing, machine learning, and deep learning. A number of collections of papers and standards provide important information to agricultural researchers and farmers.

Keywords: Deep learning, machine learning, plant disease

Introduction

Agriculture is vital since it employs 70% of the people in our country. Crop production in agriculture can be harmed by various plant pathogenic microbes and cause diseases, some of which are undetectable by the human eye. As a consequence, it reduces the yield, so, it needs to defend itself remotely and quickly (Kaur and Kang, 2015). Crop production quality and quantity are important for the country's economic success. Plant disease identification in real-time can boost production rates. so that proper management can be implemented at the right time. Many techniques have been used for detecting leaf diseases, for instance machine learning, image processing, deep learning, etc. So, frequent skilled monitoring of farmers is necessary but may be excessively costly and time-consuming. Finding a rapid, low-cost, and reliable approach to accurately identifying disease symptoms on plant leaves is essential. Botanists and the general public might benefit from an automated method for quickly recognizing plant species. Deep learning is effective in extracting features because it excels at giving more detailed information about pictures. A convolutional neural networks (CNN) based technique called D-Leaf was proposed (Wei Tan et al., 2018). Chakraborty et al. (2021) crop diseases carried on by bacteria, viruses, or fungus cost farmers 15 to 20% of their annual revenue. The second-largest producer and exporter of rice worldwide is India. In order to limit additional damage, early disease identification in vital crops is a key area for study. CNN was used to identify the brown spot disease in a rice paddy. Kumar and Kannan (2022) depicted that rice leaf disease was classified through the classifier Adaptive Boosting support vector machine (SVM) and got 98.8%.

This paper presents many techniques of machine learning (ML), deep learning (DL), and image processing used to identify leaf disease. In section 1- types of plant leaf diseases are presented. Section 2- leaf disease detection through image-processing techniques, ML and DL

Type of Diseases in Plants Leaf

Plant leaf diseases are caused mostly by three types: the first is a viral disease, which occurs as a result of viral infection to the plant. Some of the diseases are leaf curl viral diseases, leaf mosaic, stunt disease, rice tungro disease. Second, leaf infection from fungal diseases led to leaf spots, leaf blight, powdery mildew, smut, and leaf rust. Thirdly, the bacterial disease which cause due to the phytophagous bacterial microbes shown in Figure 38.1. Several diseases such as bacterial leaf blight, bacterial leaf spot and soft rot are common. Many disease infections on plant's leaves are caused by microbes that are transmitted through soil, infected sources, or insect vectors borne. It is extremely expensive and ineffective to use pesticides to manage some microorganisms when it comes to controlling diseases (Lukyanenko, 1991). Several image processing methods detected various plant diseases, like viruses, nematodes, and other organisms that cause plant

[a]priyangel24@gmail.com; [b]tarandeep.24836@lpu.co.in; [c]krishna.23363@lpu.co.in

diseases, have been developed but mainly focused on image processing-based detection of fungal infections (Pujari et al., 2015). Deep neural networks automate the detection of soybean leaf diseases with various parameters assessed for fine-tuning and transfer learning to attain high accuracy (Tetila et al., 2019).

Leaf disease detection techniques

Phadikar et al. (2013) selected the appropriate threshold value to determine the shape of the diseased region and used a region extraction method for automated rice disease detection. Many computer approaches for plant leaf disease detection may be used to classify the various diseases. Image segmentation is an important step for disease detection. The leaf disease detection process includes three main steps: 1. Image processing, 2. Feature extraction CNN, from deep learning as shown in Figure 38.2, leaves photos collected by mobile phones for image categorization. ResNet-50 was the architecture utilized for neural network image categorization and network training for leaf identification (Taslim et al., 2021). The public data set and new plant dataset were used and detected 10 diseases in 5 different types of crops (Sun et al., 2022). Durmu et al. (2017) worked on healthy leaves and sick leaves of tomato plants using the PlantVillage dataset and CNN classifiers such as VGG Net (VGG16), Shuffle Net, and Squeeze Net. As a result, a standalone, independent system model was created, which could be applied in the field to categorize and diagnose tomato plant diseases using minimum equipment (Durmu et al., 2017; Sembiring et al., 2021).

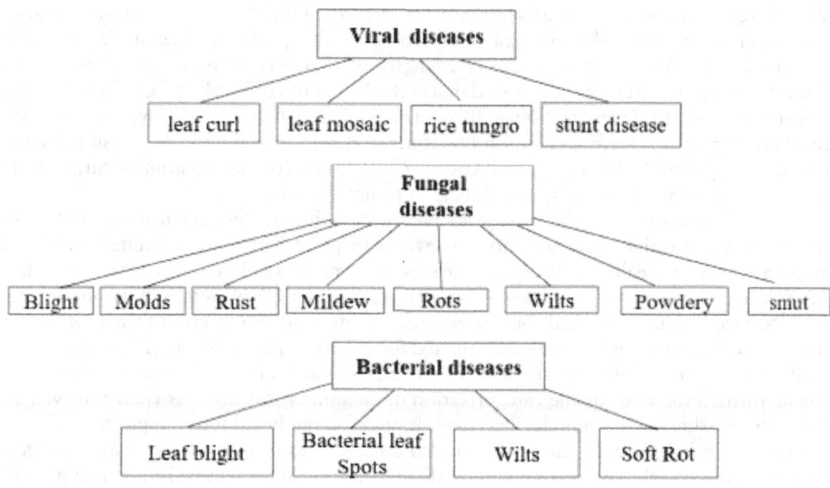

Figure 38.1 Types of diseases

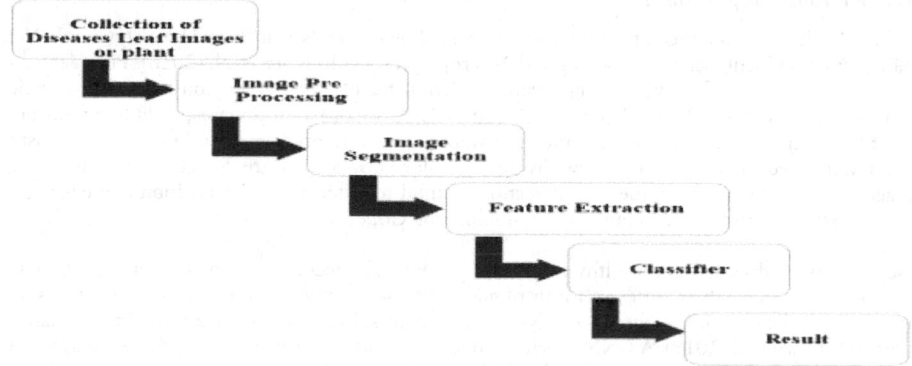

Figure 38.2 Process of leaf disease detection

Image-processing methods for detecting leaf disease

This method was created to recognize five plant diseases, including ashen mold, small whitening, cottony mold, early scorch, and late scorch. The framework was composed of k-means and pre-trained neural network techniques (Bashish et al., 2010). Automatic image processing techniques were used to examine the sugarcane leaf scorch infections (Umapathy Eaganathan et al., 2014). To efficiently and accurately identify guava leaf diseases, the author employed picture pre-processing, segmentation, and clustering using k-means and SVM (Perumal, 2021). Through image processing, the banana streak virus infection on banana leaves was detected. The hue saturation value was the method used to distinguish between impacted and unaffected leaf image areas (Karthik and Praburam, 2016).

Leaf disease detection through machine learning

Wheat disease classification has been done through ML algorithms. The result was 86.8% and 94.5% of neural network and SVM respectively (Punn and Bhalla, 2013). The histogram technique was used to diagnose wheat disease and healthy wheat. For wheat disease identification, two techniques were used: a neural network and SVM (Gaikwad and Musande, 2017). Panigrahi et al. (2020) used the SVM method for detecting maize plant diseases using plant images. Ferentinos (2018) developed a model for differentiating 13 distinct forms of plant diseases from healthy leaves and got accuracy of between 91 and 98%.

One significant fruit produced in tropical areas is the guava. There are more than 177 pathogens, of which 167 are fungi, and others, like bacteria, algae, and nematodes, attack them. To identify and categorize the most critical guava plant diseases, and 4E segmentation to produce color histograms of Red Green Blue, HSV, and texture local binary pattern descriptors for guava plants' leaves (Almadhor et al., 2021). Mengistu et al. (2016) explored coffee leaf rust, wilt, and coffee berry disease. These three significant coffee diseases damage the leaves of coffee plants. Coffee plant diseases performed 90.07% better when RBF and SOM were combined. Behera et al. (2018) identified the severity of disease, the right quantity, and concentration of pesticide were focused on the afflicted region and disease. As a result, it correctly identified the disease with an accuracy of 90%. Basavaiah and Arlene (2020) improved classification accuracy and used RF and decision tree classification algorithms to identify leaf disease in tomato plants.

Owomugisha and Mwebaze (2016) worked on the disease incidence and disease severity features and classified LinearSVC, extra trees, and KNN were trained and used for cassava crop plant leaf images. Ramesh et al. (2018) extracted 160 images of papaya leaves on healthy and diseased leaves. The model could classify with approximately 70% accuracy. A non-disease class and two typical disease classes were created by CNN using 800 photos of cucumber leaves. The suggested CNN-based system attained 94.9% accuracy using a four-fold cross-validation technique (Kawasaki et al., 2015). The leaves of a pepper plant were investigated for diseases. The neural network and backpropagation algorithms were used for improved results (Francis and Anoop, 2016). Cucumber leaf diseases were detected in the experiments. The results performed the best for the categorization of cucumber leaf diseases (Jian and Wei, 2010). In many countries throughout the world, tea is a popular beverage. It affected the healthy development of tea leaves, causing a reduction in their number and impeding tea output. It also created a technique for processing images that can distinguish between healthy leaves and the two most common diseases affecting tea leaves: brown blight and algal leaf disease. The SVM was applied to identify disorders (Hossain et al., 2018; Kaur and Kaur, 2018; Gill et al., 2022).

Leaf disease detection through deep-learning

A collection of images healthy and damaged plant leaves was trained by deep CNN such as AlexNet, GoogLeNet, and obtained 99.35% accuracy in identifying 26 diseases and 14 crop species (Mohanty et al., 2016). Plant leaf diseases affecting a variety of plants are identified and classified using modern detectors such as, Region-based Fully, Single Shot Multibox Detector and Faster Region-Based (Akila and Deepan, 2018). Six different diseases, including fusarium wilt, bacterial blight, leaf blight, micronutrient, root rot, and verticillium wilt, were predicated and using a color histogram and color descriptor were used to compute the skew divergence color variance feature. Sobel and Canny derived the shape skew divergence feature by applying the edge detection method to determine edge position and edge variance. The skew divergence texture feature was computed by combining the Gober filter and texture descriptor (Revathi and Hemalatha, 2014).

CNNs were used to classify diseased and healthy leaves and got 99.53% accuracy (Sladojevic et al., 2016). CNN's technology was applied to diagnose three different forms of maize diseases, including common rust, grey leaf spot, and northern leaf blight, using a dataset (3.854 photos) of diseased corn plants. In identifying diseases in maize plants, with a 99% accuracy rate (Hidayat et al., 2019). A CNN was used to identify and categorize whether the leaf was infected or healthy on an apple and tomato leaf image dataset of 3663 pictures and got 87% accuracy (Francis and Deisy, 2019).

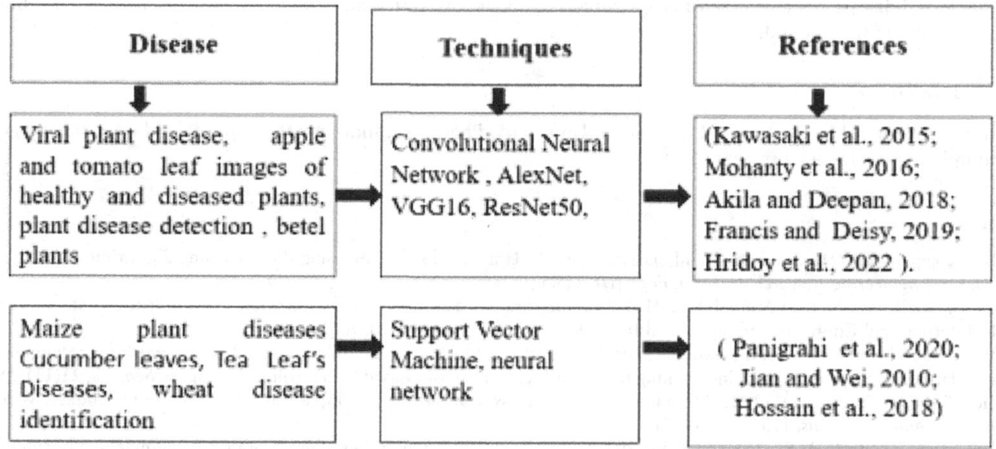

Figure 38.3 Description of disease and techniques

Table 38.1 Various techniques for identify and disease detecting

Techniques	*Crops and their disease*	*Merits*	*Demerits*	*Result*	*Refences*
SNN	Wheat different color and morphological features of wheat were extracted	classify wheat grains effectively using SVM	Neural Network was better than SVM	94.5%	Niu et al. (2014)
SVM	Diseases of brown blight in tea leaf's	The disease was identified and the best match was discovered.	SVM with a smaller number of features	93%	Hossain et al. (2018)
Deep learning	Plant Village dataset and anthracnose bacterial blight healthy leaf disease	CNNs are ideally suited for automated disease identification and diagnosis in plants using basic leaf image processing.	The training set's testing data was obtained from the same database as the training data.	98.17	Perumal (2021).
CNN	Images of healthy and diseased apple and tomato leaves	CNN significantly improved its classification accuracy	used a CNN for binary classification.	87%	Francis and Deisy (2019)

A CNN-based technique called D-Leaf was proposed for the disease of betel plants (Hridoy et al., 2022). Figure 38.3 depicts the disease and its techniques.

Comparison of Various Leaf Disease Detection Techniques

The various techniques for leaf disease detection and a comparison of their performance are shown in Table 38.1.

Conclusion

Machine learning techniques such as support vector machine (SVM) and deep learning-based techniques such as convolutional neural networks (CNN) have been shown to be reliable and practical for detecting microbial disease infections on plants. Plant leaf detection has been created by utilizing a variety of software. The two most significant qualities of plant leaf disease detection are speed and accuracy. It enables plant leaf disease identification and throughput. This publication discusses all the plant diseases and methods, including machine learning, deep learning, and image processing. It covers a variety of methods for identifying plant diseases with accurate identification and timely management programs, such as integrated disease management of crops, which can be incorporated and create a vast field of study for scholars in the fourth-coming time period.

Acknowledgment

The authors are grateful to the Lovely Professional University, Phagwara, India for the support and opportunity given for the completion of the manuscript.

References

Akila, M. & Deepan, P. (2018). Detection and classification of plant leaf diseases by using deep learning algorithm. International *Journal of Engineering Research & Technology (IJERT), 6(07).*

Al Bashish, D., Braik, M., & Bani-Ahmad, S. (2010). A framework for detection and classification of plant leaf and stem diseases. 2010 International Conference on Signal and Image Processing, (pp. 113–118). IEEE.

Almadhor, A., Rauf, H. T., Lali, M. I. U., Damaševičius, R., Alouffi, B., & Alharbi, A. (2021). AI-driven framework for recognition of guava plant diseases through machine learning from DSLR camera sensor based high resolution imagery. *Sensors*, 21(11), 3830.

Basavaiah, J. &Arlene Anthony, A. (2020). Tomato leaf disease classification using multiple feature extraction techniques. *Wireless Personal Communications*, 115(1), 633–651.

Behera, S. K., Jena, L., Rath, A. K., & Sethy, P. K. (2018). Disease classification and grading of orange using machine learning and fuzzy logic. *International Conference on Communication and Signal Processing*, (pp. 0678–0682).

Chakraborty, A., Layek, S., Sankar, R., Saha, S., Ghosh, A., & Ray, H. (2021). Early Detection of Disease in Rice Paddy: A Deep Learning based Convolution Neural Networks Approach. *12th International Conference on Computing Communication and Networking Technologies,* (pp. 1–5).

Durmuş, H., Güneş, E. O., & Kırcı, M. (2017). Disease detection on the leaves of the tomato plants by using deep learning. *6th International Conference on Agro-geoinformatics,* (pp. 1–5).

Ferentinos, K. P. (2018). Deep learning models for plant disease detection and diagnosis. *Computers and Electronics in Agriculture*, 145, 311–318.

Francis, J. & Anoop, B. K. (2016). Identification of leaf diseases in pepper plants using soft computing techniques. *2016 Conference on Emerging Devices and Smart Systems*, (pp. 168–173).

Francis, M. & Deisy, C. (2019). Disease detection and classification in agricultural plants using convolutional neural networks—a visual understanding. *2019 6th International Conference on Signal Processing and Integrated Networks (SPIN)*, (pp. 1063–1068).

Gaikwad, V. P. & Musande, V. (2017). Wheat disease detection using image processing. *2017 1st International Conference on Intelligent Systems and Information Management,* (pp. 110–112).

Gill. A, Kaur. T., & Devi, Y. K. (2022) Application of machine learning techniques in modern agriculture: A review. 2022 *14th International Conference on Contemporary Computing,* https://doi.org/10.1145/3549206.354925

Hidayat, A., Darusalam, U., & Irmawati, I. (2019). Detection of disease on corn plants using convolutional neural network methods. *Jurnal Ilmu Komputer dan Informasi,* 12(1), 51–56.

Hossain, S., Mou, R. M., Hasan, M. M., Chakraborty, S., & Razzak, M. A. (2018). Recognition and detection of tea leaf's diseases using support vector machine. *2018 IEEE 14th International Colloquium on Signal Processing & Its Applications*, (pp. 150–154).

Hridoy, R. H., Habib, T., Rahman, S., & Uddin, M. S. (2022). Deep neural networks-based recognition of betel plant diseases by leaf image classification. *Evolutionary Computing and Mobile Sustainable Networks,* (pp. 227–241). Springer, Singapore.

Jian, Z., and Wei, Z. (2010). Support vector machine for recognition of cucumber leaf diseases. *2010 2nd International Conference on Advanced Computer Control,* (5, pp. 264–266).

Karthik, G. & Praburam, N. (2016). Detection and prevention of banana leaf diseases from banana plant using Embeeded Linux board. *2016 Online International Conference on Green Engineering and Technologies*, (pp. 1-). IEEE.

Kaur, R. & Kang, S. S. (2015). An enhancement in classifier support vector machine to improve plant disease detection. 2015 IEEE 3rd International Conference on MOOCs, Innovation and Technology in Education (MITE),(pp. 135–140).

Kaur, T., and Kaur, H. (2018). Machine Learning: An internal review. Journal of Emerging Technilogies and Innovative Research, 5, 6.

Kawasaki, Y., Uga, H., Kagiwada, S., & Iyatomi, H. (2015). Basic study of automated diagnosis of viral plant diseases using convolutional neural networks. *International Symposium on Visual Computing*, (pp. 638–645). Springer, Cham.

Kumar K. K. & Kanna, E. (2022). Detection of rice plant disease using AdaBoostSVM classifier. *Agronomy Journal,* 114(4), 2213–2229.

Lukyanenko, A. N. (1991). Disease resistance in tomato. In Genetic Improvement of Tomato (pp. 99–119). Springer, Berlin, Heidelberg.

Mengistu, A. D., Alemayehu, D. M., & Mengistu, S. G. (2016). Ethiopian coffee plant diseases recognition based on imaging and machine learning techniques. *International Journal of Database Theory and Application*, 9(4), 79–88.

Mohanty, S. P., Hughes, D. P., & Salathé, M. (2016). Using deep learning for image-based plant disease detection. *Frontiers in Plant Science*, 7, 1419.

Niu, X., Wang, M., Chen, X., Guo, S., Zhang, H., & He, D. (2014). Image segmentation algorithm for disease detection of wheat leaves. *Proceedings of the 2014 International Conference on Advanced Mechatronic Systems*, (pp. 270–273).

Owomugisha, G. & Mwebaze, E. (2016). Machine learning for plant disease incidence and severity measurements from leaf images. *2016 15th IEEE international conference on machine learning and applications (ICMLA)*, (pp. 158–163).

Panigrahi, K. P., Das, H., Sahoo, A. K., & Moharana, S. C. (2020). Maize leaf disease detection and classification using machine learning algorithms. *In Progress in Computing, Analytics and Networking*, (pp. 659–669).

Perumal, P. (2021). Guava leaf disease classification using support vector machine. *Turkish Journal of Mathematics*, 12(7), 1177–1183.

Phadikar, S., Sil, J., & Das, A. K. (2013). Rice diseases classification using feature selection and rule generation techniques. *Computers and Electronics in Agriculture*, 90, 76–85.

Pujari, J. D., Yakkundimath, R., & Byadgi, A. S. (2015). Image processing based detection of fungal diseases in plants. *Procedia Computer Science*, 46, 1802–1808.

Ramesh, S., Hebbar, R., Niveditha, M., Pooja, R., Shashank, N., & Vinod, P. V. (2018). Plant disease detection using machine learning. *In 2018 International Conference on Design Innovations for 3Cs Compute Communicate Control*, (pp. 41–45).

Revathi, P. & Hemalatha, M. (2014). Identification of cotton diseases based on cross information gain deep forward neural network classifier with PSO feature selection. *International Journal of Engineering Research & Technology*, 5(6), 4637–4642.

Sembiring, A., Away, Y., Arnia, F., & Muharar, R. (2021). Development of concise convolutional neural network for tomato plant disease classification based on leaf images. *Journal of Physics: Conference Series*, 1845(1), 012009.

Sladojevic, S., Arsenovic, M., Anderla, A., Culibrk, D., & Stefanovic, D. (2016). Deep neural networks based recognition of plant diseases by leaf image classification. *Computational Intelligence and Neuroscience.*

Sun, X., Li, G., Qu, P., Xie, X., Pan, X., & Zhang, W. (2022). Research on plant disease identification based on CNN. *Cognitive Technology*, 2, 155–163.

Taslim, A., Saon, S., Muladi, M., & Hidayat, W. N. (2021). Plant leaf identification system using convolutional neural network. *Bulletin of Engineering Geology and the Environment*, 10(6), 3341–3352.

Tetila, E. C., Machado, B. B., Menezes, G. K., Oliveira, A. D. S., Alvarez, M., Amorim, W. P., & Pistori, H. (2019). Automatic recognition of soybean leaf diseases using UAV images and deep convolutional neural networks. *IEEE Geoscience and Remote Sensing Letters*, 17(5), 903–907.

Umapathy Eaganathan, D., Lackose, V., & Benjamin, F. J. (2014). Identification of sugarcane leaf scorch diseases using K-means clustering segmentation and K-NN based classification. *International Journal of Advanced Computer Science and Applications*, 3(12), 11–16.

Wei Tan, J., Chang, S. W., Abdul-Kareem, S., Yap, H. J., & Yong, K. T. (2018). Deep learning for plant species classification using leaf vein morphometric. *IEEE/ACM Transactions on Computational Biology and Bioinformatics,* 17(1), 82–90.

39 Artificial intelligence's involvement in education and student's academic performance

Kandula Neha[1,a] *and Ram Kumar*[2,b]

[1]Research Scholar, Lovely Professional University, Punjab, India

[2]Assistant Professor, Lovely Professional University, Punjab, India

Abstract

The significant addition of technology, artificial intelligence (AI), to education has always been significant. AI has invariably aided both lecturers and students, from robotic teaching to the development of an automated system for grading analysis. To summarize and highlight the importance of AI in teaching and student analysis, we did a detailed assessment of numerous analytical advances that were used globally, such as computer science methodologies used to the education sector. Our research demonstrates that all information science-enabled intelligent tutor systems are built on AI. In this research the execution of an easy-to-use programming device for anticipating the understudy execution in course which depends on a brain network classifier will be made. In this AI model for anticipating the probable exhibition of understudy will be researched. The utilization of AI has empowered the improvement of more complex and more effective understudy models which addresses and distinguish a more extensive territory of understudy conduct than was beforehand conceivable.

Keywords: Artificial intelligence, education, prediction, students models

Introduction

Artificial intelligence (AI) is a gift in our lives and is rapidly advancing in today's world. Today, AI research is carried out in cancer research, reducing the risk of plane crashes, developing self-driving cars, and more. AI-powered robots have outperformed human surgeons in artisanal incisions while keeping an eye on children, the elderly and hospital patients. Assist in fraud detection for credit card companies. AI in education is used by educational system implementations in various fields such as physics, programming, essay writing and reading. Typical AI applications in the learning domain include information presentation, intelligent tutoring, and self-governing agents. For decades, AI in education has created powerful learning environments and positive interactive experiences for students. Rapid advances in technologies such as AI and computers are making every industry, not just education, compact. Current survey by one of the business education forum that is IBM, shows that in 2020 employment opportunities for information and analytical skills will increase by his 3 lakh to 27 lakh.

Literature Review

Communication - using a smart tutoring system to provide appropriate feedback one of the most crucial responsibilities of the teacher or lecturer type is providing students with pertinent and targeted feedback. But considering the variety of researchers in this field, it might be exceedingly challenging (Wang et al.2015). Therefore, to enhance the quality of feedback and mentoring, many colleges use interactive learning environments (ILEs). ILE is a technical term that refers to the integration of interactive learning techniques with e-learning strategies to maintain a student's learning state over the course of their academic career (Zhang and Jia, 2017).

Monitoring student performance through assessment: ITS also serves as a coach for UN organizations, directing requests for assignments and study schedules. At the same time, it assists in locating learning gaps in students' performance over the course of their lives (Yang and Li, 2018). In essence, the ITS builds a model of the teacher's PC with derived rules for the teacher's scoring decisions as the teacher (Teacher) examines her set of sample student responses. Then, this approach is frequently applied to evaluate a range of student tasks (Wang et al., 2018).

Teaching method: From individualized education to learning robots, one of the difficulties she faces in instructing kids is the stark difference in learning and comprehension rates. As a result, people who are already unfamiliar with the subject matter can just get bored, while others might get totally engrossed in novel ideas and phenomena. It assists pupils in avoiding problems and assisting them with their learning (Hutchins 2017).

Prediction models: Warning system based on prediction and data identification models where quantitate analysis of students' academic prediction. The main findings are based on class performance, knowledge summary and summative performance through online engineering education (Jiao et al.2022).

[a]neha09kandula@gmail.com; [b]ram.26209@lpu.co.in

Methodology and Specifications

While selecting out of various styles of literature reviews, we have a tendency to determine to think about non-expert narrative overview because it can higher facilitate America to realize our one major target – provides a wide image of the tutorial prospect within the context of AI applications.

Paradigm framework description for a summary

With a view to create associate in nursing decent exhibition of the composition citations, we have a tendency to propose the subsequent framework of the model tutorial landscape. We contemplate four major elements of the tutorial method that would be suffering from AI: content, teaching methods, evaluation, and communication.

Dataset and processing

We have taken steps to extract predeclared values and clarify the classifier pedagogy process and parameters and Record. Students' Academic Dataset, link: https://www.kaggle.com/aljarah/xAPI-Edu-Data.

Data is obtained for building the proposed Artificial Intelligence model to predict student performance. This is an educational dataset from the learning management system known as kalboard 360. There are 500 student records in the dataset. It has 16 different characteristics nominal data type which are translated into '0' and '1' binary data. Other are transformed into numerical. All the missing values are removed and the data cleaning number is 480. Data transformation for the dataset is applied.

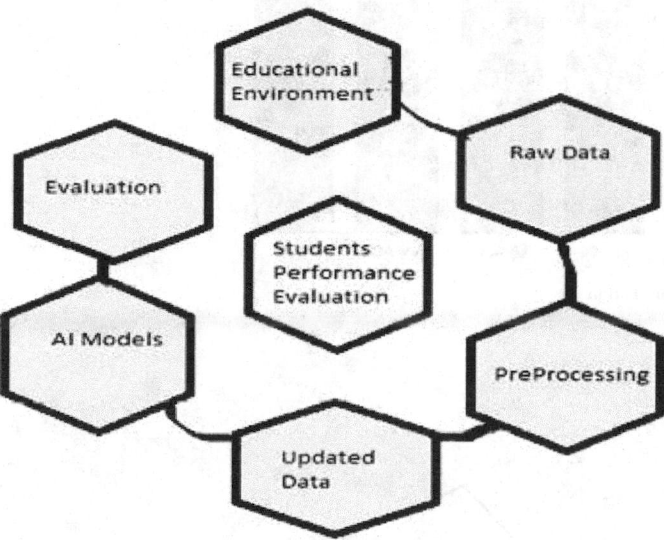

Figure 39.1 Student performance analysis model

Table 39.1 Students data set

Name	*Data type*	*Distinct values*
Gender, parent responsibility & semester	Nominal	2
Nationality and place of birth	Nominal	14
Stages and section Id	Nominal	3
Grades and topics	Nominal	12
Raised hand, visited resource, viewing announcements and group discussion	Numeric	0–100
Parent answering, parent satisfaction an student absent day	Nominal	2

Experimental Results

Evaluation of student performance is crucial for determining whether a development is viable. The student's performance is improved via daily evaluation, which also makes it clear where the student is falling short. It takes a lot of human labour to complete this operation manually. A model using artificial intelligence has been developed to make it easier, and it uses psychometric variables including student motivation, study habits, interactions, and parental support to forecast their achievement.

The designed model used Python along with multiple AI based neural networks which includes Cost function, optimization and epoch and for visualization purpose mat plot libraries has been included

After uploading the data set in the model based on different features, a graph has been generated which gives the overall accuracy of the models which has been used for performance prediction.

The performance of students have been predicted based on few metric analysis like student motivation, study behaviour, student interaction, and parent/family support with the help of pre-processed data.

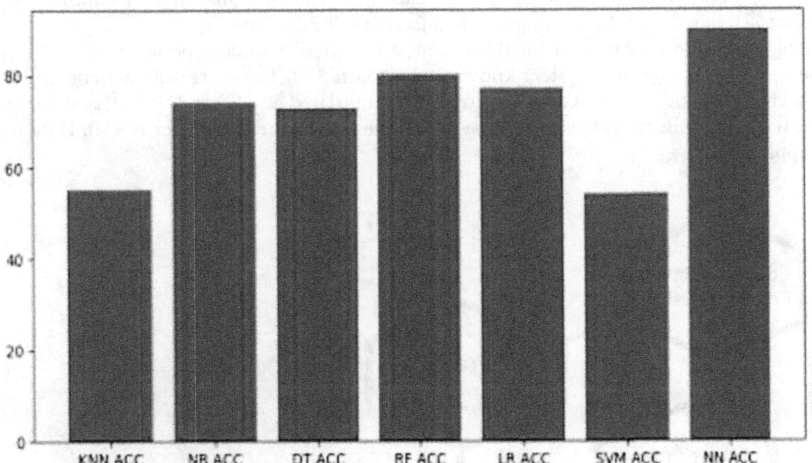

Figure 39.2 Accuracy graph of AI model prediction

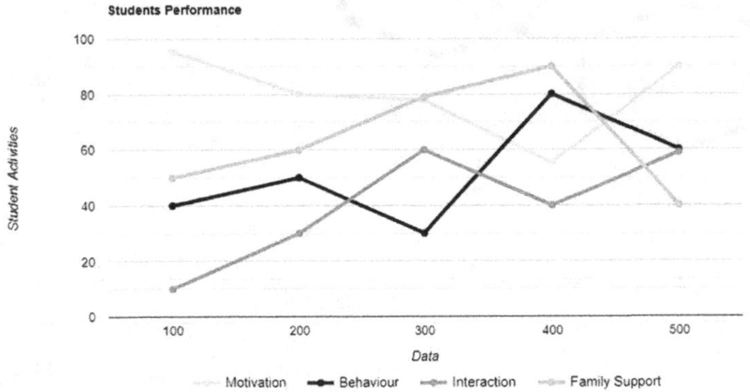

Figure 39.3 Psychometric feature analysis

Conclusion

This paper insights the impact of intelligence systems on education and provides topic-based perspectives. However, we are also considering AI. This allows you to easily rewrite student difficulties, see how to solve them, enhance collective imagination, and shape entirely new classroom knowledge. Summarizing existing clarifications and perspectives, based on clear conclusion. If you tend to collate learning environments, you won't see multiple deviations from your previous expertise. The abstract shows that AI mechanism are already being used in several elements of academic methodologies, including content evolution, pedagogy, student evaluation, and teacher-student interactions. This work contributes to existing data in the field and may be of interest to experts, faculty, students, and other universities in the field of technical reinforcement learning to predict student performance. This allows us to extend existing models for further research by conducting assessments on a large number of students.

References

Al Emran, M. & Shaalan, K. A. (2014). Survey of intelligent language tutoring systems. *Proceedings of the 2014 International Conference on Advances in Computing, Communications and Informatics.*

Chassignol, M., Khoroshavin, A., Klimova, A., & Bilyatdinova, A. (2018). Potential prediction based on data mining. *Procedia Computer Science*, 136, 16–24.

Dzikovska M. O & Moore, J. D. (2010). BEETLE II: a system for tutoring and computational linguistics experimentation. Computational Linguistics.

Frize M. & Frasson, C. (2000). Decision-support and intelligent tutoring systems in medical education. Clinical and Investigative Medicine.

Hutchins, D. (2017). AI boosts personalized learning in higher education. Ed Tech. Jiao, P., Ouyang, F., Zhang, Q. (2022). Artificial intelligence-enabled prediction model of student academic performance in online engineering education. Artificial Intelligence Review. https://doi.org/10.1007/s10462-022-10155-y

Keeler, J. D., Leow, W. K., & Rumelhart, D. E. (1991). Integrated segmentation of hand-printed numerals and recognition. *Advances in Neural Information Processing System*, 3, 557–563.

Khan, I., Ahmad, A. R., Jabeur, N., & Mahdi, M. N. (2021). An artificial intelligence approach to monitor student performance and devise preventive measures. Smart Learning Environments, 8, 17. https://doi.org/10.1186/s40561-021-00161-y.

Koedinger K. R. et al. (2013). New potentials for data-driven intelligent tutoring system development and optimization. *AI Magazine.*

Lesgold, A. et al. (1992). SHERLOCK: A coached practice environment for an electronics troubleshooting job. Computer Assisted Instruction and Intelligent Tutoring Systems Shared Goals and Complementary Approaches.

Melis, E. (2004). Active math: An intelligent tutoring system for mathematics. Seventh International Conference Artificial Intelligence and Soft Computing.

Neha, K.& Sidiq, S. J. (2020). Analysis of student academic performance through expert systems. *International Research Journal on Advanced Science Hub*, 2, 48–54.

Neha, K. (2021). A study on prediction of student academic performance based on expert systems. Turkish Journal of Computer and Mathematics Education, 12(7), 1483–1488.

Nwana H. (1990). Intelligent tutoring systems: an overview. Artificial Intelligence Review. Wang, P., Tchounikine, P., & Chao, M. Q. (2018). A framework for the development of orchestration technologies for technology-enhanced learning activities using tablets in classrooms. International *Journal of Technology Enhanced Learning*, 10.

Pedro, M. O., Baker, R., Bowers, A., & Heffernan, N. (2013). Predicting college enrolment by student interaction with an intelligent middle school teaching system. *Educational Data Mining.*

Steenbergen-Hu, S., Cooper, H. (2015). A meta-analysis of the effectiveness of intelligent tutoring systems on college students' academic learning // *Journal of Educational Psychology.*

VanLehn, K. et al. (2013). The Architecture of Why2-Atlas: A Coach for Qualitative Physics Sabo K. E. et al. Searching for the two sigma advantage: Evaluating algebra intelligent tutors // Comput. Human Behav. *2013.*

Wang D. et al. (2015). A problem solving oriented intelligent tutoring system to improve students' acquisition of basic computer skills // Computing Education.

Weerasinghe, A. & Mitrovic, A. (2011). Facilitating adaptive tutorial dialogues in EER-tutor //. Lecture Notes in Computer Science (including subseries Lecture Notes in Artificial Intelligence and Lecture Notes in Bioinformatics). 2011.

Yang, F. & Li, W. B. F. (2018). Study on student performance estimation, student progress analysis, and student potential prediction based on data mining. Computers & Education, 123, 97–108.

Zhang, B. & Jia, J. (2017). Evaluating an intelligent tutoring system for personalized math teaching // Proceedings - 2017 International Symposium on Educational Technology.

40 An experimental study of text preprocessing techniques on user reviews

Sonia Rani[1,a] *and Tarandeep Singh Walia*[2,b]

[1]Research Scholar, School of Computer Application, Lovely Professional University, Punjab, India

[2]Associate Professor, School of Computer Application, Lovely Professional University, Punjab, India

Abstract

Text preprocessing plays a vital role in extracting important information from unstructured raw data and improving the quality of raw data. Preprocessing techniques transform the raw data into a more understandable format. The popularity of online shopping has been increasing the number of product reviews on e-commerce websites. However, it is very challenging to understand these informal reviews written by non-professionals, which contain so much noise, abbreviations, and spelling errors. So, text preprocessing is a crucial and essential step to removing the noise from reviews and understanding the users' feedback about the products. This study's primary purpose is to experiment with several preprocessing techniques, such as noise removal, contractions, spelling correction, stemming, and lemmatization on text data, and analyze the challenges of some preprocessing methods.

Keywords: Product reviews, preprocessing, spell correction, tokenization, stemming, lemmatization, natural language processing

Introduction

Online shopping is exponentially increasing unstructured consumer reviews daily. These reviews are vital to understanding the user's intentions regarding product features and improving the product's cons. There are millions of reviews on e-commerce websites for several products. But the main problem is that these reviews contain so much noise and abbreviations because professionals do not write them. So, text preprocessing plays a vital role in normalizing noisy reviews. Text pre-processing is applied to text before applying feature extraction techniques to extract important information from reviews. To avoid errors in the results at later stages, preprocessing steps like tokenization, stop word removal, and stemming must be applied carefully. However, most researchers have done admirable work on text preprocessing to develop text mining systems. But still, there are some limitations in existing systems due to much noisy and abbreviated text. This study experimented with the main steps of text preprocessing techniques and analyzed their challenges to understanding the reviews. The structure of this paper is as follows. Section 1 introduces the problem definition, and related work is presented in the 2 Section. 3 Section describes the data collection and preprocessing techniques and concludes this study in the 4 Section.

Literature Review

Text preprocessing is the first and crucial step to extracting knowledge information and useful patterns from unstructured text data. Raw data contains noise, outliers, missing values, and incomplete and inconsistent information. Alasadi and Bhaya (2017) reviewed the study of text preprocessing techniques to mine the data and described the 1st step of preprocessing is to clean data by removing missing values and outliers from the text. Chai (2022) surveyed the study on various text preprocessing techniques with their pros and cons. They have also suggested the preprocessing steps must be used according to the problem statement. Etaiwi and Naymat (2017) experimented with 1600 hotel reviews collected from trip advisor and compared the results by applying (stemming, stop words removal, punctuation removal) preprocessing techniques and without preprocessing. The system improved the review classification results by applying the preprocessing steps. Gabriela et al. (2021) proposed an extractive summarization system of hotel reviews using sentence segmentation, word tokenization, pos-tagging, and case folding preprocessing techniques. Yulia (2008) described that eliminating stop words scribed that eliminating stop words can reduce the efficiency of summarizing results. Lourdusamy and Abraham (2018) surveyed the study on preprocessing tools and steps for summarization purposes. These steps are tokenization, pos tagging, grammatical parsing, chunking, stemming, document indexing, stop word filtering, word sense disambiguation, and lemmatization. Nayak et al. (2016) applied tokenization, stop words removal, and stemming preprocessing techniques to summarize the text. Tabassum and Patil (2020) surveyed the study on different preprocessing techniques. These techniques include punctuation removal, sentence tokenization, case folding, stop words removal, stemming, and lemmatization preprocessing steps.

[a]soniasimran30@gmail.com; [b]tarandeep.25153@lpu.co.in

Experiments

Data extraction through web scrapping

Data collection is the first step to experimenting with any machine learning or NLP algorithm. This study has used the Beautiful Soup library to collect reviews from an e-commerce website. Beautiful Soup crawls multiple web page information to collect multiple reviews simultaneously. For experiment purposes, this study has collected reviews in the fashion domain.

Preprocessing steps

Preprocessing is an essential and challenging task to clean the data. Almost 80% of the time is spent preprocessing the data to clean the noisy and abbreviated data. Online user reviews contain irrelevant data such as null values, noisy data, outliers, emojis, punctuations, abbreviations, non-vocab words, white spaces, informal words, spelling errors, etc.

Data cleaning

The data cleaning process finds out the errors and inconsistencies in data due to the absence, duplicate, or null values in data and cleans these errors by removing or replacing the missing values; It is known as scrubbing. Sometimes there are many null values, outliers, and Nan values in the data due to noise and data extraction methods. So, the first step is to remove or replace the null or NAN values to clean the data and remove the duplicate values to contain the unique reviews.

Removal of emojis, special characters, and punctuations

Emojis are like small digital icons or images used to express emotions. Nowadays, most people use emojis in reviews to express their feedback about products, but machine learning algorithms cannot process these emojis. So, removing the emojis is an important step of preprocessing. Emoticons library is used to detect the emojis present in the reviews. The regular expressions (re) are used to clean the alphanumeric, special characters, numbers, and punctuations.

Figure 40.1 demonstrates the many emojis in reviews that machine learning algorithms can't process. These emojis can be detected by the emoticons Python library and removed before applying any further steps.

Spell correction

When writing reviews, users write many abbreviations, wrong spelling, and non-vocab words in the reviews. The major challenge is to correct these non-vocab words and abbreviations. This study has used the Text Blob, autocorrect, and spellchecker libraries to correct spelling errors and abbreviations. Text Blob and spellchecker cannot accurately correct the non-vocab words' spelling errors due to non-vocab words not being present in these libraries. Although the Autocorrect library has given more accurate results in less time than Text Blob. Still, it is a big challenge to correct the abbreviated words.

Figure 40.2 shows the output of correcting the spelling through Text Blob, but it has changed the spelling from suprb to Supra and Drs into dry Vry changed to Cry, and Gud changed to Mud Cloth which changed the entire meaning of the sentence.

Reviews	Rating	Review Dates	Review Title
Suprb drs , Nys Looking Vry SmarT , Gud Cloth , Received the product before expected date, Same as Displayed	4.0 out of 5 stars	Reviewed in India on 23 April 2019	Suprb , Nys
Perfect fit,material ,color. Unlike other party wear stuff, the material is cotton(hoisery) material. The kids wear it comfortably.My kid is extremely fussy when it comes to wearing anything other...	5.0 out of 5 stars	Reviewed in India on 25 April 2019	Must Buy.Smart and comfortable.
Very very happy with this purchase .the product quality is really awesome with a very decent price...good color and perfect stiching...lasts long...	5.0 out of 5 stars	Reviewed in India on 2 October 2019	Super quality material nice color perfect stiching
Very soft very comfortable .it's really worth of money. I get this dress in 800 rs but it's ooking like 2000 dress very nice.♥♥♥♥.my kid very comfortable in this dress .thank u amazon to delive...	5.0 out of 5 stars	Reviewed in India on 2 August 2020	♥very very super much worth of money .so soft .
	5.0 out of 5	Reviewed in India on 9	

Figure 40.1 Presents the emojis in reviews

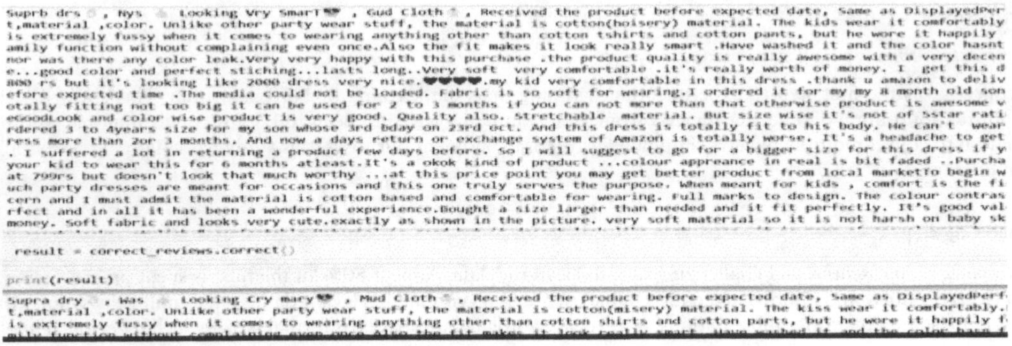

```
Suprb drs , Nys  Looking Vry SmarT , Gud Cloth , Received the product before expected date, Same as DisplayedPer
t,material ,color. Unlike other party wear stuff, the material is cotton(hoisery) material. The kids wear it comfortably
is extremely fussy when it comes to wearing anything other than cotton tshirts and cotton pants, but he wore it happily
amily function without complaining even once.Also the fit makes it look really smart .Have washed it and the color hasnt
nor was there any color leak.Very very happy with this purchase .the product quality is really awesome with a very decen
e...good color and perfect stiching...lasts long..Very soft  very comfortable .it's really worth of money. I  get this d
800 rs but it's looking like 2000 dress very nice.❤❤❤❤.my kid very comfortable in this dress .thank u amazon to deliv
efore expected time .The media could not be loaded. Fabric is so soft for wearing.I ordered it for my my 8 month old son
otally fitting not too big it can be used for 2 to 3 months if you can not more than that otherwise product is awesome v
eGoodLook and color wise product is very good. Quality also. Stretchable  material. But size wise it's not of 5star rati
rdered 3 to 4years size for my son whose 3rd bday on 23rd oct. And this dress is totally fit to his body. He can't  wear
ress more than 2or 3 months. And now a days return or exchange system of Amazon is totally worse. It's a headache to get
. I suffered a lot in returning a product few days before. So I will suggest to go for a bigger size for this dress if y
your kid to wear this for 6 months atleast.It's a okok kind of product ...colour appreance in real is bit faded ..Purcha
at 799rs but doesn't look that much worthy ...at this price point you may get better product from local marketTo begin w
uch party dresses are meant for occasions and this one truly serves the purpose. When meant for kids , comfort is the fi
cern and I must admit the material is cotton based and comfortable for wearing. Full marks to design. The colour contras
rfect and in all it has been a wonderful experience.Bought a size larger than needed and it fit perfectly. It's good val
money. Soft fabric and looks very cute.exactly as shown in the picture. very soft material so it is not harsh on baby sk

result = correct_reviews.correct()

print(result)

Supra dry , Was  Looking Cry mary , Mud Cloth , Received the product before expected date, Same as DisplayedPerf
t,material ,color. Unlike other party wear stuff, the material is cotton(misery) material. The kiss wear it comfortably.
is extremely fussy when it comes to wearing anything other than cotton shirts and cotton parts, but he wore it happily f
```

Figure 40.2 Implementation of spell correction with Text Blob

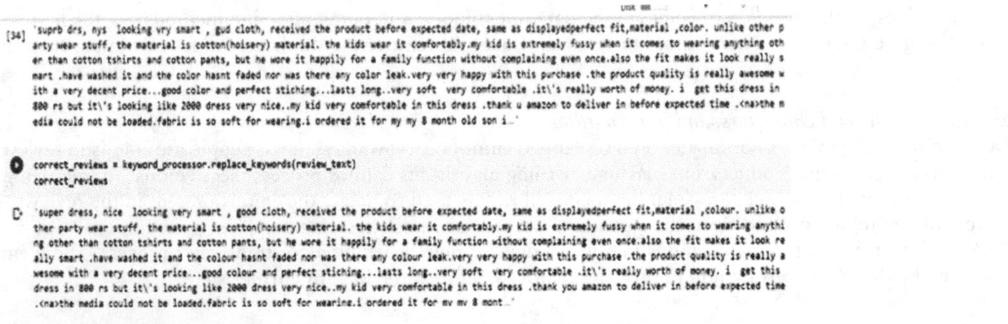

```
[34] 'suprb drs, nys  looking vry smart , gud cloth, received the product before expected date, same as displayedperfect fit,material ,color. unlike other p
arty wear stuff, the material is cotton(hoisery) material. the kids wear it comfortably.my kid is extremely fussy when it comes to wearing anything oth
er than cotton tshirts and cotton pants, but he wore it happily for a family function without complaining even once.also the fit makes it look really s
mart .have washed it and the color hasnt faded nor was there any color leak.very very happy with this purchase .the product quality is really awesome w
ith a very decent price...good color and perfect stiching...lasts long..very soft  very comfortable .it\'s really worth of money. i  get this dress in
800 rs but it\'s looking like 2000 dress very nice..my kid very comfortable in this dress .thank u amazon to deliver in before expected time .<na>the m
edia could not be loaded.fabric is so soft for wearing.i ordered it for my my 8 month old son i...'

correct_reviews = keyword_processor.replace_keywords(review_text)
correct_reviews

'super dress, nice  looking very smart , good cloth, received the product before expected date, same as displayedperfect fit,material ,colour. unlike o
ther party wear stuff, the material is cotton(hoisery) material. the kids wear it comfortably.my kid is extremely fussy when it comes to wearing anythi
ng other than cotton tshirts and cotton pants, but he wore it happily for a family function without complaining even once.also the fit makes it look re
ally smart .have washed it and the colour hasnt faded nor was there any colour leak.very very happy with this purchase .the product quality is really a
wesome with a very decent price...good colour and perfect stiching...lasts long..very soft  very comfortable .it\'s really worth of money. i  get this
dress in 800 rs but it\'s looking like 2000 dress very nice..my kid very comfortable in this dress .thank you amazon to deliver in before expected time
.<na>the media could not be loaded.fabric is so soft for wearing.i ordered it for my my 8 mont...'
```

Figure 40.3 Implementation of spell and abbreviations correction with flash text

Figure 40.3 shows the implementation of spell and abbreviations correction with Flash Text. To correct the abbreviations, we create a dictionary and replace the abbreviations and unknown words using the Flash Text library. It gives the correct output.

Case folding

Case folding helps to preprocess the data because the machine produces different outcomes after inputting the same word in upper-case and lower-case variations. It is required that all reviews must be converted into small letters to apply machine learning methods.

Contractions

Most users write reviews in short form, which cannot be processed without changing the exact form. This work has used the contraction library to expand the short words, which helps to improve the accuracy.

Stop words removal

Stop words removal in the English language, NLTK stop words list contains (a, an, the, it, my, from, and not) in the text. These stop words are removed to reduce the features. But it loses the semantic meaning of the sentence. For example, I bought it for my son. After removing stop words from and it (I bought son), it can change the entire meaning of the sentence. So, removing stop words is not a good choice for summarization, but we can delete the stop words by creating and defining a list of domain-specific stop words with the Tf-Idf scores of these words.

Tokenization

Tokenization is performed to split the paragraphs into sentences and words. A sentence or phrase tokenizer with a bigram or n-gram approach can give an accurate output rather than a word tokenizer. Because the single word (nice)

is not contained any semantics but (nice product) is useful. The phrase tokenizer can be developed to extract the multi-word expression, increasing accuracy in mining the text.

Stemming

To normalize the reviews stemming is performed, and it helps to find the similarity between text and stem the words into their root form. But the major limitation of stem words is that they can change the entire meaning of one sentence. After implementation, it is found that stemming is not a good choice for review summarization.

Lemmatization

To overcome the limitation of stemming, lemmatization is used. Lemmatization strips the words into their root form. But it does not change the entire meaning because it strips the words according to the position. For example (playing change it to play) after lemmatizing it. It maintains the exact meaning of the word. It is also used for the similarity between words.

Figure 40.4 demonstrates that after performing the stemming on reviews, excellent word change into excel, which is the inappropriate and wrong output. But lemmatization gives the correct happy, excellent words after lemmatizing the words, which can help to improve the accuracy of the reviews' summary.

Pos tagging

After lemmatization, tagging can be performed to tag the words with nouns, verbs, adjectives, proper nouns, or determiners. Tagging can be performed with the NLTK library and can also help extract the important features from reviews.

[happy purchase product quality really awesome...	happy purchase product quality really awesome ...	[happy, purchase, product, quality, really, aw...	[happi, purchas, product, qualiti, realli, awe...	[happy, purchase, product, quality, really, aw...
[soft comfortable really worth money get dress...	soft comfortable really worth money get dress ...	[soft, comfortable, really, worth, money, get,...	[soft, comfort, realli, worth, money, get, dre...	[soft, comfortable, really, worth, money, get,...
[na]	na	[na]	[na]	[na]
...	...	...	...	...
[excellent]	excellent	[excellent]	[excel]	[excellent]

Figure 40.4 Implementation of stemming and lemmatization

Summary of Existing Work

Table 40.1 Summary of existing traditional approaches with limitations

Reference	*Approaches*	*Limitations*
Gabriela et al. (2021)	Applied the four preprocessing steps-sentence segmentation, word tokenization (NLTK), case folding, and pos tagging with adjective-noun pairing phrases.	Not considering some preprocessing techniques and their system ROUGE-1 recall results, BLEU scores {0.2101, 0.7820} and {0.0670, 0.03672} were achieved.
Ramadhan et al. (2020)	Proposed the extractive summary and experimented with both conditions considered typos, without stop words and no typos, and with stop words.	Achieved less accuracy (Rouge-l- 42.29% with typos and no stop words) and (Rouge-l- 46.71% with no typos but stop words.
Singh et al. (2015)	They have corrected abbreviations, informal words, and wrong spelling manually.	Not considered the Flash Text (released in Aug 2017) Python library to replace the informal and abbreviated words.
Gautam et al. (2021)	Generated the extractive summary of Tv reviews by clustering the features and sub-features.	Informal and unnormalized words affected to clustering of the features and limit the blue scores to 0.321.

Conclusion

After experimenting with several preprocessing techniques, it is found that not every preprocessing technique can be applied to every data because each problem's solution may vary according to the problem statement. However, some research work has not considered data preprocessing techniques, but text preprocessing is a vital step in text summarization. Noise removal and spelling and abbreviations correction are the main preprocessing steps; these steps can be applied to every data. Removing the punctuation, special characters or symbols, and case folding is also an important preprocessing step for summarization. The phrase or sentence tokenization can be more helpful in improving the summary quality because single words do not express any detailed or important information. Stemming should not be performed on reviews because sometimes the wrong stemming of a word can change its entire meaning and give incorrect output. However, lemmatization is a good choice of preprocessing to find the similarity between two words but stop word removal is not an important preprocessing step for summarization purposes. Some preprocessing techniques are also demonstrated in this study. Every preprocessing technique has pros and cons, and a wrong technique can affect the whole NLP pipeline. So, preprocessing techniques must be applied wisely according to the development of the type of NLP application.

References

Alasadi, S. A. &Bhaya, W. S. (2017). Review of data preprocessing techniques in data mining. *Journal of Engineering and Applied Sciences*, 12(16), 4102–4107. https://doi.org/10.3923/jeasci.2017.4102.4107.

Chai, C. P. (2022). Comparison of text pre-processing methods. *Natural Language Engineering,* 1–45. https://doi.org/10.1017/S1351324922000213

Etaiwi, W. & Naymat, G. (2017). The impact of applying different preprocessing steps on review spam detection. *Procedia Computer Science*, 113, 273–279. https://doi.org/10.1016/j.procs.2017.08.368

Gabriela, N., Siautama, R., Claire, I. A., & Suhartono, D. (2021). Extractive hotel review summarization based on TF/IDF and adjective-noun pairing by considering annual sentiment trends. *Procedia Computer Science*, 179, 558–565. https://doi.org/10.1016/j.procs.2021.01.040

Gautam, S., Kaur, J., & Josan, G. S. (2021). Deep neural network-based multi-review summarization system. *International Journal of Next-Generation Computing,* 12(3), 461–466. https://doi.org/10.47164/ijngc.v12i3.714

Ledeneva, Y. (2008). Effect of preprocessing on extractive summarization with maximal frequent sequences. Advances in Artificial Intelligence. *Lecture Notes in Computer Science*, 5317, 123–132. https://doi.org/10.1007/978-3-540-88636-5_11

Lourdusamy, R. & Abraham, S. (2018). A survey on text pre-processing techniques and tools. *International Journal of Computer Sciences and Engineering*, 6(3), 148–157. https://doi.org/10.26438/ijcse/v6si3.148157

Nayak, A. S., Kanive, A. P., Chandavekar, N., & Balasubramani, R. (2016). Survey on preprocessing techniques for text mining. *International Journal of Advanced Trends in Computer Science and Engineering*, 5(6), 16875–16879. https://doi.org/10.18535/ijecs/v5i6.25

Ramadhan, M. R., Endah, S. N., & Mantau, A. B. J. (2020). Implementation of text rank algorithm in product review summarization. *Proceeding 4th International Conference on Informatics and Computational Sciences*, 1–5. https://doi.org/10.1109/ICICoS51170.2020.9299005

Singh, J. P., Rana, N. P., & Alkhowaiter, W. (2015). Sentiment analysis of product reviews containing English and Hindi texts. *Open and Big Data Management and Innovation*, 9373: 416–422. https://doi.org /10.1007/978-3-319-25013-7_33.

Tabassum, A. & Patil, R. R. (2020). A survey on text pre-processing & feature extraction techniques in natural language processing. International Research Journal of Engineering and Technology, 7(6), 4864–4867. www.irjet.net.

41 Implementation of gas and fire detection systems in home and industrial environment

Yogendra Bharadwaj[1,a], *Prabhdeep Singh*[2,b], *and Navneet Kumar Rajpoot*[1,c]

[1]Student, Graphic Era Deemed To Be University, Dehradun, Uttakhand, India

[2]Assistant Professor, Graphic Era Deemed To Be University, Dehradun, Uttakhand, India

Abstract

One of the main factors that hurts not only buildings but also people is fire accidents. Electrical distribution, lighting systems, cooking, etc. are the most frequent causes of house fires. Gas leakage issues cause numerous incidents that cause both financial damage and human injuries. In this technological age, using engineering is the best method to prevent such incidents. This research proposes a low-cost smoke and heat-based fire detection and control system. It combines an Arduino microcontroller with heat and fire detection sensors to identify the presence of a fire and inform people through alarms after detection. These alarms could be triggered by heat or smoke detectors that detect fire. In this paper, the design of an Arduino-based fire alarm system for homes and companies is discussed. The primary goal of the paper on home safety is to prevent fire incidents that could harm both the people and the property inside the home. The heat from the fire is detected by an MQ-5 sensor, and the flame is detected by a flame sensor. A buzzer and red light are activated and an alarm is displayed as soon as the system senses gas or flame. The test's outcomes are recorded and discussed. This technology can assist users in raising their safety standards by providing quick action to stop mishaps. The users will finally be able to safeguard both their lives and their property against these types of disasters.

Keywords: Arduino Uno, flame sensor, gas sensor

Introduction

As everyone is aware, security is a huge problem in the present day, and this includes the problem of gas leaks. The number of accidents seems to be rising steadily (Subramnian et al., 2020). In this context, we refer to incidents involving flammable gases like cylinder explosions in homes and cars are a common occurrence in the news. Many have been hurt, and some have lost their lives.

The fire problem is promising in terms of the number of accidents caused by fire and the number of fatalities and injuries, but the substantially greater proportion of deaths to injuries is concerning. This increased fatality rate may point to difficulties experienced by medical and emergency services in responding to similar incidents, which may have resulted in fewer fatalities (Kumar et al., 2019). High death rates may have additional causes, such as the extreme nature of fire incidents.

The need for an early fire detection system cannot be overstated when it comes to the protection of human life and material possessions. Damages may be mitigated, and firefighting efforts can be maximized with the help of a fire detection system. It's also a must-do in terms of basic fire prevention (Roque et al., 2020). There is no need to worry about being in danger when sleeping or working since early fire detection will alert you and give you time to escape. Having a fire detection system installed in your house or place of business is important for several reasons.

It is necessary to implement a gas deduction scheme. As the world evolves, so too does technology, ever-improving thanks to more practical ideas and harder labour. The MQ-6 semiconductor sensor is being used to detect flammable gases in this paper. Tin oxide (SnO_2) is used in this gas sensor (Jadon et. al., 2019). This sensor's conductivity drops in the open air. There is a correlation between the presence of the flammable gases of interest and an increase in the conductivity of the sensor. This sensor's conductivity is concentration-dependent; therefore, it can detect flammable gases as well as smoke, butane, isobutene, and alcohol. It also doubles as a handy tool for us to utilize when sampling new bottles of booze (Sohail et al., 2019). The output of the liquefied petroleum gas (LPG) sensor drops whenever it detects a leak from a storage tank. The microcontroller will keep an eye on this low signal to determine how much gas is released. The microcontroller's current capabilities are limited to activating an light-emitting diode (LED) and a buzzer. This paper presents a method for protecting homes and businesses from fire and gas leaks with the use of sensors like the MQ-6 gas sensor, which can detect LPG seepage while maintaining a high output under normal circumstances (Dubey et al., 2019). The material has poor conductivity to oxygen-free air and is hence very sensitive to SnO_2. The conductivity of the sensor is exactly proportional to the concentration of the gas when the target combustion gases are present.

[a]Bharadwaj.yogendra1@gmail.com,Yogendrabharadwaj_200211167.cse@geu.ac.in;[b]ssingh.prabhdeep@gmail.com,prabhdeepsingh.cse@geu.ac.in; [c]shubham151515@gmail.com

Methane, butane, ethane, propane, and LPG all register strongly on the sensor. These flame detectors can also pick up light waves between 760 nm and 1100 nm, making them useful for finding fires. Advantage - inflammable gases are the cause of dangerous fire mishaps in both industrial and home settings. We need a system that can detect leaking flammable gases and give protection against them to prevent an accident of this kind. Homes, hospitals, hostels, and factories are only some of the places where this concept has been implemented as a security system. (Zulkarnain et al., 2021).

Proposal Approach

Hardware components

Arduino Uno

The Arduino Uno is a single-board computer (MCU) based on the AVR microcontroller Atmega328 and designed by the open-source electronics company Arduino. The most up-to-date version of the Arduino Uno has a USB port, as well as other devices. There are 14 input/output pins in total, however, only six of them may be utilized for PWM generation. Designers may use it to monitor and manipulate electrical gadgets in the physical environment (Zulkarnain et al., 2021). Using the included USB connection, you may connect this board to your computer. The IDE may be used on Mac or Linux computers as well, however, Windows is recommended when compared to other boards in the Arduino family, the only difference is that the Uno doesn't have Among the available due to their 32KB of RAMand Atmega328 8-bit AVR Atmel microprocessor. When the task's nature and functionality get more sophisticated, a Micro SD card may be inserted into the boards to increase their storage capacity. Because it is built on an open-source framework, the board may be customized and optimized by every user by their desired quantity of instructions and desired job. An on-board regulator on this board controls the voltage when it is linked to an external device.

Gas sensor

MQ5 sensory interface IC by monitoring the device's current discharge, we can calculate the gas concentration. The MQ-5 gas sensor can detect concentrations of gases from 100 parts per billion (ppb) to 3000 ppb, including hydrogen, carbon monoxide, methane, and LPG. The sensor works by ionizing the gas being measured and then absorbing the resulting ions. This absorption results in a voltage differential across the element, which is sent to the central processing unit through the element's output pins. In turn, this modifies the current leaving the detecting element by changing its resistance.

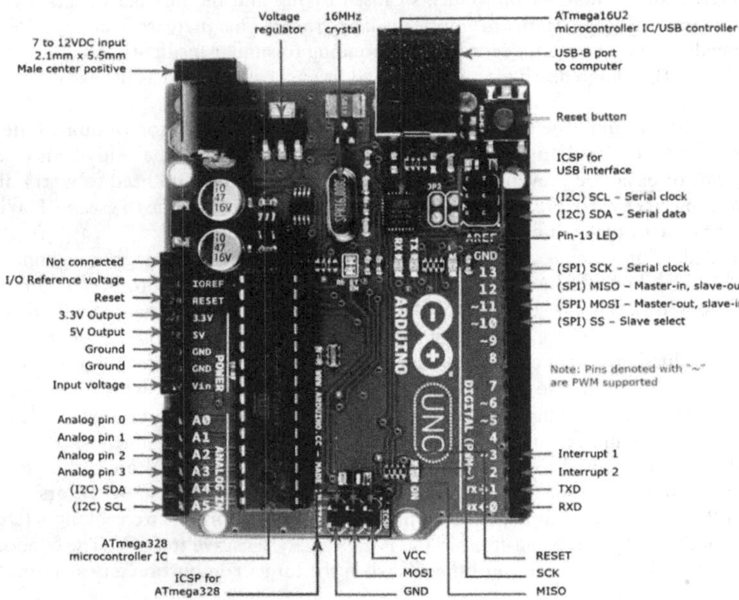

Figure 41.1 Arduino Uno

Flame sensor

The infrared flame flash method is used by it. This phototransistor-based fire detector is very specific. Commonly, this takes the shape of a black LED on the module's front panel. The wavelengths of interest for a flame detection system are in the infrared, between 4.3 and 4.4 microns. Carbon dioxide (CO_2), produced by the combustion of organic compounds, has a resonance frequency in this band (Jadon et al., 2020). By-products of the combustion process, such as greenhouse gases, emit radiation and show distinctive patterns in infrared radiation. Both may be detected using a flame sensor. More so than a smoke or fire alarm, it responds quickly and accurately. It's safe to assume that your continued interest in this article stems from a desire to learn more about its compatibility with Arduino. The sensor is like the robot's eyes in a firefighting simulation, and it's crucial to the game's success.

Complete Circuit Working

Fire alarm systems are widely used in businesses and factories; they consist of a network of sensors that keep a constant eye out for any sign of fire, smoke, or gas in the facility. (Alqourabah et al., 2021).

In this paper, we will learn how to connect and detect light, and the op-amp in the module can measure how sensitive the sensor is. It generates a HIGH signal and may be used as a smoke detector. When Arduino picks up on a signal, it activates a buzzer and an LED to warn of danger. The IR-based flame sensor is what's being used.

Figure 41.2 Gas sensor [3]

Figure 41.3 Flame sensor

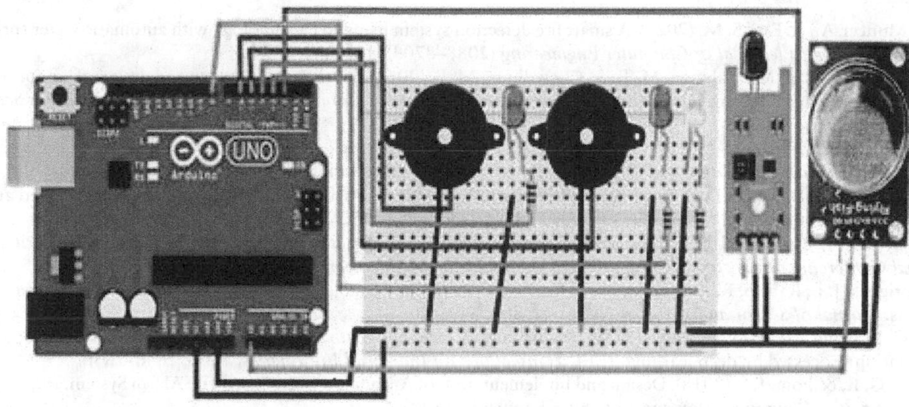

Figure 41.4 Circuit working

Experiment and Result

We have seen the paper through testing and found it to be functional. To guarantee a risk-free environment, a system has been created that accurately pinpoints the exact room or floor where a fire or gas leak has occurred (Ghosh et al., 2019). Additionally, an alarm may be shown through the system's use of a siren and a flashing red light. A microprocessor is linked to the smoke and fire sensors to manage the whole system. In this setup, two sensors are employed, each of which is programmed to respond to one of three different circumstances. To begin, a gas sensor and a fire sensor are calibrated using the specified reference value. The microcontroller will sound an alert until the gas or fire has been extinguished if the sensor value it receives is greater than the reference value it has been programmed to expect (Ilouno et al., 2021).

The application of technological innovation is certain to become a critical problem in the business sector as we enter the scientific era. (Asif et al., 2014). This invention will benefit humanity in this regard. It will lessen the possibility of theft and ensure the safety of employees (Garg et al. 2020).

If the expected result does not appear, double-check that you have uploaded the correct code to your board and that the circuit has been constructed and tested correctly (Pundir et al., 2019).

Work done	*Sensor used*		*Application*	
	MQ-2	*Flame sensor*	*Home*	*Industry*
Asif et al. (2014)	✓		✓	
Ilouno et al. (2018)		✓	✓	
Dubey et al.		✓		✓
Proposed	✓	✓	✓	✓

Conclusion

Detection of fire and toxic gases is critical in all areas of life where safety is paramount. The system is practical, straightforward, and straightforward to set up. The system's components may be purchased from a nearby shop. This device may help to save lives, livelihoods, and property by preventing fires and protecting against flammable gas leaks in a variety of commercial buildings.

Because of the many ways in which technology has been put to use, modern life has become easier, healthier, and more pleasurable for everyone. The proposed gas leak detector seems to have great potential in the field of safety. The original intention of this design was to bring a revolutionary approach to safety, drastically lowering the potential for harm from poisonous and hazardous gas leaks of any magnitude. Monitoring gas reserves and leaks in homes and factories are examples of this use case. There are several solutions to the issue, but gas leak detection has been a major one. A novel method for gas reservation and gas detectors was therefore presented in this work, one that is microcontroller-based.

References

Alqourabah, H., Muneer, A., & Fati, S. M. (2021). A smart fire detection system using IoT technology with automatic water sprinkler. *International Journal of Electrical & Computer Engineering* (2088–8708), 11(4).

Asif, O., Hossain, M. B., Hasan, M., Rahman, M. T., & Chowdhury, M. E. (2014). Firedetectors review and design of an automated, quick responsive fire-alarm system based on SMS. *International Journal of Communications, Network and System Sciences*, 7(9), 386.

Dubey, V., Kumar, P., & Chauhan, N. (2019). Forest fire detection system using IoT and artificial neural network. *International Conference on Innovative Computing and Communications,* (pp. 323–337). Springer, Singapore.

Garg, N., Wazid, M., Das, A. K., Singh, D. P., Rodrigues, J. J., & Park, Y. (2020). BAKMPIoMT: Design of blockchain enabled authenticated key management protocol for internet of medical things deployment. *IEEE Access*, 8, 95956–95977.

Ghosh, P. & Dhar, P. K. (2019). GSM based low-cost gas leakage, explosion and fire alert system with advanced security. *2019 International Conference on Electrical, Computer and Communication Engineering*, (pp. 1–5). IEEE.

Gomes, J. B., Rodrigues, J. J., Rabêlo, R. A., Kumar, N., & Kozlov, S. (2019). IoT-enabled gas sensors: Technologies, applications, and opportunities. *Journal of Sensor and Actuator Networks*, 8(4), 57.

Han, Y., Zhang, C. J., Wang, L., & Zhang, Y. C. (2019). Industrial IoT for intelligent steelmaking with converter mouth flame spectrum information processed by deep learning. *IEEE Transactions on Industrial Informatics*, 16(4), 2640–2650.

Ilouno, J., Newton, G. F., & Fom, T. P. (2018). Design and Implementation of Automatic GSM Based Fire Alarm System. *International Journal of Electronics Communication and Computer Engineering*, 9(4).

Jadon, A., Omama, M., Varshney, A., Ansari, M. S., & Sharma, R. (2019). FireNet: a specialized lightweight fire & smoke detection model for real-time IoT applications. arXiv preprint arXiv:1905.11922.

Jadon, S., Choudhary, A., Saini, H., Dua, U., Sharma, N., & Kaushik, I. (2020). Comfy smart home using IoT. *Proceedings of the International Conference on Innovative Computing & Communications.*

Kumar, P. N. S. & Kumari, A. K. (2019). Design of gas detection and monitoring system using IoT. *International Journal of Engineering Research and Technology*, 8(11), 463–468.

Pundir, S., Wazid, M., Singh, D. P., Das, A. K., Rodrigues, J. J., & Park, Y. (2019). Intrusion detection protocols in wireless sensor networks integrated to Internet of Things deployment: Survey and future challenges. *IEEE Access*, 8, 3343–3363.

Roque, G. & Padilla, V. S. (2020). LPWAN-based IoT surveillance system for outdoor fire detection. *IEEE Access*, 8, 114900–114909.

Sohail, H., Ullah, S., Khan, A., Samin, O. B., & Omar, M. (2019). Intelligent trash bin (ITB) with trash collection efficiency optimization using IoT sensing. *2019 8th International Conference on Information and Communication Technologies*, (pp. 48–53). IEEE.

Subramanian, M. A., Selvam, N., Rajkumar, S., Mahalakshmi, R., & Ramprabhakar, J. (2020). Gas leakage detection system using IoT with integrated notifications using Pushbullet-A review. *2020 Fourth International Conference on Inventive Systems and Control.*

Suwarjono, S., Wayangkau, I. H., Istanto, T., Rachmat, R., Marsujitullah, M., Hariyanto, H., Caesarendra, W., Legutko, S., & Glowacz, A. (2021). Design of a home fire detection system using Arduino and SMS gateway. *Knowledge*, 1(1), 61–74.

Waworundeng, J. M. S., Kalalo, M. A. T., & Lokollo, D. P. Y. (2020). A prototype of indoor hazard detection system using sensors and IoT. *2020 2nd International Conference on Cybernetics and Intelligent System*, (pp. 1–6).

Zulkarnain, A. F., Sari, Y., & Rakhmadani, R. (2021). Monitoring system for early detection of fire in wetlands based Internet of Things (IoT) using fuzzy methods. *IOP Conference Series: Materials Science and Engineering*, 1115(1), 012007.

42 Machine learning and artificial intelligence in the era of digital marketing

Animesh Kumar Sharma[1,a] *and Rahul Sharma*[2,b]

[1]Research Scholar, Mittal School of Business, Lovely Professional University, Punjab, India

[2]Professor, Mittal School of Business, Lovely Professional University, Punjab, India

Abstract

This research paper aims to provide an overview of machine learning and artificial intelligence in digital marketing. The current technological advancements have moved industries forward. Marketing has evolved to the point where it must now stay up with the most recent digital trends. While this may seem like a call to action for marketers, all automated applications and systems powered by artificial intelligence essentially accomplish little more than simplifying the complexity of conventional targeting and personalization procedures. Algorithms are frequently included in online promotion platforms to identify the best combinations, but occasionally companies create and use their specialized internal systems. This paper presents an overview of the current state of artificial intelligence and machine learning in digital marketing operations and suggests a model that makes use of a marketing strategy that can increase a website's visibility.

Keywords: Machine learning, artificial intelligence, marketing, digital marketing

Introduction

Artificial intelligence (AI) and machine learning (ML) are the two key digital technologies of today that are revolutionizing people's lives everywhere (Bughin ad Hazan, 2017). The way value is created in digital marketing has been changed by machine learning (Magistretti, et al., 2019; Ullal, et al., 2021). ML is the use of AI that takes advantage of the inherent ability of current machines to learn through algorithms and statistical analysis tools. Amazon and Facebook are two great examples of how machine intelligence can advance digital marketing. Starting with bringing individuals together, moving on to bringing players together, selling books, and finally building a platform where employers can find employees and vice versa (Trabucchi and Buganza, 2020). ML is being used in digital marketing to revolutionize the industry by gathering, analyzing, and recycling clicks and comments on companies to determine the emotions they elicit. With so many options available to them on digital platforms today, ML can help marketers match customers with the right products (Verganti, 2017). The wide-ranging effects of ML and AI, in all spheres of society, ML has compelled scholars to use the word the 'AI Revolution' of the present day (Makridakis, 2017). With new business models, goods, and services, machine learning is upending several industries. The impact seems to be equally significant in academia. For instance, the so-called 'replication issue,' which has impacted many of the biological and social sciences, including the domains of management and marketing, is centered on the lack of generalization of scientific discoveries (Camerer, et al., 2018). AI is now being employed in practically every facet of life as technology advances. It has been used in conjunction with digital marketing to make it simpler for firms to reach consumers at the correct time (Thilagavathy and Kumar, 2021).

Literature Review

Marketing intelligence encourages two significant advancements in digital marketing. First, it increases marketing efficiency, even in the absence of KPIs, as life-cycle marketing, automatic price adjustment, and AI-based programmatic advertising all contribute to the goal of fully standardized marketing automation with real-time, optimized customer centricity. Second, brand-new marketing disciplines like content marketing, viral marketing, and social media marketing highlight the growing significance of creative marketing (Lies, 2021). The existing research deems machine learning in the context of digital marketing as being worthy of future study. Because of developments in machine learning, businesses in the digital marketing sector are finding new prospects (Buganza, et al., 2020). ML is the ability of a machine to learn from raw data rather than from instructions from people. This implies that machines can find patterns in the data they gather from their detectors and use that data to extract significant information (Buller, et al., 2018).

Digital marketing affects consumers at a specific moment, in a specific location through a specific channel. Businesses are now able to create enormous volumes of items because of technological improvements, which they then employ

[a]animesh.41800104@lpu.in; [b]rahul.12234@lpu.co.in

to increase prospects for marketing and client sales. Digital marketing advancements have also been made possible by the integration of big data and academic research on smart apps. Artificial intelligence helps to create new company prospects and plays a significant part in digital marketing. Artificial intelligence must be included in marketing efforts by companies if they want to stay competitive (Pradeep, et al., 2018). The highest earning potential and success rates for artificial intelligence applications in marketing have been identified. Marketing is one of the areas that is seen to be among the most viable for improvement (Fagella, 2019).

One of the main forces driving innovation in marketing has been artificial intelligence. Artificial intelligence's benefits are already being used by marketers to learn more about their target audiences, rival companies, and marketplaces. Automation, cost-cutting, and better workflows are all benefits of artificial intelligence (Mitić, 2019). ML is useful for many behavioral research methods, including varying treatment effects, stimulus sampling, and imputed missing data for complicated processes being examined over time (Hagen et al., 2020). Through machine learning, online click frauds can be also identified (Minastireanu ad Mesnita, 2019).

Author	*Literature review*
De Bruyn et al. (2020)	Marketers can accelerate intelligent marketing by using AI.
Choudhury and Nur (2019)	Analyzed customer purchasing patterns for a retail superstore by implementing many ML methods, including logistic regression, decision tree, etc.
Duan et al. (2019)	AI-enabled solutions are enhancing human decision-making capacity while disrupting industries and reimagining fresh, creative business models.
S. Dimitreska et al. (2018)	discussed how AI is changing marketing in a time when machines are capable of understanding all issues and coming up with answers.
A. Aluri et al. (2018)	Demonstrated how ML may assist businesses in increasing the number of participants in their loyalty program
Olson and Levy (2018)	attempted to demonstrate a deeper connection between consumers and marketers and to enhance their capacity to create lifetime value models.
Syam and Sharma (2018)	concluded that more helpful programmes for monitoring production and the full operational structure of major firms will be necessary to understand consumer behavior.
Lindsay, (2017)	AI and ML learning are used to predict or provide calculated suggestions after studying a lot of data.
Pansari and Kumar, (2017)	The majority of companies interact with clients by using digital and AI technologies.
Stalidis, et al. (2015)	concluded that cutting-edge knowledge representation, data analysis, and neural network technology combine to produce a smart information system for promoting tourist destinations.
Plaza (2011)	AI helps predict and provide lifetime value to customers.
Al-Sukkar et al. (2008)	highlighted what may have a bearing on how AI is applied in developing marketing tactics.
Nordlander (2001)	enhanced the idea that AI has already impacted the commercial market.

Research Methodology

Based on secondary data, the present paper examines the applicability of machine learning, and artificial intelligence in the area of digital marketing using qualitative pragmatic study methodology.

Discussions

Applicability of AI and ML in digital marketing is discussed below:

AI-driven marketing

Driven by technology, big data, and competitiveness, this decade has seen the emergence of autonomous AI agents powered by machine learning techniques in every area of business and marketing (Ma and Sun, 2020; Alexander, 2022). Identifying consumer needs, matching those needs to the appropriate products and services, and persuading them to make purchases are all crucial components of marketing. Sales can be significantly increased with the help of an AI-powered marketing and business plan (Mari, 2019). Chatbot, which is responding to customer questions and inquiries as well as carries out online transactions is an example of artificial intelligence (Chaffey and Ellis-Chadwick, 2019).

Marketing automation

New technology adoption is regarded as a significant source of commercial prospects (Mero et al., 2020). The advent of Software-as-a-Service (SaaS) has aided the adoption of agile technology, which places more emphasis on iterative modifications through learning by doing than on the execution of a predesigned implementation strategy (Mero et al., 2022).

Content marketing

The process of creating and distributing pertinent, beneficial brand-related content to present or potential customers as well as to other target groups via the internet or print media is known as content marketing (Hollebeek and Macky, 2019).

Search engine optimization

Search engine optimization (SEO) refers to techniques that improve organic web traffic to a website, blog, or infographic so that they can be found and appear as the top results when an online search is made (Bala and Verma, 2018). To improve search engine ranks and attract more relevant visitors, a website should have user-friendly navigation, original content, and a well-written Meta description (Sharma and Verma, 2020).

Search engine marketing

Utilizing a variety of internet search engines, search engine marketing (SEM) is the promotion of a business. (Nyagadza, 2022). The majority of internet users click on the first website that appears on the search engine result page, which is a very natural behavior for direct response in search engine marketing.

Social media marketing

Social media has changed the approach that consumers and businesses interconnect and influence one another. When two people are in social contact, they engage in 'activities' that affect each other's choices and consumer behaviors, whether actively or inactively (Li, et al., 2021).

Conclusion

This study offers guidance to marketers working on machine learning as they create models for cross-cultural and professional profiles. The software is developed by developers in collaboration with digital marketers with an emphasis on analyzing the customer's attitude, behavior, and choices. Companies modify their operational procedures to raise their responsiveness, productivity, and competitiveness. There have always been fresh marketing prospects as a result of technological improvements. Artificial intelligence has changed how people interact with information, technology, brands, and services, just as the advent of television signaled a new phase of truly mass advertising and attainment, and the introduction of the Internet and mobile phones signaled a new level of targeting and background. Marketers are made aware of the possibility of personalization and the relevance of artificial intelligence and machine learning. Companies can reach billions of people in daily life with platforms like Facebook, YouTube, Google, and Search engines, and use digital ad platforms to achieve mass communication. Companies can tailor customized advertising in real time thanks to artificial intelligence's customization capabilities mixed with determination.

References

Alexander, L. (2022). The who, what, why, & how of Digital Marketing. Retrieved from HubSpot Blog: https://blog.hubspot.com/marketing/what-is-digital-marketing

Al-Sukkar, A. S., Hussein, A. H., & Jalil, M. A. (2008). The effect of applying artificial intelligence in shaping marketing strategies: A field study at the Jordanian industrial companies. International Journal of Applied Science and Technology, Jordan, Global Society of Scientific Research and Researchers, 3(2), 1–11.

Aluri, A., Price, B. S., & McIntyre, N. H. (2018). Using machine learning to cocreate value through dynamic customer engagement in a brand loyalty program. *Journal of Hospitality & Tourism Research*, 43(1), 78–100. https://doi.org/10.1177/1096348017753521

Bala, M. & Verma, D. (2018). A critical review of digital marketing. M. Bala, D. Verma (2018). A Critical Review of Digital Marketing. *International Journal of Management, IT & Engineering*, 8(10), 321–339.

Buganza, T., Trabucchi, D. & Pellizzoni, E. (2020). Limitless personalization: the role of Big Data in unveiling service opportunities. *Technology analysis & strategic management*, 32(1), 58–70. https://doi.org/10.1080/09537325.2019.1634252

Bughin, J. & Hazan, E. (2017). The new spring of artificial intelligence: A few early economies. *VoxEU. org*.

Buller, L., Gifford, C. & Mills, A. (2018). Robot: Meet the Machines of the Future. Dorling Kindersley Limited: London.

Camerer, C. F., Dreber, A., Holzmeister, F., Ho, T. H., Huber, J., Johannesson, M., ... & Wu, H. (2018). Evaluating the replicability of social science experiments in Nature and Science between 2010 and 2015. *Nature Human Behaviour*, 2(9), 637–644. https://doi.org/10.1038/s41562-018-0399-z

Chaffey, D., & Ellis-Chadwick, F. (2019). *Digital marketing*. Pearson uk.

Choudhury, A. M. & Nur, K. (2019). A machine learning approach to identify potential customers based on purchase behavior. *In 2019 International Conference on Robotics, Electrical and Signal Processing Techniques (ICREST)*, (pp. 242–247). https://doi.org/10.1109/ICREST.2019.8644458

De Bruyn, A., Viswanathan, V., Beh, Y. S., Brock, J. K. U., & Von Wangenheim, F. (2020). Artificial intelligence and marketing: Pitfalls and opportunities. *Journal of Interactive Marketing*, 51(1), 91–105. https://doi.org/10.1016/j.intmar.2020.04.007

Dimitrieska, S., Stankovska, A., & Efremova, T. (2018). Artificial intelligence and marketing. *Entrepreneurship*, 6(2), 298–304

Duan, Y., Edwards, J. S., & Dwivedi, Y. K. (2019). Artificial intelligence for decision making in the era of Big Data – evolution, challenges and research agenda. *International Journal of Information Management*, 48, 63–71, https://doi.org/10.1016/j.ijinfomgt.2019.01.021.

Fagella, D. (2019). Machine learning marketing - expert consensus of 51 executives and startups. Retrieved from https://emerj.com/ai-market-research/machine-learning-marketing.

Hagen, L., Uetake, K., Yang, N., Bollinger, B., Chaney, A. J., Dzyabura, D., ... & Zhu, Y. (2020). How can machine learning aid behavioral marketing research? Marketing Letters, 31(4), 361–370. https://doi.org/10.1007/s11002-020-09535-7

Hair Jr, J. F. & Sarstedt, M. (2021). Data, measurement, and causal inferences in machine learning: opportunities and challenges for marketing. *Journal of Marketing Theory and Practice*, 29(1), 65–77. https://doi.org/10.1080/10696679.2020.1860683

Hollebeek, L. D. & Macky, K. (2019). Digital content marketing's role in fostering consumer engagement, trust, and value: Framework, fundamental propositions, and implications. *Journal of interactive marketing*, 45, 27–41. https://doi.org/10.1016/j.intmar.2018.07.003

Li, F., Larimo, J., & Leonidou, L. C. (2021). Social media marketing strategy: definition, conceptualization, taxonomy, validation, and future agenda. *Journal of the Academy of Marketing Science*, 49(1), 51–70. https://doi.org/10.1007/s11747-020-00733-3

Lies, J. (2021). Digital marketing: Incompatibilities between performance marketing and marketing creativity. *Journal of Digital & Social Media Marketing*, 8(4), 376–386. https://link.springer.com/chapter/10.1007/978-3-658-29367-3_12

Lindsay, T. (2017). What is Artificial intelligence marketing and why is it powerful?

Ma, L. & Sun, B. (2020). Machine learning and AI in marketing–Connecting computing power to human insights. *International Journal of Research in Marketing*, 37(3), 481–504. https://doi.org/10.1016/j.ijresmar.2020.04.005

Makridakis, S. (2017). The forthcoming Artificial Intelligence (AI) revolution: Its impact on society and firms. Futures, 90, 46–60. https://doi.org/10.1016/j.futures.2017.03.006

Mari, A. (2019). The Rise of machine learning in marketing: goal, process, and benefit of AI-driven marketing. https://doi.org/10.5167/uzh-197751

Mero, J., Leinonen, M., Makkonen, H., & Karjaluoto, H. (2022). Agile logic for SaaS implementation: Capitalizing on marketing automation software in a start-up. Journal of Business Research, 145, 583–594. https://doi.org/10.1016/j.jbusres.2022.03.026

Mero, J., Tarkiainen, A., & Tobon, J. (2020). Effectual and causal reasoning in the adoption of marketing automation. *Industrial Marketing Management*, 86, 212–222. https://doi.org/10.1016/j.indmarman.2019.12.008

Minastireanu, E. A., & Mesnita, G. (2019). Light gbm machine learning algorithm to online click fraud detection. *Journal of Information Assurance & Cybersecurity*. https://doi.org/10.5171/2019.263928

Mitić, V. (2019). Benefits of artificial intelligence and machine learning in marketing. In Sinteza 2019-International scientific conference on information technology and data-related research (pp. 472–477). https://doi.org/10.15308/Sinteza-2019-472-477

Nordlander, T. E. & Nordlander, T. E. (2001). AI surveying: *Artificial intelligence in business. Department of Management Science and Statistics-Montfort University*.

Nyagadza, B. (2022). Search engine marketing and social media marketing predictive trends. Journal of Digital Media & Policy. https://doi.org/10.1386/jdmp_00036_1

Olson, C. & Levy, J. (2018). Transforming marketing with artificial intelligence. Applied Marketing Analytics, 3(4), 291–297.

P. J., Geisler, F. H., Schneider, J. S., Li, P. A., Fiumelli, H., & Sipione, S. (2019). Gangliosides: treatment avenues in neurodegenerative disease. *Frontiers in Neurology*, 10, 859. https://doi.org/10.3389/fneur.2019.00859

Pansari, A. and Kumar, V. (2017). Customer engagement: the construct, antecedents, and consequences. *Journal of the Academy of Marketing Science*, 45(3), 294–311. https://doi.org/10.1007/s11747-016-0485-6.

Plaza, B. (2011). Google analytics for measuring website performance. *Tourism Management*, 32(3), 477–481. https://doi.org/10.1016/j.tourman.2010.03.015.

Pradeep, A. K., Appel, A., & Sthanunathan, S. (2018). AI for marketing and product innovation: powerful new tools for predicting trends, connecting with customers, and closing sales. John Wiley & Sons.

Sharma, S. & Verma, S. (2020). Optimizing Website effectiveness using various SEO Techniques. *In 2020 7th International Conference on Signal Processing and Integrated Networks,* (pp. 918–922). https://doi.org/10.1109/SPIN48934.2020.9070893

Stalidis, G., Karapistolis, D., & Vafeiadis, A. (2015). Marketing decision support using Artificial Intelligence and Knowledge Modeling: application to tourist destination management. *Procedia-Social and Behavioral Sciences*, 175, 106–113. https://doi.org/10.1016/j.sbspro.2015.01.1180

Syam, N. & Sharma, A. (2018). Waiting for a sales renaissance in the fourth industrial revolution: Machine learning and artificial intelligence in sales research and practice. *Industrial marketing management*, 69, 135–146. https://doi.org/10.1016/j.indmarman.2017.12.019

Thilagavathy, N. & Kumar, E. P. (2021). Artificial intelligence on digital marketing-An overview. *Nveo-Natural Volatiles & Essential Oils Journal*, 9895–9908.

Trabucchi, D. & Buganza, T. (2020). Fostering digital platform innovation: From two to multi-sided platforms. *Creativity and Innovation Management*, 29(2), 345–358. https://doi.org/10.1111/caim.12320

Ullal, M. S., Spulbar, C., Hawaldar, I. T., Popescu, V., & Birau, R. (2021). The impact of online reviews on e-commerce sales in India: A case study. *Economic Research-Ekonomska Istraživanja*, 34(1), 2408–2422. https://doi.org/10.1080/1331677X.2020.1865179

Verganti, R. (2017). Design thinkers think like managers. *The Journal of Design, Economics, and Innovation*, 3(2), 100–102.

43 Comparative study of rice crop growth stages using sentinel-1 and MODIS satellite imagery

VSRNR Rao T[1,a] *and Sakshi Dua*[2,b]

[1]Research Scholar, School of Computer Applications, Lovely Professional University, Punjab, India

[2]Assistant Professor, School of Computer Applications, Lovely Professional University, Punjab, India

Abstract

The benefits of remote sensing in agriculture are currently limited to scientists, and policyholders, but have not reached most farmers or agriculturists in developing countries like India. Knowing geo-location, the study suggested an approach to infer results from multiple sources to conclude on different crop growth stages that would be useful in low-cost and time-effective agricultural management practices. The current research indicated that time-series data of Sentinel-1 (S1) SAR data agrees with patterns noticed from Normalized Difference Vegetation Index, enhanced vegetation index, FPAR, and LAI vegetation parameters. These parameters are derived from MODIS spectral bands through analysis-ready products of MOD13Q1 and MCD15A3H which are composite images of 16-day and 4-days, respectively. The false colour images of S1 have produced reliable images without cloud limitation and MODIS products are available in a ready-to-use state for comparison and deriving invaluable information.

Keywords: MODIS, MOD13Q1, MCD15A3H, rice, remote sensing, sentinel-1

Introduction

Rice is a primary cereal grain in Asian countries. Farmers involve in intense management practices at different growth stages of rice paddy to ensure the right decisions can be made at the right time. Financial institutes or insurance carriers look for more reliable trends of past growth stages or climate (Hazaymeh and Hassan, 2017) impact in a specific area which builds confidence for them to lend loans or increase/decrease insurance premiums based on the risk profile of the land.

Remote sensing brings a plethora of opportunities to monitor rice crops in a cost and time-effective manner (Gohain et al., 2021). The current research developed an approach of using MODIS spectral data along with ESA's Sentinel-1 SAR (Synthetic Aperture Radar) data. Aqua and Terra satellites of NASAcarryMODIS (Moderate Resolution Imaging Spectro Radiometer) instrument which captures the earth's surface in thirty-six spectral bands of various resolutions every 1 or 2 days. MODIS vegetation index products MOD13Q1 (Didan, 2015) and MCD15A3H (Myneni et al., 2015) products are used in the current study and they are processed at level-3 and level-4 respectively. MOD13Q1 (Didan, 2015) provides two vegetation layers Normalized Difference Vegetation Index (NDVI) (Tarpley et. a., 1984) and enhanced vegetation index (EVI) at 200 m spatial resolution (Huete, et al., 2002). Similarly, MCD15A3H (Myneni et al., 2015) has FPAR and LAI (Garrigues, et al., 2008) layers which are 500 m spatial resolution. Spectral instruments are passive sensors that capture the radiant energy of the sun from the earth's surface. Consequently, MODIS can capture images during the day and image quality would be high when cloud cover is less. SAR imagery overcomes this limitation with all-day and all-weather capabilities. ESA has introduced two satellites S1A and S1B which captures data in strip map (SM), interferometric wide (IW), extra wide (EW) and wave (WV) modes from 3.8–7.5 cm wavelength (Torres, et al., 2012). The current study leveraged level 1 GRD products which have dual-polarization capabilities of VV+VH and HH+HV. The remaining part of the document covers a literature review, satellite data acquisition process, methodology and conclusion by comparing S1 results with MODIS and discussions.

Study Area

The study area is in the Mahbubnagar district of the Telangana state in India at the coordinates 16°48'57.5"N and 78°10'42.3"E. This location is chosen remotely with the farmer's reference of crops and then analysed with Satellite imagery to study various growth stages of the rice.

[a]venkat.sunder73@gmail.com; [b]sakshi.26557@lpu.co.in

Literature Review

The current study's objective is to benefit from the S1 all-weather and all-day capabilities of GRD imagery and compare them with MODIS pre-processed data to assess crop growth stages reliably in a shorter period.

Satellite Data

Study period and sample

The study was conducted from September 2021 to December 2021 with high-resolution images from S1-GRD and MODIS pre-processed products. The following table describes the acquisition dates of satellite imagery.

Figure 43.1 The study area in Mahboob Nagar district of Telangana

Table 43.1 Literature review

No.	*Title*	*Review*	*Authors*
1	Mapping paddy rice with satellite remote sensing: A review	Numerous studies have been undertaken to map paddy rice using optical and radar sensors individually using machine learning algorithms. Optical sensors contribute to the identification of crop stages that are comparable to what is visible to the naked eye. The S1 C-band assists in overcoming cloud cover limitations with all-weather capability.	Zhao and Ma (2021)
2	Automatic mapping of rice growth stages using the integration of sentinel-2, mod13q1, and sentinel-1.	This study implemented an innovative approach to integrate S1, S2 and MOD13Q1 products from MODIS to assess the accuracy of crop growth stages. However, the accuracy assessment increases when the sensor's data is leveraged individually rather than by combining them.	Ramadhani et al. (2020)

Table 43.2 MOD13Q1, MCD15A3H and S1-GRD acquisition dates

S1-GRD	*MOD13Q1*	*MCD15A3H*	*MCD15A3H*	*MCD15A3H*
10-SEP-21	29-AUG-21	29-AUG-21	04-OCT-21	09-NOV-21
16-OCT-21	14-SEP-21	02-SEP-21	08-OCT-21	13-NOV-21
28-OCT-21	30-SEP-21	06-SEP-21	12-OCT-21	17-NOV-21
21-NOV-21	16-OCT-21	10-SEP-21	16-OCT-21	21-NOV-21
03-DEC-21	01-NOV-21	14-SEP-21	20-OCT-21	25-NOV-21
15-DEC-21	17-NOV-21	18-SEP-21	24-OCT-21	29-NOV-21
	03-DEC-21	22-SEP-21	28-OCT-21	03-DEC-21
		26-SEP-21	01-NOV-21	07-DEC-21
		30-SEP-21	05-NOV-21	11-DEC-21

Methodology

Onboard navigation of the S1 is not generally accurate. The orbit state vector file is applied on S1-GRD imagery to get proper satellite and velocity positions. A speckle filter is applied to SAR images to diminish the speckle effect. Radiometric calibration is required to properly match pixel values to the backscattered wave of a scene. Finally, terrain correction (Wegmuller, 1999) is applied to rectify geometric distortions (layover or shadow) of the SAR imagery to keep the image as close to the real world. MOD13Q1 (Didan, 2015) and MCD15A3H (Myneni et al., 2015) are already pre-processed, so they can be consumed in the available state.

Results

Figure 43.3 shows time series imagery of false color SAR data. The polygon highlighted the area of interest (AOI). VV, VH and VV/VH are assigned to respective RGB channels. VH is dominant when the crop is at the ripening stage as shown in Figure 43.3(c) in the Kharif season. The blue (VV/VH) is evident when the crop is at the vegetative stage as

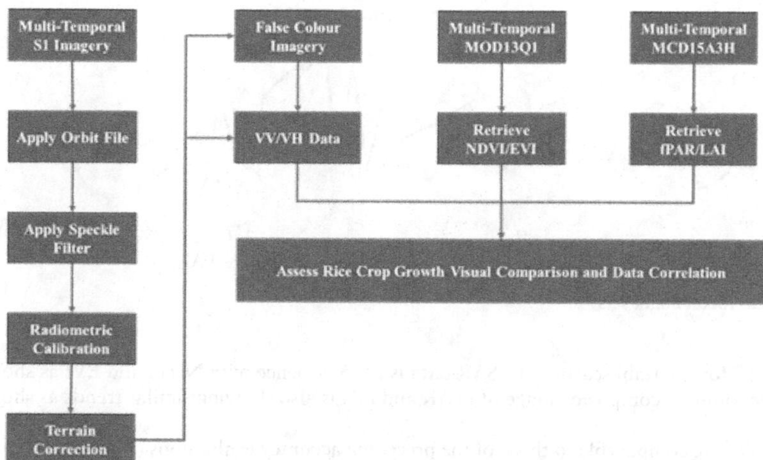

Figure 43.2 The methodology adopted for assessing rice crop growth stages

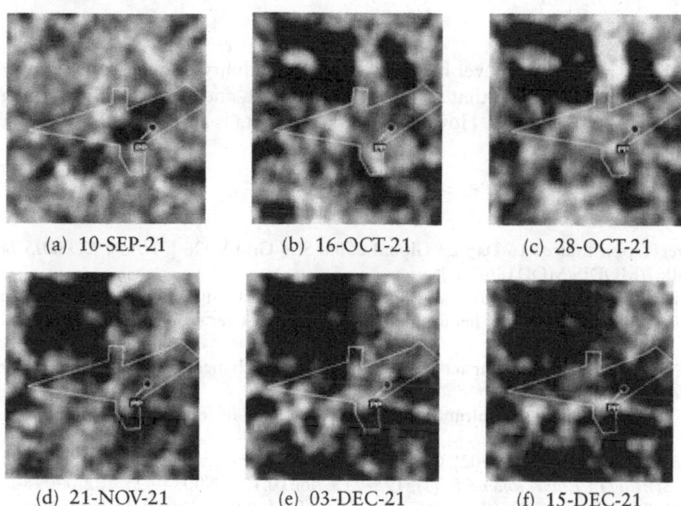

Figure 43.3 S1-SARFalse Color images of vegetation changes in the AOI

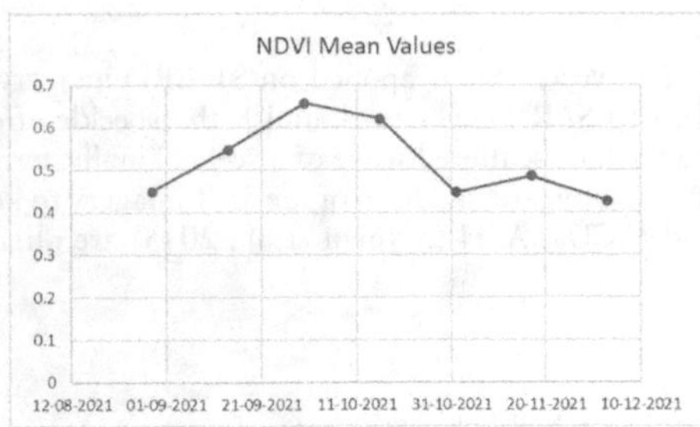

(a) MOD13Q1 - NDVI

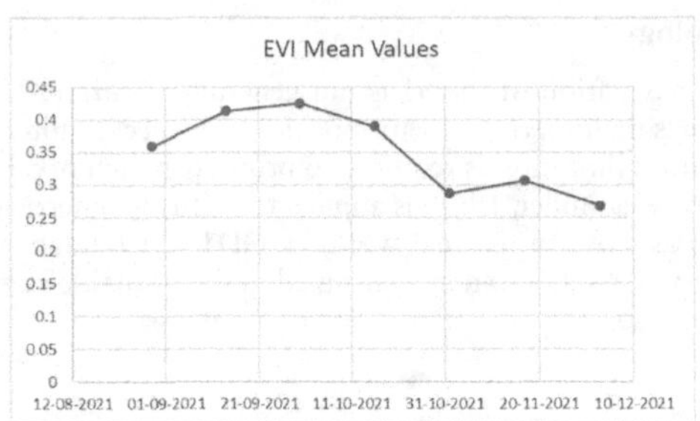

(b) MOD13Q1 –EVI

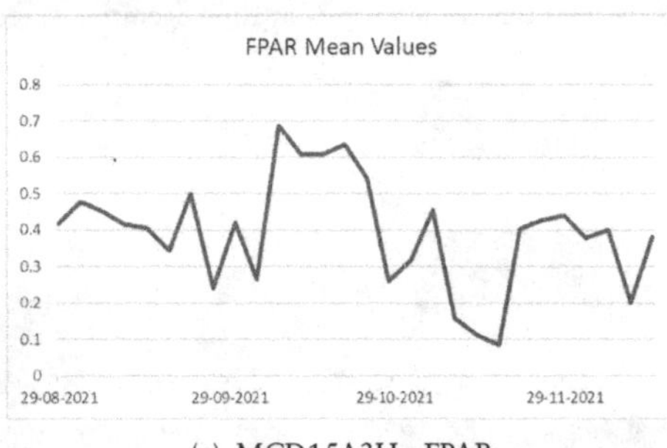

(c) MCD15A3H - FPAR

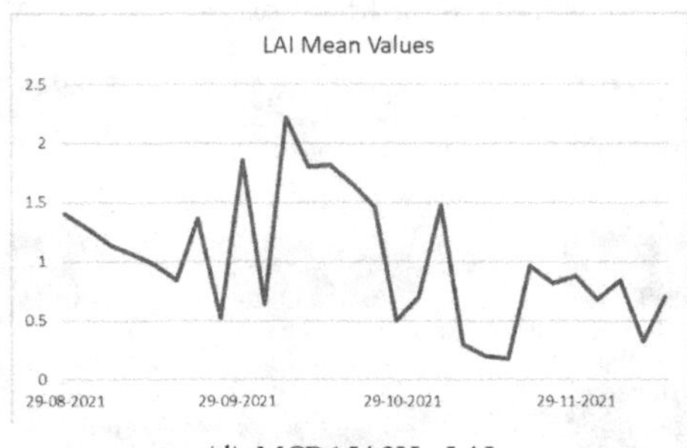

(d) MCD15A3H - LAI

Figure 43.4 MOD13Q1 and MCD15A3H data sets

shown in Figures 43.3(e) and 43.3(f) for the Rabi season. The SAR data is in congruence with NDVI and EVI as shown in Figures 43.4(a) and 43.4(b). The four-day composite image of FPAR and LAI is also showing similar trends as shown in Figures 43.4(c) and 43.4(d).

The findings of S1 and MOD13Q1 are comparable to those of the preceding accuracy evaluations (Ramadhani et al., 2020). False color pictures, FPAR, and LAI data, however, provide further details on changes in chlorophyll concentration at various crop growth stages.

Conclusion

Growth stage assessments of the rice crop are now easier than ever before with the availability of open-source imagery. Analysis-ready data from AppEEARS offers invaluable insights that save time, reduce cost, and eliminate the number of process steps involved in creating and storing fine-tuned images. However, the S1-SAR data is a trustworthy resource to overcome the limitations of cloud cover with all-day capability.

References

Didan, K. (2015). MOD13Q1 MODIS/Terra Vegetation Indices 16-Day L3 Global 250m SIN Grid V006 [. *NASA EOSDIS Land Processes DAAC*. doi: https://doi.org/10.5067/MODIS/MOD13Q1.006

Garrigues, S., Shabanov, N., Swanson, K., Morisette, J., Baret, F., & Myneni, R. (2008). Intercomparison and sensitivity analysis of Leaf Area Index retrievals from LAI-2000, AccuPAR, and digital hemispherical photography over croplands. *Agricultural and Forest Meteorology*, 148, 1193–1209.

Gohain, K. J., Mohammad, P., & Goswami, A. (2021). Assessing the impact of land use land cover changes on land surface temperature over Pune city, India. *Quaternary International*, 575–576.

Hazaymeh, K., & Hassan, Q. K. (2017). A remote sensing-based agricultural drought indicator and its implementation over a semi-arid region. *Jordan*, 9(3).

Huete, A., Didan, K., Miura, T., Rodriguez, E., Gao, X., & Ferreira, L. (2002). Overview of the radiometric and biophysical performance of the MODIS vegetation indices. *Remote Sensing of Environment*, 83(1), 195–213. doi:10.1016/S0034-4257(02)00096-2.

Myneni, R., Knyazikhin, Y., & Park, T. (2015). MCD15A3H MODIS/Terra+Aqua Leaf Area Index/FPAR 4-day L4 Global 500m SIN Grid V006. *NASA EOSDIS Land Processes DAAC*. doi:http://doi.org/10.5067/MODIS/MCD15A3H.006

Ramadhani, F., Pullanagari, R., Kereszturi, G., & Procter, J. (2020). Automatic mapping of rice growth stages using the integration of sentinel-2, mod13q1, and sentinel-1. *Remote Sensing*, 12(21). doi:10.3390/rs12213613

Tarpley, J. D., Schneider, S. R., & Money, R. L. (1984). Global Vegetation indices from the NOAA-7 meteorological satellite. *Journal of Climate and Applied Meteorology*, 23, 491–494.

Torres, R., Snoeij, P., Geudtner, D., Bibby, D., Davidson, M., Attema, E., et al. (2012). GMES Sentinel-1 mission. *Remote sensing of environment*, 120, 9–24.

Weiss, M., Baret, F., Verger, A., Lacaze, R., Ramon, D., Wandrebek, L., & Smets, B. (2014). *Near real time, global, LAI, FAPAR and cover fraction products derived from PROBA-V, at 300m and 1km resolution.* Global Vegetation Monitoring and Modeling (GV2M).

Zhao, R., Li, Y., & Ma, M. (2021). Mapping paddy rice with satellite remote sensing: A review. *Sustainability*, 13. doi:10.3390/su13020503

44 Sentiment analysis of IMDB movie review with machine learning

Sapandeep Singh Sandhu[1,a] *and Jarnail Singh*[2,b]

[1]Research Scholar, University Institute of Computing, Chandigarh University, Chandigarh, India

[2]Professor, University Institute of Computing, Chandigarh University, Chandigarh, India

Abstract

Sentiment analysis is an estimation of the people, speakers, or writers concerning any topic. Nowadays, social media is viral. People use it to interact with people and exchange their thoughts on any topic, happenings, products, and other services. IMDB, known as Internet movie database, is the most popular online source of movies, TV shows, and celebrity content. It was launched online in 1990. It is an online database providing information related to entertainment, ratings, or reviews of movies. Various machine learning algorithms may be used categories its information primarily based totally on their sentiments. This paper implements the sentiment analysis of IMDB movie review. A trained dataset from the IMDB database used. After analyzing the data, prediction of the number of negative and positive reviews based on sentiments by using different classification models. The implementation of this system Python with SKlearn, NLTK, Bags of words model, term frequency- inverse document frequency model is applied. Also, the word cloud is plotted, showing the most frequently appearing positive and negative comments in the review.

Keywords: Sentiment analysis, Naïve Bayes, support vector machine, decision tree, K-nearest neighbors, ripple role learning, random forest, stochastic gradient descent

Introduction

Opinions of people on a particular topic, activity, product is vital because it reflects their attention, behavior or satisfaction towards topic or products (Yasen and Tedmori, 2019). This will help in many ways, such as adjusting marketing and business strategies, improving customer services, monitoring performances, enhancing product quality.

A review means the evaluation of public opinion on some subjects, such as a new book or film. A movie review can be positive or negative. It will provide the public an idea well about film and assist them in selecting whether to see it. Movie feedback can affect the work of the whole crew on that movie. According to the research, the failure or success of a film depends on its review text.

The movie review is categorized into two parts negative or positive review. The words used in review texts help to understand whether it is active content or positive content. Sentiment analysis helps in understanding the review text.

Sentiment analysis is the most popular in natural language processing (NLP). It is referred to as the opinion mining or predicting the behavior, attitude, or emotion of text, sentence, or a review on a particular topic, i.e., it is negative or positive. The decision-maker further uses this to plan, an appropriate action.

The steps involve in sentiment analysis are tokenization, filtering words, stemming or lemmatization, and classification. Tokenization is taken under the pre- processing stage. The row data is split into parts called tokens. After that, words are filtered, unnecessary words are removed. Stemming is performed. It will be removing affixes and prefixes to convert the word into its stem.

This paper addresses the sentiment analysis of a movie review. Different algorithms are used and compared to see the performance of the task. The Naive Bayes, logistic regressions, support vector classifiers (SVM) are taken to compare with each other because these algorithms are supervised classified and give the efficient and reliable result in sentiment analysis.

The following is the paper's structure: The literature survey in the topic of sentiment analysis is described in section 2. Section 3 shows the method used. Section 4 includes the proposed model, i.e., the model used in the paper. Section 5 present the experiment and result. Section 6 presents the conclusion of the research.

Literature Review

In the sentiment analysis domain, a lot of research has already been done.

Yasen and Tedmori (2019) used eight classifications and five evaluation measures. Naive Bayes, SVM, decision tree (DT), Bayes network (BN), K-nearest neighbors (KNN), ripper role learning (RRL), and random forest (RF). Stochastic

[a]Sapandeep.r1079@cumail.in; [b]jarnail.e9937@cumail.in

gradient descent (SGD) on the IMDB reviews the movie dataset and compares their results. And in conclusion, the RF gives the best results to give 96.01% accuracy compared to the other classifiers.

Kumar et al. (2019) used hybrid features on the data set on a short casual text. The sentiment analysis is a different process because it has fewer characters and large dimension characteristics, so hybrid featured, and lexicon-based features are used. Their combined features are used. Four different classifiers, such as SVM, Naive Bayes, Maximum entropy, and LNN, are used to check the effectiveness, and the maximum entropy with correlation shows the best accuracy. Therefore, both in space complexity and classification precision or accuracy, the result is very positive.

Goel et al. (2016) perform the analysis using Naive Bayes on tweets of movies. Naive Bayes is used because it is fast and straightforward. Twitter provided Twitter API to access data from the database before sending the data into the classification model. First, it is pre-processed with Naive Bayes and is used to improve the accuracy of the texting model with a recent hundred to its accuracy of 58.04%.

On various time intervals, Bhardwaj et al. (2015) obtain the live server data values of sensex and nifty. This can be used to predict the stock market shares, and the Python scripting language that has the execution of environment various methodologies of sentiment analysis explained—machine learning approach and lexicon-based approach.

The author worked on a variety of classifications, including linear classification of weighted n-gram features, sentence vector, combination tree, three-model based on generative technique on TF-IDFS and continuous representation of sense, as mentioned in (Tarımer et al., 2019). And the greatest outcome comes from combining these models.

As discussed by Tripathy et al. (2016), ML and vector space method are used to analyze on movie review dataset, in first the decision tree, Naive Bayes model are performed, and second method uses the natural language processing by vector space method and the term frequency (TF) and inverse document frequency (IDF) is used on the Twitter as well as IMDB dataset. The result shows that the decision tree algorithm is performed well for both the data set.

The four classifiers are used by the author namely Naive Bayes, support vector machine (SVM), maximum stochastic gradient descent for the sentiment analysis and for evaluation recall, accuracy precision, and f-measure used (Wang and Manning, 2012). It shows that the combination of a trigram, unigram, and bigram gives better accuracy.

The author of Large Movie Review Dataset suggested using a SVM and Naive Bayes and using a modified SVM using NB log- count ratios. The outcome revealed in the short text; the NB was better than SVM. However, in more time, records were easier for SVM; its attention, the positive result was provided by the algorithm instead of using SVM. Logistic regression gave the same result. A consistent benefit in SA has been made by word by bigram.

This paper suggests a model for sentiment analysis in a movie review. Various measurement methods, such as accuracy, F-measure, precision AUC are considered. In an analysis, the model will be tested using three different well- known classifiers to determine which classifier allows us to determine which classifier outcome is better and accurate. In this logistic regression, Naïve Bayes and linear SVM classifier are used.

Method Used

Pre-processing

By using the raw data directly, we cannot get the desired output because the data contains many irrelevant things, so it isn't easy to handle it and get the desired result, so we must pre-process the data before using it, and this filtered data is fit for any machine learning model.

To implement NPL, the machine translation toolkit is utilized to create Python program and deal with human language data. NLP works on words, not on a sentence. It contains libraries for text processing such as classification tagging, tokenization, stemming.

Tokenization with NLTF

Tokenization is splitting the row data or text into small parts. It breaks the data into sentences or words called tokens. Different way to tokenize the data (Balakrishnan and Lloyd-Yemoh, 2014). Sentence tokenization divides the data into sentences. Full stop character is used to indicate the completion of a sentence, but sometimes it is used for abbreviations. To solve this problem, the table of abbreviations is used (Yasen and Tedmori, (2019). NLTK is used for sentence tokenization (Jurish & Würzner, 2013). It is trained so that it is to identify the end of the sentence and beginning of the sentence.

Filtering words with NLTK

In NLTK, word tokenization split the sentence into words. After tokenization, stop or remove the words that are not necessary and not after the classification process. Firstly, we stop words from NLTK to remove the unnecessary word secondly, manually remove the unwanted words.

Stemming

Stemming is just like cutting down the branches of a tree to its stem. Stemming is used to extract the word by removing affixes and prefixes. Porter stemming algorithm is a rule-based algorithm introduced by Martine Porter is used; it is fast and straightforward. It is useful in information retrieval (Kobayashi & Takeda, 2000).

Lemmatization

Lemmatization is the method of collecting the many lipped versions of words into an individual entity for analysis (Singh et al., 2014). Lemmatization is preferable because the stem word of stemming does not impact proper meaning. In contrast, the Lemmatization of stem words conveys meaning as it does morphological analysis of the world.

Applications: -In comprehensive retrieval system.

Bags of words: Whenever we must apply any algorithm in NLP, we must convert the raw data into numbers because it works on a number. There are many ways from where we can alter the data. It can be used to pre-process the text. it keeps the count of total occurrences of most frequently used words.

Tf-IDF vectorizer: Term-frequency – inverse document frequency (TF-IDF) is a technique in different manner to determine the subject of an article by the terms it holds with TF-IDF; terms are given weight. TF-IDF calculate fitness, not count. In other words, the sum up of word is altered with TF-IDF outcome over the entire dataset. Firstly TF-IDF calculate that how many times words occur in the document, which is allocated to this tech, but Some words recur often in all publications, such as "and", "a," "an," and "is." and these words also do not provide much information. These words much are in counted, and this is the inverse document frequency path.

To keep all the reviews to be the same length padding, and truncation is used. Most of the machine learning model expects the same number of input column in the data frame in Keras built-in functions there is a parameter to set a maximum number of words in each review.

Proposed Model

The basic workflow of the sentiment models explained as followers:

1. Load the IBDB reviews datasets.
2. Labeling the data.
3. Tokenization.
4. Removing the unnecessary words.
5. Apply stemming/lemmatization.
6. Splitting the data into training and testing.
7. Classifying the data using different classifiers

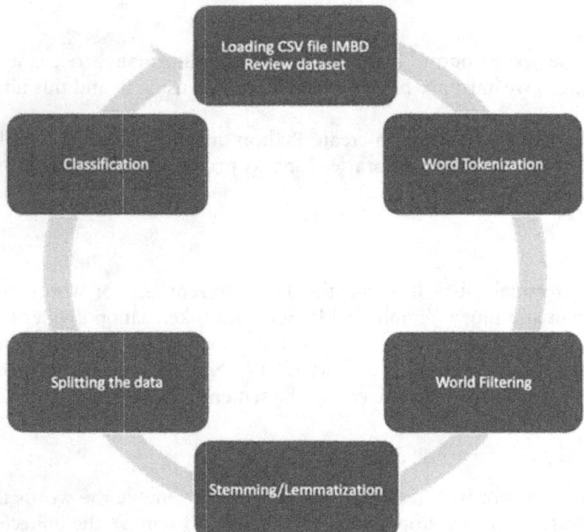

Experiment and Result

Dataset used

The suggested method's success was assessed using the IMDB review data set. This data set includes 5,000 reviews of movies and their binary classification, and it describes a community of movie review negative or positive the first row of the data set represents the header which contains the attributes description.

Experiment setting

First, import the data set to check the data set is balanced or not. The used data set is balanced. Divide the data set into two parts: a training dataset and a test dataset. After that, perform text normalization. Different algorithms and models are performed on the filtered data.

Bags of words model

This is used to convert train and test data to numerical vectors, and term-frequency-inverse document frequency modes (TF-IDF) converts data into a matrix of TF-IDF feature.

Classification

Logistic regression

It calculates the association between a categorical dependent variable and one or more independent variables using a logistic function, which is known as a cumulative logistic distribution (NLTK, 2018). Earlier, it was used in many social science applications.

The logistic regression model is built for both bags of words and TF-IDF features. This model performs on test dataset and predicting the model for a large packet of strings and TF-IDF characteristics.

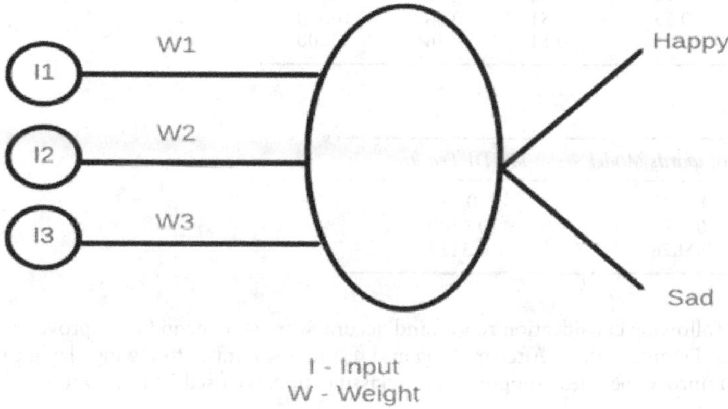

Multi-nominal Naïve Bayes:

The term frequency, or in what way numerous times a term emerge in a text, is utilize by multinomial Naive Bayes. The raw term frequency is usually divided by the document duration to normalize term frequency. To estimate the conditional probability, label frequency can be utilized after normalization to evaluate peak similarities which are estimates based on the training data (Rish, 2001).

Linear SVM: SVM stands for SVM and is a linear model for classification and regression issues. It is useful for a wide range of applications and can tackle both linear and nonlinear problems. A fundamental notion is SVM: By drawing a line or hyperplane through the data, the algorithm separates it into groups (Lin and Lin, 2003).

Table 44.1 Bags of word model classification report

Techniques	*Output*	*Precision*	*recall*	*F1-score*	*support*
Logistic regression	Positive	0.75	0.75	0.75	4993
	Negative	0.75	0.75	0.75	5007
	Macro avg	0.75	0.75	0.75	10000
	Weight avg	0.75	0.75	0.75	10000
Multinominal Navi Bayes	Positive	0.75	0.76	0.75	4993
	Negative	0.75	0.75	0.75	5007
	Macro avg	0.75	0.75	0.75	10000
	Weight avg	0.75	0.75	0.75	10000
Linear support vector	Positive	0.94	0.18	0.30	4993
	Negative	0.55	0.99	0.70	5007
	Macro avg	0.74	0.58	0.50	10000
	Weight avg	0.74	0.58	0.50	10000

Table 44.2 TF-IDF feature classification report

		Precision	*recall*	*F1-score*	*support*
Logistic regression	Positive	0.74	0.77	0.75	4993
	Negative	0.76	0.73	0.75	5007
	Macro avg	0.75	0.75	0.75	10000
	Weight avg	0.75	0.75	0.75	10000
Multinominal Navi Bayes	Positive	0.75	0.76	0.75	4993
	Negative	0.75	0.74	0.75	5007
	Macro avg	0.75	0.75	0.75	10000
	Weight avg	0.75	0.75	0.75	10000
Linear support vector	Positive	1.00	0.02	0.04	4993
	Negative	0.51	1.00	0.67	5007
	Macro avg	0.75	0.51	0.36	10000
	Weight avg	0.75	0.51	0.36	10000

Table 44.3 Accuracy table

Techniques	*Bags of words Model*	*TF-IDF Features*
Logistic regression	0.7512	0.75
Multinominal Navi Bayes	0.751	0.7509
Linear support vector	0.5826	0.5112

After training and testing the dataset following classification report and accuracy are shown, and to improve the linear support vector classification, we used Lemmatization. After training and testing the dataset following classification report and accuracy are shown, and to improve the linear support vector classification, we used Lemmatization.

Conclusion

In this paper, implementation of three model on the same data set and compare their accuracy. The first the logistic regression model, the second is multinomial Nave Bayes, and the third is linear support vector machine. It is observed that the accuracy of the first two models approximately the same, but third model linear support vector machine shows the less accuracy compared to the other two models. After using Lemmatization feature in the linear support vector, the accuracy is improved compared to the other two models. The accuracy improves from 0.5826 to 0.90296.

References

Balakrishnan, V. & Lloyd-Yemoh, E. (2014). Stemming and lemmatization: A comparison of retrieval performances. *Lecture Notes on Software Engineering*, 2(3).

Bhardwaj, A., Narayan, Y., & Dutta, M. (2015). Sentiment analysis for Indian stock market prediction using SENSEX and NIFTY. *Procedia Computer Science*, 70, 85–91.

Grefenstette, G. (1999). Tokenization. *Syntactic Wordclass Tagging*, 117–133.

Goel, A., Gautam, J., & Kumar, S. (2016). Real-time sentiment analysis of tweets using Naive Bayes. *2016 2nd International Conference on Next Generation Computing Technologies*, (pp. 257–261).

Jurish, B., & Würzner, K. M. (2013). Word and sentence tokenization with Hidden Markov Models. *Journal for Language Technology and Computational Linguistics*, 28(2), 61–83.

Kobayashi, M., & Takeda, K. (2000). Information retrieval on the web. *ACM computing surveys (CSUR)*, 32(2), 144–173.

Kumar, H. M., Harish, B. S., & Darshan, H. K. (2019). Sentiment analysis on IMDb movie reviews using hybrid feature extraction method. *International Journal of Interactive Multimedia & Artificial Intelligence*, 5(5).

Large Movie Review Dataset. http://ai.stanford.edu/~amaas/data/sentiment/

Lin, K. M. & Lin, C. J. (2003). A study on reduced support vector machines. *IEEE Transactions on Neural Networks*, 14(6), 1449–1459.

Porter, M. F. (2018). An algorithm for suffix stripping. *Program: electronic library and information systems, Program*, 14(3), 130–137.

Rish, I. (2001). An empirical study of the naive Bayes classifier. *2001 Workshop on Empirical Methods in Artificial Intelligence*, 3(22), 41–46.

Samal, B., Behera, A. K., & Panda, M. (2017). Presentation analysis of supervised machine learning techniques for sentiment analysis. *2017 Third International Conference on Sensing, Signal Processing and Security*, (pp. 128–133).

Singh, G., Kumar, B., Gaur, L., & Tyagi, A. (2019). Comparison between multinomial and Bernoulli naïve Bayes for text classification. *2019 International Conference on Automation, Computational and Technology Management*, (pp. 593–596).

Tarımer, İ., Çoban, A., & Kocaman, A. E. (2019). Sentiment analysis on IMDB movie comments and Twitter data by machine learning and vector space techniques. arXiv preprintarXiv:1903.11983.

Tripathy, A., Agrawal, A., & Rath, S. K. (2016). Using n-gram machine learning to classify sentiment reviews method. *Expert Systems with Applications*, 57, 117–126.

Wang, S. I. & Manning, C. D. (2012). Baselines and bigrams: simple, good sentiment, and topic classification. *Proceedings of the Association for Computational Linguistics' 50th Annual Meeting*, 2, 90–94.

Yasen, M. & Tedmori, S. (2019). Movies Reviews sentiment analysis and classification. *2019 IEEE Jordan International Joint Conference on Electrical Engineering and Information Technology*, (pp. 860–865).

45 A novel approach for classification of different Alzheimer's stages using pre-trained deep learning models with transfer learning and their comparative analysis

Gowhar Mohiuddin Dar[a], *Avinash Bhagat, and Sophiya Sheikh*

Department of Computer Applications, Lovely Professional University, Punjab, India

Abstract

Transfer learning has become extremely popular in recent years for tackling issues from various sectors, including the analysis of medical images. Medical image analysis has transformed medical care in recent years, enabling physicians to identify diseases early and accelerate patient recovery. Alzheimer's is a degenerative neurological condition that slowly deprives patients of their memory and cognitive abilities. Computed tomography and brain MRI scans are used to detect dementia in Alzheimer's patients. This research primarily aims to classify AD patients into multiple classes by implementing different deep learning models along with transfer learning on a large dataset as compared to existing approaches and hence improves classification accuracy. The novel approach gives results with an accuracy of 96.6%.

Keywords: Alzheimer's disease, EMCI, MCI, LMCI MRI, convolution neural networks, ResNet50, VGG16, DenseNet121

Introduction

Nearly 50 million people worldwide have been diagnosed with Alzheimer's disease (AD), a neurological condition (Mohi ud din dar et al., 2023). The malady permanently affects the brain, diminishing comprehension, recall, and other capabilities. The patient succumbs in case of brain failure. By 2050, the estimate is projected to rise to 152 million (Nawaz et al., 2021). As a result, in 2018, the expected global treatment expenses were established at almost $186 billion. In 30 years, this number is anticipated to increase by around four times (Sharma et al., 2022). Unfortunately, no precise treatment or prevention for Alzheimer's disease has yet been discovered by science (Planche et al., 2019). Early diagnosis of dementia disorders is crucial for patient recovery and treatment expenses because the cost of treating patients with EMCI, and LMCI is different. Diagnosis of Alzheimer's is best possible after the death of a patient since Alzheimer's pathology variations in patients are not assessed early. With the discovery of different biomarkers such as CSF, MRI, and PET data, the international working group devised a new approach in 2014 (Jellinger, 2006). Biomarker data is used to connect the clinical condition of dementia or mild cognitive loss to intrinsic Alzheimer's pathologic changes with the high, moderate, or low risk in the NIA-AA criteria. The physiology of dementia and its differential diagnosis have benefited greatly from structural and functional imaging, which also holds considerable potential for tracking the course of the disease (Narayanan & Murray, 2016). Numerous articles are written regarding how various imaging methods can be used to detect Alzheimer's disease. In volumetric MRI, patterns of sick and healthy subjects were identified using feature-based morphometry (FBM) (Toews et al., 2010). In computerized medical image processing, convolution neural networks (CNNs) have achieved major advancements. As a result, various CNN models, including VGG, MobileNet, AlexNet, and ResNet, are available for object detection and segmentation. Despite the fact that CNNs are a renowned deep learning technique, their effectiveness is hampered by the absence of an extensive medical imaging dataset. Transfer learning is among the efficient methods for building deep convolutional neural networks without overfitting when the amount of data is minimal (Acharya et al., 2019). A pre-trained network is the foundation of transfer learning. The proposed method can learn the most useful features instead of training a specific CNN network without preparation. To categorize AD into five classes, the proposed research study has used four pre-trained networks, comprising VGG 16, ResNet, and DenseNet121.

An automated framework was developed by U. Rajendra et al. (Acharya et al., 2019) to evaluate whether a baseline brain scan will detect any evidence of Alzheimer's disease. Lihua Wang et al. (Wang & Liu, 2019) integrated genomic data from six different brain areas using SVM machine learning techniques to find AD biomarkers. Martin Randles and Mohamed Mahyoub (Mahyoub et al., 2018) proposed that relying on characteristics including lifestyle, medical history, demography, and other considerations, Alzheimer's is predicted at various stages. Rueda et al. suggested a fusion-based image processing technique that identifies discriminative brain patterns connected to the presence of neurodegenerative

[a]dargowhar123@gmail.com

disorders (Rueda, Gonzalez, & Romero 2014). A classification approach based on multilayer brain divisions was presented by Li et al. (Li & Zhang, 2016). Using SVM, histogram-based parameters from MRI data were used to categorize various brain levels. Giraldo et al. (Giraldo et al., 2018) proposed an automated technique recently developed for identifying structural abnormalities in the thalamus, planum temporal, amygdala, and hippocampal areas. They have suggested identifying the stages of AD. Large datasets were necessary for classification and extracting deep features to avoid overfitting problems. To attain the maximum accuracy in early Alzheimer's diagnosis, they have recommended on time the depth and propagation of learning techniques compared to previous approaches. There is currently no treatment for AD using any medical reasoning approaches, and early detection of Alzheimer's disease is complicated. To attain high accuracy, KetkiTulpule et al. (Vickers, 2017) focused on nonlinear SVM for the radial base purpose when developing a computerized machine learning approach for categorizing Alzheimer's phases. Muazzam Maqsood et al. (Maqsood et al., 2019) devised a transfer learning approach to identify Alzheimer's disease. They suggested breaking down the AD category among different divisions.

Transfer Learning

The machine learning method of transfer learning uses a model developed for one job as the foundation for another. Transfer learning is learning a new activity more effectively by applying what has already been learned about a related one (Yosinski et al., 2014). For this approach to be practical, the features must be generic, i.e., applicable to both the base task and the target task (Fuse et al., 2018). Convolutional neural networks, often known as ConvNet, are a subset of deep neural networks (DNN) and are most frequently applied to the processing of medical images. The fundamental structure of the CNN is shown in Figure 45.1.

Experimental Evaluation

MRI images from the ADNI dataset are used in this study. There are 2900 images in this dataset (580 images from each class), each measuring 224 × 224. The images from each AD stage are listed in Table 45.1.

Data Balancing

Data balancing is essential for the model to predict more accurately. Unbalanced data leads to overfitting and underfitting; thus, data needs to be balanced. Here in this study, we use up sampling techniques to balance the data. The figures below show the data before and after sampling.

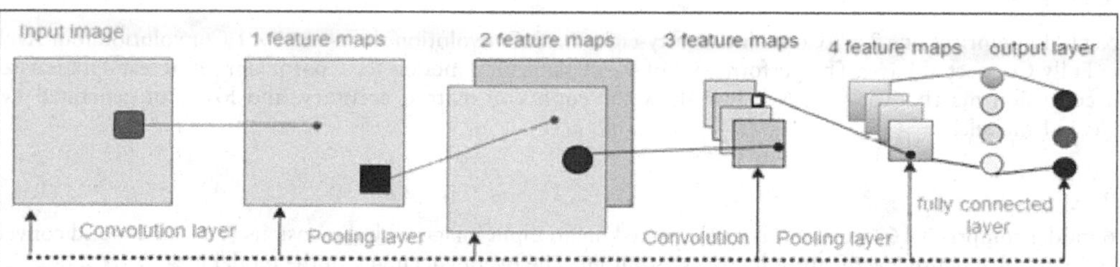

Figure 45.1 Basic CNN architecture

Table 45.1 The images given inputs to the model. 400 images from each class are used for training purposes, 90 from each class for validation, and 90 from each class for testing

AD stage	*Total images in a dataset*			
	Training data	*Test data*	*Validation data*	*Total*
NC	400	90	90	580
EMCI	400	90	90	580
MCI	400	90	90	580
LMCI	400	90	90	580
AD	400	90	90	580

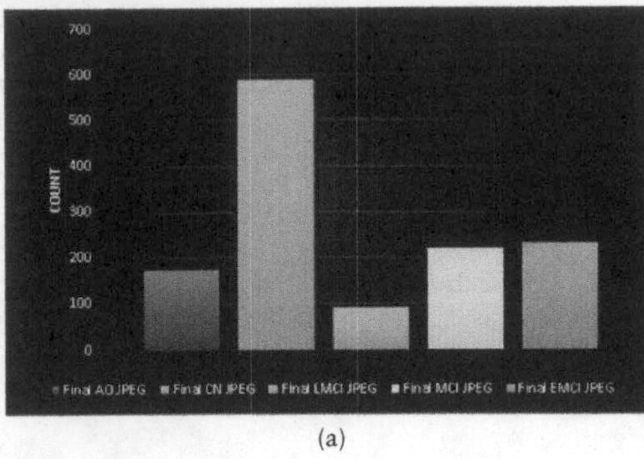

(a)

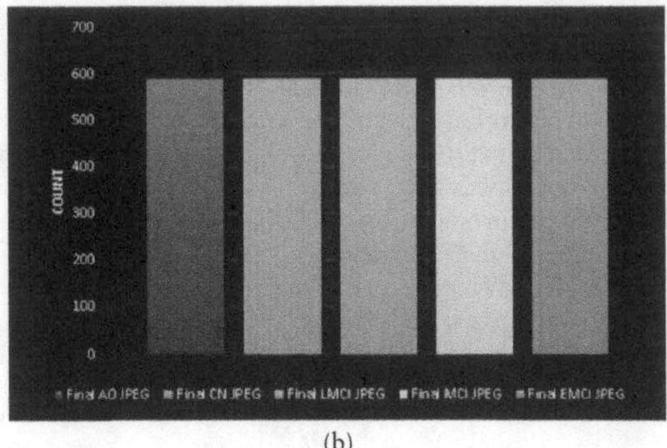

(b)

Figure 45.2 (a) shows the unbalanced data, (b) shows the balanced data

Data Augmentation

The size of the dataset is significant for deep learning models. These models predict more accurately and give better accuracy results on large datasets. The major drawback of image datasets is that they are not available in large size. Therefore, it needs to be augmented to make the dataset larger for the models. We applied different data augmentation techniques to datasets, such as horizontal filliping of the images, rotation of images by 5°, and width and shift in the images. in this study, we applied data augmentation with the help of an image data generator of Keras API.

Result Evaluation

Dataset used in this paper is divided into testing, training, and validating data. Total of 2900 images is used in this research. We applied transfer learning by applying pre-trained CNN models such as DenseNet121, and VGG16 with ImageNet weights. For multiclass classification, we are utilizing the RMSProp as our optimizer with a learning rate of 0.00001 and categorical cross-entropy as the loss metric while maintaining accuracy metrics that will provide training and validation results as well as loss and accuracy values.

DenseNet121

DenseNet121 comprises one 7 × 7 Convolution fifty-eight 3 × 3 Convolution sixty-one 1 × 1 Convolution four AvgPool an done Fully Connected Layer. The performance of the classification models for a particular set of test data is assessed using a confusion matrix. The figures below show the confusion matrix, accuracy, and loss plot generated by the DenseNet121 model.

VGG16

VGG16 model comprises 16 layers and is implemented on an input image with dimensions (224 × 224) and converts it into (7 × 7) and five dense layer feature matrices as output. The overall accuracy of the model is 96.0.

Discussion

The proposed model evaluates the efficiency of models in different performance metrics, such as the confusion matrix, accuracy, loss, F1 Score, precession, recall, ROC, and sensitivity. In the present study, 2900 images from the ADNI dataset are split into groups based on the stages of Alzheimer's. For Evolution, the whole data is divided into training, testing, and validation (500,90,90 images from each class). The performance analysis comparison of the applied models is shown in the figure below.

Conclusion

This study examined pre-trained strategies to predict the phase of Alzheimer's disease. The best accuracy of the model achieved is 97.23%. The proposed model works on ADNI data using Keras API, where the MRI image is divided into five categories: EMCI, MCI, LMCI, and Alzheimer's disease (AD). The analysis has looked at underfitting and

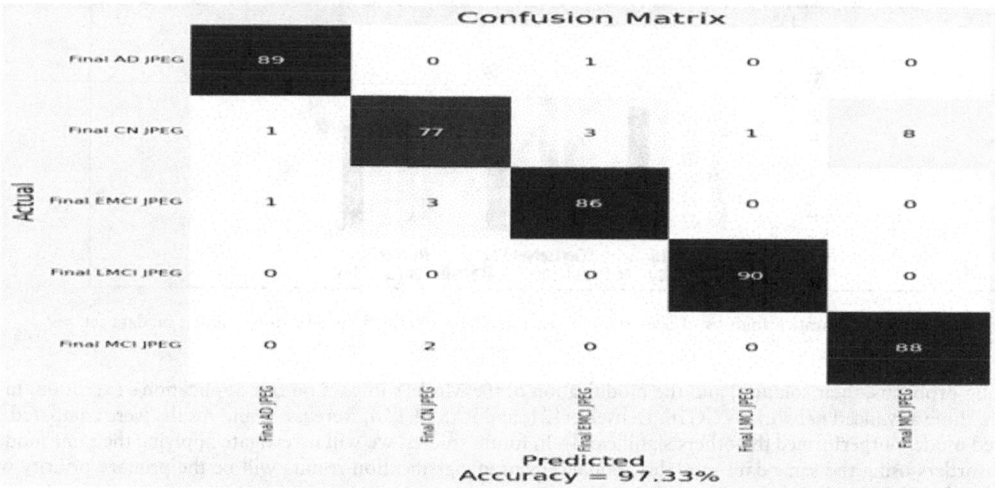

Figure 45.3(a) shows the confusion matrixgenerated by the DenseNet121 model. The overall accuracy is 97.33%

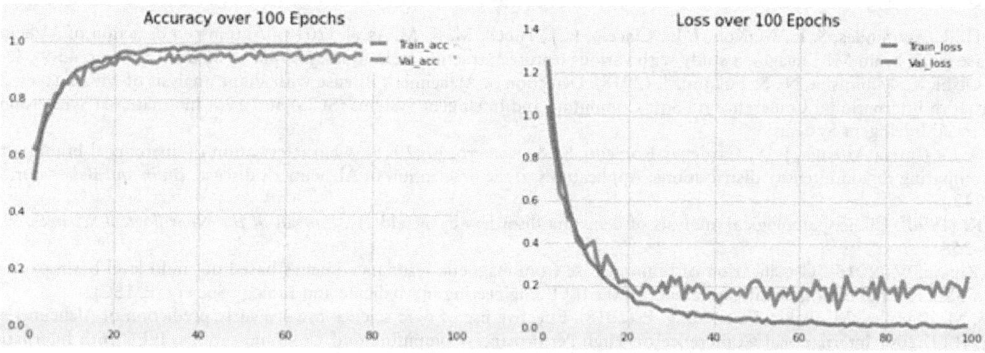

Figure 45.3(b) shows the accuracy and loss plot generated by the DenseNet121 model over 100 epochs

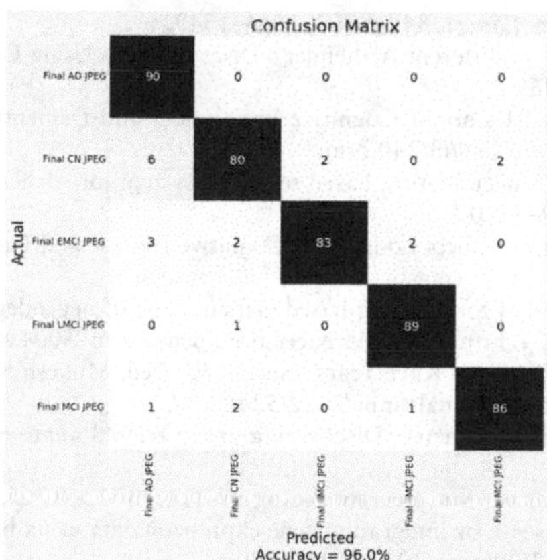

Figure 45.4 The confusion matrix generated by the VGG16 model. The overall accuracy is 96.0%

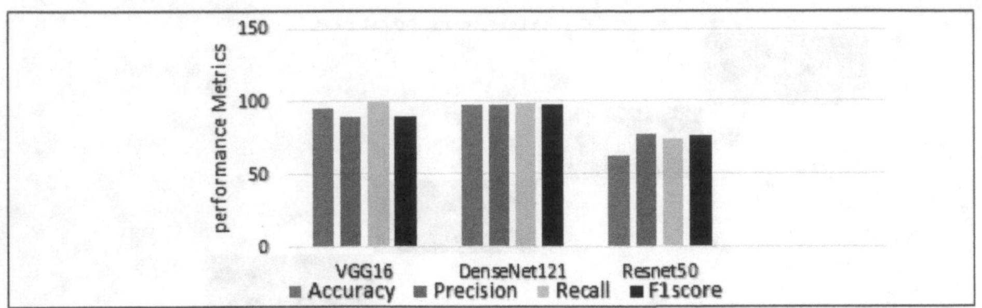

Figure 45.5 The comparative analysis of performance generated by pre-trained deep learning models on data set

overfitting problems, their solution, and the modification of the Model's impact on our application's execution. In this research, three advanced networks VGG16, DenseNet121, and RESNET50, were used, and results were compared. The suggested model outperformed the others significantly. In future studies, we will investigate applying the same model to other disorders using the same data modality. Enhancement in classification results will be the primary priority while training and testing the data.

References

Acharya, U. R., Fernandes, S. L., WeiKoh, J. E., Ciaccio, E. J., Fabell, M. K. M., et al. (2019). Automated detection of Alzheimer's disease using brain MRI images–a study with various feature extraction techniques. *Journal of Medical Systems*, 43(9), 1–14.

Fuse, H., Oishi, K., Maikusha, N., & Fukami, T. (2018). Detection of Alzheimer's disease with shape analysis of MRI images. 2018 Joint 10th International Conference on Soft Computing and Intelligent Systems (SCIS) and 19th International Symposium on Advanced Intelligent Systems.

Giraldo, D. L., García-Arteaga, J. D., Cárdenas-Robledo, S., & Romero, E. (2018). Characterization of anatomical brain patterns by comparing region intensity distributions: Applications to the description of Alzheimer's disease. *Brain and Behaviour*, 8(4), e00942.

Jellinger, K. (1990). Clinicopathological analysis of dementia disorders in the elderly. *Journal of the Neurological Sciences,* 95, 3, 239–258.

Li, T., & Zhang, W. (2016). Classification of brain disease from magnetic resonance images based on multi-level brain partitions. 2016 38th Annual International Conference of the IEEE Engineering in Medicine and Biology Society (EMBC).

Mahyoub, M., Randles, M., Baker, T., & Yang, P. (2018). Effective use of data science toward early prediction of Alzheimer's disease. IEEE 20th International Conference on High-Performance Computing and Communications; IEEE 16th International Conference on Smart City; IEEE 4th International Conference on Data Science and Systems (HPCC/SmartCity/DSS).

Maqsood, M., Nazir, F., Khan, U., Aadil, F., Jamal. H., & Mehmood, I. (2019). Transfer learning assisted classification and detection of Alzheimer's disease stages using 3D MRI scans. Sensors, 19(11), 2645.

Maurer, K., Volk, S., & Gerbaldo, H. (1997). Auguste D and Alzheimer's disease. *Lancet*, 349, 9064, 1546–1549.

Mohi ud din dar, Gowhar et al. 2023. "A Novel Framework for Classification of Different Alzheimer's Disease Stages Using CNN Model." *Electronics* 12(2): 469. https://www.mdpi.com/2079-9292/12/2/469.

Narayanan, Leela, and Alison Dorothy Murray. 2016. "What Can Imaging Tell Us about Cognitive Impairment and Dementia?" *World Journal of Radiology* 8(3): 240. http://www.wjgnet.com/1949-8470/full/v8/i3/240.htm.

Nawaz, H., Maqsood, M., Afzal, S., Aadil, F., Mehmood, I, & Rho, S. (2021). A deep feature-based real-time system for Alzheimer disease stage detection. *Multimedia Tools and Applications*, 80, 28, 35789–35807.

Planche, Vincent et al. 2019. "Evolution of Brain Atrophy Subtypes during Aging Predicts Long-Term Cognitive Decline and Future Alzheimer's Clinical Syndrome." *Neurobiology of Aging* 79: 22–29.

Rueda, A., Gonzalez, F. A., & Romero, E. (2014). Extracting salient brain patterns for imaging-based classification of neurodegenerative diseases. *IEEE Transactions on Medical Imaging,* 33(6), 1262–1274. http://ieeexplore.ieee.org/document/6750019/.

Sharma, Shilpa et al. 2022. "A ResNet50-Based Approach to Detect Multiple Types of Knee Tears Using MRIs" ed. Mukesh Soni. *Mathematical Problems in Engineering* 2022: 1–9. https://www.hindawi.com/journals/mpe/2022/5248338/.

Toews, M., Wells 3rd, W., Collins, D. L., & Arbel, T. (2010). Feature-based morphometry: Discovering group-related anatomical patterns. *Neuroimage,* 49(3), 2318–2327.

Vickers, N. J. (2017). Animal communication: when I'm calling you, will you answer too. Current Biology, 27(14), R713–R715.

Wang, L. & Liu, Z. P. (2019). Detecting diagnostic biomarkers of Alzheimer's disease by integrating gene expression data in six brain regions. *Frontiers in Genetics*, 10. https://www.frontiersin.org/article/10.3389/fgene.2019.00157/full.

Yosinski, Jason, Jeff Clune, Yoshua Bengio, and Hod Lipson. 2014. "How Transferable Are Features in Deep Neural Networks?" http://arxiv.org/abs/1411.1792.

46 A detailed survey on applications of machine learning techniques for forecasting

Jitendra Singh[1,a], *Preeti Pandey*[2,b], *and Geeta Sharma*[3,c]

[1]PhD Scholar, Lovely Professional University, Punjab, Assistant Professor, Computer Science and Engineering, GLBITM, Greater Noida, Uttar Pradesh, India

[2]PhD Scholar, Lovely Professional University, Punjab, Assistant Professor, Computer Science and Engineering, Delhi Technical Campus, Greater Noida, Uttar Pradesh, India,

[3]Assistant Professor, Lovely Professional University, Punjab, India

Abstract

Machine learning (ML) is a very popular branch of artificial intelligence (AI). In ML, machines are trained on available training data by using the appropriate mechanism (algorithm). Further a validated model is prepared. When the new data having specified feature, is passed through this model, the machines using the model responses on the basis of that learning. ML is used for different purposes. One of the most popular areas is forecasting. This is about to say (by considering available information) what will probably occur in the future. In this paper, we reviewed 8 machine learning techniques which were used specially for prediction. Every technique is not suitable for every type of applications. In the work, a collective analysis was performed on uses of these algorithms on different fields for predicting the outcomes in coming time. Reviewed work covers different sectors of applications like agriculture, stock market, sentiment analysis, COVID-19 pandemic, medicine, environment, human behavior, banking and many more.

Keywords: Machine learning, forecasting, artificial neural networks, Gaussian process, support vector regressor, random forest, generalized regression neural networks (GRNN), critical analysis

Introduction

Forecasting is all about predicting future outcomes on the basis of available concerned information at present. Forecasting help decision makers in building successful enterprise by enabling them to take relevant decisions for future based on currently available processed data.

ML has a significant impact in this regard. Procedure of ML provides such capability to systems/machines so that learning from data and appropriate outcomes could be possible.

Related engineers of this field develop a model by training algorithms on existing data. As model is trained then it can be utilized for different aspects of machine learning applications. Nowadays one of the very popular aspects of machine learning is predicting outcomes i.e., forecasting. Figure 46.1 shows the generalized process of ML forecasting. First step is includes define objective and data elicitation, second step is preprocessing and feature engineering on acquired data, third step is to data split for training and testing in needful ratio, fourth step involves building and training ML model, fifth step is to evaluation of model's effectiveness by comparing forecast with actual data and the last step is to related to performance comparison with other models and selecting the model with least weighted mean absolute error.

Role of ML algorithms comes in step four for building the ML model. Models stand on the suitable techniques. In this paper, we reviewed eight ML algorithms which are used in forecasting and collective analysis is presented in Table 46.1.

Forecasting Applications using Machine Learning Algorithms

Artificial neural network algorithm

Artificial neural network (ANN) is a type of computer modelling approach, have been developed for simulating complex real-world situations and have found its extensive use in numerous fields. Artificial neurons (or nodes) are structures that can do extremely parallel computations for data processing and knowledge representation. They are made up of densely coupled adaptable simple processing components (Hecht-Nielsen, 1990; Schalkoff, 1997). The development of mathematical algorithms that will allow ANNs to learn by imitating information processing and knowledge acquisition in the human brain is the primary goal of ANN-based computing (also known as neurocomputing) Basheer and Hajmeer, 2000).

To calculate the coupling between the EF and adsorption processes' COD and TOC removal efficiencies, an ANN model was developed. For COD and TOC removals, in both batch and continuous modes, a good correlation was

[a]jitlogic15@gmail.com; [b]preeti1986pandey@gmail.com; [c]Geeta.26875@lpu.co.in

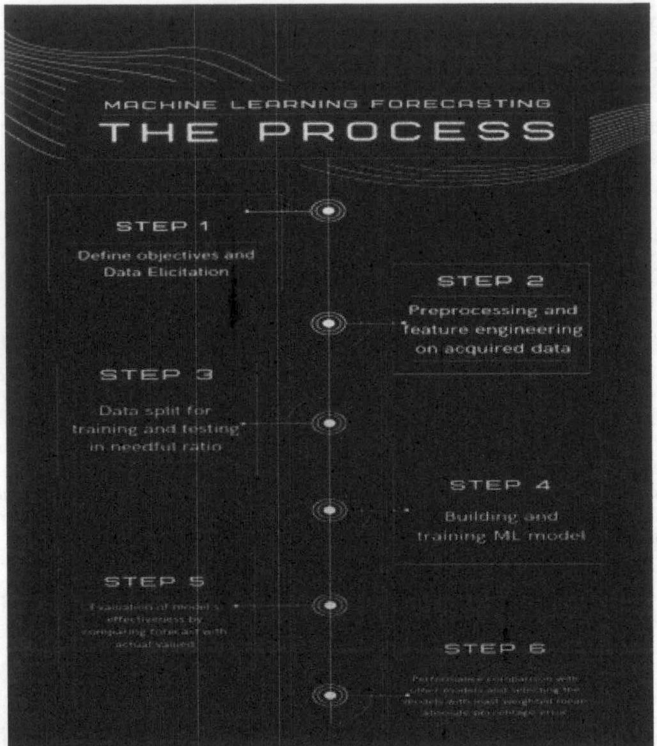

Figure 46.1 Machine learning forecasting process

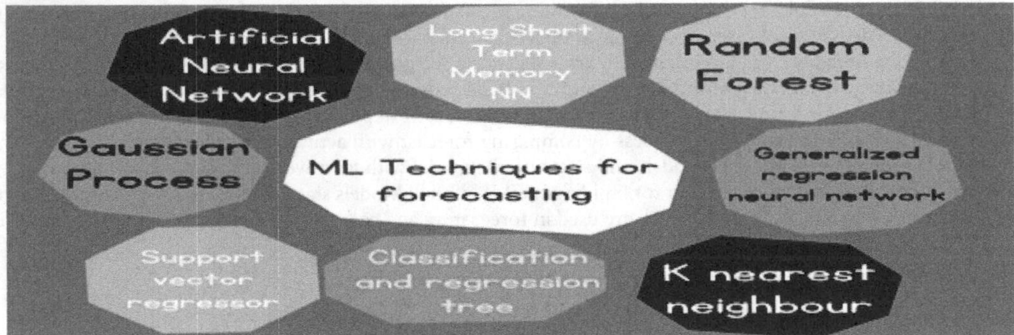

Figure 46.2 Machine learning algorithms used for applications of forecasting

discovered between the theoretical prediction made by the ANN model and the experimental data. The uniqueness of the presented work was the synergistic interaction between the EF and adsorption processes in wastewater treatment, which makes the ANN model a useful tool for explaining this under various experimental setups (Kuleyin et al., 2022). Parameters for drying experiments were drying time, variety, air velocity, initial oil content, free fatty acid content, drying temperature and storage type. In order to model these parameters, a multilayer perceptron model was used (Voca, 2022) with three layers (input, hidden, and output) for three ANNs. For the prediction of the target values, the constructed model's prediction was accurate enough. The researchers Gourabi et al. (2022) used an ANN network to forecast the TOA albedo factor and IR radiation flux using the ERB data. The obtained results accurately show that the technique is suitable for intervals of sunlight. By creating a new method to design the ANN (hybrid) while taking relationships (non-linear) into account, the study (Zhang et al., 2022) illustrated the usefulness of using ANNs in decision analysis. For forecasting the pandemic of recent COVID-19 in Egypt, statistics and AI methodologies were preferred in the study (Saba and Elsheikh, 2020).

LSTM algorithm

Specifically in the tasks where sequence prediction is involved, numerous recurrent neural networks (RNNs) are capable to learn long-term dependencies. Long short-term memory networks (LSTMs) are used in DL. LSTM networks provide superior outcomes than RNNs in DP field. Wan et al. (2020) suggested an unique LSTM variation, CTS-LSTM, for forecasting correlated time series collectively. To enhance the model's prediction accuracy, a general interface (for external elements management) was constructed and complicated non-linear are explicitly modelled and stored in cells. In order to anticipate future values for both GOOGL and NKE assets, the article by Moghar and Hamiche (2020) presented an RNN based on LSTM. The model's results have been encouraging. The testing outcome supported the claim that the model can track the development of opening prices for both assets. The study by Pathan et al. (2020) examined the overall genomic sequence mutation rate using data from patients with COVID-19 from various nations. The processed dataset was used to identify the codon mutation and nucleotide mutation independently. In the study by Huang et al (2022), an LSTM model was developed to anticipate the production performance of a carbonate reservoir in the Middle East while taking gas injection effect into account. According to the findings, the LSTM method's average error is 43.75% less than that of conventional RNS. Additionally, only 10.43% and 36.46% of RNSs are accounted for by the total CPU time and total computational power used by the LSTM approach, respectively. Therefore, it is obvious that the LSTM technique has a sizable advantage in terms of calculation.

RF algorithm

Random forest (RF), as the literals implies, is a classifier which involves various decision trees and averages them to increase the dataset's predictive accuracy. RF is a popular ML algorithm and part of the supervised learning methodology. It can be applied to ML issues involving both classification and regression. It is built on the idea of ensemble learning, which is a method of integrating various classifiers to address difficult issues and enhance model performance. In the study (Luciano, et al., 2021), researchers integrated several data sources to anticipate sugarcane yield across a large area nearly 51,000 ha more than four years using this algorithm. In the research (Harley et al., 2020), environmental data sets from numerous agencies and tribal partners were combined in order to estimate and forecast PST concentrations in Southeast Alaska from 2016 through 2019. The time of early summer blooming may be predicted using environmental variables, according to the authors. Allergies to pollen are harmful to one's health. The objective of this study (Lo et al., 2021) was to create and assess statistical models that forecast daily pollen concentrations using the RF and ML technique. Four different eco-climate zones can accurately predict the presence of four different pollen kinds over the next one to fourteen days. In the study (Borup, et al., 2022), researchers demonstrate that 'effective targeting regulates the likelihood of splitting data along powerful predictors, offering a crucial addition to RF feature sampling. Simulations employing finite representative samples substantiate this'.

Generic regression neural network algorithm

Specht (1991) proposed generic regression neural network (GRNN) first time in 1991. The GRNN () is a single-pass neural network which uses Gaussian activation function in the hidden layer. Four layers (input, hidden, summation, and division) make up GRNN. Training a GRNN is easy. The training targets are the output weights, and the input weights are the training inputs transposed. GRNN is an associative memory i.e., training samples are equal to hidden neurons (after training). This study compared the performance of the GRNN, a particular neural network architecture, against a number of forecasting methods, such as the 'multi-layered feedforward network (MLFN), the multivariate transfer function, and random walk models' (Leung et al., 2000). The research (Zhou et al., 2014), initially suggested 'a hybrid ensemble empirical mode decomposition- (EEMD) GRNN model based on data preparation and analysis for one-day-ahead PM2.5 concentration prediction'. The EEMD component breaks down the original PM2.5 data into a number of intrinsic mode functions (IMFs), and the GRNN component predicts each IMF. 50 samples were utilized to assess the chemical effects of agricultural biomass in (Huang et al., 2016). GRNN model based on the element composition and a linear model based on the high heat value were both constructed as projected models for the chemical exergy. First, an auto-refinement technique was created to enhance the regression neural network model's functionality. The experimental findings (Hariharan, et al., 2012) indicate that, when compared to MLP and TDNN, the GRNN classifier offers extremely promising classification accuracy, and the suggested technique can successfully distinguish between normal and abnormal infant screams. proposes a time-frequency analysis using a short-time Fourier transform. It is suggested to use generalized regression neural networks for classification.

K-NN regression algorithm

One of the straightforward and effective machine learning techniques is KNN. It is a non-parametric, supervised learning classifier that dictates proximity about procedure of grouping of single data point. This approach and its modified variations from earlier studies were highlighted in the work (Taunk et al., 2019). At the same time, closing status and high status of price in stock market can be predicted. In this direction researchers (Zhang et al., 2017) suggested a two-stage methodology which combines EEMD (ensemble empirical mode decomposition) with MKNN (multidimensional closest neighbor model). This research (Cheng et al., 2018) suggested an adaptive- spatiotemporal k-nearest neighbor (STKNN) model for short-term traffic prediction to address the issues of quantitatively unclear spatiotemporal dependency linkages along with fixed model structures. Based on the time, weights, AS (adaptive spatiotemporal) neighbors other variables, it thoroughly took into account the spatial heterogeneity of city traffic.

Managers of water resources and river forecasters frequently struggle to find records of previous years that exhibit the same situations of river and weather conditions (as the current year). One such ML technique is KNN algorithm, which makes no assumptions about the dataset distributions but only needs a brief (and implicit) training phase. This is particularly helpful when predicting river ice because the intricate river ice dynamics are challenging to precisely measure and indicators of river and weather conditions frequently do not follow the usual assumptions as per theory (Sun et al., 2017). By giving precise energy demand projections, the work (Gómez-Omella, et al., 2021) presented a case study of big data and ML with the aim of enhancing energy demand response (DR) programme.

CART algorithm

To create prediction models from data classification and regression algorithms are also used in forecasting. Leo Breiman coined the term 'Classification and Regression Trees (CART)' to describe decision tree methods that can be applied to classification or regression predictive modelling issues. Traditionally, this method is known as 'decision trees', however on other platforms, like R, it is known by the more contemporary moniker CART. This algorithm is having the roots of popular algorithms like boosted decision tree, RF and bagged decision tree. In the research (Erdal and Karakurt, 2013), authors optimized prediction accuracy of CART. The purpose was to perform the monthly streamflow forecast. Developed models had better performance than CART and SVRas they used bagging and boosting techniques in it. These newly involved techniques improved the performance of weak learners. Result was in in the form of findings of BRTs and GBRTs (Bagged regression trees and Gradient Boosting regression trees). In the research (Razi and Athappilly, 2005), authors suggested use of RF with CART to get more accurate risk assessment due to smoking dataset in the strained institutions. For eliciting the credit risk of banks (Li et al., 2020), these outcomes were having significant ramifications. And in research (Antipov and Pokryshevskaya, 2012), a method for identifying segments with underestimated or inflated predictions is suggested.

SVR Algorithm

Support vector machine (SVM) maintains all the key characteristics that define the algorithm and can be utilised as a regression technique (maximal margin). With only a few minor exceptions, the support vector regression (SVR) for classification follows the same concepts as the SVM' (Zhang and O'Donnell, 2020). In addressing non-linear forecasting issues, in recent years, SVR has shown to be effective in addressing non-linear forecasting issues this algorithm performs well. Selection of right parameters plays crucial role in performance of SVR. In the final simulation (Wang, et al., 2012), in annual load forecasting BPNN (Back propagation neural network outperforms. Based on two error measures, mean squared error (MSE) and mean absolute percent error, 'the proposed model (Kazem et al., 2013) outperformed genetic algorithm-based SVR (SVR-GA), chaotic genetic algorithm-based SVR (SVR-CGA), firefly-based SVR (SVR-FA), ANNs, and adaptive neuro-fuzzy inference systems (ANFIS) (MAPE)'. Multiple linear regression and tree-based models were used to apply the feature selection technique, which increased the accuracy and predictive performance of the epsilon radial basis function (R=.9925) SVR model even more. The findings (Onyekwena, et al., 2022) shown that the primary predictive variables are SAC, DS, and porosity. The work by Chang et al. (2013) used SVR in physiological emotion analysis.

GP Algorithm

An stochastic process is a collection of random variables indexed by time or space. Guassian process (GP) is one of the types of stochastic processes. In this every fixed number of linear combination of the random variables has a multivariate normal distribution. The authors in Morales-lvarez (2019) have developed two new, scalable, and effective probabilistic crowdsourcing techniques that can handle datasets that were previously prohibitively large. In the study (Velásquez and Lara, 2020), estimates overall cases of COVID-19 reported in the United States from January 21 to April 12 of 2020 were made in a timely manner. With GIS data available, writers developed a novel Bayesian system as the pandemic spread. The chosen algorithms for the chaotic dynamic system include the correlation coefficient for a reduced-space Gaussian process regression with data collected over 82 days by daily, continuous learning is 98.91%. The study (Wang, et al., 2022) presented a probabilistic method for predicting wind gusts based on the sparse GPR model, which simplifies training for the complete GPR. The suggested methodology improves the forecasting accuracy of the wind gust (in both short- and long-term horizons) by combining the 'ECMWF data' and on-site observations. The study (Ballabio, et al., 2019) produced a brand-new set of maps showing the chemical characteristics of topsoil at a baseline level at a resolution of 250 m for 26 EU countries, encompassing an area of more than 4.5 million km^2. The Gaussian Process Regression technique, on which the modelling is based, enables the estimation of prediction uncertainty.

Collective Analysis and Conclusion

Nowadays it seems that machine learning (ML) experts don't want to leave any field unexplored. Because of the data availability in huge amount and highly advantageous ML approaches, the job is on its hike. ML techniques not only having benefit of wide range of applications but are benefitting by the features of continuous improvement in accuracy, automation and identification of trends and patterns. We focused on forecasting in this paper. In forecasting, generally qualitative data is used that depend on the judgment of experts. At primary level, forecasting benefits enterprises with relevant information which is useful in making decisions about the future of the enterprises. In Table 46.1, collective

Table 46.1 Collective analysis on forecasting mechanisms by researchers

S.No.	*Algorithm*	*Forecasting Applications*
1.	ANN	• To COD and TOC removal effectiveness prediction (Kuleyin. A., et al., 2022). • Forecasting the key quality indicators of thirteen cultivars and hybrid of rapeseed (Voca. N. et al., 2022) • To forecast die infrared flux of earth albedo (Gourabi, F. N. et al., 2022) • For predicting RPV adoption behaviors (Zhang, N et al., 2022). • To predict the incidence of the pandemic COVID-19 (Saba. A. 1., and Elsheikh. A. H., 2020).
2.	LSTM	• To anticipate correlated time series collectively (Wan. FL. et al., 2020). • To forecast future stock market values (Moghar, A. & Hamiche. M. 2020) • To forecast the body's rate of mutation (Padian. R. K, et al., 2020). • To forecast the gas injection impact (Huang. R. et al., 2022),.
3.	RF	• Intelligent crack evolution prediction model (Wang. B. et al., 2022). • To forecast sugarcane yield before harvest (Santos Luciano, et al., 2021). • Prediction of paralytic shellfish toxins (PSTs) concentration (Harley. J. R. et al., 2020). • To forecast pollen concentration using environmental data (Lo. F. et al., 2021).
4.	GRNN	• Mondily exchange rates prediction of die Japanese Yen, Canadian dollar and the British pound. (Leung. M. T. et al., 2000). • A warning system for quick air quality was created. (Zhou. Q., et al., 2014) • For predicting die chemical exergy of biomass (Huang, Y. et al., 2016). • Effectively distinguishing normal and abnormal cries of a baby (Hariharan. M. et al., 2012).
5.	KNN	• To forecast the high price and closing price of the four equities in stock market (Zhang. N. et al., 2017). • For predicting die APBF of the smoky river in Canada (Sun. W. et al., 2017).
6.	(ART	• For monthly stream flow prediction (Erdal. H. L. & Karakurt. O. 2013). • To carry out a three-way evaluation of prediction accuracy on a sizable dataset of smokers (Razi. M. A. & Adiappilly. K. 2005). • To forecast credit ratings for GCC banks (Li, J. P. et al., 2020). • For mass residential estate appraisal (Antipov. E. A. & Pokryshevskaya. E. B. 2012).
7.	SVR	• Forecasting annual load for die electric power sector (Wang. J., et al., 2012). • To assess prediction in stock market datasets (Kazem. A. et al., 2013). • To predict die gas diffusion coefficient of biochar-amended soil (Onyekwena. C. C., et al., 2022). • Emotion identification approach (Chang, C. Y. et al., 2013)
8.	GP	• For crowd source learning (Morales-Alvarez. P., 2019) • To predict cases of COVID-19 (Velasquez. R. M. A. & Lara. J. V. M. 2020). • For niultistep ahead wind gust forecasting (Wang, H., et al., 2022) • By estimating prediction variance. GPR enables the creation of uncertainty maps (Ballabio. C., et al., 2019).

analysis is presented in tabular form that represents the applications of selected eight ML techniques which are rapidly used in research from 20002022. From this time frame we explored many research papers and selected around 40 out of them. In this work analysis reveals that recently ANN is used to COD and TOC removal effectiveness prediction, LSTM is used to forecast the gas injection impact, RF algorithm is used to forecast pollen concentration using environmental data, GRNN is applied for predicting the chemical exergy of biomass, KNN is used to forecast the high price and closing price of stock market, CART is applied to forecast credit ratings for some banks, SVR is used to predict the gas diffusion coefficient of biochar-amended soil, and Gaussian process is used for wind gust forecasting.

In this work, we set a goal to extract outcomes of ML techniques implemented in recent years in the field of prediction and finally achieved the same by reviewing and critical analysis on existing research.

References

Antipov, E. A. & Pokryshevskaya, E. B. (2012). Mass appraisal of residential apartments: An application of Random forest for valuation and a CART-based approach for model diagnostics. *Expert Systems with Applications*, 39(2), 1772–1778.

Ballabio, C., Lugato, E., Fernández-Ugalde, O., Orgiazzi, A., Jones, A., Borrelli, P., & Panagos, P. (2019). Mapping LUCAS topsoil chemical properties at European scale using Gaussian process regression. *Geoderma*, 355, 113912.

Basheer, I. A. & Hajmeer, M. (2000). Artificial neural networks: fundamentals, computing, design, and application. *Journal of microbiological methods*, 43(1), 3–31.

Borup, D., Christensen, B. J., Mühlbach, N. S., & Nielsen, M. S. (2022). Targeting predictors in random forest regression. *International Journal of Forecasting*.

Chang, C. Y., Chang, C. W., Zheng, J. Y., & Chung, P. C. (2013). Physiological emotion analysis using support vector regression. *Neurocomputing*, 122, 79–87.

Cheng, S., Lu, F., Peng, P., & Wu, S. (2018). Short-term traffic forecasting: an adaptive ST-KNN model that considers spatial heterogeneity. *Computers, Environment and Urban Systems*, 71, 186–198.

Dos Santos Luciano, A. C., Picoli, M. C. A., Duft, D. G., Rocha, J. V., Leal, M. R. L. V., & Le Maire, G. (2021). Empirical model for forecasting sugarcane yield on a local scale in Brazil using Landsat imagery and random forest algorithm. *Computers and Electronics in Agriculture*, 184, 106063.

Erdal, H. I., & Karakurt, O. (2013). Advancing monthly streamflow prediction accuracy of CART models using ensemble learning paradigms. *Journal of Hydrology*, 477, 119–128.

Gourabi, F. N., Kiani, M., & Pourtakdoust, S. H. (2022). Satellite Pose Estimation Using Earth Radiation Modeled by Artificial Neural Networks. Advances in Space Research.

Gómez-Omella, M., Esnaola-Gonzalez, I., Ferreiro, S., & Sierra, B. (2021). k-Nearest patterns for electrical demand forecasting in residential and small commercial buildings. *Energy and Buildings*, 253, 111396.

Hariharan, M., Sindhu, R., & Yaacob, S. (2012). Normal and hypoacoustic infant cry signal classification using time–frequency analysis and general regression neural network. *Computer methods and programs in biomedicine*, 108(2), 559–569.

Harley, J. R., Lanphier, K., Kennedy, E., Whitehead, C., & Bidlack, A. (2020). Random forest classification to determine environmental drivers and forecast paralytic shellfish toxins in Southeast Alaska with high temporal resolution. *Harmful Algae*, 99, 101918.

Huang, R., Wei, C., Wang, B., Yang, J., Xu, X., Wu, S., & Huang, S. (2022). Well performance prediction based on Long Short-Term Memory (LSTM) neural network. *Journal of Petroleum Science and Engineering*, 208, 109686.

Huang, Y. W., Chen, M. Q., Li, Y., & Guo, J. (2016). Modeling of chemical exergy of agricultural biomass using improved general regression neural network. *Energy*, 114, 1164–1175.

Kazem, A., Sharifi, E., Hussain, F. K., Saberi, M., &Hussain, O. K. (2013). Support vector regression with chaos-based firefly algorithm for stock market price forecasting. *Applied soft computing*, 13(2), 947–958.

Kuleyin, A., Gök, A., Eroğlu, H. A., Özkaraova, E. B., Akbal, F., Jada, A., & Duply, J. (2022). Combining Electro-Fenton and Adsorption Processes for Reclamation of Textile Industry Wastewater and Modeling by Artificial Neural Networks. *Journal of Electroanalytical Chemistry*, 116652.

Leung, M. T., Chen, A. S., & Daouk, H. (2000). Forecasting exchange rates using general regression neural networks. *Computers & Operations Research*, 27(11–12), 1093–1110.

Li, J. P., Mirza, N., Rahat, B., & Xiong, D. (2020). Machine learning and credit ratings prediction in the age of fourth industrial revolution. *Technological Forecasting and Social Change*, 161, 120309.

Lo, F., Bitz, C. M., & Hess, J. J. (2021). *Development of a Random Forest model for forecasting allergenic pollen in North America*. Science of The Total Environment, 773, 145590.

Loh, W. Y. (2011). Classification and regression trees. *Wiley interdisciplinary reviews: data mining and knowledge discovery*, 1(1), 14–23.

Moghar, A., & Hamiche, M. (2020). Stock market prediction using LSTM recurrent neural network. *Procedia Computer Science*, 170, 1168–1173.

Morales-Álvarez, P., Ruiz, P., Santos-Rodríguez, R., Molina, R., & Katsaggelos, A. K. (2019). Scalable and efficient learning from crowds with Gaussian processes. *Information Fusion*, 52, 110–127.

Onyekwena, C. C., Xue, Q., Li, Q., Wan, Y., Feng, S., Umeobi, H. I., & Chen, B. (2022). Support vector machine regression to predict gas diffusion coefficient of biochar-amended soil. *Applied Soft Computing*, 109345.

Pathan, R. K., Biswas, M., & Khandaker, M. U. (2020). Time series prediction of COVID-19 by mutation rate analysis using recurrent neural network-based LSTM model. *Chaos, Solitons & Fractals*, 138, 110018

Rasmussen, C. E. (2003). Gaussian processes in machine learning. In Summer school on machine learning (pp. 63–71). Springer, Berlin, Heidelberg.

Razi, M. A., & Athappilly, K. (2005). A comparative predictive analysis of neural networks (NNs), nonlinear regression and classification and regression tree (CART) models. *Expert systems with applications*, 29(1), 65–74.

Saba, A. I., & Elsheikh, A. H. (2020). Forecasting the prevalence of COVID-19 outbreak in Egypt using nonlinear autoregressive artificial neural networks. *Process Safety and Environmental Protection*, 141, 1–8.

Specht, D. F. (1991). A general regression neural network. *IEEE Transactions on Neural Networks*, 2(6), 568–576.

Sun, W., & Trevor, B. (2017). Combining k-nearest-neighbor models for annual peak breakup flow forecasting. *Cold Regions Science and Technology*, 143, 59–69.

Taunk, K., De, S., Verma, S., & Swetapadma, A. (2019, May). A brief review of nearest neighbor algorithm for learning and classification. *2019 International Conference on Intelligent Computing and Control Systems (ICCS)* (pp. 1255–1260).

Velásquez, R. M. A., & Lara, J. V. M. (2020). Forecast and evaluation of COVID-19 spreading in USA with reduced-space Gaussian process regression. *Chaos, Solitons & Fractals*, 136, 109924.

Voća, N., Pezo, L., Jukić, Ž., Lončar, B., Šuput, D., & Krička, T. (2022). Estimation of the storage properties of rapeseeds using an artificial neural network. *Industrial Crops and Products*, 187, 115358.

Wan, H., Guo, S., Yin, K., Liang, X., & Lin, Y. (2020). CTS-LSTM: LSTM-based neural networks for correlated time series prediction. *Knowledge-Based Systems*, 191, 105239.

Wang, H., Zhang, Y. M., & Mao, J. X. (2022). Sparse Gaussian process regression for multi-step ahead forecasting of wind gusts combining numerical weather predictions and on-site measurements. *Journal of Wind Engineering and Industrial Aerodynamics*, 220, 104873.

Wang, J., Li, L., Niu, D., & Tan, Z. (2012). An annual load forecasting model based on support vector regression with differential evolution algorithm. *Applied Energy*, 94, 65–70.

Zhang, F., & O'Donnell, L. J. (2020). Support vector regression. Machine Learning, (pp. 123–140). Academic Press.

Zhang, N., Hwang, B. G., Lu, Y., & Ngo, J. (2022). A Behavior theory integrated ANN analytical approach for understanding households adoption decisions of residential photovoltaic (RPV) system. *Technology in Society*, 102062.

Zhang, N., Lin, A., & Shang, P. (2017). Multidimensional k-nearest neighbor model based on EEMD for financial time series forecasting. Physica A: *Statistical Mechanics and its Applications*, 477, 161–173.

Zhou, Q., Jiang, H., Wang, J., & Zhou, J. (2014). A hybrid model for PM2. 5 forecasting based on ensemble empirical mode decomposition and a general regression neural network. *Science of the Total Environment*, 496, 264–274.

47 Sentiment analysis on mobile reviews by using machine learning models

Ameya Parkar[a] *and Rajni Bhalla*[b]

School of Computer Application, Lovely Professional University, Punjab, India

Abstract

Since the past few years, lot of people express their opinions online. A lot of people then express their views on different websites. They express about the food they eat, mobile phones they purchase and so on. Sentiment analysis is gathering a lot of attention nowadays as a lot of online data is gathered through blogs, ecommerce websites, product reviews, etc. This data is extracted by companies to judge if their products are having positive or negative outlook. We are doing sentiment analysis on reviews of mobile phones using different machine learning classifiers. We used machine learning techniques like logistic regression, decision tree classifier, gradient boosting, AdaBoost, bagging classifier, support vector machine amongst others. Logistic regression gave the best accuracy with 91.57% and F-score of 94.77%.

Keywords: Machine learning, sentiment analysis, mobile reviews

Introduction

A lot of data is gathered online as more and more people are expressing their views on day to day events and activities. Opinion mining/sentiment analysis is a process in which we can find out the sentiment behind the process/words/sentences. It is used to find out if the review given by the customer is positive or negative. We use sentiment analysis to find out what is the perception of other people about different products and about the organizations. It is important to know the perception of the people to grow the business. From the Kaggle website, we downloaded a dataset on mobile phone reviews. Sentiment analysis is used to gain valuable insights about the opinions of the people.

Rest of the paper is structured as follows. The next section reviews the literature followed by the proposed methodology, followed by the findings, challenges and the conclusion of the paper.

Literature Review

Bhalla et al. (2020) proposed a RB-Bayes method and compared it with Naïve Bayes method on a mobile phone survey. Naïve Bayes method has the problem of zero frequency which was resolved using RB-Bayes method.

Bhalla et al. (2019) compared RB-Bayes method with other machine learning classifiers and mentioned that it was having a good accuracy compared to other classifiers.

Nahili et al. (2021) took Amazon mobile phone reviews and analysed the reviews using NLTK library of Python and VADER analysis tool. They classified the reviews into five classes: very negative, negative, neutral, positive, and very positive. They achieved an accuracy of 76.80% on the dataset.

Minu et al. (2020) used Amazon mobile reviews dataset of five different mobile manufacturers from Kaggle and classified opinions using k-nearest neighbors (KNN), support vector machines (SVM), branch-and-bound (BNB), multinomial Naive Bayes. (MNB). KNN and SVM gave the best accuracy of 95%.

Rajkumar et al. (2019) took Amazon dataset which contained reviews of different products like mobile phones, cameras, etc. They used machine learning algorithms and Naïve Bayes gave an accuracy of 98.17% and Support Vector Machine gave an accuracy of 93.54%.

Yashaswini et al. (2015) proposed a lexicon-based approach on Kannada language product reviews. They used Naïve Bayes technique for judging the polarity and built a customized corpus in Kannada language. They achieved am accuracy of 65% on the dataset.

Zeenia et al. (2017) used machine language classifiers on data gathered from Amazon website of mobile reviews. Cross validation was performed on the dataset and SVM had the highest accuracy of 81.75%.

Salem et al. (2020) used machine learning classifiers on a Kaggle dataset of mobile reviews. Maximum entropy and Naïve Bayes gave the best accuracy.

Fangyu et al. (2020) introduced a novel model SenBERT-CNN to analyse mobile reviews of customers on a Chinese website. They used a combination of BERT model and CNN technique. BERT model was used for word vector coding and CNN to extract text features.

[a]parkar.ameya@gmail.com; [b]rajni.b27@gmail.com

Pandey et al. (2019) collected mobile reviews from Amazon. They used POS tagging and pre-processing techniques on the dataset to find the sentiment of the reviews.

Seema et al. (2020) improvised on the lexicon-based approaches to detect the polarity of the sentiments expressed by using an Augmented dictionary approach. Reviews were taken from online sources such as restaurants, mobiles, etc. They achieved an accuracy of 63% on the mobile phone reviews and 67% on the movie reviews.

Singh et al. (2017) took data on mobile reviews from shopping websites. They gathered opinions of users on three brands of mobile phones and carried out analysis on positive and negative reviews. They gathered the data on different aspects of a mobile phone such as battery, screen, sounds, etc. They used MATLAB as a computational tool. Table 47.1 shows the related work.

Proposed Methodology

We downloaded the dataset of Amazon mobile reviews from the Kaggle website which had 71922 reviews. We used Python as a language and used the NLTK library. The data was in an unstructured format. We cleaned the data using preprocessing techniques such as removing stop words, lemmatization, etc. Any ambiguity in the dataset was removed from the dataset. The dataset was split into 80% for training and 20% for testing.

We used bag of words module to convert text data into vectors. The model was trained on logistic regression, decision tree, gradient boost, Ada boost, random forest, Naïve Bayes, bagging classifier, extra trees classifier, support vector machine and k nearest neighbor classifiers.

Overview of Evaluation Metrics

The evaluation metrics are used to judge the quality of an algorithm/method/model in natural language processing. Different models can be compared and judged based on the evaluation metrics. The most prominent evaluation metrics are:

Accuracy

It is calculated as the ratio of the correctly predicted samples to the total number of samples. The accuracy of the model determines how well the model performs. It tells us whether the model is trained properly and how it will perform.

Accuracy = (True positive + true negative)/(true positive + true negative + false positive + false negative)

Table 47.1 Related work

References	*Name of the paper*	*Dataset Size*	*Language*	*Performance A: Accuracy P: Precision R: Recall F: F-score*
Wedjdane (2021)	Better Decision Making with Sentiment Analysis of Amazon reviews	Amazon 400000 reviews	English	Statistical Analysis A: 76.80
Abraham (2020)	Feature Based Sentiment Analysis of Mobile Product Reviews using Machine Learning Techniques	Kaggle Amazon 200 reviews	English	KNN, MNB, BNB, SVM A: 95
Jagdale (2019)	Sentiment Analysis on Product Reviews Using Machine Learning Techniques	Kaggle Amazon 13057 reviews	English	NB: A: 98.17 SVM: A: 93.54
Hegde (2015)	Sentiment Analysis for Kannada using Mobile Product Reviews A Case Study	Online reviews	Kannada	NB A: 65 P: 62.5 R: 75 F: 68.2
Singla (2017)	Sentiment Analysis of Customer Product Reviews Using Machine Learning	Amazon 400000 reviews	English	NB A: 66.95 SVM A: 81.77 DT A: 74.75
Salem (2020)	Sentiment analysis of mobile phone products reviews using classification algorithms	Kaggle 82815 reviews	English	NB A: 82.1 SVM A: 80.7 ME A: 82.7 DT A: 73.6
Wu (2020)	Sentiment analysis of online product reviews based on S.enBERT-CNN	JD.com 9600 reviews	Chinese	SenBERT-CNN A: 95.72 P: 95.21 R: 96.24 F: 95.32
Yadav (2020)	Sentiment analysis of reviews using an augmented dictionary approach	Online reviews 26988	English	Dictionary approach on mobile dataset A: 63 P: 65.3 R: 56.2 F: 60.3

(All values are in percentages)

Precision

It is calculated as the ratio of number of samples belonging to positive class to the true positive samples and false positive samples.

Precision = True positive/(true positive + false positive)

Recall

It is calculated as the ratio of correctly predicted positive samples to the number of correct positive samples and wrong negative samples. The recall of the model determines the number of correctly predicted positive samples to all the positive labels.

Recall = True positive/(true positive + false negative)

F-measure

It is calculated as the weighted average of precision and recall. It is calculated to take both false positives and false negatives into account. It is best to be used as it is a combination of precision and recall. It is particularly useful on an unbalanced dataset.

F-measure = (2 * precision * recall)/(precision + recall)

Results

We used ML classifiers on the Amazon dataset of mobile reviews and the results are summarized in Table 47.2 below:

From Table 47.2, it is evident that logistic regression with accuracy of 91.57%, precision of 94.01%, recall of 95.54%, F-score of 94.77% and SVM with accuracy of 91.12%, precision of 92.87%, recall of 96.28%, and F-score of 94.54% gave the best performance measures. The F-score of all the classifiers were above 90%.

Challenges in sentiment analysis

1. Datasets available online are largely unstructured and cleaning the text and making it structured is a tedious task.
2. Sarcasm flips the polarity of a sentence. Hence, it is necessary to detect sarcasm and get the right polarity of the sentence.
3. Ambiguity of human language.

Conclusion

Sentiment analysis is a way to judge the polarity of the user opinions. From the Kaggle website, we downloaded a dataset on mobile phone reviews. We used different machine learning classifiers to train the model and found that logistic

Table 47.2 Performance of machine learning classifiers

Techniques	*Accuracy*	*Precision*	*Recall*	*F-score*
DT	87.2	91.99	92	91.99
Gradient boost	85.91	86.48	97.64	91.72
AdaBoost	85.83	87.23	96.39	91.58
RF	85.95	90.38	97.26	93.69
Naïve Bayes	85.46	93.68	87.73	90.61
Bagging classifier	88.65	92.79	93.03	92.91
Extra trees classifier	89.89	91.18	96.71	93.86
SVM	91.12	92.87	96.28	94.54
Logistic regression	91.57	94.01	95.54	94.77
KNN	83.85	88.23	92.09	90.12

(All values are in percentages)

regression and support vector machine gave the best performance on classifying the mobile reviews. In future work, we will include deep learning algorithms as well as transformers.

References

Abraham, M. P.(2020). Feature based sentiment analysis of mobile product reviews using machine learning techniques. *International Journal of Advanced Trends in Computer Science and Engineering*, 9(2), 2289–2296. doi: 10.30534/ijatcse/2020/210922020.

Bhalla, R. & Amandeep. (2020). A Comparative analysis of application of proposed and the existing methodologies on a mobile phone survey. Commun. *Journal of Computing & Information Science*, 1206, 107–115.

Bhalla, R. & Bagga, A. (2019). Opinion mining framework using proposed rb-bayes model for text classification. *International Journal of Electrical and Computer Engineering*, 9(1), 477–484. doi: 10.11591/ijece.v9i1.

Hegde, Y. & Padma, S. K. (2015). Sentiment analysis for Kannada using mobile product reviews: A case study. *2015 IEEE International Advanced Computing Conference*, (pp. 822–827). doi: 10.1109/IADCC.2015.7154821.

Jagdale, R. S., Shirsat, V. S., & Deshmukh, S. N. (2019). Sentiment analysis on product reviews using machine learning techniques. *Advances in Intelligent Systems and Computing*, 768, 639–647. doi: 10.1007/978-981-13-0617-4_61.

Pankaj, P., Pandey, P., Muskan, M., & Soni, N. (2019). Sentiment analysis on customer feedback data: Amazon product reviews. *International Conference on "Machine Learning, Big Data, Cloud and Parallel Computing: Trends, Perspectives and Prospects*, (pp. 320–322). doi: 10.1109/COMITCon.2019.8862258.

Rekha and Singh, W. (2017). Sentiment analysis of online mobile reviews. *Proceeding International ConferenceInventory Communications technologyComputing Technology*.(pp. 20–25). doi: 10.1109/ICICCT.2017.7975199.

Salem, M. A. M., & Maghari, A. Y. A. (2020). Sentiment analysis of mobile phone products reviews using classification algorithms. *Invasive Cardiopulmonary Exercise Testing*, (pp. 84–88), doi: 10.1109/ICPET51420.2020.00024.

Singla, Z. & Jain, S. (2017). Statistical and sentiment analysis. *IEEE Xplore*, 1–6.

Wedjdane, N., Khaled, R., & Okba, K. (2021). Better decision making with sentiment analysis of Amazon reviews. *International Conference on Information Systems and Advanced Technologies*. doi: 10.1109/ICISAT54145.2021.9678483.

Wu, F., Shi, Z., Dong, Z., Pang, C., & Zhang, B. (2020). Sentiment analysis of online product reviews based on SenBERT-CNN. *Proceedings International Conference on Machine Learning Cybernetics*, (pp. 229–234).

Yadav, S. & Saleena, N. (2020). Sentiment analysis of reviews using an augmented dictionary approach. *International Conference on Computing, Communication and Security*, (pp. 0–4). doi: 10.1109/ICCCS49678.2020.9277094.

48 Investigating the impact of motivational techniques on the employee retention with special reference to telecom industry

Avinash Bhagat[1,a] *and Sonu Dua*[2]

[1]Associate Professor, Lovely Professional University, Punjab, India

[2]Associate Professor, Lyallpur Khalsa College of Technical Campus, Jalandhar, Punjab, India

Abstract

Telecom industry is very vast and spreading their wings in very fast manner. Today most of the people are dependent on the various application of telecom industry. In India, telecom industry has created big opportunities for the young and dynamic people and they are also providing good financial incentives to their employees. In this study, an attempt has been made to investigate the significant impact of motivational techniques on the retention of employees with special reference to telecom industry. For this purpose, a model has been proposed and checked with the help of various statistical tools. A sample of 150 employees has been taken and at the end, results were significant as per the reviews studied.

Keywords: Employee retention, telecom industry, analysis, factor analysis, confirmatory factor analysis

Introduction

The major challenge in the field of telecom industry is to retain competent employees for longer period in the organization. As due to significant opportunities, they are frequently switching their jobs. There could be another reason to change the job is good remuneration, perks, allowances, and better designation along with good number of facilities. This situation is good for the employees who is a having a capability, but it is an alarming situation for the organization, from where the best human resource is moving to another company and it will directly lead to increase in attrition rate, which is not a good signal for the organization.

Employee retention provides the sustainable competitive advantage to the organization in terms of better productivity and in achieving the overall goal of the organization (Almulla, 2019). Here, the motivation factors play significant role to retain the employees in the organization. Motivation factors include two types of rewards i.e., financial as well as non-financial rewards. The financial benefits are referred as extrinsic rewards and non-financial benefits are referred as intrinsic rewards. The category of financial rewards includes different components (Chiang and Canter, 2008). Moreover, one of the authors focused on work fulfilment and work environment are the major retention strategies for employees in the organization (Ganesh and Sathesh, 2021).

The environment is changing very rapidly due to the advancements and technological development (Burke and Ng, 2006). This change is affecting each aspect of the global environment. Earlier, there was no need of specialized person, but in today era we need the services of expert person, who are well equipped with practical knowledge and skills, so that the organization could gain sustainable competitive position in the competitive world. Now the role of highly skilled employees come and the corporate houses are required to retain then for their benefits in the organization. When one skilled employee leaves the organization, it creates void that need to be filled, but due to the shortage of skilled employees, it will directly lead to hamper the productivity of the organization (Hiltrop, 1999).

Review of Literature

Theoretical framework

The word motivation came from the word 'movere' which means to move ahead. Motivation is a striking force which compels the person to do the task in a desired manner and that will directly lead to the rewards (Dessler, 1980). There are different theories, which were proposed on motivation such as Maslow's theory of needs, two factor theory etc.

Maslow' need theory

As per Maslow, there were five levels of needs. Physiological needs are related with the basic requirements of human beings such as food, shelter, and clothes. Safety need is related with job security. Social needs are related with relationship

[a]Avinash.bhagat@lpu.co.in

with others. Self-esteem needs are related with power, authority, recognition, self-respect etc. Self-actualization need is related with self-fulfillment of need.

Herzberg two factor theory

Herzberg categorized their study into two significant factors: Motivation factors and hygiene factors. Various motivation factors were, achievement, growth, recognition authority etc. And various hygiene factors were Job security, HR policies, paid leaves etc.

Vroom's expectancy theory

As per the Vroom expectancy theory, the efforts of the employees directly lead to the effective performance and effective performance will be directly proportionate to the rewards. The rewards may be in the form of pay, promotion opportunities etc.

(Yousaf, 2017) Different types of research methods were adopted in this study. A structured questionnaire was developed to get the responses of employees. At the end researcher found that number of financial as well as non-financial rewards affects the employee's performance. Undoubtedly financial rewards played significant role in motivating the employees. Rainey (2001) explained that motivation is related with enthusiasm and persistence of efforts, which are required to be performed by the employees in the organization to accomplish their goals. In every organization, employees are ready to give their best for the overall achievement of organizational objectives, if their needs are satisfied. The motivated employees will be more productive and they will perform better in the organization. Even organization can attain competitive edge over the other companies by retaining the motivated employees. Fuhrman (2006) studied that by providing financial and non-financial rewards, organization can motivate the high performers employees and which will provide them greater job satisfaction. At the end, the study concluded that financial and non-financial rewards influenced the employee's motivation level but it the extent varies with age factor.

In return of their services, employees are getting the remuneration. There should be proper system pertaining to the compensation. The compensation must be related with performance as well as the basic work of the employees. Money was considered as best financial motivator in the eyes of employees (Rynes, 2004). Few other researchers believed that money was important but non-financial rewards were equally important for the growth of employees such as recognition, ranks, authority, belongingness etc. and those who are rich they are considered as more influential person in the society (Bohlander, 2004). Working environment refers to a place where employees are working (Roeloelofsen, 2002). It is place where employees find reason to work in a particular organization. Even non-financial benefits played significant role in providing greater job satisfaction to the employees working conditions includes following aspects, which motivates the employees adequate resources, better relationship with superiors and subordinates, proper training programmes, illumination facilities, cross ventilation, seating capacity, changing Room and fencing among the dangerous machinery. There were some studies which established relationship between non-financial rewards with reference to training and development programmes and employee motivation. Based on any promotion, recognition depends upon the nature of training programme.

Nowadays, it is a challenging task for HR department to retain skilled workers in their organization. Attractive salary, perks, conducive environment are the key ingredients for retaining the good employees in the organization. And Employee demands security pertaining to their job, giving respect to each one from the management (Iqbal, 2017). Even efficient HRM practices in the organization may also minimize the employee turnover and it will lead to retain the good employees in the organization (Malik, et al., 2020). Even some authors considered training is one of the important aspects to motivate and retain their employees in the organization. They have directly created a relationship between employee training and retention strategies (Elsafty and Oraby, 2022).

Objective of the Study

The main objective of this proposed study is to explore the role of motivational techniques in retaining the employees in telecom industry.

Research Methodology

Research methodology is always considered as integral part of every research, whereby the blue print of every research is prepared. In this study, sample of 150 employees have been taken to make the study more representative. It was difficult to get the official permission from the concerned telecom company, so convenient sampling (Malhotra, 2000) has been applied to get the data from the employees. Well-structured questionnaires were prepared and applied to collect the data, thereafter different statistical tools such as CFA, SEM, reliability analysis were applied to get the desired result.

Analysis

Factor: 1: Appreciation and stimulation

This is the first and foremost factor which accounted for 17.414% of the total variance. In the rotated form five statements revealed significant loadings on this factor.

Factor: 2: Leadership skills

This is another relevant factor which accounted for 11.341% of the total variance. Five statements revealed significant loadings on this factor.

Factor: 3: Pressure of work

Five statements significantly load on this factor and together accounted for 9.931% of the total variance.

Factor: 4: Following procedures

This factor contributes 9.254% of the overall variance. Five statements shared significant loadings on this factor.

Factor: 5: Learning attitude

The 5th factor accounted for 8.690% to the total variance. Five statements constituted this factor.

Factor: 6: Employee retention

The 6th factor contributed 7.704% of the total variance. six statements revealed significant loadings for this factor.

Confirmatory Factor Analysis

CFA is also known as RFA. This analysis is performed after successfully running the exploratory factor analysis:

The aforementioned cut off indices clearly indicated that the proposed model has provided the significant result towards attaining the proposed objective of the study

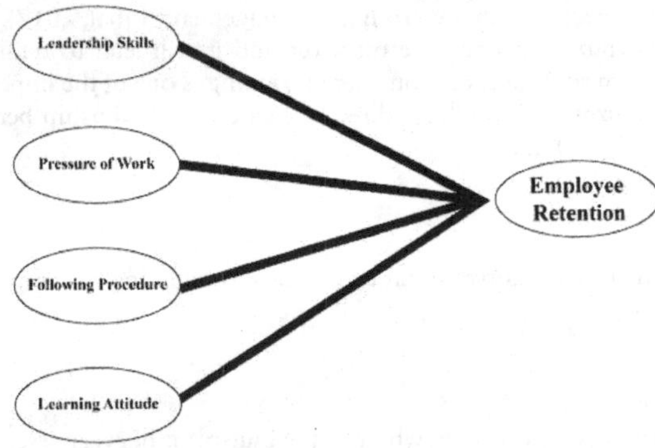

Figure 48.1 Proposed Model

Table 48.1 Goodness of fit indices for analysis

S. No	*Name of index*	*Results*
1	Chi-square	610.71
2	Degree of freedom	352
3	Chi-square/Degree of freedom	1.735
4	Comparative fit index	0.96
5	Goodness of fit index	0.93
6	Adjusted goodness of fit index	0.91
7	Normed of fit index	0.92
8	Incremental of fit index	0.96
9	Root mean square error of approximation	0.03
10	Root mean square residual	0.02

Source: Results generated from AMOS 23.0

Table 48.2 Hypothesis Testing

S. No	*Hypothesis*	*Beta Value*	*Sig. T*	*Supported or Not Supported*	*Order of Importance*
Hl	There is direct and positive effect of Appreciation & Stimulus on Employee Retention	0.528	0.001	Supported	1
H2	There is direct and positive effect of Leadership Skills on Employee Retention	0.323	0.0001	Supported	3
H3	There is direct and positive effect of Pressure of Work on Employee Retention	0.228	0.0001	Supported	5
H4	There is direct and positive effect of Following Procedures on Employee Retention	0.295	0.001	Supported	4
H5	There is direct and positive effect of Learning Attitude on Employee Retention	0.496	0.001	Supported	2

Source: Results generated from AMOS 23.0

Conclusion

This study was conducted to undertake the several aspects and it showed significant role of motivational factors in retaining the employees in the organization. Furthermore, the key feature pertaining to the study was the methodology which was used to study the aforementioned relationship. Different aspects have come out from the conclusion of the study, which were also supported by different authors. Results related with the first hypothesis significant positive influence appreciation and stimulation (Trevor, 2001; Walker, 2001). Employee recognition, interest was more important factors while working in the company. Another hypothesis leadership skill was also significant and had positive impact on retention of employees (Rowden, 2002; Rowdon and Connine, 2005). Under leadership skills, different factors were covered communication, stress free environment. Another hypothesis pressure of work, following of procedure and learning attitude were also significant and had positive impact on retention of employees (Hytter, 2007).

References

Almulla, A. & Alzoubi, H. (2019). Impact of employees motivation on employees retention: empirical evidence from UAE telecommunication industry. *Intelligent Information System Supply Chain*, 12(4), 92–99.

Bohlander, G. & Snell, S. (2004). Managing Human Resources (13thed.), Mason, Thompson.

Burke, R. and Ng, E. (2006). The changing nature of work and organizations: implications for human resource management. *Human Resource Management Review*, 16, 86–94.

Elsafty, A. & Oraby, M. (2022). The impact of training on employee retention: An empirical research on the private sector of Egypt. *International Journal of Business and Management*, 17(5), 58–74

Fuhrmann, T. D. (2006). Motivating employees. *Advances in Diary Technology*, 18, 93–101.

Ganesh, S. & Sathesh, M. (2021). *A study on employee retention strategies with special reference to karur district, International Journal of Creative Research Thoughts*, 9(5), 672–684

Hiltrop, J. M. (1999). The quest for the best: human resource practices to attract and retain talent, *European Management Journal*, 17(4), 422–430.

Iqbal, S., Guohao, L., & Akhtar, S. (2017). Effects of job organizational culture, benefits, salary on job satisfaction ultimately affecting employee retention. *Review of Public Administration and Management*, 5(3), 1–10.

Malik, W., Khan, S., & Azeem, K., (2020). The impact of Human Resource management practices on employee retention in telecom subcontractor. *International Journal of Scientific and Engineering research*, 11(8), 1466–1474.

Rainey, H. (2001). Work motivation Handbook of organizational behavior. In R. T. Golembiewski (Ed.). pp. 19–39. Marcel Dekker, New York, NY.

Roeloelofsen, P. (2002). The impact of office environments on employee Performance: The design of the workplace as a strategy for productivity enhancement. *Journal of Facilities Management*, 1(3), 247–264.

Rynes, S. L., Gerhart, B., & Kathleen, A. M. (2004). The importance of pay in employee motivation: Discrepancy between what people say and what they do. *Resource Management, Winter*, 43(4), 381–394.

Sabir, A., 2017. Motivation: outstanding way to promote productivity in employees. *American Journal of Management Science and Engineering*, 2(3), 35–45.

Shah, M & Asad, M. (2018). Effect of motivation on employee retention: Mediating role of perceived organizational support, *European Online Journal of Natural and Social Sciences*, 7(2), 511–520.

49 Federated learning: A rescue in machine learning for data privacy preservation

Pritpal Kaur[a], *Sofia*[b], *and Sakshi Sharma*[c]

Assistant Professor, University Institute of Computing, Chandigarh University, Chandigarh, India

Abstract

In the era of digitalization, machine learning (ML) has experienced a prodigious growth. Researchers have unfolded the many aspects and issues of ML. The main concern in question while implementing ML is privacy protection. Federated learning (FL) has materialized as a rescue in the case; it is a setup for training the ML algorithms or models in distributed environment without breaching the privacy. The primary goal of this study is to analyze the different aspects of FL undertaken by the researchers. The study will explore the different application aspects of FL.

Keywords: Federated learning, machine learning, IoT, distributed computing

Introduction

In the last two decades machine learning (ML) has exhibit immense growth in the province of computer science and engineering. Machine learning models are highly depended on datasets for training of models which leads to the data privacy issues (Abdellatif et al., 2021). Federated learning (FL) is a state-of-the-art technique in ML, FL has come into picture to cope up with the problem of data privacy which was a major concern while using ML. It was first introduced by Google in a paper published in year 2016. FL is a set up for training the models in distributed environment. FL implementation includes a sequence of steps to be followed; 1) Selecting the nodes/clients to take part in the training process, 2) Sending the model to the client for training, 3) Collecting the training weights from clients after locally training the model, 4) Finally aggregating the training weights to create a global model.

FL has been used to tackle many problems like healthcare systems which concerns data privacy of patients while using ML models for creating smart health care solutions. The FL has been optimized by IoT engineers to handle the extensively growing Internet of Things (IoT) data and create the privacy enhanced IoT systems like vehicular IoT systems (Bao et al., 2021). Despite from data privacy, the FL models also managed to cut the communication costs and latency in the systems, as data need not to be sent to some centralized machine for training (Wu et al., 2020).

Figure 49.1 shows the general representation of FL. From cloud, ML model is deployed on local nodes, these nodes train the model using the local data. Then training weights are shared with the cloud node. These training weights can be used to train the global ML model. It doesn't require sharing of data, instead only training weights are shared which preserve the privacy of the users.

Federated Learning

Gholizadeh and Musilek (2021) study proposes the LSTM networks consist of one hidden layer. The study was conducted on real time data collected from 75 locations of Edmonton city. The work proposed is compared with central learning and local learning methods. FL performs better for individual load forecast than centralized learning but while calculating aggregate load it does not perform well in any of the clusters. MIFL framework is proposed for improving the security of edge computing networks (Chen and Li, 2021). The framework makes use of convolutional neural networks for implementation and it secures the system against malicious node attacks. An asynchronous FL scheme for asynchronous edge selection Chen et al. (2021). The proposed framework consists of three phases namely initialization, aggregation, and parameter update. The capability of purposed scheme is compared with two baseline schemes Synchronous Federated Learning (SFL) and Random Nodes Selection Federated Learning (RNS-FL). The model is able to give better accuracy than both the schemes.

The model shows more potential as compared to the conventional learning models. The model uses block chain method (Kumar et al., 2021). Where, it collects the locally trained model' weights ensuring the privacy of the data. The framework uses time convolutional networks (TCN) is used to implement city DT and federated learning is used for

[a]kaurpritpal94@gmail.com; [b]sofia.singla97@gmail.com; [c]sakshi28sharma95@gmail.com

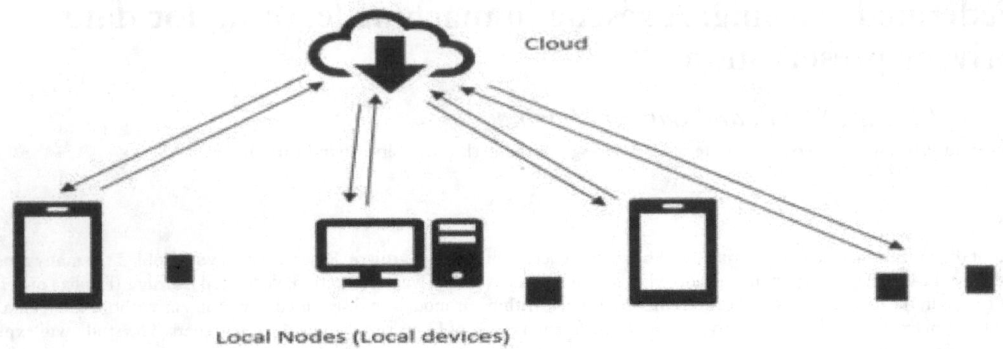

Figure 49.1 Basic representation of FL

collaborative training to minimize the privacy risks (Pang et al., 2021). Gao et al. (2020) have compared the performance of FL and SplitNN technique. It has been observed that SplitNNperforms better when deployed to imbalanced data but FL is preferred while using non- inactive ingredient database (IID) data. PELM model purposed in study ensures the privacy and security of gradients (Jiang et al., 2021). To implement the model three entities are considered namely users, TA (trusted authority) and the cloud server. The active adversary threat model is considered in this study where user and server both can be active adversaries. Sattler et al. (2020) purposed Sparse Ternary Compression a communication protocol. This approach relies on high frequent low volume communication. It has been observed that if data is non IID type than STC performs better as compared to federated averaging (Efremov and Kholod, 2021). The study focuses to create a Java language based FL framework. The base entity of the architecture is FLService which is an abstract class. The communication between different FLServices is done using descriptor. Descriptors are objects and transfer data independent of the transport used. The framework purposed only supports simulation mode currently (Ye et al., 2020). The study purposed an Edge federated learning framework named as EdgeFed. It uses stochastic gradient descent (SDG) algorithm for local training of learning models. The results after local training are aggregated at edge devices. The purposed EdgeFed framework is compared with the FedAvg framework purposed by Google inc. for evaluating the performance. The experiments are carried out using MNIST open-source dataset. EdgeFed is able to lower the total computational and communication cost of mobile devices as compared to the FedAvg (Zhai et al., 2021). The authors purposed two algorithms namely cli-max greedy and uti-positive guarantee for client selection in Dynamic federated learning for power grid mobile edge computing (GMEC). The purposed algorithms are evaluated against FedCS. The parameters like local training success ratio, utility, energy consumption and learning delay are considered while comparing the model performance. The uti-positive guarantee algorithm can achieve the lower learning delay and less energy wasting as compared to FedCS. Whereas, cli-max greedy has also achieved less learning delay as compared to FedCS. It has been observed that uti-positive guarantee algorithm outperforms cli-max greedy and FedCS in all the parameters considered for evaluation.

Application aspects and datasets for federated learning

This section will explore the various application aspects of the FL where it has been used till now and some future scopes. The federate learning has been widely used for training of IoT based models. Looking at the initial face of FL it was used by Google for improving the performance of auto-fill suggestions of android keyboards. In this FL model, training the ML models was done on local user machines and training weights to the centralized node for aggregating the weights. In this way Google improved the efficiency of android keyboards using people's personal chat data without compromising their privacy. Because of the privacy preservation scheme of this method, it got famous in many fields especially medical field where health data of the patients is quite very crucial, and privacy can't be compromised.

Healthcare: Abdellatif et al.(2021) proposed an algorithm EUs assignment and resource allocation for hierarchical federated learning model for smart health care system. The authors considered I-care system architecture where there are three layers end user layer, edge node layer and finally a centralized server layer. Each EU layer is connected to its corresponding Edge layer and all the Edge layers are connected to centralized server layer. For evaluating the model 2 datasets are used, namely heartbeat and seizure. While comparing the algorithm performance with DBA (distance-based allocation) scheme it is examined that it reduces the communication rounds by 75–85% maintaining the accuracy of the model. Study purposed a digital twin enabled collaborative training framework to handle the COVID-19 situation (Pang et al., 2021). To evaluate the results COVID-19 tracking project dataset is used.

Communication: Other than healthcare FL is also being used for different applications like an adaptive federated reinforcement learning (Mowla et al., 2020) technique to detect and defend the jamming attacks in FANET. It is also effective in preserving the secrecy and privacy of local sensory data in an FANET. The optimal path selection is done through the adaptive epsilon greedy policy. Model simulation is performed on ns-3 simulated FANET dataset and CRAWDAD which is a jamming dataset. Polap and Wozniak (2021) purposed the FL technique incorporated with meta heuristic technique to improve the accuracy of the existing technique and to lower the vulnerability to poison attack. The authors use the latest meta heuristic called Red Fox Optimization algorithm in this model. The dataset used to simulate and evaluate the model is Skin Cancer MNIST: HAM10000.

Human Activity Detection: Xiao and Xu (2021) purposes a model of federated learning for human activity recognition namely HARFLS for feature extraction. It uses perceptive extraction network (PEN) for feature extraction in HAR. To ensure the security of the system it uses two methods, firstly it shares only model weights instead of data, and to secure the communication of weights it uses homomorphic encryption. For evaluation of the model four different datasets are used. In the study (Tian et al., 2021) the authors purposed a Delay compensated Adam (DC-Adam) approach for anomaly detection.

Marketing and business: An automatic auction framework have been purposed in this study to commercialize the use of wireless federated learning (Jiao et al., 2021). The reverse multi-dimensional auction (RMA) mechanism has been designed to increase the social welfare. To improve the social welfare an automated deep reinforcement learning based auction (DRLA) mechanism using the graph neural network (GNN) has also been developed. To ensure the efficiency of the model economic properties like truthfulness, individual rationality (IR) computational efficiency (CE) has been considered. Hua et al. (2020) purposes a block chain based FL model to train the intelligent driving models in heavy haul railway without sharing any data. The model is a SVM based learning model. The authors design a hybrid kernel for SVM using polynomial and radial basis function kernels. The model uses blockchains to store and transfer the machine learning model. It has been observed that when the training period is increased, the model accuracy also increases.

Conclusion

In recent times, emphasis on data privacy and protection has escalated and federated learning (FL) is a rescue in this situation. As a proliferating technology FL is being the talk of the town but it has been observed that only Internet of Things (IoT) application has explored the field to the fullest. It is analyzed that most of the existing studies related to FL presented multiple positive impacts on the overall processing of data using distributed computing. Despite the privacy protection and burgeoning technology, it is still facing the issues in ensuring the privacy of local gradient and integrity. Dealing with IID and non-IID data is another difficulty that needs attention. From the review conducted, it is observed that FL is a revolutionary step for privacy protection and data protection.

References

Abdellatif, A. A., Mhaisen, N., Mohameda, A., Erbad, A., Guizani, M., Dawy, Z., & Nasreddine, W. (2021). Communication-efficient hierarchical federated learning for IoT heterogeneous systems with imbalanced data. *Future Generation Computer Systems*, 128, 406–419.

Bao, W., Wu, C., Guleng, S., Zhang, J., Yau, K. L. A., & Ji, Y. (2021). Edge computing-based joint client selection and networking scheme for federated learning in vehicular IoT. *Time-Critical Communication and Computation for Intelligent Vehicular Networks,* (pp. 39–52).

Chen, Z., Liao, W., Hua, K., Lu, C., & Yu, W. (2021). Towards asynchronous federated learning for heterogeneous edge-powered internet of things. *Digital Communications and Networks,* 27, 317–326.

Chen, N., Li, Y., Liu, X., & Zhang, Z. (2021). A mutual information based federated learning framework for edge computing networks", Computer Communications 176: 23–30.

Gao, Y., Kim, M., Abuadbba, S., Kim, Y., Thapa, & Kim, K., et al. (2020). End-to-End Evaluation of Federated Learning and Split Learning for Internet of Things. International Symposium on Reliable Distributed Systems (SRDS). Dedan Kimathi University of Technology, Kenya.

Hua, G. & Zhu, L., Wu, J., Shen, C., Zhou, L., & Lin, Q. (2020). Blockchain-based federated learning for intelligent control in heavy haul railway. Special Section on Blockchain Technology: Principles and Applications, (pp. 176830–176839).

Jiang, C., Xu, C., & Zhang, Y. (2020). PFLM: Privacy-preserving Federated Learning with membership proof. *Information Sciences.*

Jiao, Y., Wang, P., Niyato, D., Lin, B., & Kim, D. I. (2021). Toward an automated auction framework for wireless federated learning services market. *IEEE Transactions on Mobile Computing*, 20(10), 3034–3048.

Kumar, R., Khan, A. A., Kumar, J., Zakria, Golilarz, N. A., & Zhang, S. et al. (2021). Blockchain-Federated-Learning and deep learning models for COVID-19 detection using ct imaging. *IEEE Sensors Journal*, 21(14), 16301–16314.

Pang, J., Huang, Y., Xie, Z., Li, J., & Cai, Z. (2021). Collaborative city digital twin for the COVID-19 pandemic: A federated learning solution. *Tsinghua Science and Technology*, 26(5), 759–771.

Połap, D. & Woźniak, M. (2021). Meta-heuristic as manager in federated learning approaches for image processing purposes. *Applied Soft Computing*, 113.

Mowla, N. I., Tran, N. H., Doh, I., & Chae, K. (2020). AFRL: Adaptive federated reinforcement learning for intelligent jamming defense in FANET. *Journal of Communications and Networks*, 22(3), 244–258.

Sattler, F., Wiedemann, S., Müller, K. R., & Samek, W. (2020). Robust and Communication-Efficient Federated Learning from non-i.i.d. data. *IEEE Transactions on Neural Networks and Learning Systems*, 31(9), 3400–3413.

Tian, P., Chen, Z., Yu, W., & Liao, W. (2021). Towards asynchronous federated learning-based threat detection: A DC-Adam approach. *Computers & Security*, 108.

Ye, Y., Li, S., Liu, F., Tang, Y., & Hu, W. (2020). EdgeFed: Optimized Federated Learning Based on Edge Computing. *IEEE Access*, 8, 209191–209198.

Zhai, S., Jin, X., Wei, L., Luo, H., & Cao, M. (2021). Dynamic Federated Learning for GMEC with time-varying wireless link. *IEEE Access*, 9, 10400–10412.

50 Integration of deep neural network architecture for network intrusion detection system

Vaishnavi Sivagaminathan[a], *Manmohan Sharma*[b], *and Santosh Kumar Henge*[c]
Lovely Professional University, Punjab, India

Abstract

The extensive usage of computer system interconnection and interoperability has become an unavoidable requirement for enhancing our daily operations. Simultaneously, it opens the door for automation where human control will not play any important role. There have been huge gaps of in security where communication protocols come and managing with artificial intelligence ability is the big challenge. For this very reason for increasing high end security protocols to avoid the security threat is necessity. Deep leaning architectures has proven to categories the network threat and enhance the exiting network intrusion detection system to greater accuracy. The main aim of the proposed deep learning network will be understood by the daily network intrusion, adapts to automation learning from daily data, reduce the risk of intrusion with eradication of any intruder anomaly. The UNSW-NB15 dataset was used to show the model's performance, which reflects the working network communication behavior along with artificially produced attack operations. The novelty of this research work is the proposed algorithm can detect successfully, 40 different networking attacks as it had been given training using five different datasets which include some standard datasets like the above stated one and some created datasets which have been originated during the creation of a network model or while creation of simulation networks involved in research study. Particle swarm optimization (PSO) has been used in combination with various machine learning algorithms. The results of which have been compared with other researchers' work and it was found that PSO in combination with artificial neural networks earned best results for the considered network.

Keywords: Network intrusion detection system, deep neural network, cyber security.

Introduction

To prevent attacking and hacking of important websites and hacking of their user's confidential data and the organization's databases was the main motivation behind this research work and thus to build an efficient intrusion detection and prevention systems (IDPS) was the main aim. Man in the middle (MITM) attacks, attacks including denial of service (DoS), sinkhole attacks, floods attacks, wormhole attacks and selectively redirection are only a few examples. DoS attacks include flooding a network's server with phony messages to generate bottleneck in the network, preventing genuine traffic from reaching the server. This is especially true in the realm of big shopping website or aggregator website. A site's servers can be purposefully overburdened by false packets from a rival site. Is it also important to identify and prevent intrusions (Quincozes et al., 2021).

Literature Review

Among the most important difficulties in cloud computing is the detection of DoS or DDos attack. To solve the problem, one of the researchers suggested the opposite feedback system using optimize search algorithms (Theja and Shyam, 2021). The search optimized algorithms was integrated with recurrent neural network (RNN), which significantly improves the detection accuracy response time. The feature selection (FS) refers to the process of choosing key features, whereas classification refers to a subset of key characteristics. When it comes to accuracy, the key overall computations are critical for IDS, as the system is time dependent in real time environment (Yerriswamy and Venkatagiri, 2018).

The network system internal or internet dependent can have large volume of data rate and low detection rate; so, to combat network invasions, machine learning techniques to intrusion detection are necessary. Neural networks, Nave Bayes, k nearest neighbor algorithms, game theory logic, fuzzy logic, bagging, random forest, in addition, many other algorithms for machine learning are utilized to install an anomalous intrusion detection system (IDS) (Mebawondu, 2018; Moustafa and Slay, 2015). Anomaly IDSs are significantly better at identifying new threats, but they have a high false alarm rate. The KDD99 IDS and NSL-KDD databases investigated by Boppana and Su (2011), Vinchurkar and Reshamwala (2012); Schmidhuber [7], and employed several neural variations networks to discriminate between normal and attack traffics.

[a]vaishnavi.ganesh8@gmail.com; [b]manmohan.21909@lpu.co.in; [c]santosh24372@lpu.co.in

DoS attack

The most hazardous sorts of significant mistakes are DoS attacks, according to Chen et al. (2018) and Doshi et al. (2018). Small network services, like smart houses (Ranga and Verma, 2019) are impacted by such assaults, which target clever gadgets inside such settings (for instance, intelligent door locks, set-top boxes, and smart incandescent bulbs) and prevent the potential recipient from accessing them. In this situation, some recent research (Syed et al., 2020; Vaccari, et al., 2020; Anthi et al., 2018) have focused on safeguarding such devices to DoS attacks. DoS attacks have an advantage of being easy to launch by creating bespoke packets.

Control area network

The controller area network (CAN) is a common communication protocol, particularly when genuine information is communicated. Message scheduling on the CAN corresponds to giving identifiers (IDs) to messages based on their priorities, with the CAN message ID being broken into two parts: the first is assigned based on the text's dynamic priority, while the other identifies the message itself. The number of bits allotted to the adaptive routing component.

Intrusion detection system

Intrusion detection is the process of evaluating and analyzing computer or network events for signals of likely incidents, such as breaches or threats to computer security laws, permitted usage guidelines, or basic security processes (Mohamed, 2013). A software-based IDS facilitates the attack identification process (Anthi et al., 2021). The process of doing intrusions and seeking to avoid discovered probable occurrences is known as antivirus software. IDPS detects potential security breaches, logs information about them, tries to prevent them, and notifies security professionals (Girdler and Vassilakis, 2021).

Intrusion prevention system

An intrusion prevention system's (IPS) primary responsibilities are to identify malicious behavior, log information about all this, continue to prevent or halt it, and report it. By deploying detection devices in-line, IPS were created to overcome ambiguity in passive network scanning. IPS may now make user access choices based upon the type content instead than IP addresses or ports, as classic firewalls could. IPS systems and intrusion detection systems are still connected (Birkinshaw et al., 20119), since IPS systems were initially a literal development of intrusion detection systems. Web filtering systems can also be used to halt potentially harmful behavior at the host level.

Network intrusion detection system

A network intrusion detection system (NIDS) is a security mechanism made up of application and/or hardware that detects cyber-attacks on networks and servers (Tidjon et al., 2019; Khraisat et al., 2019). Apart from a datagram sorting firewall, which would only access and filter connections packets based on partial information contained in the datagrams, a NIDS can use deep packet inspection (DPI) to describe the details of cyberattacks from the packet of datagrams, revealing their hidden agenda of affecting the PC to which they would be addressed. To identify intrusions and irregularities, a NIDS channels all network traffic via its sensors.

Technology limitations

Despite being effective at detection and analysis [28, 29], wireless IDPSs have a few significant disadvantages that need to be addressed. The utilization of evasion strategies, particularly those directed against gauge channel scanning methods, is a problem that exists with a number of wireless IDPS sensors (Ahmad et al., 2022). One instance is launching attacks in brief bursts on channels that aren't being watched right now (Ganesh and Sharma, 2021). An attacker might potentially conduct simultaneous strikes on two systems (Basati and Faghih, 2022).

Data-set

For user-defined datasets and the pre-partitioned UNSW-NB15 train and test datasets, the architecture is combined with a semi-dynamic hyper-parameter tuning strategy.

UNSW-NB15 datasets used for model testing for pre-partitioned

Deep learning benchmarks using the pre-partitioned UNSW-NB15 dataset and a complete set of features range from 74.3–98.54% when using a wrapper-based strategy like the one described by Anthi et al. (2018) and Chen et al. (2018) respectively. The proposed architecture and hyperparameter method led to significant improvements in model performance, with the testing dataset obtaining an accuracy of 95.3% (Zhang et al., 2022). The method suggested integrating categorical cross entropy via momentum-based Adam optimization (Zhao, et al., 2022). This was done to prevent the problem of overfitting. The learning rate of the approach is 0.001, and its initial two double-stacked layers have a reduced dropout rate (Simon et al., 2022), whereas the dropout rate for the last layer is significantly higher. The rate of detection for each form of assault is shown in Figure 50.1, which can be seen here. As was established, the identification rate for underrepresented groups was substantially lower than the overall rate.

UNSW-NB15 datasets used for model testing for user define

When compared to the pre-partitioned data, the benchmarks obtained by applying deep learning models to a user-defined UNSW-NB15 dataset partition that contains a complete set of features achieve significantly better results.

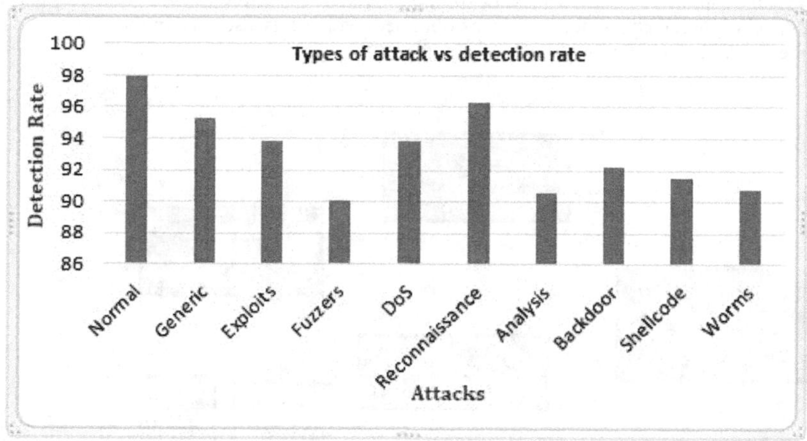

Figure 50.1 Types of attacks vs detection rate for case A

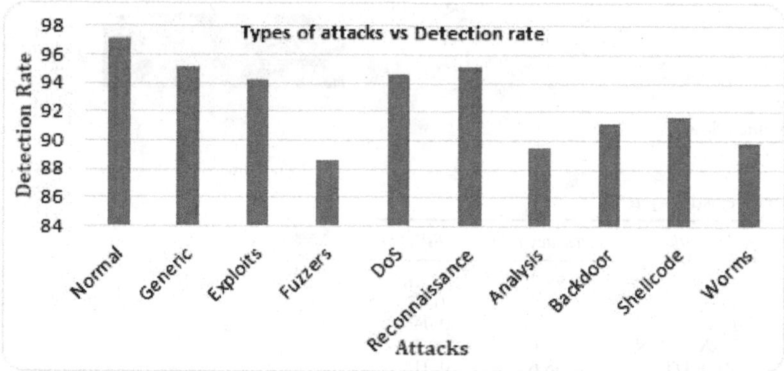

Figure 50.2 Types of attacks vs detection rate for case B

Applying the suggested architecture and hyper parameter technique to the testing dataset, which made up 25% of the total, resulted in a model that performed well, with 95.6% accuracy. The technique suggests using momentum based Nadam optimization and 'categorical cross entropy', much like it did with the prior datasets, in order to prevent overfitting. To avoid overfitting, this was done. Even with the identical dropout rate pattern, the approach results in a slightly greater learning rate of 0.005%. The rate of detection for each form of assault is shown in Figure 50.2, which can be seen here. The identification rate for the underrepresented classes was much lower, similar to the pre-partitioned datasets model.

Proposed system flow diagram

This proposed system flow is shown in figure below which involves dataset from KDD -CUP 99. Then feature selection is done using PSO algorithm which is used initially during pre-processing stage also and in the last stage during performance evaluation of various Machine learning algorithms. Here three ML algorithms have been evaluated i.e., DT, KNN and ANN. So, this research work includes PSO combination along with all three above stated ML algos and it was found that PSO in combination with ANN earned highest efficient results as compared to other algos. Comparative study with other research work is shown below.

Simulated network was created using NS2 and a model of network consisting of mobile phone, laptop and six node MCUs, was created for this research study. Through Wireshark tool, datasets involving the various attributes involved in the communication of data packets in the above networks, was obtained, which was also used in the training of neural networks in addition to the available datasets in Github and Kaggle.

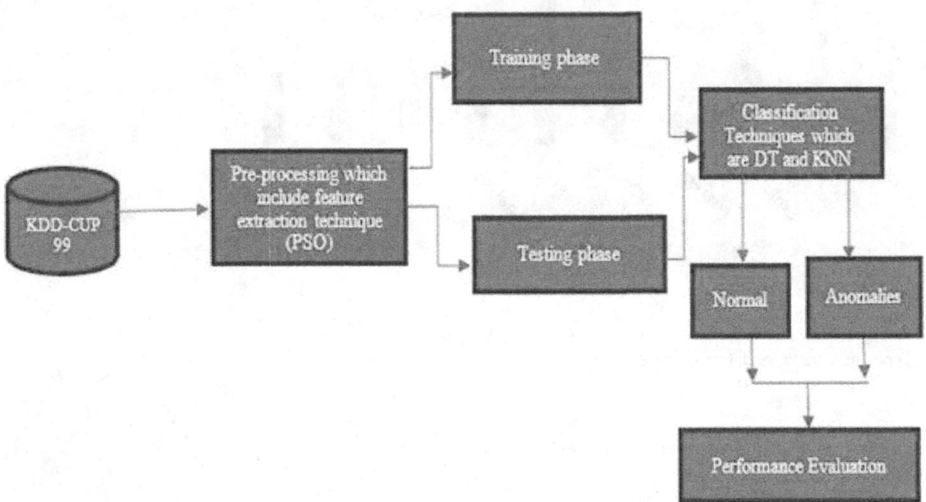

Figure 50.3 Proposed system block flow

Table 50.1 Comparative analysis with existing system

Authors	*Algorithm*	*Accuracy (%)*	*FPR*
Sindhu, Geetha & Kannan [31]	DT	98.2	0.016
Mohammad Sazzadul Hoque [32]	GA	96.4	0.05
Guo [33]	KNN	98.45	0.048
	TCM+KNN	99.4	0.1
Proposed Classifier	**PSO+DT**	**98.6**	**0.011**
	PSO+KNN	**99.6**	**0.004**
	PSO+ ANN	**99.78**	**0.003**

Conclusions and Future Work

This article addressed network intrusion detection systems by utilizing the most recent simulated network traffic dataset. It included both important components as well as typical cyber security defects and exposures. The paper also used the dataset. In addition to that, the most recent dataset was used to simulate network traffic throughout the research. The deep learning classification architecture that was proposed along with the hyper-parameter showed the higher degree of improvement in accuracy, precision, efficiency and rate of detection. According to the models, the proposed method possesses an accuracy of 96.3% for pre-partitioned multiclass classification and 96.2% for user-defined multiclass classification overall.

Even if the models that are currently available have shown results that are encouraging, we know that there is potential for improvement, mainly in the form of the application of techniques that include feature reduction. We want to apply transfer learning in near future to improve model categorization by making use of the UNSW-NB15 dataset. This will, in turn, strengthen the capacity of our models to withstand zero-day attacks. Its highly recommended to integrate computer intelligent or optimization technique to further increase the accuracy and intrusion detection rate specially on higher order datasets.

References

Ahmad, J., Shah, S. A., Latif, S., Ahmed, F., Zou, Z., & Pitropakis, N. (2022). DRaNN_PSO: A deep random neural network with particle swarm optimization for intrusion detection in the industrial internet of things. *Journal of King Saud University—Computer and Information Sciences.* https://doi.org/10.1016/j.jksuci.2022.07.023.

Anthi, E., Williams, L., Malgortzata, G., Theodorakopoulos, G., & Burnap, P. (2018). A supervised intrusion detection system for smart home IoT. *IEEE Internet Things Journal*, 78, 477–90.

Anthi, E., Williams, L., Rhode, M., Burnap, P., & Wedgbury, A. (2021). Adversarial attacks on machine learning cybersecurity defences in Industrial Control Systems,. *Journal of Information Security and Applications*, 58, 102717. https://doi.org/10.1016/j.jisa.2020.102717.

Basati, A. & Faghih, M. M. (2022). PDAE: Efficient network intrusion detection in IoT using parallel deep auto-encoders. *Information Sciences*, 598, 57–74. https://doi.org/10.1016/j.ins.2022.03.065.

Birkinshaw, C., Rouka, E., & Vassilakis, V. G. (2019). Implementing an intrusion detection and prevention system using software-defined networking: Defending against port-scanning and denial-of-service attacks. *Journal of Network and Computer Applications*, 136, 71–85. https://doi.org/10.1016/j.jnca.2019.03.005.

Boppana, R. V. & Su, X. (2011). On the effectiveness of monitoring for intrusion detection in mobile ad hoc networks. *IEEE Transactions on Mobile Computing*, 10(8), 1162–1174.

Chen, Q., Chen, H., Cai, Y., Zhang, Y., & Huang, X. (2018). Denial of service attack on IoT system. *2018 9th International Conference on Information Technology in Medicine and Education,* (pp. 755–758).

Doshi, R., Apthorpe, N., Feamster, N. (2018). Machine learning DDoS detection for consumer internet of things devices. arXiv preprint arXiv:1804.04159

Ganesh, V. & Sharma, M. (2021). Intrusion detection and prevention systems: A review. In G. Ranganathan, J. Chen, & Á. Rocha (Eds). Inventive communication and computational technologies. *Lecture Notes in Networks and Systems*, Springer, Singapore

Girdler, T. & Vassilakis, V. G. (2021). Implementing an intrusion detection and prevention system using Software-Defined Networking: Defending against ARP spoofing attacks and Blacklisted MAC Addresses. *Computers & Electrical Engineering*, 90, 106990. https://doi.org/10.1016/j.compeleceng.2021.106990.

Khraisat, A., Gondal, I., Vamplew, P., & Kamruzzaman, J. (2019). Survey of intrusion detection systems: techniques, datasets and challenges. *Cybersecurity,* 2(1), 20.

Mebawondu, J. (2018). Development of a network intrusion detection system using neural network. M.Tech, Federal University of Technology.

Mohamed, A. A. (2013). Design intrusion detection system based on image block matching. *International Journal of Computer and Communication Engineering*, 2(5).

Moustafa, N. & Slay, J. (2015). UNSW-NB15: a comprehensive data set for network intrusion detection systems (UNSW-NB15 network data set). *Military Communications and Information Systems Conference IEEE*, (pp. 1–6).

Quincozes, S. E., Albuquerque, C., Passos, D., & Mossé, D. (2021), A survey on intrusion detection and prevention systems in digital substations. *Computer Networks*, 184, 107679. https://doi.org/10.1016/j.comnet.2020.107679.

Simon, J., Kapileswar, N., Polasi, P. K., & Elaveini, M. A. (2022). Hybrid intrusion detection system for wireless IoT networks using deep learning algorithm. *Computers and Electrical Engineering*, 102, 108190. https://doi.org/10.1016/j.compeleceng.2022.108190

Sivagaminathan, V. & Sharma, M. (2021). Dynamic Communication Protocol Modelling for Intrusion Traces Using Cisco Packet Tracer Integration with Wireshark. *Design Engineering*, 4583–4599. http://thedesignengineering.com/index.php/DE/article/view/3853.

Syed, N. F., Baig, Z., Ibrahim, A., & Valli, C. (2020). Denial of service attack detection through machine learning for the IoT. *Journal of Information and Telecommunication,* 4(4), 482–503

Theja, R. S. S. & Shyam, G. (2021). An efficient metaheuristic algorithm based feature selection and recurrent neural network for DoS attack detection in cloud computing environment. *Applied Soft Computing*, 100, 106997. doi:10.1016/j.asoc.2020.106997.

Tidjon, L. N., Frappier, M., & Mammar, A. (2019). Intrusion detection systems: A cross-domain overview. *IEEE Communications Surveys & Tutorials*, 21(4), 3639–3681.

Vaccari, I., Aiello, M., Cambiaso, E. Slow, T. T. (2020). A slow denial of service against IoT networks. *Information*, 11(9), 452.

Verma, A. & Ranga, V. (2019). Machine learning based intrusion detection systems for IoT applications. *Wireless Personal Communications*, 1–24.

Vinchurkar, D. P. & Reshamwala, A. (2012). A review of intrusion detection system using neural network and machine learning technique. *International Journal of Innovative Technology and Exploring Engineering*, 1(2), 54–63.

Yerriswamy, T. & Venkatagiri, J. (2018). Ant colony optimization based traffic analysis for finding shortest path in mobile ad hoc networks. *International Journal of Pure and Applied Mathematics*.

Zhai, B. & Chena, J. (2017). Development of a stacked ensemble model for forecasting and analyzing daily average PM2.5 concentrations in Beijing China. *Science of The Total Environment*, 635, 644–658.

Zhang, Z., Zhang, Y., Guo, D., Yao, L., & Li, Z. (2022). SecFedNIDS: Robust defense for poisoning attack against federated learning-based network intrusion detection system. *Future Generation Computer Systems*, 134, 154–169. https://doi.org/10.1016/j.future.2022.04.010.

Zhao, X., Huang, G., Jiang, J., Gao, L., & Li, M. (2022). Task offloading of cooperative intrusion detection system based on Deep Q Network in mobile edge computing. *Expert Systems with Applications*, 206, 117860. https://doi.org/10.1016/j.eswa.2022.117860.

51 A load balanced approach for smart agriculture system based on IoT- cloud framework

Prerna Rawat[1,a], *Prabhdeep Singh*[2,b], *and Dr. Devesh Pratap Singh*[3,c]

[1]M.Tech(CSE), Department of Computer Science & Engineering, Graphic era deemed to be University, Dehradun, Uttarakhand, India

[2]Assistant Professor, Department of Computer Science & Engineering, Graphic era deemed to be University, Dehradun, Uttarakhand, India

[3]Professor, Department of Computer Science &Engineering, Graphicera deemed to be University, Dehradun, Uttarakhand, India

Abstract

The agricultural sector is among the most significant sectors in the primary industry, but it is also an unstable, sensitive, complicated, dynamic, and the fiercely competitive sector as well. As stated by the Food and Agriculture Organization (FAO) of the United Nations, agricultural production must be boosted by 60% to provide a safe and sufficient food supply for the rapidly expanding global population. There are several ways that climate-smart agriculture may be implemented, including resource sharing, cost-saving, and efficient agricultural system building. Climate-smart agriculture may benefit from agricultural informationization, which can be achieved by adopting new technology trends like cloud computing or the Internet of Things (IoT). Research in cloud computing and the IoT for agricultural applications is of particular interest, especially in agricultural automation and digital management. In both rich and emerging countries, the reappearance of the global crisis has sent waves of anxiety and uncertainty. To achieve global food security, the agricultural industry will need to be more efficient and robust. Larger farms, advanced technology, commerce, and government laws all put Indian farmers at a disadvantage. Using IoT and cloud computing, the notion of load balancing may be used to remarkable effect in smart agriculture. Data from many kinds of sensors used in agriculture will be handled by the intelligent load balancer. All the data acquired will be utilized to its fullest potential, as well as all the methods used. A three-tier architecture for smart agriculture has been proposed in this research paper.

Keywords: Smart agriculture, Internet of Things, load balancing, cloud computing

Introduction

Sharing knowledge on traditional sustainable farming practices and techniques would be made possible via the crowd-sourcing platform's affordability and accessibility as well as its interactivity and offline data input for aggregated information upload (Lipper et al., 2014). The answer to food and water security must include more information and services for farmers, such as micro-finance, third-party agriculture, etc. Conventional sustainable agricultural techniques, crop diseases, and other information from various sources must be centralized in a single location that can be accessed via a variety of devices including cell phones, IVR, computers, and kiosks, as well as offering multi-lingual assistance of practices with modern value (Kalyani and Collier, 2021). An urgent need for more research exploration in the smart-agricultural field to move toward a more sustainable and food-secure future motivated us for this study. We contributed our thoughts and ideas to this paper after a regressive study of the already present research paper related to this field of interest. Seventy percent of the world's poorest people depend on agriculture to fulfil their basic requirements and support their livelihoods. Agriculture has the potential to reduce poverty, boost incomes, and improve food security for most of the poor population of the world who live in rural areas and work largely in farming (World Bank). Climate change mitigation, adaptation, and food security will have a major effect on the world's poorest farmers (Sinha and Dhanalakshmi, 2022). According to leading international organizations, a transition toward climate-smart agriculture (CSA) is vital to ensure that there will be enough food for the predicted nine billion people by 2050. Smart agriculture is an automated and directed information technology that makes use of the Internet of Things (IoT). IoT is expanding quickly and is used extensively in all wireless settings. IoT sensors' ability to offer information about agricultural areas and then act on it depending on user input makes smart agriculture an emerging idea. By 2050, the country's economy will have a billion people, thus growth in the agriculture sector is essential. Over the previous ten years, rainfall patterns have fluctuated due to climate change (Adil et al., 2021). Agriculture is poised to undergo a radical transformation thanks to emerging technologies like the robots, IoT, artificial intelligence (AI) and cloud computing, and. There is no lack of applications for these technologies; smart farming techniques are being employed to improve the precision of the administration of fertilizer, pesticides, and herbicides. The best times to sow crops are presently being determined

[a]Prerna7rawat@gmail.com; [b]prabhdeepsingh.cse@geu.ac.in; [c]Devesh.geu@gmail.com

using smart farming techniques, such as Microsoft's Cortana Intelligence Suite, in countries like India and Colombia. Drones are being utilized to help identify weeds, and robots are assisting farmers with weed removal and milking their livestock. The IoT signals the next stage in communication and computer growth because of its adaptability. For the sake of this discussion, a network of goods is referred to as 'booting' and is frequently a wireless network in preparation for usage. Food security in the digital era requires a unified global digital market, the future internet, and information sharing through social media, as well as data protection and free access to information. As the IoT advances, agriculture should place a higher priority on the development of smart systems based on geomatics (RS/GIS/GPS), sensor technology, WLANs, RFID, and cloud computing. Farmers are reaping the benefits of geomatics in the agricultural sector while maintaining their financial viability thanks to the rising use of this technology in the field. Satellite and aerial photographs play a major role in modern agriculture (Yang et al., 2021). Farmers will be able to better manage animal and plant pests because of the widespread deployment of the IoT. In agriculture and forestry, the IoT is essential to enhancing research efforts. IoT technology has lately been used in agriculture and forestry. A fundamental Internet technology trend has arisen since cloud computing was first proposed in the 1960s, allowing for the development of new services while reducing ownership costs and simplifying resource management. Climate-smart agriculture will benefit from the convergence of these two technologies since it will be easier to experiment with new services and improvements. The IoT is on the verge of a paradigm shift with the virtualization of everything. The paper organization for this paper goes as mentioned in the upcoming paragraph. After a short abstract of the paper in section 1, we have introduced the ideas given in the paper along with what motivated us to move into this area of research. Section 2 explains about literature review of past research papers, section 3 explains our proposed framework for smart agriculture section 3.1 explains about agriculture- IoT unit, and section 3.2. explains load balancing unit, section 3.3 explains cloud layer, section 3.4 explains Name Node, and Data node, section 3.5 explains map reducer, section 3.6 explains servers and section 4 concludes our proposal.

Literature Review

The IoT is based on a dynamic, global network architecture with nodes (things) that are intelligent and self-configuring. It's a game-changer because it opens the possibility of ubiquitous and pervasive computing. As an alternative, cloud computing is a well-established technology with almost unlimited storage and processing power potential; most IoT issues have been at least partly addressed. Crop fields might be monitored via a wireless sensor network, as discussed in publications (Keerthi and Kodandaramaiah, 2015). Temperature and humidity sensors are included in these systems, as well as an image sensor that takes photos of crops for comparison purposes. Temperature, humidity, and images all play a role in making an educated decision on a healthy crop. Sensor stability is much improved while power consumption is reduced thanks to these methods. All these have been concluded after a considerable amount of time spent observing. IoT-based cloud monitoring systems for greenhouses were suggested by the study paper (Keerthi and Kodandaramaiah, 2015). Sensor devices, such as light, temperature, relative humidity, and soil moisture sensors, may be used by greenhouse managers to monitor a wide range of environmental data. Internet of Things and cloud computing are utilized to store data collected by sensors in the agricultural field area every 30 s. It was suggested in the paper (Kaur et al., 2016) to use a sophisticated drip irrigation system. This employs an Android smartphone app to manage and monitor the crop area remotely to reduce the need for human interaction. There may be less water waste when using drip irrigation. Sensors that monitor water levels are used in this system. Wireless sensor networks automatically analyze data from agricultural fields and provide a judgment to the farmer for a healthy crop using sophisticated software applications (Srisruthi, et al., 2016). The author of this study proposes low-maintenance, high-gain agriculture that makes use of cutting-edge sensor technology that is both environmentally benign and energy-efficient. Automatic farm monitoring and irrigation systems employ a range of sensors to remotely detect soil temperature, moisture, and fertility while also regulating the quantity of water and fertilizer given to the field, as explained in this article. Automated irrigation systems may be maintained without the need for human intervention by using IoT sensors (Kansara et al., 2015).

A proposal for smart agriculture using cloud computing and IoT

We are proposing a three-tier model framework for the smart agricultural system. These include three layers namely the agriculture-IoT unit, the load balancing unit, and the cloud layer. All the data collected from the agricultural field will be stored in an agriculture-IoT unit using the use of different types of sensors. Then the load balancing unit layer will ensure the optimized uses of all the computing resources along with giving us the best result. The whole data then will be forwarded to the cloud layer, where it will be analyzed and then the analyzed data can be used to achieve the goal of smart agriculture in the most optimized way leading us towards a more sustainable and secure future.

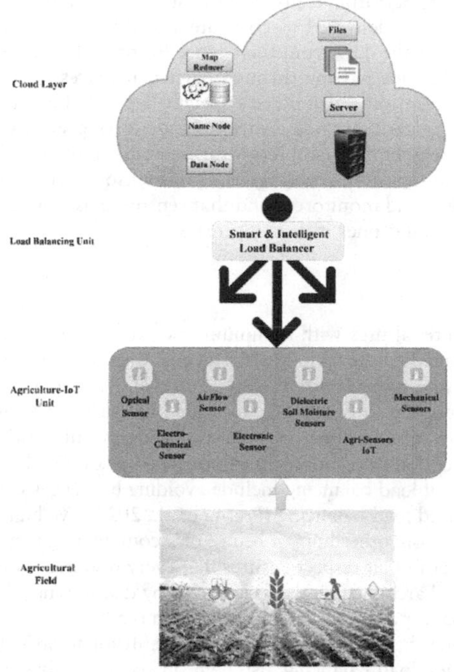

Figure 51.1 Proposed framework for smart agriculture using IoT and cloud computing

Agriculture- IoT unit

This unit in our proposed model consists of different types of agricultural sensors. They offer information that enables farmers to monitor and improve crops considering changing environmental circumstances and difficulties. The weather stations, drones, and robots used in agriculture all have these sensors installed and fastened. Mobile apps created specifically for this may control them precisely. A sensor is a portable device that measures or detects physical phenomena like motion, heat, or light and transforms them into analog or digital representations.

The following sensors have been used in this framework.

- ***Agricultural use of optical sensors:*** It employs a variety of wavelengths to determine the quality of the soil. Plant color and soil reflectance data may be collected and processed using these sensors, which can be placed on vehicles or drones. Optical sensors can be used to assess organic matter, soil moisture, and clay.
- ***In-soil electrochemical nutrient detection sensors:*** Data about the soil's chemical composition is beneficial. Sensors for soil nutrient monitoring that uses electrochemical technology are called information sensors. soil samples are sent for testing in the respective department. The pH is calculated using an ion-selective electrode, which is used for a variety of other tests. Sodium, potassium, and nitrate ions may all be detected using these electrodes.
- ***Agriculture's mechanical soil sensors:*** To record the force exerted by pressure scales or load cells, these sensors use a device that pierces the ground. Soil cutting, breaking, and displacement forces are measured when a sensor is pierced by the soil and penetrated by the sensor. Soil mechanical resistance is the ratio of the force required to penetrate the soil medium to the instrument's frontal area engaged with the soil. It is given in units of pressure.
- ***Sensors for soil moisture dielectric:*** Soil moisture content is determined using this device. Several rain check stations are used in combination with moisture sensors on the property. Soil moisture conditions may be studied when there are few plants present.
- ***Agricultural use of GPS location sensors:*** These sensors detect the range, distance, and height of any point within the required zone. To help them do this, they depend on the GPS satellites that orbit the Earth.

- ***Sensors based on electronic components:*** Inspection of equipment performance is accomplished by mounting it on tractors and other outside machines. As a result, the information is delivered to computers or through email via cellular and satellite networks. The field executive may then access the data from their office PC or mobile phone.
- ***Airflow detectors:*** It's possible to take measurements of air while it's passing through particular places. The targeted output is the pressure needed to push a given volume of air into the ground at a specific depth. Different soil features, such as compaction, structure, soil type, and moisture content, provide a variety of identifying signatures.
- ***IoT sensors for agriculture:*** Measurement and recording of air temperature, soil temperature at different depths as well as rainfall as well as chlorophyll, and wind speed and direction are done regularly using this sensor. Greenhouses and crops must be mechanized so that livestock can be controlled and monitored, and that sensor be used in smart precision agriculture. It is possible to increase productivity by using drones in agriculture.

Load balancing unit

The basic aim of cloud computing, like in any other recourse, is optimal uses with minimum cost. To achieve the best utilization of resources in cloud computing, the concept of load balancing plays a vital role. The goal of load balancing is to reduce the amount of time it takes for activities to be completed and to maximize the use of available resources. This will result in improved system performance at a reduced cost. In addition to this, the goal of load balancing is to offer scalability and flexibility for applications the size of which may grow in the future, hence necessitating the allocation of more resources, and to prioritize activities that need immediate execution in comparison to other processes. In addition to decreasing energy consumption and carbon emissions, other goals of load balancing include avoiding bottlenecks, providing resources, and meeting quality of service standards for improved load balancing (Prerna et al., 2022). We humans by nature want a quick response to every action of ours. Whether it's from other human beings or a computer system, we need a quick response to be engaged in any task. So, the load balancer in that respect ensures that every resource is made to do the same quality of work at a given point in time. In cloud-based architecture, this is achieved by distributing a load of request traffic among multiple servers and resources. The load balancer also ensures that no system is either overloaded or underloaded. The elasticity feature of cloud computing has made the technology extremely useful for today's data storage and analysis problem. Along with these tech-savvy advantages, load balancing also helps in accomplishing green cloud computing by limiting power usage and carbon emission reduction. This fits almost perfectly with the present need of establishing a balance between the desire for never-ending development and environmental conservation. A smart and intelligent load balancer will ensure all the above advantages are collected by the user. This concept is used in the cloud layer of our proposed framework in this framework. Table 1 Pre-crisis summary statistics.

Cloud layer

Cloud computing enables high-capacity data storage for large-scale data and information. A cloud-based database may be used to store a variety of farming-related data, including crop and weather data, market data, farmer experiences with agricultural operations, pesticide and prescription information, and more. It's easy for farmers to save and retrieve data from the cloud for individual farms (Friha et al., 2021. Cloud computing may be used to disseminate knowledge on new agricultural practices and instruments produced by researchers from a wide range of agricultural institutions. Otherwise, cloud computing provides a good platform for farmers throughout the world to exchange knowledge and experiences. Data on the current market conditions of various crops helps determine which crops to grow. IT resources may be accessed at little cost with cloud computing. It employs a pay-as-you-go model. The agricultural community does not need to invest in owning IT resources but may instead get the resources they need via the cloud. To keep track of all the data about agriculture, the cloud-based agro system was developed (Mekala and Viswanathan, 2017). The agricultural community is dispersed around the globe, hampered by cultural and linguistic differences. The online language translation procedures are provided by current IT systems. As a result, the cloud agricultural system may offer information in the farmer's local language. The world's land records are becoming digitized due to the availability of large-scale storage technology. The land records are stored in a cloud computing storage facility that includes information about the property, such as soil analysis results and production history.

NameNode and DataNode

An HDFS file system would be incomplete without a NameNode. It maintains the directory structure of all files in the file system and records where the data is stored throughout the cluster. It does not keep these files' data on its servers. Client programs use NameNode to identify files and perform operations on them, such as adding, copying, moving, and deleting. The NameNode returns a list of appropriate DataNode servers for successful queries. DataNodes hold the real data. There are several DataNodes in a working filesystem.

Map reducer

The use of Map-Reduce processing, allows data from various IoT nodes to be analyzed locally and then condensed into a few nodes as much as feasible.

Server

It is the job of a server to deliver a service to another computer program and its user or clients.

Conclusion

The importance of more research exploration in the field of smart agriculture is very prominent today. The Internet of Things (IoT) has several applications in agriculture. Connecting sensors and picture-capturing equipment to the internet in agricultural areas is a viable option that may be done using IoT, to increase the efficiency of all the resources. Fertilizers and pesticides may be utilized more efficiently with the data collected and analyzed using IoT. Intensive farming is made possible by cloud technology in the agricultural industry. The cutting-edge technology has simplified and streamlined agricultural management and monitoring. Data storage, administration, access, and dissemination can all be done quickly and cheaply thanks to cloud computing. Farmers profit from the use of cloud computing in the context of increased production, marketing, and selling. Various government programs for agriculture may be made available to farmers using cloud computing.

In this paper, we proposed a three-tier framework for smart agriculture, which we believe can better optimize the whole smart-agri system. The load balancer plays a very essential and critical role in this framework. There are multiple issues still unresolved in this field like more result accuracy using smart devices for better decision making, better and optimized storage and access of collected data, and security of that data collected from sensors. The battery life of sensors is also one of the necessary fields that require more research exploration and innovation. These must be explored to make smart agriculture more sustainable. The same framework can be used in different sectors of the economy for better management of collected data.

References

Adil, M., Khan, M. K., Jamjoom, M., & Farouk, A. (2021). MHADBOR: AI-enabled administrative-distance-based opportunistic load balancing scheme for an agriculture internet of things network. *IEEE Micro*, 42(1), 41–50.

Dhaya, R., Ahanger, T. A., Asha, G. R., Ahmed, E. A., Tripathi, V., Kanthavel, R., & Atiglah, H. K. (2022). Cloud-based IoE enabled an urban flooding surveillance system. *Computational Intelligence and Neuroscience*.

Friha, O., Ferrag, M. A., Shu, L., Maglaras, L. A., & Wang, X. (2021). Internet of Things for the future of smart agriculture: A comprehensive survey of emerging technologies. *IEEE/CAA Journal of Automatica Sinica*, 8(4), 718–752.

Kalyani, Y. & Collier, R. (2021). A systematic survey on the role of cloud, fog, and edge computing combination in smart agriculture. *Sensors*, 21(17), 5922.

Kansara, K., Zaveri, V., Shah, S., Delwadkar, S., & Jani, K. (2015). Sensor-based automated irrigation system with IOT: A technical review. *International Journal of Computer Science and Information Technologies*, 6 (6).

Kaur, B., Inamdar, D., Raut, V., Patil, A., & Patil, N. (2016). A survey on smart drip irrigation system. *International Research Journal of Engineering and Technology*, 3(2).

Keerthi. V. & Kodandaramaiah, G. N. (2015). Cloud IoT based greenhouse monitoring system. *International Journal of Engineering Research and Applications*, 5(10), 35–41.

Lipper, L., Thornton, P., Campbell, B. M., Baedeker, T., Braimoh, A., & Bwalya, M. (2014). Climate-smart agriculture for food security. *Nature Climate Change*, 4(12), 1068–1072.

Mekala, M. S., & Viswanathan, P. (2017). A Survey: Smart agriculture IoT with cloud computing. *2017 International Conference on Microelectronic Devices, Circuits, And Systems,* (pp. 1–7).

Sinha, B. B. & Dhanalakshmi, R. (2022). Recent advancements and challenges of Internet of Things in smart agriculture: A survey. *Future Generation Computer Systems*, 126, 169–184.

Pant, M. B. & Arora, M. (2017). All you want to know about Internet of Things (IoT). *2017 International Conference on Computing, Communication and Automation*, (pp. 1306–1311). doi: 10.1109/CCAA.2017.8229999.

Prerna, R., Singh, P., & Tripathi, V. (2022). Load balancing in cloud computing leading us towards green cloud computing. https://ssrn.com/abstract=4031990/http://dx.doi.org/10.2139/ssrn.4031990

Rayabharapu, V. K., Rampur, V., Tripathi, V., Bhaskar, T., & Glory, K. B. (2022). IOT sensor-based pollution management control technique. *Measurement: Sensors*, 100513.

Srisruthi, S., Swarna, N., Susmitha Ros, G. M., & Elizabeth, E. (2016). Sustainable agriculture using eco-friendly and energy efficient sensor technology. *IEEE International Conference on Recent Trends in Electronics Information Communication Technology.*

Yang, J., Sharma, A., & Kumar, R. (2021). IoT-based framework for smart agriculture. *International Journal of Agricultural and Environmental Information Systems*, 12(2), 1–14.

52 Computational intelligence methods for predicting breast cancer

Vivek Kumar Pandey[1,a], *Chandan Kumar*[2,b], *and Monica Sankat*[3,c]

[1]Research Scholar, SAGE School of Advanced Computing, SAGE University Bhopal, Madhya Pradesh, India

[2]Assistant Professor, SAGE School of Advanced Computing, SAGE University Bhopal, Madhya Pradesh, India

[3]Assistant Professor, School of Computer Applictaion, Lovely Professional University, Punjab, India

Abstract

Breast cancer is the most prevalent condition and the main cause of mortality for most women worldwide. Women who have blood relatives who have the same condition are more likely to develop breast cancer, even though many people who have the disease have no family history. A high risk of breast cancer also involves becoming older, having dense breast tissue, being extremely overweight, and exposure to radiation. Tumors can be either malignant (harmful) or benign (harmless), and clinicians require a reliable disease-identifying process to distinguish between the two. The mammography is utilized to find breast cancer however, X-ray specialists have noticeably distinct understandings. The detection of a disease or its cause of breast cancer is frequently done using fine needle aspiration cytology (FNAC). Furthermore, for a treatment to have a higher probability of success, early diagnosis of a disease or its cause is crucial. Results can be separated and labelled efficiently and effectively using classification and data mining attributes, utilizing machine learning models, which will be crucial in making early predictions about a possibility. We discuss the potential for breast cancer in the future in this research and compare the accuracy of several machine learning sets of computer algorithms. We obtained database from the Wisconsin Dataset of Breast Cancer (WDBC) Following examination, the various model with parameter optimization has an AUC of 99.6% and an accuracy of 97.36%. Additionally, the mathematical models for these sets of computer instructions can be changed to improve the accuracy of detecting breast cancer.

Keywords: Machine learning, breast cancer, prediction, supervised learning, genetic programming

Introduction

Breast cancer is the second-most lethal type of cancer after lung cancer. The breast cells of the mortal body are where the hazard of breast cancer first manifests itself, and these altered cells can easily spread to neighboring Apkins. Cancer, the threat level, and the age of the cases may all affect how the illness manifests. Breast cancer can be classified categorically or visually, such as by looking for a lump in the breast. There are many different categories of categorical data, and to create colorful orders, you require categorical variables. The lump might be benign or unpleasant excrescences, which are aberrant cell growths. If the problem is identified ahead, made more accessible, and prevented from spreading, people's lives will be protected. The sole method for describing breast cancer was the X-ray. Although fine needle aspiration cytology (FNAC) is widely advocated in the context of breast cancer, the average rate of accurate diagnosis is just 90. However, several models have been developed and put out for finding a method that is more effective than X-ray treatments, comparable to artificial intelligence and data mining. A subfield of artificial intelligence (AI) and machine literacy (ML) is the study of the creation and improvement of data-based algorithms. It is also possible to properly evaluate the provided data automatically to establish the threat-specific characteristics and breast cancer survival rate. These computerized models support croakers in providing accurate case predictions based on their collected database of parameters. Machine literacy is widely used to diagnose, prognosticate, and treat serious, common ailments like cancer, hepatitis, and heart conditions. ML algorithms are divided into supervised and unsupervised categories. A function called supervised literacy converts inputs into output-affair dyads. A labelled training data set is utilized to examine the training data and provide an inferred function that can be applied to the mapping of new examples. Unsupervised machine learning is a kind of ML that searches for previously unnoticed patterns in data with the least amount of human interaction and without pre-defined markers. Top factors and cluster analysis are the unsupervised literacy styles employed.

Literature Review

ML is a branch of computer science that is constantly growing and has a wide range of applications (Rubinger, 2022). It is a technique for taking valuable information out of a lot of data (Massari, 2022). Naive Bayes (NB) with standard and

[a]vivek.pandey1379@gmail.com; [b]Chandan.k@sageuniversity.edu.in; [c]monica.28744@lpu.co.in

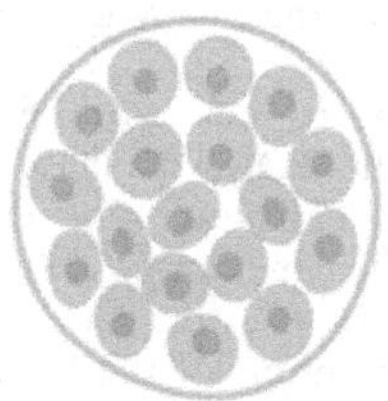

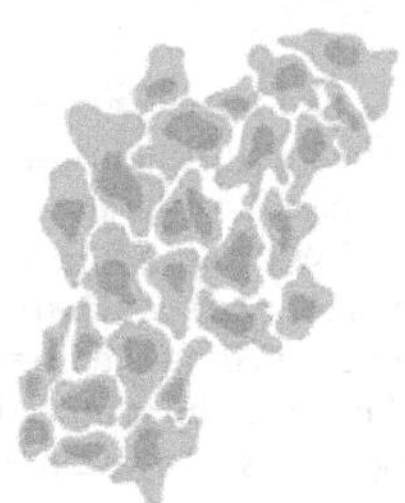

Figure 52.1 Malignant and benign breast cancer

kernel functions (Fatima, 2020). It's a probability classifier that counts on the independence of every variable. The Bayes theorem estimates the likelihood of an event based on previously known, potentially relevant conditions. The Bayesian theorem is employed in machine literacy outcomes acquired from this model with a delicacy of 92.1% since it is demonstrated to be superior to all other probabilistic approaches. To accomplish bracket rigor, random forest (RF) Aggarwal (2019) use a number of DT. Ho originally suggested the arbitrary timber in 1995. The advantage of this algorithm's improved delicateness is that it exhibits 'randomness', meaning that as more DT grow out of the system, the algorithm's delicateness grows even more. Decision trees, an advanced system of arbitrary timbers, are very rigid in comparison to one another. Each DT has a number of splint bumps, and tree depth ensures that each decision tree's output produces separate conclusions. Train each decision tree to produce outcomes, then choose the appropriate outcome based on those results. Results from this model were 94.90% accurately produced. By simulating random wood and presenting an alternative-style LibSVM of support vector machine (SVM), several classifiers are analyzed and the stylish results are described. The proposed model for brackets (Alghunaim, 2019) that may be applied to mammography pictures promotes methods of image processing for point birth. The suggested model includes a cost function that, after numerous number duplications, returns the ideal value. The suggested model prognosticates with 93.7% delicacy and combines LR and BPNN. In this method of constructing a system, binary logistic regression (BLR) may distinguish between harmful and benign excrescences. With a delicacy of 98.9%, the model will quantify a smaller variety of aspects with those who have the fashionable separation between the two classes. The suggested SVM is dependent on the separation of classes. Grid hunt and F-score computation were suggested by the SVM model to be used to optimize parameters and choose input features, respectively. These subset values are learned using the subset that was produced by the grid hunt utilizing the ten-fold. The process is repeated until every feature is present in the subset. Application of the suggested model and point selection (Mao, N. 2019) produced the highest delicacy of 99.51% with an 80–20% split of training and testing data.

Machine Learning Algorithms for Breast Cancer Prediction

These are the algorithm we used for breast cancer prediction comparison are:

Logistics regression (LR)—It's a supervised literacy algorithm that includes further dependent variables. The response of this algorithm is in the double form. Logistics retrogression can give the nonstop outgrowth of a specific data. This algorithm consists of a statistical model with double variables.

K-nearest neighbor (KNN)—This algorithm is used in pattern recognition. It's a good approach for bone cancer vaccination. In order to fete the pattern, each class has given an equal significance. K Nearest Neighbor prize the analogous featured data from a large dataset. Based on the similarities in the features, we classify a big dataset.

Decision tree (DT)—Decision tree is grounded on bracket and retrogression model. Dataset is divided into a lower number of subsets. These lower sets of data can make vaticination with the loftiest position of perfection.

Naive Bayes algorithm (NB)—This model is used to make a supposition of a large training dataset. The algorithm is used to calculate Page 2 the probability through the Bayesian system. It provides the loftiest delicacy while calculating the chances of noisy data that's used as an input. It's an analogy classifier that's used for comparing training dataset with training tuples.

SVM—It's a supervised literacy algorithm which is used for both bracket and retrogression problems. It consists of theoretical and numeric functions to break the retrogression problem. It provides the loftiest delicacy rate while doing vaccination of large datasets. It's a strong machine learning fashion that's grounded on 3D and 2D modeling.

Random forest (RF)—Random forest algorithm is grounded on supervised literacy that's used to break both bracket and retrogression problems. It's a structured block of machine literacy that's used for validation of new data on the base of a former dataset.

Methodology

Dataset for analysis - The Wisconsin Bone Cancer dataset used in this study was sourced from the UCI ML repository. This is the same dataset that Bennett used to distinguish between bad and good.

The characteristics that describe the nexus of the present image were uprooted from digitized images of a fine needle aspirate of a bone mass. A total of 569 cases in Wisconsin hospitals were impacted by the WDBC database, which also linked 357 benign and 212 malignant cases. Each observation reflects the results of the FNA test. "The identifier number and the opinion status are represented by the first two attributes for this dataset. The remaining values are the thirty genuine properties, including, the mean, the standard error, and the worst of 10 cell nexus features. The compass, texture, border, area, smoothness, conciseness, concave points, dint, harmony, and fractal dimension are the 10 genuine values that are measured."

Stage 1: Pre-processing—The Standard Scaler module was used to handle the raw bone cancer data as part of this investigation to evaluate the features. Many machine learning estimators frequently request the standardization of datasets. "It transforms the attributes to a standard Gaussian distribution grounded on (xi – mean (x))/ stdev (x) where

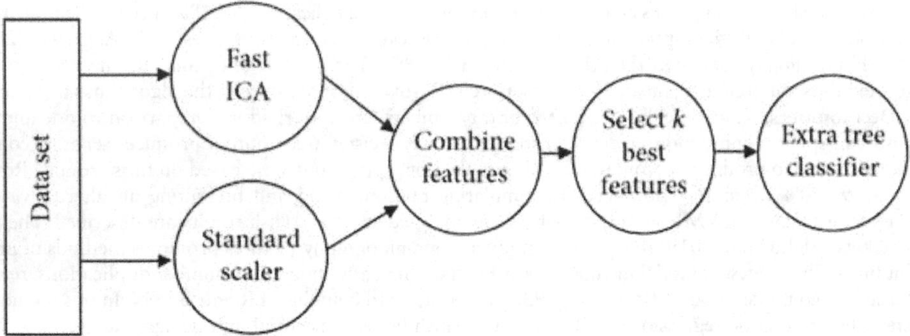

Figure 52.2 Pipeline

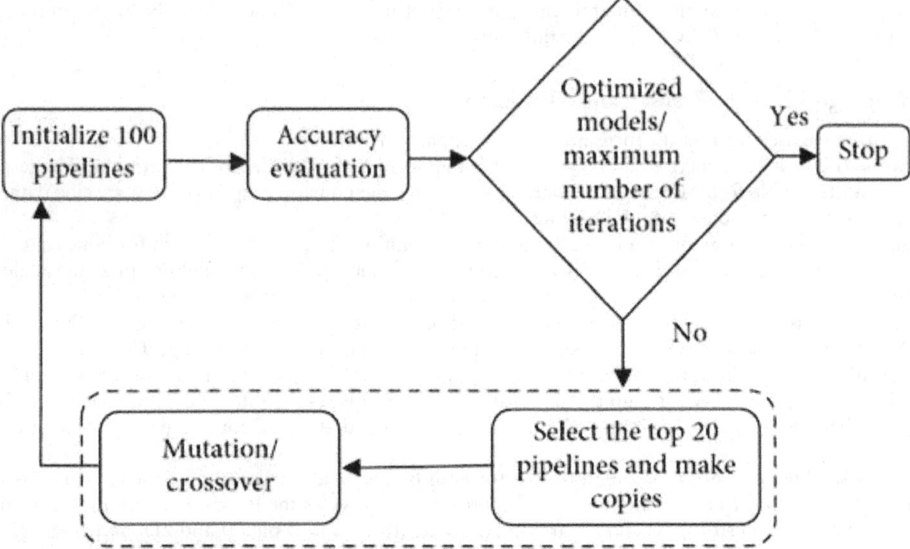

Figure 52.3 Flowchart of genetic programming

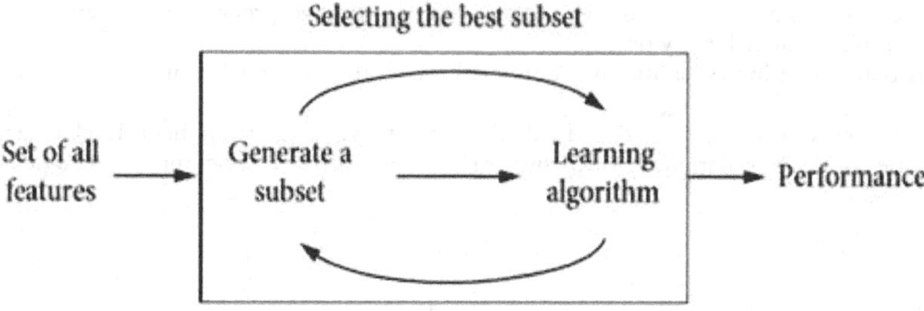

Figure 52.4 Wrapper methods

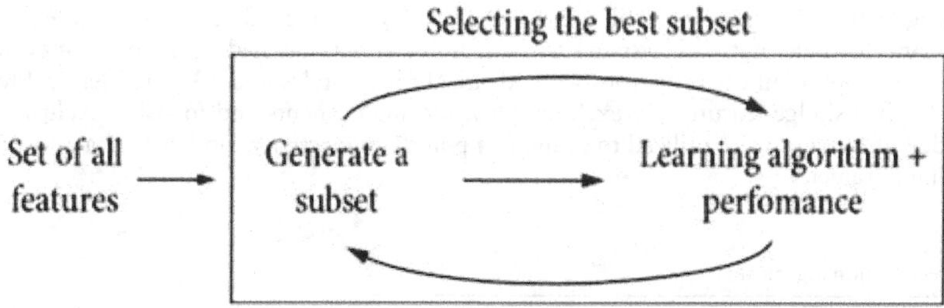

Figure 52.5 Embedded methods

stdev is the standard divagation. The Robust Scaler depends on the interquartile range to transfigure the features using (xi – Q1 (x))/ (Q3 (x) – Q1 (x)), where Q1, Q2 and Q3 represent quartiles. All the metamorphoses used are included in scikit- learn machine literacy library."

Stage 2: Features selection—Point selection is frequently used as a pre-processing stage prior to factual literacy. However, no algorithm can produce accurate predictions without instructive and discriminative features. As a result, we used randomized SVD to enforce PCA in order to preserve the most important features and shrink the Page 2 dataset (28). When utilizing the Python scikit-learn package, the point selection module was enforced. All selection methods were based on a number of factors that valued the fashionable traits. In our research, point selection was based on the following modules: univariate point selection and recursive point elimination, which remove features with little resistance.

Stage 3: Machine learning algorithm—In general, compared to a single model, ensemble machine literacy algorithms enable greater prophetic performance. This might be viewed as a machine literacy contest, with the winning outcome serving as a guide for public perception of bone cancer. The SVM, KNN, DT, grade boosting classifier (GB), arbitrary timber, logistic retrogression, AdaBoost classifier (AB), Gaussian Naive Bayes (GNB), and direct discriminant analysis (LDA). were utilized in this study to categorize the given data set.

Stage 4: Parameter optimization—A type of evolutionary algorithm (EA) known as inheritable programming (GP) generalizes the inheritable algorithm. GP serves as a model for evaluating findings and selecting the chic option. GP produces a result based on natural elaboration and its abecedarian medium (mutation, crossover, and selection). The usage of GP accounts for its rigidity; it can model systems even when the details of the requested models' structures and essential characteristics are unknown. For the bracket problem in this study, GP enabled the system to choose models from a variety of potential model structures and optimize the channels represented in tree topologies. In a similar manner to feature selection corruption, GP initially creates a predetermined number of channels based on the previously mentioned features. In other words, the order of the drivers evolves to build channels of machine literacy that are predicted to maximize the delicacy of the bracket. An illustration of a machine learning channel is shown in Figure 52.1. A new generation is founded on the highest former channels after evaluating the current channels' machine literacy. Every channel is regarded as an element of GP.

The GP is formed by the three main operators:

Mutation operator: Changing hyperparameters or adding or removing a primitive preprocessing step similar as Standard Scaler or the number of trees in an arbitrary timber."

Crossover operator: Assumes that 5% of individualities will cross with each other using a 1- point crossover named at arbitrary.

Selection operator: Its main purpose is to elect the top 20 individualities and make clones from them. To change information between the individualities of the population, the crossover or mutation driver can be applied. The posterior stages of GP are given in Figure 52.3.

Expected Outcomes

Three trials were set up for training the input data. The point of interest in the first instance was the phase of point selection. The type of model was the main focus of the alternative trial. In the end, automating the earlier experiments into a single tone-regulating mechanism was the main emphasis of the third trial. In other words, the goal was to automate the creation and improvement of machine learning algorithms. First, an open-source machine learning package named WEKA was used to evaluate the EA's features, which comprised flyspeck mass optimization (PSO), inheritable algorithm (GA), evolutionary programming (EP), and voguish first (BF). Table 52.1 displays the named attributes for the previous hunt styles. It was concluded from the table that each system's list of features about matched the amount of evaluated styling options. We deduced that just 60 of all the properties were identical for all styles and 80 were identical for the EA from the outcomes of the applied sludge features. By excluding low-scoring elements and focusing exclusively on the point connection core, sludge techniques were utilized to estimate a point's connectivity. Similar to that, every hunt style employed required a tuning parameter.

Table 52.1 Comparison of feature-selection algorithm

Search algorithm	*Number of selected attributes*	*Numbers*
PSO	1, 9, 10, 16, 21, 23, 24, 25, 26, 27, 30, 31	12
Evolutionary search	1, 3, 9, 10, 11, 15, 23, 24, 25, 26, 27, 29, 30	13
Genetic algorithm	1, 7, 9, 10, 16, 21, 23, 24, 25, 26, 29, 30	12
Best first	1, 4, 9, 10, 16, 21, 23, 25, 26, 27, 29, 30	12

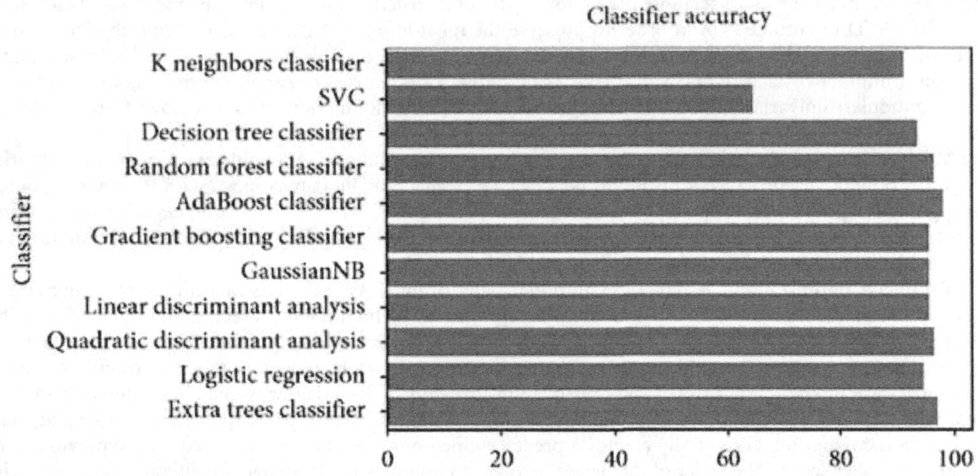

Figure 52.6 Comparison of classifier accuracy

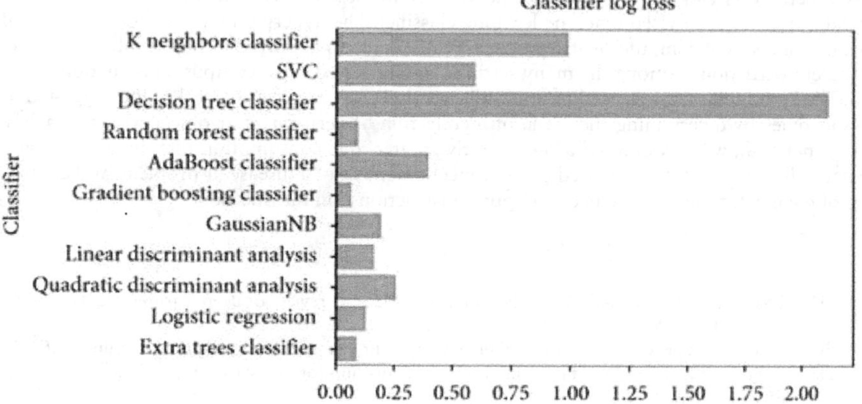

Figure 52.7 Comparison of log-loss classifier

Table 52.2 F1-measurements for breast cancer results

	GB	*DT*	*RF*	*GBN*	*SVM*	*KNN*	*AB*	*LDA*	*QDA*	*LR*	*ET*
Benign (%)	96.69	95.36	97.37	96.69	78.72	93.42	98.67	96.73	0.97.26	96.10	98.01
Malignant (%)	93.51	90.91	94.74	93.51	0	86.84	97.44	93.33	95.12	91.89	96.10
Average (%)	95.57	93.80	96.45	95.57	51.10	91.11	98.23	95.33	96.51	94.63	97.34

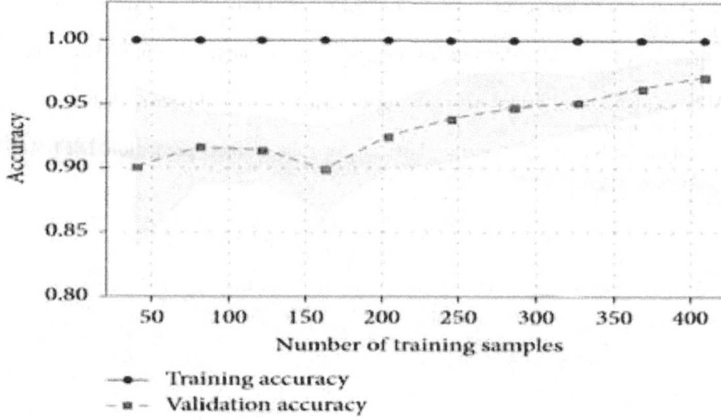

Figure 52.8 Validation accuracy

Conclusion

This work uses a set of machine learning computer instructions to try to solve the issue of automatic breast cancer diagnosis. The current set of computer commands advance/move forward in stages. Using the breast cancer dataset, three different experiments were organized and carried out.

In the first test, we established that the three most well-liked sets of computer instructions, which are concerned with things gradually getting better over time, can achieve or gaining the same performance with effort after a successful setup. The second experiment was centered on the idea that combining features selection techniques enhances performance in terms of being very close to the truth or true number. In the final experiment, we succeeded in figuring out how to automatically create a supervised machine learning classifier. The hyperparameter problem, which offers a challenge for machine learning sets of computer instructions, was attempted to be solved using the inheritable programming (GP) set of computer instructions. Among the many settings, the suggested set of computer instructions choose the proper set for the job. The Python library was used to finish all experiments. Despite the fact that the suggested method produced significant outcomes by determining the value of a collection of performers or objects of approaches using a full machine learning approach, we encountered a significantly greater time consumption rate. Finally, the suggested model appears to be naturally adapted for automated breast cancer diagnosis of a disease or problem, and control limit/guideline establishing of the machine learning sets of computer instructions, on the one side.

References

Abdel-Jaber, H., Devassy, D., Al Salam, A., Hidaytallah, L., & ELAmir, M. (2022). A review of deep learning algorithms and their applications in healthcare. *Algorithms*, 15.

Aggarwal, G. & Jain, S. (2019). Analysis of genes responsible for the development of cancer using machine learning. *IEEE Xplore*.

Alghunaim, S. & Al-Baity, H. (2019). On the scalability of machine-learning algorithms for breast cancer prediction in big data. *IEEE Xplore*.

Alickovic, E. & Subasi, A. (2017). Breast cancer diagnosis using GA feature selection and rotation forest. *Neural Computing and Applications*.

Banaie, M., Soltanian-Zadeh, H., Saligheh-Rad, R., & Gity, M. (2018). Spatiotemporal features of DCE-MRI for breast cancer diagnosis. *Computer Methods and Programs in Biomedicine*.

Charateand, A., Jamge, S. (2017). The preprocessing methods of mammogram images for breast cancer detection. *International Journal on Recent and Innovation Trends in Computing and Communication*.

El Massari, H., Mhammedi, S., Gherabi, N., & Nasri, M. (2022). Virtual OBDA mechanism ontop for answering SPARQL queries over couchbase. *Advanced Technologies for Humanity*.

Fatima, N., Liu, L., Sha, H., & Ahmed, H. (2020). Prediction of breast cancer. *Comparative Review of Machine Learning Techniques and their Analysis*.

Jha, D., Kim, J., & Kwon, G. (2017). Diagnosis of alzheimer's disease using dual-tree complex wavelet transform, PCA, and feedforward neural network. *Journal of Healthcare Engineering*.

Mao, N., Yin, P., & Wangetal, Q. (2019). Added value of radiomics on mammography for breast cancer diagnosis: a feasibility study. *Journal of the American College of Radiology*.

Rubinger, L., Gazendam, A., Ekhtiari, S., & Bhandari, M. (2022). Machine learning and artificial intelligence in research and healthcare. *Injury*.

Valvano, G., Santini, G., & Martini, N. (2019). Convolutional neural networks for the segmentation of micro calcification in mammography imaging. *Journal of Healthcare Engineering*.

Waseem, H., M. (2019). On the feature selection methods and reject option classifiers for robust cancer prediction. *IEEE Access*.

53 A fault-tolerant resource reservation model in cloud computing

Sheikh Umar Mushtaq[1,a] *and Sophiya Sheikh*[2,b]

[1]Research Scholar, Lovely Professional University, Punjab, India

[2]Assistant Professor, Lovely Professional University, Punjab, India

Abstract

Making scheduling fault proof is one of the critical challenges in any dynamic environment like the cloud. Fault tolerance makes the system more efficient and thereby continues the processing of any task till completion without any disruption. This paper proposes Advance Reservation Fault Tolerance Model (ARFTM), which minimizes the Makespan in combination with making the system fault-proof. ARFTM uses a resource reservation strategy and reserves the virtual machines (VMs) in advance for the certainly predicted timeslot. In case of fault, the system provides an alternative VM to the affected task for successful task execution. Here, the alternative VM is chosen based on the previous workload history. The proposed ARFTM was compared with traditional MCT on various parameters like Makespan, flowtime, and average VM utilization. The results show that the proposed ARFTM overpasses the compared approach.

Keywords: Virtual machines reservation, cloud computing, scheduling, Makespan, flowtime, virtual machines utilization

Introduction

The cloud is a global distribution of huge applications and computing resources like memory, network, and processor virtually over the internet. These distributed applications and resources are globally provided and shared with the users based on a 'pay as you go' approach. The cloud environment assists as a request-response model, which allows clients to make requests for the different available services on a 'pay as you go' basis. The virtual machines (VMs) are scattered over the bulky geographical site and are interconnected by a well-organized network to form a cloud environment. The collective power of all the scattered VMs is used to accomplish user requests. The cloud environment offers a dynamic and flexible phenomenon of VM allocation. To provide guaranteed and unfailing services, there must be a resourceful scheduling mechanism that proficiently maps each task to the VM to satisfy the user's needs. Moreover, there are various features of the cloud which must be considered for providing guaranteed and reliable services. These features are based on availability, security, scalability, and fault tolerance. The provisioning of services provided by cloud providers is mainly based on service level agreement (SLA). SLA is the contract between cloud providers and customers which mainly defines the levels or quality of services being provided by the service providers. However, quality of service (QoS) also play a significant role in a cloud environment (Gautam and Yadav, 2015). Cloud is a dynamic environment; hence, the services can be requested by any number of clients. Therefore, the cloud providers should be able to bag the corresponding requests from the clients, which can be attained by efficient scheduling and arranging applications on suitable VMs. Cloud scheduler accounted for four main tasks:

- Finding an adequate and efficient order of task execution.
- Finding an efficient and appropriate allocation schedule of VMs for the tasks.
- Making the schedule fault-proof by incorporating any fault tolerance mechanism and thereby preventing the immature termination of tasks.
- Skilled and effective migration.

Advance reservation (AR) is a firm and settled concept for VM allocation and is having many advantages (Burchard, et al., 2005). Since applications are mainly installed in VMs, which can be displaced or shifted easily anywhere to squeeze out sufficient MS for reservation by employing some virtual machine migration techniques (Zhao and Figueiredo, 2007). In a dynamic system like the cloud, the scheduler is unaware and has no accurate idea about the task size and time. Moreover, in a dispersed environment like a cloud, the VM may step into and depart the system at any time throughout the execution of any task. Likewise, there can be multiple possible cases for the VMs to depart the system. Therefore, it is not requisite that the task will finish its execution after being assigned to the VM without any interruption. Faults in the VM may lead to interruption in the execution (Foster et al., 2001; Foster and Kesselman, 2006;

[a]Shiekhumar12@gmail.com; [b]sophiyasheikh@gmail.com

Haider and Nazir, 2016; Olteanu et al., 2012). The faults can occur in case any of the VM changes its state from active to inactive or to offline without being instructed resulting in an unexpecting result. Furthermore, faults can be of two types i. e., permanent faults or transient faults. The permanent faults reside in the environment until the damaged VM is restored. While the transient faults could not be accessed once they arrive in the system. To handle this fault situation, some alternate VMs are required that need to be assigned to the tasks in case any of the VM fails to make the environment fault-tolerant (Liu and Buyya, 2018).

In this paper, an Advance Reservation Fault-Tolerant Model (ARFTM) has been proposed for minimizing task execution time while maximizing Average Utilization and ensuring guaranteed task execution in case of any VM failure by employing the Advance Reservation mechanism. For allocation, this algorithm prefers the available VM having the minimum load history and lowermost execution time over others. The reservation of VMs is done in advance for the required time slots with VM configuration. Moreover, an alternative VM is allocated to carry through the task execution which is interrupted in case of VM failure. In the proposed ARFTM, the Makespan of tasks was mainly optimized. However, average utilization and flowtime are also taken into consideration while the performance evaluation of the model. The model was compared with MCT and the model was evaluated for varying the number of tasks.

The rest of the paper is structured as follows: section 2 presents a review of related proposed work reported in the literature. Different notions used in the proposed work are symbolized in section 3, Moreover, section 3 also discusses the problem formulation and proposed algorithm and architecture, and section 4 presents the results and discussion. Section 5 concludes the work.

Related Work

In the case of unexpected failures, the current fault tolerance approaches often compromise resource reliability and the efficiency of resource management in a job. However, the cloud is unstable and fault-prone due to the dynamic nature of its VMs, which might result in immature termination of the tasks. This instability can arise when any VM fails or leave the system without any prior notice. Additionally, even when system defects or mistakes are notified, fault tolerance tends to provide the anticipated services at the proper time. The AR technique is one of the techniques which we can employ to make the cloud fault-proof. In the AR technique, we bind the VM to a particular task for a certain precalculated period/time slot. On reviewing the literature, it has been found that advance reservation has been employed for different categories of tasks given different scenarios i.e., static, dynamic, and distributed systems. However, the proposed fault tolerant techniques considered VM reliability and efficiency under normal conditions. Still, due to dynamism, the system will be volatile and prone to faults which leads to the shocking termination in the execution of the task. The related literature review is presented as follows:

On reviewing the entire literature, AR has been reported. the live migration framework was described for multiple virtual machines with changed resource reservation methods (Ye et al., 2011). Then a sequence of experimentations was performed to examine the effect of changed resource reservation methods on the act of live migration in both the source machine and target machine. Moreover, the efficiency of the parallel migration and workload-aware migration strategies were analyzed. Parameters like downtime, workload performance overheads, and total migration time are measured. Later, virtual machine reservation scheduling was done in cloud data centers by considering energy efficiency (Tian et al., 2018). The objective is to schedule all reservations non-pre-emptively keeping in mind the constraints of the capacity of PM and running time interval spans to minimize the total energy consumption of all PMs termed or abbreviated as Mine. MinTEC problem generally being an NP-complete, two approximation algorithms were considered for two cases, i.e., the 5-approximation algorithm was used for special illustrations by employing the First-Fit-Decreasing algorithm. In the second case, 3-approximation was used for the general offline scheduling of parallel machines in unit demanding. The optimal and workload features in interval spans are combined and the general method for finding the optimal solution having a minimum number of job migrations was proposed, the best-known bound 3-approximation algorithm was improved to the 2-approximation algorithm by introducing the LLIF algorithm. Furthermore, an elastic reservation technique was involved in conventional 'on-demand provisioning' (He, 2015). This inclusion allows the cloud providers to accept over-reservation requests under certain conditions which will lead to improved resource effective utilization (REU) and user satisfaction. Reactive or post-migration of VMs next to the allocation is one of the widespread ways of achieving load-balancing objectives and traffic consolidation. However, this type of migration makes it difficult to grasp the predefined objectives of load balancing. Though, reactive migration can cause interrupts in services and other associated costs. Considering this view, a new paradigm-pre-partition was proposed (Tian et al., 2014), where the processing time on PM for each request is set proactively. The preparation of migrating the VMs is done proactively in advance to reduce the processing time and instability in services and thereby achieve the desired goal of load balancing. Apart from the cloud, AR has also been used in grid computing and has been applied for various categories of tasks such as batch of tasks (BoT), priority tasks, independent tasks, workflow applications, etc. Furthermore, different environmental conditions have been considered such as static, centralized, dynamic, and distributed environments. Additionally, some of the methods implemented by AR are associated with the optimization of various QoS parameters of the grid while others are related to resourceful job scheduling. The FTHRM was proposed (Sheikh, et al., 2021) which was based on an advanced reservation technique, where the main focus has been carried on turnaround time and the model was proposed wholly on grid computing. In the batch scheduling strategy, a review of the resource reservation has been drafted by the GRAAP survey. However, AR is limited to providing the resources for a specific period after negotiation in a static environment (MacLaren, 2003). Additionally, the author presents a general model for scheduling a batch of computational tasks that have reservation requests for resources to accomplish the job on time (Park, 2004). Moreover, the author proposed an online scheduling policy that minimizes the drawbacks of the AR technique on the schedule's quality and enhances resource utilization, flowtime, and tardiness. Besides, this research considered a static system model for the purpose that could not deal with the dynamic behavior of the resources or a dynamic system. Apart from this, a few more tasks in grid computing have been declared in the literature using AR. Initially, AR was implemented using Gridsim simulator (Sulistio and Buyya, 2004). Later in similar model has been proposed by Depoorter et al. (2014) for scheduling both the batch of computational tasks and tasks with AR requests.

In previous research on reservations, some AR negotiation strategy is introduced, which depends upon the selection of a backup resource from the cluster to ensure the quality of service for the request.

The Proposed Model

This section contains the illustration of the proposed ARFT fault tolerant model in a dynamic cloud environment which employs the advanced reservation technique to handle the faults. The notions used in the paper are mentioned below:

Notions used

K: Number of VM	AR^s_{ij}: AR slot t_i on VM_j	v_f: fth failed resource in V_f
N: Number of tasks	EST_{ij}: Early start time of t_i on VM_j	T_f: Set of failed tasks
T: Set of tasks	AFT_{ij}: Actual finish time of t_i on VM_j	VM_f: Set of failed VMs
t_i: ith task of T	MCT: Minimum completion Time	q: Number of failed tasks in T_f
VM_j: jth resource of R	p: Number of failed VMs in V_f	$d(T_f)$: Order of T_f
VM: Set of VMs	m: Mapping between T and VM	$d(V_f)$: Order of V_f

The VM set is available for executing the various tasks. These VMs are having different processing speeds and are located in different geographical locations. Out of the available VMs, the VM broker selects the suitable VM for task execution. The VMs are managed locally and at the cloud level by local resource management and cloud scheduler respectively. The resource allocation is performed in a manner to minimize Makespan.

Proposed architecture

The architecture of the proposed work is carrying three main layers as shown in Figure 53.1.

- Application layer: The main interface for communication is provided by application layer. Moreover, requests for VMs are also generated by the user in this layer. Application layer consists of users and requests.
- Middleware: Middleware is the main component of this architecture and is mainly responsible for VM reservation. The generated schedule by scheduler is further sent to VM Broker for further processing of schedule.

  Advance time manager: This is responsible for reservation-related details such as, AR slot, VM allotment, fresh reservations, cancellation of request etc.

  Reservation producer: This component checks the schedule for user requirement and state of VM. The required reservation is provided to the user if the user requirement matches with the schedule for the AR slot produced by tTime manager.
- *VM layer/Host layer:* This layer contains different VMs which are used by user to execute their tasks.

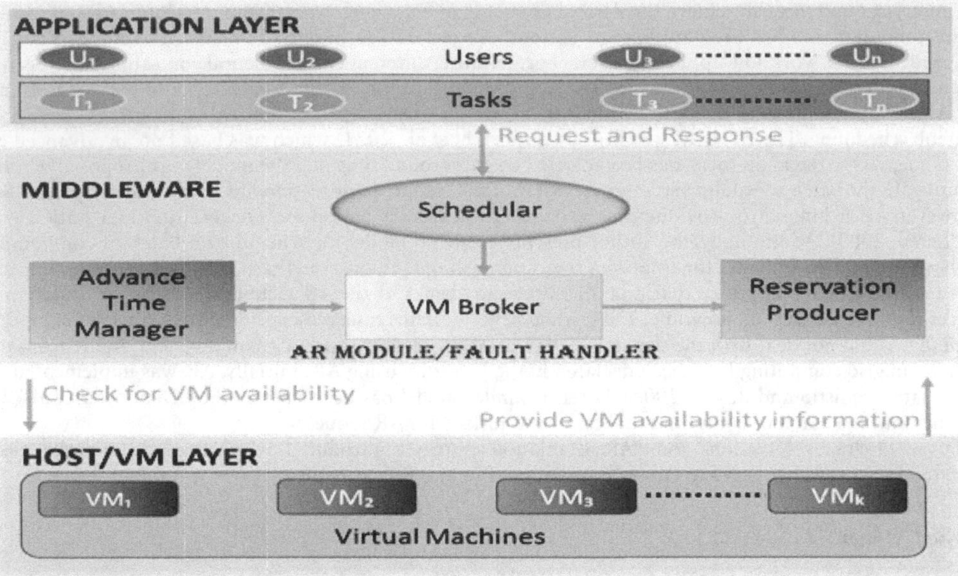

Figure 53.1 Architecture of the proposed work

Problem formulation

The allocation is performed according to MCT heuristic. MCT is the allocation heuristic that performs task allocation with a minimum Makespan. i. e., on the arrival of any task $t_i$in the system, the available VM_l will be assigned to t_i by employing the MCT allocation strategy. The allocation problem can be illustrated mathematically as an efficient mapping (m) (Maheswaran, et al., 1999) of each task and VM to optimize the Makespan. The mapping is presented as follows:

$$m{:}T \rightarrow VM \tag{1}$$

Due to the dynamic nature of the cloud, the overall processing of the tasks may get affected because of the various kinds of faults occurring in the system. To handle this situation, one of the precautions is to estimate the execution time slot on the suitable VM and reserve the calculated slots in advance. Hence, making the system capable of providing an alternative VM to the affected task. In the advance reservation technique, the advance reservation slot (AR^s_{ij}) is calculated for each task t_i execute on some resource VM_j. This AR^s_{ij} is calculated by subtracting EST_{ij} from AFT_{ij}. After the execution of ti is completed, The AFTij of ti executed on VMj is computed by adding the total processing time of ti on VMj to the ESTij.

If the advance reservation strategy is not employed, the task tu may fail to execute on VMf i.e., the failed VM or if the VM will leave the system for a certain time will result in the suffering of the corresponding task. To handle this situation, p failed VMs are defined as $VM_f = \{v_f{:}v_f \in V \,\&o(VM_f) = p\}$ and q corresponding affected tasks are defined which were executing on these failed VMs. Now, these failed tasks need to be reallocated to some other available suitable VMs. The set of failed tasks is defined as $T_f = \{t_f{:}t_f \in T, o(T_f) = q \& q <= N\}$. On reallocating, all the failed tasks Tf are migrated from VMfto VMj such that VMj∉VMf.

Makespan is taken as the highest or maximum among all AR slots. Flowtime can be calculated as the sum of all Makespans. Finally, the Average VM utilization of the system can be obtained by dividing the flow time with Makespan.

Proposed algorithm

The proposed ARFTM guarantees effective mapping between Virtual Machines and tasks by employing an MCT approach escorted by the advance reservation of VMs. The VMs are reserved for the computed time slot to ensure task execution. ARFTM wins fault tolerance in case any of VMs fail to execute the task at any point of time. The schedule generation for allocating the VMs and reservations in ARFTM is done according to the following Pseudocode:

ARFTM () //Advance reservation fault tolerant model

1. Initialize the Input parameters i.e., the task number, size of the task, number of VMs, the capacity of VM, etc.
2. Schedule or mapping is generated for tasks according to the MCT heuristics.
3. Calculate EST and AFT as discussed in the problem formulation.
4. ARM matrix is calculated by taking EST, AFT, and Status as input.
5. Update Makespan after every allocation.
6. Reserve VMs for a predicted timeslot to continue the processing of the task in case of VM failure.
7. Status=1 i.e., VMs are reserved for the calculated AR slot.

Repeat steps 2 to 7 for all t_i

See the results in parameters like Makespan, flowtime, and average utilization.

Results and Observations

The clever features of the proposed model optimized Makespan. It shows 11–29% of enhancements when compared to traditional MCT. Further, the proposed ARFTM enhanced the flowtime from 16–29% than that of existing MCT. Apart from this, when ARFTM is compared based on overall VM utilization, it was observed that the obtained VM utilization increased from 13–22% of the original MCT. The statistical results of the model are shown in Figure 53.2–53.4.

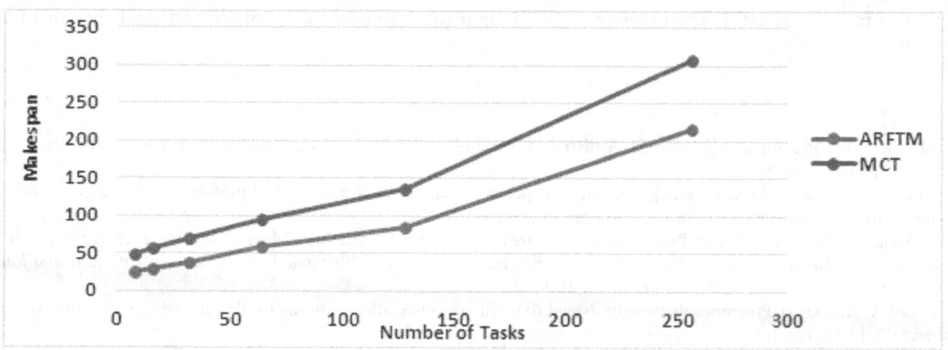

Figure 53.2 Makespan

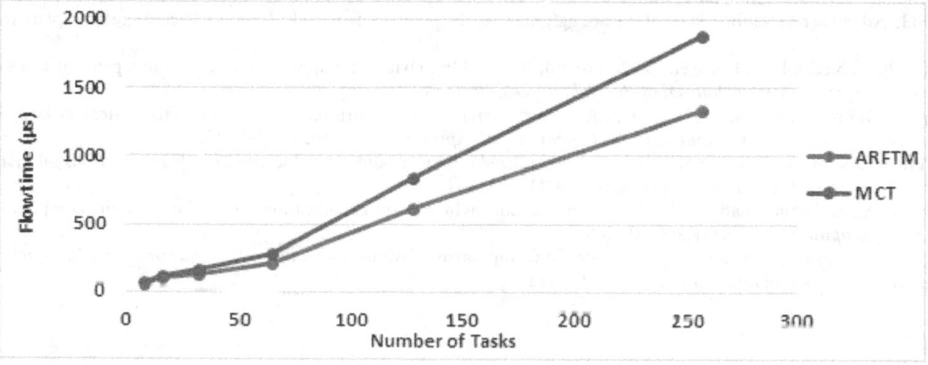

Figure 53.3 Flowtime

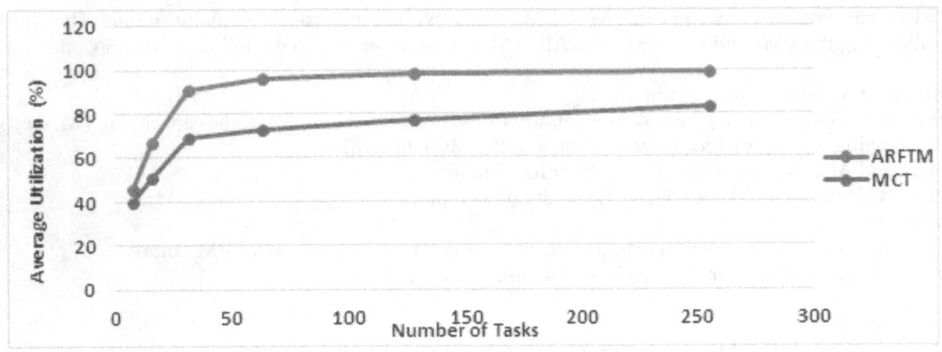

Figure 53.4 Average resource utilization

Conclusion

In the proposed work, the failure of any virtual machine (VM) in the cloud is managed by reserving the VMs in advance for the computed AR slot. The proposed Advance Reservation Fault-Tolerant Model (ARFTM) provides an alternative VM to tarry the interrupted task till completion even in presence of failure in the originally allocated VM. ARFTM has been evaluated based on Makespan, flowtime, and UT and was compared with MCT. The proposed ARFTM was implemented in C language. In comparison, ARFTM shows lower Makespan, lower flowtime and higher aAverage utilization than that of traditional MCT. The extension of this algorithm can be done by predicting the behavior of VMs to make the results more optimal.

References

Burchard, L. O. Linnert, B., & Schneider, J., (2005). A distributed load-based failure recovery mechanism for advance reservation environments. (pp. 1071–1078).

Depoorter, W., Vanmechelen, K., & Broeckhove, J. (2014). Advance reservation, co-allocation and pricing of network and computational resources in grids. *Future Generation Computer Systems*, 41, 1–15.

Foster, I. & Kesselman, C. (2006). The Grid2: Blueprint for a future computing infrastructure, Morgan Kauffman, San Francisco, CA.

Foster, I., Kesselman, C., & Tuecke, S. (2001). The anatomy of the grid: Enabling scalable virtual organizations, *International Journal of High Performance Computing Application*, 15(3), 200–222.

Goutam, S. & Yadav, A. K. (2015). Preemptable priority based dynamic resource allocation in cloud computing with fault tolerance. *2015 International Conference on Communication Networks.*

Haider, S. & Nazir, B. (2016). Fault tolerance in computational grids: perspectives, challenges, and issues. *SpringerPlus*, 5(1), 1991.

He, H. (2015). Virtual resource provision based on elastic reservation in cloud computing. *International Journal of Networking and Virtual Organisations*, 15(1), 30–47.

Liu, X. & Buyya, R. (2018). Resource management and scheduling in distributed stream processing systems: A taxonomy, review and future directions. *ACM Computing Surveys*. 1(1).

MacLaren, J. (2003). Advance reservations: state of the art, ggfgraap-wg. http://www. fz-juelich. de/zam/RD/coop/ggf/graap/graap-wg. html

Maheswaran, M., Ali, S., Siegel, H. J., Hensgen, D., & Freund, R. F. (1999). Dynamic mapping of a class of independent tasks onto heterogeneous computing systems, *Journal of Parallel and Distributed Computing*, 59(2), 107–131.

Olteanu, A., Pop, F., Dobre, C., & Cristea, V. (2012). A dynamic rescheduling algorithm for resource management in large scale dependable distributed systems. *Computers & Mathematics with Applications*, 63(9), 1409–1423.

Park, J. (2004). A deadlock and livelock free protocol for decentralized internet resource coallocation. *IEEE Transactions on Systems, Man, and Cybernetics-Part A: Systems and Humans*, 34(1), 123–131.

Sheikh, S., Nagaraju, A., & Mohammad, S. (2021). A fault-tolerant hybrid resource allocation model for dynamic computational grid. *Journal of Computational Science*, 48, 101268.

Sulistio, A. & Buyya, R. (2004). A grid simulation infrastructure supporting advance reservation. *16th International Conference on Parallel and Distributed Computing and Systems*, 11, 9–11.

Tian, W., He, M., Guo, W., Huang, W., Shi, X., Shang, M. et al. (2018). On minimizing total energy consumption in the scheduling of virtual machine reservations. *Journal of Network and Computer Applications*, 113, 64–74.

Tian, W., Xu, M., Chen, Y., Zhao, Y. (2014). Prepartition: A new paradigm for the load balance of virtual machine reservations in data centers. *2014 IEEE International Conference on Communications*.

Ye, K., Jiang, X., Huang, D., Chen, J., & Wang, B. (2011). Live migration of multiple virtual machines with resource reservation in cloud computing environments. *2011 IEEE 4th International Conference on Cloud Computing*.

Zhao, M. & Figueiredo, R. J. (2007). Experimental study of virtual machine migration in support of reservation of cluster resources. *Experimental Study of Virtual Machine Migration*, 1–8.

54 Twitter sentiment analysis for depression detection using machine learning algorithms

Rajvir Kaur[a], *Sarneet Kaur*[b], *and Syed Mufassir Yassen*[c]
Assistant Professor, GNA University, Phagwara, Punjab, India

Abstract

Social media sites like Facebook, Instagram, and Twitter have transformed our world forever because there are more internet users in the present era. The most prevalent mental health conditions affecting people globally throughout time are stress, anxiety, and depression. This work uses support vector machine, random forest, and logistic regression among other machine learning methods to identify depression on Twitter. Tweets are first downloaded from Twitter in order to build the model, and preprocessed tweets are then used for sentiment analysis. The resulting dataset is then split into 80:20 ratios in order to use machine learning methods to identify the number of depressed and non-depressed tweets. The performance of machine learning algorithms is then analyzed and compared using various evaluation matrices such as accuracy, precision, recall, and F1 score. The results showed that the random forest algorithm achieves the highest prediction accuracy of 90%.

Keywords: Depression, logistic regression, support vector machine, sentiment analysis, random forest algorithm.

Introduction

Depression is a common and fatal medical condition that affects one's mental health. People's minds are being psychologically impacted by today's way of life, causing emotional distress and depression. Depression is a common mental disorder that has an impact on a person's thinking and mental development. According to WHO, approximately 1 billion people worldwide suffer from mental disorders, with over 300 million suffering from depression (Mali and Sedamkar, 2021). There are three types of depression symptoms: psychological, social, and physical. Although it is unlikely that a patient will experience all of these symptoms, they can aid in predicting the severity of depression (Aleem et al., 2022).

Social media is an excellent virtual community for people to connect with one another by sharing personal thoughts these days. People have begun to use online forums, microblogs, and tweets to discuss their struggles with mental health illnesses as internet usage has increased (Alsagri and Ykhlef, 2020). This study focuses on the detection of depression using the Twitter social media platform. Twitter is now the most popular social media platform for sentiment analysis research (Angskun et al., 2022). An uncountable number of tweets are posted on Twitter every second, with over 400,000 tweets sent per minute, nearly two hundred billion tweets posted annually, and approximately five hundred million tweets posted per day. According to the researchers, analyzing Twitter posts can help them identify depression and other mental health issues (Asad et al., 2019).

Researchers are increasingly turning to advanced intelligent techniques for detecting depression as technology advances. Machine learning (ML) algorithms learn automatically and identify patterns in large amounts of data to make predictions. This research focuses on three ML algorithms - support vector machine (SVM), random forest (RF), and logistic regression - for detecting depression on Twitter.

Based on detection performance, this study selects and compares three ML algorithms (SVM, RF, and logistic regression). SVM is a supervised ML technique that is used to solve classification and regression problems. This classification method divides data using hyperplanes, which are straight lines connecting two classes (Babu and Kanaga, 2022). The logistic regression algorithm is a supervised ML technique for classification problems that predicts the categorical dependent variable using independent variables (lsagri and Ykhlef, 2020). The RF algorithm is another supervised learning technique that can be used to solve classification and regression problems (Choudhury et al., 2019). This classifier applies many decision trees to the data samples before selecting the best prediction from each to produce the best solution. The second section reviews the existing research on detection of depression. The research methodology is described in section 3. The section 4 shows the results related to study and section five describes the conclusion.

[a]rajvir_kaur@gnauniversity.edu.in; [b]sarneet.kaur@gnauniversity.edu.in; [c]syed.yassen@gnauniversity.edu.in

Literature Review

Aleem et al. (2022) used ML algorithms to diagnose depression. The authors divided the machine learning algorithms into three categories: classification, deep learning, and ensemble. A general model for diagnosing depression is also presented, as well as an overview of various limitations and goals for detecting depression.

Islam et al. (2018) used Twitter data to identify the characteristics that indicate depressive symptoms. They trained the data using ML approaches and NLP techniques.

Uddin et al. (2022) created an LSTM-RNN-based approach for detecting depression from public online information sources. They used symptom-based feature extraction and demonstrated that symptom-based feature extraction performs well.

Choudhury et al. (2019) used a survey conducted by consulting psychologists, professors, and counsellors to predict depression in Bangladeshi undergraduates. Various ML algorithms were used for this purpose, and they discovered that random forest was the best algorithm.

Kumar et al. (2022) used tweets from tweeter to predict depression. They applied deep learning algorithms such as CNN and LSTM to a Kaggle dataset of various tweets. Alsagri and Ykhlef (2020) focused on microblogging sites like Reddit.com for data collection in 2021, processing the data with sentiment analysis and using various algorithms like SVM, Multinomial Naive Bayes, and KNN for final classification. Asad et al. (2019) used Facebook and Twitter posts to detect depression in 2019. For NLP, they used SVM and the Naive Bayes algorithm.

Research Methodology

The primary goal of this study is to detect depression using Twitter data. To accomplish this, tweets are first downloaded from Twitter and then sentiment analysis is performed. Following that, various ML algorithms such as SVM, RF, and

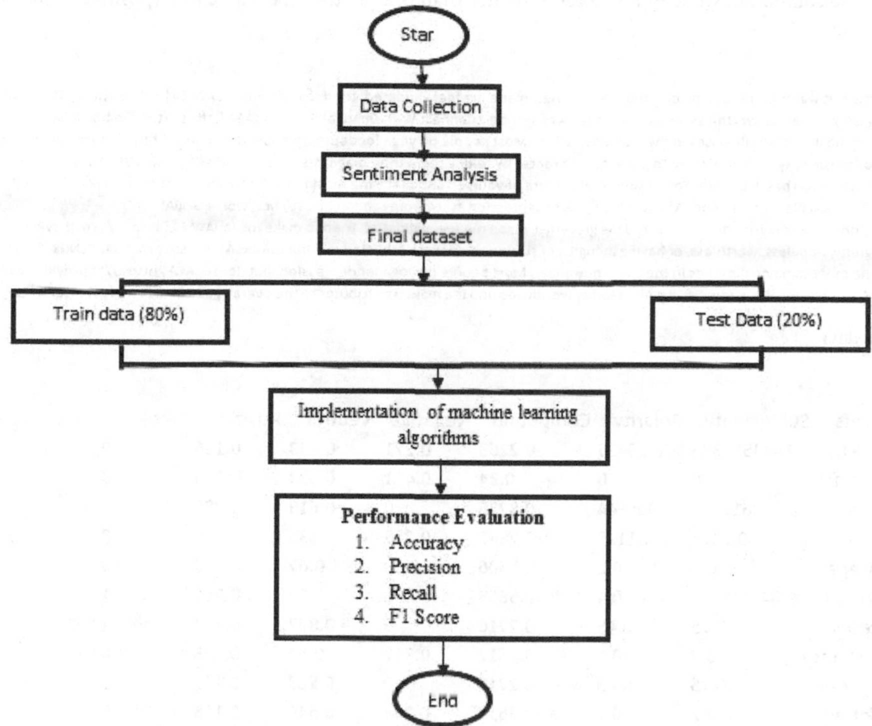

Figure 54.1 Flow chart

logistic regression are applied to the collected tweets, and their performance is compared using different evaluation parameters such as accuracy, precision, recall, and F1 score to determine the best algorithm for depression detection. This section describes each step used in depression detection system, which is depicted in Figure 54.1.

Data collection

To distinguish between depressed and non-depressed tweets, the tweets are first downloaded from Twitter using the Twitter Application Program Interface (API) in Python. The nodexl tool is also used to download the more than 2000 tweets.

Data preprocessing

Data preprocessing is the process of converting raw data into a more understandable, useful, and effective format. Preprocessing is used to remove noise and other irregularities from data. Special characters from downloaded tweets, such as user names, hashtags (#), unwanted symbols ("/", "@", "|"), stopwords ("of", "in", "and", "the", "is", "are", etc), duplicate tweets, and uniform resource locators (URLs), must be preprocessed before using machine learning algorithms (Naresh and Krishna, 2021).

Sentiment analysis

Sentiment analysis determines whether a piece of writing is neutral, negative, or positive. Positive sentiment is represented by the number 1, negative sentiment by the number -1, and neutral sentiment by the number 0 (Kaur et al., 2020). For sentiment analysis, the polarity, subjectivity, and compound value of each tweet in the dataset were calculated using the Python TextBlob module.

The label value is set after performing sentiment analysis on Twitter data to determine whether the tweet is positive, negative, or neutral. If the compound value of the tweet is greater than 0.2, set the label value to 1 (positive), otherwise

Tweets
b'In my deepest depression, it was the friends who ordered me groceries, made me feel validated, tried to make me lauÃ¢Â€Â¦ https://t.co/j1lfyPQehL'
b"If you're also feeling guilty, hopeless, worthless, or having thoughts of suicide...Connect With Dr. Vivek PratapÃ¢Â€Â¦ https://t.co/Bn4UCLNG80"
b'Depression is one of the most common illnesses in the world nowadays. Most people do yoga for depression, but doesÃ¢Â€Â¦ https://t.co/nyKBhh9J6p'
b'"The unfounded fear of causing psychological harm to patients with cancer by telling them their diagnosis should noÃ¢Â€Â¦ https://t.co/hQN7oxj3pR'
b"Don't ever feel selfish when you need to write. You're simply taking care of yourself and that's the most importantÃ¢Â€Â¦ https://t.co/MxHCIQLBV7"
b"Depression and anxiety is real please let's knock Ã°ÂŸÂ˜Â" them out #depression #sucideprevention https://t.co/w6FngGFI0A"
b'In my deepest depression, it was the friends who ordered me groceries, made me feel validated, tried to make me lauÃ¢Â€Â¦ https://t.co/j1lfyPQehL'
b"If you're also feeling guilty, hopeless, worthless, or having thoughts of suicide...Connect With Dr. Vivek PratapÃ¢Â€Â¦ https://t.co/Bn4UCLNG80"
b'Depression is one of the most common illnesses in the world nowadays. Most people do yoga for depression, but doesÃ¢Â€Â¦ https://t.co/nyKBhh9J6p'
b'RT @WHOWPRO: #DYK: Depression is a leading cause of disability worldwide and is a major contributor to the overall global burden of diseaseÃ¢Â€Â¦'

Figure 54.2 Twitter data

Preprocessed tweets	Subjectivity	Polarity	Compound	Negative	Neutral	Positive	label
Guys loosing battle bee	0.414583333	0.20625	-0.2263	0.271	0.543	0.186	0
deepest depression fri	0	0	-0.34	0.411	0.333	0.256	0
also feeling guilty hope	0.673611111	0.006944	0.8225	0	0.619	0.381	1
Depression most comm	0.2875	-0.1125	-0.7845	0.365	0.635	0	0
Vlad Does want prepare	0.3	0.2	-0.7506	0.33	0.67	0	0
Does want prepare Joh	0.844444444	0.4	0.5859	0.08	0.66	0.259	1
know many noticed Sta	0.75	0.45	0.2716	0	0.827	0.173	1
Mental illness much mc	0.2	-0.1	-0.3612	0.312	0.52	0.168	0
Quotes About Depressi	0.75	0.45	0.2716	0	0.827	0.173	1
perspective week Happ	0.2	-0.1	-0.3612	0.295	0.546	0.158	0

Figure 54.3 Final dataset

set it to 0. (negative). The remaining tweets have been assigned a neutral value. Label value 0 indicates that the person is depressed, while label value 1 indicates that the person is not depressed. After considering all of these parameters, the final dataset is created, which divides the data into 80% training data and 20% testing data. The label column is regarded as the target or dependent variable, while the combined sentiment analysis of Twitter data is regarded as an independent variable. The performance of machine learning algorithms is evaluated using various metrics such as accuracy, precision, recall, and F1 score. Figure 54.3 depicts a sample of the completed dataset.

This study selects and compares three machine learning algorithms (SVM, RF, and logistic regression) based on their detection performance. SVM is a technique for supervised machine learning that is used to solve classification and regression problems. This method of categorizing data divides it using hyperplanes, which are straight lines connecting two classes (Naresh and Krishna, 2021). The logistic regression algorithm is a supervised machine learning technique for classification problems that uses independent variables to predict the categorical dependent variable. Another supervised learning technique that can be used to solve classification and regression problems is the random forest algorithm. This classifier applies many decision trees to the data samples and then selects the best prediction from each one to produce the best solution.

Results and Discussion

There are numerous criteria for evaluating and comparing machine learning algorithms. The following are the various evaluation parameters used to assess the performance of machine learning algorithms:

Confusion matrix: The confusion matrix describes the performance of a classification model (or 'classifiers') for a given set of test data, which can only be determined if the true values of the test data are known (Shetty et al., 2020). It compares actual depression tweets to predictions made by machine learning algorithms.

The logistic regression algorithm's confusion matrix is shown in Table 54.1. The classifier has made a total of 2098 predictions, of which 1562 are correct and 536 are incorrect.

The SVM algorithm's confusion matrix is shown in Table 54.2. The classifier has made a total of 2098 predictions, of which 1568 are correct and 530 are incorrect.

The RF algorithm's confusion matrix is shown in Table 54.3. The classifier has made a total of 2098 predictions, of which 1822 are correct and 276 are incorrect.

Classification accuracy simply refers to the rate of correct classifications. It is defined as the proportion of correct predictions to total forecasts (Wang et al., 2013). Precision is defined as the proportion of true positives among positives. It is determined by dividing the total number of true and false positives by the number of true positives. Recall is defined

Table 54.1 Confusion matrix for logistic regression

		Predicted	
	SVM	*Depression*	*Non-Depression*
Actual	Depression	1364	130
	Non-depression	406	198

Table 54.2 Confusion matrix for SVM

		Predicted	
	SVM	*Depression*	*Non-Depression*
Actual	Depression	1391	103
	Non-depression	427	177

Table 54.3 Confusion matrix for RF

		Predicted	
	Random forest	*Depression*	*Non-depression*
Actual	Depression	1455	39
	Non-depression	237	367

Table 54.4 Machine learning algorithms performance

	Accuracy	*Precision*	*Recall*	*F1*
Logistic regression	74%	74%	61%	72%
SVM	74%	74%	61%	72%
Random forest	90%	90%	81%	90%

as the proportion of true positives among all positive events in the data. It is determined by dividing the total number of true positives and false negatives by the total number of true positives (Uddin et al., 2022) intervention, and relapse prevention. With an increase in data sets with relevance for depression, and the advancement of machine learning, there is a potential to develop intelligent systems to detect symptoms of depression in written material. This work proposes an efficient approach using long short-term memory (LSTM). The F1-score is a metric that combines precision and recall. F1 is frequently more advantageous than precision (Zogan et al., 2022) especially in the medical domain. Model explainability is important for building trust by providing insight into the model prediction. However, most existing machine learning methods provide no explainability, which is worrying. For instance, in the task of automatic depression prediction, most machine learning models lead to predictions that are obscure to humans. In this work, we propose explainable Multi-Aspect Depression Detection with Hierarchical Attention Network (MDHAN), for automatic detection of depressed users on social media and explain the model prediction. We have considered user posts augmented with additional features from Twitter. Specifically, we encode user posts using two levels of attention mechanisms applied at the tweet-level and word-level, calculate each tweet and words' importance, and capture semantic sequence features from the user timelines (posts.) The performance of machine learning algorithms is shown in Table 54.4.

According to the above classification models, random forest clearly outperforms the other classifiers in terms of all performance evaluation parameters, while SVM and logistic regression performed the worst for the input dataset. The results showed that the z algorithm achieves the highest prediction accuracy of 90%.

Conclusion

This research study used various machine learning algorithms to detect depression on Twitter. Three machine learning algorithms are used to detect depressed and non-depressed tweets: logistic regression, support vector machine (SVM), and random forest. The performance of the chosen machine learning algorithms is evaluated using various evaluation parameters such as accuracy, precision, recall, and F1 score, and then these algorithms are compared to determine the best algorithm. According to the findings of this study, the random forest algorithm outperforms the other classifiers across all performance evaluation parameters, while SVM and logistic regression performed the worst for the input dataset. The results showed that the random forest algorithm achieves the highest prediction accuracy of 90%.

References

Aleem, S., Huda, N., Amin, R., Khalid, S., Alshamrani, S. S., & Alshehri, A. (2022). *Machine Learning Algorithms for Depression: Diagnosis.*

Alsagri, H. S. & Ykhlef, M. (2020). Machine learning-based approach for depression detection in twitter using content and activity features. *IEICE Transactions on Information and Systems*, E103D(8), 1825–1832. https://doi.org/10.1587/transinf.2020EDP7023

Angskun, J., Tipprasert, S., & Angskun, T. (2022). Big data analytics on social networks for real-time depression detection. *Journal of Big Data*, *9*(1). https://doi.org/10.1186/s40537-022-00622-2

Asad, N. Al, Mahmud Pranto, M. A., Afreen, S., & Islam, M. M. (2019). Depression Detection by Analyzing Social Media Posts of User. *2019 IEEE International Conference on Signal Processing, Information, Communication and Systems, SPICSCON 2019*, 13–17. https://doi.org/10.1109/SPICSCON48833.2019.9065101

Babu, N. V. & Kanaga, E. G. M. (2022). Sentiment analysis in social media data for depression detection using artificial intelligence: A review. *SN Computer Science*, 3(1), 1–20. https://doi.org/10.1007/s42979-021-00958-1

Choudhury, A. A., Khan, M. R. H., Nahim, N. Z., Tulon, S. R., Islam, S., & Chakrabarty, A. (2019). Predicting Depression in Bangladeshi Undergraduates using Machine Learning. *Proceedings of 2019 IEEE Region 10 Symposium, TENSYMP 2019, June*, 789–794. https://doi.org/10.1109/TENSYMP46218.2019.8971369

Govindasamy, K. A. L., & Palanichamy, N. (2021). Depression detection using machine learning techniques on twitter data. *Proceedings - 5th International Conference on Intelligent Computing and Control Systems, ICICCS 2021, Iciccs*, 960–966. https://doi.org/10.1109/ICICCS51141.2021.9432203

Islam, M. R., Kabir, M. A., Ahmed, A., Kamal, A. R. M., Wang, H., & Ulhaq, A. (2018). Depression detection from social network data using machine learning techniques. *Health Information Science and Systems*, *6*(1), 1–12. https://doi.org/10.1007/s13755-018-0046-0

Kaur, R., Kaur, R., Singh, M., & Ranjan, S. (2020). Twitter sentiment analysis of the Indian union budget 2020. *International Journal of Advanced Science and Technology*, *29*(4 Special Issue), 2282–2288.

Kumar, P., Samanta, P., Dutta, S., Chatterjee, M., & Sarkar, D. (2022). Feature Based Depression Detection from Twitter Data Using Machine Learning Techniques. *Journal of Scientific Research*, *66*(02), 220–228. https://doi.org/10.37398/jsr.2022.660229

Mali, A. & Sedamkar, R. R. (2021). Prediction of depression using Machine Learning and NLP approach. *International Journal of Intelligent Communication, Computing and Networks*, *2*(1), 9–19. https://doi.org/10.51735/ijiccn/001/16

Naresh, A. & Venkata Krishna, P. (2021). An efficient approach for sentiment analysis using machine learning algorithm. *Evolutionary Intelligence*, *14*(2), 725–731. https://doi.org/10.1007/s12065-020-00429-1

Shetty, N. P., Muniyal, B., Anand, A., Kumar, S., & Prabhu, S. (2020). Predicting depression using deep learning and ensemble algorithms on raw twitter data. *International Journal of Electrical and Computer Engineering*, *10*(4), 3751–3756. https://doi.org/10.11591/ijece.v10i4.pp3751-3756

Uddin, M. Z., Dysthe, K. K., Følstad, A., & Brandtzaeg, P. B. (2022). Deep learning for prediction of depressive symptoms in a large textual dataset. *Neural Computing and Applications*, 34(1), 721–744. https://doi.org/10.1007/s00521-021-06426-4

Wang, X., Zhang, C., Ji, Y., Sun, L., Wu, L., & Bao, Z. (2013). A depression detection model based on sentiment analysis in micro-blog social network. *Lecture Notes in Computer Science (Including Subseries Lecture Notes in Artificial Intelligence and Lecture Notes in Bioinformatics)*, 7867 LNAI, 201–213. https://doi.org/10.1007/978-3-642-40319-4_18

Zogan, H., Razzak, I., Wang, X., Jameel, S., & Xu, G. (2022). Explainable depression detection with multi-aspect features using a hybrid deep learning model on social media. *World Wide Web*, *25*(1), 281–304. https://doi.org/10.1007/s11280-021-00992-2

55 Technology in food industry: Effect of website quality, perceived risk and subjective norms on consumer trust and purchase intention

Narinder Kaur[1], Shamily Jaggi[2], and Harvinder Singh[3]

[1]Research Scholar Mittal School of Business, Lovely Professional University, Punjab, India

[2]Professor Mittal School of Business, Lovely Professional University, Punjab, India

[3]Professor, School of Management, Maharaja Agresen University, Baddi, India

Abstract

The objective of this academic paper is to look at the connection between purchase intention and the factors that influence trust in using online food applications. It looks at the relationship between perceived website quality, subjective norms and perceived risk connection to online purchase intention. Data collection was done using an online survey (304 valid responses). A model was proposed using AMOS 22 (SEM). Data was gathered between July and September 2022. Results indicate a considerable relationship between subjective norms and perceived website quality and trust in online food services. The slope of the association between purchase intention and online shopping trust indicates a strong connection, although perceived risk indicates a negligible relationship between trust and perceived risk. This study enhances decision makers' knowledge of the important role that trust plays in online food services.

Keywords: Online food services, purchase intention, perceived risk, subjective norms, trust, website quality

Introduction

The rapid use of mobile devices and tablets is one of the key factors fueling the e-commerce market's explosive expansion. An expansion of e-commerce, mobile commerce involves the use of mobile devices for transactions. The explosive growth of online food services (OFS) has become a worldwide trend, and numerous nations already have at least one significant food distribution network. The advantages of OFS were made clear during the COVID-19 epidemic because these channels made it simple for customers to get ready-to-eat meals. Digital platform purchases are a crucial component of OFS. Customers place orders through a mobile app for food delivery from a variety of restaurants of serving as a bridge between consumers and restaurants, assists restaurants by managing delivery logistics. Prior studies on OFS focused on determining how different features of online food services affect consumer behavioral intentions, with particular attention paid to the courtesy of the delivery people, the hygiene of the prepared food, the food safety, the quality of the product received, the experience of consumers by Yeo et al. (2017), and online comments and opinions (Alalwan, 2020). Performance expectation is one of the most crucial aspects that customers consider when deciding whether to adopt OFS (Yeo et al., 2017). In addition, found that social influence and enjoyment are significant determinants of intention to use OFS.

Customers are still hesitant to order food online in some countries, despite the increase in internet usage and online food services around the world, because of security concerns by Regner and Riener, (2017), perceived risk by Pelaez et al. (2019), perceived website quality and trust by Hasan (2016). On the other hand, time savings and lower prices by Yeo et al. (2017), convenience, subjective norms by Hasbullah et al. (2016) professional guidance, and increased access to information are the driving forces behind online purchasing.

The limited research of the trust-building process and its linkages (Chang et al., 2013). Its considerable influence on internet culture, and intention toward online purchasing are some of the reasons for doing this study. Theoretically, this research contributes to the body of literature by offering information about the role of trust in the relationship between perceived website quality, perceived risk, subjective norms, and purchase intention.

Literature Review

Perceived risk

For the first time, Bauer (1960) outlined the two-dimensional structure of risk perception, notably uncertainty and negative outcomes. Previous study shows that the desire to purchase online things is negatively impacted by perceived risk.

[a]narinder.kaur500@gmail.com; [b]shamily.18688@lpu.co.in; [c]hsingh_07@hotmail.com

Additionally, researchers looked at the connection between perceived risk and trust straight and discovered a negative correlation (Damghanian et al., 2016).

H1:*Perceived risk has negative effect on consumer trust.*

Perceived website quality

Websites are essential to businesses' success because they serve as a route for consumer and business communication (Liang and Chen, 2009). Website design as a predictor of perceived service quality, whereas the majority of earlier researchers used perceived website quality as one of the predictors of the quality of an e-service, researchers used perceived website quality. of e-service quality. These investigators discovered a strong link between perceived website quality, and customer belief in online ordering (Gregg and Walczak, 2010).

H2: *Perceived website quality has positive effect on consumer trust.*

Subjective norms

The term "person's belief that most people who are significant to him believe that he should or shouldn't perform the action in issue" is used to describe subjective norms (Ajzen, 1991). Number of previous studies show relationship between subjective norms and trust (Hitosugi, 2011).

H3: *A subjective norm has positive effect on consumer trust.*

Trust

According to (Morgan and Hunt, 1994), trust indicates that a person has confidence in and perceives their transactional partners as trustworthy and reliable. Consumers may overcome their perceptions of fear and insecurity with the support of the trust (Harrison et al., 2002). Trust is therefore a crucial variable to consider when examining online consumers' purchase intentions.

H4:*Trust has positive effect on consumer purchase intention.*

Methodology and Sample Selection

Convenience sampling is used in this study, and measurement items are taken from earlier, established studies for assessing latent constructs. The measurement scale items of subjective norms and purchase intention were adopted from (Ajzen, 1991). The measurement scale items of trust and perceived website quality factors are adopted from Harrison et al. (2002) and perceived risk from Mitchell (1999). A total of 316 responses were received. A sample size of 304 acceptable replies was employed for data analysis. A seven-point Likert scale was adopted, with 1 signifying 'strongly disagree' and seven signifying 'strongly agree'. AMOS 22 was used to conduct confirmatory factor analysis on the measurement model. The structural model and the theoretical hypotheses were both tested using the AMOS.

There were 304 responses that were useful. Among all 47.3% of respondents were female and 52.6% were men in the sample. Ages ranged from 18–25%, 26–35%, 36–45%, and 46–55%. 43.75% users of 18–25 years use online food services. In term of order value 48.68% users of Rs. 101–500 spend on per orders through online food apps and 35.85% users were students.

Reliability and validity

Table 55.1 demonstrates that all reliability and validity met the suggested cut-off, CR > 0.7 and AVE > 0. 0.5.

Table 55.1 Validity metrics

	CR	*AVE*	*MSV*	*TR*	*PR*	*PWQ*	*SN*	*PI*
TR	0.775	0.538	0.052	**0.734**				
PR	0.763	0.519	0.017	0.131	**0.720**			
PWQ	0.811	0.589	0.052	0.228	0.244	**0.767**		
SN	0.840	0.567	0.024	0.155	0.049	0.092	**0.754**	
PI	0.850	0.655	0.037	0.193	-0.114	0.055	0.043	**0.810**

Source: Author's compilation

Note: TR-Trust, PR-Perceived risk, PWQ- Perceived website quality, SN- Subjective norms, PI-Purchase intention.

Fronell-Larcker criterion states that the correlation between the construct must be greater than the square root of the average variance extracted. In Table 1 all AVE values in bold are higher than the correlation coefficient between the constructs, so there is no discriminant validity issue in the study.

Cronbach's coefficients ranging from 0.714–0.857 confirmed the internal consistency of the measurements within each construct.

The link between the observed and unobserved parameters and the constructs was then identified using a first order CFA to determine if the chosen measures give a satisfactory fit to the data. Using AMOS 22, CFA was conducted on 17 items in the current investigation. A reasonable goodness of fit index was observed in the CFA data, degree of freedom is 1.285, GFI = .948, CFI = 0.983, TLI = 0.979, IFI = .983, RMSEA = 0.031) (Anderson and Gerbing, 1988). All the results are above the limits, which show the good fit between model and data collected from field.

Modling of Structural Equations

Hypothesis testing came after CFA as the next phase with the help of path analysis. In order to assess the model fit, six metrics were utilized, degree of freedom is 1.301, GFI = .946, CFI = 0.982, TLI = 0.978, IFI=.982, RMSEA = 0.032 evidence by Anderson and Gerbing (1988) all value are higher than the limits, which show good fit.

Table 2 describes the finding of path analysis to determine factors influencing trust and purchase intention in OFS measures among Delhi-NCR. As seen in Table 2, (hypotheses 1) were not support: perceived risk on trust (hypothesis 2, 3 and 4); perceived website quality and subjective norms on trust and trust on purchase intention supported.

Discussion and Conclusion

The study shows the perceived website quality and subjective norms significant influence among online food services. According to Gregg and Walczak (2010), key predictor of trust was found to be perceived website quality. The finding suggests that online shops have prioritized design, colors and real-time services while providing all necessary details to remove any uncertainty. The study finds no significant results between perceived risk and trust. As these results were in opposition to those of other research, it was demonstrated that perceived risk has no negative impact on trust in the context of online food services evidence by Damghanian et al. (2016). Further this insignificant output between perceived risk and trust was supported by (Bulsara and Vaghela, 2022). Previous studies also supported the subjective norms positive and significant towards trust (Hitosugi, 2011). Further study highlights that trust significantly and positive influence the purchase intention for online food application users for ordering food (Chiu et al., 2012).

Practical Contribution

In order to assist owners, executives, managers, and potential customers (decision-makers) understand the substantial impact of trust in online buying food, this paper presents a comprehensive view of important indicators against the context of a discussion on trust, perceived risk, perceived website quality, and subjective norms. This research enhances our knowledge of how website quality improvements may affect how potential consumers interact with the site and how website content can influence visitors' trust and intention to buy. For instance, the findings show that trust significantly influences the likelihood that a consumer would make a purchase in terms of website visits, rising online orders, sign-up, "rush to a website," favorable reviews, and marketing for online retailers on social media. Additionally, trust in online buying reduces the perceived risk.

Shortcomings and Future Road for Further Research

As a result, it may be viewed as a restriction when just a small number of factors are involved. Additionally, the size of the sample of prospective customers can be seen as a restriction. In future study may be extended to know the effect of demographic factors (gender and age) among online food services.

Table 55.2 Hypotheses results

Hypotheses		*Estimate*	*P-value*	*Results*
H1	PR→TR	.112	.124	**Not Support**
H2	PWQ→TR	.139	.003	Support
H3	SN→TR	.130	.044	Support
H4	TR→PI	.169	.003	Support

Source: Author's compilation

Note: PR-Perceived Risk, PWQ-Perceived website quality, SN- Subjective Norms, TR-Trust, PI- Purchase Intention

References

Ajzen, I. (1991). The theory of planned behavior. *Organizational Behavior and Human Decision Processes*, 50(2), 179–211.

Alalwan, A. A. (2020). Mobile food ordering apps: An empirical study of the factors affecting customer e-satisfaction and continued intention to reuse. *International Journal of Information Management*, 50, 28–44

Anderson, J. C. & Gerbing, D. W. (1988). Structural equation modeling in practice: A review and recommended two-step approach. *Psychological Bulletin*. 103(3), 411–423

Bulsara, H. P. & Vaghela, P. S. (2022). Millennials' online purchase intention towards consumer electronics: Empirical evidence from India. *Indian Journal of Marketing*, 52(2), 53–70.

Chang, M. K., Cheung, W., & Tang, M. (2013). Trust online: Interactions among trust building mechanisms. *Information and Management*. 50(7), 439–445.

Chiu, C. M. (2012). Re-examining the influence of trust on online repeat purchase intention: The moderating role of habit and its antecedents. *Decision Support Systems*. 53(4), 835–845.

Constantinides, E. (2004). Influencing the online consumer's behavior: The Web experience. *Internet Research*. 14(2): 111–126.

Damghanian, H., Zarei, A., & Siahsarani, M. A. (2016). Impact of Perceived Security on Trust, Perceived Risk, and Acceptance of Online Banking in Iran. *Journal of Internet Commerce*. 15(3): 214–238.

Gregg, D. G. & Walczak, S. (2010). The relationship between website quality, trust and price premiums at online auctions. *Electronic Commerce Research*, 10(1): 1–25.

Harrison, M. D., Choudhury, V., & Kacmar, C. (2002). The impact of initial consumer trust on intentions to transact with a web site: A trust building model. *Journal of Strategic Information Systems*, 11(3): 297–323.

Hasan, B. (2016). Perceived irritation in online shopping: The impact of website design characteristics. *Computers in Human Behavior*, 54, 224–230.

Hasbullah, N. A. (2016). The relationship of attitude, subjective norm and website usability on consumer intention to purchase online: An evidence of Malaysian youth. *Procedia Economics and Finance*, 35, 493 – 502

Hitosugi, C. (2011). Trust on the web: The power of subjective norm across cultures. *Proceedings of the 15th Cross-Cultural Research Conference*. Brigham Young University, Hawaii.

Liang, C. J. & Chen, H. J. (2009). A study of the impacts of website quality on customer relationship performance. *Total Quality Management and Business Excellence*, 20(9), 971–988

Mitchell, V. (1999). Consumer perceived risk: conceptualizations and models. *European Journal of Marketing*, 33, 163–195.

Morgan, R. M. & Hunt, S. D. (1994). The commitment-trust theory of relationship marketing. *Journal of Marketing*. 58(3), 20–38.

Pelaez, A., Chen, C. W., & Chen, Y. X. (2019). Effects of perceived risk on intention to purchase: A meta-analysis. *Journal of Computer Information Systems*, 59(1), 73–84

Regner, T. & Riener, G. (2017). Privacy is precious: On the attempt to lift anonymity on the internet to increase revenue. *Journal of Economics and Management Strategy*, 26(2), 318–336

Yeo, V. C. S., Goh, S. K., & Rezaei, S. (2017). Consumer experiences, attitude and behavioral intention toward online food delivery (OFD) services. *Journal of Retailing and Consumer Services*, 35(2), 150–162.

56 Artificial intelligence as a tool in the visual effects and film industry

Hardeep Singh[1,a], *Ajay Rastogi*[2,b], *and Kamaljeet Kaur*[3,c]

[1]Research Scholar, Chandigarh University, India

[2]Assistant Professor, Lovely Professional University, Punjab, India

[3]Professor, Chandigarh University, India

Abstract

With the advancements in artificial intelligence (AI) technology, it has become an important factor in visual effects (VFX) production and the film industry. AI when combined with machine learning has the potential to transform VFX production to the next level. In this study, we aim to analyze and summarize the current use of artificial intelligence in the Film Industry and VFX. Artificial intelligence has helped film directors and producers in areas running from script writing, motion picture, and character animation to final film composition and tracking. This research summarizes the different areas, be it pre-production, production, or post-production, where AI has been extensively applied in the filmmaking process. In addition, we have also done a survey which consists of a questionnaire indicating how AI is useful for VFX and the film industry in present and future. The results show that AI in filmmaking can help in improving the quality of film production and can ensure better box-office returns.

Keywords: Artificial intelligence, visual effects, filmmaking, film production process

Introduction

The current digital revolution in the visual effects (VFX) industry is artificial intelligence (AI) and machine learning (ML). Recent advancements have witnessed AI's dramatic coming of age in the film industry, from 3D modeling to VFX, ultra-realistic CGI to box office predictions. AI and VFX are extensively used in tracking and match moving, 3D simulation, rendering, Mocap, animation, image processing, roto, paint, and compositing (Qu et al., 2021).

"Autotune", which automatically corrects voice into nation mistakes, is one of the AI-based solutions that has existed for more than two decades. (Pataranutaporn et al., 2021). In the 1980s and 1990s, films such as "Star Wars", "Superman III", "Wargames", and 'Star Trek' featured AI technology. However, the invention of CGI in the 2000s sparked an Artificial intelligence explosion in the film industry (Krishna, 2022). Artificial Intelligence (2001), Matrix Reloaded (2003, Transformers (2007), Iron Man (2008), Eagle Eye (2008) and Her (2013) are among the films that captured the public's attention with their memorable depictions of AI. Indian Cinema didn't keep out of the contest either, as it produced Robot (2010) and Ra. One (2011), Bahubali (2017), Zero (2018) and RRR (2022) use AI technology in graphics

Figure 56.1 shows the application of AI in the VFX film industry at different steps of the filmmaking process. Be it pre-production, production, or post-production step, AI has shown its importance in easing almost every task involved in the film industry including from script writing to final film production and promotion.

Since AI has been applied in various aspects of the film industry, it is of utmost relevance to summarize the role of artificial intelligence as a tool in the filmmaking process. To the best of our knowledge, none of the studies in the existing literature has summarized this work so far. Therefore, in this paper, the role of AI in VFX technology for making films is highlighted to understand the current trends and needs of the film industry. Moreover, a brief analysis of some of the films is performed to summarize how AI and VFX gained popularity in making films (Song, 2021). In addition, to validate the role of AI in VFX and the film industry, we have gone through a survey which consists of several questions indicating how AI has been used in films to improve the quality, production, and future of the film industry. Results of this survey show that majority of the respondents are in agreement that AI has the power to improve production quality which results in the growth of film making industry.

The remaining parts of this paper are structured in the following manner. In section 2, the researcher conducts a concise literature review. Section 3 discusses the utilization of AI in various areas of filmmaking. Section 4 describes survey methodology. In section 5, results and findings are presented. Section 6 finally concludes this work.

[a]hardeepvfx1@gmail.com; [b]ajay.27859@lpu.co.in; [c]kamaljeet.7384@cumail.in

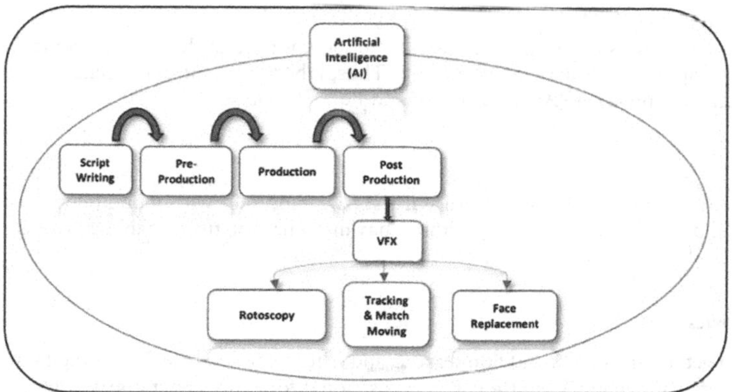

Figure 56.1 AI in different areas of the filmmaking production process

Literature Review

Rotoscoping is still mainly a manual procedure that requires time and equipment. Recent machine learning and image segmentation research claim to speed up or automate digital roto and paint. Intel and Laika teams found a technique to leverage data from five finished images combined with renderings (Stringer et al., 2020).

At the level of data analysis, a prediction of a movie's profitability is made to help support investment choices made during early phases of film production. The proposed system can extract multiple different sorts of features by using data from a wide variety of data sources. It is shown how it may be used to provide recommendations for a cast to maximize the amount of money made (Lash and Zhao, 2016).

Recent years have seen the development of AI-based business models for media companies. The 'AI activity model' has been considered in this topic. It is recommended to apply AI to turn conventional media companies into effective digital media enterprises. Activities that make up the efficiency model are personalization based on home equipment and suggesting media content (Song, 2019).

As AI is a broad term, its definition depends on the application and public perception. Wang recommends four requirements for a 'good functioning definition': simplicity, correctness, adherence to mainstream use, and constructive research. Artificial intelligence is a system designed to interact with complex environments by receiving and processing data (Samoili et al., 2021).

If AI can automate the majority of the process, filmmakers will be able to focus on more creative and human-centered aspects. This article analyses the movie-making pipeline or process, demonstrating that most film directors take on the most onerous and complex pre-production tasks. The advancement of artificial intelligence and its applications in the film business are examined. It also assesses the purpose, sorts, contents, styles, and technological advancements of movies. (Datta and Goswami, 2021).

AI as a Tool in VFX and Filmmaking

In this section, we discuss various areas where AI has been applied effectively and successfully in the filmmaking process. Many recent movies have used AI along with machine and deep learning and were nominated for prestigious awards in VFX category. AI is in fact considered the *future of image synthesis* which has revolutionized the VFX industry.

AI in script writing

Choosing an efficient script is key to the success of a movie. AI helps filmmakers design new screenplays. Machine learning algorithms scan enormous volumes of movie screenplays to create unique scripts. Using this technique, filmmakers can easily save time and money (Sweetser and Wiles, 2002)

AI is a facilitator for pre-production

AI may assist manage timetables, discovering storyline-appropriate venues, and other pre-production tasks. AI will automate filming schedules based on actor availability, saving time, and increasing efficiency. AI algorithms can assess script settings and propose real filming spots, saving time and money (Song, 2021).

AI in production

Film professionals are constantly seeking methods to shorten the tedious production process. Robots can control cameras depending on settings, handle 3D printing, and carve items and sets. Thus, laborious, time-consuming procedures are automated, synchronized, and completed precisely (Anantrasirichai and Bull, 2021).

AI in post-production

Post-production requires innovative and repetitive mechanical procedures. AI might help with monotonous tasks in post-production. Deep learning, NLP, and picture recognition algorithms may minimize job time, enabling professionals to focus on creativity (Jayanthiladevi et al., 2020).

AI is useful for the success of VFX movies

In the modern era, everybody wants to get about success and flop reasons and features of a movie. In this digital world, AI can evaluate a film's script to estimate its revenue. Even though computational forecasts aren't always right, major VFX film studios are interested. Warner Bros. uses Cinelytic's AI engine to predict box office performance. Sony Pictures employed Script Book, an AI-based film prediction system, to examine 62 movies.

AI is best for the casting of actors

AI auditions help speed up casting performers. AI systems search for actors based on criteria and visual descriptions. When given huge volumes of data detailing actors' facial characteristics in different moods, the computer may overlay the actor's digital face on a body double to keep authentic expression (Momot, 2022).

AI for character replacement face in VFX

Deep fakes are the most recent development in computer imagery. A deep fake program is an AI that is built from convolutional neural networks (CNN), autoencoders, and generative adversarial networks (GAN). It is designed to replace the facial characteristics of one person in a recorded video with those of another person (Anantrasirichai and Bull, 2021).

AI in rotoscopy

Rotoscoping extracts objects from a shot's backdrop and sometimes we use green and blue screens that have been utilized to divide items since the early animation days. Without these tools, computers can now extract text and objects from a photo. Others achieve this by scanning the photo for faces and identifying people. Then, the program tracks the individual from the photo (Kudrle et al., 2020).

AI in tracking and match moving

Tracking and matching moving is a vital part of VFX movies because without it we are not able to do Camera track, object track and body tracking. The use of deep learning technology for camera tracking, object tracking and body tracking has proven more successful, especially when monitoring lots of thing sat once in a video (Condorelli et al., 2020).

Table 56.1 provides a summary of some selected films released in past where AI has been used along with VFX technology at different production steps. It can be seen from this Table 56.1 that movies which use AI and VFX have got higher rating from critic and audience as compared to those which do not use this technology. Moreover, AI and VFX have been applied at almost all the production steps in almost all the top rated films as shown below in Table 56.1.

Research Methodology

To know about the current interest of our target audience towards the VFX film industry, we perform a survey which consists of a questionnaire filled by those respondents who know very well about VFX, Film and AI. The sample of 108 respondents was taken into consideration with random sampling throw Google Forms.

Survey questionnaire and data collection

Data is collected using a well-structured questionnaire by an online survey throw google forms, as well as secondary data, has been used. The following questions were asked from the respondents:
Q1: Do you agree that the use of AI in VFX and filmmaking results in the growth of the film industry?
Q2: Do you agree that the use of AI enhances the quality of VFX Film making?
Q3: Do you agree that AI is the future of the VFX film industry?
Q4: Which of the following technology would you like to see in movies?
Q5: Do you agree that AI and VFX have the power to change the sentiments of the audience towards a movie?
Q6: Do you agree that AI and VFX are preferred over the story of a movie?

Results Summarization and Findings

This section presents the findings of our survey. Overall, 95% of people agree that the use of AI and VFX can result in better box-office returns for film professionals, out of which 45% were in strong agreement (Figure 56.2A). It is evident

Table 56.1 AI and VFX technology used in selected films (RTR: Rotten Tomatoes Rating, CR: Critic Rating, AR: Audience Rating)

Name of film	*Artificial intelligence*	*Rotoscopy*	*Tracking & Match moving*	*Face replacement*	*VFX technology*	*RTR*		*Year*
						CR	*AR*	
Green Zone	✗	✓	✓	✗	✓	53%	56%	2010
How Do You Know	✗	✗	✗	✗	✗	31%	25%	2010
Her	✓	✓	✓	✓	✓	94%	82%	2013
Ex Machina	✓	✓	✓	✓	✓	92%	86%	2014
The Jungle Book	✓	✓	✓	✓	✓	94%	86%	2016
BEIRUT Beirut	✗	✓	✓	✗	✓	82%	56%	2018
Destroyer	✗	✗	✗	✗	✓	74%	50%	2018
Avengers: End Game	✓	✓	✓	✓	✓	94%	88%	2019
I am Mother	✓	✓	✓	✓	✓	91%	75%	2019
Spider- Man: No Way Home	✓	✓	✓	✓	✓	93%	98%	2021

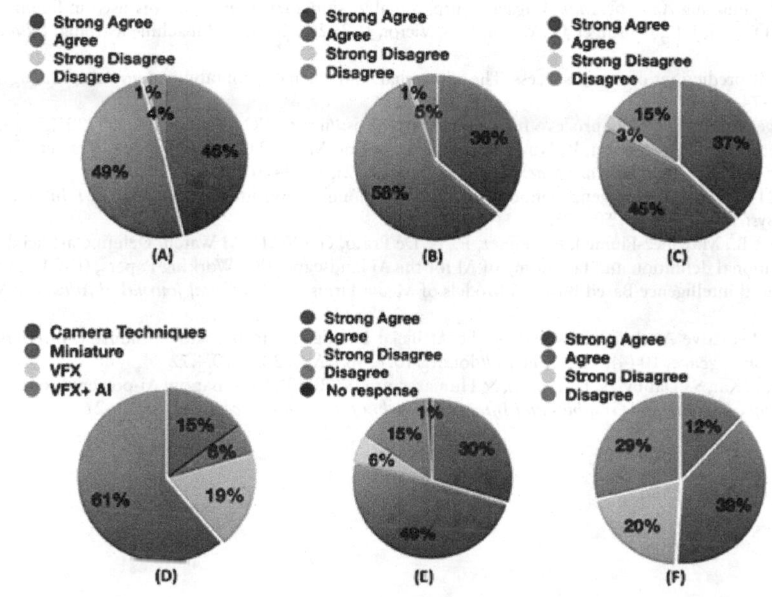

Figure 56.2 Results analysis of survey ((A) to (F) represents the responses of respondents on questions Q1 to Q6)

from Figure 56.2(B), that a large proportion of people are looking forward to the use of AI in VFX as it delivers quality output in less amount of time. People believe that AI will do better in every aspect of filmmaking. The results also indicate that the audience is excited to witness the wonders created by AI and believes that AI is the future of VFX (Figure 56.2 C). The technology that most people would like to prefer in future movies is none of the other, but VFX+AI, as can be verified from Figure 56.2(D). When asked whether AI and VFX are preferred over a story, more than half of our respondents choose AI and VFX over a story (Figure 56.2F). However, a significant number of respondents (49%) disagreed about Q6 of our questionnaire, they believe that story also has equal importance in a good quality film production. We are in an era where visual effects decide the fate of the film. The impact of the VFX on the audience is so significant that an excellent visual effect at the right time brings out the audience's emotions (Figure 56.2E). From the above results, we can say that AI is helping the film industry by enhancing the overall filmmaking process, saving time and resources, and ultimately results in increasing profits. The movie business is expanding much faster than we could have ever imagined with the aid of such cutting-edge technology.

Conclusion

This study discusses various applications of AI in visual effects and filmmaking. Film professionals can leverage AI is used in many different parts of making movies, from pre-production to production to post-production. The role of artificial intelligence at various stages of filmmaking is summarized and explained. To know about the current interest of the audience towards AI, VFX and the film industry, a survey is taken, results of which indicate that the majority of the respondent's favor AI and VFX for better quality films and growth in film production. Respondents from our survey also confirmed that AI and VFX are the future of the film industry.

References

Anantrasirichai, N.& Bull, D. (2021). Artificial intelligence in the creative industries: a review. *Artificial Intelligence Review*, 168.

Condorelli, F., Rinaudo, F., Salvadore, F., & Tagliaventi, S. (2020). A match-moving method combining AI and SFM algorithms in historical film footage. *International Archives of the Photogrammetry, Remote Sensing & Spatial Information Sciences*, 43.

Datta, A. & Goswami, R. (2021). The film industry leaps into artificial intelligence: Scope and challenges by the filmmakers. *Rising Threats in Expert Applications and Solutions*, (pp. 665–670). Springer, Singapore.

Jayanthiladevi, A., Raj, A. G., Narmadha, R., Chandran, S., Shaju, S., & Prasad, K. K. (2020). AI in video analysis, production and streaming delivery. *Journal of Physics: Conference Series*, 1712(1), 012014.

Krishna,S.(2022).HowAIisusedinfilmmaking.*AnalyticsIndiaMagazine*.https://analyticsindiamag.com/how-ai-is-used-in-filmmaking/.

Kudrle, S., Belton, J., Edwards, T., O'Neal, J. E., Pensinger, G., Welch, J., & Victor, J. (2020). 14 AI and machine learning. *Education*, 914, 205–2379.

Lash, M. T. & Zhao, K. (2016). Early predictions of movie success: The who, what, and when of profitability. *Journal of Management Information Systems*, 33(3), 874–903.

Momot, I. (2022). Artificial intelligence in filmmaking process: future scenarios. https://urn.fi/URN:NBN:fi:amk-2022052712497

Pataranutaporn, P., Danry, V., Leong, J., Punpongsanon, P., Novy, D., Maes, P., & Sra, M. (2021). AI-generated characters for supporting personalized learning and well-being. *Nature Machine Intelligence*, 3(12), 1013–1022.

Qu, M., Liu, Y., & Feng, Y. (2021). Artificial intelligence empowered visual communication graphic design. *2021 International Conference on Networking Systems of AI*, (pp. 50–53).

Samoili, S., Cobo, M. L., Delipetrev, B., Martinez-Plumed, F., Gomez, E., & De Prato, G. (2021). AI Watch. Defining artificial intelligence 2.0. towards an operational definition and taxonomy of AI for the AI landscape. JRC Working Papers, (JRC126426).

Song, M. (2019). A Study on Artificial Intelligence Based Business Models of Media Firms. *International Journal of Advanced Smart Convergence*, 8(2), 56–67.

Song, M. (2021). A Study on the Predictive Analytics Powered by the Artificial Intelligence in the Movie Industry. *International Journal of Advanced Smart Convergence*, 10 (4), 72–83. https://doi.org/10.7236/IJASC.2021.10.4.72

Stringer, J., Sundararajan, N., Pina, J., Kar, S., Dabby, N. L., Lin, A., & Hilmarsdottir, S. (2020). Rotomation: Ai-powered rotoscoping at laika. *Special Interest Group on Computer Graphics and Interactive Techniques Conference Talks*, (pp. 1–2).

57 A systematic review on performance enhancement methods in LTE-A downlink

Mandeep Singh Ramdev[1,a] *and Rohit Bajaj*[2,b]

[1]Research Scholar, Department of CSE, Chandigarh University, India

[2]Associate Professor, Department of CSE, Chandigarh University, India

Abstract

The evolution of LTE to LTE-Advanced (LTE-A) (version 10) is motivated by the need to provide faster data rates, improved radio resource utilization, reduced distribution costs, decreased latency, and unbroken mobility. In order to improve user connectivity with the ultrafast 4G multi-class traffic network, such as VoIP, video streaming, video conferencing, online gaming, etc., backward compatibility and conventional technology have been combined to create converged IP architecture. This study intends to review the downlink performance of the LTE-A network by applying the best solutions for efficient CSI information, resource management, load balancing, and CBR during hand-off, exponential, and video traffic. By dividing performance enhancement techniques in the LTE-A networks into four groups, these research issues are highlighted.

Keywords: LTE-A, scheduling, downlink, resource allocation

Introduction

In order to meet the requirements, set forth by ITU-R for International Mobile Telecommunication-Advanced (IMT-A), LTE has started to evolve in the form of LTE-Advanced (LTE-A) (Shin et al., 2013). The LTE Release-10 also refers as LTE-A. The goal is to link the network closer to the user in order to provide high speed peaks, more output and coverage, low latency, and lower costs while also enhancing user experience. A backward-compatible version of LTE is LTE-A (Parikh and Basu, 2011). In contrast, LTE Advanced UE can run in the LTE Release 8 network, allowing LTE Version 8 UE to operate in the LTE-A 10 network versions. A self-organizing network, higher latency, better power efficiency, sophisticated multi-antenna technology, and other aspects will allow LTE to provide some level of security in the future without typically conflicting with the necessity for backward compatibility.

LTE-A was supposed to accomplish a number of objectives, including improved spectrum flexibility, decreased latency, increased data throughput, increased reliability of data transmission, and improved communication efficiency. When we need more internet speed, the data rate needs to be raised. The time it takes for data to travel from its source to its destination and be processed is known as latency. Reduced latency implies that less time should be needed for data to travel and process. Spectrum allotment should be more flexible, if not more so. This implies that data transmission must be dependable, and we want dependable data transfer, particularly near cell boundaries.

LTE-A Architecture

LTE-A promises to boost network capacity and user experience by bringing the network closer to the user. In order to offer end customers a higher quality of service (QoS), LTE-Enhanced depends on advanced topology. The E-UTRAN and EPC are the two main parts of the LTE-A Evolved Packet System (EPS), which are shown in Figure 57.1. The Developed Terrestrial Universal Access Network consists of two primary parts (E-UTRAN). The only components of E-UTRAN are eNodeBs, which support user plane and control planes for UEs and perform all tasks related to the air interface, such as access control and radio resource planning. The user plane means a group of protocols used to support network-wide user data transfers, whereas the control plane refers to the group of protocols used for monitoring user data transfers and for managing the UE-Network connection. Certain functions include delivery, service set-up, resource management, etc.

The evolved universal terrestrial radio access network (eUTRAN), or eNodeB, is the only node that makes up the LTE architecture. It derives from the word 'NodeB', which initially referred to the UMTS (3G) base station and contained a 'e' that stood for 'evolved'. Figure 57.1 shows how the eNodeB interacts with the UE directly on one side and the Evolved packet Core (EPC), which is made up of the MME, PGW, SGW, and PCRF on the other.

The base station, or eNodeB, is the most intricate LTE-A node. The Remote Radio Head (RRH), which is made up of antennas, is one of the two main components of the eNodeB. The most noticeable components of the mobile network go by the name Remote Radio Unit (RRU). All signals sent or received over the air interface must also be modulated

[a]mandeep.singh.phd@gmail.com; [b]rohit.rick@gmail.com

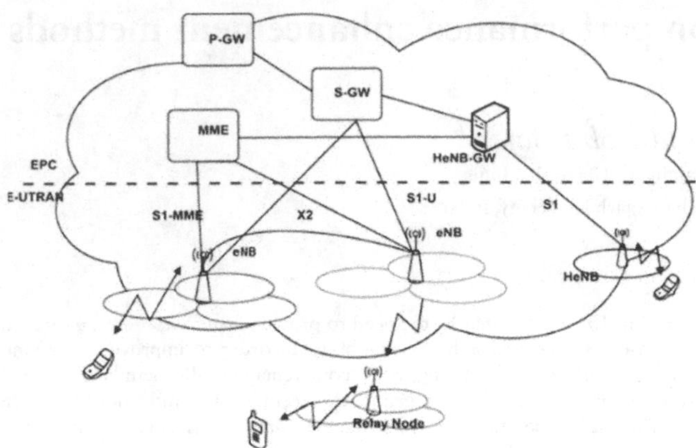

Figure 57.1 LTE-Advanced architecture

and demodulated by them. The second component is the Base Band Unit (BBU), which is made up of digital modules and serves as the interface to the core network via a fast backhaul link. It processes all signals sent and received over the air interface.

Performance Enhancement Techniques

The purpose of this study is to improve the downlink functionality of LTE-A networks. In order for the system to adapt to the limitations of a radio channel and dramatically improve performance, LTE-A heavily relies on MU-MIMO, which necessitates some amount of channel state information (CSI) at the base station. In a multi-user setting, the goal of multi-antenna techniques is to provide spatially multiplexed data streams to a number of users while utilizing all of a MIMO's free levels. The information is based on the stations that collect CSIs from each UE in order to allocate resources. The suggestions for enhancing the performance of LTE-A based networks are provided below.

Channel State Information Estimation

Lu et al. (2010). proposed the framework for feedback, along with related precoding and scheduling schemes that enhanced the SU and MU-MIMO feedback accuracy. The most accurate measurement is the challenge. The suggested technique is not responsive to the codebook's lower peak level and could offer added benefits when combined with spatial information, albeit it will add a little extra expense.

Caire et al. (2010) studied the multi input-multiple output (MIMO) transmission channel and determined ergodic speeds that could be obtained from receivers by means of the downlink learning and forwarded the transmitter for channel feedback.

The performance and efficiency of the MU-MIMO downlink network were studied by Kumai et al. (2017). A new SINR approximation method was proposed to improve speed matching and make MU-MIMO technology more effective by utilizing the quantized CSI available at the base station. Badic et al. (2012) attempted to familiarize CQI MU-MIMO prediction for LTE networks. The topic under discussion is the accurate prediction of CQI. A detailed analysis and presentation of the connection between channel conditions and CQI signalization. Regarding the CQI MU-MIMO prediction, the balance between performance enhancement and feedback overload is also looked at.

The reduced complexity, optimal CSI feedback algorithm proposed for LTE by Singh et al. (2013). Identify and manipulate the LTE precoder codebook structure such that the precoder array computation is best optimized for the lemma of the reversal array.

In LTE-A downlink multi-user transmission, the dynamic switch from single-user (SU) transmission to multi-user transmission (MU) occurs without the usage of higher-level signals, according to Määttänen et al. (2012). Dynamic switchover between SU-MIMO and MU-MIMO is the problem at hand. The interference will be lessened if the quantization takes place slowly.

Vertical Handoff Decision Making

The various needs for a vertical transfer process in the LTE network were identified by Gondara and Kadam (2011). The different transmission requirements include higher bandwidth, less transmission time, less power consumption, less price, load balance, protection, RSS, the customer preferences, and throughput. The author assesses existing vertical transfer techniques against the different specified requirements.

The transmittal approach in femtocell networks is investigated by Ulvan et al. (2013) taking both kinds of transmission into account: horizontal and vertical. Three scenarios: handover, handover and interFAP evaluate the distribution process based on 3GPP LTE.

The technique for calculating the transmission necessities in two stages of WiFi cell was proposed by Abdoulaziz et al. (2012). By using this method, the estimate threshold and journey time are set. Based on the RSS and MT speed readings, the distance travelled is calculated. The time threshold is determined using network characteristics such the WLAN cell range, the transmission delay, and the likelihood of a permissible transmission failure or the chance of an unnecessary transmission.

The description of mobility was given by Ismail and Nordin (2014). A management framework for a multi-home mobility protocol that emphasizes decision-making methods, details some air interface specifications, and evaluates various handoff techniques.

The handoff management technique proposed by Meetei and George (2011) included a predictor of the next cell of the UE and the best handover time. A predictive model uses the previously saved mobility model for the implementation of the forecast is used to construct the forecast portion.

In the LTE-A networks, Huang et al. (2015) focuses on the multi-traffic equilibrium threshold process. These algorithms are built to resolve the inconsistency between the need for broad network bandwidth and the lack of spectral resources by reconfiguring the transfer thresholds to cell load.

The algorithm for vertical transfer decision for wireless 4G networks has developed by Sun et al. (2011). Link time, QoS settings, mobility and location information, network access, and signal load are all taken into consideration in this work. The network makes the decision on the vertical transition.

In the light of the vertical transmission characteristics from UMTS to WiMAX networks, Janevski et al. (2011) were testing various real-time video streams in different wireless networks, and the reverse. The IEEE 802.21 protocol is used for vertical transmission and the measurement of output statistics by means of real-time video. The consequence is that the delivering time and the output between UMTS and WiMAX networks increase as the mobile user speed increases.

Load balancing

Cooperative's inter-domain traffic balancing technique sought to lower the Het-Net multi-effective domain's resource cost and lower interference in the same channel (Kumar et al., 2017). First, the idea of multidomain in Het-Net is introduced, and the suggested traffic balancing system incorporates interference on the same channel. In order to reduce the actual cost of resources, the traffic balancing problem is therefore represented as an optimization problem for multi-domain traffic sources. The average cell efficiency and the cell edge efficiency, however, are not actually improved.

Dynamic hysteresis control was proposed by Li et al. (2012). Load balancing and transfer parameter optimization are regarded in this approach as facets of the self-organizing network (SON) that can allow better coordination. This strategy, however, suffers from a lack in transmission.

Li et al. (2012) introduced an LTE virtualization platform allowing spectrum sharing) and a multi-eNB and multi-VO (virtual operator) dynamic load balancing framework. Network virtualization and load balances strategies may support LTE networks.

The min-max load balancing system was designed by Min et al. (2012) to minimize the radio resources needed by the cell fully loaded. Multicast services are distributed in single frequency network (SFN) mode and unicast services in point-to-point (PTP) mode for hybrid mixed multicast and unicast services.

Kaur and Bajaj (2015) proposed to include a clear handover for broadcast/multi-channel sessions via heterogeneous networks and extensions via the new Media Independent Broadcast Multicast Service Center (MIBM-SC) network including 27 architectural changes to the MBMS and MIIS architectures.

Wang et al. (2010) proposed the restrained network structure and a functional algorithm known as Heaviest-First Load Balancing (HFLB). The network can achieve a much better charge balancing using the HFLB algorithm while retaining the same network output at a slightly higher price than the normal signal strength-based transfer algorithm. Although in the mobile scenario, the load balance index is minimal, this approach only takes into account a load balance between cells, leading to a multitude of transmissions.

Altrad and Muhaidat (2013) suggested a universal load balance technique to dynamically help overloaded cells. It is built on cluster methods and appropriate for LTE, WiMAX, and GSM as well as all other wireless technologies. For each system cell, the algorithm can be automatically activated and tested as needed. It can be fully or partially dispersed. It's also conceivable. The activation time of this algorithm will be set by the operator; because changes below are gradual, quick SON techniques are not required. Signal overload is drastically reduced since the load from an overloaded cell is distributed in the following cells in a single step.

Hao et al. (2013) suggested a 3GPP SON mobility load balancing (MLB) approach where a user's cell could be selected to perform the load balancing, not function as the cell with a maximum power obtained. A single MLB algorithm for the LTE network is presented in this article. However, the load would be more unbalanced at higher arrival rates.

Resource allocation for multiclass traffic

Zhou et al. (2013) introduced the dynamic resource allocation method to enhance performance, low-latency machine-type communications (LTE/LTE-A) with a contention-based random access (CBA). In this procedure, the likelihood of an event being caused by a CBA transmission has first been assessed, and the latency has then been ascertained by measuring the unit. When the approximate latency of the CBA resources met the application's QoS criteria, the CBA resources were enhanced.

In order to detect the efficiency of the allocation of resources for real time/delay tolerant applications Rezaei et al. (2015) suggested a new equity index. A new approach to the distribution of capital could be suggested by 25. A variety of methods are available for allocating mobile network resources using an honesty index to assess performance. For each application, an acceptable utility function is identified and the necessary QoS is met by resolving the related optimization issue.

In order to boost the QoS of multimedia services in the LTE downlink networks, Iturralde et al. (2012) suggested a two-tier resource allocation system. This is a solution which combines cooperative theory of games, a virtual token mechanism and the EXP-RULE algorithm. The system is structured to create coalitions between power groups, using cooperative game theory, as in the case of the bankruptcy and Shapley's value, to allocate bandwidth equally.

Abdel-Rahman et al. (2015) proposed new joint stochastic channels and BS allocation schemes that take the uncertainty of channel accessibility into consideration. First, two static joint assignment models were created. It is recognised as Het-SMKP1 and Het-SMKP. The adaptable model helps you to correct the initial allocation of resources.

Chadchan and Akki (2011) proposed priority ladder technology (PS) with priority assignment and retention (ARP). This approach indicates that the minimum level of services (QoS) of all low priority active PABs must be prevented on a priority scale (PS) (LPPs). The sacrifice of QoS by high-priority PABs is restricted to the minimum QoS (Singh et al., 2022).

Samia et al. (2016) proposed an algorithm focused on cooperative theory of games, intended to increase efficiency and fairness in radio distribution. The simulations show that as the users guarantee a minimum QoS requirement, the proposed algorithm increases the QoS level of the system more effectively than all other algorithms.

Serge and Liu (2016) made recommendations for the best resource distribution. In this method, two variations of the Queue Based Control (QBC) technique are given. Version 1 and Version 2 of QBC are both in use. When QBC versions 1 and 2 are compared to one another, QBC version 1 is more efficient at data loss and has higher latency than QBC version 2 and QBC version 2. Better power consumption efficiency when compared to QBC 1 edition (Paware, 2019).

Qian et al. (2009) focused on a RAC scheme for the control of long-term evolutionary systems multi-class facilities (LTE). The capability of the device is evaluated by optimizing the number of registered users. Furthermore the author introduced a combined complete model of sharing and virtual resource partitioning, and built a resource restriction consumption scheme in the proposed RAC scheme, in order to address the optimization problem (Ramdev et al., 2019). Nevertheless the user preferences are not considered and the equal distribution of resources to users is not relevant to this system.

An effective algorithm for assessing applicants and choosing the optimum user set has been offered by Ferdosian et al. (2016) to maximize device efficiency without having to increase the bandwidth capacity that is available. The greedy backpack method, which is based on the fractional backpack issue, is regarded as the best way to allocate resources. A balance between performance and QoS is achieved by offering the class-specific classification feature, which combines throughput and service quality characteristics defined for each application.

A proportional fair based iPF algorithm was also proposed by authors which increased the performance of existing systems by a considerable amount while scheduling is being used in Remote Radio Head in eNodeB. The following graph shows the performance comparison of existing and proposed work at 100 TTL.

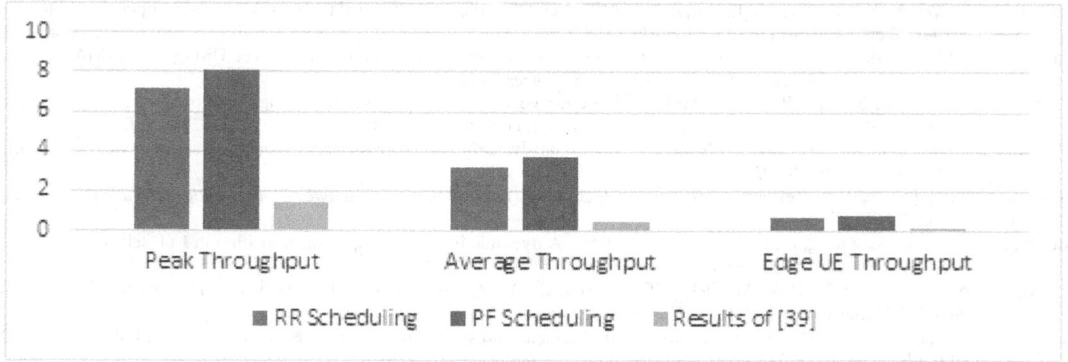

Figure 57.2 Performance comparison of existing and proposed work in RRH scheduling

Conclusion

After the extensive literature review, it can be concluded that using the CSI hierarchical feedback method, this method minimizes the overload of feedback if the channel slowly changes. The number of levels defined in the hierarchical structure increases coded library size, which in turn improves the MU-MIMO system's performance effectively. The network also provides the best modulation and coding rates for the user using the SINR approach technique. However Vertical Handoff Decision Making also provides good support in the terms of lower power consumption and less transmission time but it always needs a higher bandwidth otherwise the end user experience will be below par. Load Balancing techniques can also help improve the output of the LTE-A based networks but optimization of Load Balancing algorithms is a bottleneck. Resource allocation for multiclass traffic is a very effective strategy for network optimization. It is very successfully used in other wireless networks too. The results of this algorithm in LTE-A based networks are promising (Ramdev et al., 2022).

References

Abdel-Rahman, M. J., Raheem, A. B., & MacKenzie, A. B. (2015). Stochastic resource allocation in opportunistic LTE-A networks with heterogeneousself-interference cancellation capabilities. *IEEE International Symposium on Dynamic Spectrum Access Networks*, (pp. 200–208).

Abdoulaziz, I. H., Renfa, L., & Fanzi, Z. (2012). Handover necessity estimation for 4G heterogeneous networks. *International Journal of Information Sciences and Techniques*, 2(1), 1–13.

Ali, A. H. & Nazir, M. (2019). Finding a pareto optimal solution for a multi-objective problem of managing radio resources in LTE-A systems: A QoS aware algorithm. *Wireless Personal Communications*, 107(4), 1661–1685.

Altrad, O. & Muhaidat, S. (2013). Load balancing based on clustering methods for LTE networks. *Journal of Selected Areas in Telecommunications*, 3(2).

Badic, B, Balraj, R, Scholand. T, Bai. Z. & Iwelski. S. (2012). Analysis of CQI prediction for MU-MIMO in LTE systems. *IEEE 75th Vehicular Technology Conference*, (pp. 6–9).

Caire, G., Jindal, N., Kobayashi, M., & Ravindran, N. (2010). Multiuser MIMO Achievable Rates With Downlink Training and Channel State Feedback. *IEEE Transactions on Information Theory*, 56(6).

Chadchan, S. M. & Akki, C. B. (2011). Priority-Scaled Preemption of Radio Resources for 3GPP LTE Networks. *International Journal of Computer Theory and Engineering*, 3(6).

Ferdosian, N., Othman, M., Ali, B. M., Kweh, & Lun, Y. (2016). Greedy-knapsack algorithm for optimal downlink resource allocation in LTE networks. *Wireless Networks*.

Gondara, M. K. & Kadam, S. (2011). Requirements of vertical handoff mechanism in 4G wireless network. *International Journal of Wireless & Mobile Networks*, 3(2), pp. 18–27.

Hao, W., Nan, L., Zhihang, L., Ping, W., Zhiwen, P., & Xiaohu, Y. (2013). A unified algorithm for mobility load balancing in 3GPP LTE multi-cell networks. *Science China Information Sciences*, 56(2).

Huang, Z., Liu, J., & XiaoyingGan, Q. S. (2015). A threshold based multi-traffic load balance mechanism in LTE-A networks. *IEEE Wireless Communications and Networking Conference*, (pp. 1273–1278). doi:10.1109/WCNC.2015.7127652.

Ismail, M. M. & Nordin, R. (2014). Vertical handover Solution over LTE-Advanced Wireless Networks: An overview", wireless Personal Communications, 77(4), pp. 3051–3079, August 2014. DOI: 10.1007/s11277-014-1695-1.

Iturralde, M., Wei, A., Yahiya, T. A., & Beylot, A. L. (2012). Resource allocation for real time services using cooperative game theory and a virtual token mechanism in LTE networks *IEEE Consumer Communications and Networking Conference*, (pp. 879–883).

Janevski, T. & Jakimoski, K. (2011). Improving vertical handovers for real-time video traffic between UMTS and WiMAX networks. *International Journal of Research and Reviews in Next Generation*, 1(1), 1–6.

Kumai, N., Kumar, R., & Bajaj, R. (2017). Mobile ad hoc networks and energy efficiency using directional antennas: A review. In 2017 international conference on intelligent computing and control systems (ICICCS) (pp. 1213–1219). IEEE.

Kumar, R., Bajaj, R., & Pawar, L. (2017). Advanced replicated hardware architecture for smartphones and smart devices. *International Journal of Computational Intelligence Research*, 13(5), 805–813.

Kaur, H., & Bajaj, R. (2015). Review on localization techniques in wireless sensor networks. *International Journal of Computer Applications*, 116(2).

Li, W., Duan, X., Jia, S., Zhang, L., Liu, Y., & Lin, J. (2012). A dynamic hysteresis-adjusting algorithm in LTE self-organization networks. *75th IEEE Vehicular Technology Conference.*

Li, M., Zhao, L., Li, X., Li, X., Zaki, Y., Giel, A. T., & Görg, C. (2012). Investigation of network virtualization and load balancing techniques in LTE networks. *75th IEEE Vehicular Technology Conference.*

Lu. D, Yang. H., & Wu. K. (2010). On the feedback enhancement and system performance evaluation of downlink MU-MIMO for 3GPP LTE-advanced. *IEEE 71st VehicularTechnology Conference*, (pp. 6–19).

Määttänen, H. L, Koivisto, T., Enescu, M., & Tirkkonen, O. (2012). CSI feedback for dynamic switching between single user and multiuser MIMO. *Wireless Personal Communications,* 64, 33–49.

Meetei, K. P. & George, A. (2011). Handoff management in wireless networks using predictive modelling. *National Conference on Communications*, 28–30.

Min, W. Chun-yan, F., & Tian-kui, Z. (2012). Min-max load balancing scheme for mixed multicast and unicast services in LTE networks. *The Journal of China Universities of Posts and Telecommunications.*

Parikh, J. & Basu, A. (2011). LTEAdvanced: The 4G Mobile Broadband Technology. *International Journal of Computer Applications*, 13(5), 17–21.

Paware, L. (2019). Smart city IoT: Smart architectural solution for networking, congestion and heterogeneity. *ICCS, IEEE*, 124–129.

Pawar, L., Bathla, G., & Bajaj, R. (2021). CoMP based Tri sector tilted antenna in lte advanced networks. *2021 2nd Global Conference for Advancement in Technology*, (pp. 1–6).

Qian, M., Huang, Y., Shi, J., Yuan, Y., Tian, L., & Dutkiewicz, E. (2009). A novel radio admission control scheme for multiclass services in LTE systems. *IEEE Global Telecommunications Conference.*

Ramdev, M. S., Bajaj, R., Gupta, R. (2019). A CQI based novel shared channel downlink scheduler for LTE networks. *International Journal of Engineering and Advanced Technology*, 8(6), 4422–4426, doi: 10.35940/ijeat.F8971.088619

Ramdev, M. S., Bajaj, R., & Sidhu, J. (2022). Remote radio head scheduling in LTE-advanced networks. *Wireless Personal Communications*, 122(1), 621–644.

Rezaei, M. J., Sabahi, M. F., Shahtalebi, K., Mahin Zaeem, R., & Sadeghi, R. (2015). New fairness index and novel approach for qos-aware resource allocation in lte networks based on utility functions. *Amirkabir International Journal of Science& Research, Electrical & Electronics Engineering*, 47(2), 19–25.

Samia, D., Ridhay, B., & Weiz, A. (2016). Resource allocation using nucleolus value in downlink LTE networks. *IEEE International Workshop on Urban Mobility & Intelligent Transportation Systems.*

Serge, M. T. & Liu, Y. (2016). Dynamic and efficient power efficient bandwidth allocation method for LTE networks. *International Journal on Recent and Innovation Trends in Computing and Communication*, 4(7).

Shin, O-S., EddineElayoubi, S., Jeong, Y. K., & Shin, Y. (2013). Advanced technologies for LTE Advanced. *Journal on Wireless Communications and Networking, Springer*.

Singh, G., Singh, A., & Bajaj, R. (2022). Analysis of energy optimization approaches in internet of everything: An SDN prospective. *Software Defined Internet of Everything*, (pp. 119–133).

Singh, J., Pi, Z., & Nguyen, H. (2013). Low-complexity optimal CSI feedback in LTE. *IEEE ConsumerCommunications and Networking Conference, (*pp. 11–14).

Sun, C., Navarro, E. S., & Wong, V. W. S. (2011). A constrained MDP-based vertical handoff decision algorithm for 4G heterogeneous wireless networks. *Wireless Network.*

Ulvan, A., Bestak, R., &Ulvan, M. (2013). Handover Procedure and decision strategy in LTE-based femtocell network. *Telecommunication Systems-Springer*, 52(4), pp, 2733–2748.

Wang, H., Ding, L., Wu, P., Pan, Z., Liu, N., & You, X. (2010). Dynamic load balancing and throughput optimization in 3GPP LTE networks. *Proceedings of the 6th International Wireless Communications and Mobile Computing Conference.*

Zhou, K., Nikaein, N., & Knopp, R. (2013). Dynamic resource allocation for machine-type communications in LTE/LTE-A with contention-based access. *IEEE Wireless Communications and Networking Conference*, (pp 256–261).

58 Investigating the scope of semantic analysis in natural language processing considering accuracy and performance

Deepender[1,a] *and Tarandeep Singh Walia*[2,b]

[1]Research Scholar, School of Computer Applications, Lovely Professional University, Punjab, India

[2]Associate Professor, School of Computer Applications, Lovely Professional University, Punjab, India

Abstract

Semantic analysis refers to the study of language and the way words are understood. Natural language processing is a branch of computer science that tries to make machines capable to comprehending human speech. Scientific and mental health professionals should have the ability to get information from web content using appropriate terminology and methods. This study's findings will be beneficial in this regard. Considering limitation of existing research in the field of natural language processing and semantic analysis it has been observed that there should be more accurate, high performance and reliable semantic analysis mechanism in existence.

Keywords: Semantic analysis, natural language processing, Lexicon, Grammar, AI

Introduction

Analysis of language and how words are interpreted is known as semantics. In computer science, natural language processing (NLP) is a discipline that aims to help computers understand human speech. Use suitable vocabulary and procedures to extract information from online material for scientific and mental health experts. The results of this investigation are going to be useful in this respect. According to current research in NLP and semantic analysis, there should be a more accurate and high-performance semantic analysis mechanism in existence.

Natural Language Processing

In computer science, a subject known as NLP deals with artificial intelligence (AI), which is used to make computers capable of comprehending and processing human language. The area of NLP tries to offer robots, the capacity to

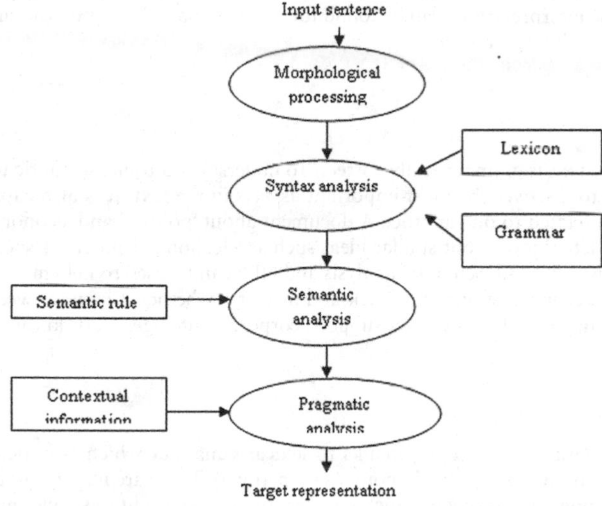

Figure 58.1 Semantic analysis

[a]deependerduhan6@gmail.com; [b]tarandeep.25153@lpu.co.in

interpret natural languages in their own words and sentences. Semantic analysis is one of the several sub-topics in this subject that are explored. A simple definition of semantic analysis is determining the text's meaning. Various methods are used to do this.

NLP is depicted in the figure by a series of stages or logical steps. Several stages are addressed in detail in the following paragraphs.

Morphological processing

NLP begins with morphological processing. In this phase, chunks of linguistic input are broken down into sets of tokens corresponding to paragraphs, phrases, and words. Uneasy can be divided into two sub-word tokens, 'un-easy', as an example.

Syntax analysis

The second phase of NLP is syntax analysis. In this step, the goal is to determine whether a sentence is well-formed or not as well as to break it down into its syntactic components. Syntax analyzers and parsers would reject a statement like 'The school goes to the boy'. It considers both the vocabulary and grammar.

a. Grammar: The syntactic structure of a well-formed program can be described using grammar. Natural language syntactic rules are denoted by the literary term. Since the origin of natural languages like English, Hindi, etc., linguists have endeavored to define grammars.
b. Lexicon: Lexical meaning refers to the definition of a word (or lexeme) in a dictionary.

Semantic analysis

NLP's semantic analysis is the third stage. At this stage, the goal is to extract the text's precise meaning or dictionary definition. The text's meaning is double-checked. A statement like 'Hot ice-cream' would be rejected by a semantic analyzer.

Pragmatic analysis

NLP's fourth phase is known as pragmatic analysis. Contextual information is the focus. Pragmatic analysis is a simple fit between the real objects and events in a particular context and the object references that were gathered in the previous step (semantic analysis). Two possible semantic interpretations can be found for 'Put banana in basket on the shelf'. The pragmatic analyzer will choose one of these two interpretations.

Finally, target representation is attained.

Semantic Analysis

The job of a semantic analyzer is to ensure that the text is grammatically correct. To understand a topic, semantic technology analyses the logical structure of sentences to discover the most important aspects in the text. It is also capable of figuring out how the many ideas in the text are related to one another. A document about 'politics' and 'economics' can be understood even if it does not contain the actual terms, but similar ideas such as 'election', 'democrat', 'speaker of the house', or 'budget, tax, or inflation' can be used instead. Semantic analysis and NLP can be used to help machines and understand text. This furthers the goal of converting customer feedback and insight – whether it be in a tweet or in a customer service log – into information that can be used in customer support, corporate intelligence, or knowledge management.

Working of Semantic Analysis

Machines can grasp lexical associations (words, phrasal verbs, etc.), thanks to lexical semantics which is critical to semantic analysis. Specific synonyms of a general synonym are called hyponyms (hypernym). There are many fruit hyponyms, such as orange (hypernym). An instance of polysemy is one in which two or more words or phrases have similar but distinct meanings e.g., writing a paper was a two-step process for me. Joyful, pleased, delighted, and euphoric are all synonyms (words that have the same or almost the same meaning as one another0. Antidote: a word that has a nearly opposite connotation to the one it describes. The color orange is a homonym with the term orange (color), however the two words have different meanings (fruit). Semantic analysis also considers signs, symbols (semiotics), and collocations (words that often go together).

A machine learning (ML) algorithm is used to perform automated semantic analysis. You may teach computers to make accurate predictions based on prior observations by feeding them semantically enhanced machine learning algorithms with text samples. Word sense disambiguation and association extraction are just two of the many sub-tasks required in a semantic-based approach to machine learning.

It is the automatic method of determining the sense a word is used in given context, based on that context. It's not uncommon for a word to have multiple meanings depending on how it's used in a sentence. The term 'date', which can signify a specific day of the month, a fruit, or a meeting, is another example. Using word sense disambiguation, computers can identify which interpretation is right in a particular situation. It is necessary to identify the semantic linkages in a piece of writing. Two or more people are often involved in a relationship (which can be names of people, places, company names, etc.). Semantic categories, such as 'worked' or 'lived' or 'is the CEO' or 'headquartered' are used to connect these entities.

Semantic Analysis Techniques

You can use one of two methods for semantic analysis: a text classification model (which assigns predetermined categories to text) or a text extractor (which extracts text from a database and pulls out specific information from the text).

Semantic classification models

Predefined categories are used to categorize text according to its content. It is possible for customer care personnel to categorize support tickets as soon as they arrive at the help desk. A "payment issue" or a "shipping difficulty" can be identified using semantic analysis by ML methods. Negative or neutral emotions can be detected in a text to indicate urgency by using sentiment analysis. Customers can be identified in real time by tagging Twitter mentions by sentiment to obtain a sense of how they feel about your company. Text classification based on what customers intend to do next is called intent classification. There are a number of ways you may utilize this to identify potential customers who could be interested in your product.

Semantic extraction models

Textual analysis is the process of extracting keywords and phrases from a document. With this method, you may get a more granular understanding of your data. This can be done by analyzing many tweets that have been classed as 'negative' and identifying the most frequently used terms and subjects.

Entity extraction is the process of identifying identified entities in a given piece of text. Automated extraction of product names, shipment numbers, and email addresses from customer support tickets may be valuable for customer service teams. Agents are freed up to focus on more valuable activities and the customer experience when they use semantic analysis technologies to automatically classify tickets. Shorter response times and higher customer satisfaction levels can be achieved by routing tickets to the proper people and prioritizing critical concerns. Data insights also aid teams in identifying areas for improvement and making more informed decisions. For example, you may want to build a robust knowledge base by identifying the most frequently asked questions from your customers.

Literature Review

Studying NLP's many research articles on semantic analysis and NLP provided us with a solid foundation for our thesis on 'semantic analysis in NLP'. A brief outline of the papers that serve as the foundation and guide our study will be provided in the coming weeks.

As early as possible, Zait and Zarour (2019) developed a strategy to ambiguity identification and resolution using NLP and semantic web tools. In this way, the unclear terms were identified and all the interpretations and clarifications of the requirements were provided. By using POS tagger, we were able to identify user requirements that contained syntactically problematic ideas and then use linked data to clear up any semantic ambiguity.

Question answering (QA) is one of the most common tasks in NLP, according to Jaydeb Sarker et al.(2019). Semantic parsing is a common tool for deciphering natural language. As a means of generating syntactic and semantic structures of texts, synchronous frameworks were extensively employed. They proposed a strategy based on semantic parsing of texts to take advantage of semantic information in order to answer queries quickly. Semantic parsing was performed using a lambda calculus method, and the logical forms of sentences were derived as a result. Finding the correct responses from the facts was done by analyzing the questions. Despite this, the proposed approach was only used for basic sentences.

Lütfi An atlas of cross-lingual semantic similarity was developed by Senel et al. (2019) by quantifying representational similarity analysis of cross-linguistic semantic similarities between 76 languages from around the world. The languages were represented by pre-trained fastText word vectors trained on Wikipedia. Linguists discovered that languages spoken in close proximity to one another have a high degree of semantic homogeneity.

According to Sadhuram and Soni (2020), a technique called NLP has been applied, which deals with the processing of information in any form. An AI system employed this NLP, which falls under the category of NLP. Their efforts were devoted to building a factoid QA system that would answer the questions that the users had requested. In order to answer queries based on a given collection of articles, their method made advantage of lexical chaining and keyword analysis. The validity of the response was checked using the reasoning approach. The SQUAD dataset was used in this investigation. TFIDF's passage retrieval accuracy was measured at 69.69% in their testing. It was found that 69.93% of people correctly predicted the answer.

In the appropriate format and context of a sentence or paragraph, Maulud, et al. (2021) indicated this. Regarding the study of linguistic importance, semantics. Considering the interdependence between linguistic classes, the vocabulary chosen here communicates the importance of the subject. NLP was used to do semantic interpretation in this article. Sentiment analysis and prediction inaccuracy were found to be of low importance in the best-achieved accuracy of the papers that were checked.

Definite clause grammar (DCG) was created by Dagerman (2013) to explain how sentences may be compared to DCG semantics. As a bonus, it demonstrated the potential advantages of DCG capabilities. Openly accessible NLP frameworks were used to combine statistical parsing, part-of-speech tagging, and word-sense disambiguation into a single strategy. In order to determine the degree of semantic similarity, they used a massive lexical and conceptual-semantic thesaurus. Additionally, the COactive Language Definition (COLD) enhanced an existing programming language for multimodal interfaces that makes use of static specified DCGs. Consequently, every word that is acceptable to COLD must be specified in detail. By implementing their method, it was demonstrated how DCG-based systems can eliminate reliance on word definitions while simultaneously improving grammatical definitions.

The approach proposed by Hassan et al. (2017) utilized a semantic framework specifically created for the interpretation and analysis of natural language software requirement specifications in detail on the level of the semantic level. Semantic technology was used to build the framework, which included knowledge gleaned from current software requirement documents and from already developed applications. An ontology-based strategy to enabling knowledge management, designing a system, and conducting experiments on the requirements of real-world software systems is provided in this paper. Starting with the formulation of software requirements, they remove the extraneous ones and transform the cleaned ones into a graph depicting the interconnectedness of various aspects. They used the OntoGen programme to convert the requirement graph into a sparse matrix, following which they created an ontology.

They conducted a survey on semantic analysis and looked at the work done by various researchers in semantic analysis. A famous statistical model known as the LSA model and another area of active research known as ontology, which represents a set of primitives of domain of knowledge, were also noted throughout their investigation. According to the findings, LSA was used to compare automated results to human ones, as well as to extract semantic information from text. Unstructured data was analyzed using the ontology technique to extract structural information, which was then employed in the database and in semantic web applications.

NLP systems, such NLTK, have fewer knowledge requirements for skills like neural network competency and cosine similarity, while text mining systems necessitate skills like Perl or Python expertise, according to Tyagi (2021). Text mining needed a thorough understanding of statistical methods.

The work of Pande and Karyakarte (2019) has been reviewed to propose different strategies for text annotation. Natural Language Pre-processing has been used for the pre-processing of document text. Before any pre-processing procedures, such as tokenization and POS tagging, are implemented, certain NLP tasks must be completed. SVO triples are formed via syntactic analysis to convey significant information about the sentence. A variety of additional text annotation techniques are used to analyze a document's text and offer semantic information automatically, such as ML, KWBA, OBA, and WSD.

Problem Statement

There have been several research in area of semantic analysis. But the issue with those research was that they did limited work on performance. Moreover, there was lack of scalability and flexibility. The lack of accuracy was other issue that was faced in those researches. If you're a human, you can easily connect a misspell word with its correct spelling and understand the rest of a sentence. When it comes to misspellings, though, a computer may have a harder time catching them. NLP technology is required to identify and proceed past the typical misspellings of phrases. NLP will be necessary. If you feed the system with incorrect or distorted data, it will learn the wrong things or learn in an ineffective manner. NLP systems may carry the biases of their programmers and the data sets from which they were developed. It is possible for an NLP to exploit or propagate certain societal preconceptions, or to deliver a better experience to specific types of users than others, depending on the app. It's hard to come up with a solution that works in every situation and with every person.

Need of Research

Programming declarations and statements must be semantically accurate to be analyzed by semantic analysis. This collection of processes is invoked by the parser whenever grammar dictates that it is necessary. Syntax tree of previous phase and symbol table are utilized to verify code coherence. In many downstream applications, such as speech recognition or text analytics, NLP helps resolve ambiguity in language and adds helpful quantitative structure to the data.

Challenges faced by semantic analysis

Issues of semantic analysis has been discussed in this section.

Preparation period

The time it takes to build an NLP system should also be taken into consideration. In order to train an AI, it is necessary to analyze millions of data points; this process may take a lifetime with an underpowered PC. It could take just a few hours of training with a shared deep network and a large number of GPUs working together. When developing an NLP product from scratch, you must account for the time it will take to construct it from the ground up.

Asserting confidence

However, another human being has a hard time deciphering what someone is trying to convey when they say something unclear. There will be no obvious, succinct meaning to be found in their statements even after a thorough examination. When dealing with this issue, an NLP system must be able to search for context that will help it understand the word. Asking for clarification may be required at times.

Differences in language

Even though English is widely spoken in the United States, if you want to appeal to a wide range of individuals, you'll need to offer support for many languages. Varied languages not only have vastly different vocabularies, but they also use different phrasing, inflections, and cultural standards to express themselves. To get around this, use 'universal' models, which allow you to transfer some of what you've learned to languages other than your own. However, each additional language will necessitate the update of your NLP system.

Preliminary research results

Language is at the heart of NLP, which focuses on learning to better understand it. Developing fluency in a language requires years of constant exposure; even the most advanced artificial intelligence must devote significant time to reading, listening to, and speaking the target language. NLP systems are only as good as the data used to train them.

Scope of Research

With the advancement of technology, voice assistants have grown increasingly popular. In order to effectively communicate with humans, they make use of voice recognition, NLP, and speech synthesis technology. Using a voice assistant, we can do a slew of things like make phone calls, get information from the web, play our favorite song, and more. The use of NLP for Sentiment Analysis can help businesses gain insight into their customers' purchasing behaviors, likes, dislikes, and more. When you learn more about your customers, you can gain valuable information. Sentiment analysis has benefited greatly from the rise in social media use. Marketing and sales decisions can be made based on the customer's behaviors. Our inboxes are organized according to the tone of the emails we receive, thanks to the usage of NLP algorithms. Many emails are automatically placed in the Spam folder by NLP algorithms after a thorough examination.

Automatic email sorting saves a great deal of time and effort. We've come a long way since the days when we had to look through every email one by one. Gmail and Yahoo Mail are two of the most popular email systems that employ these strategies. An NLP tool can provide useful information to financial traders and firms by analyzing people's comments and perspectives on a specific topic. Tracking news and global events is possible with this app. Businesses can increase their profitability by utilizing algorithms that take advantage of this data.

Conclusion

There has been a rise in the number of people using social media to spread fake news. There has been a lot of concerns about the prevalence of fake news, which has resulted in people feeling anxious and stressed out. The language can be analyzed by natural language processing algorithms to see if it is reliable or not. When the world is faced with global pandemics or natural disasters like cyclones, this is a lifesaver. Writing a blog post or sending an email necessitates proper grammar. When an article or email is well-written, it has an impact on the reader. People used to carefully check for grammatical and spelling errors in the past. Nowadays, thanks to the rise of NLP, automated grammar and spelling checks are becoming more prevalent. When it comes to producing big essays or sending crucial emails, they are considerably more efficient, accurate, and instrumental. User-friendly and useful Grammarly is one example of an automatic grammar checker.

References

Asogwa, T. C., Fidelis, E., Obodoeze, C., & Obiokafor, I. N. (2007). IJARCCE wireless sensor network (WSN): Applications in oil & gas and agriculture industries in Nigeria. *International Journal of Advanced Research in Computer and Communication Engineering,* 3297, 146–149. doi: 10.17148/IJARCCE.

Dagerman, B. (2013). Semantic analysis of natural language and definite clause grammar using statistical parsing and thesauri.

Hassan, T., Hassan, S., Yar, M. A., & Younas, W. (2017). Semantic analysis of natural language software requirement. *2016 Sixth International Conference on Innovative Computing Technology*, (pp. 459–463). doi: 10.1109/INTECH.2016.7845013.

Maulud, D. H., Zeebaree, S. R. M., Jacksi, K., Mohammed Sadeeq, M. A., & Sharif, K. H. (2021). State of art for semantic analysis of natural language processing. *Qubahan Academic Journal*, 1(2). doi: 10.48161/qaj.v1n2a44.

Pande, N. & Karyakarte, M. (2019). A review for semantic analysis and text document annotation using natural language processing techniques. *SSRN Electronic Journal.* doi: 10.2139/ssrn.3418747.

Sadhuram, M. V. & Soni, A. (2020). Natural language processing based new approach to design factoid question answering system. *Proceedings of the 2nd International Conference on Inventive Research in Computing Applications*, (pp. 276–281). doi: 10.1109/ICIRCA48905.2020.9182972.

Shadrach, F., Lacey, B., Roberts, A. S., Akbari, A., Thompson, A., Ford, S. et al. (2019). Using natural language processing to extract structured epilepsy data from unstructured clinic letters. *International Journal of Population Data Science*, 3(4).

Sarker, J., Billah, M., & Al Mamun, M. (2019). Textual question answering for semantic parsing in natural language processing. 1st Int. Conf. Adv. Sci. Eng. Robot. Technol. (pp. 1–5). doi: 10.1109/ICASERT.2019.8934734.

Senel, L. K., Utlu, I., Yucesoy, V., Koc, A., & Cukur, T. (2019). Generating semantic similarity atlas for natural languages. (2018). *IEEE Spok. Lang. Technol. Work.* (pp. 795–799). doi: 10.1109/SLT.2018.8639521.

Tyagi, A. (2021). A Review study of natural language processing techniques for text mining. *International Journal of Engineering Research & Technology*, 10(9), 586–589.

Weston, J. E., Bordes, A., Lebrun, A., &Raison, M. J. (2017). Techniques to predictively respond to user requests using natural language processing.

Zait, F. & Zarour, N. (2019). Addressing lexical and semantic ambiguity in natural language requirements. *2018 Fifth International Symposium on Innovation in Information and Communication Technology,* (pp. 1–7). doi: 10.1109/ISIICT.2018.8613726.

Printed in the United States
by Baker & Taylor Publisher Services